BLUE GUIDE

SICILY

Ellen Grady

A&C Black • London
WW Norton • New York

Sixth edition 2003
Published by A & C Black Publishers Limited
37 Soho Square, London W1D 3QZ

© Ellen Grady 2003

First edition 1975, Second edition 1981, Third edition 1988, Fourth edition 1993, Fifth edition 1999 by Alta Macadam

Maps and plans drawn by H.B.C. Consultants Ltd and Robert Smith © A & C Black
Illustrations © Colin Ross
'Blue Guides' is a registered trade mark

A CIP catalogue record of this book
is available from the British Library.

ISBN 0–7136–6278–6

Published in the United States of America by
WW Norton and Company, Inc
500 Fifth Avenue, New York, NY 10110

Published simultaneously in Canada by
Penguin Books Canada Limited
10 Alcorn Avenue, Toronto, Ontario M4V 3B2

ISBN 0–393–32470–2 USA

The author and the publishers have done their best to ensure the accuracy of all the information in *Blue Guide Sicily*; however, they can accept no responsibility for any loss, injury or inconvenience sustained by any traveller as a result of information or advice contained in the guide.

Cover pictures. Top: House with orange tree, © Riccardo Lombardo. Bottom: Temple of Selinunte, © Giacomo Mazza
Title page illustration: San Giovanni dei Lebbrosi, Palermo

A&C Black uses paper produced with elemental chlorine-free pulp, harvested from managed sustainable forests.

Printed and bound in Great Britain by Butler and Tanner Ltd, Frome and London.

BLUE GUIDES

Please write in with your comments, suggestions and corrections for the next edition of the Blue Guide. Writers of the most helpful letters will be awarded a free Blue Guide of their choice.

Contents

Trapani province

Agrigento province and the Pelagian islands

Caltanissetta province

Enna province

Ragusa province

Syracuse province

Maps and plans

Introduction

Sicily, the largest island in the Mediterranean, and the southernmost part of Italy, has had a remarkable history and many superb archaeological sites and beautiful buildings survive from the past. It also has lush sub-tropical vegetation around the coast, with wonderful mountain scenery in the interior. It is famous above all for its Greek remains, only rivalled by those in Greece itself, including the superb temples at Agrigento, Segesta and Selinunte, and the spectacular theatres at Taormina, Syracuse and Segesta. Palermo has fascinating Arab Norman buildings, especially famous for their wonderful mosaics (which also decorate the cathedrals of Monreale and Cefalù). Sicily has its own delightful Baroque architecture in the east and in the southeast corner of the island, where the towns were all rebuilt after an earthquake in 1693, resulting in the splendours of Noto, Ragusa, Militello, Catania and Acireale.

The two main cities of the island, Palermo and Catania, after a period of decline in the 1960s and 1970s, have in the last few years become much more pleasant places to visit since the standard of living here has greatly improved. They are better kept and numerous restoration projects are in progress, more churches are open and there is more to do in the evenings. Palermo is a fascinating city with numerous large street markets in the old city centre, and Catania is a very elegant Baroque city which is awakening to new life after many years of shameful neglect.

The natural beauty of the island is at last being preserved; there are many wildlife reserves as well as several regional parks which ensure protection for Mount Etna, the Nebrodi Mountains and the Madonie Mountains and some of the most beautiful offshore islands; Ustica, the Aeolians and the Egadi islands. The Roman villa at Piazza Armerina, the temples of Agrigento, the Aeolian Islands, the Baroque monuments of Noto, Militello, Scicli, Modica, Caltagirone and Ragusa are all now recognised by UNESCO as world heritage sites.

The food of Sicily is extremely good and inexpensive, and local specialities ensure an interesting variety. The sweets and cakes, using pistachios, almond paste and ricotta as basic ingredients, are particularly delicious, and ice cream is always superb. Excellent fresh fish is served all over the island. Sicily is catching up with the rest of Italy in the provision of good small hotels, and very good accommodation is now available in farmhouses and country homes all over the island. A recent law has made it possible for people to open their homes to guests on a bed-and-breakfast arrangement, and this is certainly one of the most interesting and rewarding ways of visiting Sicily, allowing closer contact with the Sicilian people.

Although the island has long been notorious as the birthplace of the Mafia, professional criminals who have subjected the population to a 'protection' system, which has for years controlled almost every business transaction on the island, both private and state, it is necessary to emphasise that travellers to the island are in no way exposed to this problem. Sicilians are famous for their hospitality and are extremely kind and helpful to visitors. Sicily is as safe a place to visit as any other part of Italy, if not safer. After the courageous stand taken by a number of Sicilians against the Mafia there are signs that it is fast losing two of its greatest strengths, its legitimacy and its invisibility.

Acknowledgements

Ellen Grady expresses her grateful thanks to the staff at all the tourist offices of Sicily, for their competence and enthusiasm while she was updating this guide, and to Alta Macadam, author of previous editions of the guide. She also received a lot of help from Grazia Barbagallo, Giusi Belfiore, Salvo Buffa, Fabio Bonaccorsi, Rosario Cassaro, Laura Cassataro, Claudio Castiglione, Santi Correnti, Salvatore Cucuzza Silvestri, Franco D'Angelo, Michele Gallo, Diana Mazza Rampf, Giacomo Mazza, Margherita Perricone, Emilia Poli Marchese, Franco Purpura, Carmelo Paci, Bruno Ragonese, Costanza Schacht and the Touring Club Italiano.

How to use the Guide

The guide is divided into nine **chapters** covering the nine provinces of Sicily: Palermo, Trapani, Agrigento, Caltanissetta, Enna, Ragusa, Syracuse, Catania, Messina. Within each province, sections are devoted to the provincial capitals and their immediate environs, and then to other places of interest; towns, villages, areas known for their distinctive landscape and any offshore islands. A number of walks are provided around the major cities and towns, with separate descriptions for the major monuments and museums.

An indispensable section at the beginning of the book lists all the **practical information** (see p 13) a traveller is likely to need or want to know before visiting Sicily and while on holiday. Local information, for those travelling by public transport or by car, suggestions on where to stay and places to eat, is integrated both at the beginning of each chapter and of each town or island. For more information on price categories see also under 'Where to stay' and 'Food and Drink'.

The most **important monuments or works of art** in Sicily have been highlighted in bold letters throughout the guide. Major places of interest in the island which should not be missed are listed in the 'Highlights' section (see p 11).

All **churches** are taken as being orientated with the entrance at the west end, and the altar at the east end, the south aisle on the right and the north aisle on the left. In the larger towns all the main monuments have a map reference to the grid on the double-page **town plans**. On the ground plans of museums, figures or letters have been given to correspond with the description in the text.

The **local tourist boards** (*APT* or *Azienda di Promozione Turistica, Azienda di Soggiorno* and *Pro-Loco*), are usually extremely helpful and it is only through them that it is possible to secure up-to-date information on the spot about accommodation and opening times of museums and monuments (see below). The nine provincial offices have been listed with their telephone numbers on p 30, and the local information offices are listed at the beginning of each province section and in each town. On the town maps they are marked with the letter **i**, the symbol which is used on local signposts throughout Italy. For information on maps of the island see p 15.

Opening times of museums and monuments are listed throughout the guide (i.e. 09.00–14.00; Sun & PH 09.00–13.00). However, opening times vary and often change without warning, so it is best to consult the local *APT* for up-to-date information on your arrival. Almost all churches close at 12.00 noon and do not re-open again until 16.00 or 17.00. For further information, see p 32 in the Practical information section.

Abbreviations and symbols

ACI	Automobile Club Italiano
APT	Azienda di Promozione Turistica (official local tourist office)
b.	born
c	century
d.	died
DOC	Denominazione d'Origine Controllata
ENIT	Ente Nazionale per il Turismo
FAI	Fondo per l'Ambiente Italiano (modelled on Britain's National Trust)
fest.	*festa*, or festival (ie. holiday, including Sunday)
fl.	*floruit* (flourished)
FS	Ferrovie dello Stato (Italian State Railways), now also known as Trenitalia
PH	public holidays
S. and SS.	Saint and Saints (San, Santo, Santa, Santi etc.)
TCI	Touring Club Italiano
WWF	World Wide Fund for Nature

▨	email and/or website	✿	nature or wildlife reserves
€	euro		
☎	telephone		
🗐	fax		

The terms *Quattrocento*, *Cinquecento*, abbreviated in Italy as '400, '500, etc., refer not to the 14C and 15C but to the 'fourteen hundreds' and 'fifteen hundreds', i.e. the 15C and 16C.

Planning a visit

As many days as possible should be devoted to the city of **Palermo** and its environs (notably Monreale). **Selinunte** may then be reached via Segesta and the west coast (Trapani, Erice, the island of Mozia, and Marsala), or, if you have very little time, direct from Palermo (in this case Segesta can be visited on a detour or in a day from Palermo). **Agrigento**, reached from Selinunte along the south coast via Eraclea Minoa, deserves a visit of at least two days. The numerous medieval hill towns and spectacular countryside in the interior of the island can be explored from Enna (reached via Caltanissetta from Agrigento). **Piazza Armerina**, with the famous mosaics in its Roman villa, and the ruins of Morgantina are between Enna and Caltagirone, another inland town.

In the southeast corner of the island are the fine Baroque towns of Ragusa, Modica and Comiso. The exploration of **Syracuse** and its environs (the Castello Eurialo, Noto, Palazzolo Acreide and the necropolis of Pantalica) requires at least three days. **Catania**, which can be visited in a day, is a good centre for the ascent of **Etna** and a circular tour of the foothills. The road between Catania and Messina passes Giardini Naxos and **Taormina**, where at least one night should be spent. On the road along the north coast, Tindari and **Cefalù** should not be missed.

Acireale, Milazzo and Syracuse are ideal bases for spending a few days touring in eastern and central Sicily and they all offer excellent accommodation. The most spectacular farmhouses for a restful holiday are in the province of Messina, on the Nebrodi Mountains. This area is also very good for birdwatching.

Highlights

Prehistoric Sicily

Some of the earliest traces of habitation on the island can be seen in the caves on Monte Pellegrino and on the island of Levanzo. Excavations on Lípari have revealed the presence of man on the island from the Neolithic age onwards, and there are other prehistoric sites in the Aeolian Islands (Panarea, Salina and Filicudi). In the eastern part of the island is the most impressive of all the prehistoric sites in Sicily where the upland plateau of Pantalica has thousands of tombs cut into the rock face. The beautiful Cava Grande del Cassibile and Cava d'Ispica also have prehistoric tombs.

Ancient sites

The most famous Greek buildings on the island are at Agrigento, Syracuse, Selinunte and Segesta. Other archaeological sites of great interest and in splendid positions include: Morgantina, Eraclea Minoa, Naxos, Mozia, Palazzolo Acreide and Tindari. The Cave di Cusa provide a unique view of an ancient quarry. The Roman villa at Piazza Armerina has some of the most extensive and beautiful mosaics known, and the ancient theatre of Taormina has a spectacular view. Extremely important Greek fortifications are to be seen at Gela and the Castello Eurialo, on the outskirts of Syracuse. Lesser known sites include Jetae, Solunto, Eloro, Halaesa and Kamarina.

Norman buildings

Palermo has the greatest concentration of Norman architecture, including the Cappella Palatina, the Zisa, the Ponte dell'Ammiraglio (Admiral's Bridge), Roger's Room in the Palazzo dei Normanni and the wonderful churches of La Martorana, S. Cataldo, S. Giovanni degli Eremiti, La Magione and S. Giovanni dei Lebbrosi. The mosaic decoration of the Cappella Palatina and La Martorana is particularly splendid, and just outside the city at Monreale, the Norman cathedral has one of the greatest mosaic cycles ever produced. The presbytery of the cathedral of Cefalù also has very fine mosaics. Smaller, lesser known churches of this period can be seen on the east coast near Casalvecchio Siculo (SS. Pietro e Paolo d'Agro) and Itala (S. Pietro), and not far from Castelvetrano near Marsala.

Baroque towns

The most famous and best preserved Baroque town in Sicily is Noto, but other towns in the southeast corner of the island worth visiting, which were rebuilt after an earthquake in 1693, include Ragusa, Modica, Ispica, Scicli, Comiso, Militello, Catania and Acireale. Ortygia, the old part of Syracuse, also has some interesting Baroque buildings.

Archaeological museums

Perhaps the most impressive archaeological museum on the island is the one in Syracuse. The regional archaeological museums in Palermo and Agrigento also have very fine collections with finds from all over Sicily. Particularly interesting local collections can be seen in Marsala, Gela, Lipari and Centuripe.

Small, well preserved towns in picturesque positions

Polizzi Generosa, Petralia Soprana, Nicosia, Leonforte, Sperlinga, Sclafani Bagni, Castelbuono and Contessa Entellina are all well preserved towns in the interior. Erice on the west coast is a particularly enchanting place in a wonderful position. Other very small and little known places include Forza d'Agro in the Monti Peloritani and S. Marco d'Alunzio in the Monti Nebrodi.

Offshore islands

The Aeolian islands are very beautiful, and each one has a distinctive character. Here the two islands with active volcanoes, Stromboli and Vulcano, are also very interesting. Ustica has a particularly beautiful coastline and seabed, and Marettimo, one of the Egadi islands, is unspoilt. Remote Pantelleria, the biggest of Sicily's islands and closer to Africa than to Sicily, has no beaches but some fine scenery.

PRACTICAL INFORMATION

 Planning your trip

When to go

Travelling in Sicily is possible year round. It is, after all, a kind of paradise on earth. But travellers should bear in mind that there can be heavy rainstorms in October and November and that it is usually very hot in July and August; when the *scirocco* blows the temperature can reach 40°C and higher. Springtime is lovely and February–March is the best time to see the wild flowers.

In March, April and May school parties can often descend on historical sites and museums but with a little careful planning one can avoid them. Often the best time to visit the Roman Villa at Piazza Armerina or the Greek Theatre in Taormina, for example, is at lunch time (between 13.00 and 15.00) when it can be quite peaceful.

The *maestrale*, the prevailing wind around Messina and the Aeolian Islands, blows from the northwest, often making it difficult for the hydrofoils to reach the offshore islands in winter, and sometimes even the ferryboats have problems. Strong winds sometimes affect communications between Trapani and the Egadi Islands. But the advantages of travelling in Sicily during the winter are fewer crowds, cloudless skies, mild weather, and the incomparable spectacle of Mount Etna covered in snow.

Passports

Passports are necessary for all visitors from America and Canada, Australia and New Zealand entering Italy (citizens of EU countries can enter with a valid identity card). Travellers from North America, Australia and New Zealand can stay in Italy for a maximum of 3 months without a visa. A lost or stolen passport can be replaced by the relevant embassy in Rome (see below). Travellers must carry a valid identity card or passport with them at all times. It is a good idea to make a photocopy of your passport or ID card and keep it in a separate place.

Embassies in Rome

Australia 25/c Corso Trieste, ☎ 06 852 721. Open Mon–Thur 09.00–12.00 and 13.30–17.00; Fri 09.00–12.00.
Canada 30 Via Zara, ☎ 06 4459 8421. Open Mon–Fri 08.30–12.30 and 13.30–16.00.
Republic of Ireland 3 Piazza Campitelli, ☎ 06 697 9121. Open Mon–Fri 10.00–12.30 and 15.00–16.30.
Netherlands 8 Via M. Mercati, ☎ 06 321 5827.
New Zealand 28 Via Zara, ☎ 06 440 4035. Open Mon–Fri 08.30–12.45 and 13.45–17.00.

South Africa 14 Via Tanaro, ☎ 06 852 541. Open Mon–Fri 08.30–12.00.
United Kingdom 80/A Via Venti Settembre, ☎ 06 4890 3777. Open Mon–Fri 09.30–13.30.
United States of America 121 Via Veneto, ☎ 06 46741. Open Mon–Fri 08.30–12.00.

Italian tourist boards

General information can be obtained abroad from the Italian State Tourist Office (*ENIT, Ente Nazionale Italiano per il Turismo*), which provides detailed information on Sicily at ✉ www.italiantourism.com.

Australia c/o Italian Chamber of Commerce and Industry, Level 26, Market St, Sydney, ☎ 0061 292 662 1666, 🖷 0061 292 621 677.
Canada 1 Place Ville Marie, Suite 1914, Montreal, Quebec H3B 2CR ☎ 001 514 886 7667, 🖷 001 514 392 1429, ✉ www.initaly@ucab.net.
Netherlands Stadhoudestrade 2, 1054 ES Amsterdam, ☎ 003 616 120 8244, 🖷 003 618 120 8515.
UK 1 Princes Street, London WIR 8AY, ☎ 020 7408 1254 or 020 7355 1557, 🖷 020 7493 6695, ✉ enitlond@globalnet.co.uk
USA New York: 630 Fifth Avenue, Suite 1565, NY 10111, ☎ 001 212 245 5633, 🖷 001 212 586 9249, ✉ www.enitny@italiantourism.com. **Chicago**: 500 North Michigan Avenue, Suite 2240, ☎ 001 312 644 0996, 🖷 001 312 644 3012. **Los Angeles**: 12400 Wiltshire Blvd, Suite 550, Los Angeles, CA 90025, ☎ 001 310 820 1898, 🖷 001 820 6357.

Addresses of official local tourist boards (*APT*) in Sicily are given on p 30.

Websites for Sicily

- ✉ www.regione.sicilia.it/turismo/web_turismo/
- ✉ www.bestofsicily.com
- ✉ www.dionysosmagazine.com (specializing in history, current affairs, entertainment)

Tour operators

A selection of tour operators offering package holidays to Sicily from the UK are

Ace Study Tours, Babraham, Cambridge CB2 4AP, ☎ 01223 835055, ✉ ace@study.tours.org, ✉ www.study-tours.org
Alternative Travel Group Ltd, 69–71 Banbury Rd, Oxford OX2 6PE, ☎ 01865 315678, 🖷 01865 315697, ✉ www.atg-oxford.co.uk. Specialises in walking holidays.
Citalia (CIT Holidays Ltd), Marco Polo House, 3–5 Lansdowne Rd, Croydon, Surrey CR9 1LL, ☎ 020 8686 5533; 🖷 020 8681 0712, ✉ www.citalia.co.uk.
Cottages to Castles, Tuscany House, 10 Tonbridge Rd, Maidstone, Kent ME16 8RP, ☎ 01622 775217, 🖷 01622 775217, ✉ www.cottagestocastles.com
Andante Travels, The Old Barn, Old Road, Alderbury, Salisbury SP5 3AR, ☎ 01722 713800, 🖷 01722 711966, ✉ tours@andantetravels.co.uk, ✉ www.andantetravels.co.uk.
International Chapters, 47–51 High St, St John's Wood, London NW8 7NJ, ☎ 020 7722 0722; 🖷 020 77229140l; ✉ www.villa-rentals.com.

Italia nel Mondo, 6 Palace St, London SW1E 5HY, ☎ 020 7828 9171; 020 7630 5184.

Magic of Italy, King's House, 12–42 Wood Street, Kingston upon Thames, Surrey KT1 1JF, ☎ 02700 270 500 (reservations); ☎ 0900 462 442 (brochures); www.magictravelgroup.co.uk.

Martin Randall Travel Ltd, 10 Barley Mow Passage, London W4 4PH, ☎ 020 8742 3355, 020 8742 7766, www.martinrandall.com. Cultural tours specialising in art, history, archaeology and music.

Prospect Music and Art Tours Ltd, 36 Manchester Street, London W1V 7LH, ☎ 020 7486 5704; 020 7486 5686; enquiries@prospecttours.com.

SAGA Holidays, The Saga Building, Enbrook Park, Folkestone, Kent CT20 3SE ☎ 0800 300 456; 01303 771 010, www.saga.co.uk.

Specialtours (National Art Collections Fund Tours), 2 Chester Row, London SW1W 9JH, ☎ 020 7730 2297; 020 7823 5035, info@specialtours.co.uk.

Sunvil Holidays, Sunvil House, Upper Square, Isleworth, Middlesex TW7 7BJ, ☎ 020 8568 4499; 020 8568 8330, www.sunvil.co.uk.

The Italian Connection, ☎ 020 7486 6890, 020 7486 6891, www. italian-connection.com. Hotel accommodation or self-catering apartments.

Tuscany Now, 276 Seven Sisters Rd, London N4 2HY, ☎ 020 7272 5469, 020 7272 6184; brochure@tuscanynow.com; www.tuscanynow.com.

Maps

Detailed town plans are included throughout the book, providing easy navigation around towns and ancient sites. The colour map on the inside front and back covers of the book and the province maps within the text are useful when planning an itinerary. For those requiring a more detailed map, the *Italian Touring Club (TCI)* publishes several sets of excellent maps which are constantly updated; these are indispensable to anyone travelling by car in Italy.

The *Grande Carta Stradale d'Italia*, on a scale of 1:200,000 is divided into 15 maps covering the regions of Italy, Sicily included. The road maps are also published in the handier form of a three-volume atlas (with a comprehensive index) called the *Atlante Stradale d'Italia*. The one entitled *Sud* covers Sicily. These maps can be purchased from *TCI* offices and at many booksellers: in London they can be purchased from *Stanfords*, 12–14 Long Acre, London WC2E 9LP, ☎ 020 7836 1321, www.stanfords.co.uk.

The *Istituto Geografico Militare* of Italy has for many years been famous for its map production (much of it done by aerial photography). Their maps are now available at numerous bookshops in the main towns of Italy. They publish a map of Italy on a scale of 1:100,000 in 277 sheets, and a field survey partly 1:50,000, partly 1:25,000, which are invaluable for the detailed exploration of the country, especially its more mountainous regions; the coverage is, however, still far from complete at the larger scales, and some of the maps are out-of-date.

Health and insurance

British citizens, as members of the EU, have the right to claim health services (free treatment and prescriptions) in Italy if they are in possession of the E111 form (available from all post offices). There are also a number of private holiday health insurance policies. Remember to keep the receipt (*ricevuta*) and medical report (*cartella clinica*) to give to your insurer if you need to make a claim.

Currency and banks

In Italy the monetary unit is the euro. Notes are issued for 5, 10, 20, 50, 100, 200 and 500 euros, and coins for 1, 2, 5, 10, 20 and 50 cents, and 1 and 2 euros. Travellers' cheques are the safest way of carrying money when travelling. Most credit cards are now generally accepted in shops, hotels and restaurants (and at most petrol stations). In town centres and at airports there are automatic teller machines (ATMs) called Bancomat and also machines which change foreign bank notes. To order your travellers' cheques online in the UK contact:
Thomas Cook: ✉ www.thomascook.co.uk
American Express (UK): ✉ www.americanexpress.co.uk
American Express (USA): ✉ www.americanexpress.com.

Disabled travellers

Italy is catching up slowly with the rest of Europe in the provision of facilities for the disabled. All new public buildings are now obliged by law to provide access for the disabled, and specially designed facilities within. In the annual list of hotels published by the local APT offices, hotels which are able to give hospitality to the disabled are indicated. Airports and railway stations now provide assistance and certain trains are equipped to transport wheelchairs. Access for cars with disabled people is allowed to town centres normally closed to traffic where parking places are reserved for them. For all other information, contact the local APT offices.

Getting there

By air

From the UK

The two international airports are at Palermo and Catania. Air services between Sicily and London are operated by *Alitalia*, ☎ 0870 544 8259, ✉ www.alitalia.co.uk. Flights to Palermo and Catania usually operate via Milan or Rome (direct flights in summer). *Meridiana* operates flights from London to Catania via Florence, and to Palermo via Naples, UK office: 15 Charles II Street, London SW1, ☎ 020 7839 2222, ✉ info.london@meridiana.uk.com, ✉ www.meridiana.it (flight information only, no online booking for international flights). ✉ www.ebookers.com and ✉ opodo.com are both worth checking for special offers. There are also charter flights (often much cheaper) to Palermo and Catania. Details of these are available through travel agencies and listings sections in many of the national newspapers, especially the Sunday newspapers and the *London Evening Standard* and *Time Out* magazine. Teletext and the Internet also advertise flights and package holidays at competitive prices (see below). Scheduled services offer special fares which are available according to season; there are reduced fares for students and fly-drive schemes can also be arranged.

From the USA

Alitalia flies to Rome or Milan (☎ 1 800 223 5730; ✉ www.alitaliausa.com), non-stop from New York, Boston, Chicago and Los Angeles. Flights from New York to Rome are also operated by *Continental* (☎ 1 800 231 0856; ✉ www. continental.com), *Delta* (☎ 1 800 241 4141) and *TWA* (☎ 1 800 892 4141; ✉ www.twa.com). *United Airlines* (☎ 1 800 5382 929) operate between Washington DC and Rome. *British Airways, Air France, Air Malta* and *Air Europe* offer flights connecting through London, Paris, Malta and Amsterdam and these are often more economical than direct flights.

From the Italian mainland
Flights are operated by *Alitalia, Air Europe/Volare Airlines, Air Sicilia* (✉ www. sntweb.it) *Alpieagles* (✉ www.alpieagles.com), *Meridiana* (✉ www.meridiana.it) and *Air One* (✉ www.flyairone.it). There are many daily services from Rome and Milan to Palermo and Catania. Flights also operate from Naples, Pisa, Florence, Bologna, Turin, Venice, Verona, Brescia, Cagliari and Olbia to Palermo and Catania, and from Malta.

By rail
There are numerous rail services between Sicily and the Italian mainland. From Turin, Genoa and Milan mainline trains (via Rome and Naples) run to Villa San Giovanni and Reggio Calabria, and through carriages for destinations in Sicily (Palermo, Catania, and Syracuse) continue via the ferry to Messina. Overnight trains (with sleeping accommodation) run daily from Milan and Turin via Rome to Palermo and Syracuse.

Italy can be reached by a direct train from Paris Gare de Lyon overnight (by sleeper); there are frequent *Eurostar* trains from London Waterloo through the Eurotunnel via Calais to Paris Gare du Nord (in c 3hrs). For more information, contact *European Rail Ltd.* ☎ 020 7387 0444; 🖷 020 7387 0888 and see websites below.

> ### Rail websites
> ✉ www.raileurope.co.uk
> ✉ www.europeanrail.com
> ✉ www.fs-on-line.it (gives Italian timetables and ticket prices).
> ✉ www.freedomrail.co.uk
> ✉ www.itwg.com/home.asp
> ✉ www.railchoice.co.uk (arranges travel between London and Italy via Paris, and will also supply tickets for travel within Italy).
> ✉ www.trenitalia.com (Italian State Railways)

By coach
There is no direct service from London to Sicily but *National Express* run a coach service (48 hr journey, reduction for students) between London (Victoria Coach Station) and Rome (piazza della Repubblica) daily June–September, and once or twice a week for the rest of the year. From Rome, *SAIS* runs a daily coach service to Messina (going on to Catania, Syracuse and Agrigento) and to Palermo (in c 12–13hrs). *Segesta* also run an overnight coach service from Rome to Palermo.

For further information contact the National Express office at Victoria Coach Station (☎ 0870 580 8080; ✉ www.gobycoach.co.uk), local National Express agents, or *Eurolines* (☎ 01582 404511; ✉ www.eurolines.com). In Italy, the offices of *SITA* will be able to advise on international coach travel.

By car

From northern Italy the motorway known as the *Autostrada del Sole* (A1) runs south to Rome, which is now bypassed well to the east, avoiding the congested ring-road around the capital. At Caserta, just north of Naples, the A30 motorway forks left to bypass Naples. At Salerno the A3 motorway (toll free) continues south via Cosenza to Reggio Calabria, where the ferry for Messina departs from Villa San Giovanni. Messina can be reached comfortably in a day from Naples using the A3 motorway.

Car sleeper train services operate from Paris and Boulogne, Hamburg, Vienna and Munich to Milan, Bologna, Rome, etc. Car transport by train in Italy is available from Turin, Milan, Bologna, Genoa and Rome to Villa S. Giovanni. Overnight car sleepers run once a week between Calais and Bologna, May–September, information on ☎ 0272 544 350 or ☎ 051 630 3589.

  Driving from the UK British drivers taking their own cars need the vehicle registration document and a valid national driving licence. If you have the old-style green one you will also need an International Driving Licence from the *AA* with a translation (issued free of charge by the *Italian State Tourist Office*), insurance cover and a nationality plate attached to the car. If you are not the owner of the vehicle you must have the owner's written permission for its use abroad. *AA* or *RAC* membership entitles you to use of many of the facilities of affiliated societies on the Continent. Temporary membership of the *Automobile Club Italia* (*ACI*) can be taken out on the frontier or in Italy. They provide a breakdown service: Soccorso *ACI*, ☎ 116.

By sea

The shortest sea approach is across the Straits of Messina from Villa S. Giovanni and Reggio Calabria to Messina.

Ferries to Messina car ferries on the Straits of Messina operate from Villa S. Giovanni (c every 20 min.) in 20 minutes to Messina. The ferries are run both by the State Railways (*Trenitalia*) and two privately owned companies, *Caronte*, ☎ 090/3718 324, ✉ www.carontespa.it/caronte, and *Tourist Ferry Boat*, ☎ 090/3718510, ✉ www.paginegialle.it/touristfb. There is a frequent service, but there can be delays and long queues in the height of summer.

Hydrofoil to Messina *SNAV* operates a frequent service between Reggio Calabria and Messina (takes 15mins). For further details, see p 394.

Ferries to Palermo there are overnight car ferries from Naples, Cagliari, Tunis and Genoa operated by *Tirrenia*, ☎ 091/6021111. Services from Livorno, Genoa, Tunis and Malta by *Grandi Navi Veloci* (Palermo office: Calata Marinai d'Italia, ☎ 091/587404; London agent: *Viamare Travel Ltd*, Graphic House, 2 Sumatra Road, London NW6 1PU, ☎ 0207 4314560, ✉ www.viamare.com; the website also gives information on car rental from many towns across Sicily). Advance reservation is advised, particularly for a cabin or if with a car.

Catamaran to Palermo there is a daily service from Naples mid-April–early October (4hrs) run by *SNAV*, ☎ 090/364045, ✉ www.snavali.com.

Where to stay

Hotels

There are now quite a few good small hotels in Sicily. The nine provincial capitals all have adequate hotels (although Enna, Caltanissetta, and Trapani have only a very small selection) but the hotels in Erice and Taormina are particularly good.

Hotels in Italy are classified by stars as in the rest of Europe. However, the grading is not standard and prices can vary considerably, even within the same star category. A 3-star hotel in Taormina for example may be better (and more expensive) than a 3-star hotel in a less fashionable town. So the prices given below can only be a guideline. The five official categories, from luxury to a simple 1-star hotel (*pensioni* were abolished in 1985), are now established by the services offered (television in each room, swimming pool, private telephone, minibar, etc.) and do not necessarily reflect quality. The prices below usually include breakfast. ✩✩✩✩✩ L: single 200 euros, double 300 euros; ✩✩✩✩✩ single 180 euros, double 250 euros; ✩✩✩✩ single 150 euros, double 180 euros; ✩✩✩ single 85 euros, double 130 euros; ✩✩ single 30 euros, double 50 euros; ✩ single 25 euros, double 40 euros.

Bed and breakfast accommodation is about 15–20 euros per person per night.

An up-to-date selection of different types of accommodation in Sicily is listed in the Guide. The selection favours well located, smaller hotels either in town centres or in particularly picturesque rural situations. Small hotels often have no restaurant, and are only able to serve breakfast, but there are usually plenty of places where you can eat nearby.

Provincial tourist boards (*APT*s) issue a free annual list of accommodation giving category, price and facilities. Local tourist offices help you to find accommodation on the spot. It is, however, advisable to book in advance, especially at Easter and in the summer. To confirm the booking you are usually asked to send a deposit (or give a credit card number and details); you have the right to claim this back if you cancel the booking at least 72 hours in advance. Hotels equipped to offer hospitality to the disabled are indicated in the *APT* hotel lists.

Breakfast (which can be disappointing and costly) is by law an optional extra charge, although a lot of hotels try to include it in the price of the room. When booking a room, always specify if you want breakfast or not. If you are staying in a 2-star or 3-star hotel in a town, it is usually well worthwhile to go round the corner to the nearest pastry shop (*pasticceria*) or *caffè* for breakfast, as Sicilians themselves do. However, in the more expensive hotels some good buffet breakfasts are now provided, but even here the standard of the 'canteen' coffee can be poor: you can always ask for an espresso or cappuccino instead. There is a large supplement if you order breakfast in your room.

In all hotels the service charges are included in the rates. The total charge is exhibited on the back of the door of the hotel room. You should beware of **extra charges** added to the bill. The drinks in the *frigo bar* in your room are extremely expensive (it is always best to buy drinks outside the hotel). Telephone calls are also more expensive if made from your room; if you are not able to use a mobile phone there is usually a pay telephone in the lobby which is the most economical way of telephoning (avoiding noisy public telephones in the streets). Hotels are now obliged by law (for tax purposes) to issue an official receipt to customers, you should not leave the premises without this, or you risk a fine.

Agriturismo, farmhouse accommodation and self-catering

Recently developed throughout Italy, *agriturismo* provides accommodation on working farms (*aziende agrituristiche*) or in country houses. Sicily now has some 200 authorised farms which offer this type of hospitality. Terms vary greatly from bed and breakfast, to full board or self-contained flats, and is highly recommended for travellers with their own transport, and for families, as an excellent (and usually cheap) way of visiting the country. Some farms require a stay of a minimum number of days. Cultural or recreational activities are sometimes also provided, such as horse riding, bowls, trekking or archery. On some farms it is possible to help with the work on a voluntary basis, milking sheep, gathering olives or fruit, harvesting wheat etc. The local *APT* offices provide information, and *agriturismo* accommodation is now also usually listed in the annual lists of hotels published by the *APT* (and a selection has been given in the main text).

Terranostra publish an annual list of *agriturismo* accommodation under the title *Vacanze e Natura*.

Paese albergo

Homeowners offer accommodation in places bereft of hotels; this is organized by the town council or the *pro loco* when there is one.

Renting accommodation

Renting villas, farmhouses, and apartments for holidays or short periods through specialised agencies has become easier and better organised in the last few years. Information from *ENIT* offices abroad, and *APT* offices in Italy.

Camping

Camping is well organised throughout Italy. An international camping carnet is useful. In Sicily, campsites are included in the local *APT* hotel lists, giving their official category (from the most expensive 4-star sites to the simplest and cheapest 1-star sites) and details of all services provided, size of the site, etc. Their classification and rates charged must be displayed at the campsite office. Some sites have been indicated in the text, with their star ratings. Caravans and campers are allowed at some sites.

Full details of the sites in Italy are published annually by the **Touring Club Italiano** (*TCI*) in *Campeggi e Villaggi Turistici in Italia*. The **Federazione Italiana del Campeggio** has an information office and booking service at 11 via Vittorio Emanuele, Calenzano, 50041 Florence, ☎ 055 882 391, 📠 055 882 5918. **Useful websites**: *Easycamping* at ✉ www.icaro.it/. *Faita* at ✉ www. camping.it/italy/.

Hostels

Religious organisations sometimes run hostels or provide accommodation at extremely advantageous prices (for example, at Caltabellotta, Piazza Armerina, Erice, etc. Information from local *APT* offices.

Youth hostels

The *Italian Youth Hostels Association (Associazione Italiana Alberghi per la Gioventù*, 44 via Cavour, 00184 Rome, ☎ 06/487 1152, ▤ 06 488 0492) publishes a free guide to the 61 hostels in Italy. A membership card of the *AIG* or the *International Youth Hostel Federation*, ▨ www.hostels-aig.org is required for access to Italian youth hostels. Details from the *Youth Hostels Association*, Trevelyan House, 8 St Stephen's Hill, St Albans, Herts AL1 2DY, ▨ www.yha.com and the *American Youth Hostel Inc*, National Offices, PO Box 37613, Washington DC 20013 7613. In Sicily youth hostels are open at present in Palermo, Catania, Taormina, Trapani, Castroreale (April–Oct), and Erice (summer only).

Food and wine

Sicilian food is generally excellent and carefully prepared, using basic ingredients of superb quality.

Bread is made either with durum wheat, *pane di semola*, or with tender wheat, *pane doppio zero*, and is often sold with a topping of sesame seeds. Wholemeal bread is called *pane integrale*. Bread is frequently made without yeast, using the sour dough method, and baked in the traditional stone ovens using lemon wood as fuel. The flavour, consistency and shapes of the bread vary from town to town and even from village to village, but it is always superlative and can be eaten quite happily by itself. In Japan, where a loaf of bread is a luxury, Sicilian bread is thought to be the best in the world, and young bakers are sent over to attend courses in Palermo. The wheat fields of Sicily provide a large amount of the durum wheat necessary for the other Italian basic food, which is of course pasta: spaghetti, macaroni and so on.

Pasta dishes include *pasta con il matarocco*, served with fresh raw tomatoes, garlic, basil and almonds mixed with olive oil; *pasta con le sarde* with fresh sardines, wild fennel, pine nuts and raisins; *spaghetti alla Norma* or *maccheroni alla Norma*, with fresh tomato, basil, fried aubergine, and grated salted ricotta cheese; pasta with courgettes or broccoli; *spaghetti al peperoncino* with red pepper and garlic (very spicy), *pasta all'arrabbiata* with a dry anchovy sauce. You are usually given dry toasted breadcrumbs instead of grated parmesan cheese to sprinkle on the pasta dishes with fish sauces. *Pasta con la mollica* is spaghetti with capers, anchovies, green olives, garlic and toasted breadcrumbs. *Bottarga*, dried tuna fish roe, is also sometimes used as a condiment for pasta, and so is cuttle-fish ink, *pasta col nero di seppia*.

Olive oil Sicilian olive oil is excellent. So many different soil types, and slight local variations in climate mean that many different varieties of olive tree can be cultivated, some of which can be traced back thousands of years, and may be native to the island. Sicily provides only 10 per cent of the entire national production of oil, but by far the largest quantity of olives for salting, both black and green. The finest groves are probably those of the province of

Trapani, around **Castelvetrano**. Here the trees are pruned to stay very small, almost bonsai size, and the olives are carefully gathered by hand, resulting in perfect oil and sublime pickles. Oil to rhapsodise over is also produced at **Caronia** (Messina), **Ragalna and Mineo** (Catania), **Syracuse**, and of course **Chiaramonte Gulfi** (Ragusa), where the precious liquid is the linchpin of the economy, and there is even an olive oil museum.

First courses A characteristic **hors d'oeuvre** or *antipasto* dish is *caponata* which contains aubergines, tomatoes, olives, capers, celery, and onion, served cold in a sweet-sour dressing. The olives of Sicily are renowned. Broad beans (*fave, fagioli*) chick peas (*ceci*) and lentils (*lenticchie*) are also often served (sometimes with pasta). *Maccu di fave* is a rich dish made with mashed broad beans. On the west coast of the island (Trapani and Erice) *cuscus con pesce* is a traditional Arab dish (couscous) made from coarse semolina steamed in an earthenware pan with spices and onion, to which a *zuppa di pesce* (fish stew) is added.

Second courses The fish in the seaside towns and villages (and on the islands) is usually extremely good, but, as elsewhere in Italy, it is generally much more expensive than meat. It is often best served simply *alla griglia* (grilled) or *arrosto* (roasted). *Zuppa di pesce* in Sicily usually consists of a wide variety of fish cooked in a herb and tomato sauce. Shellfish is abundant, and is often served fried, in a *fritto misto di mare*. *Calamari ripieni alla griglia* are grilled whole squid filled with capers, salted anchovies, olives, garlic, pine nuts, raisins, pecorino cheese and breadcrumbs. Tuna fish (*tonno*, caught off the Egadi islands) and swordfish (*pesce spada*, abundant near Messina in May, June and July) are delicious cooked *alla griglia*, *in bianco* (in oil, water and herbs) or *alla siciliana* (with capers, red pepper and herbs). *Involtini di pesce spada* are grilled roulades of swordfish covered with breadcrumbs and oil. Sardines are cooked in a variety of ways, including *sarde a beccafico* with breadcrumbs, grated cheese, pine nuts, salted anchovies, parsley, oil, sultanas, and lemon, and the exceptional fresh anchovies from the Gulf of Catania are often dressed with lemon and eaten raw as an appetiser. Meat dishes include *farsumagru*, a laborious dish to prepare, which was intended in the old days to make the most of a small amount of meat eked out with breadcrumbs, cheese, eggs, salami and herbs, to feed a large and hungry family. Delicious even today, but not the restaurant version, which is simply a meat loaf.

Desserts Fruit which is full of flavour is available throughout the year. A Sicilian orange, the *tarocco di Francofonte*, was voted the best in the world recently. It is available in February and March, but there are other varieties covering quite a large part of the year. Mandarins, tangerines, citrons, prickly pears, peaches, table grapes and melons, apricots, cherries, mulberries and medlars; the variety is astonishing. The ice creams and sorbets (*granite*) are famous, and can be made from roses and jasmine (*scorsunera*) as well as the more traditional flavours. The confectionery of Sicily is justly renowned, and ricotta cheese, almond paste and pistachio nuts are widely used. Particularly good and decorative are the marzipan fruits (*frutti di martorana*, or *pasta reale*); biscuits made with egg whites, almonds and lemon rind (*dolci di mandorla*), and *cannoli* (rolls of thin, deep fried pastry, made with red wine or Marsala, filled with ricotta, candied fruits, cinnamon, bitter chocolate and chopped pistachio). The *cassata alla siciliana* is a delicious light cake filled with ricotta and candied fruits, thought to be the oldest cake in the world. *Torrone alla giuggiulena* or *cubbaita* is made with sesame seeds, honey, toasted almonds and orange rind. Biscuits are often flavoured with sesame seeds, or filled with a rich *conserva* of figs, almonds and candied fruit. Every town and village in Sicily has its own particular cakes and nougat. The confectionery of Modica (including chocolate), Erice, Catania and Acireale is particularly good.

Sicilian wines

The local wines are usually excellent, and it is often advisable to accept the house wine (*vino della casa*), white and red are usually available. This varies a great deal but is normally a *vino da tavola* of average standard and reasonable price. Sicily now produces eighteen different DOC wines of excellent standard. DOC means *Denominazione di Origine Controllata* and is a guarantee of quality. The most famous (but not necessarily the best) Sicilian wines, widely known outside the island, are *Corvo di Salaparuta* (red and white) and *Regaleali* (red, white and rosé). The best Corvo (and the most expensive) is *Duca Enrico*. The most widely consumed white wine is *Bianco d'Alcamo*. Excellent red wines include *Donnafugata*. The Donnafugata estate has recently started producing a white wine called *Mille e una notte* which has won international prizes. The distinctly different aroma is due to the fact that the harvesting is carried out at night when the fruit is cool, the way the ancient Greeks used to do. Another newcomer which has astonished wine experts is *Cometa* from the Planeta estate near Menfi. It is a white wine produced exclusively from Fiano grapes.

A famous red wine is *Cerasuolo* produced around Vittoria, Ragusa and Comiso, and *Faro* still made by a few wine-growers near Messina. A white wine called *Capo Bianco* is also produced near Messina. The wines made from grapes cultivated on volcanic soil, can be white, red or rosé. The best known is *Etna Rosso*, which is a DOC red. *Ciclopi* is also found around Etna. *Mamertino Bianco* is produced near Castroreale. Near Catania the red *Terreforti* is sold, and near Syracuse, *Anapo* (white), *Eloro* and *Pachino* (red). In the west of the island, wines produced near Agrigento include *Menfi*, *Akragas* and *Belice*, and near Trapani the white *Capo Boeo* is produced. In the Palermo area *Casteldaccia* and *Partinico* (white) can be found. Famous dessert wines produced in Sicily are *Marsala*, still made in large quantities around Marsala; *Malvasia* from Salina in the Aeolian Islands, bottled locally by Hauner; and *Moscato* (white Muscatel) from Pantelleria or Noto. Pantelleria is also the only area to produce *Zibibbo*, truly the nectar of the gods.

Eating out

Restaurants in Italy are called *ristoranti* or *trattorie*; there is now usually no difference between the two, although a *trattoria* used to be less smart (and usually cheaper) than a *ristorante*. The least pretentious restaurant almost invariably provides the best value. Almost every locality has a simple (often family run) restaurant which caters for the local residents; the decor is usually very simple and the food excellent value. This type of restaurant does not always offer a menu and the choice is usually limited to three or four first courses, and three or four second courses, with only fruit as a sweet. The more sophisticated restaurants are more attractive and comfortable and often larger and you can sometimes eat at tables outside. They display a menu outside, and are also usually considerably more expensive. In all restaurants it is acceptable to order a first course only, or skip the first course and have only a second course. Note that fish is always the most expensive item on the menu in any restaurant. Service is slow, but that does not upset Sicilians at all. Part of the fun of eating out is to dress up a little, talk to one's friends, admire the other people, be admired in one's turn, all in the comfortable knowledge that the food is being prepared especially for you, and not being warmed up in the microwave.

Meal times Lunch is normally around 13.00 or 13.30, while dinner is around 20.00 or 21.00. Prices include service, unless otherwise stated on the menu. **Tipping** is therefore not necessary, but a few euros can be left on the table to convey appreciation. Restaurants are now obliged by law (for tax purposes) to issue an official receipt (*ricevuta fiscale*) to customers, you should not leave the premises without this document, or you risk a fine.

Restaurant prices

A small up-to-date selection of restaurants has been given in each chapter, which is by no means exhaustive. The restaurants have been divided into three categories (€€€, €€, and €) to reflect current price ranges:

€€€ luxury restaurants, where the prices are likely to be over €30 a head (and sometimes well over €50 a head). These are among the most famous restaurants in Sicily and are well worth a visit, at least once in the course of a holiday.

€€ first class restaurants where the prices range from €20 and above. These are generally comfortable, with good service, but are not cheap.

€ simple establishments where you can eat for around €15 a head, or less. Although simple, and by no means 'smart', the food in this category which often includes local specialities, is usually the best value.

Restaurant and wine guides

Some of the best annual guides to eating out in Italy (only available in Italian) are published by **Gambero Rosso**, *Ristoranti d'Italia* and **Slow Food** *Osterie d'Italia*, (a guide to cheaper eating). There is also an annual guide to Italian wines published jointly by **Gambero Rosso** and **Slow Food**. Specialised annual guides to restaurants (mostly in the €€€ and €€ price ranges) include the red **Michelin** guide (*Italia: hotel-ristoranti*); *I Ristoranti di Veronelli*, and *Alberghi e Ristoranti* by the *TCI* ▣ www-e-ristoranti.it.

Pizzerie and self-service restaurants

Pizza (a popular and cheap food throughout Italy), always flash-baked on order, usually in a stone oven which in Sicily uses lemon wood as fuel, is served in a *pizzeria*. They are usually open only in the evening. Excellent **hot snacks**, including ready-cooked pizza in large rectangular pans, are served in a *rosticceria* or *tavola calda*. Some of these have no seating accommodation and sell food to take away or eat on the spot. Typical **Sicilian snacks** are *arancini di riso*, rice balls fried in breadcrumbs and filled with cheese, or meat, tomato and peas.

For **picnics**, sandwiches (*panini*) are made up on request (with ham, salami, cheese, anchovies, tuna fish, etc.) at *salumerie* and *alimentari* (grocery shops) and *panifici* (bakeries). Bakeries often also sell delicious individual pizzas, *focacce* or *schiacciate*, bread or puff pastry topped or filled with cheese, spinach, tomato, salted anchovies, ham, etc., they also usually sell good sweet buns, rolls and cakes. Some of the best places to picnic in towns have been indicated in each section in the main text.

Cafés, bars and pastry shops

Cafés and bars (*caffè* or *pasticcerie*) are comfortable and pleasant places to sit and have a tasty snack, and soft drinks, wines and spirits are also available. A selection of these has been given in each section in the main text. They are open all day, and most Italians eat the excellent refreshments they serve standing up. You pay the cashier first and show the receipt to the barman in order to get served. In almost all bars, if you sit at a table you are charged considerably more and are given waiter service (you should not pay first). However, some simple bars have a few tables which can be used with no extra charge (it is always best to ask before sitting down). Black coffee (*caffè* or *espresso*) can be ordered diluted (*alto*, *lungo* or *americano*) or with a dash of milk (*macchiato*), with a liqueur (*corretto*), or with hot milk (*cappuccino* or *caffè latte*). In summer iced coffee (*caffè freddo*) is served. A popular summer drink is almond milk (*latte di mandorla*), made with crushed almonds and sugar diluted with water and chilled (the best will be found in Catania and Modica). Very sweet, it is surprisingly refreshing. In town centres kiosks serve inexpensive drinks; freshly squeezed lemon juice with soda water and a pinch of salt is one of the most popular. Kiosk owners also make their own syrups which are diluted with soda water.

Sicily is particularly famous for its cakes and ice creams. A pastry shop (usually also a café) always sells the best cakes since they are made on the premises. Delicious local specialities are still produced (see above). Ice creams are nearly always made on the premises and are fresh and imaginative.

Getting around

By car

The standard of roads on the island has improved in recent years. However, some of the main roads have rough stretches, while the condition of secondary roads can be unexpectedly good. The roads through the beautiful country in the mountainous interior of the island, with wonderful views, carry very little traffic but are often very tortuous and slow. In the larger towns the traffic tends to be chaotic (with excessive use of car horns), the roads congested and parking difficult. You are strongly recommended to park outside the centre and explore towns on foot. Signposting is erratic and can be virtually non-existent especially in large towns. However, hotels are almost always clearly signposted (yellow signs). Information offices are marked with a black and white '*i*' symbol throughout Italy, on a brown, yellow or blue background. Monuments of interest are also often signposted (yellow or brown signs).

Motorways (*autostrade*) are indicated by green signs (and normal roads by blue signs). At the entrance to motorways, the two directions are indicated by the name of the most important town (and not by the nearest town) which can be momentarily confusing. Not only are they a convenient and fast way of travelling if you are restricted for time, they often provide panoramic views of the countryside, crossing difficult terrain by means of viaducts and tunnels, and in places they are spectacularly beautiful.

Motorways link Messina to Catania, Catania to Palermo, Palermo to Trapani, and Palermo to Mazara del Vallo. The convenience of being able to reach Palermo from Catania in under three hours has transformed communications between the western and eastern half of the island. The motorway from Messina to Palermo is now almost completed, some sections are absolutely stunning. The project to build a motorway from Catania to Syracuse and from there to Gela is now under way again at last. **Tolls** are charged according to the rating of the vehicle and the distance covered, although no tolls are charged on the last stretch of the motorway on the mainland from Salerno to Reggio Calabria, and in Sicily the motorways from Palermo to Catania, and from Palermo to Mazara del Vallo, are also toll free.

Petrol stations and service areas exist on most motorways and are open 24 hours a day. If purchasing fuel or oil at a motorway service station you are strongly advised to check that you have been given the right amount, that the seal on the oil can is intact and that you have been given the correct change. Unscrupulous service station staff know that it is difficult for a tourist to go back if a fraud is discovered. Some of the main motorways have SOS points every two kilometres. Petrol stations in towns are also open 24 hours but otherwise their opening times are: 07.00–12.00, 15.00–20.00; winter 07.30–12.30, 14.30–19.00. There are now quite a number of self-service petrol stations open 24hrs operated by euro bank notes. Petrol in Italy costs more than in England, and a lot more than in America.

Car parking Although most towns on the Italian mainland have at last taken the wise step of closing their historic centres to traffic, many town centres in Sicily (including Palermo) are still open to cars. This makes driving and parking extremely difficult. On approaching a town, the white signs for *centro* (with a bull's eye) should be followed towards the historic centre. Car parks are also sometimes indicated by blue P signs; where parking is a particular problem, the best places to park near the centre have been mentioned in the main text. Some car parks are free and some charge an hourly tariff. In the larger towns it is usually a good idea to look for a garage which provides parking space (these usually have a blue P sign and a blue and white striped entrance); tariffs are charged by the hour, by the day, or overnight. It is forbidden to park in front of a gate or doorway marked with a *passo carrabile* (blue and red) sign. Always lock your car when parked and never leave anything of value inside it.

Car hire is available in the main Sicilian towns and at Palermo and Catania airports. Arrangements for car hire in Italy can also be made through *Alitalia* or *British Airways* (at specially advantageous rates in conjunction with their flights). Website: ◪ www.holidayautos.co.uk. Firms include:
Sicily by Car Palermo ☎ 091/328531; Rome ☎ 06/8840235; Milan ☎ 02/29403525
Maggiore Catania, ☎ 095/536927
Avis Catania ☎ 095/340500; Palermo ☎ 091/591684
Hertz Catania ☎ 095/341595; Palermo ☎ 091/591682
Breakdown services Temporary membership of the *Automobile Club d'Italia* (*ACI*) can be taken out on the frontier or in Italy. The headquarters of *ACI* in Palermo is at 6 viale delle Alpi (branch offices in all the main towns). They provide a breakdown service (*Soccorso ACI*, ☎ 116).

Rules of the road Italian law requires that you carry a valid driving licence and identity card or passport when travelling (see p 13). It is obligatory to keep a red triangle in the car in case of accident or breakdown. This serves as a warning to other traffic when placed on the road at a distance of 50 metres from the stationary car. It is now compulsory to wear seat belts in the front seat of cars in Italy, and children should sit in the back. Driving in Italy is generally faster (and often more aggressive) than driving in Britain or America. Road signs are now more or less standardised to the international codes, but certain habits differ radically from those in Britain or America. Unless otherwise indicated, cars entering a road from the right are given precedence. If a driver flashes his headlights, it means he is proceeding and *not* giving you precedence. In towns, Italian drivers are very fond of changing lanes without much warning. Some crossroads in small towns have unexpected 'stop' signs. Italian drivers tend to ignore pedestrian crossings. In towns, beware of motorbikes, mopeds and scooters, the drivers of which seem to consider that they always have right of way. At least, Sicilians never drink and drive, but their driving style is fierce. When not behind the wheel, however, the motorists are quite kind people. Stress and road rage are unknown. A little patience and a little practice, and newcomers will find that driving in this way is really quite pleasant after all.

The police (see p 35) sometimes set up road blocks to check cars and their drivers: it is important to stop at once if you are waved down by a policeman at the side of a road and you must show them your driving licence, your identity card and the car documents.

By rail
Sicilian trains are quite comfortable but notoriously slow and in some places the service is infrequent. The two main lines, Messina to Palermo, and Messina to Catania and Syracuse run a frequent service, but almost all the fast trains are through trains from the Italian mainland (Naples, Rome, Milan, etc.) and more often than not subject to considerable delays. Some of the minor secondary lines on the island have recently been closed and substituted by bus connections. With careful planning and with the help of the regional timetables (see below) it is still possible to reach many places by rail, and details of the lines have been given in the Guide, although local buses are now often quicker and more frequent than train services.

The Italian State Railways, *FS; Ferrovie dello Stato, Trenitalia,* ✉ www.fs-on-line.it; ✉ www.trenitalia.com, run various categories of trains: *ES* (*Eurostar*), international express trains (with a special supplement, approximately 30 per cent of the normal single fare) running between the main Italian and European cities (with obligatory seat reservation since no standing passengers are permitted), with first- and second-class carriages; *EC* and *IC* (*Eurocity* and *Intercity*), international and national express trains, with a supplement (but cheaper than the Eurostar supplement); *Espressi*, long-distance trains (both classes) not as fast as the Intercity trains; *Diretti*, although not stopping at every station, a good deal slower than *Espressi*; *Interregionali*, local trains stopping at most stations; and *Regionali*, local trains stopping at all stations, mostly with second-class carriages only.

Buying tickets and booking a seat Tickets (valid for two months after the day sold) must be bought before the journey, otherwise a fairly large supplement has to be paid to the ticket-collector on the train. In order to validate your ticket it has to be stamped at an automatic machine in the railway station before starting the journey (there is always a machine at the beginning of each platform and sometimes half-way up the platform). If, for some reason, you fail to do this, try to find the ticket conductor on the train before he finds you. Once the ticket has been stamped it is valid for 6 hours for distances up to 200km, and for 24 hours for distances over 200km.

The most convenient way of buying rail tickets (and making seat reservations) is from a travel agent (but only those who are agents for the Italian State Railways), as there are often long queues at the station ticket offices. Some trains charge a special supplement (see above), and on some seats must be booked in advance (*prenotazione obbligatorio*): when buying tickets you therefore have to specify which category of train you intend to take as well as the destination. Trains in Italy are usually crowded especially at holiday time and in summer; and it is now always advisable to book your seat for long-distance journeys when buying a ticket for a *Eurocity* or *Intercity* train. There is a booking fee and the service is available from 2 months to 3 hours before departure. In the main stations the better known credit cards are now generally accepted and there is a special ticket window (*sportello*) which must be used when buying a ticket with a credit card.

Discounts and railcard options In Italy fares are still much lower than in Britain. Children under the age of 4 travel free, and between the ages of 4 and 12 travel half price, and there are certain reductions for families. For travellers over the age of 60 (with Senior Citizen Railcards), the **Carta Res** (valid one year) offers a 30 per cent reduction on international rail fares. The Inter-rail card (valid 1 month) which can be purchased in Britain by young people up to the age of 26, is valid in Italy (and allows a reduction of 50 per cent on normal fares). In Italy the **Carta d'Argento** and the **Carta Verde** (valid for one year) allow a reduction on rail fares for those over 60, and between the ages of 12 and 26. A **Chilometrico** ticket is valid for 3000km (and can be used by up to five people at the same time) for a maximum of 20 journeys. A **Eurodomino** ticket is valid for one month's travel in a number of European countries (for 3, 5, or 10 days). You can claim reimbursement (on payment of a small penalty) for unused tickets and sleepers not later than 24 hours before the departure of the train. Bicycles are allowed on most trains (except Eurostar trains): a day ticket costs €3.50 on slow trains, and €7 on *Intercity*. A **Carta Blu** is available for the disabled, and certain trains have special facilities (information from the main railway stations).

Timetables The timetable for the train services changes on about 26 September and 31 May every year. Excellent timetables are published twice a year by the Italian State Railways (*In Treno*; one volume for the whole of Italy) and by Pozzorario in several volumes (*Sud e Centro Italia* covers Sicily). These can be purchased at newsstands and railway stations.

Left luggage offices are usually open 24 hrs at the main stations; at smaller stations they often close at night, and for a few hours in the middle of the day.

Porters are entitled to a fixed payment (shown on noticeboards at all stations) for each piece of baggage, but trollies are usually available in the larger stations.

Restaurant cars (sometimes self-service) are attached to most international and internal long-distance trains. Also, on most express trains, snacks, hot coffee and drinks are sold throughout the journey from a trolley wheeled down the train.

At every large station snacks are on sale from trolleys on the platform and you can buy them from the train window.

Sleeping cars with couchettes, or first- and second-class cabins, are carried on certain trains from the mainland, as well as 'Sleeperette' compartments with reclining seats (first-class only).

By bus

In Sicily it is now easier to reach some destinations by bus rather than by train, since the buses are sometimes quicker and almost always more punctual than trains. Local buses, run by numerous different companies, abound between the main towns in Sicily. It is, however, difficult to obtain accurate information about these services outside Italy. Some information is available from *Citalia*, London, or from the local tourist offices (*APT*) in Italy. The names of the local bus companies and their town termini have been given where possible in the Guide. The fastest way by public transport from Palermo to Catania is by the direct bus service operated by *SAIS* along the motorway (service c every hour in 2 hrs 40 mins.) Other comfortable express coaches run direct by motorway from Palermo to Trapani and from Messina to Catania. Fares are normally comparable to rail fares and luggage is carried free of charge.

Island bus services The main bus companies operating on the island include: *AST*, piazza Marina, Palermo, ☎ 091/620811; piazza delle Poste, Syracuse, ☎ 0931/462711; 230 via Sturzo, Catania, close to railway station, ☎ 095/7461096. *SAIS/INTERBUS*, via Balsamo, Palermo (☎ 091/6166028); 28 via Trieste, Syracuse, ☎ 0931/66710; 185 via D'Amico, Catania, ☎ 095/536168. *Segesta*, 26 via Balsamo, Palermo, ☎ 091/6167919.

Town buses It is almost always necessary to purchase tickets before boarding (at tobacconists, bars, newspaper kiosks, information offices, etc.) and stamp them on board at automatic machines. It is usually best to explore towns on foot as the buses in the big cities tend to be overcrowded, infrequent, and slow, but it is well worth taking a bus to the places of interest on the outskirts of towns (and details of these have been given in the Guide).

Taxis

Taxis (painted white) all have taximeters: it is advisable to make sure these are operational before setting off. Taxis are hired from ranks or by telephone, there are no cruising taxis. When you telephone for a taxi you are given the approximate arrival time and the number of the taxi. A small tip of about €1 can be given to the driver, but is often not expected. A supplement for night service and for luggage is charged. There is a heavy surplus charge when the destination is outside the town limits (ask roughly how much the fare is likely to be). In Sicily taxis are noticeably more expensive than in most other places in Italy, usually with a minimum charge of €5.

Local tourist offices

Regional State Tourist Office
This is in Palermo: *Assessorato Regionale del Turismo*, 11 via Notarbartolo (☎ 091/6968033).

Provincial tourist boards
The nine provinces of Sicily each have their own tourist boards, called *APT* (*Aziende di Promozione Turistica*). These provide invaluable help to travellers, supplying a free accommodation list (revised annually), including hotels, farm holidays, and campsites; up-to-date information on museum opening times and annual events; and information about local transport. The *APT* usually distribute, free of charge, illustrated pamphlets about the province, sometimes with good town plans, etc. The headquarters in Palermo are normally open Monday–Saturday 08.00–14.00, but nearly all the provinces also have separate *APT* information offices which often open in the afternoon. Subsidiary information offices are sometimes open in railway stations, airports, or ports (usually in summer only). Some local tourist boards (*Aziende Autonome di Soggiorno e Turismo* or AAST) still operate in the main tourist centres. Addresses for all of these offices are given in the practical information sections in the Guide.

APT offices in Sicily
Palermo 35 piazza Castelnuovo, ☎ 091/6058351; 🖷 091/586338; ✉ www.palermotourism.com; ✉ www.aapit.pa.it.
Trapani 27 via S. Francesco d'Assisi, ☎ 0923/29000; 🖷 0923/29430; ✉ www.cinet.it/apt.
Agrigento 255 viale della Vittoria, ☎ 0922/401352; 🖷 0922/25185; ✉ www.provincia.agrigento.it.
Caltanissetta 109 corso Vittorio Emanuele, ☎ 0934/21089; 🖷 0934/21239; ✉ www.aapit.cl.it.
Catania 10 via Domenico Cimarosa, ☎ 095/7306233; 🖷 095/316407; ✉ www.apt-catania.com; ✉ www.apt.catania.it.
Enna 411 via Roma, ☎ 0935/528228; 🖷 0935/528229, ✉ www.apt_enna.com.
Ragusa 33 via Capitano Bocchieri, Ragusa Ibla, ☎ 0932/621421; 🖷 0932/623467, ✉ www.ragusaturismo.com.
Syracuse 45 via S. Sebastiano, ☎ 0931/67710; 🖷 0931/67803, ✉ www.apt_siracusa.it.
Messina 301 via Calabria (corner of via Capria), ☎ 090/674236, 🖷 090/6411047; ✉ www.aapitme.it.

Language

Although many people speak a little English, some basic Italian is helpful for everday dealings. If you are able to say a few words and phrases your efforts will be much appreciated. See also the Food and Wine section for relevant vocabulary.

good morning *buon giorno*
good afternoon/good evening *buona sera*
good night *buona notte*
goodbye *arrivederci*
hello/goodbye (informal) *ciao*
see you later *a più tardi*
what is your name? *come si chiama/ come ti chiami?* (informal) my name is *mi chiamo ...*

yes/no *si/no*
okay *va bene*
please *per favore*
thank you *grazie*

today *oggi*
tomorrow *domani*
yesterday *ieri*
now *adesso*
later *più tardi*
in the morning *di mattina*
in the afternoon/evening *di pomeriggio/di sera*
at night *di notte*
what time is it? *che ore sono?*
at what time? *a che ora?*
when? *quando?*

I would like *vorrei*
do you have ...? *ha ...?/avete ...?* (plural)
where is ...? *dov'è ...?*
how much is it? *quanto è?*
the bill *il conto*
where are the toilets? *dove sono i gabinetti?*

do you speak English? *parla inglese?*
I don't understand *non capisco*

cold/hot *freddo/caldo*
with/without *con/senza*
open/closed *aperto/chiuso*
cheap/expensive *economico/caro*

left/right/straight on *sinistra/destra/ diritto*
railway station *stazione ferroviaria*
bus station *stazione degli autobus*
airport *aeroporto*
ticket *biglietto*
police station *ufficio di polizia/questura*
hospital *ospedale*
doctor *medico*
dentist *dentista*
aspirin *aspirina*

town council/town hall *comune*
municipality/town hall *municipio*
old town (centre) *centro storico*
café (which sells cakes) *pasticceria/e*
ice cream parlour *gelateria*

Monday *lunedì*
Tuesday *martedì*
Wednesday *mercoledì*
Thursday *giovedì*
Friday *venerdì*
Saturday *sabato*
Sunday *domenica*

spring *primavera*
summer *estate*
autumn *autunno*
winter *inverno*
January *gennaio*
February *febbraio*
March *marzo*
April *aprile*
May *maggio*
June *giugno*
July *luglio*
August *agosto*
September *settembre*
October *ottobre*
November *novembre*
December *dicembre*

Museums and churches

Museums

The opening times of museums and monuments have been given in the text but they vary and often change without warning: when possible it is always advisable to consult the local tourist office (*APT*) on arrival about the up-to-date times. Many museums and archaeological sites in Sicily are now open seven days a week. State-owned museums and monuments are usually open 09.00–14.00, Sun & PH 09.00–13.00 and are sometimes closed on Mondays. However, they are extending their opening times; some now open in the afternoon on certain days and others stay open seven days a week. There is no standard timetable and you should take great care to allow enough time for variations in the hours shown in the text when planning a visit to a museum or monument. Some museums are closed on the main public holidays: 1 January, Easter, 1 May, 15 August and Christmas Day (although there is now a policy to keep at least a few of them open on these days in the larger cities, information has to be obtained there and then).

Admission charges and discounts Admission charges vary but are usually around €4.50 euros for the main regional museums and archaeological sites, and €3.00 for local museums.

British citizens under the age of 18 and over the age of 65 are entitled to free admission to state-owned museums and monuments in Italy (because of reciprocal arrangements in Britain), but must exhibit a valid ID card or passport.

For non state-owned museums there is a reduced rate for young people between the ages of 18 and 25, and in some cities tickets can be purchased which allow entrance to several monuments at a lower cost. During Museum Week, the *Settimana per i Beni Culturali e Ambientali*, entry is free to all state-owned museums, and others are specially opened: traditionally in early December, for the last few years it has been held instead in March.

Churches

Churches are almost always closed for a considerable period during the middle of the day (11.30 or 12.00 to 16.00 or 17.00), although they usually open very early in the morning (at 07.00 or 08.00). Small churches and oratories are often open only in the early morning, or just for services, but it is sometimes possible to find the key by asking locally. The sacristan will show closed chapels, crypts, etc. and sometimes expects a tip. Many pictures and frescoes are difficult to see without lights which are sometimes provided (operated by coins); a torch and binoculars are always useful. Some churches now ask that sightseers do not enter during a service, but normally you may do so, provided you are silent and do not approach the altar in use. An entrance fee is becoming customary for admission to cloisters, bell towers, etc. You are not allowed to enter churches wearing shorts, even the knee-length Bermuda style, miniskirts, or with bare shoulders. It is unseemly to eat or drink inside the churches, even water. Photography is permitted, even with flash, but obviously not when the priest is saying Mass.

Festivals and public holidays

Traditional festivals and feast days

There are a number of traditional festivals and feast days in Sicily which are of the greatest interest. The towns become extremely lively and the central procession or competition is always accompanied by numerous celebrations on the side; local markets are usually held at the same time and there are magnificent fireworks. They are particularly exciting events for children. The local *APT* offices will provide particulars, and some of the most important have been described in the main text. Further details are available on ✉ www.festedisicilia.it. The following list groups some of them according to season.

January The Epiphany is celebrated in Piana degli Albanesi (on 6 January). On 20 January festivities in honour of **S. Sebastiano** take place at Acireale, Syracuse and Mistretta.

February and March In the first week in February the **Sagra del mandorlo in fiore** is held in Agrigento. From the 3–5 February **S. Agata** is celebrated in Catania. On 19 February there are more festivities in honour of **S. Corrado** at Noto. **Carnival celebrations** at Acireale, Palazzolo Acreide, Termini Imerese and Sciacca. The Feast of St Joseph (19 March) is celebrated with the preparation of special banquets (originally for the poor) called '**cene di S. Giuseppe**' and elaborate loaves of bread which are hung to decorate the streets, at Salemi and Santa Croce Camerina.

Easter week is particularly important at S. Biagio Platani, where the people plan the '**archi di Pasqua**' for a whole year; arches and chandeliers, columns and pinnacles, all made of palm leaves, dates, bread, oranges, canes and flowers decorate the streets of the little town. Caltanissetta (Maundy Thursday), Trapani (Good Friday), Erice (Good Friday), Noto (**S. Spina**; Good Friday), Castelvetrano (Easter Sunday), Prizzi (Easter Sunday; 'dance of the devils'), Modica, Caltagirone, Adrano, Enna, Piana degli Albanesi, S. Fratello (Maundy Thursday and Good Friday; **Festa dei Giudei**) and Castroreale.

After Easter The **Palio di S. Vincenzo** is run at Acate, and on 23 April Castelmola and Modica hold the **Festa di S. Giorgio**.
May At Isnello, on 30 April–1 May there is a feast in honour of the Santissimo Crocifisso. On the first and second Sunday in May Syracuse celebrates St Lucy, and on the third Sunday in May the **Infiorata** is held in Noto. On 10 May there is a feast at Trecastagni and S. Alfio. On the last Sunday in May Ragusa Ibla commemorates **S. Giorgio** and Casteltermini holds the **Tataratà** feast. Also in May **S. Gandolfo** is celebrated at Polizzi Generosa, and the **Settimana delle Egadi** usually takes place at the end of May. **Corpus Domini** (May or early June) is celebrated in Cefalù with the **Festa della Frottola**.

June On 3 June Messina has celebrations in honour of the **Madonna della Lettera**. At the end of June **S. Pietro** is celebrated in Modica, **S. Paolo** in Palazzolo Acreide, and the **Ecce Homo** in Sclafani Bagni. The summer solstice (24 June) is celebrated at Alcara Li Fusi with the pagan **Festa del Muzzuni**.

July Enna honours the **Madonna della Visitazione** (2 July). The famous **Festino di S. Rosalia** takes place in Palermo from 10–15 July. The **Scala** is illuminated at Caltagirone on 24–25 July.

August From 2–6 August there are festivities in honour of S. Salvatore at Cefalù, and on 13–14 August the Palio dei Normanni is held in piazza Armerina. Messina has processions of the Giganti and the Vara on 13–15 August, and 15 August is also celebrated at Randazzo. Mistretta celebrates S. Sebastiano on 18 August, and Ragusa celebrates S. Giovanni on 29 August. There is an historical pageant in August at Castelbuono. On the last Sunday in August and the first Sunday in September the feast of S. Corrado takes place in Noto.

September A hazelnut fair is held at Polizzi Generosa and the **Madonna della Luce** is celebrated at Mistretta. There is a pilgrimage to the sanctuary of Gibilmanna on 8 September, and on 8–9 September **S. Giacomo** is celebrated at Gratteri.

October A pistachio festival is held in early October at Bronte, and an autumn festival at Zafferana Etnea on each Sunday in October.

December In Syracuse the **Immacolata** feast takes place on 8 December and the feast in honour of St Lucy on 13 December. A feast is held on 26 December in Polizzi Generosa.

Music and theatre festivals
Music festivals are held in summer at Agrigento, Erice, Noto, Taormina, Tindari and Trapani. Summer theatre festivals include those at Segesta, Syracuse, Gibellina and Catania. There is often a festival of plays by Pirandello at his birthplace near Agrigento. In Taormina in June or July an international film festival takes place. In November a music festival is held in the cathedral of Monreale, and in December a festival of international folk music is played on popular instruments in Erice.

Public holidays
Italian national holidays when banks, offices, shops and schools are closed are: 1 January (New Year), 25 April (Liberation Day), Easter Monday, 1 May (Labour Day), 15 August (Assumption), 1 November (All Saints' Day), 8 December (Immaculate Conception), Christmas Day and 26 December (St Stephen). Each town keeps its patron saint's day as a holiday.

 # Additional information

Banks
In general, banks are open Monday–Friday 08.30–13.30, 14.45–15.45 (or 14.30–15.30); closed Saturday, Sunday and public holidays. Nowadays, in large towns the central banks do not close at midday and are also open on Saturday mornings. The commission on cashing travellers' cheques can be quite high. Money can also be changed at exchange offices (*cambio*), in travel agencies, some post offices and main railway stations. Exchange offices are usually open seven

days a week at airports and main railway stations. At hotels, restaurants, and shops money can sometimes be exchanged (but usually at a lower rate).

Crime and personal security

For all emergencies, ☎ 113. Pickpocketing is a widespread problem in large towns all over Italy: it is always advisable not to carry valuables in handbags and to be particularly careful on public transport. Cash and documents etc. can be left in hotel safes. It is a good idea to make photocopies of all important documents in case of loss. You are strongly advised to carry some valid means of identity with you at all times while in Italy, since you can be held at a police station if you are stopped and found to be without a form of identification.

There are three categories of policemen in Italy: *vigili urbani*, the municipal police (who wear blue uniform in winter and white during the summer and hats similar to London policemen); *carabinieri*, the military police who have local offices in every town and village (and who wear a black uniform with a red stripe down the side of their trousers); and the *polizia di stato*, State police (who wear dark blue jackets and light blue trousers).

Crime should be reported at once. A detailed statement has to be given in order to get an official document confirming loss or damage (essential for insurance claims). Interpreters are usually provided.

Dress codes

If you are wearing shorts or miniskirts, or have bare shoulders, you can be refused admission to some churches.

Electric current

The electricity supply is 220 watts. Visitors may need round, two-pin Continental plugs for some appliances.

> ### Emergency services
> All emergencies ☎ 113. The switchboard will connect you to the necessary service.
> Ambulance and first aid services ☎ 118
> Fire brigade ☎ 115
> Police ☎ 112 or ☎ 113
> Road assistance ☎ 116

Local handicrafts

The range and the quality of handicrafts available in Sicily is almost unbeliev-able, and probably unique in Europe. **Baskets** are still made in a style distinctive to the island and a few local basket-makers' workshops can still be found. Sicilian baskets are also sometimes sold at weekly markets and in some hardware shops or *ferramenta*, and these are the best places for finding hand-wrought **copper pots and pans**. Splendid **pottery** can be found everywhere. The colours and the designs vary from place to place. Caltagirone, Santo Stefano di Camastra, Patti, Burgio and Sciacca are renowned for this art, while a late starter, Monreale, is fast catching up with the others.

The shepherds of Maletto still make the **bagpipes**, *ciaramedda*, which they bring down to the towns to play the lullabies for Baby Jesus at Christmas. Hand-made **pipes for smokers** are made in Caltanissetta. In Syracuse there are many artisans who make paper from **papyrus**, in different qualities, and near Acireale there is a craftsman who makes high quality **paper** using cotton fibre, receiving orders from artists all over the world. Colourful **rag rugs**, called *frazzate*, are woven in Erice and in the villages of the Nebrodi Mountains.

The unique and traditional **marionette puppets** called *pupi* are beautifully made by the local people, often using very simple materials—for example, until a few years ago, the armour was made out of flattened pieces of tin cans.

Coral (imported) is still worked in Trapani and amazing **coral-look jewellery** is also made here out of salt paste. Obsidian jewellery is made on the island of Lipari. High quality **soap**, made with olive or almond oil, wild flowers, herbs, spices and even lava, is made in Acicastello, and can be found in the shops of Taormina and Mount Etna. In Agrigento there is a place where they make **model temples** out of cork.

Huge bronze **church bells** are still cast in Tortorici, while one of the last craftsmen in Europe to make **church clocks** works in Bisacquino.

Hand-made lace and embroidery, made by the women of Mirabella Imbaccari, Santa Caterina Villermosa, Collesano, Castelmola and Taormina, are expensive but every piece is a work of art. **Wrought iron bedsteads**, **candlesticks**, **lamps** and other objects testify to the skill of the blacksmiths, while if the beautiful carved stone doorways are a little too heavy to take home, lovely souvenirs in **lava or limestone** can be found in Catania and on Mount Etna.

The last word goes to the **confectioners**, whose wondrous mastery of their craft can be seen in every pastry shop on the island.

Newspapers

The most prestigious national daily newspapers are *Il Corriere della Sera* and *La Repubblica*. *La Sicilia* is the most important Sicilian daily, with separate editions for each of the provinces, ▨ www.lasiciliaweb.com. *Il Giornale di Sicilia*, issued in Palermo, and *La Gazzetta del Sud* (Messina) are useful for local listings and bus and train timetables, ▨ www.gds.it.

Opening hours

Shops are generally open 09.00–13.00 and 16.00–19.30, including Saturday, and for most of the year are closed on Monday morning. Food shops usually open at 07.30/08.00–13.00 and 17.00–19.30/20.00, and for most of the year are closed one afternoon a week (usually Wednesday). In summer (mid-June to mid-September) some shops close on Saturday afternoon instead. In towns, some of the big stores now stay open all day and on Sunday morning. Government offices usually work Mon–Fri 08.00–13.30 or 14.00. For bank opening hours see p 34.

Pharmacies

First-aid services (*pronto soccorso*) are available at all hospitals, railway stations and airports. **Chemists** (*farmacie*) are usually open Mon–Sat 09.00–13.00, 15.30–19.30, but they all close one day a week, usually Saturday or Thursday. They take turns to keep at least one open in every neighbourhood on Thursdays, Saturdays, Sundays and public holidays (listed on the door of every chemist).

In every town there is also at least one chemist open at night (opening times are shown on the door). For emergencies ☎ 113.

Public toilets

Public toilets are scarce in Italy but bars, cafés and restaurants should have toilets, including those for disabled patrons (generally speaking the larger the bar, the better the facilities). Nearly all museums now have toilets.

Sport and nature

Cycling, Trekking and Hiking *Siciclando Bike Tour Service*, ☎ 091/495065, ☒ www.siciclando.com. Maps, information and tours, either by bike or on foot.

Climbing and speleology *Club Alpino Siciliano*, ☎ and 🖷 091/581323; *Club Alpino Italiano* ☎ and 🖷 091/329407, ☒ caipalermo@palermoweb.com.

Paragliding, Hang gliding and Microlighting *Angelo d'Arrigo*, ☒ www.etnacenter.net (Eastern Sicily); *Accademia Siciliana Volo Libero*, Piana degli Albanesi ☎ 091/6640535, ☒ www.asvl.it (Western Sicily).

Birdwatching *LIPU* (*Lega Italiana Protezione Uccelli*) ☎ 091/6117898, 🖷 091/323804, ☒ www.lipusicilia.it.

Nature and the environment *WWF* (*World Wide Fund for Nature*) ☎ 091/583040, 🖷 091/333468, ☒ www.wwf.it; *Ente Fauna Siciliana* ☎ 338/4888822, ☒ www.entefaunasiciliana.it; *Lega Ambiente* ☎ 091/301663, 🖷 091/6264139, ☒ www.legambiente.sicilia.it; *Forestry Commission* (runs many of the parks) *Azienda Foreste Demaniali Della Regione Siciliana* ☎ 091/6274235, ☒ www.regione.sicilia.it/agricoltura/azforeste.

Telephone and postal services

There are numerous public telephones all over Italy in kiosks, bars, restaurants etc. These are operated by telephone cards (*schede telefoniche*) which can be purchased from tobacconists (*tabacchi*, displaying a black 'T' sign), bars, newsstands and post offices. Telephone numbers in Italy can have from four to eight numbers. All numbers have an area code, which always has to be dialled, even if making a local call. If calling Italy from abroad, the full area code (ie. 091 for Palermo) now has to be used after the international code for Italy.

Directory assistance (in Italian) is available by ☎ 12. Most cities in the world can now by dialled direct from Italy. To make a collect call, or for a translator service in English, French, German or Arabic, the number is ☎ 170; for a range of information on telephone services, ☎ 176 will connect you to a multilingual operator. Numbers beginning with 800 are free; those beginning with 848 or 840 are low cost for the caller. 'Columbus' cards (for 19 countries including western Europe and North America) and *schede telefoniche internazionali* (for the rest of the world) have a set value and are valid for 3 years from the date of purchase; access is obtained by dialling a pin code.

Central post offices in large towns are now often open seven days a week 08.10–19.25. Other post offices are open Mon–Sat 08.10–13.25. **Stamps** are sold at tobacconists as well as post offices.

Tipping

Hotels and restaurants usually include a service charge in their bill, so tipping is not so common in Italy as it is in North America. If in doubt, check whether service has been included. In hotels, porters who help you find a taxi, carry your luggage and show you to your room usually expect a small tip.

BACKGROUND INFORMATION

 ## Sicilian landscape

Called *Trinacria* by the ancients because of its triangular shape, Sicily is the largest and most important of the Mediterranean islands (25,708 sq km), a place of spectacular scenery and vibrant colours. Mauve and purple mountains rise behind the hills of the interior, planted with grain since time immemorial. Renowned for its fertile soil, this is the place where it is said the goddess Demeter gave wheat to mortals. The writer Tomasi di Lampedusa compared the interior of the island to a stormy sea, suddenly frozen; a sea which changes colour constantly according to the cycle of the durum wheat: tender green in winter, gold in spring, ochre in summer. Shepherds pasture their flocks of sheep and goats on the hillsides, dotted here and there with clumps of prickly pears (*fichi d'India*), the plant symbol of the island. There is an abundance of colours: deep green citrus groves studded with orange and yellow fruits; shimmering grey-green olive trees, delicate hues in the almond orchards, and a rich fecundity in the vineyards. In early February, when they are about to explode into blossom, the peach orchards are flushed with crimson. Even the soil changes colour according to location, ranging from a reddish-orange in the west, to a yellowish-grey in the south, light brown in the interior and dark chocolate to black in the east and southeast.

Flowers are in abundance throughout the year (Persephone, Demeter's daughter, gathered flowers here). Wild chrysanthemums and bright yellow broom festoon the countryside in spring, punctuated with scarlet poppies and swathes of fuchsia-coloured clover, while the pink and white oleanders growing along the highways lift the spirits of weary travellers.

Dramatically positioned castles and ancient columns, witness to past civilisations, stand out against the often intense blue skies. Honey-coloured historic city centres survive amazingly intact. Hilltop towns bask in the sun, the old stone walls covered by a veil of starry jasmine, or a profusion of purple bougainvillea. The humblest balcony is never without a few geraniums.

A sprinkling of wondrous little islands surrounds Sicily, each with its own particular character. Mount Etna, the largest active volcano in Europe, called locally the *muntagna* (mountain) dominates everything, sometimes brooding, sometimes snow-capped, sometimes fiery, never to be taken for granted.

Physically, the island is both a continuation of the Apennine mountain chain running down the centre of mainland Italy, and of the Atlas mountains. Recent studies on the relative position of Sicily to Calabria have revealed that the Straits of Messina are actually narrower now than in former times. Lying as it does at the formation point of several fault lines in the earth's crust, caused by the continental drift, Sicily is particularly subject to earthquakes. *Fumaroles* (diminutive mud-volcanoes) and *maccalube* (thermal springs) occur frequently. Since its deforestation, the island has suffered from a shortage of water. Many of the rivers, the largest of which are the Simeto, Salso and Belice, were once navigable, but it is hard to believe that today. Most of the smaller streams are torrents and therefore dry in summer. The sea around Sicily is still rich in fish, especially in the Straits of Messina where over 140 species are known, including unusual deep-sea varieties.

Nature reserves

Some of the most beautiful parts of the island are at last becoming protected areas. The two excellently run coastal reserves of the Zingaro on the north coast, and Vendicari on the east coast, stand out not only as areas of extraordinary beauty and interest for their scenery, vegetation and birdlife, but also as examples of the success of the local population's efforts to preserve them from 'development'. They are both only accessible on foot.

There are nature reserves at the mouths of the Simeto and Fiumefreddo, at the southern and northern borders of the province of Catania. The wooded areas of the island include the Nebrodi, Madonie and Peloritan mountain ranges on the north coast, and the Bosco della Ficuzza, south of Palermo, one of the largest forests left on the island. Beautiful walks (and rides) can be taken in the Madonie Mountains south of Cefalù. Etna, one of the most fascinating areas on the island, and the Alcantara Valley are both protected regional parks.

Smaller areas, but with their own particular interest, which have also been protected, where lovely countryside can be explored, include the **Valle dell'Anapo** and the **Cava d'Ispica**. The remote plateau of **Pantalica** is also very beautiful as is the **Cava Grande**, a similar area at Cassibile. The **salt marshes** between Trapani and Marsala, interesting for their birdlife, are protected, as is the island of **S. Pantaleo** (Mozia). **Capo Bianco** and **Torre Salsa**, near Eraclea Minoa on the south coast, is another lovely stretch of coastline, purchased by the *WWF (World Wide Fund for Nature)* in 1991, with interesting vegetation and birdlife. The islands off the Sicilian coast are all of great natural beauty, particularly the **Aeolian Islands**, **Marettimo** (one of the Egadi group of islands which all now form part of the Marine Reserve) and **Pantelleria**. A well-run marine reserve protects the splendid seabed off the shore of **Ustica**.

Beaches

The sea around Sicily has suffered from pollution over the past 100 years as it has around the rest of Italy, and much of the coastline has been spoilt by new building. The industrial zones of Augusta and Gela should be avoided by visitors at all costs. An excellent guide to the best beaches in Italy, *Guida Blu*, is published by *TCI/Legambiente*. Some of the prettiest beaches can be found south of Syracuse at Cala Bernardo and Noto Marina. The south coast is generally the least spoilt part of the island, with good beaches especially around Porto Palo (south of Menfi, near Selinunte) and at Torre di Monterosso, south of Siculiana. Further east are the small resorts with some good beaches at Marina di Ragusa, Donnalucata, Cava d'Aliga and Marina di Modica. The rocky coast around Acireale and Taormina is popular for sea bathing. On the north coast there are rocky beaches at Capo di Milazzo and fine (if crowded) beaches at the resorts of Cefalù and Mondello. North of Castellammare del Golfo there is a remarkable stretch of unspoilt rocky coastline (only accessible by paths) at Cala Bianca, Cala Rossa and Baia Guidaloca, and sea bathing is allowed in the beautiful nature reserve of Zingaro and on the promontory of Capo S. Vito. The seaside resort of S. Vito lo Capo has good beaches but the best sea bathing of all is to be found on the islands, especially the Aeolian Islands, Marettimo and Pantelleria.

Historical summary

The geographical position of Sicily in the centre of the Mediterranean has, in the past, made her not only the prized possession of foreign powers but also a battle-ground between warring nations. But her long history of foreign domination has often been coloured by a brilliant mixture of traditions and cultures which has produced some of the most remarkable art in the Mediterranean world.

The earliest prehistoric finds on the island are the Palaeolithic cave paintings on Levanzo and Mount Pellegrino. The first Neolithic culture so far recognised in Sicily is that known as *Stentinello*, named after one of its typical fortified villages near Syracuse. The Aeolian Islands became important to traders for their supplies of obsidian (a volcanic glass from which sharp blades can be obtained) which was much sought after by the Mediterranean peoples around 3000 BC. In the Bronze Age, the islands were on the trade route between the Aegean Islands and the western Mediterranean.

Early settlers

The earliest recorded inhabitants of Sicily are the **Sicels** in c1700 BC (hence the modern name Sicilia for the island) in the east and the Sicans in the west. The Elymians are known to have occupied Segesta, Erice and Entella but evidence of their civilisation has so far only been found at Segesta. All of these peoples, between the 15C and 10C BC, were in close commercial touch with the Aegeo-Mycenaean peoples of Greece. Archaeological evidence has suggested that the **Phoenicians** visited the west coast of Sicily to establish trading outposts at Mozia (S. Pantaleo), and later Palermo even before the Greek settlers began to arrive in the 8C BC. The **Greeks** established strongholds on the east coast at Naxos (c735 BC) and Syracuse (734), and continued to settle in the next century at Lentini, Catania, Megara Hyblaea, Zancle (Messina) and Gela. Most of these settlements were separate from the Sicel villages, although in some cases (such as Morgantina, from the mid-6C BC) the two communities merged.

The 6C BC saw the beginning of the **heroic age of tyrants** with the notorious, if shadowy, figure of Phalaris who ruled in Akragas (now known as Agrigento) probably from 570–555. The brothers Cleander and Hippocrates were succeeded in Gela by Gelon, who captured Syracuse in 485. He and his father-in-law, Theron, tyrant of Akragas, soon controlled nearly all of Greek Sicily, and Gelon became the most powerful figure in the Greek world after his decisive victory over the Carthaginians at the Battle of Himera in 480. This supremacy aroused the jealousy of Athens, but a massive Athenian attack on Syracuse (415) met with fatal disaster.

In the late 5C BC **Dionysius the Elder**, the most powerful tyrant in Sicilian history, dominated the island's affairs for 38 years. The Corinthian Timoleon brought greater prosperity to the island, while **Agathocles** (the first King of Sicily) extended control over Carthaginian Sicily and into North Africa.

The Punic Wars and Roman domination (212 BC–5C AD)

Hieron II, his successor, brought Sicily under **Roman influence**, and in 264 the **First Punic War** broke out between Rome and Carthage, with Sicily as one of the main battlegrounds. Continuous destructive fighting continued until the Carthaginian surrender in 241. In the **Second Punic War** Sicily again found herself in an important strategic position between Italy and North Africa. In 212 Syracuse finally fell to the Roman Marcellus, and by 210 Rome controlled the whole of the island including the former Carthaginian territories in the west.

Under Roman domination the Greek cities lost some of their autonomy. Extensive rural estates were established in the interior, and luxurious villas were built (typified by the villas found at Piazza Armerina, Patti and Eloro). In the coastal towns public buildings were erected. The huge slave population on the island (increased by prisoners-of-war taken by the Romans in their battles in the east), led by Eunus in Enna and Cleon in Agrigento, revolted c 139. A second revolt (c 104) led to cruel repressions by the Romans. In the early Imperial period (1C AD) Sicily lost importance as a Roman province.

Vandals, Ostrogoths, Byzantines and Arabs (5C–1060)

During the 5C Sicily fell prey first to the Vandals then the Ostrogoths, but in AD 535 it was conquered for **Byzantium** by Belisarius. Although Syracuse became the capital of the Byzantine Empire for five years in the 7C, the Eastern Emperors relaxed their hold, under pressure from the Saracen invasion in 827; fierce fighting for possession of the island continued for 50 years. Palermo fell to the **Arabs** in 831, Syracuse in 878. Muslim rule, accompanied by vast numbers of North African and Spanish settlers, was marked by a spirit of tolerance. Palermo in the 9C was one of the great centres of scholarship and art in the world, surpassed in size only by Constantinople in the Christian world. The island's fertility was exploited to the full, and cotton, rice, oranges, lemons and sugar cane were first cultivated at this time, thanks to the introduction of terracing and irrigation.

Normans, Swabians and Angevins (1060–1282)

In 1060 the Norman **Count Roger de Hauteville** (1031–1101) seized Messina and by 1091 he was in control of the island. The newly-established Sicilian Parliament first met at Mazara del Vallo in 1097. Norman rule was characterised by its efficiency and willingness to adapt to the Arabic, Greek and Latin traditions which already existed on the island. In 1130 Roger's son (1093–1154) was crowned King of Sicily as **Roger II**. At that time he was probably the wealthiest ruler in Europe and his court in Palermo the most opulent. Meanwhile Messina flourished as a supply base for the Crusaders.

In 1194 the crown was claimed by the **Emperor Henry VI of Swabia**, son of Barbarossa, in the name of his wife, Constance (daughter of Roger II), and the last of the Norman Hautevilles were put to death. He was succeeded as Emperor and King of Sicily by his son **Frederick II** ('*stupor mundi*'), whose reign was marked by a prolonged struggle with the Papacy. His court in Palermo, drawing on Islamic and Jewish, as well as Christian cultures, was famous throughout Europe for its splendour and learning.

The Sicilian Vespers, Aragonese and Bourbon rule

The Swabian line ended with the beheading of Conradin in 1268. Charles of Anjou, as brother to Louis IX of France (who was considered a saint) had the backing of the French Pope and was invested with the crown of Sicily and Naples. The hated Angevin rule was, however, soon terminated by the famous rebellion known as the **Sicilian Vespers**, which broke out in Palermo at the hour of vespers on Easter Tuesday in 1282. A French officer, who had insulted a Sicilian bride on her way to church by insisting upon searching her for concealed weapons, was immediately killed and every Frenchman in Palermo was massacred. Every Sicilian town, except Sperlinga, followed suit by killing or expelling its French garrison, and as there were no Hohenstaufens or Hautevilles to provide an alternative ruler, the Sicilians summoned **Peter of Aragon** to be their king. He was renowned for his sense of justice and good government; in fact he agreed to take the position on condition that after his death Sicily and Aragon would be ruled as separate kingdoms. Unfortunately, this did not come to pass: in the course of time Sicily became a province of Aragon. From that day Sicily was ruled for over four centuries by Aragonese princes and Spanish and Bourbon kings, a period in which the rebellious spirit of the islanders lay dormant. But by the 16C Charles V had moved the centre of power west of the Mediterranean and Sicily lost much of her strategic importance.

Garibaldi, the Unification of Italy and Civil War

After Napoleon failed to invade the island in 1806, the British took control of Sicily in the first years of the 19C and established a constitution for a brief time. Then in 1848 revolution broke out against the Bourbons of Naples because of their ferocious tyranny. In 1860 **Garibaldi** fired the imagination of the Sicilian people and led an attack against Naples, thus paving the way for Italian Unification. But hard Piedmontese rule by Cavour soon proved unpopular. The northern Italian cities took up a dominant position over the south, and the economic position of Sicily was to remain a long way behind that of the rest of Italy for a century. Violence increased in the ungovernable interior of the island. In 1931, 40 per cent of Sicilians were illiterate.

The geographical position of Sicily meant that the Allies chose the island for their first important attack on Hitler in Europe in 1943. During the Italian administration in 1944 civil war broke out on the island because there was a strong desire for independence; failing that, many Sicilians wanted to see Sicily become one of the United States of America. Regional administration was approved by Rome in 1946 and the first Assembly was elected in 1947 which quietened things down, although it has not given the results originally hoped for.

Contemporary Sicily

Since the election of the Assembly, Palermo has been the regional capital and Syracuse, Agrigento, Messina, Catania, Caltanissetta, Trapani, Enna and Ragusa the provincial capitals. Although Sicily remains one of the poorest regions in Italy, with the highest level of unemployment in the country, recent surveys conducted by the EU indicate a glowing future for Sicily, and improvements can be seen in all fields. Probably in the course of the 21C the island will make up for a lot of lost ground, especially if the struggle against the Mafia continues.

In the 1960s and 1970s much ugly new building work took place around the coast of the island, including the Conca d'Oro on the outskirts of Palermo.

Huge industrial plants at Gela and Augusta brought serious pollution problems. As in the rest of Italy, almost every town, large and small, is now surrounded by ugly new buildings, and some of these towns have recently mistakenly been 'tidied up' with anonymous urban 'furnishings'. However, in the last few years there have been important signs of change in the island. Nature reserves have been created to safeguard the landscape and the coast; restoration of historic monuments has been undertaken; longer opening hours introduced for museums, and more churches are being kept open. Palermo and Catania are becoming much more attractive cities and after many years of neglect they both now have enlightened local administrations. Although the problems affecting the island are generally ignored by the rest of Italy, and the Sicilian regional government remains an obstacle to many attempts by local administrators to bring about much needed changes, there is no doubt that the standard of living of many Sicilians, especially in the larger towns, has greatly improved over the last few years. These optimistic signs have gone largely unnoticed by the rest of the country. Much could be done to encourage tourism on the island where the mild climate makes it an excellent place to visit throughout the year. Sicily now has about 5,200,000 inhabitants.

Emigration

Because of the poverty in Sicily at the end of the 19C many inhabitants of the island, especially from the villages in the interior, emigrated to northern and southern America and by 1900 Sicily was one of the chief emigration regions of the world. When their vineyards were destroyed by blight, thousands of peasants from the Aeolian Islands went to Australia. Some one and a half million Sicilians had left the island by the outbreak of World War I. The émigrés sent money back to their families and some eventually made enough money overseas to return. One of the most famous emigrants was Lucky Luciano (Salvatore Lucania born at Lercara Friddi in 1897) who emigrated with his family as a child to New York where he later became head of 'Cosa Nostra'. Condemned to 30 years' imprisonment in 1936, he helped the Americans during their landings in Sicily in 1943 by arranging for their reception by the local Mafia (the American secret servicemen wore yellow scarves with 'L' for Luciano printed on them in order to be recognised when disembarking). As a result the combined British and American forces occupied the island in just 38 days (known as Operation 'Husky'). In return Luciano was released from prison by the Americans in 1946 and extradited to Italy, where he died in Naples in 1962. As a consequence of America's dependence on the Mafia during the war, it unfortunately grew in prestige and power during subsequent decades.

After World War II many more artisans and peasants left the island to settle permanently in the Americas and Australia. Another exodus from rural Sicily began in the 1950s and early 1960s, this time mostly for a limited period to the industrial cities of northern Italy such as Turin, or to Switzerland, and later Germany and the coal mining areas of Belgium. Many of these Sicilians returned in the boom years of the 1960s to build houses. However, a subsequent economic downturn meant that they were never able to finish them and in numerous towns, including Gela and Palma di Montechiaro, these half-constructed houses are still abandoned shells.

The Mafia

The last century saw the power of the Mafia on the island steadily increase. Giovanni Falcone, the magistrate who investigated the Mafia and was assassinated in 1992, estimated that there were more than 5000 'men of honour' in Sicily, chosen after a rigorous selection process. He saw these men as true professionals of crime, who obeyed strict rules. Through a rigid 'protection' system they have controlled Sicilian business transactions for many years.

In the 1980s a number of men in key positions, including magistrates, politicians, and members of the police force who stood up to the Mafia, were killed by the organisation: General Carlo Alberto Dalla Chiesa, sent to Palermo as the prefect in 1982 to deal with the problem of the Mafia, was assassinated after only a few months in office. Rocco Chinnici, one of a group of investigating magistrates in Palermo, was murdered in 1983. The journalist Giuseppe Fava, who became known for his outspoken opposition to the Mafia through his newspaper *I Siciliani*, was killed in 1984. In 1991 Libero Grassi, an entrepreneur who ran a small factory in Palermo and who had spoken out against the Mafia racket in the city, was murdered. In the same year a courageous group of shopkeepers and tradesmen in Capo d'Orlando formed an association and stood up in court against those accused of extortion, and their example has been followed by other Sicilians.

A sentence passed in 1987, at the end of the largest trial ever held against the Mafia (the evidence for which had been collected by Giovanni Falcone), condemned hundreds of people of crimes connected with the Mafia. But this achievement in the battle against the Mafia was soon overshadowed when the anti-Mafia 'pool' of judges, created by Antonino Caponnetto in 1983 and led by Giovanni Falcone, disintegrated because of internal conflicts and a belief on the part of Falcone that his attempt to fight the Mafia was being obstructed. In 1992 this courageous Sicilian, who had raised the hopes of so many honest Italians, was assassinated together with his wife and bodyguards outside Palermo. Just a few months later his friend and fellow magistrate Paolo Borsellino was also murdered by the Mafia in Palermo. These tragic events were seen by many as a desperate blow in the battle against the Mafia and the response from Rome was to send in the army.

In 1993 the arrest of Totò Riina, the acknowledged boss of *Cosa Nostra*, after more than 20 years 'in hiding' in Palermo, closely followed by the capture of Nitto Santapaola outside Catania, the head of the Mafia in that city since 1982, was greeted, with some scepticism, as a step in the right direction.

However, since 1992, the whole question of the power of the Mafia has been placed on a different level. In 1992 the murder by the Mafia of Salvo Lima, Christian Democrat member of the European parliament and the most powerful politician on the island, was interpreted by many as a sign that he was no longer able to guarantee judicial immunity for Mafia bosses. In 1993 Giulio Andreotti, the most famous political figure in the country over the past four decades, was accused of collaboration with the Mafia. The trial ended with an acquittal, so the connection between the Mafia and the national political scene up to this decade has not yet been proved. In 1996 Giovanni Brusca, who detonated the bomb which killed Giovanni Falcone, was arrested. In 1997 many Mafia bosses were condemned (and most of them given life imprisonment) for their part in the murder of Falcone. Meanwhile, a group of courageous magistrates in Palermo continues the struggle against the power of the Mafia. Following the example of Falcone they also make use of *pentiti*, members of the Mafia who have decided to collaborate with the law in return for reduced jail sentences. The organisation is still strong, but continuous and determined opposition from the authorities and from the people of Sicily themselves is bearing fruit. The beginning of the end of this terrible phenomenon could be in sight at last.

Art and architecture

by Helen Hills

Sicily's strategic position, lying between Europe and Africa, linking the eastern and western Mediterranean and the Latin world with the Greek, resulted not only in its tumultuous history of successive invasions and conquests, but also in a unique cultural mixture which, in turn, stimulated the creation of rich and original works of art. The powers which ruled Sicily, and those which traded with it, each left their distinctive cultural imprints, and individual artists, both foreigners working in Sicily and Sicilians who had trained abroad, enriched these patterns. Yet the art history of Sicily is not simply a succession of disconnected impositions from foreign cultures; a strong local or Sicilian pride and conservatism nourished the development of insular and regional traditions which, during the most inventive periods, were fused with ideas coming from outside to create distinctive forms and styles quite peculiar to Sicily.

Sadly, the richness of Sicily's cultural heritage has not inspired the scholarly interest or political commitment it deserves. Many buildings which have survived the ravages of earthquakes, volcanic eruption and the bombardment of World War II now stand in desolate ruin, without hope of restoration, closed to the public and wasted. Paintings and sculpture have not fared much better: sales abroad, scandalous thefts, and over-restoration or poor conservation have dispersed or destroyed many irreplaceable and outstanding works. This pattern will continue so long as the necessary political will is lacking.

Prehistoric art

Some of the finest manifestations of Palaeolithic art yet known have been discovered in Sicily. In a small cave at Cala dei Genovesi on the island of **Levanzo,** one of the Egadi islands off the west coast, are two distinct series of figures, one set incised, and the other painted, of c 8700 BC. The incised figures, of red deer, oxen, equids and other animals, are particularly vivacious. Another series of incised drawings (c 8000 BC), in one of the Addaura caves of **Monte Pellegrino,** is of particular interest because it features not only figures of animals of the kind usually depicted in Quaternary art, but human figures as well, sometimes isolated and sometimes arranged in groups and drawn with the same naturalistic liveliness as the animals.

The earliest Neolithic culture known in Sicily, the *Stentinello*, may have covered much of the island by 3000 BC. Its pottery, decorated by impressions or incisions often made with the edges of shells, is finer and more compactly decorated than similar pottery of the same period elsewhere in the Mediterranean. In some of the sites of this civilisation (Stentinello, Lipari and especially Megara Hyblaea) more spirited pottery has been found, painted with red bands or flames on a light background, recalling the early painted ware of the Greek mainland. Painted wares were followed by others with incised spirals or complicated rolled handles. Each of these styles reflects an impact from outside, either casual landings or settlements, whose local nature accounts for the regional variations. The main sources were Anatolia, the Aegean, Cyprus and Syria, but contacts with North Africa and Egypt can occasionally be inferred. This rather disjointed development lasted throughout the so-called Copper Age (3rd millennium). Examples of pottery, idols and jewellery are in the Archaeological Museums in Palermo and Syracuse.

Cultural influences from Anatolia and the Aegean created the rock-cut chamber tombs which became ubiquitous in Sicily with little variation until the 5C BC. Most of the tombs are very simple, small oval, mitten-shaped rooms but a few are more complicated architecturally with recessed doorways, pilasters and pillars in front of a prepared façade. Some fine tombs at **S. Angelo Muxaro**, in use from the 8C to the mid-5C BC, attain very grandiose dimensions and are comparable with Mycenean examples. At **Castelluccio**, near Noto, spiral motifs in relief of the 3rd or 2nd millennium BC sometimes decorate the stone slabs closing the tomb doorways, and these are the only examples of prehistoric stonecarving so far known in Sicily. As the population centres expanded in the Late Bronze and Iron Ages, so their necropoleis became larger and more conspicuous, giving rise to the thousands of tombs which honeycomb the hills at Pantalica, most of which date from the 13C to the 11C BC. Mycenean influences manifested themselves at Pantalica in the architecture of the so-called 'Anaktoron', or prince's palace, and in the form and decoration of pottery. However, in spite of its dolmens, strongholds, the variety of chamber tombs and Mycenean influence, Sicily does not display cultural or architectural sophistication until the arrival of the Greeks in the 8C BC.

Hellenic Sicily

Architecture

Early Greek settlements were focused on the southeastern part of Sicily, especially at Syracuse, founded 734 BC (*Naxos*, on the east coast, was founded in c 735 BC). At first, Greek pottery was imported, but soon a flourishing pottery industry producing decorated 'red-figured' ware sprang up. New buildings and graves were created on Sicily in the Greek architectural style. Greek Sicily was, and felt itself to be, fully Greek, not just a rude distant outpost.

From the 6C BC Greek cities like *Megara Hyblaea* and *Selinus* (Selinunte) were planned in a rational way and had the characteristic Greek central square or agora, temples and cemeteries. But the Greeks' most magnificent and influential monuments—built hundreds of years earlier—were the Doric temples which still stand, noble and unforgettable, in the dry Sicilian hills. The oldest of these, the temple of Apollo, or of Apollo and Artemis (c 575 BC) at **Syracuse**, characterised by an enormous heaviness, is obviously a pioneer building. It was followed in the course of the next one and a half centuries at *Himera*, *Akragas* and elsewhere, but most grandly of all at **Selinunte** where at least nine temples were built in the long period of peace c 580–480 BC.

Sicilian Greeks were able to keep in step with old Greece through the continuous traffic between Sicily and the old Greek world; documentary evidence suggests the arrival of skilled craftsmen and architects summoned by Sicilian patrons. But distinctive Sicilian peculiarities also developed in the temples: sculpted reliefs on friezes and pediments are much rarer here than in Greece and the rule that a *pteron* (an external colonnade) should be more closely spaced along the sides than at the ends was gradually abandoned, as at Selinunte (Temple C). Aesthetic considerations often prompted these changes, for instance the unorthodox elements of the unfinished temple at Segesta were designed to give the building a squat appearance in keeping with its situation in a wide valley.

The most remarkable Sicilian Greek building is the temple of Olympian Zeus at **Agrigento**, the largest of all the Doric temples and never finished. Its structure, plan and elevation, with its enormous engaged half columns and colossal Atlas figures, were all revolutionary. At Gela, Timoleon founded a whole new city in 339, and the fortifications on Capo Soprano, which were completed during the reign of Agathocles (early 3C BC), were recovered from the sand in almost perfect condition in 1953–54. But the most impressive example of Greek defence works is at the Castello Eurialo, Syracuse, the strategic position of which encouraged the creation of exemplary solutions to the defensive problems of the 4C BC.

Most of the Greek theatres in Sicily were modified or completely rebuilt when Sicily belonged to Rome. For example, at **Segesta**, the best preserved of all the Hellenistic Sicilian theatres (3C BC), the unusually high *scena frons* with architectural decoration was probably added early in the 1C, and at *Tyndaris* the theatre was drastically altered by the Romans, first by the addition of a magnificent *scena*, to make it suitable for spectacular plays, and then by the removal of the lowest rows of seats to allow the presentation of circus performances. Nevertheless, it is clear that these buildings were conceived as part of a wonderful natural stage, taking careful advantage of dramatic views and slopes of the land around.

Sculpture

The rarity of sculpted reliefs on temples in Sicily in comparison with ancient Greece is most arresting and has not yet been convincingly explained. Of all the Greek cities in Sicily, Selinunte is the only one whose temples are decorated with sculptured *metopes*. (Agrigento might have had sculptured reliefs on the pediments of the Temple of Heracles, but this has not been conclusively proved.) The metopes of Selinunte, therefore, are very important in the story of archaic sculpture. While the oldest, belonging to Temple C (early 6C BC), are in flat relief, others are almost in the round, and those of Temple E, dated between 460 and 450 BC, abound with life and movement.

The Roman period

Architecture

After Hieron II's switch away from Carthage to a partnership with Rome in 263 BC, the culture and civilisation of Sicily absorbed much from Rome. Most of the monuments of this era were public. The theatre of **Catania**, the aqueduct of **Termini Imerese**, the theatre and the naumachia of **Taormina** are representative. Only the central powers were willing to fund such expensive projects and consequently a number of similar buildings went up simultaneously in the most important towns of Sicily, as in the rest of Italy and the provinces. For instance, amphitheatres (which were sometimes converted theatres), in use until the late empire with gladiatorial games and jousting, frequently date from the Augustan age, from 27 BC to 1C AD. However, the most spectacular sign of Roman wealth and luxury is the villa in the wooded valley at Casale not far from **Piazza Armerina**, near Enna. Probably built in the early 4C as the country retreat of Diocletian's colleague Maximian, it had nearly 50 rooms, courts, galleries, baths and corridors arranged in five complex groups and approached by an imposing entrance. Little remains of the sculpture, murals or marble architectural elements, but the **mosaic floors** surpass in extent and inventiveness any others of their kind. Ranging from geometrical patterns to scenes of bathing, dancing, fishing, from theatrical performances to scenes of animal life and complicated narrative compositions drawn from Greek mythology, the mosaics create a wonderful display of trompe l'oeil effects, colours and designs. Despite their Roman imperial style, they are almost certainly the work of craftsmen imported from North Africa. Indeed, Roman Sicily did not develop a distinctive culture of its own: the marble portrait busts of local dignitaries, Roman emperors and Greek philosophers are exactly like those of Italy or Gaul.

The early catacombs in Syracuse also date from this period and the grandest of them exceed those of Rome in size and embellishment. The oldest, that of S. Lucia, was in continuous use for at least a century during the period of illegality before Constantine. There was little attempt at decoration during this period, but after the Edict of Toleration, the Syracusan Christians enlarged their underground cemeteries, and introduced new architectural and decorative elements. Higher social class was expressed by more carefully cut chambers with arched entrances and the creation of 'rotundas' in which sculpted sarcophagi were placed in groups.

The Byzantine period

Of the years of Byzantine rule very little architecture, painting or sculpture remains and the fragmentary pieces in the Palazzo Bellomo, Syracuse and elsewhere are a sorry contrast to the long duration of the dominion. A sketchy picture of architectural developments can be constructed, however, from the few surviving churches. Up until the 6C most churches were basilican in plan, ending in one or more semicircular apses, as at S. Pietro, Syracuse. Then the eastern provinces began to favour the centralised church in variations on the Greek cross. A few of these were erected in Sicily too, but the basilica seems to have remained the most common form. Hardly any fresco painting of this period has survived, although the remains in **S. Pietro, Noto; S. Maria della Rotonda, Catania** and elsewhere show that painted decoration was the rule. The most important surviving frescoes, although severely damaged, are the six half-length figures of the saints covering the walls and ceiling of an oratory built in the cat-acombs of **S. Lucia, Syracuse**. Their style and spirit are Byzantine and their date is probably 8C. Paradoxically, Byzantine art is better represented in the Norman period.

The Norman period

Architecture

King Roger II de Hauteville (1093–1154; king, 1130–54) and his two successors were guided above all by a political desire not to antagonise unnecessarily any of their subjects, be they Latins, Orthodox or Muslims. As art tended to be con-trolled by the royal court, this tolerance manifests itself as a fascinating heterogeneous mixture of styles in the architecture, mosaics and woodwork, in the sculpture, coins and vestments of this period. Their architecture absorbed alien elements with particular grace, producing monuments of composite style, harmony and dignity. Secular, especially court, architecture, naturally inclined to Muslim models whose levels of refinement were unknown in the north. In Palermo the palaces of Favara, La Zisa and La Cuba, built or adapted to house royal and aristocratic families in splendour, show remarkable cultural hetero-geneity: Muslim, Romanesque and Byzantine forms rub shoulders; Norman interlaced round arches, Muslim domes, honeycomb roofs and stilted pointed arches occur in compositions carrying Byzantine mosaics and classically pro-portioned columns. La Zisa is a particularly beautiful example.

The ecclesiastical architecture of the Norman period is its most celebrated achievement today. Indeed the interiors of Cefalù and Monreale cathedrals and of the Palatine chapel in Palermo are without equal in Europe. The first of these great Norman churches was **Cefalù**, begun in 1131 in a newly-founded bishopric and intended to reinforce monarchical, as opposed to papal, power. It is largely a northern, Romanesque church: tall, adorned with chevron patterning, and with a projecting transept and deep choir, flanked by chapels. But traditional Sicilian forms such as stilted pointed arches and columns set into angles were used.

A more complicated stylistic syncretism occurred at the **Palatine Chapel** in the **Royal Palace** in **Palermo**, built 1132–40. The ground plan is a combina-tion of the Byzantine, centralised, inscribed cross plan and the south Italian longitudinal plan. The cupola, with its high drum and stepped squinches which oversail the wall, is of Egyptian Islamic derivation; and the wooden honeycomb ceiling of the nave, probably erected under William I (1154–66), belongs to the North African Islamic world. Its paintings include Cufic inscriptions, Hellenistic scenes, and images traceable to Persian and Indian legends. It has been given many attributions, but it was probably executed by local Sicilians. The effect of the interior of this chapel is extraordinarily harmonious and tranquil, its rich-ness is never strident because of the careful balancing of the colours and spatial rhythms.

La Martorana, Palermo, completed in 1143, is the only important church of this period which was not built for the Hautevilles, although its founder Admiral George of Antioch (d. 1151) was an important figure at Roger II's court. His Greek Orthodox religion probably explains why the plan is of the Byzantine inscribed cross type. This seems to have been especially popular for Basilian monasteries: it occurs at **Trinità di Delia** near Castelvetrano and at **S. Antonio, Palermo**.

The climax of Sicilian Romanesque architecture is **Monreale Cathedral**, built by William II as his mausoleum and as a counterpoise to the power of the Archbishop of Palermo. Like the Palatine Chapel, it is a combination of a southern Italian basilica and a Byzantine cross-in-square church, but its great size compelled the architect to do without vaults. As before, no attempt was made to fuse the Latin, Byzantine and Islamic ideas, but they are all handled on an unprecedentedly large and exhilarating scale.

It is the mosaic decoration of these buildings which contributes most to their splendour and constitutes Sicily's main claim to fame in the visual arts of the 12C. The Pantocrators in the choirs of Cefalù and Monreale with their ascetic reserve and haggard beauty attain a particularly deep spiritual intensity. The presence of Byzantine decoration in these Latin churches is explicable by the fact that they were royal foundations and the Norman kings were seeking to rival the Byzantine emperors. They were executed by important Byzantine craftsmen. Two styles are discernible: the elegant, humane, classical style of Cefalù and the Palatine Chapel; and the dynamic, late Comnenian style of Monreale (decorated 1185–90). Both styles profoundly influenced 12C Western painting, such as the Winchester Bible (c 1150–80). They are not, however, completely Byzantine. Their iconography reflects the outlook of their patrons (hence the early appearance of St Thomas Becket at Monreale). Whereas in a Byzantine church mosaic decoration consisted of an image of the world, the places sanctified by Christ's life and the feasts of the Church, in Sicily such decoration was didactic. At Monreale, for example, the Christian story from the Fall to the Last Judgement unfolds from the entrance eastwards (typically the Last Judgement is represented at the west end). This is the largest and most important Greek mosaic decoration of the 12C which exists anywhere.

Very few secular mosaics have survived and, of those that have, hardly any have been dated. Most of the palaces built in the Conca d'Oro by Roger and his followers probably contained mosaic decorations. The Sala Terrena at La Zisa, probably set at the beginning of William II's reign, displays beautiful interlaced roundels, pairs of peacocks and other characteristic motifs, but the Norman Stanza, usually called the *Sala di Ruggero* or Roger's Room, in the Royal Palace at Palermo far exceeds this in sumptuousness. Despite clumsy restorations, the mosaics still glimmer brilliantly in greens and golds in this evocative room.

The fall of the Hauteville dynasty, however, put an end to these developments. A court art, fostered by kings who were strangers in their country and executed by foreign artists, the mosaic work flourished and died with the Hautevilles and did not lead to subsequent developments in mosaic art in Sicily.

Sculpture

The largest and most impressive group of sculpture of this period is the cloister of the Benedictine monastery at **Monreale**, created between 1172 and 1189. Here over 200 paired colonnettes, with twin capitals treated in single compositions, display an astonishing variety of styles and subjects. Sources of the styles and iconography include Arabic, Byzantine (the mosaics of Monreale Cathedral and Byzantine caskets were drawn upon), north French, Tuscan, Lombard and Campanian; but a general stylistic harmony exists because of the dominance of the classicising style of Campania. The royal porphyry tombs, free-standing under monumental aedicula, in the cathedrals of Palermo and Monreale are equally outstanding, but very different, examples of the sculpture of this period. The unique forms of their sarcophagi were derived from antique models, in fact some scholars believe them to be Roman and brought to Sicily at an unknown date; Roman craftsmen achieved mastery in working the notoriously hard porphyry stone. Besides, the sources of porphyry in Egypt were already exhausted in the early Middle Ages. Some monuments reflect the style of contemporary Byzantine sculpture, such as the relief slabs from Messina cathedral, now in the Museo Regionale, Messina.

Manuscripts

A particularly fine group of illustrated manuscripts was produced at Messina under the patronage of Richard Palmer, the English archbishop of Messina (1182–95). This exceptional work provides a tantalising glimpse of the patronage of one of the highly educated foreign prelates.

Thirteenth and fourteenth centuries

Architecture

Unlike his predecessors, Frederick II did not endow monasteries or bishoprics; instead he devoted his building energies to creating a line of fortifications running from Germany to southern Italy and Sicily. In Sicily this line tended to favour the east coast and internally towards Enna. Castles dominated the cities in this area and fortresses were erected at strategic points inland. The most characteristic of the Swabian castles are **Castello Maniace**, Syracuse (1239), **Augusta** (begun 1232) and **Castello Ursino**, Catania (begun 1234) ; the contemporaneity of their construction—or reconstruction—conveys an efficient technical organisation and illustrates Frederick's personal control over the castle building programme; in addition to their military function the castles were designed to house Frederick on his journeys through Sicily. The castles consist of quadrangular curtain walls with corner towers, a plan and spatial form derived from Byzantine and Muslim architecture. Castello Maniace, for instance, is square with round towers at the corners. Others, like the castle at Augusta, have towers in the middle as well as at the corners. Their original internal arrangement is best seen at Castello Maniace. Here, the ground floor was originally unpartitioned but was divided by square bays with rib vaults resting on robust round columns, except for the central bay, which formed a small atrium. The atrium acquired a dominant role because of its swollen size and luminosity, evident in the castles of Catania and Prato in Tuscany. The Swabian castles are remarkable above all because they encase elegant apartments built in the Gothic style, as at Castello Maniace and Castello Ursino. Although these 13C castles in their remote location, are still awe-inspiring sights, little detailed research on them has been carried out or published. Thus we know very little about **Castello di Paternò**, an austere tower of volcanic rock commanding the wide Simeto valley, or the **Castello di Garsiliato** (recorded 1240) which rises in forbidding solitude in the immense valley of Gela; indeed, many buildings generally attributed to the Swabian period could date from other periods.

Frederick II did not devote much energy to the development of religious architecture. His direct involvement was restricted to the Murgo basilica near Lentini; but religious orders initiated some important buildings like the Badiazza near Messina, a Cistercian church and the Franciscan foundation at Messina. The **Murgo**, founded c 1225, demonstrates the continuity of Norman architectural forms in the use of Byzantine and Islamic motifs, but its plan is typical of Cistercian buildings and it has elements in common with contemporary castles:

the side aisles of the basilica strongly recall the arcades of Castello Maniace. Similar elements occur in the Badiazza, whose rib vaults are among the most beautiful of 13C buildings and whose capitals include Byzantine, Burgundian and Cistercian types. Burgundian Gothic rib vaults, responds and portal capitals also appear in another important church, **S. Maria degli Alemanni** (c 1220) in Messina. They are combined with Romanesque elements which persist in the portal and interior capitals. Among the most remarkable churches is **S. Francesco** (founded 1254), Messina, whose architectural sophistication is illustrative of the axiom that the finest achievements of Italian Gothic architecture are often obtained by the simplest forms. Its eight nave chapels create interesting effects: too shallow to disturb the spatial unity of the nave, their undecorated pointed arches give the appearance of internal buttressing (a feature which originated among the mendicants in Catalonia and southern France). Its apse is unexpectedly animated by the introduction of Gothic decoration elements not found elsewhere in the church.

With the fall of the Swabian monarchy and the break up of its central authority, 14C Sicily became tormented by factional struggles. As a result, the dominating 14C structural feature is the tower. The great feudal lords continued the well-tried building traditions established in the Swabian castles: the castle at **Naro** near Agrigento, for instance, echoes the constructive style of Frederick II's castles in its use of round and quadrangular towers. Swabian forms also persist in the castle at Mussomeli, built by Manfredo Chiaramonte towards the mid-14C, and in that at Venetico, erected by the Spadafora in the first half of the 15C.

Castle building in the country was echoed in the towns by the erection of 'strong' houses, such as those of the Chiaramonte (begun 1307) and Sclafani (1329–30) at Palermo, or the tower houses of the 15C and early 16C still visible at Enna, Randazzo, Taormina and Alcamo. Of these the **Palazzo Steri** (Chiaramonte) in Palermo is the most interesting. Its lava inlay decoration and large windows belie the impression of a fortified castle given by the exterior. Inside, the painted ceiling, full of verve, dated 1377–80 and signed by three Sicilians, is the only surviving example of what may have been a widespread vernacular decoration.

Painting

Our knowledge of 14C painting is very cloudy because of the loss of many paintings and the inadequacy of research to date. Most important paintings executed in Sicily during the 14C were by foreigners and show Sienese influence. For instance, the elegant early 14C *St Peter Enthroned* in the Chiaramonte Collection, outstanding for the decorative brilliance of its design, recalls the work of Lippo Memmi and has been attributed to him. The important panel of 1346, signed by **Bartolomeo da Carmogli** (fl. 1346–after 1358) in the Galleria Regionale, Palermo, which shows the Virgin feeding Christ at the breast, is the earliest dated example of what became one of the key symbols of Italian painting for the rest of the 14C. Its predella is also interesting. It shows kneeling members of a flagellant confraternity, four of whom wear the hooded robes with circles cut into the backs to bare the body to the scourge, reflecting the fashion of violent self-mortification.

Sculpture

In sculpture as in painting the Sienese influence was marked in 14C Sicily.

The wall tomb of Archbishop Guidotto de' Tabiati, dated 1333, in the cathedral at Messina, signed by **Goro di Gregorio** (fl. 1324–43), a Sienese, shows the weaknesses and strengths characteristic of this period: in places the composition is swallowed up by the narrative and crowded figures make a hectic impression, but in the Annunciation the composition is more controlled and the clear lines and careful balance of the masses are most eloquent. Throughout the Gothic period, Sicilian sculpture betrays a certain clumsiness. Figure sculpture in particular is often coarse and shows little appreciation of the living form. Ornament and relief display the continuing influence of Byzantine work. Not until the Gagini family came down from Ticino, some time in the late 1450s, was a group of able sculptors established in Sicily.

Fifteenth and sixteenth centuries

Architecture

Soon after 1400, Catalan art, often combined with Gothic forms from other sources, began to make its mark in Sicily. In architecture Catalan influences appeared throughout Sicily, but especially at Trapani, Syracuse, Ragusa, Modica and Palermo. The most significant building of the period occurred at **Palermo Cathedral**, and, as the capital was in closer contact with Barcelona than other towns, orthodox Catalan style was used for the sacristy (begun 1430) and the south loggia (1440s), and for the Flamboyant window added to the archipiscopal palace by Archbishop Simone da Bologna (1458–62); but on the whole Catalan influence in church architecture was limited to superficial details: doors and windows of typical shapes and with distinctive forms of vegetal ornament, in particular, of bands of leaves serving as capitals for a group of colonnettes, as in S. Pietro and S. Martino in Syracuse. **S. Giorgio Vecchio**, in Ragusa, is a perfect example of a Catalan Gothic façade transplanted to Sicily (compare with, for example, S. Martí Provençals, Barcelona), but usually doors and windows were plainer than comparable examples in Catalonia and Valencia. Elements associated with florid Gothic became increasingly evident during the 15C. Flowing tracery in place of a tympanum appears at S. Maria del Gesù in Palermo, in a chapel doorway, built by a family of Catalan origins, probably in the second half of the 15C. But unlike cities where Gothic had taken stronger root, these elements never produced a thoroughly Flamboyant style.

In secular architecture the **Palazzo Aiutamicristo** (c 1495) and **Palazzo Abatellis** (1488–95, by M. Carnelivari), both in Palermo, best represent the peculiar blend of southern Italian and Spanish forms; their courtyards are closely akin to the courtyard of Palacio Velado, Avila; and the massive portal of the Palazzo Abatellis, like a rope-bound raft, combines Castilian and Catalan designs. Secular architecture of this period reflects the metamorphosis of the ruling class. The castle-tower of the 14C, closed and defensive, hostile to the urban scene and reflecting the military power of its owner, was replaced by the 15C palace, open and outward-looking, expressive of the civil and economic power of the aristocracy. Bankers were the patrons of the Palermitan palazzi Aiutamicristo and the Afflitto, both begun in the 1490s. On the whole, 15C palace architecture tended towards the solid block marked by a strong, but not over-stressed, horizontality. This was the result of the three distinct vertical divisions: the ground floor was for the services, stables and kitchens; the grand *piano nobile* for the owner and reception rooms; and the attic housed the servants or cadet members of the family.

Other characteristics of 15C Sicilian palaces include the vaulted entrance passage, patio, sunken garden and a regular grid of rooms.

Sicilian architecture of the 15C was not sustained by humanism and remained somewhat inaccessible to Renaissance ideas; but great changes were wrought by two artists working in a mature Renaissance style who arrived in Palermo in the middle years of the century. **Francesco Laurana** (c 1420–79) had worked for Alfonso I in Naples, and was in Palermo from 1467–71 (and he may have returned later: the tomb relief of Abbot Speciale now in the Galleria Regionale, Palermo, is dated 1495). His most significant work, the arch to the **Cappella Mastrantonio** in the church of S. Francesco d'Assisi, Palermo, executed in 1468, was the earliest important Renaissance work in Sicily. However, his advanced style was too aloof to take root and it was the sculptor-architect **Domenico Gagini** (fl. 1448–92)—founder of a dynasty of craftsmen which dominated Sicily for the next century—who effectively introduced the new style. Gagini, who had been trained in Genoa and worked in Naples on the triumphal arch of the Castelnuovo, arrived in Palermo in 1458/9 and stayed there until his death in 1492. Among his first documented works is the door to the church of S. Agostino (c 1470) in Palermo. It is a competent, if crudely executed, version of the style current in central and northern Italy, and soon doors of this type appeared all over Sicily, persisting long after the type had become old-fashioned in Lombardy and Tuscany. Domenico's gifted son, **Antonello** (1478–1536), carried on his tradition into the 16C. The gulf between him and local architects is well illustrated in the church of **S. Maria di Porto Salvo** (Palermo), which he began in c 1527 in a Tuscan Quattrocento style, its chapels being articulated with orthodox pilasters and round-headed arches with more or less correct mouldings. But when Antonello died in 1536, it was impossible to find an architect able to complete it in the Renaissance style and it was finished in the Gothic tradition by Antonio Scaglione, a local architect.

S. Maria di Porto Salvo is one of a most interesting group of churches, almost all near the port of Palermo, dating from the last years of the 15C and the early 16C, which demonstrate that the juxtaposition of Gothic and Renaissance forms, which is so disconcerting to us, was not regarded as inappropriate by contemporaries. At **S. Maria della Catena** in Palermo, which was probably begun soon after 1502, columns crowned by 15C Florentine-style capitals stand on late Gothic pedestals, to which they are joined by French High Gothic bases, and carry Gothic rib vaulting; and a similar combination of Gothic and Renaissance elements appears in S. Maria Nuova.

The persistence in Sicily of certain architectural forms is particularly striking in this period. The unusual rustication and diamond-cut blocks of 16C buildings such as the Giudecca, Trapani and Palazzo Steripinto, Sciacca, may derive from the prestigious rustication of the Hohenstaufen castles. However, the most obvious of these persistent architectural elements is the squinch. Inherited from Arab architecture and frequently found in Norman buildings in Sicily, the squinch was still being used in the 16C: the **Cappella Naselli** (built between 1517 and 1555) in S. Francesco, Comiso, and the remarkable **Cappella dei Marinai** in the Santuario dell'Annunziata, Trapani, are two instances out of many. In these later buildings the squinch is used with compelling conviction, not as an overworn cliché to be inserted where inspiration failed, and this raises questions about the significance it must have had for the architects.

Another Norman practice which survived into the 16C was the use of two or three superimposed columns for the pier of the crossing of a church. The most remarkable example of this occurs at S. Giorgio dei Genovesi, Palermo, built in an otherwise full Renaissance style between 1576 and 1591. These Sicilian forms have no bearing on the ideas developed in the rest of Italy.

Sculpture

A surprising amount of late 15C and early 16C sculpture survives in churches and museums scattered throughout Sicily. Quite unlike the pattern of development in northern Italy, where ducal workshops provided focuses of development, in Sicily a single style tended to spread over the whole coastal area of the island. As in architecture, the main impetus came from **Francesco Laurana** and **Domenico Gagini**, both marble sculptors working in a style deriving from late Quattrocento Florence. Indeed, the similarity of their styles has created problems in attributing some works like the reliefs on the holy-water stoups in Palermo Cathedral and portrait busts (now in the Galleria Regionale, Palermo). Domenico Gagini's style reflects that of late 15C Florence and particularly his interest in the work of Ghiberti and Buggiano, Brunelleschi's protégé. His 'Madonnas' are exceptional for their suggestion of delicate movement: in his later works he departs from his early rigid frontal presentation of the image, creating a greater dynamic tension as in the figure on the tomb of Pietro Speciale in S. Francesco d'Assisi, Palermo, but on the whole his work and especially his portraits lack the sensitivity of Laurana's. Laurana produced an influential series of standing polychrome Madonnas, beginning with the one in Palermo Cathedral modelled on a 14C *Virgin* by Nino Pisano in Trapani; others can be seen in the church of the Crocifisso in Noto and in the museum at Messina. They demonstrate Laurana's ability to fuse late Gothic and Renaissance ideas.

Antonello Gagini developed his father's work. He came to be considered the most significant Sicilian Renaissance sculptor and his vast amount of work reflects his popularity. The period between 1510 and 1536 was particularly busy: not only did he have his usual studio work of statues, tombs and altars, but also the vast tribuna of Palermo Cathedral, remarkable for its combination of old and new styles and ideas, and for the introduction to Palermo of stucco as a material for sculpture. Indeed, Antonello and his workshop sculpted in marble, terracotta, *mistura* (plaster and papier mâché mixed) and stucco, which meant that their work was available at a range of prices. Antonello's search for an ideal beauty, evident in the roundels in the Gancia, Palermo, of c 1500, was related to the contemporary classicising trend in Lombardy, and tended to produce rather sickly sweet Madonnas, such as the *Madonna della Scala* (1503) in Palermo Cathedral.

Just as the ambivalence between Gothic and Renaissance forms persisted in architecture into the 16C, so it did in sculpture. A relief in the church of the Magione, Palermo, produced in the workshop of the Gagini in the late 15C or early 16C illustrates this well. Florentine Quattrocento-style figures stand between late Gothic twisted colonnettes and snuggle into shell niches below Gothic gables.

Painting

During the early 15C, Sicilian painting was markedly Spanish in character and showed little awareness of developments in the north. The most important paintings were by foreigners and most were in a Catalan style of which the early 15C polyptych in the church of S. Martino, Syracuse, by the so-called **Maestro di S. Martino**, is representative. The only major work in an independent 'Sicilian' style is the *Triumph of Death* in the Galleria Regionale at Palazzo Abatellis, Palermo.

However, **Antonello da Messina** (c 1430–79) dramatically altered the character of Sicilian painting in the late 15C. As no strong Sicilian stylistic tradition existed, he turned to movements abroad: three separate foreign experiences deeply affected his work. These were a training (probably in Naples) in the Flemish style and in the technique of oil painting; the influence of Giovanni Bellini during a stay in Venice; and the influence of the work of Piero della Francesca. The first half of Antonello's career is well documented, but almost entirely devoid of extant works. He seems to have been working from 1457–65 in and around Messina. Paintings of this period are dominated by Flemish forms, but show signs of his experimentation with the representation of spatial depth that had been developing in central Italy. During his most active period, 1473–77, Flemish influences, such as the work of Robert Campion, Petrus Christus or Hans Memling, remained keen: the interior setting, decorated drapery and the fascination with precise rendering of reflected light in both the polyptych for the church of S. Gregorio of 1473 (now in the Regional Museum, Messina) and in the *Annunciation* of 1475 (now in the Galleria Regionale at Palazzo Bellomo, Syracuse) are good examples of this; but Italian influences make themselves felt in the column dividing the Annunciation which recalls Piero della Francesca's Annunciations, and in the shape of the polyptych itself. In Venice, Antonello learned how to handle architectural space, especially from Bellini. His *Virgin Annunciate* (Galleria Regionale, Palermo) displays this new mastery in the placing and perspectival treatment of the lectern and the Virgin's hand, which give a dramatic depth and solidity to the picture.

The influence of Antonello da Messina was widespread, especially amongst his descendants and relations who included **Jacobello di Antonello** (c 1455–90), **Antonello de Saliba** (1466/7–after 1535), **Salvo di Antonio Giovanni** (fl. c 1493–1525) and **Marco di Costanzo** (15C).

16C sculpture

Because of its geographical position, Messina was in closer contact with the mainland than other towns in Sicily, and during the 16C artists from Florence and Rome frequently travelled there, attracted by its political and social importance. Of these, a pupil of Michelangelo, the Florentine **Giovanni Angelo Montorsoli** (1507?–63), who came to Messina in 1547, was the most important. He established in Sicily the Tuscan style of the mid-century in both sculpture and architecture, reinstating the use of human and monstrous figures in sculpture, which had been lost largely because of Arab influence. Montorsoli's **Orion fountain** (begun 1547), with its Michelangelesque forms, was particularly influential both in Sicily and mainland Italy, and his **Neptune fountain** (begun 1557) was hardly less so. He left behind a long line of followers at Messina, principal among whom was **Martino Montanini** whose work, exemplified by the St Catherine statue in the church of SS. Annunziata (1558/9) at Forza d'Agro, is a frostier version of Montorsoli's.

In Palermo, the influence of Tuscan Mannerism was much weaker and, except for piecemeal scatterings, is restricted to one monument. In 1570 it was decided that the square in front of the Palazzo Municipale should be embellished with a fountain, and in 1574 the Fontana Pretoria, by the Florentine sculptor **Francesco Camilliani** (d. 1586), originally intended for a Florentine villa, was duly installed, with the necessary additions by Francesco's son, **Camillo** (fl. 1574–1603) and **Michelangelo Naccherino** (1550–1622). With this, Palermo tasted, albeit belatedly, the new language of Mannerist sculpture; but, unlike in Messina, no new school of sculptors formed here, and the fountain remained an isolated example, even though its unusual figures were sometimes copied or adapted in later works of art.

16C architecture and town planning

These fountains were part of flamboyant attempts to modernise the urban environment, by opening new streets, creating vistas marked by prestigious buildings or gates, improving the water supply, and so on, with which ambitious viceroys, courting popularity, sought to link their names. Religious orders also played an important role, demonstrating their power by building churches and convents. This process of renewal of the urban fabric, which was to be most significant at Palermo, began in Messina, where **Andrea Calamech** (1514–78) and Camillo Camilliani were entrusted with much of the work. A great deal of their work has been destroyed, but what survives reveals a new sturdy monumentality. Temporary architecture, designed for special religious or political occasions, was probably very influential. In Palermo, for instance, when the road to Monreale was opened between 1580 and 1584, the new gates of Porta Felice and Porta Nuova were erected, and the latter perpetuated ideas of the temporary triumphal arch put up for Charles V's celebrated visit of 1535.

Two of the finest streets of Palermo took their names from viceroys, the via Toledo in the 1560s and the via Maqueda in the 1590s, and ten years later another viceroy built a fine Baroque octagon at their intersection, the Quattro Canti, in imitation of Rome's Quattro Fontane. Begun by the Florentine architect, **Giulio Lasso**, most of the work was completed by **Smiriglio**. Monarchical, heavenly, and local references were combined in a ponderously impressive work, which hid, as it still does today, the slums of the poor behind its proud screens.

The return to Sicily of the Messinese **Giacomo Del Duca** (fl. 1540–1600), who had worked in Rome under Michelangelo in his later years, also contributed to the new phase of late 16C architecture in Messina. His understanding of Michelangelo's late style is visible in the remarkable church of **S. Giovanni di Malta**, Messina, on which he began work with Camilliani from about 1590: the use of giant pilasters and deep triangular *guttae* had repercussions in Sicilian architecture until the 18C. His establishment of a mature late 16C Roman style in a country with very different architectural traditions is unparalleled anywhere else in Italy. The vigour and monumentality of the tradition was perpetuated by **Natale Masuccio** (fl. 1560–70), a Jesuit architect, who had trained in Rome at the turn of the century and absorbed there a mixed Tuscan-Roman style from Bartolomeo Ammanati and Giuseppe Valeriani. Their influence can be seen in his Jesuit Novitiate in Trapani (begun before 1614) and the ruins of his Monte di Pietà in Messina.

Baroque architecture

This is one of the most exciting periods of the architectural history of Sicily.

The exuberant vivacity and inventiveness, the variety and exhilarating beauty of Sicilian Baroque architecture (including vernacular architecture) are unparalleled. In the more sophisticated buildings architects familiar with current styles in Rome worked to create, not slavish copies of Roman Baroque, but vigorous interpretations of that style from within Sicilian traditions. This is best seen in the work of **Rosario Gagliardi** (?1700–70). At their best Sicilian buildings occupy positions of dignity and authority in the field of European Baroque architecture.

The earthquake of 1693 which devastated most of the towns of south and east Sicily deeply affected the development of Baroque architecture on the island and our picture of it. Little remains of pre-1693 architecture in the earthquake zone, but that which does, such as **S. Sebastiano**, Acireale, suggests that it was highly decorated with scrolls, rustication and grotesque masks. This strange anthropomorphised architecture was rarely taken up again after 1693. The abruptness of this break and the inevitable self-consciousness of the new style makes the architecture of the east unlike that of the west where, particularly at Palermo, local traditions persisted as the most powerful force.

The new towns in the earthquake zone often enjoyed the benefits of new sites and plans. At Avola, **Angelo Italia** created a regular grid with large open piazzas, designed for safety in the event of another quake; but here and at Grammichele these new ideas were encased in a dramatic hexagon, derived from traditional military treatises. This approach, which cannot be appreciated from within the town, contrasts strongly with the ideas used at Noto where the grid arrangement of the streets was exploited to create beautiful vistas punctuated by fine buildings to be enjoyed from within the city.

The buildings around the cathedral square in Catania illustrate well the first style which evolved after the earthquake. Its main characteristics were vigorous superficial decoration and multiform rustication. **G.B. Vaccarini** (1702–68), who arrived in Catania c 1730, introduced a completely different style which was to dominate Catanese architecture for several decades. From Rome, where he had trained in the early 1720s, he brought a number of new church plans and architectural features, especially windows, which show a thorough study of the great Roman Baroque architects and of Borromini in particular. In his best buildings, such as the **Palazzo Valle** (c 1740–50) or **S. Agata alla Badia**, Vaccarini stretched out from these Roman ideas and created a unified movement and play of curves unthinkable in contemporary Rome. His introduction of certain Roman church plans to Sicily was seminal, but he always developed the Roman plans to achieve new effects. S. Agata, based on S. Agnese in piazza Navona, is less centralised than its model (and its interior is lighter as a result of using stucco rather than marble). In contrast, the most active mid-18C local architect, **Francesco Battaglia** (fl. 1732–78), created in the salone of **Palazzo Biscari**, Catania, the most liberated Rococo decoration to be found in Sicily or southern Italy. Vaccarini's later classicising style was continued by Stefano Ittar in S. Placido and the Collegiata; but the move towards the neo-classical use of orders and decoration is most marked in Antonio Battaglia's new staircase at the monastery of the Benedettini, 1749.

The most original architect in the southeast was **Rosario Gagliardi**, engineer to the town and district of Noto. Several churches have been grouped around his documented works, whose distinctive traits can perhaps best be appreciated at **S. Giorgio**, Ragusa Ibla, of 1744. Both here and at **S. Giorgio**, Modica, the hillside site is brilliantly exploited, and underlined by the façade design, in which the tower seems to burst from the central bay, itself a solution to the Sicilian belfry façade problem. The columns, canted boldly against the curved centres, and the pediments, flicked above the doorways, exploit a freedom never tasted by the Roman followers of Bernini and Borromini (if hinted at in some Roman façades, such as Martino Longhi's SS. Vincenzo ed Anastasio) and add dynamism to the design. The interiors of Gagliardi's churches, unlike those of the Roman architects and his fellow countryman and contemporary Filippo Juvarra, do not display great commitment to spatial experimentation, but they are full of fascinating details, some of which reveal an interest in Gothic forms. In Syracuse the masterpiece of Baroque architecture is **Andrea Palma**'s (1664–1730) cathedral façade (begun in 1728) which uses broken masses within a columnar façade to create a jagged and dramatic effect.

In Palermo ecclesiastical Baroque architecture shows greater continuity with insular architectural traditions. The basilican plan remained popular and the local (Norman) tradition of columnar arcades persisted, of which **S. Giuseppe dei Teatini**, begun 1612 by **Giacomo Besio**, is the most awe-inspiring example. Greater attention was given to plans consisting of a simple hall with shallow side chapels and apses, such as **Giacomo Amato**'s (1643–1732) **S. Teresa alla Kalsa**; this plan type was readily taken up by the many confraternities which blossomed in post-Tridentine Sicily. As in Catania, centralised plans were created more frequently but spatial experimentation was less important than in Rome.

A few Palermitan churches show that their architects were familiar with Roman Baroque architecture. **Paolo Amato**'s (1634–1714) SS. Salvatore (begun 1682), an elongated oval plan, is a much more spacious and flatter version of Rainaldi's S. Maria di Montesanto; and Giacomo Amato, who was in Rome from 1670 to 1687, derived the magnificent façades of S. Teresa (begun c 1686) and La Pietà (begun 1689) from Rainaldi's S. Maria in Campitelli and S. Andrea della Valle. These bold and majestic façades also incorporate traditional Sicilian elements, such as the circular window at the centre of the design, which would never have been used on a church on the mainland. This interest in Sicily's own traditions is shown equally in Angelo Italia's exceptional (if not wholly satisfactory) little church, **S. Francesco Saverio** (1684–1710), whose pierced hexagonal chapels were derived from Guarini's churches in Messina (tragically destroyed in 1908).

One of the most fascinating and peculiar aspects of Palermitan (and, to a lesser extent, Messinese) Baroque architecture is the use of cut and polished inlaid stones, known as *marmi mischi*, to cover the walls in a fabulous display of motifs, sometimes religious and symbolic, sometimes purely decorative. The practice seems to have begun with the use of flat panels of coloured marble on tombs; white reliefs were subsequently introduced and the rigid geometric forms were discarded: an early example is a tomb of 1637 in S. Domenico. Particularly fine examples of the fully developed form include the Cappella dell'Immacolata (c 1650) in S. Francesco d'Assisi, and the churches of the Casa Professa and S.Caterina, which incorporate low and high reliefs and statuary in complex iconographic programmes. Small biblical scenes were frequently depicted in marble on chapel walls and altarpieces in the 18C. The technical virtuosity in the *Flight out of Egypt* in S. Maria Miracoli is characteristic.

The exquisite stuccowork by **Giacomo Serpotta** (1656–1732) and his descendants displays similar concerns. Although indebted to earlier traditions of stucco work, the celebrated oratories of Serpotta surpass them by far in artistic sensibility and technique. In the Oratorio di S. Zita (1685–88), the walls appear to be draped in cloth, against which are set the *Mysteries of the Rosary* and the *Victory at Lepanto*, all delicately modelled in stucco. The paintings and frescoes around which Serpotta conceived his stuccowork still exist in the Oratorio del SS. Rosario di S. Domenico (c 1710–17), showing how harmonious and elegant these interiors must have been. Giacomo Serpotta's son, **Procopio**, allowed architecture a greater importance in his compositions, as in his masterpiece, the Oratorio of S. Caterina (1719–26). Although he strove to achieve his father's elegance and perfect finish of modelling, his figures are elongated and languid and lack his father's verve and energy.

Palace architecture has suffered from disgraceful neglect in Palermo, and only in recent years has any attempt been made to halt the degradation but enough survives for us to appreciate the diversity of plans, the character of the façades and the most important features, such as doors, windows and staircases. Giacomo Amato's **Palazzo Cutò** (begun 1705) and **Palazzo Cattolica** (c 1720) combine innovative planning with the creation of impressive spaces and vistas. Similar theatrical effects are created by the most spectacular of Palermitan staircases at **Palazzo Bonagia** by **Andrea Giganti** (18C), probably executed in the 1760s. The interiors of 17C and 18C palaces have almost all been destroyed, but surviving examples show an imaginative gaiety rarely found outside Sicily. **Palazzo Gangi**, (c 1770–90) for instance, boasts a spectacular suite of rooms culminating in the diaphanous Sala degli Specchi, whose unique ceiling is composed of a deeply coved upper shell, painted with allegorical frescoes, and a pierced lower ceiling suspended below. This creates an effect of shifting worlds, like a magic lantern.

Built by an extravagant and feckless aristocracy as retreats from the feverish capital during hot weather, the villas of Bagheria and Piana dei Colli are among the most inventive of Sicilian 18C buildings. Their simple façades, in keeping with their rustic setting, contrast with the grand and complex exterior staircases, which reflect the sophisticated life-style of the owners. Almost all these staircases are double, some are curved, as at the Villa Spina, others are jaggedly contorted, as at the Villa Palagonia. The latter was built by **Tomaso Napoli** (17C) who emerges as an outstanding architect here and at the Villa Valguarnera (begun c 1709). He combined unusual forms, concave and convex curves, with ingenious and inventive planning involving the creation of many different shaped rooms, to achieve an overall effect of grace and flowing line.

It is important to remember that our picture of Baroque architecture in Sicily is very fragmentary, for two main reasons. First, in the 17C and 18C, temporary architecture and decoration, erected to celebrate church festivals and political events, were at least as important as permanent architecture. Although they are recorded in drawings and engravings, our impressions of these *apparati* are necessarily imperfect without being able to experience them in the round and bedecked with lights and colour. Second, much Baroque architecture has been destroyed. The ravages caused by the earthquake of 1693 prompted much fertile rebuilding; but much of the damage caused by subsequent earthquakes and by the bombing of World War II has never been attended to. Consequently, many 17C and 18C palaces and churches stand as empty shells, their once splendid features crumbling into meaningless rubble. This is the result of political irresponsibility and it is horrifying to see.

Seventeenth century painting

Seventeenth century painting is illuminated by the contributions of two outstanding foreign artists, Caravaggio and Van Dyck. **Caravaggio** (1571–1610), fleeing arrest in Malta, landed in Syracuse in 1608/9 and executed in Sicily at least five paintings, mainly for private patrons. His first work in Sicily, the *Burial of St Lucy* (now in the Galleria Regionale, Syracuse), probably begun in early 1609, concentrates on the human aspects only of the divine drama, making an eloquent contrast between the helpless passivity, even distraction, of the mourners, and the empty but self-confident gestures of the officials. The *Adoration of the Shepherds* (1609, Museo Regionale, Messina), commissioned by the Messinese Senate as the high altarpiece of the church of S. Maria degli Angeli, is one of Caravaggio's most deeply felt and impressively simple works. Here the dignity he recognised in the poor and simple is intensely conveyed; even the resonant space accentuates the silent devotion of the shepherds.

Van Dyck's (1599–1641) visit to Palermo in 1624, although cut short by his fear of the plague raging in west Sicily, produced a remarkable group of pictures of S. Rosalia (now in New York, Houston and Ponce) and his grandest Italian altarpiece, the *Madonna of the Rosary* 1624–28 (finished in Genoa) which is still in the Oratorio del Rosario in S. Domenico. Although Sicily has retained only one of Van Dyck's Sicilian paintings, his influence is frequently apparent in local 17C painting, and in the work of **Pietro Novelli** (1603–47) above all.

Eighteenth and nineteenth century architecture

During the 18C neo-classical architecture gradually took root all over Sicily, but particularly in Palermo, as a result of its close links with Naples, Rome and France. **Venanzio Marvuglia** (1729–1814), a Palermitan who had become deeply imbued with neo-classicism during his stay in Rome (1747–59), was the most significant architect of this style. With his Benedictine monastery, **S. Martino delle Scale**, near Palermo (1762–76), the curvaceous middle bays and flowing lines of Palermitan Baroque palaces are shrugged off and replaced by straight lines and planes. Of great significance is Marvuglia's use of a flat impost, rather than the traditional arcade, above the columns of the nave in the Oratory of S. Filippo Neri, in Palermo, built 1769. This was in accordance with Laugier's influential idea that the ancient Greek form is the only true standard in architecture. However, Marvuglia's obvious feeling for the effect of simple masses and carefully thought-out proportions and his use of characteristic Sicilian balconies in the palaces of Riso-Belmonte and Constantino in Palermo push him far from the inflexible rigidity of some neo-classicists. Sicily's antiquity was very fashionable in 18C Europe and it was a Frenchman, **Léon Dufourny**, who first used again in Sicily the Greek Doric style when he built his pavilion in the Palermo Botanic Gardens in 1787. This style was taken up all over Sicily for 19C public buildings, such as the theatre at Castelvetrano and the Ministry of Finance offices in Palermo.

Art Nouveau

Palermo is an important centre of Art Nouveau architecture, surpassed in Italy only by Turin and Milan. Its importance reflects the concentration of upper middle-class families gravitating around the Florio financial empire whose patronage provided the mainstay of Ernesto Basile's commissions. For it was **Ernesto Basile** (1857–1932), whose father, **G.B. Basile** (1825–91), had created the heavy Corinthian Teatro Massimo, Palermo, who dominated the Art Nouveau style in Sicily. He was an able architect, keenly aware of Sicily's architectural traditions, without feeling bound to copy them slavishly. He borrowed heavily from Sicilian 15C motifs for the exteriors of his buildings, such as the **Palazzo Bruno**, Ispica, and the **Villino Florio** in Palermo. Here Carnelivari, of whose work he had made careful measured drawings, was particularly important. By contrast, Sicilian Norman motifs are the predominant source for his interiors. Basile's characteristic fusion of structural and ornamental elements is best seen today in the **Villa Igiea** (1899), Palermo, whose dining room is the epitome of Basile's fantastic medievalism. Although most of his work was for private patrons, Basile also designed the theatre in Canicattì and the Palazzo Municipale in Licata (1930s). The interest of Basile's workshops in the revival of the applied arts contributed to the spread of Art Nouveau throughout Sicily, and to Catania in particular, where a number of good examples survive in the Viale Regina Margherita. Sadly, however, many fine Art Nouveau style villas have been demolished in recent decades.

Twentieth and twenty-first century

Twentieth century architecture in Sicily is a dispiriting subject. Political irresponsibility has allowed ugly speculative schemes to stampede unhindered into the countryside and to smother the coastlines with blocks of flats, tourist villages and holiday villas. Awareness of Sicilian traditions and of the distinctiveness of Sicilian culture, which were for centuries such important and invigorating forces in the island's architecture, has been cast aside, and the language these new buildings speak is the same inarticulate grunting that occurs everywhere in Europe where speculative gain has triumphed over artistic and social concerns.

Further reading

Sicilian writers

Sicilians have always been good writers. In the Middle Ages the multi-ethnic character of the population had brought about the birth of a new language as a means of communication among the people; a mixture of Latin, Arabic, Greek, Hebrew and French. This language was also adopted as the language of literature, and the court of Palermo became a place of learning and culture which had no equal in Europe at the time. Dante was using a version of this new language when he wrote his *Divine Comedy*. Two Sicilians have won the Nobel prize for literature: **Luigi Pirandello** in 1934, and the poet **Salvatore Quasimodo** in 1959. Many of Italy's top journalists are Sicilian (one of them, Maria Grazia Cutuli, was killed in Afghanistan in 2001). Possibly the most widely read Italian author today, Andrea Camilleri, is Sicilian; he writes in a mixture of Sicilian and

Italian and is available in translation: *La Forma dell'Acqua* (*The Shape of Water*) and *Il Cane di Terracotta* (*The Terracotta Dog*). Both belong to a series about a feisty police superintendant called Salvo Montalbano. Camilleri also writes on 19C Sicilian history in his personal style (not yet available in translation).

A very influential 20C writer was **Giovanni Verga** from Vizzini. His master-pieces: *Mastro-don Gesualdo, I Malavoglia* (*The House by the Medlar Tree*) and *Vita dei Campi* (*Life in the Fields*) influenced other writers of his time and are quite impressive even today; they are usually available in translation (some of them were translated by D.H. Lawrence in 1925 and 1932).

A shy, introvert intellectual wrote a book in the 1950s that shook the Italian literary scene. Published with some difficulty, it was immensely popular from the start. The author was a Palermitan prince, **Giuseppe Tomasi di Lampedusa**, and the novel, *Il Gattopardo*, (*The Leopard*, translated in 1960) tells the story of his aristocratic family's fortunes during a period of painful transition for Sicily after 1860 in which the island had to adapt to the reality of being part of Italy. On the strength of the success of his book, another collection of writings was published, called *I Racconti* (two stories and a memoir, translated in 1962), but he died before knowing of his success.

Many of the plays by **Luigi Pirandello**, born in Agrigento, are usually avail-able in translation, for example, *Sei Personaggi in cerca d'autore* (*Six Characters in Search of an Author*; 1921). He also wrote very good short stories and a couple of novels, but his true genius is as a playwright. Another 20C Sicilian writer was **Elio Vittorini** author of *Conversazione in Sicilia, Uomini e no* (*Men and not Men*) and *Il Garofano Rosso* (*The Red Carnation*).

Comiso has also produced a great author: **Gesualdo Bufalino** (1920–96) is known for his six novels which include *La Diceria dell'Untore*, (*The Plague Sower*; 1981) and *Le Menzogne della Notte* (*Night's Lies*; 1988).

Leonardo Sciascia (1921–89) from Racalmuto was famous both for his nov-els and his unprejudiced writings on the Mafia: *Il Giorno della Civetta* (*The Day of the Owl*), *Il Consiglio d'Egitto* (*The Council of Egypt*), *A ciascuno il Suo* (*To Each his Own*, translated 1992), *Il Mare Colore del Vino* (*The Wine-coloured Sea*), *La Sicilia come Metafora* (*Sicily as Metaphor*). Other English translations of his works include: *Candido, A dream dreamed in Sicily* (translated 1995), and *Sicilian Uncles; four novellas* (translated 1986).

Art and architecture

Blunt, Anthony, *Sicilian Baroque** (1968).

Borsook, Eve, *Messages in Mosaic* (Boydell Press, 1998).

Demus, Otto, *The Mosaics of Norman Sicily* (Hacker Art Books Inc, 1987).

Garstang, Donald, *Giacomo Serpotta and the Stuccatori of Palermo, 1560–1790* (Zwemmer, 1984).

Guido, Margaret, *Sicily: an archaeological guide* (Faber, 1967, 1977)

Leighton, Robert, *Sicily before History: an archaeological survey from the Palaeolithic to the Iron Age* (2002).

Sitwell, Sacheverell, *Southern Baroque Revisited* (Weidenfeld & Nicholson, 1967).

Tobringer, Stephen, *The Genesis of Noto, an eighteenth-century Sicilian city* (1982).

Sicilian food

Carluccio, Antonio, *Southern Italian Feast* (BBC Books, 1998).

Grammatico, Maria and Simeti, Mary Taylor, *Bitter Almonds** (William Morrow, 1994). Cookery and autobiography.

Harris, Valentina, *Southern Italian Cooking* (1993).

Pomar, Anna, *La Cucina Tradizionale Siciliana* (Ital. Brancato).

Tasca Lanza, Anna, *The Flavors of Sicily* (Ici LA Pr).

Tasca Lanza, Anna, *Heart of Sicily: Recipes and Reminiscences of Regaleali, a Country Estate* (Cassell Illustrated, 1993).

Simeti, Mary Taylor, *Sicilian Food* (Grub Street, 1999).

Simeti, Mary Taylor, *Pomp and Sustenance* (Ecco Press, 1998). Cookery/autobiographical.

Tornabene, Wanda & Giovanna, and Evans, Michele, *Gangivecchio's Sicilian Kitchen* (*La Cucina Siciliana di Gangivecchio*), (Knopf, 2001).

General

Amman, Peter, *Landscapes of Sicily* (Sunflower Books, 2001). Walking guides.

Cronin, Vincent, *The Golden Honeycomb* (1954; Harvill Press, 1992). Travel and art guide.

Dolci, Danilo, *Poverty in Sicily* (1966 translation) and *Sicilian Lives* (1981 translation). Social essays.

Lewis, Norman, *In Sicily* (Picador, 2001).

Lewis, Norman, *The Honoured Society* (Eland Books, 1984).

Lewis, Norman, *The March of the Longshadows** (Secker & Warburg, 1987). Novel.

Maggio, Theresa, *Mattanza: Love and Death in the Sea of Sicily* (Perseus, 2000). Autobiography.

Maraini, Dacia, *The Silent Duchess** (Peter Owen; Feminist Press, 1998) Novel.

Maraini, Dacia, *Bagheria, A childhood memoir* (Peter Owen; Dufour).

Maxwell, G., *God Protect me from my Friends* (1956; Pan 1972); *The Ten Pains of Death* (1959; Sutton, 1986). Autobiographical.

Price, Gillian, *Walking in Sicily* (Cicerone Press, 2000).

Simeti, Mary Taylor, *On Persephone's Island* (Bantam, 2001). Autobiographical.

Robb, Peter, *Midnight in Sicily* (Harvill Press, 1999), a chilling and factual account of the Mafia.

History

Ahmad, Aziz, *A History of Islamic Sicily* (Edinburgh University Press, 1975).

Falcone, Giovanni, *Men of Honour; the truth about the Mafia* (Fourth Estate, 1992).

Finley, M.I., Mack Smith, Denis, and Duggan, Christopher, *History of Sicily* (Viking, 1987).

Hibbert, Christopher, *Garibaldi and his Enemies** (Penguin, 1987).

Matthew, Donald, *The Norman Kingdom of Sicily* (Cambridge University Press, 1992).

Norwich, John Julius, *The Normans in the South* (1967) and *The Kingdom in the Sun* (1970), published in 1 volume as *The Normans in Sicily* (Penguin, 1992).

Runciman, Stephen, *The Sicilian Vespers* (Cambridge University Press, 1992).

Stille, Alexander, *Excellent Cadavers* (Vintage, 1996).

Trevelyan, Raleigh, *Princes under the Volcano* (Phoenix Press, 2002).

* denotes titles currently out of print.

Palermo province

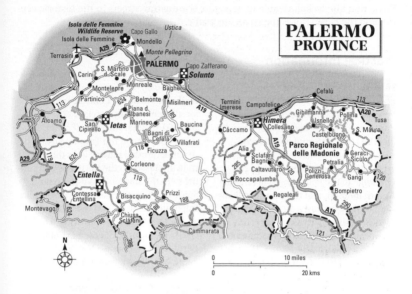

PALERMO

Palermo (population 720,000), the capital of Sicily and a fascinating city, is built on a bay on the north coast at the foot of Mount Pellegrino, a beautiful headland. It has a superb climate. One of the largest and most important cities in the world from the 9C to the 12C, Palermo still possesses some of the great Arab-Norman buildings erected at that time: the **Cappella Palatina**, **La Martorana**, **S. Giovanni degli Eremiti**, the **Zisa**, and, a few kilometres outside the city, the Cathedral of **Monreale**. Numerous delightful Baroque churches and oratories survive from later centuries. The **Archaeological Museum** and the **Regional Gallery** contain outstanding collections.

The bustling streets and animated markets give the town an oriental atmosphere. The centre, suffering from depopulation, was neglected for decades after World War II and numerous decaying slum areas grew up around the bomb sites; a large proportion of the houses were in danger of collapse. This disastrous situation finally changed in 1988–90 when detailed plans to restore and renovate the centre of the city were drawn up. Conspicuous restoration work is now in progress, at last giving the city the careful attention it deserves. Churches and palaces are being restored and the Opera House has been reopened. The spectacular restoration of the former church and convent of Lo Spasimo as a cultural centre is perhaps the most significant project completed to date.

Despite stricter control over illegal parking, a chaotic traffic system and consequent noise levels is still a major problem. Because of the congestion (not helped by the numerous weddings which take place in the churches in the city centre throughout the year) public transport functions with difficulty. However, there are signs of improvement, with the introduction of two mini-bus services (Linea Rossa and Linea Gialla), able to negotiate the narrow streets in the historic centre, and the closure of some streets to traffic.

Practical information

Getting there
By air

Falcone Borsellino **airport** at Punta Raisi, 32km west (motorway). ☎ 091/591698. Internal and international services. Coach services about every 30 minutes run by *Prestia & Comandé* to the Politeama (via Emerico Amari; **map: 7**), and the central railway station; the taxis are a lot more expensive. The *Trinacria Express* train runs between Palermo Central station and the airport hourly (04.45–21.40 from Palermo and from 05.40–00.05 from the airport).

By sea

For general enquiries contact the port at Molo Vittorio Veneto (**map: 8**), ☎ 091/6043111 or ☎ 091/6277111, ✉ www.autoport.pa.it. Several companies operate car ferries (*traghetti*) to mainland Italy and Sardinia and others run a hydrofoil service to the islands.
Car ferries to mainland Italy and Sardinia. *Tirrenia*, via del Mare, beside the port; ☎ 091/6021111. Overnight ferry service to Naples and Cagliari (Sardinia).
Grimaldi Grandi Navi Veloci, Cal. Marinai d'Italia, Porto, ☎ 091/587404, ✉ www.forti.it/grandinavi. From Molo S. Lucia to Livorno, Genoa, and Salerno.
Hydrofoil and ferry services to the islands. *Siremar*, 120 via Crispi; ☎ 091/582403. To Ustica.
SNAV, ☎ 091/6118525. To Naples and the Aeolian Islands in summer.

By rail

Railway stations. Centrale (**map: 16**) for all state railway services ☎ 091/6165914; Notarbartolo (off map), subsidiary station on the Trapani line.
An underground railway links the central railway station to the northwestern suburbs via the stations of Vespri (near S. Spirito dei Vespri), Orleans, Notarbartolo, Imperatore Federico (at the southern end of the Parco della Favorita), Fiera, Giachery, Francia, S. Lorenzo Colli, Cardillo and Tommaso Natale. It runs c every 25 minutes from 06.00–20.35.

Getting around
By bus

Around town. City buses run by *AMAT*, ☎ 091/7291111, tend to be overcrowded, infrequent and very slow because of the traffic congestion in the city centre. Tickets must be purchased at tobacconists or newsagents and stamped at automatic machines on board. There are now two excellent mini-bus circular services, both of which penetrate some of the narrower streets and pass many of the city's most important monuments (see below). Buses to monuments beyond the city centre and on the outskirts, are given in the city description.
Mini-buses. **Linea Gialla (yellow)**: railway station • corso dei Mille • Orto Botanico • Kalsa • via Alloro (Regional Art Gallery in Palazzo Abatellis) • via Maqueda • Ballarò • corso Tuköry • S. Spirito • via Oreto • railway station.

Linea Rossa (red): via Alloro (Regional Art Gallery in Palazzo Abatellis) • Quattro Canti • Cassaro (corso Vittorio Emanuele) • Cathedral • via Papireto • via S. Agostino • via Maqueda • Vucciria • Cala • piazza Marina • via Alloro (Palazzo Abatellis).

Other buses stopping at the railway station and following the corso, via Maqueda, or via Roma for part of their route: **No. 107** from the railway station. Via Roma (north side) • Giardino Inglese • terminating near the Parco della Favorita. **No. 101** Via Roma (north side) • via the Politeama (piazza Ruggero Settimo) it follows viale della Libertà. **No. 109** Corso Tuköry • piazza Indipendenza (for the Palazzo dei Normanni and Cappella Palatina). **No. 108** links piazza Indipendenza and the Cathedral to the Politeama. **No. 105** follows corso Vittorio Emanuele east to west from the seafront and piazza Marina • past the cathedral • piazza Indipendenza • corso Calatafimi.

Inter-city bus services from Palermo are run by various companies. Daily services from **via Balsamo** (beside the railway station; **map: 16**): *INTER-SAIS* c every hour to Catania (via the motorway in c 2hr 40mins), and, less frequently to Enna (in c 2hrs); also to Cefalù and Messina. They also run services to many mainland destinations, such as Bari, Taranto, Rome, Bologna, Pisa, Florence, Naples and Salerno. *Segesta* to Trapani (via Alcamo); *Cuffaro* to Agrigento, and *Randazzo* to Piazza Armerina. From **piazza Marina** (**map: 12**): *Trepanum* to Segesta; *Stassi* to Erice, and *AST* to Ragusa and Syracuse. *Segesta* also run a daily overnight coach service to Rome. For services to the environs of Palermo, see chapters below.

Parking

Parking is extremely difficult in the centre of Palermo. Most 3- and 4-star hotels have parking facilities or garages (at extra cost). Pay car parks (with parking attendant) are situated near piazza Castelnuovo, the station and via Stabile. There are some garages and *ACI* car parks in and near piazza Castelnuovo (**map: 6**) and piazza Verdi (**map: 11**). Elsewhere there are blue line areas, for which tickets are purchased at tobacconists or newsagents and then displayed inside the windscreen. If you want to stay longer, you can leave two tickets at once. If your car is illegally parked and towed away, telephone the city police (vigili urbani), ☎ 091/6954111, or ask a taxi driver to help you.

Information offices

APT Palermo, 35 piazza Castelnuovo (see **map: 6**) ☎ 091/6058111, or 091/583847, ✉ www.palermo-tourism.com. Subsidiary offices at the railway station and airport (they always have up-to-date information on opening times and what's on in the city). *Azienda Autonoma di Turismo*, Villa Igiea, 43 salita Belmonte, ☎ 091/540122. *Assessorato Regionale del Turismo* (Sicilian Regional Tourist Board), 11 via Notarbartolo. *Agenzia Sole Blu Sicilia*, 10 via Mariano Stabile, ☎ 091/323064 or 091/6122735, 🖷 091/6122736; ✉ soleblusicilia@tin.it. If the idea of planning a trip to Palermo seems too daunting, the agency will assist in finding accommodation, organizing excursions, hiring cars, yachts or motorcycles, finding guides or interpreters, and suggesting itineraries.

Visitors to Palermo are given a free **tourist card** on arriving at their hotel. The card allows discounts in shops and museums, plus many services, ✉ www.touristcardpalermo.com.

 Where to stay
Hotels

PALERMO ✮✮✮✮✮ *Villa Igiea* (beyond **map: 3**), 43 salita Belmonte, ☎ 091/ 543744, 🖷 091/547654, ✉ www. thi.it. In a remarkable Art Nouveau building on the sea at Acquasanta, 3km north of the city in a large park. Built as a sanatorium for the wealthy, it was transformed into a luxury hotel by Ernesto Basile in 1900, The dining room (*Sala Basile*) is a masterpiece. with walls painted by Bergler, and matching furniture. Tennis courts and pool.

✩✩✩✩ *Centrale Palace Hotel* (**map: 11**), 327 corso Vittorio Emanuele, 90139. ☎ 091/336666, 📠 091/334881, 📧 www. bestwestern.it. One of the oldest hotels; rooftop terrace, lovely rooms and lounges, excellent restaurant.

✩✩✩✩ *Excelsior Palace* (**map: 2**), 3 via Marchese Ugo, ☎ 091/6256176, 📠 091/ 342139, 📧 www. excelsiorpalermo.com. Delightful Belle Epoque atmosphere, central position, excellent service and good restaurant.

✩✩✩✩ *Grande Albergo Sole* (**map: 11**), 291 corso Vittorio Emanuele, 90133. ☎ 091/6041111, 📠 091/6110182, 📧 www.market.thecity.it/albergosole. Newly overhauled, historic hotel where many of the famous have stayed. Very central but not easy if you are driving.

✩✩✩✩ *Grand Hotel et des Palmes* (**map: 7**), 398 via Roma, 90139. ☎ 091/ 583933, 📠 091/331545, 📧 www. thi.it. In the former Palazzo Ingham. Luxurious. Good restaurant.

✩✩✩✩ *Jolly* (**map: 16**), Foro Italico, 90133. ☎ 091/6165090, 📠 091/ 6161441, 📧 www.jollyhotels.it. Lovely hotel on the seafront close to the Villa Giulia park. Excellent restaurant; pool; free use of bicycles.

✩✩✩✩ *Politeama Palace* (**map: 6**), 15 piazza Ruggero Settimo, 90139. ☎ 091/322777, 📠 091/6111589, 📧 www. hotelpoliteama.it; modern hotel in city centre, opposite Politeama Theatre. Comfortable rooms, obliging service, good restaurant.

✩✩✩✩ *President* (**map: 3**), 228 via Crispi, 90139. ☎ 091/580733, 📠 091/ 6111588. Situated in front of the port,

comfortable rooms and good restaurant.

✩✩✩✩ *Principe di Villafranca* (**map: 2**), 4 via Turrisi Colonna, ☎ 091/ 6118523, 📠 091/588705, 📧 www.principedivillafranca.it. Small, refined hotel. Central position in the new city; good restaurant, cosy library and lounge with open fireplace, garage and fitness centre. Elegant bedrooms.

✩✩✩ *Athenaeum*, 4 via Giannettino (off map), ☎ 091/6523529, 📠 091/ 6523456, 📧 www.tin.it/athenaeum. No-nonsense hotel near the University. Breakfast is dreary but the set meals in the restaurant (for guests only) are surprisingly good and not expensive. Longish walk into town.

✩✩✩ *Casena dei Colli*, 20-22 via Villa Rosato (off map), ☎ 091/6889771, 091/6889779, 📧 www. vol.it/ target.turismo/casena. Pleasant, characterful hotel close to the Favorita park. Good restaurant.

✩✩✩ *Europa*, 3 via Agrigento (**map: 2**), ☎ & 📠 091/6256323, 📧 www. abeuropa.com. Efficient, modern, comfortable. In new town centre. Small restaurant (for guests only).

✩✩✩ *Hotel Tonic* (**map: 7**), 126 via Mariano Stabile, ☎ 091/581754, 📠 091/585560, 📧 www.hoteltonic. com. Small, well-run, comfortable hotel in the modern city centre.

✩✩✩ *Massimo Plaza*, 437 via Maqueda (**map: 11**), ☎ 091/325657, 📠 091/325711, 📧 www.massimo plazahotel.com. Opposite the Opera House. Luxurious rooms, courteous management, no restaurant. Classy.

✩✩✩ *Villa D'Amato*, 180 via Messina Marine (off map), ☎ 091/6212767, 📠 091/6112767, 📧 www. hotelvilladamato.it. Restored villa on the old road to Messina. Private beach at Mondello; breakfast with a view; pleasant restaurant.

✩✩ *Joly*, 11 via Amari (**map: 7**), ☎ & 📠 091/6111766. Good value. Central.

✩✩ *Posta*, 77 via Gagini (**map: 11**), ☎ &

🗐 091/587347. Modern hotel with nice rooms and good service. Garage available.

☆☆ *Villa Archirafi*, 30 via Abramo Lincoln (**map: 16**), ☎ & 🗐 091/6168827. Comfortable hotel with garden, close to Villa Giulia and the Botanical Gardens; impeccable service.

☆ *Ariston*, 139 via Mariano Stabile (**map: 7**), ☎ 091/332434. Centrally situated, small hotel with clean, comfortable rooms and good management.

☆ *Letizia* (**map: 12**), 30 via Bottai, ☎ & 🗐 091/589110, ✉ www.hotelletizia.com. Small, friendly hotel close to corso S. Francesco and the Vucciria.

☆ *Petit*, 84 via Principe di Belmonte (**map: 7**), ☎ 091/323616. Tiny hotel on what is now Palermo's most fashionable street. Book early.

☆ *Orientale*, 26 via Maqueda (**map: 15**), 90134. ☎ 091/6165727, 🗐 091/6165180. Among the oldest hotels in town (1890). Quaint, large rooms, no restaurant, but you can park your car in the once beautiful courtyard.

MONDELLO ☆☆☆☆ *Mondello Palace*, 1953 viale Principe di Scalea, 90151, ☎ 091/450001, 🗐 091/450657. In a beautiful park with minigolf and private beach, pool, good restaurant.

☆☆☆ *Addaura*, 4452 lungomare Cristoforo Colombo, ☎ 091/6842222, 🗐 091/6842255, ✉ www.addaurahotel.it. New hotel on the beach, with diving centre, windsurfing, waterskiing, pool, garden and good restaurant; comfortable rooms.

☆☆☆ *Splendid Hotel La Torre*, 11 Piano Gallo, 90151, ☎ 091/450222, 🗐 091/450033, ✉ www.latorre.it. On the promontory close to the old watchtower, very comfortable hotel with garden, pool, good restaurant.

☆☆☆ *Conchiglia d'Oro*, 9 viale Cloe, 90151, ☎ 091/450359, 🗐 091/450032. Just right for families, a quiet hotel with private beach and pool.

☆☆ *Villa Esperia*, 53 via Margherita di Savoia, ☎ & 🗐 091/6840717. Attractive Art Nouveau building in central position, close to the beach; garden and restaurant.

Bed and breakfast

PALERMO ☆☆☆☆☆ *Palazzo Conte Federico*, 4 via dei Biscottari (**map: 14**), ☎ & 🗐 091/6511881, ✉ www.cd-net.it/contefederico. For a unique experience, why not stay in an ancient palazzo with the last descendant of Frederick of Hohenstaufen and his countess? Very exclusive and expensive. English, French and German spoken.

☆☆☆ *Ai Cartari*, 62 via Alessandro Paternostro (**map: 12**), ☎ 091/6116372, 🗐 091/589395, ✉ www.aicartari.com. House near S. Francesco church. English and French spoken. Very friendly owners.

☆☆☆ *Castiglione*, 3 piazza Stazione Lolli (**map: 6**), ☎ & 🗐 091/335300, ✉ www.primitaly.it. Central position for this 19C apartment, good breakfasts are served in the rooms; guests can use the fridge. English and French spoken.

☆☆☆ *St Thorn House*, 210 via Spinasanta (off map), ☎ 091/532987, 🗐 091/6916347, ✉ www.bedandbreakfast.pa.it; on the hills overlooking Mondello, modern home with pool, car park, air conditioning, private bathroom, TV, internet access and use of kitchen on request.

MONDELLO ☆☆☆ *Il Banano*, 3 via Stesicoro, ☎ 091/454011, 🗐 091/546872, ✉ www.ilbanano.com. A lovely 19C villa with garden, close to beach and main square; pick up from airport at small extra cost, English and Spanish spoken.

Accommodation agency

PALERMO *Casa Giuditta*, 10 via Savona (**map: 16**, piazza Kalsa), ☎ 328/2250788, 🗐 02/700401920, ✉ casagiuditta@ yahoo.com. Organizes B&B accommodation in old Palermo, also villas and apartments. Many additional services on offer such as babysitters, car and cell phone hire, cooks and personal tour guides.

Youth hostel

PALERMO Casa Marconi, 140 via Monfenera (off the map, near the Hospital), ☎ 091/ 6451116, ✉ www.casamarconi.it.

Campsites

The following sites are quite a way from Palermo, at Sferracavallo, west of the city after Mondello and Tommaso Natale, but there is nothing closer.

☆☆ *Trinacria*, 23-25 via Barcarello, Sferracavallo, ☎ & 🖷 091/530590. On the sea with plenty of amenities.

☆ *Campeggio degli Ulivi*, 25 via Pegaso, Sferracavallo, ☎ & 🖷 091/533021. Rather spartan structure on the sea.

Eating out
Restaurants

PALERMO €€€ *Osteria dei Vespri*, 6 piazza Croce dei Vespri (**map: 2**), ☎ 091/6171631. Right under the palace where Visconti filmed the ballroom scenes of *The Leopard*, a tavern where you can sample the exciting fusions of Sicilian and Parma cuisine. Ravioli stuffed with mussels served with potato purée, rock fish and sea urchins, for example. Extensive wine list including most Sicilian and Italian wines. Closed Sun.

€€€ *Ristorantino*, 19 piazza dei Gasperi, (stadium) ☎ 091/512861. Refined little restaurant where Pippo Anastasio takes great care of his guests. Many surprising dishes: *insalata di seppie con pesto e fave* (cuttlefish salad with pesto and broad beans) and unusual desserts: *semifreddo al gorgonzola*. Exceptional wine list. Closed Mon.

€€€ *Santandrea*, 4 piazza Sant'Andrea (**map: 11**), ☎ 091/334999. In a square close to the church of S. Domenico. Delightful restaurant; special atmosphere; delicious food; extensive wine list. Peter Robb wrote much of his *Midnight in*

Sicily here. Closed Tues; Sun. in summer.

€€ *Capricci di Sicilia*, 8 piazza Sturzo (**map: 7**; Politeama) ☎ 091/327777 takes pride in presenting the very best cuisine of Palermo, served with only the best Sicilian wines. Closed Mon.

€€ *Delizie di Cagliostro*, 150 corso Vittorio Emanuele (**map: 11**), ☎ 091/332818. Refined menu; an almost Baroque atmosphere. The *pasta al cartoccio* (cooked in a little paper parcel) is renowned. Closed Sun. evening.

€€ *Maestro del brodo*, 7 via Pannieri (**map: 11**, Vucciria), ☎ 091/329523. One of the oldest restaurants in town. Their broths (brodo); antipasti and pasta are superb. Closed Wed.

€€ *Mamma Carmela*, via Principe di Scordia (**map: 7**), ☎ 091/6112701. Friendly, casual restaurant (so better for lunch than for dinner). Realistic prices, good simple dishes. Excellent *pasta con broccoli alla Palermitana*.

€€ *Stella* (Hotel Patria), 104 via Alloro (**map: 12**), ☎ 091/6161136. Charming trattoria. Very popular with the locals. Meals are served in the cool courtyard. The antipasti are good, so are the grilled meats. Closed Sun.

€€ *Trattoria Biondo*, 15 via Carducci (**map: 7**, Politeama), ☎ 091/583662. Charming, intimate atmosphere, so better for dinner than lunch. The list of Sicilian wines is superb; impeccable cuisine. Closed Wed.

€€ *Trattoria Lo Sparviero*, 23 via Sperlinga (**map: 7**, Opera House), ☎ 091/331163. Very good Sicilian food, reasonable prices. Marvellous grilled vegetables, the best in Palermo, and superb desserts.

€€ *Dal Pompiere*, 107 via Bara all'Olivella (**map: 11**), ☎ 091/325282. Eating here is great fun; the food is simple and satisfying. Right in the centre of the 'arts and crafts' area of the city.

€€ *La Mensa del Popolo*, 58 via Mariano Stabile (**map: 7**). Yassine from Tunisia offers local and North African specialities. Pizzeria in the evenings.

Pizzerie and self-service

PALERMO *Antica Pizzeria Venezia*, 75 via Venezia (**map: 11**), ☎ 091/586038, Tasty home cooking, and excellent pizza in the evenings.

Bar Mazzara, 15 via Generale Magliocco (**map: 6**, Opera House). Excellent self-service lunches and the best *cotoletta palermitana* (breaded grilled steak) of the city. Tomasi di Lampedusa wrote *The Leopard* here. Great sweets too (see under *cafés*).

Bellini, piazza Bellini (**map: 15**). Popular with the locals. Pizza at lunchtime.

Pizzeria Italia, 54 via dell'Orologio (**map: 11**), ☎ 091/589885. The oldest and best-loved pizza restaurant in Palermo, superb pizzas, evenings only.

Renna Self-Service, 29/A via Principe di Granatelli (**map: 7**), ☎ 091/580661. Fresh, simple food in a clean, tidy setting. Very inexpensive.

Vegetarian restaurants

PALERMO *Il crudo e il cotto*, 45 piazza Marina (**map: 12**), ☎ 091/6169261. Closed Tues.

Il mirto e la rosa, 30 via Principe di Granatelli (**map: 7**). Imaginative vegetarian dishes, meat also on the menu.

Alla fermata di Porta Carini, 108 via Volturno (**map: 10**), ☎ 091/586024. A good assortment of vegetarian dishes on offer as well as meat and fish. Closed Sun.

MONDELLO €€€ *Charleston*, viale Regina Elena, ☎ 091/450171. Opulent Art Nouveau establishment jutting out over the sea. Very expensive. probably the best cuisine and wines of Sicily, with suitably professional service. Closed Wed.

€€€ *Sapori di Mare*, 52 via Mondello, ☎ 091/6840623. Refined restaurant, excellent seafood; *pepata di cozze* (mussel soup) is delicious. Closed Tues in winter.

€€ *Bye Bye Blues*, 23 via del Garofalo, ☎ 091/6841415. Fish dishes a speciality, but magnificent vegetable antipasti; superb desserts. Good wine list. Closed Tues.

€€ *La Locanda*, 26 via Torre, ☎ 091/6840127. Historic restaurant (1865) in front of the harbour. Local dishes and some very special recipes; good wine list. Closed Thurs.

SFERRACAVALLO Palermitans often go to the village of Sferracavallo when they want to spend an evening eating seafood. There are lots of inexpensive restaurants here which serve a series of seafood dishes, usually for a fixed price. One of the best, offering an experience of life Palermo-style is *Temptation*, in the main square, ☎ 091/6911104.

Snack bars and sandwiches

PALERMO *Antica Focacceria di S. Francesco*, 58 via Alessandro Paternostro (**map: 12**), ☎ 091/320264. Sample traditional Palermitan snacks and sandwiches: bread with *panelle* (chick pea fritters), *meusa* (grilled beef spleen), *purpu* (boiled octopus), *stigghiole* (stuffed intestines of kid or lamb, seasoned and wound around a cane and grilled). Closed Mon.

Caffè Opera, 62 piazza Verdi (Opera House). Ideal for lunch or a snack.

Da Filippo, 38 via Porta Carini (**map: 11**). Excellent, simple, full of locals.

Focacceria Basile, 76 via Bara dell'Olivella. Opposite the Opera House; the best *arancini* (rice balls).

Minà, 28 via Pannieri (Vucciria). A good choice for robust sandwiches.

Pani ca' meusa, 60 via Porta Carini (**map: 10**). Very, very basic and very, very good; Franco has been preparing typical Palermo goodies here since 1943.

Special Sandwich, 54 via Mazzini (**map: 2**), elegant sandwich bar.

Cafés, ice cream parlours and pastry shops

PALERMO *Aluia*, via Mazzini, corner 27 via Libertà (**map: 2**). One of the best pastry shops for local specialities.

Antico Caffè Spinnato, 111 via Principe di Belmonte (**map: 7**). Elegant open-air café, for rubbing shoulders with glitzy Palermitans.

Bar Alba, 7 piazza Don Bosco (off map, Stadium area), is worth a trip for its famous ice cream and pastries.

Bar Mazzara, 15 via Generale Magliocco (**map: 6**, Opera House). Try their famous ricotta tart, rum baba or cassata. Great lunches too (see under *self-service*).

Bar Santoro, piazza Indipendenza (in front of the Royal Palace). A good choice for breakfast or an afternoon break.

Caffè Oriente (usually called **Caffè Arabo**), 8 piazza Gran Cancelliere (**map: 11**; Quattro Canti), for a Middle Eastern lunch or a glass of mint tea, accompanied by belly dancers and perhaps a hookah.

Da Ciccio, 73 corso dei Mille (near Central Station). Memorable ice creams.

Golden, 38 piazzale de Gasperi (Stadium). Popular place for Sicilian breakfast.

Il Golosone, 22 piazza Castelnuovo (**map: 6**). Very good ice cream or *panna cotta*.

Il Rintocco, 14 via Orologio (**map: 11**, Opera House). Charming old-fashioned coffee house. Unusual coffee, herb teas and hot chocolate. Closes early (20.00).

Malavoglia, 5 piazzetta Speciale (**map: 15**, behind piazza Bologni). Literary café with foreign language books and magazines, besides Italian.

Nino Matranga, kiosk at 1 piazza Gentili (off map; at crossroad between via Libertà and via Notarbartolo), prepares famous *cremolate*, a kind of creamy, squashy sorbet. Now very fashionable. 32 flavours.

Pasticceria Ruvolo, 121 via Bara all'Olivella (**map: 11**). Comfortable tea room serving the very best cakes and pastries.

Ristoro del Massimo, 364 via Maqueda (**map: 11**). Tiny coffee bar not far from the Opera House. Many snacks and sandwiches; delicious *spumoni* (fluffy ice cream) and the best espresso in Palermo.

Scimone, 18 via Miceli (**map:10**). Good confectionery, Apostle's finger biscuits

(*dita d'apostolo*).

Caffè Vannucci, 197 corso Vittorio Emanuele (**map: 11**), old-fashioned tea room.

MONDELLO **Renato** and **Antico Chiostro**. Two ice cream parlours side by side in the main square. Both make fantastic ice creams and cakes.

Wine bars and pubs

PALERMO *I Grilli Giù*, 9 piazza Valverde (**map: 11**, behind S. Domenico). Fashionable cocktail bar which serves delightful Middle Eastern style snacks. Hot music.

Kursaal Kalsa, 21/A Foro Umberto (also called Foro Italico, **map: 12**). Wine and coffee bar. Wonderful atmosphere, often live music, an open fire in winter, foreign language newspapers.

Mi Manda Picone, 59 via Alessandro Paternostro (**map: 11**), ☎ 091/6160660. Near S. Francesco church. Welcoming little bar; vast choice of wines, delicious freshly cooked food.

The Navy, 46 via Cala (**map: 12**). An English-style pub serving British beers.

Picnics

Public parks pleasant for picnics near the centre of Palermo include the Villa Giulia (**map: 16**), Villa Trabia (**map: 1, 2**) and the Giardino Inglese (**map: 2**).

 ## Shopping
Arts and crafts

Via Bara all'Olivella is fast becoming the street for arts and crafts. At no. 38, Antonio Cuticchio makes **puppets** for his brother Mimmo, famous *puparu*, who has his theatre close by. At no. 60 is the **Bottega Ippogrifo**, where Paolo Seminara makes beautiful **toys** from wood and papier maché. **Storie Sognate** is at no. 28, where three artists: Pietro Sciortino, Giuseppinella Tedesco and Adele Papa, paint on wood, glass and wax, creating novel works of art. At no. 70, Gabriella Ingrassia makes irresistible **lamps**, using agate, clay, scraps of cloth, string, rope and wood. At no. 64, Enzo Scerrino paints **vases**, while Alfio Ferlito makes **miniature houses** complete with furniture, perfect down to the tiniest detail. Laura Plaja, at no. 97, makes original **jewellery** using silver and semi-precious stones, while at no. 105 is *Caleidoscopio*, with the distinctive **pottery** of Silvana Donelli.

De Simone, 698 **via Lanza di Scalea** (velodromo) ☎ 091/6711005 is one of the best known names in Sicilian **pottery**, at once recognisable from the naif design and distinctive colours: orangey-red, turquoise blue and lemon yellow.

In **via della Loggia** (map: 11, between via Roma and the Cala) **silk fringes** are made for curtains and tablecloths. There are **silversmiths** at Piazza Meli (map: 6, near the Cala) and **coppersmiths** near ponte dell'Ammiraglio (off map).

I peccatucci di mamma Andrea, 67 via Principe di Scordia (map: 7), ☎ 091/334835. Andrea De Cesare sells exquisite **home-made sweets**, jams and marmalades all made by hand and beautifully displayed and packaged. Nougat, almond biscuits, marzipan filled with pistachio paste and chocolate-covered fruit.

At *Domus Artis*, 6 via Nino Basile (Casa Professa, map: 15) Luigi Arini still makes exquisite religious articles using wax, silver and coral, as established by a Vatican ruling in 1566 which indicated the materials, colours and symbolism that artists and craftsmen could use.

Markets

The street markets of Palermo are justly famous, and should not be missed even by the most hurried visitor. The stalls are set up in the morning around 08.30 or 09.00 and stay open all day until around 19.30. The biggest are: **Vucciria** (map: 11), for produce (especially fish); **Ballarò** (map: 15), for produce and household goods; **Capo** (via S. Agostino; **map: 10, 11**), for clothes, cloth and shoes; **Papireto** (piazza Peranni; **map: 10**), for antiques and bric-a-brac, usually called *Mercato delle Pulci*. Another **food market** opens in the afternoon and evening in corso Scinà (**map: 3**).

Opening times of museums and monuments

These have been extended but often change: for the latest list of times contact the *APT*. Numerous churches are now kept open (usually weekdays 09.00–17.00, Sat 09.00–13.00) through a scheme (Cento Chiese Aperte) promoted by the local council and the Curia whereby groups of young people act as guides and custodians. The final goal is to open 100. For information, contact the *Alba Chiara Association*, ☎ 091/6884302. Cumulative tickets are available, grouping various monuments and museums, and are valid two days.

 ## Annual festivals

Festino di S. Rosalia (10–15 July), with celebrations including theatre performances, concerts, fireworks and a street procession with the statue of St Rosalie on a huge cart drawn by horses; pilgrimage (with a torchlight procession) to the shrine on Monte Pellegrino, 3–4 September.

Entertainment
Theatre, opera, concerts, cabaret

Massimo Opera House, piazza Verdi (**map: 10**), ☎ 091/6053111. Music and opera.

Politeama Garibaldi, piazza Ruggero Settimo (**map: 7**), ☎ 091/6053315. Concerts and ballet.

Biondo, 258 via Roma (**map: 11**) ☎ 091/582364, prose.

Teatrino Ditirammu, 6 via Torremuzza alla Kalsa (**map: 16**), ☎ 091/6177865. The smallest theatre in Italy (25 seats).

Popular music, dance, Mancuso's puppet shows. **Concerts** are also held at S. Maria dello Spasimo, in via dello Spasimo in the Kalsa district and in the churches of La Gancia, S. Salvatore and S. Giuseppe, and in the Sala Scarlatti of the Conservatorio, 45 via Squarcialupo. *Teatro di Verdura*, Villa Castelnuovo, information from the Tourist Office or in the daily newspapers. Open-air concerts and ballets in the beautiful gardens of this aristocratic dwelling in summer. *Candelai* (65 via dei Candelai, ☎ 091/327151, 🖳 www.candelai.it), an old furniture warehouse near the University; art shows, dance, live music and cabaret.

Puppet theatres

Performances at the *Museo Internazionale delle Marionette* (see below), 1 via Butera (**map: 12**), ☎ 091/328060, and periodically at various small theatres in the city including *Cuticchio*, 52 via Bara (**map: 11**) ☎ 091/323400; *Opera dei Pupi Ippogrifo*, 4 vicolo Ragusi (**map: 11**), ☎ 091/329194; *Compagnia Argento*, 1 via Novelli, (**map: 14**) ☎ 091/6113680, 🖳 www.digilander.iol.it/argentopupi; performances every day 18.00. Ring theatres to check performance times.

Internet points

Aboriginal Internet Café, 51 via Spinuzza (**map: 11**), ☎ 091/662222.
Accademia Internet, 64 via Cala (**map: 12**), ☎ 091/6118483. Falcone and Borsellino airport internet; 3rd floor).
@Internet Point, 5 via Dante (**map: 6**), Politeama.
I Candelai Internet Café, via Candelai (**map: 11**), ☎ 091/327151 (except Mon).
Informatica Commerciale, 23 via

Notarbartolo (off map), ☎ 091/343646
Internet Shop, 32/34 via Napoli, (10.30–20.00).
Internettamente, 3/A via Sammartino, ☎ 091/6121174.
Navigando, 73 via Libertà (**map: 2**), ☎ 091/345332. (During office hours).
Palazzo Ziino, 53 via Dante (**map: 6**), ☎ 091/7407621, Tues–Sun 09.30–18.30.
Villa Niscemi, piazza Niscemi (Favorita park), ☎ 091/7404805, Mon–Sat 09.00–15.00, 15.30–19.00.
Villa Trabia, (**map: 1,2**) 3 via Antonio Salinas, ☎ 091/7405905, 09.00–18.00, closed Sun afternoon.

Consulates

UK   117 via Cavour, ☎ 091/326412.
USA   1 via Vaccarini, ☎ 091/305857.
Netherlands   489 via Roma, ☎ 091/581521.
Malta   55 via Principe di Belmonte, ☎ 091/586533.

Foreign language newspapers and periodicals

Newsagents in piazza Verdi (Opera House), piazza Castelnuovo (Politeama), piazza Vittoria (Cathedral), 326 via Maqueda, Falcone Borsellino Airport, 2nd floor, Central Railway Station.
MONDELLO In Viale Regina Elena and at 2, viale Margherita di Savoia.

Police station (Questura)

11 piazza della Vittoria (**map: 14**) ☎ 091/210111; office for foreigners, ☎ 091/6514330.
For all emergencies ☎ 113.

English church

(Holy Cross; **map: 7**), 118 via Stabile; services in winter only.

History

Traces of Paleolithic settlements have been found in grottoes on Monte Pellegrino. The carsic mountains which surround the plain ensured the fertility of the Conca d'Oro which was important to the inhabitants of Palermo throughout her history. *Panormus*, a Phoenician colony of the 8C–6C BC, was never a Greek city, despite its Greek name signifying 'all harbour'. It was, instead, an important Carthaginian centre, hotly disputed during the First Punic War, and not finally acquired by Rome until 254 BC. It became a municipium, and after 20 BC, a flourishing colony. After the invasions of the Vandals and Ostrogoths it was reconquered for the Byzantine emperors in 535 and remained in their possession until 831, when the Saracens captured it after a prolonged resistance.

Under Muslim rule it was made capital of an emirate (and named *al Medina*) and rivalled Cordoba and Cairo in oriental splendour. It became an important trading post and cosmopolitan centre which showed tolerance towards Christians and Jews, even though hundreds of mosques were built in the city at this time.

Taken by Count Roger de Hauteville in 1072, it again reached a high state of prosperity under his son King Roger II (1130–54), and became the centre of trade between Europe and Asia. Under the brilliant court of the Emperor Frederick II of Hohenstaufen (1198–1250), *stupor mundi*, the city became famous throughout Europe for its learning and magnificence.

The famous rebellion of the '**Sicilian Vespers**' (see p 118) put an end to the misrule of Charles of Anjou in 1282. A long period of Spanish domination, which became increasingly tyrannical, led to the gradual decline of the city, despite an insurrection of 1646. By the **Treaty of Utrecht** (1713) Sicily was allotted to Vittorio Amedeo of Savoy, who was, however, forced to exchange it for Sardinia (1718) in favour of the Neapolitan Bourbons. Under their rule the island suffered more than ever, though Ferdinand IV established his court at Palermo in 1799 during the French occupation of Naples. The island was granted a temporary constitution in 1811 while under British protection. In the 18C Palermo was the largest town in Italy after Naples. The city rebelled against misgovernment in 1820 (when Sir Richard Church was relieved of his governorship), 1848, and in April 1860. On 27 May 1860 **Garibaldi and the Thousand** made a triumphal entry into the city.

Much of the centre of Palermo was badly damaged during air raids in World War II. The city was virtually governed by the Mafia in the following decades, when much illegal new building took place in the Conca d'Oro which spoiled the once beautiful surrounding area. In the 1960s and 1970s it was perhaps the most neglected city in Italy, when a vast number of houses in the historical centre were in danger of collapse, and the population of this area dwindled to some 35,000 (from 125,000 in 1951), representing a mere five per cent of the total population of the municipal area. But in 1997, an enlightened city government finally approved a detailed plan to restore and revitalise the old city centre and numerous restoration projects are now under way if not already completed.

Art and architecture

Norman domination, with its architecture showing a strongly oriental influence, has left many magnificent buildings, including the Palazzo della Zisa and Palazzo dei Normanni, the Cappella Palatina, La Martorana, and, on the outskirts, Monreale Cathedral. All these buildings also have especially remarkable mosaic decoration. Architecture and painting in the early 15C was influenced by Catalan masters, as can be seen from the south porch of the Cathedral and at Palazzo Abatellis.

Matteo Carnelivari was the most important architect working in Palermo at this time. Francesco Laurana, the Renaissance sculptor, came to work in Palermo in the middle of the 15C. Another extremely influential sculptor here in the second half of the 15C was Domenico Gagini; his style was continued into the following century by his son Antonello. If the dramatic 15C fresco of the *Triumph of Death* (now in the Regional Gallery) is by a Sicilian master, it is the most important Sicilian work of this period.

Numerous splendid Baroque churches were erected in Palermo, many of them by the local architect Giacomo Amato (1643–1732). From the mid-17C to the end of the 18C the interiors of many churches were lavishly decorated with coloured marbles and mosaic inlay. The delightful stuccoes of Giacomo Serpotta (1656–1732) are best seen in the oratories of S. Cita, S. Domenico and S. Lorenzo. Pietro Novelli of Monreale was the greatest 17C Sicilian painter. Venanzio Marvuglia (1729–1814) produced some fine neoclassical buildings in Palermo, and the city is particularly rich in Art Nouveau architecture. There are also a number of monumental edifices in eclectic styles by Ernesto Basile (1857–1932).

Topography

The ancient town, bounded by two small rivers which run into the sea, the Kemonia and the Papireto, occupied an elliptical area centering on the present Cathedral. Its main street (now the western half of the corso Vittorio Emanuele) was known as the *Cassaro Vecchio*, a name derived from Castrum or the Arabic '*Kasr*' (meaning castle). The Saracen citadel, called *Halisa*, the Elect (now Kalsa) grew up to the south of the harbour, in an area thought to have been occupied also by the Neapolis, or new town, another fortified area which was created in the Roman era nearer the port.

By the mid-16C the rivers had silted up and the harbour was reduced to its existing proportions and the plan of Palermo from then on hinged on two main thoroughfares: the **Cassaro**, extended to the east in 1565 and prolonged to the sea in 1581, and the **via Maqueda** (laid out c 1600), running roughly parallel with the coast. These bisect one another at the Quattro Canti. In the 19C and 20C the city expanded northwards, with its focus at piazza Verdi (**map: 10**).

In present day Palermo very few street names are written up, even though they all have an official name on the maps. This is being rectified, and in the Jewish Quarter (Giudecca) of the historic centre, roughly corresponding to the area just south of S. Agostino (**map: 11**), you will notice that the street signs are written in Italian, Arabic and Hebrew, to underline the cosmopolitan character of old Palermo.

Famous residents

These include the composer Alessandro Scarlatti (1660–1725), the chemist Stanislao Cannizzaro (1826–1910), and Vittorio Emanuele Orlando (1860–1952), prime minister of Italy (1917–19) and a brilliant jurist. Though educated in Palermo, Sergius I (pope, 687–701) is now thought to have been born at Antioch.

1 • The city centre

The monumental crossroads known as the **Quattro Canti** (map: 11) was laid out in 1608–20 by Giulio Lasso at the central intersection of the four longest and straightest streets of the city. It was named piazza Vigliena after the Duke of Vigliena, Spanish viceroy in 1611, and is often called Teatro del Sole or Theatre of the Sun, because in the course of the day the sun illuminates the four corners in turn. The decorative façades bear fountains with statues of the four seasons, the four Spanish kings of Sicily, and the four patron saints of Palermo (Cristina, Ninfa, Oliva and Agata). It is now a confined and busy road junction, but is still used as a meeting place by the locals. At either end of corso Vittorio Emanuele, Porta Nuova and the sea beyond Porta Felice can be seen, while via Maqueda has a vista of the hills surrounding the Conca d'Oro.

Piazza Pretoria

A few steps along via Maqueda to the southeast, piazza Pretoria (**map: 11**) is almost entirely occupied by a fountain designed by the Florentine Francesco Camilliani (1554–55) and later reassembled here by his son Camillo and Michelangelo Naccherino (1573). The great basin is decorated with numerous statues of monsters, harpies, sirens and tritons, all with very little in the way of clothes; for this reason the fountain is often called the *Fontana della vergogna*, or Fountain of Shame.

A tale of two fountains

There has always been rivalry between Palermo and Messina, both of which through the centuries have strived to emerge as the foremost city on the island. Messina was the first, however, to supply citizens with water coming from a nearby river by means of a modern acqueduct in 1547, and to celebrate this, a beautiful fountain was situated by the side of the Cathedral (see Messina chapter), which caused quite a stir in Sicily. The envious citizens of Palermo thought they should have something equally gorgeous; and having decided that 'bigger is better', they were fortunate enough to snap up the enormous fountain which had been designed for the garden of a Tuscan villa by Francesco Camilliani. Thought to be too cumbrous, the owners were only too glad to get rid of it, and it ended up in Palermo, where it looks perfectly at ease. The Palermitans even went to the point of copying the idea of the four rivers, in this case Oreto, Papireto, Kemonia and Gabriele, while instead of Orion, the figure on the summit represents the Genius of Palermo. Both Palermo and Messina can be well satisfied with the results of this competition; definitely a draw.

Palazzo delle Aquile

Palazzo delle Aquile, named after the eagles which decorate its exterior (and usually referred to as Palazzo Pretorio ☎ 091/7401111), is the Town Hall. It was built in 1470, enlarged in the 16C, and over-restored in 1874. On the top of the façade is a statue of St Rosalie by Carlo D'Aprile (1661). Visitors are admitted without formality when it is not in use. This was formerly the seat of the Senate which governed the city from the 14C until 1816, senators being elected from the local aristocracy.

In the **atrium** is a Baroque portal by Paolo Amato and a Roman funerary monument with statues of a husband and wife. At the foot of the 19C staircase is part of a 16C fountain of the Genius of Palermo, one of a number of allegorical statues in the city with the figure of a king, personifying civic rule, entangled in a serpent, representing wisdom, sometimes with a dog at his feet, for loyalty, or a lion, for strength, and an eagle on his shoulder, representing the empire. On the **first floor**, the assembly room, which has a 16C painted wooden ceiling, is covered with numerous inscriptions relating to events which have taken place in the room. The other rooms, including that of the mayor, were decorated by Damiani Almeyda in 1870 and contain mementoes of Garibaldi and Napoleon.

Another side of the piazza is closed by the flank and dome of the church of **S. Caterina** (1566–96).The interior, especially the choir, is an elaborate example of Sicilian Baroque, with its striking effects of sculptural decoration and marble veneering (executed in the early 18C). In the right transept is a *St Catherine* by Antonello Gagini (1534). The frescoes in the cupola are by Vito D'Anna (1751).

San Giuseppe dei Teatini

Across via Maqueda is the side of the church of S. Giuseppe dei Teatini (**map: 15**). The upper church, built by Giacomo Besio of Genoa (1612–45), was the scene of two popular assemblies called by Giuseppe D'Alessi during the revolt of 1647 against the Spanish governors.

In the lavish Baroque **interior** (open 07.00–12.00, 17.00–20.00), in addition to the 14 monolithic columns in the nave, eight colossal columns of grey marble support the well-proportioned central dome. The frescoes of the nave roof are copies of the originals by Filippo Tancredi; those in the dome are by Borremans; the stuccoes are remarkable. The two large angels holding the stoups on either side of the entrance are by Marabitti.

In the fourth south chapel, with pretty marble decoration, is a statue of the *Madonna* by the school of Gagini.

In the south transept, beneath the altarpiece of *St Andrew of Avellino* by Sebastiano Conca is a charming frieze of child musicians, and the altar has a bas-relief of a *Madonna amidst angels*, both by Federico Siragusa (1800).

In the choir vault are fine reliefs, with full-length figures, by Procopio Serpotta. In the chapels flanking the choir are (right) a *Crucifix* by Fra Umile da Petralia and (left) reliefs by Filippo Pennino, and an 18C statue of *St Joseph*. In the north transept, above an altar of marble mosaic (probably late 17C), is a painting of *St Cajetan* by Pietro Novelli.

Next to the church is the former Convent of the Teatini di S. Giuseppe, now occupied by the university (the building was modified in the 19C). The small Geological Museum founded here in the early 19C is now at no. 131 corso Tuköry (**map: 15**), and open to students.

La Martorana and San Cataldo

Adjoining piazza Pretoria is piazza Bellini where the majestic campanile of La Martorana stands next to the three little red domes of S. Cataldo, raised above part of the east wall of the Roman city and surrounded by a few trees; it is fitting that these two beautiful churches, founded by two of Norman Sicily's greatest statesmen, should survive together in the centre of the city.

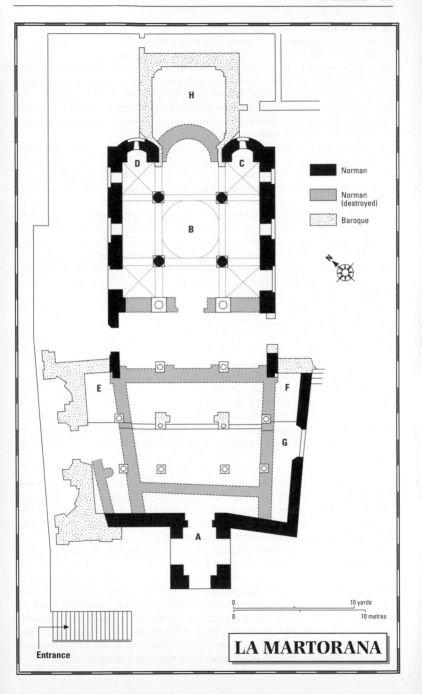

Norman

Norman
(destroyed)

Baroque

N

LA MARTORANA

0   10 yards
0   10 metres

Entrance

La Martorana

La Martorana (**map: 15**; open 08.00–13.00, 15.30–17.30; Sun & PH 08.30–13.00, ☎ 091/6161692) or S. Maria dell'Ammiraglio, is a Norman church founded c 1146 by George of Antioch, a Syrian of the Greek Orthodox faith who became admiral under Roger II. It was presented in 1433 to a convent founded in the 12C by Eloisa Martorana, wife of Goffredo de Martorana. The Sicilian Parliament met here after the Sicilian Vespers. Since 1935 it has shared Cathedral status with S. Demetrio in Piana degli Albanesi, a small town in the province, with offices according to the Greek rite.

Exterior. The Norman structure survives on the north and south sides, although a Baroque façade was inserted in 1588 on the north side when the Norman narthex was demolished and the atrium covered. The present entrance (**A**) is beneath the splendid 12C campanile which survived the alterations (only its red dome is missing).

Interior. The central Greek cross plan of the tiny original church can still be detected, despite the Baroque alterations at the west end and the prolongation of the chancel in 1683. The walls at the west end are heavily decorated with Baroque marble and frescoes which at first overpower the original mosaic decoration which remains on and around the central cupola. The mosaics, probably by Greek craftsmen from Constantinople, date from the first half of the 12C; *Christ and four angels* is depicted in the dome (**B**) and, in Arabic lettering, a quotation from a Byzantine hymn; around the drum, *Prophets and Evangelists*; on the triumphal arch, the *Annunciation*; in the south apse (**C**) *St Anne*, in the north apse (**D**), *St Joachim*; and in the side vaults, *four evangelists*, the *Nativity* and the *Dormition of the Virgin*. The transennae in front of the apses and the mosaic pavement are also Norman.

At the west end are two more original mosaic panels (restored; set in Baroque frames) from the destroyed portico: to the left (**E**), *George of Antioch at the feet of the Virgin*, and, to the right (**F**), *Roger crowned by Christ*. This is the only known portrait of Roger II of Sicily. Also here are frescoes by Borremans (1717), and in the embrasure of the south portal (**G**) is a carved wooden door of the 12C. Above the main altar (**H**) is a fine painting of the *Ascension* (1533) by Vincenzo da Pavia.

Southeast of the church some arches survive of the cloister of the 12C **Casa Martorana**, the Benedictine convent founded by Eloisa Martorana. Although the convent has disappeared, the marzipan fruits which used to be made by the nuns here are immortalised by the name *frutti di martorana*, and are still produced by numerous confectioners all over the island.

In the courtyard, opposite the campanile, is the **Church of S. Cataldo** (open Mon–Fri 09.00–15.30, Sat 09.00–12.30, Sun & PH 09.00–13.00). It was founded by Maio of Bari, William I's chancellor, because of his early death in 1160 the interior was never decorated. After 1787 it served as a post office and was restored in 1885. The fine exterior has blind arcading round the windows and crenellations at the top of the wall. In the centre three small red domes rise, pierced by little windows. The simple plan of the interior has three aisles ending in apses and three domes high up above the central aisle. The beautiful old capitals are all different. The original mosaic floor and lattice windows survive.

2 • Corso Vittorio Emanuele to the Cathedral

The busy **corso Vittorio Emanuele** (map: 11,14), the main street of the town, was once called the Cassaro Vecchio (from the Arab '*Kasr*' meaning castle) because it led from the port to the royal castle. It now has numerous bookshops. On the left-hand side (with the port behind you) it passes **piazza Bologni** (map: 11,15) with an unsuccessful statue of Charles V by Scipione Li Volsi (1630), and some fine palaces.

From the far end of the piazza a detour can be made: beside Palazzo Ugo delle Favare with attractive balconies, the interesting old via Panormita leads to piazzetta Speciale where the **Palazzo Speciale** has an 18C staircase in its pretty courtyard. Further on is piazza S. Chiara where the church, with a delightful little campanile, was recently restored. Via Puglia continues (with a view left down via Benfratelli to the 14C tower of S. Nicolò), and tunnels under a massive arch to emerge in piazza S. Giovanni Decollato beside the impressive **Palazzo Sclafani** (map: 14), built by Matteo Sclafani in 1330. Part of the original façade here has attractive lava decoration around the windows. The fine portal has sculptures by Bonaiuto da Pisa. Opposite is the ruined church of S. Giovanni Decollato, with a huge ficus tree growing through its façade. The piazza beyond, known as the Piano del Palazzo, is described below.

Facing piazza Bologni (see above), across the corso, is the façade of **Palazzo Riso-Belmonte**, once the grandest of all Marvuglia's buildings (1784) in the city. Further west along the corso is the church of **S. Salvatore** (map: 14; open 09.30–12.30, except Tue), built in 1682 by Paolo Amato. Damaged in the war, its oval interior has been well restored. It is frequently used for weddings.

On the opposite side of the corso the narrow via Montevergini leads to the church of **Montevergini** (map: 10; open 08.30–20.00) with a fine façade by Andrea Palma and a little campanile with an onion-shaped dome decorated with early 18C tiles, beside an 18C loggia for the nuns. After its deconsecration in 1866 it became a school for artisans, then the seat of the Fascist party, and was later used (until 1955) as a law court. The trial of Gaspare Pisciotta, who murdered his brother-in-law, the bandit Salvatore Giuliano, took place here (see p 151). In the interior there are some vault frescoes by Borremans, and a neo-classical east end decorated by Emanuele Cordona with frescoes by Giuseppe Velasco. The sacristy also has a neo-classical vault.

Further along the corso is the **Biblioteca Centrale della Regione Siciliana**(Central Library). It occupies the former Jesuit college, and is entered by the portal of the adjacent church of S. Maria della Grotta. It owns over 500,000 volumes and many ancient manuscripts (particularly of the 15C and 16C).

Just beyond is piazza della Cattedrale, with the elaborate flank of the Cathedral on the other side of a garden enclosed by a balustrade bearing statues of saints.

The Cathedral

The Cathedral (**map: 10**; Assunta; open daily 07.00–19.00, PH 08.00–13.30, 16.00–19.00; ☎ 091/334376), a building of many styles not too skilfully blended, is still a striking edifice with its golden coloured stone and its sharp contrast of light and shade.

The present Cathedral, on the site of an older basilica which did duty as a mosque in the 9C, was founded in 1185 by Walter, Archbishop of Palermo.

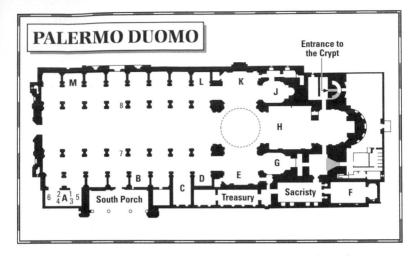

PALERMO DUOMO

Entrance to the Crypt

M   L   K   J

H

G

B   D   E

C

6 2 A 5   South Porch   Treasury   Sacristy   F
4 3

Building continued for many centuries and in the 15C much of the exterior acquired a Catalan Gothic style. The incongruous dome was added by Ferdinando Fuga in 1781–1801. Baroque and neo-classical elements predominate in the interior.

Exterior

The façade, turned towards the southwest on via Matteo Bonello, is a fine example of local Gothic craftsmanship (13C–14C). The doorway dates from 1352. Two powerful Gothic arches span the road to a Norman tower transformed into the campanile in the 19C. The east end, with three apses and two towers matching those at the west end, is practically original 12C work.

The usual entrance is from the garden through the great **south porch**, a splendid Catalan Gothic work of 1429 by Antonio Gambara. In the tympanum there is a delicate relief of the *Redeemer between the archangel Gabriel and Mary*. Beneath is a frieze of saints in polychrome relief. The remarkable painted intarsia decoration above the three arches, which probably dates from 1296, was rediscovered during recent restoration work. It represents the *Tree of Life* in a complicated geometric composition showing Islamic influence. The twelve roundels are decorated with a great variety of symbolic animals (including fish, cockerels, serpents, crabs, mice, camels, lions, wolves, bears, peacocks, dragons, doves and owls), as well as fruit and flowers and human figures. Intended to be read from left to right, the last roundel seems to represent the sun with the head of Christ in the centre.

Beneath the porch, the column on the left, probably preserved from the earlier mosque, is inscribed with a passage from the Koran. The fine doorway by Antonio Gambara (1426) has wooden doors by Francesco Miranda (1432).

Interior

The aisled nave has been spoilt by Fuga's alterations. In the **south aisle** the first two chapels (**A**) enclose six splendid **royal tombs** including that of the first king of Sicily, Roger II (d. 1154), who was crowned in this Cathedral in 1130. His daughter Constance (d. 1198) is also buried here with her husband, Henry VI (d.

1197), Emperor of Germany and son of Frederick Barbarossa. Their son, Frederick II (d. 1250), Emperor of Germany and King of Sicily, lies nearby with his wife, Constance of Aragon (d. 1222). The Emperor died in Apulia but his body was embalmed and transported here since he had expressed the wish to be buried beside his father and grandfather. The later Aragonese royalties buried here are Duke William (d. 1338), son of Frederick II of Aragon, and (in Frederick II's sarcophagus) Peter II (d. 1342), King of Sicily.

The tombs have been enclosed. On the left in front is the porphyry sarcophagus (1) of Frederick II and Peter II; the similar tomb on the right (2) contains the ashes of Henry VI. At the back, beneath mosaic canopies (3,4), are the tombs of Roger II and his daughter Constance. The two fine porphyry sarcophagi which Roger had had installed in the Cathedral of Cefalù where he wished to be buried, were later moved here. On the left (5), is the sarcophagus of Duke William. The Roman sarcophagus on the right (6) contains the body of Constance of Aragon.

In the **nave** are statues of saints from a high altar by the Gagini and (7) a canopied stoup by Giuseppe Spadafora and Antonio Ferraro (1553–55). In the fourth chapel (B), altarpiece by Pietro Novelli, and in the sixth chapel (C), reliquary urns of saints of Palermo, and, used as an altar frontal, the tomb slab of St Cosmas (d. 1160). The seventh chapel (D) has a fine altar of *marmi mischi* (1713). In the **south transept** (E) there is an altarpiece by Giuseppe Velasquez and, above the altar, a bas-relief of the *Dormition of the Virgin* by Antonello Gagini (1535).

The **treasury** (open Mon–Sat 09.30–17.30, groups only on Sun & PH) contains the crown of Constance of Aragon (wife of Frederick II), made by local craftsmen in the 12C, found in her tomb (see above) in the 18C. Also displayed here are the contents of some of the other royal tombs, 18C and 19C copes, chalices and altar frontals.

The **crypt** (open at the same time as the treasury but with a separate ticket) is approached through the **sacristy** which has two fine portals by Vincenzo Gagini (1568). The inner sacristy (F: usually closed) has a *Madonna* by Antonello Gagini (1503). To the left is a tower with a fine Catalan doorway and the remains of a little Arab stalactite vault. It is now necessary to cross the east end of the choir which has a *Resurrection of Christ* on the altar, high reliefs, and (in niches), statues of the apostles, all fragments of Antonello Gagini's high altar. Stairs lead down to the interesting crypt which preserves 23 tombs, many of them Roman sarcophagi (all of them numbered and labelled). The tomb (no. 12) of archbishop Giovanni Paternò (d. 1511) has a very fine effigy by Antonello Gagini, resting on a Greek sarcophagus. The tomb (no. 16) of the founder of the Cathedral, Archbishop Walter (d. 1190), has a beautiful red, green and gold mosaic border. No. 7 is a splendid large Roman sarcophagus with a scene of the coronation of a poet accompanied by the nine muses and Apollo. The tomb of Frederick of Antioch (d. 1305) has a Gothic effigy of the warrior with his helmet.

In the chapel (G) to the right of the choir is a silver coffer containing the relics of St Rosalie by Francesco Rivelo, Giancola Viviano and Matteo Lo Castro (1631). The reliefs on the walls are by Valerio Villareale (1818). In the **choir** (H) the stalls date from 1466. In the chapel on the left (J) is a large domed ciborium in lapis lazuli (1663) and the funerary monument of Bishop Sanseverino by Filippo and Gaetano Pennino (1793).

North transept (K). At the foot of an early 14C wooden Crucifix donated by Manfredi Chiaramonte are marble statues of the mourners by Gaspare Serpotta and Gaspare Guercio. On the altar are fine reliefs with scenes of the *Passion* by Fazio and Vincenzo Gagini.

North aisle. In the seventh chapel (**L**), there is a statue of the *Madonna* by Francesco Laurana and his pupils. In the nave (**8**) is a stoup attributed to Domenico Gagini (damaged) of finer workmanship than the one opposite. The second chapel (**M**) has an *Assumption* and three reliefs by the Gagini, once part of the high altar.

Palazzo Arcivescovile(Archbishop's Palace), across the busy via Bonello, has a portal of 1460 which survived the rebuilding in the 18C. The **Diocesan Museum** was founded here to house fragments from the Cathedral and works of art from destroyed churches. It has been closed for many years.

Behind Palazzo Arcivescovile, in an alley, is the **Oratorio dei SS. Pietro e Paolo** (usually closed) which contains stuccoes by Giacomo Serpotta and Domenico Castelli (1698) and a 17C ceiling fresco by Filippo Tancredi. The entrance can be seen from via Bonello. On the other side of via Bonello is the **Loggia dell'Incoronazione** (map: **10**), erected in the 16C–17C using earlier columns and capitals. It takes its name from the tradition that the kings used to show themselves to the people here after their coronation. Behind is the Cappella dell'Incoronata, a Norman building partly destroyed in 1860.

3 • Palazzo dei Normanni and the Cappella Palatina

Piazza della Vittoria, or **Piano del Palazzo** (map 14) is occupied by Villa Bonanno, a well kept public garden. At the centre of the old city and in front of the royal palace the piazza has been used throughout Palermo's history for public celebrations. Partially protected by a roof are some remains of three Roman houses, the only buildings of this period so far found in the city. The garden adjoins piazza del Parlamento with a monument to Philip V of Bourbon, at the foot of the Palazzo dei Normanni. Spanning the corso is the **Porta Nuova**, a triumphal gateway celebrating Charles V's Tunisian victory (1535), reconstructed after damage by lightning in 1667 (with a conical top).

Palazzo dei Normanni and the Cappella Palatina

Palazzo dei Normanni or Palazzo Reale (**map: 14**) stands on the highest part of the old city. It was built by the Saracens, enlarged by the Normans, and later restored by the Spaniards who added the principal façade.

It has always been the palace of the rulers of the island, and here the splendid courts of Roger II and Frederick II, *stupor mundi*, held sway over Europe. Since 1947 it has been the seat of the Regional Assembly. The long façade (1616) hides the apse of the famous Cappella Palatina: at the right end is the massive Torre Pisana, part of the Norman palace.

• **Admission** When not in use the **palace** (Royal apartments) is open Mon, Fri and Sat 09.00–12.00, ☎ 091/7057003. The **Cappella Palatina** is open Mon–Fri 09.00–11.45, 15.00–16.45; Sat 09.00–11.45; Sun 09.00–09.45, 12.00–12.45, closed for most PH.

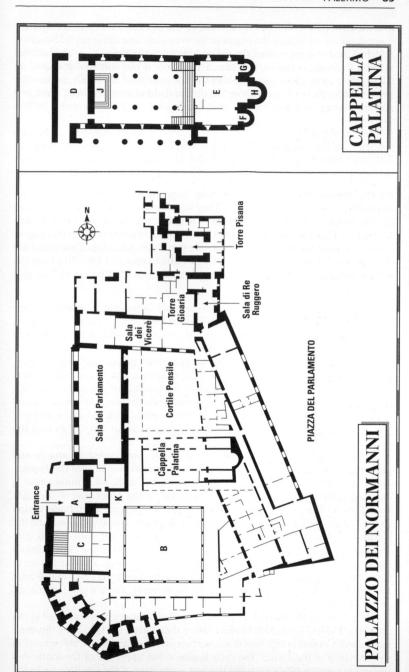

CAPPELLA PALATINA

PALAZZO DEI NORMANNI

Torre Pisana

Sala di Re Ruggero

Torre Gioaria

Sala dei Viceré

Sala del Parlamento

Cortile Pensile

Cappella Palatina

PIAZZA DEL PARLAMENTO

Entrance

N

The **entrance** for visitors is at the back of the palace: this is reached by steps down from the left side of the piazza to the very busy and noisy via del Bastione, which skirts the great wall of the palace around to the right. From the bastions a ramp leads up to the back entrance (**A**). Here a monumental staircase (**C**; 1735) leads up to a loggia overlooking the fine courtyard (**B**; 1600). Set into the wall of the loggia is a pillar with an inscription (behind glass) in Greek, Latin and Arabic relating to a water clock built for Roger II in 1142, probably in Fez, Morocco.

Beneath the portico of seven columns with modern mosaics, is the side entrance to the **Cappella Palatina** (Palatine Chapel), a jewel of Norman-Saracenic art built by Roger II c 1132–40. The **interior** is famous for its wonderful mosaics, one of the finest works of art of its kind in the world.

> The **mosaics** were commissioned by Roger II and completed by his son William I at an unknown date. They follow a carefully worked out design intended to celebrate the monarchy of Roger II, and the subjects seem to have been chosen with particular reference to the Holy Spirit and the theology of light. The earliest and finest mosaics are in the east part of the chapel and are thought to have been the work of Byzantine Greeks (c 1140–50). Here the splendour of the mosaics is increased by the use of silver as well as gold tesserae.

The light changes constantly so the chapel should, if possible, be visited at different times of the day. A small aisled basilica in form, with a raised choir and a cupola above the central bay, it shows the perfection reached by this style of architecture. Every detail of the decoration is exquisite.

The ten antique columns of the nave are made from granite and cipollino marble; the ceiling is a splendid Saracenic work in carved and painted cedar wood from Lebanon, with rich and varied designs. The ambo and paschal candlestick are good examples of the richest Norman marble decoration. The pavement and lower part of the walls are made of white marble inlaid with red, green and gold patterns, which combine in a delightful harmony of colour and design with the mosaics of glass and plaster on a gold ground above.

In the cupola of the **Sanctuary** (**E**) is *Christ surrounded by angels and archangels*; on the drum, *David, Solomon, Zachariah and St John the Baptist*; on the pendentives, *Evangelists*. On the triumphal arch, an *Annunciation* is depicted. Above the right apse (**F**) is a *Nativity*; on the upper part of the right wall, *Joseph's Dream* and the *Flight into Egypt*; on the nave arch, *Presentation in the Temple*; in the middle of the right wall, *Baptism, Transfiguration*, and the *Raising of Lazarus*; and on the lower part of the right wall, *Entry into Jerusalem*. On the lower part of the left wall, five bishops of the Greek church (among the best preserved mosaic figures in the building), and, on the arch, three female saints. Above the left apse (**G**), are a *Madonna and Child* and *St John the Baptist*. In the main apse (**H**) is *Christ Pantocrator*, above a late 18C mosaic of the *Virgin*.

The mosaics in the **nave** were probably the last mosaics to be executed in the chapel (c 1150–71) and are Roman rather than Greek in style. They illustrate the book of Genesis in two tiers of scenes between the clerestory windows and in the spandrels of the arches. The cycle begins in the upper tier of the south wall nearest to the sanctuary, showing the first seven days of the *Creation* up to the

Creation of Eve. The sequence continues in the upper tier of the north wall (beginning at the west end) with the *Fall* up to the *Building of the Ark*. The lower tier of the south wall (from the east end) illustrates the *Flood* up to the *Hospitality of Lot*, and continues in the lower tier of the north wall (west end) with the *Destruction of Sodom* and continues up to *Jacob's Dream* and his *Wrestling with the Angel*, which is the last scene in the sequence (nearest to the sanctuary).

In the **aisles** are scenes from the lives of Sts Peter and Paul, also executed after the mosaics in the east part of the church, possibly by local artists. The sequence begins at the east end of the south aisle with *Saul leaving Jerusalem for Damascus* and the last scene in this aisle shows *St Peter's escape from Prison*. The cycle continues at the west end of the north aisle with *Sts Peter and John healing the lame man at the temple gate*, and the last scene in this aisle, nearest to the sanctuary, shows the *Fall of Simon Magus*.

Above the recomposed Norman throne on a dais at the **west end** (J) is a 15C mosaic of *Christ enthroned between Sts Peter and Paul*. The original **narthex** (D), now the baptistery with a mosaic font, has two beautifully carved mosaic doorways with bronze doors. The sacristy and treasury are usually closed.

Royal apartments

The staircase leads up to the top floor of the palace and the former Royal apartments (for admission, see above), mostly decorated in the 19C. The **sala del viceré** has a series of portraits of viceroys from 1754 to 1837. The **Torre Gioaria** (from the Arabic *al johara*, the pearl, meaning the centre of the building), or Tower of the Winds, preserves part of the Norman building, with four columns. The most interesting room is the so-called **Sala di Re Ruggero** (Roger's room) with delightful mosaics of 1140, including centaurs, birds, palm trees, lions and leopards. In the vault are heraldic beasts. The lower parts of the walls with marble and mosaic decoration, and the floor all survive intact. The **Sala da Ballo** has a fine view over the piazza to the sea.

Other parts of the palace, which are not usually shown, include the **Sala del Parlamento** decorated in 1700 by Giuseppe Velàzquez where the Regional Assembly meets. The vaulted armoury, treasure-chamber and dungeons survive from the Norman period. From the observatory at the top of the Torre Pisano, Giuseppe Piazzi discovered the first asteroid (Ceres) on 1 January 1801.

Across corso Re Ruggero is **Palazzo d'Orléans** (map: 14), now the seat of the Regional President. This was the residence of the exiled Louis Philippe d'Orléans (1773–1850), eldest son of the Duke d'Orléans and King of France, at the time of his marriage in 1809 to Marie Amélie, daughter of Ferdinand IV, the Spanish King of the Two Sicilies. Their son Ferdinand Philippe (1810–42) was born here in the following year.

In piazza della Pinta (map: 14) is the little **Oratorio della Compagnia della Madonna della Consolazione** (S. Mercurio). The stucco decoration in the interior has recently been attributed, as an early work, to Giacomo Serpotta. Via dei Benedettini leads from here to the church of S. Giovanni degli Eremiti.

San Giovanni degli Eremiti

The church of S. Giovanni degli Eremiti (map: 14; open Mon–Sat 09.00–19.00, Sun & PH 09.00–13.00, ☎ 091/6515019) is perhaps the most romantic building of Norman Palermo, because of its small, carefully tended luxuriant garden. It was built by Roger II in 1132–48, and has now been deconsecrated. Paths lead

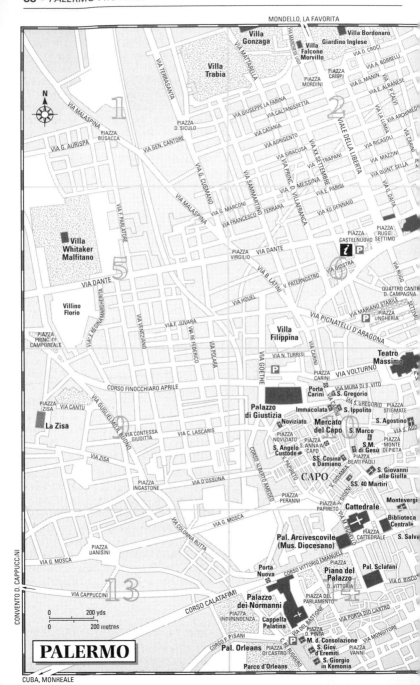

PALERMO

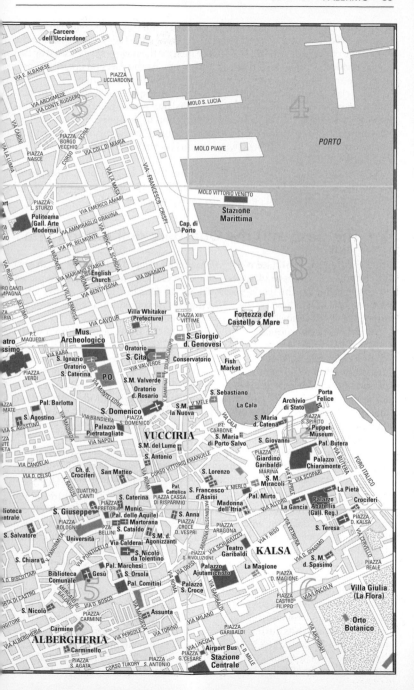

up through the beautiful garden, with splendid palm trees, cactus and flowering jasmine, overshadowed by five charming red domes, the tallest one crowning the campanile of the little church. In the bare interior the nave is surmounted by two domes divided by an arch (pierced by a window). At the east end are three apses and three smaller domes, the one on the left part of the campanile.

To the right is an older structure, probably a **mosque**, consisting of a rectangular hall with cross vaulting and once divided by a row of pillars. Adjoining this (seen from the right of the entrance to the church) is a portico of five arches, whose inner wall is now the right wall of the church, and an open courtyard. The little cloister of the late 13C has twin columns bearing pointed arches which surround a delightful garden.

Next to the church, in via dei Benedettini, is the church of **S. Giorgio in Kemonia**, of ancient foundation, rebuilt in 1765. The interior has rococo and neo-classical elements and paintings by Giuseppe Tresca.

4 • The Gesù and the Quartiere dell'Albergheria

From the Quattro Canti (see p 77) via Maqueda (**map: 11,15**) leads south past the church of S. Giuseppe (described above) to via del Ponticello which branches off to the right. On the left is piazza dei SS. 40 Martiri. Here the sturdy tower (with a Catalan window) of the 15C **Palazzo Marchesi** forms the base of the campanile of the Gesù. The palace garden is sometimes open.

Via del Ponticello continues to the church of the **Gesù** or the church of the Casa Professa (**map: 15**; open 07.30–11.30, 17.00–18.30, Sun 07.00–12.30), the first church to be erected in Sicily by the Jesuits (1564–1633). The spendid interior was beautifully decorated in the 17C and 18C with colourful marble intarsia and sculptures (especially good in the nave chapels, 1665–91). The inside façade has very fine 18C sculptural decoration. In the south aisle, the second chapel has paintings of two saints by Pietro Novelli, and the fourth chapel has a statue of the *Madonna* by the school of Gagini. The presbytery also has remarkably good marble decoration.

Beside the church is the fine Baroque atrium of the Casa Professa, now partly occupied by the **Biblioteca Comunale** (town library), founded in 1760. It has over 250,000 volumes, and more than 1000 incunabula and manuscripts.

Via Casa Professa continues straight on to piazza Ballarò, the centre of the colourful market known since the Arab period as the **Mercato di Ballarò** (from the Arab *Suq al Bahlara*), when fruit and vegetables were brought into town through the nearby Porta S. Agata. This is part of the **Quartiere dell'Albergheria** (**map: 15**), one of the poorest districts in the city, which was devastated by bombing in 1943. Beyond, the church tower of **S. Nicolò** (**map: 15**) can be seen, once part of the 14C town fortifications.

Via Ballarò continues left through the market to piazza del Carmine, with more stalls, above which towers the fantastic dome of the church of the **Carmine** with its telamones and colourful majolica tiles (1681). The interior (open Mon–Fri 08.30–13.30, no visits during Mass) contains altars in the transepts by Giuseppe and Giacomo Serpotta (1683–84), paintings (in the sanctuary) by Tommaso de Vigilia (late 15C), a statue of *St Catherine* by Antonello Gagini, and a *Madonna* by the Gagini School. Behind the church in via delle Mosche, Giuseppe Balsamo was born in 1743. Under the assumed title of Count Cagliostro, he travelled all over Europe professing skills as a physician and an alchemist until he was sentenced to life imprisonment for freemasonry by the Inquisition six years before he died in 1795. His story fascinated Goethe when he was in Palermo in 1787.

Via Musco and via Mugnosi lead to the church of the **Carminello** (open 09.00–17.00; Sat 09.00–13.00, closed Sun & PH), built in 1605 and decorated with stuccoes at the end of the 17C and the beginning of the 18C. Those on the entrance wall have recently been attributed to Procopio Serpotta.

The straight via del Bosco leads away from the market back towards via Maqueda past some fine palaces. On the corner of via Maqueda is **Palazzo Comitini** by Nicolò Palma (1771), open Mon–Fri 09.30–13.30, Sat and Sun by prior arrangement, ☎ 091/6628368; seat of the province of Palermo. The 18C rococo interior has fine frescoed ceilings, Murano chandeliers and decorative mirrors.

On the opposite side of via Maqueda (to the right) is the long façade (mid-18C) of Palazzo S. Croce. Just beyond is the **Assunta** (open 09.00–12.00, 16.00–18.30; Sat & Sun mornings only), a convent church built in 1625–28 and richly decorated in the 18C with stuccoes by a Giacomo Serpotta (the high altar and angels) at the very height of his skill. The vault frescoes are by Filippo Tancredi. The marble intarsia floor dates from 1638.

Returning towards the Quattro Canti via Maqueda passes, next to Palazzo Comitini, the church of **S. Orsola** (open daily 09.00–13.00), built in 1662. The interior was redecorated in the late 18C. The two last chapels on either side of the nave contain stuccoes by Giacomo Serpotta (1692), and (in the left chapel) an altarpiece of *St Jerome* by Zoppo di Gangi. A fine painting of the *Madonna and Child* (as Salvator Mundi) by Pietro Novelli is kept in the sacristy.

Further on, on the opposite side of the road is the church of **S. Nicolò da Tolentino** (open weekdays 09.00–17.00; Sat 09.00–13.00), in the centre of a district where Jews lived freely from the 9C onwards. However, Ferdinand of Spain expelled them from the city in 1492 and the synagogue here was destroyed, on the site of which the building of the church was begun in 1609. The two altarpieces in the transepts are by Pietro Novelli. The convent houses the city archives.

Just beyond, via dei Calderai diverges right from via Roma. It leads to via Giovanni da Procida where the church of **S. Maria degli Agonizzanti** is situated (open 09.00–17.00; Sat & Sun mornings only), rebuilt in 1784. The polychrome marble high altar has reliefs by Ignazio Marabitti.

5 • San Francesco d'Assisi and the Regional Gallery

Corso Vittorio Emanuele leads east from the Quattro Canti towards the sea. A short way along on the left is the fine Baroque church of **S. Matteo** (map: 11; open Mon–Sat 09.00–17.00, Sun & PH 10.00–11.00, ☎ 091/334833). It was begun in 1633 by Mariano Smiriglio. It contains stucco statues by Giacomo Serpotta and frescoes by Vito D'Anna (1754).

The corso intersects with **via Roma**, one of the main thoroughfares of the city running north from the station.

San Francesco d'Assisi

Beyond via Roma, the narrow via Paternostro (with numerous shops selling and repairing luggage) curves right towards the attractive piazza in front of the 13C church of S. Francesco d'Assisi (**map: 12**; open 09.00–12.00, ☎ 091/582370). The **façade** has a beautiful portal with three designs of zig-zag ornamentation (1302) and a lovely rose window.

Interior

The church was damaged by an earthquake in 1823 and again during air raids in 1943, after which it was well restored (with lights for most of the chapels). The Franciscan nave of 1255–77 is flanked by beautiful chapels added in the 14C–15C. Eight statues by Serpotta (1723) decorate the west door and nave.

South aisle. Above the door is a fine sculpted arch of 1465; in the second chapel there is an altarpiece of *St George and the dragon* in high relief and carved roundels by Antonello Gagini (1526); in the third chapel there is a *Madonna* attributed to Antonio Gagini flanked by 15C statues of saints. The Gothic fourth chapel contains a beautiful 15C *Madonna* by a Catalan sculptor and the sarcophagus of Elisabetta Omodei (1498) attributed to Domenico Gagini. Beyond the side door and another Gothic chapel is the sixth chapel with three bas-reliefs by Ignazio Marabitti (including the altar frontal). The seventh chapel has interesting 14C lava decoration on the arches.

The chapel to the right of the **sanctuary** has a fine polychrome marble intarsia decoration (17C–18C; carefully restored after war damage). The eight figures of Sicilian saints are by Giovanni Battista Ragusa (1717). The altarpiece of the *Immacolata* in mosaic is on a design by Vito D'Anna and below is an elaborate marble altar frontal. The sanctuary has fine choir stalls carved and inlaid in 1520 by Giovanni and Paolo Gili. The chapel to the left of the sanctuary has intricate marble decoration and an 18C wooden statue of *St Francis*.

North aisle eighth chapel: a bust of *St John* in polychrome terracotta, attributed to Antonello Gagini, has been replaced by a cast (it will be exhibited in the museum when it opens, possibly in 2004). The four statuettes of the *Virtues* are attributed to Pietro da Bonitate.

By the door into the sacristy there is a tomb effigy of the young warrior Antonio Speciale attributed to Domenico Gagini (1477) with a touching inscription above it. The fifth chapel has a 14C portal with zig-zag ornamentation and remains of early frescoes on the intrados. The fourth chapel, the **Cappella Mastrantonio** has an arch superbly sculpted by Francesco Laurana and Pietro da Bonitate (1468; restored in 1992), the earliest important Renaissance work in Sicily. On the left wall of the chapel, the *Madonna and saints* has been attributed to Vincenzo da Pavia.

In the second chapel a highly venerated silver statue of the *Immaculate Virgin* (1647) is hidden by a curtain, and a fresco of *St Francis* is on the left wall. In the first chapel (light on the right), with a fine 16C portal, is a *Madonna and Child with St John*, by Domenico Gagini (with a beautiful base), and a relief of the *Madonna*.

San Francesco d'Assisi, Palermo

To the left of the church is the **Oratorio di S. Lorenzo** (entrance at no. 5 via Immacolatella; closed for restoration). The interior, designed by Giacomo Amato is decorated with stuccoes illustrating the lives of *St Lawrence* and *St Francis*, perhaps the masterpiece of Giacomo Serpotta (1699–1707). Ten symbolic statues, eight vivacious little reliefs, and the *Martyrdom of St Lawrence* situated above the door, the whole encircled by a throng of joyous cherubs, make up a well balanced and animated composition. The modelling of the male figures above the windows is especially skilful.

The *Nativity*, by Caravaggio (1609; his last known work), which was stolen from the altar in 1969, has never been found. It has been asserted that the Mafia was responsible for the theft and that the painting may subsequently have been destroyed. The superb 18C mahogany benches with carved supports and beautiful mother-of-pearl inlay, have been removed until the repairs are complete (probably 2004).

In via Paternostro, opposite S. Francesco, is the *Antica Focacceria di S. Francesco*, a snack bar founded in 1834, with a charming old-fashioned interior. Palazzo Cattolica nearby (no. 48) has a double courtyard by Giacomo Amato (c 1720).

Palazzo Mirto

Via Merlo leads out of the piazza to the right of the façade of S. Francesco. At no. 2 an 18C gateway leads into Palazzo Mirto (**map: 12**; open daily 09.00–18.30; Sun & PH 09.00–13.00, ☎ 091/6164751). The main façade on via Lungarini, with a double row of balconies, dates from 1793. The residence of the Lanza-Filangeri family since the early 17C, it was donated by them, together with its contents, to the region of Sicily in 1982. The well-kept interior is interesting as a typical example of a princely residence in Palermo with 18C and 19C decorations, including a little 'Chinese' room. The contents include furniture (mostly 18C and 19C), Capodimonte porcelain and Murano glass. On the ground floor, near the delightful stables (1812), the funerary stele of Giambattista and Elisabetta Mellerio (c 1820) by Antonio Canova are displayed, purchased by the region of Sicily in 1978 to prevent them being exported.

Beyond, opposite Palazzo Rostagno is the Renaissance church of **S. Maria dei Miracoli** (1547; open Mon–Fri 09.00–17.00, Sat 09.00–13.00. Sun & PH closed), the interior is impressive for its graceful architecture.

Piazza Marina

S. Maria dei Miracoli overlooks piazza Marina (**map: 12**), which was once a shallow inlet of the sea, and reclaimed in Saracen times. Here 16C Aragonese weddings and victories were celebrated by jousting. Later, in the proximity of two prisons (the Vicaria and that of the Inquisition), public executions were held here. The centre is occupied by the **Giardino Garibaldi**, with fine palms and enormous *Ficus magnoloides*. The garden has recently been restored; it is now surrounded by new railings and elegant lamp-posts and the piazza is lively once again with several open-air restaurants and pizzerie. **Palazzo Galletti Marchesi di S. Cataldo** is a reconstruction incorporating some windows of a Renaissance palace (in the side street).

At the seaward end of Piazza Marina is **Palazzo Chiaramonte**, known as **Lo Steri** (i.e. hosterium, or fortified palace), which was occupied by the law courts from 1799 until 1972. The building was restored in 1984 by the University to serve as Rectorate (sometimes open for concerts or exhibitions). Begun in 1307 by the Chiaramonte family, it became the palace of the Spanish viceroys. From 1605–1782 it was the seat of the Inquisition; the graffiti which survive on the prison walls provide a fascinating historical record of the persecutions. The exterior, though deprived of its battlements, retains several of its original windows. Inside are two rooms with wooden ceilings painted by Simone da Corleone and Cecco di Naro (1377–80), in Saracenic style.

Beyond the last side of the square is **La Cala**, a shallow basin used as a mooring by the fishing fleet and all that remains of the ancient harbour which, until Norman times, extended far into the old town. There are three churches here. On the corner by the corso is the church of **S. Giovanni dei Napoletani** (1526–1617; open only on some days, usually Tues and Thurs afternoons). The harmonious interior has a magnificent contemporary **organ** by Raffaele La Valle, with its choir-loft decorated with 15 panels, perhaps the work of Vincenzo da Pavia, and a *St John the Baptist* by Zoppo di Gangi.

On the other side of the corso is the late 15C church of **S. Maria della Catena** (**map: 12**; open Mon–Fri 09.00–13.00; Sat Sun & PH closed), probably the work of Matteo Carnelivari (1502–34). Its name *catena* (chain) probably comes from the chain that used to close the old port: it stretched from this bank across the harbour to Castello a Mare. There is also a legend that three innocent people were condemned in 1391 and as custom demanded, were sent to spend the night in this church in prayer; as they prayed their chains dropped from them and they were spared. A flight of steps leads up to the three-arched porch, which, with its two corner-pilasters, provides an ingenious combination of Gothic and Renaissance styles. The delicate carving of the three doorways is attributed to Vincenzo Gagini.

The elegant interior has been beautifully restored. In the chapel on the right, under a 16C canopy, is a lovely 14C fresco of the *Madonna and Child*, discovered in the 1980s. The four statues are by the school of the Gagini. In the second chapel is a late 15C relief of the *Madonna and Child with angels* from the church of S. Nicolò alla Calza. In a chapel with a 16C relief are frescoes by Olivio Sozzi. The east end is particularly beautiful with elaborate Gothic decoration and double columns. There is a Roman sarcophagus here.

The Renaissance church of **S. Maria di Porto Salvo** (closed), was mutilated in the replanning of 1564. It was begun in c 1527 by Antonello Gagini and the interior was completed by Antonio Scaglione.

In the corner of the piazza is the outstanding **Fontana del Garraffo** (designed by Paolo Amato in 1698), recently restored and surrounded by a little garden. The slender little figure on the top represents *Abundance* chasing away the Hydra monster; the fountain is a typical example of Baroque taste for sumptuous street furnishings.

The lower end of the corso, the Cassaro Morto, was virtually destroyed in 1943; the **Fontana del Cavallo Marino**, with a seahorse by Ignazio Marabitti, is now surrounded by palm trees. The reconstructed **Porta Felice** (1582–1637) has no arch between the two monumental pillars to allow the tall *vara* (or 'float') of St Rosalie to pass through it on her feast day. The long 17C façade of **Palazzo Butera** stands above the terraced **Mura delle Cattive**, or 'Wall of the Bad Women' (open daily 08.00–19.00). The name may refer to a time when women caught in adultery were exposed to public ridicule. Alternatively, it may refer to the widows who, for reasons of decorum, could not take their *passeggiata* with other ladies along the Foro Italico, so they passed the time here in malicious gossip.

The busy, broad **Foro Italico** (map: 12) which runs outside the walls along the seafront offers a splendid view of Monte Pellegrino.

International Marionette Museum

Just out of piazza S. Spirito, at no. 1 via Butera, is the Museo Internazionale delle Marionette (**map: 12**; ring the bell; open Mon–Fri 09.00–13.00, 16.00–19.00; Sat Sun & PH closed, ☎ 091/328060, ✉ www.museomarionettepalermo.it), founded in 1975. There is a delightful collection of puppets from Sicily and Naples, as well as puppets from Africa, the New Hebrides, Vietnam, Korea, Burma, China, and India (particularly Rajasthan), shadow puppets from Malaysia, Cambodia, and Java and even Professor Jingles' Punch and Judy theatre from England, all beautifully displayed. There is also a room where children can play and make their own puppets.

Opra dei Pupi

Sicily has long been famous for its puppet theatres, known as the *opra dei pupi*. In the 18C and 19C, at the height of their popularity, the most important puppet theatres on the island were in Palermo, Trapani, Sortino, Syracuse, Acireale and Catania. In the 1960s, puppet theatres languished and many closed down, but recently there has been a revival of this traditional entertainment.

The plays focus on chivalrous episodes in the lives of the paladins of Charlemagne's court, portrayed through the various heroic deeds of Orlando, Rinaldo, Astolfo and others who challenge the Saracens. The key moment in every play is the battle, enacted in the traditional style, with much foot stamping and blood spurting, even the occasional dragon or wizard putting in an appearance. Garibaldi is also a source of inspiration for the *pupari*, as is King Arthur of the Round Table. UNESCO has recently declared that the Sicilian puppet theatre is a world heritage.

Santa Maria della Pietà

Via Butera continues (past a plaque on a wing of Palazzo Butera recording Goethe's stay here in a hotel on this site in 1787) to the church of S. Maria della Pietà, with a splendid Baroque **façade** by Giacomo Amato (1678–84). The interior (map: 12; open Mon–Fri 08.00–17.00, Sat Sun & PH 08.00–13.00; ☎ 091/6165266) is a particularly striking example of local Baroque architecture. The delightful vestibule has stuccoes by Procopio Serpotta and frescoes by Borremans: it supports a splendid nuns' choir. Four choir screens in gilded wood decorate the nave. The fresco in the vault is by Antonino Grano (1708). On the south side, the first altar has a painting of Dominican saints by Antonio and Francesco Manno, and the second altar a *Madonna of the Rosary* by Olivio Sozzi. The high altar has a tabernacle in lapis lazuli. On the north side, the third altar has a *Pietà* (in the beautiful original frame) by Vincenzo da Pavia and the second altar, *St Dominic* by Olivio Sozzi.

Regional Gallery of Sicily

At no. 4 via Alloro is Palazzo Abatellis (**map: 12**), designed in 1488–95 by Matteo Carnelivari for Francesco Abatellis, appointed 'master-pilot' (or admiral) of Sicily by the Spaniards, in a style combining elements of the Renaissance with late Catalan Gothic. Much altered internally during its occupation by Dominican nuns from 1526 until 1943, when it was damaged by bombs, the palace was freely restored in 1954 as the home of the Galleria Regionale della Sicilia (open daily 09.00–13.30; Tues and Thurs also 15.00–19.30; Sun & PH 09.00–13.00, ☎ 091/6230011). This is a fine collection of Sicilian sculpture and paintings, well documented and beautifully arranged.

Ground floor

A doorway of original design leads out to the pleasant courtyard. The ground floor is devoted principally to **sculpture**. A door on the left leads into **room 1**. On display here are some 16C wooden sculptures, a 12C Arab door frame carved in wood and a painting of the *Madonna with saints* from the workshop of Tommaso de Vigilia. Beyond, **room 2**, the former chapel, is dominated by a famous large fresco of the *Triumph of Death*, detached from Palazzo Sclafani. Dating from c 1449 it is of uncertain attribution, thought by some scholars to be a Sicilian work and by others to be by Pisanello or his school. Death is portrayed as an archer on a spectral horse, piercing the contented and successful (right) with his arrows, while the unhappy and aged (left), among whom are the painter and a pupil, pray in vain for release. The painting has provided inspiration for several artists, among them Pablo Picasso.

A corridor (**3**) containing Saracenic ceramics, including a magnificent majolica vase of Hispano-Moresque type (13C–14C), thought to come from Malaga and kept for centuries in the Cathedral in Mazara del Vallo, and a fragment of a wooden ceiling (Siculo-Arabic, 12C) from Palazzo dei Normanni, leads to three rooms devoted to **late 15C and early 16C sculpture**. Room 4 contains works by **Francesco Laurana**, principally a bust of *Eleonora of Aragon*, his masterpiece. The bust of a young boy here has recently been attributed to Domenico Gagini (c 1469), who also sculpted (with assistants) the *Madonna of the Milk*. Room 5 is devoted to the Gaginis; notable are a marble statuette of the *Madonna and Child*, the *Tabernacle of the Ansalone*, the *Madonna of the Good Rest* (1528), and the head of a young boy, all by Antonello Gagini, and the *Madonna of the Snow* (1516) by his workshop. In **room 6** there are architectural fragments, including carved capitals.

First floor

The first floor is reached by a staircase from room 6 or from the courtyard. It contains the **Picture Gallery** (*pinacoteca*), with its wonderful series of Sicilian paintings, including 13C–14C works, still in the Byzantine manner, and later works showing the influence of various schools (Umbrian, Sienese, Catalan, and Flemish). Room 7 (left) contains the *Raising of Lazarus* and *Christ in Limbo*, two small paintings, perhaps Venetian, of the 13C; a painted 13C *Crucifix*; *Madonna* in mosaic in a Byzantine style (early 14C); Antonio Veneziano, *Madonna and Child*; Bartolomeo da Camogli, *Our Lady of Humility* (1346). In **room 8** (left) are paintings of the late 14C and early 15C. Giovanni di Pietro, *St Nicholas*; Turino Vanni, *Madonna and saints*; Master of the Trapani Polyptych, *Our Lady of the Flower*; Gera da Pisa, *Sts George and Agatha*.

Beyond a short corridor is **room 9** which contains **early 15C Sicilian paint-ings**, including several *Coronations of the Virgin* by the same unknown master, and works by the 'Master of the Trapani Polyptych'. **Room 10. Late 15C paint-ings and frescoes** by Tommaso de Vigilia; Pietro Ruzzolone, *Crucifix*; *Coronation of the Virgin*, a polyptych from Corleone, by an unknown hand. In a little room off the hall, a 16C custodia (case) from Palermo. Beyond, in room 11, is a precious collection of works by **Antonello da Messina**, including the stun-ning portrait universally considered to be his masterpiece, *Virgin Annunciate*, and *Sts Gregory, Augustine and Jerome*; also, *Madonna*, attributed to Marco Basaiti.

Room 12, the upper half of the chapel, overlooks the *Triumph of Death* (see above), and is devoted mainly to Riccardo Quartararo, notably *Sts Peter and Paul* and *Coronation of the Virgin*. Also here is a 15C–16C wooden *Pietà*. A number of 16C works of uncertain attribution are displayed in **room 13**: these include *Master of the Pentecost*, *Pietà* and *Pentecost*; Andrea da Salerno's *Sts John the Baptist and John the Evangelist*; and a copy (1538) by Antonello Crescenzio of Raphael's *Spasimo* (formerly in the church of S. Maria dello Spasimo, see below).

Room 14 is devoted to **15C–16C Flemish paintings**: an *Annunciation*, in the style of the master of Flémalle; Mabuse, Malvagna Triptych of the *Virgin and Child between Sts Catherine and Barbara* (on the outside, *Adam and Eve*), a painting of extraordinary detail; works of the 16C Antwerp and Bruges schools. **Room 15** (left). Jan van Scorel, *St Mary Magdalen*; Tuscan school (dated 1563), portrait of a young man. **Room 16** is devoted mainly to works by Vincenzo da Pavia: *Deposition*, *St Conrad the Hermit* and two scenes from the *Life of the Virgin*. **Room 17**: Giuseppe Cesari, *Andromeda*; Mattia Preti, *Christ and the Centurion*; Pietro Novelli, *Communion of St Mary of Egypt*; Van Dyck (copy), *Madonna*, his early masterpiece; Leandro Bassano, *Portrait of a Man*; Palma Giovane, *Deposition*.

La Gancia

Next to Palazzo Abatellis is the 15C church called La Gancia (**map: 12**), or S. Maria degli Angeli, entered by the side door (open Mon–Sat 09.00–17.00, Sun & PH 10.00–12.30, ☎ 091/6165221). The fine exterior dates from the 15C.

In the **interior** (lights in each chapel) the wooden ceiling and fine organ (over the west door; perhaps by Raffaele La Valle) date from the transformation begun in 1672. **South side**: in the second chapel (right) are Antonello Crescenzio, *Madonna with Sts Catherine and Agatha* (signed and dated 1528), Pietro Novelli (attributed), *Holy Family*; in the fourth chapel: Antonello Gagini (attributed), seated *Madonna* (the head of the Christ Child is modern); fifth and sixth chapels, inlaid marble panels with scenes of the *Flight into Egypt*: outside is a pulpit made up of fragments of sculpture by the Gagini. The chapel on the right of the choir has fine marble decoration and stuccoes by Giacomo Serpotta. On the choir-piers are two delicately carved *Annunciations* attributed to Antonello Gagini.

In the chapel to the left of the choir are more stuccoes by Serpotta, and a *Marriage of the Virgin* by Vincenzo da Pavia (removed for restoration). **North transept**: on the wall (high up), *St Francis* by Zoppo di Gangi. **North side**: in the sixth chapel are two fine reliefs (one of the *Descent into Limbo*) by Antonello Gagini; in the third chapel, Pietro Novelli's *St Peter of Alcantara* and in the sec-ond chapel, Vincenzo da Pavia's *Nativity*.

The adjoining convent is famous in the annals of the revolution of 4 April 1860 against Neapolitan rule. The convent bell gave the signal to the insurgents; Francesco Riso, their leader, was mortally wounded, 13 were captured and shot while two hid for five days in the vaults of the church, before escaping through the '*Buca della Salvezza*', a hole in the wall next to Palazzo Abatellis.

The nearby Kalsa district with the church of Lo Spasimo, Villa Giulia and the Orto Botanico, are all described in the next walk. **Via Alloro**, a narrow medieval street with some aristocratic palaces, continues back from the church of La Gancia towards the centre of the city. At no. 54, some way along on the left, stood **Palazzo Bonagia**, which was almost totally destroyed in the last war. The remarkable Baroque staircase in the courtyard, attributed to Andrea Giganti, survives, propped up by scaffolding behind a closed gateway.

Beyond, on the right, is the church of the **Madonna dell'Itria dei Cocchieri** (map: 12; open 08.30–15.30; Sat 09.00–13.00, Sun & PH closed), once the seat of the confraternity of coachmen. Built in 1596, it has a crypt with 18C frescoes (closed). The confraternity, dressed in coachmen's livery (examples of which are preserved in the church) still carry the statue of the *Madonna Addolorata* (kept here) through the streets of Palermo in the Good Friday procession. Via Alloro ends in piazza Aragona, described below.

6 • The Kalsa district

From the seaward end of via Alloro (see above) via Torremuzza leads past the church of the **Crociferi** or **S. Mattia** (map: 12), by Giacomo Amato. Further on is the façade (1686–1706) of the **church of S. Teresa** (map: 16), also by Amato, and one of his best works (open daily 08.00–11.00, 16.30–18.00, ☎ 091/6171658). In the interior, on the south side: the first altar contains Giovanni Odazzi's *Holy Family* (1720); and the second altar Ignazio Marabitti's marble *Crucifixion* group (1780–81). The high altarpiece is by Gaspare Serenario (1746) and the two statues of female saints in the sanctuary are by Giacomo Serpotta. North side: the second altarpiece is by Guglielmo Borremans (1722) and the first altarpiece by Sebastiano Conca.

The church faces piazza della Kalsa (from the Arabic *al halisa*, meaning 'the elect'). This was one of the oldest parts of the city, fortified by the Arabs in 938. The stately 17C Oratorio dei Bianchi, incorporating the church of Victory, built over one of the gates of the Kalsa citadel has been restored and will now be used as an exhibition venue. The **Quartiere della Kalsa** (map: 16) is a very poor district, badly damaged by bombs in World War II and now under repair.

Villa Giulia and the Botanical Gardens

Via Niccolò Cervello ends at viale Lincoln across which is the entrance to **Villa Giulia** (map: 16; open daily 08.00–20.00, ☎ 091/7404028), or **La Flora**, a delightful garden laid out in 1777, with beautiful trees and flowers, much admired by Goethe in 1787. In the centre are four *prospetti*, or niches in the Pompeian style, and a sundial fountain; towards the sea is another statue of the *Genius of Palermo*, by Marabitti.

The **Botanical Garden**, adjoining the Villa, is remarkable for its subtropical vegetation (open Mon–Fri 09.00–17.00; Apr–Sept closes 18.00, Sat & Sun 08.30–13.30, closed PH; entered by the side gate, ☎ 091/6238241). The entrance pavilion was built in the Greek Doric style in 1789 by Léon Dufourny; Marvuglia worked on the decoration and added the side wings. The garden, one of the finest in Europe, was laid out by Filippo Parlatore, the important Italian botanist who was born in Palermo. It was opened to the public in 1795. It has ficus trees, bamboo, date palms, lotus trees and tropical plants from all over the world. The circular water-lily pond dates from 1796.

Church and convent of Lo Spasimo

From beside the church of S. Teresa (see above) via S. Teresa and via dello Spasimo lead away from the sea through the Kalsa district to the former church and convent of S. Maria dello Spasimo, beautifully restored as a cultural centre for exhibitions, concerts and theatre performances (open daily 09.00–24.00 by a group of young Palermitans, ☎ 091/6161486). It has justly become the symbol of the city's 'rebirth' in the last decade.

Founded in 1509, the church and convent were never completed as the area was taken over by the Spanish viceroy in a general plan of strengthening the city's defences. In 1573 the convent was sold to the Senate and the church was used as a theatre after 1582, and again at the end of the 17C. Part of the convent became an isolation hospital for plague victims in 1624, and in the 19C and 20C it was used as a general hospital. Over the centuries the buildings have been adapted as warehouses, a deposit for the snow brought down from the mountains used for making ice creams, and as storage for the débris after the bombardments of World War II. After the hospital was finally closed in 1986 a remarkable restoration programme began in 1988.

Beyond the 16C cloister is the church of S. Maria dello Spasimo (roofless except for the beautiful Gothic apse vault) which has been cleaned up, leaving a few trees growing in the nave. It is used for theatre performances and concerts. In 1516 Raphael was commissioned to paint an altarpiece of Jesus falling beneath the Cross (which came to be known as *Lo Spasimo di Sicilia*) for this church. After an adventurous journey, during which, according to Vasari, the painting was lost at sea in a shipwreck, but subsequently discovered on the shore near Genoa, it was finally installed here in 1520. However, the Spanish viceroy presented it to Philip IV of Spain in 1661 and it is now in the Prado in Madrid. A copy was made of the painting and some art experts believe that at some point the paintings were swapped so that the original is now in the Prefecture of Catania. The original frame by Antonello Gagini is to be re-installed here, having been found recently in a villa garden in Bagheria and restored by the *Fondo per l'Ambiente Italiano*. Beyond the church is a little public **garden** on the bastions, and another chapel used for exhibitions.

Piazza Magione

Just beyond Lo Spasimo is piazza Magione. In the centre, between two agaves, is a small memorial plaque to Giovanni Falcone, who was born in this area in 1939. It was set up by the city of Palermo in 1995 'in gratitude and admiration' for this courageous magistrate who was assassinated by the Mafia in 1992.

At the beginning of via Castrofilippo is the little **Teatro Garibaldi**, built in 1861, and visited by Garibaldi himself in 1862. Once used for the performance of popular comedies, it was acquired by Palermo Town Council in 1983 and is being rebuilt.

Also on this side of the piazza is the fine Norman apse of the church of **La Magione** (map: 16; open daily 08.30–11.30, 15.00–18.30, Sun & PH 08.30–12.00, ☎ 091/6170596) which stands in majestic isolation, painstakingly restored after bombs in World War II devastated the neighbourhood. It was founded for the Cistercians by Matteo d'Aiello before 1151 as the Chiesa della Trinità, but transferred to the Teutonic knights in 1193 by the Emperor Henry VI as their mansion, from which it takes its name. It is a precious example of Arab-Norman architecture.

The façade has three handsome and very unusual doorways. The beautiful tall **interior** has a fine apse decorated with twelve small columns. Above the 14C stone altar hangs a painted *Crucifix*. The contents include statues of *Christ and the Madonna and Child* by the Gagini school, a 15C marble triptych, and a tabernacle of 1528. The custodian will show you the charming little Cistercian cloister of c 1190 around a garden (open daily except Sun & PH 09.30–19.00); one walk with twin columns and carved capitals has survived. A room off the cloister contains a detached 15C fresco of the *Crucifixion* with its sinopia. Outside is a delightful garden and a monumental 17C gateway on via Magione.

Via Magione leads to **via Garibaldi**, a dilapidated street with some handsome palaces and graceful balconies. Here is **Palazzo Ajutamicristo**, built by Matteo Carnelivari in 1490, with Catalan-Gothic elements (the courtyard is entered from no. 23; visits can be arranged for small groups by previous arrangement, ☎ 091/6161894, ✉ www.palazzoajutamicristo.com). Charles V was entertained here on his return from Tunis in 1535. Via Garibaldi, and its continuation northwards, corso dei Mille, mark the route followed by Garibaldi on his entry into the city. At the end is **piazza della Rivoluzione**, the scene of the outbreak of the rebellion of 1848, inspired by Giuseppe La Masa. Here is another bizarre fountain depicting the *Genius of Palermo*. Near the 16C Palazzo Scavuzzo is the church of **S. Carlo** (1643–48) with an elliptical interior.

The west end of piazza Aragona just north of here leads into **piazza della Croce dei Vespri**, where the graves of many French victims of the Sicilian Vespers were marked in 1737 by a cross. Two sides of the piazza are occupied by the fine 18C **Palazzo Valguarnera-Ganci**, still owned by the family. Visconti used the sumptuous Salone degli Specchi as the setting for the scene of the great ball in his film *Il Gattopardo*, based on the novel by Giuseppe Tomasi di Lampedusa.

Nearby is the church of **S. Anna**, with a fine Baroque façade begun in 1726 by Giovanni Biagio Amico, with sculptures by Giacomo Pennino and Ignazio Marabitti, on designs by Giacomo Serpotta. The **interior** dates from 1606–36. On the west wall are two paintings by Giuseppe Albina. South aisle: the second chapel contains a 17C altarpiece of the *Holy Family* and two good paintings from the *Life of the Virgin*. The third chapel has a 17C painting of St Rosalie with a view of Monte Pellegrino and the port. In the south transept there are frescoes by Filippo Tancredi. In the sanctuary is a 16C organ case.

Via Roma leads back (right) to corso Vittorio Emanuele and the Quattro Canti.

7 • San Domenico and the Regional Archaeological Museum

From the Quattro Canti (**map: 11**) corso Vittorio Emanuele (described above) leads eastwards to the sea. Take via Roma left past (right) the church of **S. Antonio** (**map: 11**) which occupies the highest point of the eastern part of the old city. The 14C campanile was lowered in height at the end of the 16C, and the church reconstructed after the earthquake of 1823 in the Chiaramonte style of the original.

The maze of small streets around piazza Caracciolo, piazza Garraffello, etc. is the scene of a busy daily market known as the **Vucciria** (**map: 11**), one of the most colourful sights in the city. All kinds of produce is sold on the streets here, including fish. In **piazza Garraffello** is **Palazzo Lo Mazzarino**, where the father of the famous Cardinal Mazzarino was born in 1576.

The market extends along via dei Cassari passing the 18C church of **S. Maria del Lume**, designed by Salvatore Marvuglia. From piazza Garraffello via Materassai leads to the piazza in front of the 16C church of **S. Maria la Nuova** (open Mon–Sat 08.30–13.00, Mon Tues Fri also 15.30–17.30, Sun & PH closed, ☎ 091/326597) with a Catalan-Gothic porch (the upper storey was added in the 19C in neo-Gothic style). The fine interior contains stuccoes in the presbytery and 18C paintings. Close by, towards the sea, you can see the well-sited late Renaissance façade of **S. Sebastiano**. Inside are 18C polychrome marble altars, stuccoes by Giacomo Serpotta (1692) and 18C frescoes.

Via G. Meli leads away from the sea back up towards via Roma and piazza S. Domenico, in the middle of which rises the **Colonna dell'Immacolata** by Giovanni d'Amico (1724–27), crowned by a *Madonna* by Giovanni Battista Ragusa.

San Domenico

The large church of S. Domenico (**map: 11**; open 09.00–11.30; Sat and Sun also 17.00–19.00, ☎ 091/329588), rebuilt in 1640, has a tall façade of 1726. Since the middle of the last century the church has served as a burial place for illustrious Sicilians.

Interior. South aisle: on the left wall of the first chapel is the funerary monument of Francesco Maria Emanuele di Villabianca by Leonardo Pennino(1802). In the second chapel, there is an altarpiece of the Crucifixion by Paolo Fondulli (1573); in the third chapel there is a fine marble decoration on a design by Gaspare Serpotta and a very fine statue of St Joseph by Antonio Gagini. Beyond is the fourth chapel with an altarpiece attributed to Rosalia Novelli. The fifth chapel has the funerary monument of Emerico Amari, by Domenico Costantino (1875). The sixth chapel has a painting of St Vincent Ferrer by Giuseppe Velasquez (1787).

South transept. The altarpiece of *St Dominic* is by Filippo Paladino, and on the left wall there is a monument to Giovanni Ramondetta by Giacomo Serpotta and Gerardo Scudo (1691). In the chapel to the right of the sanctuary is a good bas-relief of *St Catherine* attributed to Antonello Gagini, a neo-classical monument by Benedetto de Lisi (1864), a relief of the *Trinity* (1477) by Rinaldo Bartolomeo, a small *Pietà* in high relief by Antonello Gagini and a pretty little stoup. The two fine organs date from 1781; beneath the one on the right is a small Turrisi Colonna funerary monument, with a female figure by Antonio Canova.

The **sanctuary** has 18C choir stalls. The chapel to the left of the sanctuary has Gaginesque reliefs including a roundel of St Dominic, and the tomb of Ruggero Settimo (1778–1863), who convened the Sicilian parliament in this church in 1848. **North transept**. On either side of the altarpiece by Vincenzo da Pavia are funerary monuments by Ignazio Marabitti.

North aisle. The tomb of the painter Pietro Novelli, (1608–47), is here. In the fourth chapel is an altarpiece of *St Raymond* by Filippo Paladino; third chapel: on the left is a statue of *St Catherine* by Antonello Gagini (1528), with reliefs on the base, and on the right, a statue of *St Barbara* by his school. The second chapel has a terracotta statue of *St Catherine of Siena*, and the first chapel an altarpiece by Andrea da Trapani. On the left is the funerary monument of Lancellotto Castelli, prince of Torremuzza by Leonardo Pennino (1870), and on the right a tomb by Valerio Villareale. The fragmentary 14C cloister, which was part of the first church built on this site by the Dominicans, has been restored (ask sacristan for access (tip), though it is safer to ring first).

Behind the church, in an area with numerous jewellery shops, in via Bambinai, is the **Oratorio del Rosario di S. Domenico** (open Mon–Fri 09.00–13.00, 14.00–17.30, Sat 09.00–13.00, Sun & PH closed). It contains an **altarpiece** by Van Dyck, representing the *Virgin of the Rosary with St Dominic and the patronesses of Palermo*. The artist painted it in Genoa in 1628 having left Palermo because of the plague. The wall-paintings of the *Mysteries* are by Novelli, Lo Verde, Stomer, Luca Giordano and Borremans. Giacomo Serpotta's graceful **stuccoes** (1720) display amazing skill. Statues of elegant society ladies represent various allegorical virtues. The black and white ceramic floor is also well preserved.

In its fine piazza the church of **S. Maria di Valverde** was built in 1635 (open Mon–Fri 09.00–13.00, 14.00–17.30, Sat 09.00–13.00, closed Sun & PH) by Mariano Smiriglio. It has a grey marble side portal, and a campanile rebuilt in 1723. Its sumptuous Baroque interior (1694–1716), decorated with polychrome *marmi mischi*, was designed by Paolo Amato and Andrea Palma. On the high altar is an 18C wooden statue of the *Madonna of the Rosary*.

The church and oratory of the Rosary of S. Cita

The street continues as via Squarcialupo. The next large church on the left is **S. Cita** or S. Zita: (map: 11; open Mon–Fri 08.00–12.00, Sat 09.00–13.00, Sun & PH closed, ☎ 091/332779), rebuilt in 1586–1603 (but damaged in 1943). The interior contains fine but damaged **sculptures** by Antonello Gagini (1517–27). In the apse behind the altar is a marble tabernacle surrounded by a magnificent arch, both superbly carved. In the second chapel on the left of the choir is the sarcophagus of Antonio Scirotta, also by Gagini; and more sculptures by the same artist are in the second chapel (Platamone) on the right of the choir. The chapel of the Rosary has splendid polychrome marble decoration (1696–1722) and sculpted reliefs by Gioacchino Vitaliano.

Adjoining the left side of the church is the **Oratorio del Rosario di S. Cita** (or Zita; usually entered through the church, opening times the same), reconstructed in the early 17C. It is approached through a little garden and loggia.

The stucco decoration of the exquisite **interior** is one of Giacomo Serpotta's finest: between 1685 and 1688 he worked on the nave and in 1717 on the apse. On the entrance wall there is an elaborate representation of the Battle of Lepanto which commemorates the victory over the Turks in which the Christian fleet was protected by the Madonna of the Rosary (the confraternity of the Rosary had been founded just before the battle in 1571). On the two side walls are New Testament scenes in high relief representing the 15 *Mysteries of the Rosary* between numerous seated allegorical statues. The decorative frames and stucco drapes are supported by hundreds of delightful cherubs, for which Serpotta used the street urchins of Palermo as models. The altarpiece of the *Madonna of the Rosary* (1702) is by Carlo Maratta. The ebony benches were decorated with mother-of-pearl inlay in 1702.

Nearly opposite S. Cita is the fine 14C doorway of the Conservatorio di Musica. Beyond is the isolated church of **S. Giorgio dei Genovesi** (map: 7/8; deconsecrated and at present only open for exhibitions), a church built for the Genoese merchants by Giorgio di Faccio in 1576–91. It has a graceful façade. The aisled interior is in the purest Renaissance style. Marble tomb-slabs (17C and 18C) cover the floor of the nave. It contains paintings attributed to Luca Giordano, Bernardo Castello of Genoa and Palma Giovane.

Beyond lies piazza delle Tredici Vittime, where an obelisk commemorates 13 patriots shot by the Bourbons on 14 April 1860. A huge steel stele, 30m high, was set up here in 1989 to commemorate victims of the struggle against the Mafia. A fence protects recent excavations of 10C Arab buildings, and part of the Norman fortifications of the city (restored in the 16C).

To the southeast lies the Cala (see above). Across the busy via Francesco Crispi are remains of the fortress of **Castello a Mare**, used in the 12C as a prison, and from the 13C onwards as a barracks. It was partially restored in 1988–91 (visits can be arranged by calling ☎ 091/6961319). Nearby there are remains of an Arab tower.

In via Cavour, on the other side of piazza XIII Vittime, is **Villa Whitaker** (1885; now used by the Prefecture), surrounded by a garden. This was one of two properties in Palermo owned by the Whitaker brothers.

In front of piazza S. Domenico (see above), across via Roma, the narrow via Monteleone leads up behind the post office (1933) to (no. 50) the **Oratorio di S. Caterina d'Alessandria**. The oratory has been owned by the Knights of the Holy Sepulchre of Jerusalem since 1946 and is at present only open on Thurs (12.00–14.45). The interior has fine stuccoes by Serpotta's son, Procopio (1719–26). It also contains two paintings by Zoppo di Gangi, and a *Madonna and Child* by Vincenzo da Pavia above a bench inlaid with ivory and mother of pearl. The polychrome marble floor dates from 1730.

The church and oratory of S. Ignazio all'Olivella

Just beyond is the church of S. Ignazio all'Olivella (map: 11; open 08.30–11.00, 17.30–18.30; Sun & PH 09.00–13.00, ☎ 091/586867), begun in 1598, with a good 17C façade. The fine **interior** has a barrel vault designed by Venanzio Marvuglia (1772) with frescoes by Antonio Manno (1790). **South aisle**: first chapel, Filippo Paladino, *St Mary of Egypt*; the second chapel has beautiful 17C decorations in *marmi mischi*. In the south transept, altarpiece by Filippo Paladino. The high altarpiece of the *Trinity* is by Sebastiano Conca and in the sanctuary are two statues by Ignazio Marabitti. In the north transept is an interesting altarpiece, of unusual design, of the *Martyrdom of St Ignatius* by Filippo Paladino (1613).

North aisle: the fifth chapel was sumptuously decorated in 1622 and has an altarpiece of *St Philip Neri* by Sebastiano Conca (1740) and two statues by Giovanni Battista Ragusa. The third chapel is also elaborately decorated with polychrome marble and precious stones and an altar frontal in relief. The small fresco in the vault of the *Pietà* is by Pietro Novelli. In the first chapel the altarpiece of the *Archangel Gabriel* is by Pietro Novelli.

In the piazza is the façade, by Filippo Pennino, of the **Oratorio di S. Ignazio Olivella** or di S. Filippo Neri (open Mon–Fri 08.30–17.30, closed Sat, Sun & PH). It has an interesting neo-classical interior of 1769 by Venanzio Marvuglia, with splendid columns and good capitals by Filippo Pennino. In the presbytery there is an elaborate sculpture with angels and cherubs by Ignazio Marabitti.

Regional Archaeological Museum

Adjoining the church is the former monastery of the Filippini, now the seat of the Museo Archeologico Regionale (**map: 7**), one of the most interesting collections in Italy, illustrating the history of western Sicily from prehistoric times to the Roman era (open Mon–Sat 09.00–13.45; Tues, Wed and Fri, also 15.00–18.30; Sun & PH 09.00–13.00, ☎ 091/6116805).

The rooms are numbered in the text and on the plans in their logical sequence. The collection was formed at the beginning of the 19C when it belonged to the university. During the century it acquired various collections, including that of Casuccini, the most important collection of Etruscan material outside Tuscany. It also houses finds from excavations in the western part of the island, notably those of Selinunte.

Ground floor

In the centre of the small cloister is a triton from a 16C fountain. Off this cloister (right) **room 2** is used for exhibitions. Rooms 3 and 4 contain Egyptian and Punic sculpture. In **room 3** are two Phoenician sarcophagi of the 5C BC found near Palermo. In the centre of **room 4** is a male torso of the 6C BC; on the wall, the *Pietra di Palermo*, a black diorite slab whose hieroglyphic inscription records the delivery of 40 shiploads of cedarwood to Pharaoh Snefru (c 2700 BC), and which has proved invaluable in dating ancient Egyptian history; Punic inscription to the sun god Baal-Hammon, on white stone from Lilybaeum; male figure (4C BC) of Egyptian type.

The large cloister (**5**) has a papyrus pool in the centre. In the arcades are Roman fragments: in niches: Zeus enthroned (**6**), derived from a Greek type of 4C BC, and a colossal statue of the emperor Claudius (**8**), both restored by Villareale; also an interesting funerary stele with three portrait busts (40–30 BC). On the right: sarcophagi, cippi (inscribed stones) and stelae. At the far end, **room 9** has Greek inscriptions, the majority from Selinunte. **Room 10** contains stelae from Selinunte, and a dedicatory inscription to Apollo from Temple G. Steps lead down to **room 11** in which fragments of Temple C have been gathered; part of the entablature has been assembled. **Room 12** contains a cornice of lion-head water spouts from the Doric temple of Victory at Himera (2nd quarter of 5C BC), discovered by Pirro Marconi in 1929–30.

Room 13 contains the famous **metopes of Selinunte**, the most important treasures of the museum. These sculpted panels once decorated the friezes of the temples at Selinunte, and they show the development in the skill of the local sculptors from the early 6C BC to the end of the 5C BC. On either side of the entrance are three delicate female heads and fragmentary reliefs from Temple E.

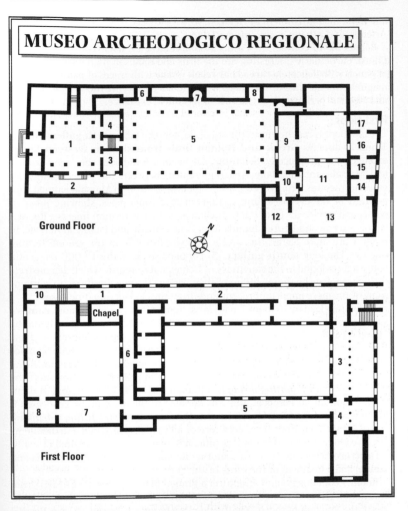

MUSEO ARCHEOLOGICO REGIONALE

Ground Floor

First Floor

Chapel

Beneath the windows are six small Archaic metopes, sculptured in low relief, from an early 6C temple, perhaps destroyed by the people of Selinunte themselves to repair their citadel, in the time of Dionysius the Elder (397–392 BC). They represent scenes with *Demeter and Kore* (one with a quadriga), three deities, a winged sphinx, the *Rape of Europa*, and *Hercules and the Cretan bull*. Facing the windows is a reconstruction, incorporating original fragments, of a frieze and cornice with three triglyphs and three fine **Archaic metopes** from Temple C (early 6C), representing the four-horse chariot of Apollo; *Perseus, protected by Athena, beheading the Gorgon*; and *Herakles punishing the Cercopes*. Also on this wall are parts of two metopes from Temple F, with scenes from the *gigantomachia* (5C BC). Opposite the entrance, four splendid **Classical metopes** from Temple E (early 5C) show *Herakles fighting an Amazon*, the *Wedding of Zeus* *and Hera*, the *Punishment of Actaeon*, who is attacked by dogs in the presence of Artemis, and *Athena overcoming a Titan*.

Rooms 14–17 contain the Casuccini collection of **Etruscan antiquities** from Chiusi. Particularly interesting are the urns and tombs in high relief, a number of panels with delicately carved bas-reliefs (many with traces of painting), and a magnificent oinochoe of bucchero ware (6C BC) portraying the story of Perseus and Medusa, perhaps the finest vase of its kind in existence.

First floor

The first floor is reached from the small cloister. The long **north gallery** (rooms **1 and 2**) displays **Greek and Roman finds from sites in western Sicily**, arranged topographically. Selinunte, Lilybaeum, Randazzo, the Lípari Islands and Marsala are especially well represented. Between the cases, containing vases, terracottas, bronzes, etc., are sepulchral stelae from Marsala painted with portraits of the deceased, and sections of lead water-pipes, showing junction points and stop-cocks from the Cornelian aqueduct at Termini Imerese. **Room 3** contains terracotta figures, mainly from Gela, Himera, and Palazzolo Acreide. In **room 4** are more terracottas and a 5C kylix fished from the sea off Termini Imerese. The long **south gallery** (5) contains some of the 12,000 terracotta votive figures found in the sanctuary of Demeter at Selinunte which demonstrate their chronology by the evolution of their design. The **west gallery** (6) contains some of the more important recent finds from sites in Palermo (fine vases).

A few steps lead up to **room 7** with large Roman bronzes. The famous **ram** is a superb sculpture dating from the 3C BC, probably modelled on an original by Lysippos (some scholars believe it to be the work of Lysippos himself) and formerly one of a pair. Up until 1448 they were on the front of the Castello Maniace in Syracuse; in the 18C they were admired by Jean Houel and Goethe in the Royal Palace in Palermo. The second ram was destroyed in 1848 by a cannon shot. The very fine *Hercules fighting a stag* is a Roman copy of a 3C BC original. It decorated a fountain at Pompeii, and was donated to the museum by Francesco I. **Room 8** is devoted to Greek sculpture: in the centre is a *Satyr filling a drinking cup*, a Roman copy from Torre del Greco of a Praxitelean original. Further items displayed here are a portrait of Aristotle, a Roman copy of an original of c 330 BC; a herm of a bearded Dionysus, another Roman copy; beautiful **5C reliefs** and **stelae**, and a fragment of the frieze of the Parthenon.

Room 9 contains Roman sculpture: a Roman matron; a priestess of Isis (from Taormina); reliefs of vestal virgins, and Mithras killing the bull; and a sarcophagus of the 2nd half of the 2C. On the floor is a mosaic pavement (3C AD). Beyond a vestibule (10), with Roman fragments, is the landing at the head of the stairs. Nearby is a small chapel (usually closed), which is part of the 17C convent.

The **second floor** (opened on request) surrounds the Large Cloister. It contains a superb collection of Greek vases (see p 457 for vase types). At the top of the stairs to the right is the short gallery with proto-Corinthian pottery of the 7C BC. In the central wall case is a 6C plate with horses and a fragment of an amphora with elaborately dressed figures. In the second central case is a 6C *oinochoe* from Selinunte and various *aryballoi*.

Long gallery

The long gallery has a splendid series of Attic black-figure vases (580–460 BC). Among the *lekythoi* with figures on a white ground is one (second central case) showing the *Sacrifice of Iphigenea*, signed by Douris (see below). In the third central case is a large krater with a quadriga and dionysic scenes, and two amphorae with Hercules. In the fifth central case is a red-figure stamnos with *Hercules and the Hydra* (480–460 BC).

Douris

Douris, active in Athens from 500–470 BC, was one of the most prolific vase-painters. He collaborated with a potter called Python, but he would occasionally try his hand at making his own pots. He liked to depict cavorting satyrs, preferring the red-figure technique on a black ground. In the museums of the world there are about 300 vases painted by this artist; if, as experts believe, only about 3 per cent of the total production of ancient Greek vases has survived to the present day, Douris would have painted about 10,000 in his career, allowing for one a day with a few high days and holidays, and all of high artistic quality.

In the room at the end (right) red-figure **vases** are displayed, including a kylix decorated by Oltos, a hydra with the *Judgement of Paris*, and a bell-shaped krater with dionysic scenes. Another room displays mosaic floors (1C BC–4C AD), mostly from piazza Vittoria in Palermo.

The **wall-paintings** here include five from the 1C BC from Solunto and a fragment (1C AD) from Pompeii. The room at the end of the next long corridor contains Italiot vases (4C–3C BC), many with reliefs and traces of painting from Puglia, Campania and Sicily. The last **long gallery** contains the collection of **prehistoric and Early Bronze Age material** which comes mainly from northwest Sicily. Here are displayed casts of the fine incised drawings (late Palaeolithic) of masked figures and animals from Cave B at Addaura on Mount Pellegrino. Nearby are the bones of elephants, rhinoceros and hippopotami found in via Villafranca, Palermo.

The narrow via Bara, in front of the museum, leading to piazza Verdi (see below) is one of the liveliest streets in Palermo, with craft shops, cafés, traditional restaurants and a puppet theatre. Here, Via Maqueda leads back to the Quattro Canti.

8 • Sant'Agostino and the Quartiere del Capo

From the Quattro Canti via Maqueda runs gradually uphill to the north, passing a large bombed site where remains of the 14C church of S. Croce and a few neighbouring buildings were demolished in 1981. Plans for the Quartiere del Capo, an important area in the centre of the city, owned by the church, are uncertain. On its far side is **via S. Agostino** home to the Mercato del Capo, a fascinating street market for cloth, clothes and household goods, not unlike the *suqs* in Damascus or Cairo.

Sant'Agostino

Beyond, on the right, hidden by the market stalls, is the church of S. Agostino (**map: 11**; open Mon–Sat 07.00–12.00, 16.00–17.30, Sun & PH 07.00–12.00, ☎ 091/ 584632). The unusual tall side portal (restored) is attributed to

Domenico Gagini. The beautiful **façade**, on via Maestri dell'Acqua, has a late 13C portal decorated with lava mosaic and a 14C rose window.

The **interior**, consisting of a huge single nave, was decorated with gilded stuccoes by Giacomo Serpotta and assistants from 1711, including numerous cherubs, statues and lunettes over the side altars. South side: first altar, panel painting by Simon de Worbrecht (16C) of *Blessed William of Aquitaine*; second altar, 17C *Flight into Egypt*; fourth altar, Antonino Grano (17C), *St Nicholas of Tolentino*; beyond the passage of the south entrance is the chapel of the Madonna del Soccorso, with a bas-relief of the *Eternal Father*. The organ dates from the 18C. Left of the high altar is the chapel of the Crucifix, with a precious 17C reliquary. North side: fourth altar, Giuseppe Salerno Zoppo di Gangi, *St Thomas of Villanova* and stories from his life. On the left of the second altar is a monument to Francesco Medici, with his bust (1774; surmounted by a cockerel) by Ignazio Marabitti. The pretty 16C cloister, with tall pulvins above its capitals, surrounds a little garden. The fine Gothic entrance to the chapterhouse was exposed here in 1962 and restored.

Via S. Agostino, now a little wider, continues uphill past the church dedicated to the **Crocifisso di Lucca**, with another very ruined but interesting façade dating from the early 17C. Just beyond on the left is a little piazza in front of the former church of **S. Marco** with a handsome early 16C façade. It has been restored as an old people's home run by nuns. The next crossroads is the centre of the **Mercato del Capo**, a colourful market. The **Quartiere del Capo (map: 10)** is a maze of narrow streets.

Via Porta Carini, with stalls selling fish, fruit and vegetables, leads to three churches. **S. Ippolito Martire** (1583), with a façade of 1728, has pretty columns, a chapel off the south aisle with numerous ex votos, and in the north aisle a damaged 14C Byzantine fresco of the *Madonna*. The 18C paintings include the high altarpiece of the *Martyrdom of St Hippolyte* by Gaspare Serenario.

Opposite is the **Immacolata Concezione** built in 1612. The **interior**, one of the most beautiful in the city, was elaborately decorated in the course of the 17C with polychrome marble, sculptures, singing galleries and marble intarsia altars. On the gilded stucco ceiling is a fresco by Olivio Sozzi.

Beyond S. Ippolito is the church of **S. Gregorio**, built in 1686–88. It contains some interesting wooden statues. At the end of the street is the **Porta Carini**, the only one of the three gateways to have survived at the northern limit of the old city, although even this was reconstructed in 1782.

From the crossroads of the Mercato del Capo (see above) via Cappuccinella continues through the food market and piazza S. Anna al Capo in a very rundown area of the city. In via Quattro Coronati (right) is the little church of the **Quattro Coronati** built in 1674. At the next crossroads, via Matteo Bonello and via del Noviziato lead right to the church of the **Noviziato dei Gesuiti**, in the area behind the law courts. Built in 1591, the interior preserves some fine 18C stuccoes and *marmi mischi* decoration, as well as an effigy of *St Stanislaus* by Giacomo Pennino (1725).

In the other direction, via Matteo Bonello leads to the church of **S. Angelo Custode** (on the corner of via dei Carrettieri), preceded by an outside stair. It dates from the early 18C. To the west is the wide and busy via Papireto across which is piazza Peranni, where Palermo's famous **flea market** is held.

Via Carrettieri (see above) returns down to the Mercato del Capo in via Beati Paoli which leads right to piazza Beati Paoli. This is named after a much feared secret society which operated in this area in the 17C. The church of **SS. Cosma e Damiano** was built after the plague of 1575 and that of **S. Maria di Gesù** was founded in 1660 (it contains a large 18C vault fresco, restored in 1884). Via Beati Paoli continues past the church of S. Giovanni alla Guilla, rebuilt in 1669 and badly damaged in World War II. On the right vicolo Tortorici leads into piazza SS. 40 Martiri with the church of **SS. Quaranta Martiri alla Guilla** (open 09.00–17.00; Sat 09.00–13.00), founded by some Pisan nobles in 1605 and rebuilt in 1725. It contains frescoes by Guglielmo Borremans. The word *guilla* derives from the Arabic *wadi*, or river, meaning the church was built on the banks of the river Papireto.

From via Beati Paoli via S. Agata alla Guilla leads steeply uphill past **Palazzo S. Isidoro** (with a fine Mannerist portal) to join corso Vittorio Emanuele near the Cathedral, while the interesting old via del Celso, in which the church of S. Paolino has recently been converted into a **mosque**, forks left for via Maqueda.

9 • The nineteenth century city

Bus **no. 101** from the railway station follows via Roma northwards as far as the Politeama and then goes up viale della Libertà north past the Giardino Inglese to piazzale de Gaspari, near La Favorita.

At the north end of via Maqueda is **piazza Verdi** (map: 10, 11), laid out at the end of the 19C, now one of the most central squares in the city. It is dominated by the **Teatro Massimo Opera House** (open Tues–Sun 10.00–15.30, ☎ 091/6053515), a huge Corinthian structure begun by Giovanni Battista Basile and finished by his son Ernesto (1875–97). Among the historic late 19C opera theatres in Europe its stage is exceeded in size only by that of the Paris Opéra and the Vienna opera house. It was inaugurated in 1897 with Verdi's *Falstaff*. In the piazza in front of the theatre are two decorative little kiosks which used to be the ticket offices, also designed by Basile.

From the piazza, via Maqueda continues north by via Ruggero Settimo, a street named not after the seventh King Roger, who never existed, but the much-loved patriot Ruggero Settimo, president of a short-lived independent Sicily in 1848, proclaimed in defiance of the Bourbons. The road is lined with clothes shops as far as the double piazza Ruggero Settimo and piazza Castelnuovo, home to the **Politeama Garibaldi Theatre** (map: 7). A 'Pompeian' structure (1874, by Giuseppe Damiani-Almeyda) crowned by a bronze quadriga by Mario Rutelli. it is now used mostly for concerts, but the building was designed to accommodate the circus, which is why Rutelli chose a victorious chariot as his theme.

In part of the building the **Gallery of Modern Art** is housed, founded in 1910, with 19C and 20C works, mostly by artists from Sicily and southern Italy (open 09.00–20.00; Sun & PH 09.00–13.00, closed Mon), including Domenico Morelli, Antonio Mancini, Giovanni Boldini, Corrado Cagli, Carlo Carrà, Felice Casorati and Gino Severini.

To the east, in via Roma, is the **Grande Albergo e delle Palme** (formerly Palazzo Ingham). Here Richard Wagner stayed with his family and completed *Parsifal* in 1882. The building was modified in 1907 by Ernesto Basile.

Viale della Libertà (**map: 2**), a wide avenue laid out in 1860, with trees and attractive Art Nouveau houses, leads north. Beyond the double piazze Mordini and Crispi and the Excelsior Hotel, the road narrows. On the left it passes a statue of Garibaldi in a garden recently renamed after Giovanni Falcone and his wife Francesca Morvillo, who were assassinated by the Mafia in 1992. Opposite is the larger **Giardino Inglese** (**map: 2**), a delightful well-kept nineteenth century public garden. It is bordered on the far side by via Generale Dalla Chiesa which commemorates General Carlo Alberto Dalla Chiesa who was assassinated by the Mafia here in 1982 (plaque), along with his wife and chauffeur, after just five months in office as Prefect of Palermo.

Further east towards the sea is the **Ucciardone** (**map: 3**), built in 1837–60, and now a maximum security jail, and the modern port of Palermo.

On the other side of via Libertà is **Villa Trabia** (**map: 1,2**), seat of the Lanza di Trabia family, an elegant 18C building (now used as local government offices), with beautiful gardens (open 07.00–19.00 daily, ☎ 091/7405905).

Across via Notarbartolo viale della Libertà passes (left; no. 52) the head office of the Banco di Sicilia with the **Mormino Foundation Archaeological Museum** (open Mon to Fri 09.00–13.00, 15.00–17.00, Sat morning only, ☎ 091/6259519, ▨ www.aesnet.it/fondasicilia), which contains archaeological material from the excavations financed by the Bank; a precious collection of Greek vases, Sicilian pottery dating from 15C–19C, prints, maps and water-colours, numismatic and philatelic collections (representing the Kingdom of the Two Sicilies, and thought to be among the finest in the world).

Viale della Libertà ends in the circular piazza Vittorio Veneto. From here via d'Artigliera (right) leads shortly to piazza dei Leoni at the south entrance (c 4km from the Quattro Canti) to La Favorita, described below.

10 • The Zisa, the Convento dei Cappuccini and the Cuba

Since these monuments are outside the central area of the city they are best reached by car or bus. For the **Zisa** (**map: 9**), take bus **no. 124** (infrequent service) from via Mariano Stabile (**map: 7**); near the Zisa there is an inconspicuous request stop in via Mulini (**map: 9**) beside the church of the Annunziata and four little trees. On the return to the centre the bus runs along via Volturno and terminates in piazza Verdi. For the **Cappuccini convent** (just off **map: 13**), take bus **no. 327** from piazza Indipendenza. For **La Cuba** (just off **map: 13**), Cubula and Villa Tasca, bus **no. 389** runs from piazza Indipendenza (**map: 13, 14**) along corso Calatafimi.

La Zisa

The palace of La Zisa (**map: 9**; open 09.00–19.00, Sun & PH 09.00–13.30, ☎ 091/6520269) takes its name comes from the Arabic *al aziz* (or magnificent) and it is the most important secular monument of Arab-Norman architecture to survive in Sicily, purely Islamic in inspiration.

History

La Zisa was one of a group of palaces built by the Norman kings in their private park of Genoard (used as a hunting reserve) on the outskirts of Palermo. It was begun by William I c 1164–65 and completed by his son. The palace is known to have been used by Frederick II, but it was already in disrepair in the late 13C. It was fortified by the Chiaramontes in the 14C. By the 16C it was in a ruined state and was drastically reconstructed by the Spanish Sandoval family who owned it from 1635 to 1806. It was expropriated by the Sicilian government in 1955 but then abandoned until part of the upper floors collapsed in 1971. After years of neglect, a remarkable restoration programme was begun in 1974 and it was finally opened to the public in 1990. The structure had to be consolidated throughout, but the astonishing architecture has been preserved.

The fine **exterior** has a symmetrical design, although the two-light windows on the upper floors were all destroyed in the 17C by the Sandoval, who set up their coat of arms on the façade and altered the portico.

In William's day the sandstone was faced with plaster decorated in a red and white design. The small pond outside, formerly part of a garden in Arab style, collected the water from the fountain in the ground floor hall, which was fed by a nearby Roman aqueduct. A damaged inscription in Cufic letters at the top of the east façade has not yet been deciphered.

The beautiful **interior** of the palace, on three floors, can be visited. The exceptionally thick outer walls (1.9 metres on the ground floor), the original small windows and a system of air vents (also found in ancient Egyptian buildings) kept the palace protected from the extremes of heat and cold. The rooms were all vaulted: the square rooms with cross vaults and the oblong rooms with barrel vaults. Amphorae were used in the structure of the vaults in order to allow for the foundations of the floors above. Some of the vaults have had to be reconstructed in reinforced concrete. The pavements (very few of the original ones remain) were in tiles laid in a herring-bone pattern, except for the ground floor hall which was in marble. The miniature stalactite vaults (known as *mouqarnas*) which decorate niches in some of the rooms and the recesses of many of the windows are borrowed from Arab architectural styles.

On the **ground floor** are explanatory plans and a display illustrating the history of the building. A model in plexiglass shows the parts where it had to be reconstructed and where iron girders have been inserted to reinforce the building. The small rooms here were originally service rooms or rooms used by court dignitaries. The splendid **central hall**, used for entertainments, has niches with stalactite vaults derived from Islamic architecture. Around the walls runs a mosaic freize which expands into three ornamental circles in the central recess. The Norman mosaics (which recall those in King Roger's Room in the Royal Palace), show Byzantine, Islamic, and even Frankish influences. A fountain gushed from the opening surmounted by the imperial eagle in mosaic and flowed down a runnel towards the entrance to be collected in the fish pond outside. A majolica floor survives here and the faded frescoes were added in the 17C. The little columns have beautiful capitals. On the inner side of the entrance arch is a damaged 12C inscription in large stucco letters.

Two symmetrical staircases used to lead up to the **first floor** (replaced by modern iron stairways). Here the living rooms are connected by a corridor along the west front. Numerous fine vaults survive here and a series of air vents (see above). Egyptian Muslim objects, including metalwork, ceramics, and wooden lattice work, which served as windows, are displayed in some of the rooms, as well as amphorae found in the vaulting. On the **top floor** is a remarkable central hall with columns and water channels which was originally an open atrium surrounded by loggias, used in the summer. The small rooms on either side were probably a harem.

To the north of the Zisa, in via dei Normanni, is the **church of Gesù, Maria e S. Stefano** which incorporates a Norman chapel built at the same time as the palace. Nearby is an auditorium and exhibition centre, known as the **Cantieri Culturali della Zisa** (open daily 09.00–18.00, ☎ 091/ 7403430). In piazza Zisa is the 17C church of the Annunziata, with Sandoval family funerary monuments.

Villa Whitaker Malfitano

From the Zisa, via Whitaker and via Serradifalco lead north to Villa Whitaker Malfitano (**map: 5**), built for Joseph (Pip) and Tina Whitaker by Ignazio Greco in 1887. The house was the centre of English society in Palermo at the beginning of the twentieth century, and the Whitakers were visited by Edward VII in 1907 and by George V and Queen Mary in 1925. Pip Whitaker, descendant of the famous Marsala wine merchants, was owner and excavator of Mozia (see p 201) and the house was left by his daughter on her death in 1971 to the Joseph Whitaker Foundation. There is a small private museum, and the villa is sometimes used for exhibitions. It is surrounded by a magnificent park (nearly 7 ha) of rare trees and plants collected by the owners, an orangery and an orchid nursery. Both museum and park are open daily 09.00–13.00, closed Sun & PH; last tickets 12.30, ☎ 091/6816133)

To the south of Villa Whitaker, at no. 38 viale Regina Margherita, is the **Villino Florio**, one of Ernesto Basile's best works (1889), perfect Art Nouveau style down to the smallest detail, and furnished by Ducrot. It has been lovingly restored after a fire in 1962, and is now open daily to the public (09.00–13.00). A number of Art Nouveau houses are situated in via Dante, which was the fashionable area to live at the time.

To the south (see Palermo environs map) is the **Convento dei Cappuccini** (open 09.00–12.00, 15.00–17.00, ☎ 091/212117), famous for its **catacombs**. Here, the bodies of wealthy citizens, aristocrats, priests and friars, even children, were dried by the Capuchins, dressed in their best finery, and hung up along the macabre underground passages in full view; this continued until 1881. There are still more than 6,000 bodies, including that of a little girl who died nearly a hundred years ago, and was illegally mummified by a friar who died immediately afterwards, taking the secret of her perfect conservation to his tomb.

From piazza Cappuccini via Pindemonte leads (right) to via La Loggia where the scant ruins of the Norman **Palazzo dell'Uscibene** (or Scibene, formerly Mimnermo) are found, built at the time of William II as a summer residence for the archbishops of Palermo. A hall with niches decorated with stucco shells has all but disappeared.

Outside Porta Nuova (**map: 14**) Corso Calatafimi begins, which leads to Monreale. On the left is a huge charitable institute built in 1735–38 by Casimiro Agretta; the church façade is by Marvuglia (1772–76).

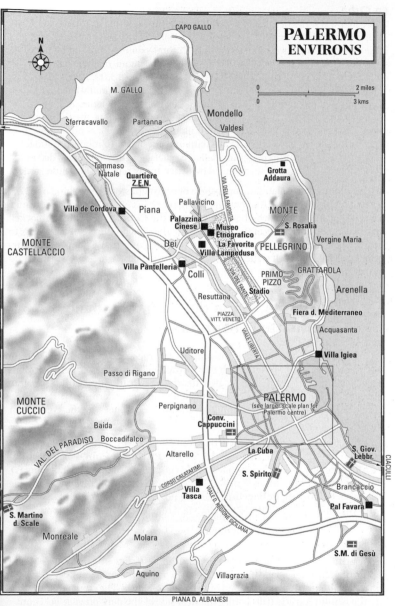

PALERMO ENVIRONS

N

0 — 2 miles
0 — 3 kms

CAPO GALLO

M. GALLO

Mondello

Sferracavallo   Partanna   Valdesi

Tommaso Natale

Quartiere Z.E.N.

Grotta Addaura

Villa de Cordova

Piana

Pallavicino

MONTE

Palazzina Cinese

Museo Etnografico

S. Rosalia

MONTE CASTELLACCIO

Dei

La Favorita

Villa Lampedusa

PELLEGRINO   Vergine Maria

Villa Pantelleria

Colli

PRIMO PIZZO

GRATTAROLA

Stadio

Resuttana

Arenella

PIAZZA VITT. VENETO

Fiera d. Mediterraneo

Uditore

Acquasanta

Villa Igiea

Passo di Rigano

MONTE CUCCIO

Perpignano

PALERMO
(see larger scale plan for
Palermo centre)

Conv. Cappuccini

Baida

Boccadifalco

La Cuba

S. Giov. Lebbr.

Altarello

CIACULLI

S. Spirito

Brancaccio

Villa Tasca

S. Martino d. Scale

Pal Favara

Monreale

Molara

S.M. di Gesù

Aquino

Villagrazia

PIANA D. ALBANESI

On the corner is a fountain of 1630 (recently restored), the only one to survive of the many which used to line the road. Opposite is the vast Albergo dei Poveri (**map: 13**), an interesting building by Orazio Furetto (1746–72), built as the Poor House, recently restored and now used for important exhibitions.

La Cuba

There follow a series of barracks including (on the left) the Caserma Tuköry (no. 100; c 1km from the gate) where excavations since 1989 have revealed part of a huge Punic necropolis (no admission), with tombs dating from the 6C BC. Here, separated from the barracks by a wall with a charming modern mural, is the entrance to La Cuba (open 09.00–19.00, Sun & PH 09.00–13.00, ☎ 091/590299).

This was a Norman palace built by William II (1180) in imitation of the Zisa. The name Cuba comes from the Arabic *kubbeh*, meaning dome. A copy of the Arabic inscription at the top of the outer wall and a model of the Cuba are displayed in a restored stable block. The building is now roofless and a few trees grow inside the walls. In one part are remains of a hall with miniature stalactite vaults, typical of Arab architecture, delicate reliefs, and a small cupola decorated with stuccoes. It was once surrounded by water, today replaced by a little garden.

Further along corso Calatafimi, opposite a department store and behind no. 575, a short road leads right to the remains of a derelict 17C villa. Here is the entrance to the delightful orchard which still surrounds the **Cubula**. The gate is unlocked by the custodian who lives at the house beside the villa on the left; a path leads to the little pavilion with its characteristic red dome, built by William I. Once surrounded by a fishpond, it is the only survivor of the many which used to decorate his private park in this area (see above).

11 • La Favorita, Piana dei Colli, Mondello and Monte Pellegrino

La Favorita (see Palermo environs map) is a large park at the foot of Monte Pellegrino. The **Pitré Museum**, an ethnographical museum with an outstanding collection is conveniently located nearby. At **Piana dei Colli**, the area between Monte Pellegrino and Monte Castellaccio (see Palermo environs map), there are numerous 18C villas, built as summer residences by the Palermitan nobility.

• For **La Favorita** take bus **no. 107** from the railway station to piazzale de Gasperi and from there the **no. 615** for the **Pitré Museum**. For **Piana dei Colli**, take bus **no. 619** from piazzale de Gasperi. For Mondello, take **bus GT** from piazza Verdi and viale della Libertà and the **no. 615** from piazzale de Gasperi. For **Monte Pellegrino**, take the **no. 812** from piazza Sturzo and the **no. 603** from piazza Vittorio Veneto, via Arenella and Addaura (terminating at Mondello).

La Favorita

La Favorita's extensive area of woods and gardens lies at the foot of Monte Pellegrino. The public park (nearly 3km long), is crossed by a one-way road system and contains a hippodrome and other sports facilities. The city stadium (right) and the Istituto Agrario (left) border the west side of the park on viale del Fante.

Just beyond piazza Niscemi is the main entrance (c 7km from the Quattro Canti) to the formal **Parco della Favorita**, an estate bought by Ferdinand of Bourbon in 1799, and laid out by him according to the taste of the times. The **Palazzina Cinese**, a charming building in a Chinese style by Venanzio

Marvuglia was occupied by Ferdinand and Maria Carolina in 1799–1802 during their enforced exile from Naples. The collection of English prints was a gift from Nelson, when the king declared him Duke of Bronte.

The **Museo Etnografico Siciliano Pitrè** (open daily 08.30–20.00, closed Fri, Sun & PH, ☎ 091/7404893) at the north end of La Favorita, was founded in 1909 by Giuseppe Pitrè. The museum has a wonderful collection illustrating Sicilian life through its customs, costumes, popular arts (painted carts, ex-votos, etc.), musical instruments, implements and typical everyday objects.

Piana dei Colli

The 18C summer villas built by the Palermitan nobility to escape the heat of the city between Monte Pellegrino and Monte Castellaccio are notable for their ingenious design (often with elaborate outside staircases). In the twentieth century many of them were engulfed by new buildings or left to decay, although more recently some interest has been shown in their preservation.

In piazza Niscemi (see above) is the 18C **Villa Niscemi**, acquired by the Council of Palermo in 1987. (**park** open daily 08.00–19.00, and the **villa** on Sun & PH 09.00–12.30, ☎ 091/7494801). Across via Duca degli Abruzzi is the small early 18C Villa Spina which also has its own park. Nearby is **Villa Lampedusa**, built in 1770 and now used for concerts and exhibitions (☎ 091/7541690). This was bought by the Principe di Lampedusa, Giulio Tomasi c 1845, and described in *Il Gattopardo* by his great-grandson Giuseppe Tomasi.

Further west, off via Nuova, is **Villa Pantelleria** (c 1730), now the seat of the *Centro Internazionale di Musica, Cultura e Arte Popolare 'Django Reinhardt'*. In the district of S. Lorenzo is the **Convitto Nazionale** (now used by the Red Cross), the grandest of this group of villas, built in 1683. Near here is the district of 'Z.E.N.', which contains a 1960s' housing estate once notorious for its social problems. Off via S. Lorenzo is **Villa Amari** built in 1720 by Count Michele Amari di S. Adriano and **Villa Boscogrande** (1756). Across via Tommaso Natale is the well-preserved **Villa De Cordova**.

In the district of Resuttana, nearer the Parco della Favorita, is **Villa Terrasi** with early 18C frescoes by Vito D'Anna. Also in this district is the **Villa Sofia** (now a hospital), purchased by Joseph Whitaker in 1850. He, and one of his sons, also called Joseph but nicknamed Pip (see p 201), created a splendid garden here famous for its palms. Only a few palms, yuccas and Turkey oaks survive.

At **Acquasanta**, on the coast, reached by via Imperatore Federico from the south entrance of the Favorita, is the **Villa Igiea** (see Palermo environs map; reached by buses from the centre of Palermo), now a 5-star hotel in a large park. A remarkable Art Nouveau building, it was built as a sanatorium by the Florio at the end of the 19C and transformed into a hotel in 1900 by Ernesto Basile. Nearby is **Villa Belmonte**, a neo-classical building by Venanzio Marvuglia (1801).

Fabulous Florios and the Belle Epoque

If Palermo in the 1890s was a capital city of the Belle Epoque, and if Mondello was the most fashionable bathing resort in the world, credit is certainly due to the Florio family; rich, good-looking and successful. In 1893, when Ignazio married Donna Franca Jacona di San Giuliano, the most beautiful and fascinating woman in Sicily, he owned the Egadi Islands with the tunny fisheries, the Marsala wine company, and a fleet of 99 merchant ships. His brother Vincenzo launched the *Targa Florio* (✉ www. targaflorio.tv) in 1906, a gruelling motor-race over 700km of hair-raising roads in the Madonie Mountains.

Donna Franca's home in Palermo was a magnet for poets, artists, royalty and heads of state, while her Cartier jewellery was envied by Queen Mary. Although not untouched by personal tragedy, the Florios glittered on the social horizon of Palermo for a while, the very epitome of Belle Epoque. Of course, this way of life did not last long; by the 1920s, governmental decisions had left their mark on the family's fortunes and Fascism put paid to the rest of it.

Mondello

From the north end of the Parco della Favorita (see above) a road runs through the suburb of Pallavicino and beneath the western slope of Mount Pellegrino, reaching the shore and numerous villas of Mondello. This is one of the most noted bathing resorts in Sicily, whose sandy beach extends for 2km from Mount Pellegrino to Monte Gallo. The opulent Art Nouveau restaurant, the *Charleston* (1910), which juts out over the sea, was originally the bathing establishment from which society ladies could discreetly lower themselves into the water.

A garden city was laid out here by an Italo-Belgian society in 1892–1910. It also had a license to use the beach as a lido which is still valid, but now the people of Palermo are tired of the ugly iron barrier which keeps them away from the sands, and the hundreds of little cabins which block the view, so in the near future it will probably be revoked. At the north end is the old fishing village of Mondello which has a medieval tower. To the south is Valdesi from which Lungomare Cristoforo Colombo returns towards the centre of Palermo following the rocky coast at the foot of Monte Pellegrino via Vergine Maria, Arenella and Acquasanta. Inland from Mondello is Partanna where the unusual Villa Partanna survives from 1722–28. Above the beautiful headland **Capo Gallo** rises (527m) vertically from the sea (now a protected area).

Monte Pellegrino

Between the Mondello road and the sea is Monte Pellegrino (606m), described by Goethe as the most beautiful headland in the world: it rises sharply on all sides except the south. The rock, in places covered with trees and cacti, has a remarkable golden colour.

Almost certainly the ancient *Heirkte*, the headland was occupied by Hamilcar Barca in the First Punic War and defended for three years (247–244 BC) against the Romans. The Arabs called it *Gebel Grin*, hence the modern name Pellegrino. In the **Addaura Caves** (closed due to rock falls) on the northern slopes **prehistoric rock carvings** were discovered in 1952. The incised human and animal figures date from the Upper Palaeolithic period: they include an exceptionally interesting scene of uncertain significance with 17 human figures, some with animal masks, who appear to be carrying out a cruel ritual or dance. Plaster casts of the carvings can be seen in the Regional Archaeological Museum.

The most direct approach to Monte Pellegrino from Palermo is from piazza Generale Cascino, near the fair and exhibition ground (Fiera del Mediterraneo). From here via Pietro Bonanno ascends to the Santuario di S. Rosalia, crossing and recrossing the shorter footpath used by people making the annual pilgrimage on 3–4 September. A flight of steps zig-zags up the 'Scala Vecchia' (17C) between the Primo Pizzo (344m; left) and the Pizzo Grattarola (276m). The terrace of Castello Utveggio (built as a hotel in 1932) provides the best view of Palermo.

The Santuario di S. Rosalia

A small group of buildings marks the sanctuary (428m; open 07.00–20.00, ☎ 091/540326), a cavern converted into a chapel in 1625. It contains a statue of the saint by Gregorio Tedeschi, and a bas-relief of her coronation, by Nunzio La Mattina. The water trickling down the walls is held to be miraculous and is carefully captured by strange metal conduits. The outer part of the cave is filled with an extraordinary variety of ex-votos.

> This was the hermitage of St Rosalie, daughter of Duke Sinibald and niece of William II. She died here in 1166, and is supposed to have appeared to a hunter on Monte Pellegrino in 1624 to show him the cave where her remains were, since she had never received a Christian burial. When found, her relics were carried in procession through Palermo and a terrible plague, then raging in the town, miraculously ceased. She was declared patron saint of Palermo and the annual procession in her honour (14–15 July), with a tall and elaborate float drawn through the streets by oxen, became a famous spectacle.

A steep road on the farther side of the adjoining convent climbs up to the summit, from which there is a wonderful view extending from the Aeolian Islands to Etna. Another road from the sanctuary leads to a colossal 19C statue by Benedetto De Lisi of *St Rosalie*, high on the cliff edge.

13 • The southern districts of the city

For S. Spirito bus no. 108 (terminating at the Ospedale Civico); or underground from the railway station to the first stop, piazza Vespri. For Ponte dell'Ammiraglio and S. Giovanni dei Lebbrosi, any bus which follows corso dei Mille from Porta Garibaldi near the railway station.

From the station corso Tuköry leads west to Porta S. Agata (follow the signs for Policlinico/Ospedale). Here via del Vespro forks left; beyond the Policlinico and just across the railway are the flower stalls and stonemasons' yards outside the cemetery of **S. Orsola**, in the midst of which is the church of **S. Spirito** or dei Vespri (which is a 15–20 minute walk from the station, open 08.00–12.00, ☎ 091/422691).

This fine Norman church (1173–78) was founded by Walter, Archbishop of Palermo. It has a pretty exterior with arches and bands of volcanic stone and lattice-work windows. The interior has a restored painted wood ceiling and a painted wooden crucifix of the 15C.

> On 31 March 1282 at the hour of vespers, a French soldier offended a young Sicilian girl in front of this church: her husband retaliated by strangling the soldier and the crowd immediately showed their sympathy by killing the other

French soldiers present. Their action sparked off a rebellion in the city against the Angevin overlords and by the next morning some 2000 Frenchmen had been killed. The revolt spread to the rest of the island and in the following centuries the famous **Sicilian Vespers** came to symbolise the pride of the Sicilians and their struggle for independence from foreign rule. The revolt also had important consequences on the course of European history, as from this time onwards the political power of Charles of Anjou, who had the support of the Papacy, dwindled and he lost his ambition to create an Empire.

From Porta Garibaldi near the station, corso dei Mille (**map: 16**) leads south to the Oreto; this ancient thoroughfare was used by Garibaldi and his men on their entrance to the city. Just across the river is the **Ponte dell'Ammiraglio**, a fine bridge built by George of Antioch in 1113, and extremely well preserved. Since the river has been diverted it is now surrounded by a well kept garden and busy roads. Here the first skirmish between the Garibaldini and the Bourbon troops took place on 27 May 1860.

A short way beyond is piazza Scaffa. On the left of the corso, hidden behind crumbling edifices (and now approached from no. 38 via Salvatore Cappello), is **S. Giovanni dei Lebbrosi**, one of the oldest Norman churches in Sicily (open Mon–Sat 09.30–11.00, 16.00–17.00, closed Sun & PH, ☎ 091/475024). Traditionally thought to have been founded by Roger I in 1072, it was more probably erected at the time of Roger II when a leper hospital was built here. From piazza Scaffa (see above) via Brancaccio leads south through the unattractive suburb of Brancaccio. Via Conte Federico continues to the **Castello del Maredolce** (or **Favara**), which is now in ruins and almost totally engulfed by apartment blocks. The palazzo, once surrounded on three sides by an artificial lake, was built by the emir Jafar in 997–1019, and was later used by the Norman kings and Frederick II. A chapel was built here by Roger II.

To the south, across the motorway, is the ruined 18C church of S. Ciro near which the Grotta dei Giganti yielded finds of fossil bones. A road leads from here to the suburb of **Ciaculli**, where a huge estate once owned by the Mafia boss Michele Greco, is now farmed by a group of young people. Greco, known as *il Papa* (the Pope), was found guilty of some 100 murders and is now in prison. The vegetation and landscape of the park is typical of the Conca d'Oro which once surrounded Palermo.

San Giovanni dei Lebbrosi, Palermo

On the slopes of Monte Grifone, beyond ugly new suburbs and the ring road and motorway (at present very difficult to find by car) is the restored church of **S. Maria di Gesù**, preceded by a terraced graveyard (if closed, ring the bell at the convent). The simple chapel of 1426 was enlarged laterally in 1481 and a presbytery was added, with two fine Gothic arches. Here are the arcade and colonnettes of the tomb of Antonio Alliata, by Antonello Gagini (1524), and a monument to a lady of the Alliata family, by the workshop of Domenico Gagini (1490–1500). In a chapel off the nave is a wooden statue of *St Francis*, by Pippinico; a Baroque niche contains a wooden statue of the *Madonna* (late 15C).

The atrium, the funerary chapel of the Bonet family, has a wooden ceiling from the late 12C. The main doorway, with a frieze of the *Apostles*, dates from c 1495, and is from the workshop of Domenico Gagini. Outside the presbytery is the Gothic **Cappella La Grua**; the frescoes are probably by a Spanish artist of the late 15C. There is a magnificent view from the Belvedere.

Monte Grifone (832m), the hill overlooking Palermo from the southeast, may be reached either from S. Maria di Gesù or from S. Ciro (see above). On its northern slope is the ravine of the Discesa dei Mille (Descent of the Thousand), above which an obelisk (337m) marks the site of Garibaldi's encampment of 26 May 1860.

MONREALE

'*Cu va a Palermu, e non va a Murriali, ci va sceccu, e torna animali*' says an old proverb: 'he who goes to Palermo without visiting Monreale, goes as a donkey, and returns as a beast'. On a hill overlooking the Conca d'Oro, on the slopes of the mountain behind Palermo, it is now quite a large dormitory town (pop. 26,000) but its saving grace is the cathedral. One of the most superb churches in the world, it is certainly the most important Norman building in Sicily, with a unique series of splendid mosaics. Pietro Novelli (1603–1647), one of Sicily's finest painters, was born here.

Practical information

 ### Getting there
By bus
Monreale is 8km southwest of Palermo. Bus **no. 389** from piazza Indipendenza (see Palermo **map: 13**; frequent service in 20–30 minutes).
By car
The town is approached by corso Calatafimi (see Palermo **map:13**).

Information offices
Azienda Autonoma del Turismo, 34 piazza Castelnuovo, Palermo, ☎ 091/058111).
Tourist Information Bureau, piazza Vittorio Emanuele, ☎ 091/6564501.

Monreale on line: ✉ www.comune.monreale.pa.it.

 ### Where to stay
Hotels
☆☆☆ *Carrubbella Park*, 233 via Umberto I, ☎ 091/6402188, 🖷 091/6402189. Comfortable hotel with restaurant.
S. MARTINO DELLE SCALE
☆☆ In the hill resort of *Ai Pini*, Villaggio Montano, ☎ 091/418198. Small hotel located in pinewoods.
Farm accommodation
☆☆☆ *Casa Mia*, contrade Malvello e Patria, Monreale, ☎ 091/8463512

091/8462922, ▤ 091/8463197, ✉ www.principedicorleone.it. Large farm in the hills a long way (35km) from Monreale but with easy access to the town, producing excellent wine, wheat, olives; abundant spring of mineral water, nice climate; pool, tennis, bowls, minigolf, seven-a-side football, children's playground, excellent restaurant.

Eating out
Restaurants
€€€ *La Botte*, 416 contrada Lentizzi, ☎ 091/414051. Out of town, on the road to S. Martino, this well-known tavern is unfortunately closed from mid-June to mid-September; it is very picturesque and serves excellent local fare, accompanied by a good wine list; cheerful open fire in winter.

€€ *Taverna del Pavone*, 18 vicolo Pensato, ☎ 091/6406209. A short distance from the cathedral, tiny trattoria which serves *caciocavallo fritto* (fried cheese), *tagliolini alla messinese* (noodles with swordfish), and delicious homemade almond parfait with hot chocolate

sauce. Closed Mon.

€ *Mizzica*, 6 via Cappuccini. Down the little street to the left of the cathedral, a small and simple restaurant with an inexpensive tourist menu and nice pizza in the evenings.

Entertainment
Puppet theatres
Munna, 15 cortile Manin, ☎ 091/6404542. The traditional shows are on Sunday evenings (summer only). *Sanicola*, 33 via D'Acquisto, ☎ 091/6409441.

Handicrafts

As might be expected, there is an excellent school for **mosaics** in the town where young people learn the art. Examples can be purchased in piazza Guglielmo II. **Pottery** is also attractive; here they specialize in applying glazed fruits and flowers on to earthenware vases. Elisa Messina has a boutique here, she is also well known locally as a painter.

The Cathedral

Monreale grew up around William II's great church. Begun c 1174, and already near to completion by 1182, it was one of the architectural wonders of the Middle Ages. On piazza Vittorio Emanuele is the north side of the Cathedral, dedicated to the Madonna and called S. Maria la Nuova, alluding to a new archbishopric created in her honour (open 08.00–12.00, 15.30–18.00). It was the last and most beautiful of the Norman churches built in Sicily, as much for political as for religious motives.

> The king needed to create a new archbishopric and ensure the sympathy of its new encumbent archbishop (the crafty English archbishop of Palermo, Walter of the Mill, was clearly too much hand-in-glove with the Pope and with the barons for William's liking). By handing over the cathedral to the Cluniac Benedictines, the king made a clever move. The abbot was automatically an archbishop in rank and therefore his appointment needed no further approval, either from the Pope or from the clerics in Sicily.

The **façade**, facing the adjoining piazza Guglielmo, flanked by two square towers (one incomplete) and approached by an 18C porch, has a fine portal with a beautiful bronze **door** signed by Bonanno da Pisa (1186). The splendid apse, decorated with interlacing arches of limestone and lava, can be seen from via del Arcivescovado (see below). The entrance is beneath the portico along the north side built in 1547–69 by Gian Domenico and Fazio Gagini, with elegant benches.

Here the portal has a mosaic frieze and a fine bronze door by Barisano da Trani (1179).

Interior

The interior (102m by 40m), remarkably simple in design but glittering with golden and coloured mosaics, covering a surface of over 6400sq m, gives an immediate impression of majesty and splendour. Its design is similar in concept to that of the Cappella Palatina, only carried out on a much greater scale. Beyond the rectangular crossing, surmounted by a high lantern, with shallow transepts, is a deep presbytery with three apses, recalling the plan of Cluniac abbey churches. The stilted arches in the nave are carried on 18 slender columns with composite capitals, of Roman origin, all of granite except the first on the south side, which is of cipollino marble, to represent the archbishop. The ceiling of the nave was restored after a fire in 1811, and then restored again in the 1980s when the 19C timber proved to be full of termites; that of the choir bears the stamp of Saracenic art.

The magnificent series of **mosaics** tell in pictures the Old and New Testaments (coin-operated lights are essential to see the exquisite details). It is not known whether only Greek, or local craftsmen trained by Byzantine artists were involved in this remarkable project, and the exact date of its completion, thought to be around 1182, is uncertain. The large scenes chosen to illustrate the theme of *Christ's Ascension* and the *Assumption of the Virgin* fit an overall scheme designed to celebrate the Norman monarchy and to emphasize its affinity with Jerusalem. Under the rich decoration of the upper walls runs an elegant marble and mosaic dado in Arab style.

Above the arcade in the **nave** the Genesis cycle in a double tier begins, starting on the upper tier at the eastern end of the south side with the *Creation* and continuing round the western wall and along the northern side to end (on the lower tier) with the *Jacob's Dream* and *Jacob wrestling with the Angel*. In the **crossing** and **transepts** the story of Christ is illustrated from the *Nativity* to the *Passion*. The piers in the transept are covered on all sides with tiers of saints.

In the **aisles** scenes show the *Ministry of Christ*. On either side of the **presbytery** are scenes from the lives of *Sts Peter and Paul*, whose figures are represented in the side apses. In the main apse is the mighty half-length figure of *Christ Pantocrator*, looking rather like an oriental pasha (which is undoubtedly what the craftsmen had in mind) with a solemn and rather severe expression on his face. Below is the enthroned *Madonna with Angels and Apostles*, and lower still, on either side of the east window, figures of saints including *Thomas Becket*, made within ten years of his martyrdom; Henry II of England was William II's father-in-law. Above the original royal throne (left; restored) *William II receives the crown at the hands of Christ*; above the episcopal throne (right; reconstructed) *William offers the cathedral to the Virgin*. The floor of marble mosaic dates in its present form from 1559, but that of the transepts is the original 12C one.

Chapels The transept south of the choir contains the porphyry sarcophagus of William I (**1**; d. 1166) and that of William II (**2**; d. 1190) in white marble (1575). Here is the Cappella di S. Benedetto (1569), with a relief of the saint by Marabitti (1760). To the north of the choir are the tombs (**3**) of Margaret, Roger and Henry, the wife and sons of William I, and an inscription (**4**) recording the resting-

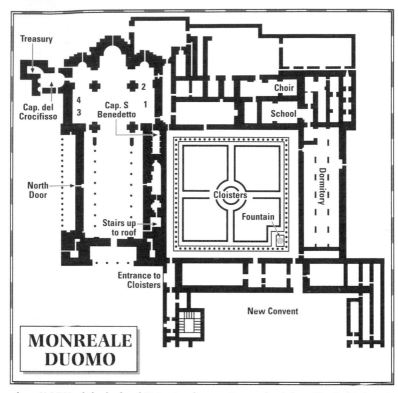

Treasury

Cap. del Crocifisso

Cap. S Benedetto

4
3
2
1

Choir

School

North Door

Cloisters

Dormitory

Fountain

Stairs up to roof

Entrance to Cloisters

New Convent

MONREALE DUOMO

place (1270) of the body of St Louis when on its way back from Tunis; his heart remains buried here.

The **treasury** (admission fee), which contains precious reliquaries, is entered through the splendid 17C Baroque **Cappella del Crocifisso**, by whose entrance is

Cloisters of Monreale Cathedral

a marble tabernacle by the school of the Gagini. In the southwestern corner of the nave is the entrance (admission fee) to the **roof** which is well worth visiting. Stairs (180 steps) and walkways lead across the roof above the cloisters and round the apses of the cathedral. The view of the Conca d'Oro and the coast is now marred by modern apartment buildings; it is nevertheless very colourful, like an enormous Turkish carpet.

On the south side of the church are the lovely **cloisters** (open 09.00–19.00, Sun & PH 09.00–13.00; ☎ 091/6404403); a masterpiece of 12C art, with Arab-Norman arches borne by 228 twin columns, with carved Romanic capitals, of which very few are alike. Many of the columns are also decorated with mosaics or reliefs. Art experts have recognized the hand of five master craftsmen, each of whom made some of the capitals, assisted by several apprentices, but only one capital is signed. A prolific confusion prevails of birds, animals, monsters, plants and people, representing religious scenes, mythology, Christian symbolism, and even the sacrifice of a bull to Mithras. The monks grew fruit trees in the enclosure (or *hortus conclusus*): trees symbolizing Paradise—palms, olives, figs and pomegranates. In the southwest corner, a stylized palm tree in a little enclosure of its own forms a charming fountain, used by the monks to wash their hands before entering the refectory; the symbolism of the various elements here alludes to the rite of baptism.

The mysteries of Monreale

Once the initial shock of the sumptuous beauty of the cathedral has passed, inevitably questions arise on just how such a construction could have been possible in the 12C. Where did the money come from, for one thing? William II justified the expenditure by telling of a dream he had had while sleeping under a carob tree during a hunting expedition. The Madonna told him to dig under the tree and use the treasure he would find to build her a great church. It must have been an enormous treasure chest—it is estimated that the mosaics were made with 2200kg of pure gold. In order to finish quickly, the king must have called hundreds of the finest craftsmen from Byzantium, a very expensive operation. Where did the granite columns in the church come from? Obviously from a pagan temple or temples, but the stone is northern European in origin. Some of these monolithic columns have been sawn in two, perhaps to get a complete set from a larger number of damaged columns. And what about the slender little marble columns in the cloisters? Some scholars believe the Benedictine monks brought them from the sunken Roman city of Baia, near Naples, where they would have formed the portico of a villa, because a few of them, especially on the east side, show traces of having spent many years under the sea—the marble has been bored in places by a mussel, *Lithophaga mytiloides*. Baia, being subject to a volcanic phenomenon which causes the area to rise and sink alternately, may have been easily accessible at that time. And lastly, it is instantly noticeable that the columns with their capitals do not fit the arches they support; a last-minute adaptation made by the architects, to allow for their use?

A pleasant public garden, called **Belvedere**, with lovely trees and views, is entered on the right of the façade of the new convent (1747), now a school. In **piazza Vittorio Emanuele** is a fountain with a triton by Mario Rutelli. The restored 18C town hall occupies part of the Norman royal palace (remnants of which can be seen from behind). In the council chamber is a *Madonna with two saints* (terracotta), attributed to Antonello Gagini (1528), and an *Adoration of the Shepherds*, by Mathias Stomer (17C). Behind is via Arcivescovado, from which the magnificent exterior of the east end of the cathedral can be seen. The choir school here incorporates some arches and windows of the Norman palace which originally had an entrance to the cathedral.

The little town also possesses some fine Baroque churches. The **Chiesa del Monte** in via Umberto I contains stuccoes by Serpotta and his school, and the *Madonna of the Constellation*, by Orazio Ferraro (1612). Higher up, on the left, is the **Collegiata**, with large 18C paintings in the nave by Marco Benefial, and an exquisite wood and tortoiseshell *Crucifixion* by Omodei (16C; on the high altar). On the external wall of the apse is an outstanding panel of majolica tiles, showing the Crucifixion with the town of Monreale in the background; it is probably the work of Giuseppe Mariani (early 18C). In piazza Vaglica, is the 18C **Collegio di Maria** close to the church of the **Santissima Trinità**, with a very elegant interior, and, in via Venero, the church of **S. Castrense**, the patron saint of Monreale, a pretty 18C building with stuccoes by the school of Serpotta and a high altarpiece by Antonio Novelli (1602). High above Monreale is the 19C church of Madonna delle Croci, with a fine view.

San Martino delle Scale

The road between Monreale and S. Martino delle Scale ascends to Portella S. Martino. Here a path climbs up through a pinewood to (c 20 minutes) the **Castellaccio** (766m; temporarily closed), the southwestern summit of Monte Cuccio and a splendid viewpoint. The castle was a fortified monastery built by William II as a hospice for the convent of Monreale. It then passed to the Benedictines and was badly damaged by Manfredi Chiaramonte in the 14C. Towards the end of the 18C it was abandoned and fell into ruin until in 1899 it was purchased by the *Club Alpino Siciliano*, ☎ 091/581323.

S. Martino della Scale (500m) is a hill resort in pinewoods. The huge Benedictine **Abbey of S. Martino**, possibly founded by St Gregory the Great, was rebuilt after 1347 by Archbishop Emanuele Spinola and the Benedictine Angelo Sisinio, and enlarged c 1762 by Venanzio Marvuglia. It is now occupied by a college. The church (closed 12.30–16.30), dating from 1561–95 (with part of the 14C masonry in the north wall) contains carved **choir stalls** by Benvenuto Tortelli da Brescia (1591–97); *St Benedict* and the *Madonna with Saints Benedict and Scholastica* are both by Pietro Novelli; six altarpieces by Lo Zoppo di Gangi; and *St Martin*, by Filippo Paladino. The fine organ in the apse was made in 1650 by Raffaele La Valle. The sacristy contains vestments of 16C–18C, paintings attributed to Annibale Carracci and Guercino and a reliquary by Pietro di Spagna.

The carved doorway into the convent dates from the 15C, and nearby is a stoup dated 1396. In the convent, at the foot of the splendid grand staircase (1786) by Marvuglia, is a group of *St Martin and the beggar*, by Marabitti. A statue of *St Benedict*, by Benedetto Pompillion, stands in the graceful monastic cloister (1612; altered and enlarged in the 18C). The Oreto fountain is by Marabitti (1784). The refectory ceiling (*Daniel in the Lions' Den*) is frescoed by Pietro Novelli.

Baida is an isolated hamlet backed by a crescent of hills that rise in Monte Cuccio to 1050m. The Convento di Baida (for admission ring at no. 41 via del Convento) was built in 1377–88 by Benedictine monks, expelled by Manfredi Chiaramonte from the Castellaccio (see above), on the site of a 10C Saracen village (*baidha*, white). The foundation was already in decline in 1499 when Giovanni Paternò took it over as a summer residence for the archbishops of Palermo; in 1595 it passed to the Observantine order. The church, its original Gothic façade pierced by a portal of 1507, has a fine 14C apse, and a statue, by Antonello Gagini, of *St John the Baptist*; traces of the 14C cloister remain.

BAGHERIA AND SOLUNTO

Bagheria, although surrounded by a mass of intrusive suburbs, is still worth visiting for its villas, in particular the Villa Palagonia. Solunto, close by, is a beautiful archaeological site in a very fine position on a mountainside overlooking the coast.

Practical information

Getting there from Palermo
By bus

Bagheria is about 14km from Palermo, and Solunto 18km from Palermo. Bus services run by *AST* , ☎ 091/6800031, from Palermo (piazza Lolli and the railway station) to Bagheria.

By train

A few trains a day on the Messina line stop at Bagheria (14km in c 10 mins) and 'S. Flavia–Solunto' (16km in c 15 mins). The Palermo–Bagheria line was the first to be opened on the island in 1863.

By car

Bagheria and Solunto are best approached from Palermo by the coastal road via Ficarazzi (and not by the motorway).

Information offices
APT Palermo, ☎ 091/583847.
Centro Informazioni Turistiche, corso Umberto, ☎ 091/909020; can also arrange guided tours. Bagheria on line: ✉ www.comune. bagheria.pa.it.

Where to stay
Hotel

☆☆ *Da Franco il Conte*, via Vallone de Spuches, Aspra, ☎ 091/966815, ▤ 091/966816, ✉ www.dafrancoilconte.it. Friendly little hotel with an excellent restaurant, not far from the sea at Aspra, a marine suburb of Bagheria. Count Franco is quite a personality.

Comfortable hotels on the coast can be found at **Trabia** and **Santa Flavia**.

Eating out
Restaurants, cafés and pastry shops

BAGHERIA €€ *Aries*, 69 via Dante, ☎ 091/965688. Specializes in seafood. Closed Sun evening, all day Mon.
€ *Don Ciccio*, 87 viale del Cavaliere, ☎ 091/932442. A popular, reasonably priced restaurant with appetizing local dishes. Closed Wed and Sun.
€ *Pizzeria La Caravella*, palazzo Puleo, via d'Amico (near sports ground). Serves appetizing simple meals and pizza.
€ *Pizzeria Mata Hari*, via Dante (corner via Città di Palermo), also doubles as a pub. *Bar Ester*, 83 via Palagonia. Famous for ice cream and *cannoli di ricotta*.
PORTICELLO (SANTA FLAVIA) Santa Flavia, between Palermo and Bagheria, is just the place to stop for lunch.
€€€ *La Muciara*, 103 via Roma, ☎ 091/957868. Owner Nello 'El Greco' is Roman, his basic ingredients are the fish, pasta and vegetables of Sicily. Superb simple dishes, overlooking the port. Closed Mon.
S. ELIA (SANTA FLAVIA) €€ *Le Nasse*, 30 via dei Cantieri, ☎ 349/1714237. Like Porticello, S. Elia is a charming little fishing port. Simple restaurant, excellent seafood dishes, Exclusively Sicilian wines. Closed Wed.
Picnics

Solunto is a lovely place to picnic.

Bagheria

Bagheria (population 47,100), birthplace of the contemporary and controversial artist Renato Guttuso and the Oscar-winning film director Giuseppe Tornatore, is a country town famous for its 18C Baroque villas set amidst lemon groves and vineyards. But it has been suffocated by frenzied, uncontrolled building in the last 40 years, which has devoured the parks and gardens of the villas, even encroaching on the ancient constructions themselves. Today it is hard to believe the old Sicilian proverb: '*Baaria, sciuri ppi la via*', ('in Bagheria the flowers grow on the streets'), a reference to the great fertility of the area. The villas themselves are disgracefully neglected, and only two of them, Villa Cattolica and Villa Palagonia, are now usually open to visitors. The gardens of Villa San Cataldo are open at weekends.

The conspicuous **Villa Cattolica**, a fine building of c 1737, houses the Bagheria Civic Library and Art Gallery, which has a large collection of paintings by Renato Guttuso (1912–87) and other contemporary artists. (☎ 091/905438; open daily 09.30–19.00, closed Mon.) Guttuso's bright blue marble tomb by Giacomo Manzù is in the garden.

Near the villa, beyond a railway crossing (right), is the start of the long corso Butera which passes the fine **Palazzo Inguaggiato**, attributed to Andrea Giganti (1770) before reaching the piazza in front of the 18C cathedral. **Villa Butera** is visible at the far end of the corso, built in 1658 by Giuseppe Branciforte (façade of 1769).

In front of the cathedral is the beginning of corso Umberto which ends at piazza Garibaldi beside (left) a garden gate (guarded by two monsters) of **Villa Palagonia** (☎ 091/932088, open daily 09.00–12.30, 15.30–17.30). The garden, and vestibule and hall on the first floor are open. The fine building was erected in 1705 by Francesco Gravina, Prince of Palagonia (and his architect Tommaso Maria Napoli). His eccentric grandson Ferdinando Gravina Alliata lived in rooms decorated in a bizarre fashion, including the hall with its ceiling covered with mirrors set at strange angles (now very damaged) and its walls encased in marble with busts of ladies and gentlemen. The oval vestibule has frescoes of *Four Labours of Hercules*.

The villa is famous for the grotesque statues of monsters, dwarfs, and strange animals set up on the garden wall by Ferdinando (their effect now sadly diminished by the houses which have been built just outside the wall). At the time these carved figures were not to everyone's taste; when Goethe visited the villa in 1787 he was appalled by them.

Opposite is the entrance gate to the avenue which leads up to **Villa Valguarnera** (not visible from here and closed to the public). Built by Tommaso Napoli c 1713–37, this is the most handsome of the Bagheria villas. The statues above the parapet are by Marabitti.

Off via IV Novembre is Villa Trabia (mid-18C), perhaps by Nicolò Palma, with a façade of 1890. It is surrounded by a neglected park. Near the railway station is the early 18C **Villa Cutò**, which is sometimes shown by appointment on guided tours (☎ 091/905438), and a little further on is **Villa San Cataldo**, which received a neo-gothic facelift in the early 19C. The gardens can be visited (Sat and Sun 09.30–18.00), and the little church in the grounds is open for Mass on Sundays.

Solunto

The solitary ruins of Solunto are in a beautiful position on the slopes of Monte Catalfano (374m) close to the sea. The archaeological site and museum are open daily (09.00–16.30, Sun & PH 09.00–13.30, ☎ 091/904557).

History

The ancient town of *Solus* is thought to have replaced a Phoenician settlement in the vicinity of the same name (perhaps at Cozzo Cannita where traces of walls have been found) which was destroyed in 397 BC by Dionysius of Syracuse. Solus was built in the 4C BC on an interesting grid plan similar to the urban layout of some Hellenistic sites in Asia Minor. It fell to the Romans, who named it *Soluntum*, in 254 BC and had been abandoned by the beginning of the 3C AD. It was discovered in 1825 and still much of the site remains to be excavated.

The entrance is through a small museum with good plans of the site, and Hellenistic capitals, two female statues, architectural fragments, etc. A Roman road, beside terraces of prickly pear, mounts the side of the hill past via delle Terme (with the remains of **baths**) and curves round to the right into the wide **via dell'Agora**. This, the main street, traverses the town to the cliff edge overlooking the sea; it is crossed at regular intervals by side streets with considerable remains of houses on the hillside above. Beyond via Ciauri and via Perez is the stepped via Cavallaro on which are some of the columns and architrave of the so-called **gymnasium** (restored in 1866), really a sumptuous house. This stretch of via dell'Agora is beautifully paved in brick.

The next stepped road, via Ippodamo da Mileto, links the main hill to another small hill towards the sea. Here on the slope of the hill above is the so-called **Casa di Leda** on three levels: above four small shops on via dell'Agora, is an oblong cistern and courtyard with a fountain off which are rooms with mosaic and tiled floors and traces of red wall-paintings. Further up via Ippodamo da Mileto there are more interesting houses.

Further on in via dell'Agora, beyond a large **sanctuary** (on the corner of via Salinas), the road widens out into the large **agora** with brick paving in front of nine rectangular exedrae along the back wall thought to have been used as shelters for the public. On the hillside above are traces of the **theatre** and a small **bouleuterion** probably used for council meetings. The hillside higher up may have been the site of the **acropolis**. Via dell'Agora next passes a huge public **cistern**, still filled with water, part of a complex system of storage tanks (many vestiges of which are still visible), made necessary by the lack of spring water in the area.

On the edge of the cliff, looking towards Cape Zafferano, in via Bagnera is a small **Roman villa** with mosaics and wall-paintings.

The view along the coast towards Cefalù, of the Aeolian Islands and Etna, is magnificent. In the foreground are the medieval castle of Solanto and the bay of Fondachello with the villas of Casteldaccia amid luxuriant vegetation on the slopes behind.

The return to the entrance can be made by taking via Ippodamo da Mileto (see above) which passes a second museum building under construction.

At the foot of Mount Catalfano a few lemon groves survive but the area is becoming very popular for up-market holiday homes, as can be seen around the fishing village of **Porticello** (where a popular fish market opens in the very early morning). **Capo Zafferano** is an isolated crag of dolomitic limestone, of great geological interest. On the cape dwarf palms and (in spring) wild orchids grow.

TERMINI IMERESE, CACCAMO, HIMERA AND ALIA

Termini Imerese's proximity to the motorway makes it a good centre for visiting places in the eastern part of the province of Palermo, including the Madonie Mountains (see p 139). It is also a town of some interest. **Caccamo** is a little hill town dominated by a huge castle with a number of interesting churches. Remains of the ancient city of **Himera** include an important Doric temple, traces of a sacred area and houses on the top of a hill and a very interesting antiquarium. Near **Alia** is a group of enormous caves entirely carved out by hand. A fascinating museum dedicated to the victims of a cholera epidemic of 1837 can be found in the nearby town.

Practical information

 ### Getting there from Palermo

Termini Imerese is 37km from Palermo; Caccamo is 10km south of Termini Imerese; and Himera is 49km from Palermo.

By train

Train services on the main Palermo–Messina line run about every hour from Palermo to Termini Imerese (in c 20 mins).

By bus

Buses run by *SAIS* from Palermo (via Balsamo) to Termini Imerese. *Randazzo* bus services from Palermo and Termini Imerese to Caccamo.

By car

Termini Imerese and Himera are easily reached by the Palermo–Messina motorway (A19), with exits at Termini Imerese and Buonfornello (for Himera). It is best to reach Alia by car: proceed from Caccamo along SS 285 to Roccapalumba, then turn left onto SS 121 to Alia, which lies 30km from Caccamo. Alternatively, take SS 121 directly from Palermo (70km).

 ### Information offices

APT Palermo, ☎ 091/583847.
Tourist Information Bureau, palazzo Monte di Pietà, piazza Duomo, Caccamo, ☎ 091/8103248, Mon–Sat 09.00–13.00.
Sicilia & dintorni, 8 via del Castello, Caccamo, ☎ 091/225035 091/545423, ✉ www.siciliaedintorni.it
Associazione Culturale Jridos, Caccamo, ☎ 091/8148171.
Tourist Information Bureau, Termini Imerese, ☎ 091/8128253, ✉ www.comune.termini-imerese.pa.it.
Tourist Information Bureau, via Vittorio Emanuele, Alia, ☎ 091/8210913, ✉ www.comune.alia.pa.it.

 ### Where to stay
Hotels

CACCAMO ☆☆ *La Spiga d'Oro*, 74 via Margherita, ☎ 091/8148968, ▤ 091/814968, small, simple hotel, in town centre, with restaurant.
TERMINI IMERESE ☆☆☆☆ *Grand Hotel delle Terme*, 2 piazza Terme, ☎ 091/8113557, ▤ 091/8113107.

Comfortable; in a good position for touring the area; spa, gym and excellent restaurant, in a lovely Art Nouveau building.

☆☆☆ *Il Gabbiano*, 221 via Libertà, ☎ 091/8113262, 📠 091/8114225, 📧 www.ilgabbianohotel.neomedia.it. Well-run; comfortable position; no restaurant.

H I M E R A ☆☆☆☆ *Polis Himera*, on main road (SS 113) at Buonfornello, ☎ 091/8140566, 📠 091/8140567, 📧 www.wel/h.polis.it. Modern; pleasant; gym.

Paese Albergo

A L I A many private homes in the old centre offer tourist accommodation. Information: *Associazione Ro.My travel*, 8 via Trieste, ☎ 091/8219808, 📠 091/8219921.

Farm accommodation

A L I A *Villa Dafne*, contrada Cozzo di Cicero, ☎ 091/8219174 or 091/489818, 📠 091/8219928. Ancient wheat farm a short distance from the town; sheep and olives; guests can help on the farm. Tennis court, pool, bowls, seven-a-side football and horseriding. Excursions are organized on horseback or mountain bike.

Cookery lessons on request. Excellent traditional local dishes and good local wines.

Campsites

☆ *Torre Battilamano*, località Buonfornello, ☎ & 📠 091/8140044.

 ### Eating out
Restaurants, cafés and pastry shops

C A C C A M O €€ *La Castellana*, 4, piazza del Monumento, ☎ 091/8148667. Restaurant in the old grain stores of the castle. Inexpensive set menu and good pizza in the evening. Superb pasta: try *farfalle al limone* (with lemon) or *penne al finocchietto* (with wild fennel); Sicilian wines.

€€ *La Spiga d'Oro*, 74 via Margherita, ☎ 091/8148968. Pizzas in the evenings.

T E R M I N I   I M E R E S E € *Bar del Duomo*, via Belvedere (near the cathedral), Cakes and pastries. Also an inexpensive restaurant on the first floor. *Crystal*, 11 via Torino. Snack bar; delicious ice creams.

€ *Da Giovanni*, 4 via Nogara (in the lower city, near piazza Terme). Friendly trattoria.

Termini Imerese

Termini Imerese (population 26,000) is built on the slopes of a hill (113m) and divided into an upper and lower town. Much new building has taken place here in the last few decades, to accommodate people working in the nearby industrial area. There is now a commercial port.

History

Thermae Himerenses received its name from the two neighbouring Greek cities of *Thermae* and *Himera*. It was captured by the Carthaginians after their sack of Himera in 408 BC and the inhabitants of the destroyed city of Himera were resettled in Thermae. In 307 BC it was ruled by Agathocles (361–289 BC), a native of the town and the most ferocious of the Greek tyrants of Syracuse. Its most prosperous period followed the Roman conquest. The thermal mineral waters were praised by Pindar.

Outside the town are conspicuous remains of a Roman aqueduct built in the 2C AD to bring water to the town from a spring 7 kilometres away. In the upper town there is a spacious main square, with an old-fashioned men's club. From the belvedere behind the cathedral there is a fine view of the coast and the modern port.

The 17C **cathedral** has a façade dating from 1912. The four statues (see below) have been replaced here by copies. Beneath the tower (right) is a fragment of a Roman cornice. The interior has huge columns and capitals. The third north chapel has a pretty tiled floor. Here are sculptures by Giuliano Mancino and Bartolomeo Berrettaro (followers of the Gaginis), including a statue of the *Madonna*, bas-reliefs, and four statues of saints (1504–06) from the façade. The chapel also has two 17C funerary monuments. In the sanctuary is a *Crucifix*, painted on both sides, by Pietro Ruzzolone (1484). In the chapel to the left of the choir are reliefs by Marabitti and Federico Siragusa. In the fourth south chapel is a marble oval relief of the *Our Lady of the Bridge*, by Ignazio Marabitti.

The 17C **Palazzo Comunale** (Town Hall) is approached by an outside stair-case. Just out of the piazza is the **Civic Museum** (☎ 091/8128279, open daily 09.00–13.00, 15.30–17.30, Mon closed), founded in 1873. On the ground floor are prehistoric finds from Termini; red- and black-figure vases from Himera; coins; and Roman capitals, a bust of a lady (c 115 AD), statues, inscriptions, architectural fragments, and glass. The last room contains Arab-Norman material and a Renaissance doorway. On the first floor is a chapel frescoed in the 15C by Nicolò da Pettineo, paintings (16C–19C) and a natural history collection. It is thought that the prestigious *mesomphalos phiale*, the solid gold libation bowl found in 1980 at Caltavuturo, will be housed here.

In via Mazzini which leads out of piazza Duomo are the **Chiesa Santa Croce al Monte** containing 16C and 17C Sicilian paintings, and **S. Maria della Misericordia** (1600), with a beautiful triptych (*Madonna with Saints John and Michael*), ascribed to Gaspare da Pesaro (1453).

Viale Iannelli leads west from piazza Duomo to the church of **S. Caterina**, whose frescoes of the life of the saint are probably by Nicolò and Giacomo Graffeo (15C–16C; much damaged) of Termini.

In the public **gardens** laid out in 1845 are remains of a Roman public building, known as the **Curia**, dating from the 2C AD.

From behind the cathedral there is a good view down to the pretty tiled dome of the church of the **Annunziata**. A road winds down from here to the lower town and, on the site of the Roman baths, the Grand Hotel delle Terme, begun in 1890 on a design by Giuseppe Damiani Almeyda). The **thermal waters** (43°C) still in use here provide natural steam baths and bathing pools.

Caccamo

Caccamo (population 8600) is a little town of ancient origins in a fine position above olive groves in the hills (521m). There is a tradition that the Carthaginians took refuge here after their defeat at Himera in 480 BC. The castle was one of the major Norman strongholds on the island, and, never captured, it remained the residence of the dukes of Caccamo up until the twentieth century.

The impressive 12C **castle** stands at the entrance to the town (open daily 09.15–12.15, 15.15–17.30), the largest castle in Sicily and one of the largest in Italy. Here in 1160 Matthew Bonellus organised a revolt of the barons against William the Bad; after the failure of the rebellion, Bonellus was captured and taken to Palermo, where he was hamstrung and blinded, and left to languish in a dungeon. The castle was enlarged by the Chiaramonte in the 14C, and was sold to the region of Sicily in 1963 by the De Spuches family. It is now used for conferences and exhibitions. The main tower of the castle was 70 metres high but toppled in an earthquake in the 19C. The empty interior has been heavily restored.

From the main road (Corso Umberto I) steps and narrow streets lead down to **piazza del Duomo**, an attractive and unusual square with a fine view over the valley. Above the raised terrace, with a balustrade decorated with four statues of the town's patron saints, is the Monte di Pietà (the palace is now used for exhibitions) flanked by the twin façades of two churches. The one on the right is dedicated to the Souls in Purgatory. It contains charming gilded stuccoes at the east end and an 18C organ. The custodian shows the crypt below, also beautifully decorated with stuccoes, with the crumbling, but fully-clothed, skeletons of past inhabitants.

The Duomo

The Duomo (ring if locked) has a fine 17C façade. Founded in 1090, it was altered in 1477 and 1614. There is a lovely relief (1660) of *Saint George* above the door by Gaspare Guercio. The tall campanile was built above a 14C tower of the castle.

In the **interior** St George features in a number of fine works of art. In the south aisle is a 15C triptych with *St George* and a charming processional statue of the saint with his dragon. In the south transept the architrave of the door into the sacristy has delicate carvings of the *Madonna and Child with angels and Sts Peter and Paul* attributed to Francesco Laurana. The roundels of the *Annunciation* and relief of the *Madonna and Child* are by the Gagini school. The rich treasury and sacristy are shown on request. They contain 16C–19C church silver, a precious collection of vestments and Flemish paintings. In the chapel to the right of the sanctuary is a statue of the *Madonna and Child* by the Gagini school. By the high altar is an unusual **font** (1466) with four large heads, perhaps representing *Matthew, Mark, Luke* and *John*. In the sanctuary are two polychrome wooden statues: *St John the Baptist* by Antonino Siragusa (1532) and *St Lucy* (16C). An exquisite silver processional statuette of St Rosalie is also kept here. On the high altar are three very fine alabaster carvings (16C–18C).

In the north transept are two painted terracotta sculptures: a *Madonna and Child* by the Gagini school and a *Pietà* group by the early 15C Sienese school. The altar here has 16C and 17C reliquary busts and an early 18C neo-classical carved and gilded altar frontal. In the north aisle an altar decorated with *marmi mischi* has a 14C painted *Crucifix*, and the first altarpiece of the *Miracle of St Isidore* is a fine painting by Mattia Stomer (in need of restoration). A sedan chair and armour belonging to the De Spuches family are also kept in this aisle.

There are good views of the castle from the old streets behind the Duomo. In the other direction via Cartagine leads to the deconsecrated church of San Francesco and, beyond, the church of **SS. Annunziata**, its Baroque façade flanked by two earlier towers. Inside is a carved 16C organ case, and the east end has stuccoes by the Serpotta school. The church of **S. Benedetto alla Badia** (1615) was attached to a former Benedictine convent. The charming interior has a splendid majolica tiled floor in the nave and choir, once attributed to Nicolò Sarzana, but now thought to date from before 1701. There are also fine wrought-iron grilles. The two graceful female figures in stucco on either side of the sanctuary are by the school of Serpotta.

S. Maria degli Angeli (1497; ring at the convent) has a fine relief of the

Madonna and Child over the door. Inside its original wooden ceiling is preserved (with 15C paintings of Dominican saints) and a statue of the *Madonna* by Antonello Gagini.

30km southeast of Caccamo is **Alia** at 726m, a remote town founded by the Arabs, surrounded by spectacular hills and wheatfields. Later, under Spanish rule, it became the seat of the Santa Croce barons, who built their palace next to the **church** of Madonna delle Grazie (1639). Not far from the town (4km), in a dramatic isolated sandstone outcrop, is a group of caves called **Grotte di Gurfa**, entirely carved out by hand during ancient times, and successively used as dwellings. The caves include a mysterious tholos, which induces scholars to date the complex to the beginning of the Bronze Age, about 5,000 years ago. The well-kept little town has two museums, the **Ethno-anthropological Museum** housed in the biblioteca comunale (Public Library), open 09.00–13.00 Mon–Sat, with a collection of farm implements, and the **Anthropological Museum** in the Botanical Gardens (open daily 10.00–12.15, 15.30–17.30) dedicated to the discovery in 1996 of a mass grave containing 400 people killed by cholera during the 1837 epidemic. Recent research has revealed much information about the inhabitants of this area during a period of intense poverty. The helpful staff at the tourist office can organize free excursions to see the local sights, including a fully functioning water-mill, still used for grinding wheat.

Himera

Beyond a large industrial area, including a power station and an important Fiat factory, which occupies the low coastal plain east of Termini Imerese is the site of Himera (open 09.00–18.30, PH 09.00–13.00). It is near the 'Buonfornello' exit of the motorway and on the bank of the Fiume Grande (or Imera Settentrionale), but is very poorly signposted. On the right of the road, just across the busy railway line are remains of a temple. On the hillside above the road is a conspicuous modern museum, and on the top, the site of the ancient city.

History

This was a colony of *Zancle* (now Messina), founded in 648 BC near the mouth of the River Himera and at the head of the valley which provided access to the interior of the island. It was the westernmost Greek colony on the north coast of Sicily, and scene of the famous defeat of the Carthaginians by Theron of Agrigento and Gelon of Syracuse in 480 BC. This was important as it was the Carthaginians' first decisive defeat in the Mediterranean. Their leader Hamilcar committed suicide by throwing himself on the funeral pyre of his dead soldiers, having ordered that his ships be burned. The survivors were taken prisoner, some took refuge where Caccamo now stands. However, the Carthaginians returned under Hannibal, nephew of Hamilcar, in 409 BC and got their revenge; they crucified 300 of the strongest men to vindicate Hamilcar, and then utterly destroyed the city. The inhabitants who survived the battle were moved to *Thermae* (now Termini Imerese). Himera was the home city of the lyric poet Stesichorus (born c 630 BC).

On the right of the main road (just across the railway line; beware of trains) are the ruins of a **Doric temple**, peripteral and hexastyle, probably built around 470 BC. This is the only building which remains here of a sanctuary probably dedicated to Athena, on the banks of the River Himera. It is still known as the 'Temple of Victory', although some scholars no longer believe it was built to celebrate the victory over the Carthaginians. In any case it seems to have been burnt and destroyed by the Carthaginians in 409 BC.

Only the basement and lower part of the columns and part of the cella walls survive. It measured 22 x 55m and had 14 columns at the sides and six in front. The cella had a pronaos and opisthodomos in antis. In the Middle Ages the site was built over and it was only rediscovered in 1823 and excavated by Pirro Marconi in 1929–30 when the splendid lion head water-spouts from the cornice were taken to the Archaeological Museum in Palermo.

Off the main road, just beyond, a byroad (left; signposted) leads up to the museum and the areas of the city excavated since 1963. The **museum** (☎ 091/8140128, 09.00–18.30, Sun & PH 09.00–13.00) is a striking modern building, and there are good plans and descriptions of the site. The first section displays finds from the temples in the sacred area on the hill top, including a votive deposit with fragments of metopes. The second section has material from the city and necropoli, including ceramics, architectural fragments and votive statues. There is also a section devoted to finds from recent excavations in the surrounding territory, including Cefalù and Caltavuturo.

Just above the museum are excavations of part of the city. Steps continue up to a plateau on the edge of the hill overlooking the plain towards the sea. Here is the Area Sacra with a temenos enclosing the bases of an altar and four temples (7C–5C BC). There are also traces of houses here. The view extends along the coast as far as Solunto. In the other direction you can see the village of Gratteri, nestling in the Madonie mountains (see p 139).

Away from the sea more excavations are under way. Three necropoli have been identified in the surrounding area and the extensive site will soon become an archaeological park.

CEFALÙ

Cefalù (population 18,000) with its stunning Norman cathedral and ruins of an ancient acropolis on the rock above the city is a very picturesque, small, feisty town with a lovely beach. The old town is still medieval in character, with many enticing shops, restaurants and cafés along its well-kept cobbled streets. An important little museum houses the collection of Baron Mandralisca.

Practical information

Getting there
By rail
Railway station, via Gramsci, 500m southwest of corso Ruggero. Trains on the Palermo–Messina line c every hour from Palermo (67km) in 50–60 mins.

By bus
SAIS buses from Palermo (3 a day, weekdays only). **Local buses** to Gibilmanna and small towns in the Madonie mountains leave from the railway station.
Parking
At the far end of the seafront. *ACI* multi

storey car park, with an hourly tariff, in via Verga; elsewhere blue line parking with an hourly ticket.

Information office
Azienda Autonoma, 77 corso Ruggero (corner of via Amendola), ☎ 0921/421050 or 0921/421458.

Cefalù on line
✉ www.cefaluonline.com.

Where to stay
Hotels

☆☆☆☆ *Alberi del Paradiso*, 18 via dei Mulini, ☎ 0921/423900, 🖷 0921/423990, ✉ paradisoclub@libero.it. Newly restructured old hotel on the hillside in a pleasant position, good restaurant, pool, shuttle service to private beach.

☆☆☆ *Astro*, 105 via Roma, ☎ 0921/421639, 🖷 0921/423103. Slightly pretentious hotel in the modern quarter, with restaurant.

☆☆☆ *Baia del Capitano*, contrada Mazzaforno. ☎ 0921/420003, 🖷 0921/420163. Nice hotel surrounded by olive trees, out of town but with access to the beach, comfortable rooms with sea view.

☆☆☆ *Le Calette*, 12 via Cavallaro, ☎ 0921/424144, 🖷 0921/423688, ✉ www.lecalette.it. Elegant hotel on a tiny bay out of town, also apartments to rent. Windsurfing, diving and horseriding available.

☆☆☆ *Tourist*, via Lungomare, ☎ & 🖷 0921/421750. Family hotel on the seafront.

☆☆☆ *Villa Belvedere*, 43 via dei Mulini, ☎ 0921/421593, 🖷 0921/422512. Just out of town; pool, bicycles for hire, good restaurant.

☆☆ *Mediterraneo*, 2 via Gramsci, ☎ & 🖷 0921/922606 or 0921/922573, ✉ www.htlmediterraneo.it. Convenient (opposite the railway station), modern, clean hotel with lovely cool quiet rooms

and attentive service.

☆☆ *Pink*, località Kaldura, ☎ 0921/422275, 🖷 0921/423122. Comfortable hotel just out of town overlooking Kaldura bay; restaurant, pool, hospitable management.

Farm accommodation

☆☆☆ *Pianetti*, contrada Pianetti, Gratteri, ☎ 0921/421890 or 339/7697089, 🖷 0921/422060 (Cefalù 14km). Farm in the Madonie Mountains which raises horses, cows and goats. Very peaceful; ideal for ramblers and naturalists. Good restaurant.

☆☆☆ *Villa Catalfamo*, Piana San Nicola, Cefalù, ☎ & 🖷 0921/911012 or 091/6112438 (Cefalù 6km). Farm on the coast, producing citrus, olive oil and carobs, offering self-catering accommodation in cottages. No restaurant but breakfast is provided. English spoken.

Bed & breakfast

Ale Robi, 17 via Porpora, ☎ 328/8412239 or 338/4921521, ✉ www.alerobi.it. In the old quarter, close to the bastions.

Masseria Abazia, ☎ 091/6167839 or 360/406016, ✉ abaziafloris@hotmail.com. Beautifully restored old farmhouse in the hills behind Cefalù amidst a large olive grove. Guests can use the kitchen, bicycles for hire, horse riding. French and English spoken.

Residence

☆☆☆ *Calanica*, contrada Vallone di Falco, ☎ 0921/420413. Self-catering accommodation in little Polynesian huts not far from the town; private beach (sand and shale). Excellent restaurant overlooking the bay; tennis, pool, seven-a-side football, diving centre. Bicycles, scooters, canoes etc. for hire.

Campsites

☆☆☆ *Costa Ponente Internazionale*, contrada Ogliastrillo, ☎ 0921/420085, ☎ 0921/424492.

☆☆ *Plaia degli Uccelli*, località Plaia degli Uccelli, ☎ & 🖷 0921/999068.

Sanfilippo, contrada Ogliastrillo, ☎ & 🖷 0921/420184.

Eating out
Restaurants

€€€ *La Brace*, 10 via XXV Novembre, ☎ 0921/423570. Elegant; delicious fish. Closed Mon.

€€€ *Ostaria del Duomo*, 5 via Seminario, ☎ 0921/421838. Carefully prepared Sicilian food, good wine list. Near cathedral. Closed Mon in winter.

€€ *Al Gabbiano*, 17 lungomare Giardina, ☎ 0921/421495. Traditionally known for its good seafood dishes, also pizza. Closed Mon in winter.

€€ *Kentia*, 15 via N. Botta, ☎ 0921/423801. Good seafood risotto and pasta.

€€ *L'Antica Corte*, 193 corso Ruggero (cortile Pepe), ☎ 0921/423228. Traditional dishes and pizza served in a tiny courtyard. Closed Thurs.

€€ *Nasca 3*, 1 via Bellini (corner of via Roma), ☎ 0921/424946. Very good antipasti and pasta in the modern quarter. Closed Mon.

€€ *Arkade Grill*, 9 via Vanni, ☎ 0921/424646. Interesting Arab-Norman cuisine.

€ *Il Covo del Pirata*, 59 via Vittorio Emanuele (next to the Lavatoio). Delicious sandwiches and salads; lunch only (becomes a hot music club evenings).

Pizzerie, snack bars, bistros

Ciao Pizza, 116 via Roma, ☎ 0921/921396. In the modern quarter. Closed Mon.

Trappitu, 96 via Bordonaro, ☎ 0921/921972. An old olive press, where imaginative fare and pizza are served on a terrace overlooking the sea.

Zazà Slow Food, 7 via Pasquale.

Gallo D'Oro, 51 via Gramsci.

L'Unico, 15/19 lungomare Giardina.

Le Chat Noir, 17 via XXV novembre.

Le Petit Tonneau, 66 via Mandralisca.

Be Bop, 4 via Botta.

L'Arca di Noé, 7–8 via Bazzana (internet point).

Cafés, pastry shops and ice cream parlours

La Martorana, 5 piazza Duomo. Local specialities; very good ice cream.

Antica Porta Terra, 6 piazza Garibaldi, exceptional ice cream or Sicilian breakfast.

La Pergola, 1 corso Ruggero; good ice cream and granita.

Irish pub

Murphy's, 5 lungomare Giardina; part of a friendly restaurant and pizzeria, the *Ragno D'Oro*; ☎ 0921/422588.

Picnics

On the Rocca above the town, Capo Marchiafava, or on the seafront near the port.

Internet points

Bacco on line, 38 corso Ruggero, ☎ 0921/421753.

Kefaonline Internet Provider, 1 piazza S. Francesco, ☎ 0921/923091.

Ziga infotel, piazza Garibaldi, ☎ 0921/423875.

L'Arca di Noé, 7–8 via Bazzana.

Italian language courses

Kulturforum, 55 corso Ruggero, ☎ & 🖷 0921/923998, 🖳 www.kulturforum.it. Lessons in Italian, French or German.

Foreign language newspapers and periodicals

Antica cartolibreria del Corso, 98 corso Ruggero, ☎ 0921/423096.

Totosystem 2000 ricevitoria, 126 via Roma, ☎ 0921/420895.

Local specialities

Anchovies in olive oil with capers or chillies, are prepared by the fishermen of Cefalù. Try **Antica Lavorazione Pesce Azzurro Cefalù**, contrada Presidiana, ☎ 0921/424333 or **Ankora Delicius**, contrada Piana Marsala, ☎ 0921/

427396. Some retired fishermen make model boats. At 34 via della Giudecca Don Giuseppe's lovely boats are just like the real ones he used to make years ago.

Paraflying and water scooter hire

Lido Poseidon, lungomare Giardina, ☎ 0921/424646.

Boat trips

Trips to the **Aeolian Islands** are run by

SMIV Sicilia Cruises every day in summer from Cefalù, ☎ 0921/420601 or 0921/421264. **Hydrofoil services** run to the Aeolian islands (June–Sept). Information from the *APT*. Giuseppe will take you **fishing** with him, ☎ 0921/420683 0921/420339 or 380/5142939; also *Pesca turismo*, ☎ 338/2309141, ✉ www. cefaluturismo.it.

History

Founded at the end of the 5C or early 4C BC, its name *Kephaloidion* comes from the head-like shape of the rock which towers above. In 307 BC it was taken by Agathocles of Syracuse. In 857 it was conquered by the Arabs. In 1131 Roger II rebuilt the town on the sea, and constructed the magnificent cathedral which became head of a powerful bishopric.

In the 1920s the necromancer Alistair Crowley lived near Cefalù, transforming a cottage into the Temple of Thelema ('Do as thou wilt, shall be thy creed'), and scandalizing the locals to the point where he was arrested, found guilty of immoral behaviour, and expelled from Italy.

Corso Ruggero leads through the town. At the beginning on the right is the sandstone façade of **Maria SS. della Catena** (1780; closed) preceded by a high portico with three statues. On the right of the façade are a few large blocks from the old walls (late 5C BC) on the site of the Porta Terra, the main entrance to the old town. The corso continues past (right) vicolo dei Saraceni (signposted for the Tempio di Diana) beyond which begins a path up to the Rocca (described below), and then runs slightly downhill. On the left is the **Osterio Magno**, once Roger's palace and now used for exhibitions, with a fine 13C triple window high up on its façade and (in via Amendola) windows decorated with black lava.

On the left are a series of nine picturesque, straight, parallel streets which lead downhill to corso Vittorio Emanuele, with a view of the sea beyond. They possibly reflect the grid plan of the ancient city. The corso continues past the tall, plain façade of the 16C church of the Annunziata. To the right opens the little piazza in front of the 15C church of the Purgatorio (formerly S. Stefano Protomartire), Inside is the tomb of Baron Mandralisca.

The Duomo

The piazza beyond on the right, planted with palm trees, leads up to the splendid Duomo (open daily 08.00–12.00, 15.30–19.00, ☎ 0921/922021; entrance from the south door, no shorts or bare shoulders). The setting is dramatic, with the formidable rocca rising immediately behind it and the small town at its feet.

Begun by Roger II in 1131, and intended as his burial place, it was still unfinished at the time of his death in 1154. His successors lost interest in the project and it was not consecrated until 1267; Frederick II of Hohenstaufen even removed the royal porphyry tombs—officially for safety—and took them to Palermo, but to carry out this scandalous act he waited until the bishop was away on a mission in the East. Excavations during restoration work have revealed Roman remains on this site. The church is preceded by a raised terrace, part of the original Norman design, surrounded by a balustrade with statues (this gate is closed; entrance from the south door).

The unusual **façade** is flanked by two massive towers with fine windows. Above the narthex built by Ambrogio da Como in 1471 is a double row of blind arcades. The beautiful exterior of the south side and transept are visible from via Passafiume.

The basilican **interior** has 16 ancient columns with Roman capitals, probably from the Temple of Diana, supporting Arab-Norman arches. The open timber roof of the nave bears traces of painting (1263). The contemporary stained glass **windows** high up in the nave are the work of the Palermo artist Michele Canzoneri and were installed in 1985–90. The work is still unfinished; the windows will eventually be 72 and represent episodes from the Old and New Testaments. The crossing is approached through an arch borne by huge columns. In the sanctuary is a 15C painted Cross attributed to Tommaso de Vigilia.

The presbytery is decorated with exquisite **mosaics**—the best preserved and the earliest of their kind in Sicily—on a background of dusky gold. They were carried out for Roger II in a careful decorative scheme, reflecting Byzantine models, but much more relaxed and spontaneous than anything seen before from those workshops. The king probably intended them to line the whole interior of the building. It is thought that they are the work of Greek craftsmen, summoned from Constantinople by Roger himself. In the apse is the splendid colossal figure of *Christ Pantocrator* holding an open book with the Greek and Latin biblical text from John 8:12 ('I am the Light of the World, he who follows me will not walk in darkness'). His compassionate expression is that of a friend we can trust, someone wiser and more experienced: the wayward locks of hair falling over his forehead add to his humanity. Many art experts believe this to be the finest portrait of Christ in existence, and it has been noted that it is the closest in resemblance to the image on the the the Shroud (Sindone), which is kept in Turin.

On the curved apse wall below are three tiers of figures: the *Virgin in prayer between four archangels* (dressed as Byzantine dignitaries; holding loaves of bread symbolizing Salvation), and the *Apostles* in the two lower registers, quite informal in their stance, as if we had suddenly interrupted their conversation. In the vault of the presbytery are angels and seraphims and on the walls below are (left) prophets, deacon martyrs, and Latin bishop saints, and (right) prophets, warrior saints, and Greek patriarchs and theologians. An inscription beneath the window states that the mosaics of the apse were completed in 1148. The soft folds of the robes, the gentle expressions, the marvellous texture and subtle colour of the angels' wings, are certainly the work of very accomplished artists.

The south aisle and transepts were stripped of their Baroque decoration in the 1970s, in order to restore the building to its Norman aspect, as far as possible. The work is still in progress, but already the effects are breathtaking. In the chapel to the right of the sanctuary is a statue of the *Madonna* by Antonello Gagini. On the left pilaster of the sanctuary, high up in a niche, is a statue of the annunciatory angel. In the neo-classical chapel to the left of the sanctuary is an elaborate 18C silver altar.

From the north aisle is the entrance to the beautiful little **cloister** (temporarily closed) which shows the remains of three galleries of twin columns with carved capitals (including *Noah's Ark* and the *Trinacria* symbol) supporting pointed Arab-Norman arches.

In **piazza del Duomo** is Palazzo Maria, with medieval traces, and the 17C Oratorio del Santissimo Sacramento beside the neo-classical Palazzo Legambi. Opposite is Palazzo Vescovile (1793), next to the 17C Seminary with a hanging garden. Opposite the Duomo is the former monastery of S. Caterina, drastically restored a few years ago by the architect Gae Aulenti (who designed the Musée d'Orsay in Paris) as the Town Hall.

Museo Mandralisca

Via Mandralisca leads down to the Mandralisca museum (open daily 09.00–19.00, closes at 24.00 in summer). The palace cellars, containing huge terracotta jars for storing oil, can be seen from the road. Enrico Pirajno, Baron Mandralisca (1809–64) once lived here and he left his remarkable collection to the city as a museum (now run by a private foundation). The Baron was a member of the first Italian parliament and he took a special interest in archaeology (participating in excavations on Lípari and an area near Cefalù) and natural history. He also endowed a local school.

On the **ground floor** is a mosaic from Cefalù (1C BC). Stairs lead up to the first floor. **Room 1** contains a famous vase from Lípari showing a vendor of tuna fish (4C BC) and a numismatic collection dating from the Greek period up to the 19C, with about 400 pieces. The collection is particularly important for its coins from Lipari, Cefalù and Syracuse. **Room 2** has Veneto-Cretan paintings and other 15C–18C works.

In **room 3** is the famous *Portrait of a Man* by Antonello da Messina (c 1465–72), the jewel of the collection and one of the most striking portraits of the Italian Renaissance. Mandralisca apparently bought this small painting from a pharmacy in Lípari, where he discovered it in use as part of a cupboard door. The sitter, with his enigmatic smile, has never been identified. The influence of the Flemish school of painting is evident in this exquisite work. Also displayed here is a sarcophagus in the form of an Ionic temple which dates from the 2C BC. **Room 4** has Mandralisca's remarkable collection of c 20,000 shells. **Room 5** has archaeological material, including Italiot vases from Lípari (320–300 BC), and a well-preserved kylix.

The **second floor** contains more archaeological finds, and miscellaneous objects including a 19C dinner service, arms, reliquaries, paintings (*Madonna and Child* attributed to Antonello da Saliba), and an ornithological collection. Mandralisca's important library, which has been added to over the years, is also kept here.

Corso Ruggero continues down to end at via Porpora which leads right to a restored square tower in a gap between the houses. Outside the tiny postern gate a fine stretch of the megalithic walls (5C BC) built onto the rock can be seen. In the other direction via Carlo Ortolani di Bordonaro leads past (right) piazza Francesco Crispi with the church of the Madonna del Cammino. Modern steps lead up to a 17C bastion (Capo Marchiafava) where a 14C fountain has been placed (good view). Via Ortolani continues down towards the sea and ends beside a terrace overlooking the little **port**, with picturesque old houses on the seafront.

From here via Vittorio Emanuele leads back past the church of the Badiola (12C–17C), next to its convent (the old portal survives on the corner of via Porto

Salvo). Opposite is the 16C Porta Pescara with a lovely Gothic arch through which the sea can be seen. It is now used to display fishermen's tackle and nets. Beyond, the discesa Fiume, with wide steps curving down past a few trees, leads to a picturesque medieval **Lavatoio**, where a spring of slightly salty water, said to be the tears of Daphnis, was converted into a wash house by the Arabs and was still in daily use until quite recently.

> The shepherd Daphnis loved the nymph Nomia: she made him promise to be faithful to her, on pain of being blinded. Crafty Chimaera enticed him into the woods, where she gave him wine to drink and seduced him. Nomia immediately guessed what had happened, and blinded him; he wept bitter tears at his folly, but to no avail; Hermes turned him into stone, on the orders of Hera, to whom Nomia was particularly dear. His stone head is the Rock of Cefalù, and his copious tears form the spring which supplies the ancient wash house.

From corso Ruggero and vicolo dei Saraceni steps and a path lead up (in c 1 hour) to the **Rocca**, the summit (278m) of which commands a wonderful view. Here the so-called Temple of Diana has walls made out of huge polygonal blocks and a carved architrave over the entrance. It was probably a sacred edifice built in the 5C–4C BC over an earlier cistern. Stretches of castellated walls can also be seen here as well as numerous cisterns and ovens, but only vague traces remain of the original castle where Charles of Salerno was imprisoned.

THE MADONIE MOUNTAINS

The Madonie Mountains which lie between the Imera Settentrionale to the west and the Pollina river to the east have extensive woods and fine views. The small hill towns here, particularly **Polizzi Generosa**, **Petralia Soprana** and **Castelbuono**, are of great interest. The Pizzo Carbonara (1979m) is the second highest mountain on the island (after Etna). This area of some 40,000 ha is protected as a nature reserve known as the **Parco Naturale Regionale delle Madonie**. The vegetation in the upland plains and mountains includes beech, enormous holly trees some 14m high and centuries old, manna ash (manna is still extracted from the bark in the Pollina and Castelbuono area), chestnuts, oaks, poplars, ilexes, cork trees and ancient olives. A rare species of fir, *Abies nebrodensis*, only found here, distinguished by the terminal twigs on the branches which form a neat cross, was saved from extinction in 1969. Apart from these extensive woods the landscape has spectacular rock formations and there is still some pastureland where sheep and cattle are grazed. For more information on the flora and fauna of the Madonie visit the museum in Castelbuono.

Practical information

Getting there
By car

The northern part of the Madonie can be visited from Cefalù and the byroads which lead inland from the main coastal road between Palermo and Messina. The southern part of the area is best approached from the Palermo–

Catania motorway ('Scillato' and 'Tremonzelli' exits). The roads within the park are generally good and well signposted.

By bus

Bus services are run by *SAIS* (☎ 091/ 6166028) from Palermo and Cefalù to most of the hill towns and villages.

Information offices

Tourist Information Bureau, 16 corso Paolo Agliata, Petralia Sottana (main office; ☎ 0921/ 684011).

Pro loco, Petralia Sottana, ☎ 0921/ 641680.

Tourist Information Bureau, Petralia Soprana, ☎ 0921/680806.

Tourist Information Bureau, Isnello, ☎ 0921/662795 or 0921/662737.

Tourist Information Bureau, Caltavuturo, ☎ 0921/541012.

Pro loco, via Umberto, Castelbuono, ☎ 0921/673467.

Tourist Information Bureau, via Umberto, ☎ 0921/671124, ✉ www. welcome.to/castelbuono.it; ✉ www. comune.castelbuono.pa.it.

Tourist Information Bureau, Collesano, ☎ 0921/661104.

Capuchin Friars, Gibilmanna, ☎ 0921/ 421835.

Tourist Information Bureau, piazza Umberto, Polizzi Generosa, ☎ 0921/ 649018. *Tourist Information Bureau*, Sclafani Bagni, ☎ 0921/541097.

Getting around
By bicycle, horse or on foot

Marked trails provide beautiful routes for walkers, riders and cyclists with mountain bikes. The road which runs through the centre of the park across the Piano Zucchi (1085m) and up to Piano Battaglia (1646m), which lies below the Pizzo della Principessa (1975m), one of the highest of the range, provides a good view of the landscape.

Where to stay
Hotels

CASTELBUONO ☆☆☆ *Milocca*, contrada piano Castagna, ☎ 0921/671944 or 0921/676162, ▤ 0921/671437). Above the town in the woods; pool, excellent restaurant, bowls. The hotel organizes trekking or horseriding in the Madonie park.

☆ *Ariston*, 2 via Vittimaro, ☎ 0921/ 671321. Simple, basic accommodation in the town centre; no restaurant.

ISNELLO ☆☆☆ *Piano Torre Park*, località Torre Montaspro, ☎ 0921/ 662671, ▤ 0921/662672. Recently restored 18C castle about 15km from Isnello. Restaurant, pool, tennis and plenty of activities for guests.

PETRALIA SOTTANA ☆☆ *Madonie*, 81 corso Pietro Agliata, ☎ & ▤ 091/641106. Charming old hotel in the town centre. Good restaurant. Excursions into the Madonie park and skiing trips.

Bed & breakfast

CASTELBUONO ☆☆ *Abbate*, 14 via Mariano Raimondi, ☎ 0921/676153. In the old city.

COLLESANO ☆☆☆ *Gargi di Cenere*, contrada Gargi di Cenere, ☎ & ▤ 0921/ 428431, ✉ gargidicenere@libero.it. Charming old country house with a farm next door, which supplies the ingredients for breakfast. Guests can use the kitchen; dinner on request; garden and small pool; French spoken.

POLIZZI GENEROSA ☆☆☆ *Rinaldi*, 19 via Dogana, ☎ 0921/649374.

☆☆ *Dolce*, contrada Pietà Alta, ☎ 0921/649501. Just outside town.

Paese albergo

PETRALIA SOTTANA Many houses in the old centre offer accommodation for tourists. Information from the *Pro Loco*, ☎ 0921/641680 or from the town council ☎ 0921/641032.

Farm accommodation

CASTELBUONO ☆☆☆☆☆ *Villa Levante*, contrada Vignicella, ☎ 335/6394574, 🖪 095/7462378. A beautiful castle (open Apr–Oct) with sweeping views over the valley. Self-catering apartments in the corner towers, Restaurant within walking distance at Castelbuono. Activities include trekking and mountain biking. Expensive.

☆☆☆ *Masseria Rocca di Gonato*, contrada Rocca di Gonato, ☎ & 🖪 0921/672616, 📧 www.roccadigonato.it. Remote 12C Basilian monastery, rather heavily restored. Good base for botanists (orchids) and bird watchers (birds of prey, shrikes, dipper, kingfisher and blue rock thrush). The farm raises cattle, sheep, goats, donkeys and horses. Restaurant is crowded at weekends with locals. Many activities available.

COLLESANO ☆☆☆☆☆ *Arione*, contrada Pozzetti, ☎ & 🖪 0921/427703, 📧 www.agriturismoarione.it. In a lovely part of the Madonie park, this farm raises thoroughbred horses and sheep and produces olive oil. The food is particularly good; everything is home-made, including the bread and the pasta.

GANGI ☆☆☆☆ *Gangivecchio*, contrada Gangi Vecchio, ☎ 0921/644804, 🖪 0921/689191. Converted monastery. The farm produces olive oil and runs highly recommended courses in Sicilian cookery for guests.

PETRALIA SOTTANA ☆☆☆☆ *Monaco di Mezzo*, contrada Monaco di Mezzo, ☎ 0934/673710, 🖪 0934/673949, 📧 www.monacodimezzo.com. Ancient farm in lovely countryside, in the Madonie park; organic food; pool; paragliding.

POLIZZI GENEROSA *Giardino Donna Lavia*, contrada Donna Laura, ☎ 0921/551037, 🖪 0921/551104, 📧 www.italiaabc.it/a/donnalavia. Beautiful farm surrounded by hazelnut groves, offering comfortable rooms or cottages. Walking tours in the Madonie park and horseriding. Good restaurant serving local products.

SAN MAURO CASTELVERDE ☆☆☆☆ *Flugy Ravetto*, contrada Ogliastro, ☎ 0921/675121, 🖪 0921/674128, 📧 www.aziendeflugyravetto.com. Historic farmhouse with very comfortable accommodation, surrounded by ancient olive groves, belonging to one of the oldest aristocratic families of Sicily. Impeccable hospitality, excellent food. Trekking, pool, children's play area.

SCLAFANI BAGNI ☆☆☆ *Case di Cardellino*, contrada Cardellino, (SS 120), ☎ 339/790620 or 347/0306182. Restored farmhouse with good restaurant, popular with local people at weekends, ideal position for exploring the hilltop villages of this area; activities include bowls, archery, mountain biking.

Alpine refuges

CASTELBUONO ☆ *Francesco Crispi* (1300m), località Piano Sempria, ☎ 0921/672279.

ISNELLO ☆ *Lo Scoiattolo*, (1105m) località Piano Zucchi, ☎ & 🖪 0921/662831.

☆ *Luigi Orestano*, (1105m) località Piano Zucchi, ☎ & 🖪 0921/662159.

PETRALIA SOTTANA ☆ *Giuliano Marini*, (1,680m) Piano Battaglia, ☎ 0921/649994.

Youth Hostel

PIANO BATTAGLIA *Ostello della gioventù Piero Merlino*, (1660m) contrada Mandria Marcate, ☎ 0921/649995, 0921/649996 or 0921/420151.

Eating out
Restaurants

CASTELBUONO €€ *Nangalarruni*, 5 via Alberghi delle Confraternite, ☎ 0921/671428.

Renowned in this part of the world, people come a long way to feast on wild fungi, delicious grills, home-made desserts. Closed Wed.

€ *Il Bistrot*, 32 via S. Anna, ☎ 0921/671679.

€ *La Tavernetta*, 7 via Garibaldi, ☎ 328/5790642. Excellent local dishes and a wide selection of Sicilian and Italian wines.

POLIZZI GENEROSA €€ '*U Bagghiu*, 3 via Gagliardo, ☎ 0921/49546. Traditional mountain fare.

Cafés and pastry shops

CASTELBUONO *Fiasconaro*, 10 piazza Margherita, 🖅 www.fiasconaro.com. The Fiasconaro brothers produce nougat, liquors and a very particular cake called *mannetto*, a light textured sponge cake iced with manna, which served warm, is the ideal accompaniment for tea or hot chocolate. It keeps for weeks, so you can take it home!

Antica Gelateria del Corso, 46 corso Umberto. Another sweet unique to Castelbuono is t*esta di turco*, a kind of blancmange with a layer of flaky pastry in the middle, sprinkled with chocolate and cinnamon. Antonio also makes marvellous almond cakes, ice cream, and chocolate-covered roasted almonds. All of these Castelbuono confections are made by hand.

 ### Annual festivals

GIBILMANNA pilgrimage on 1st Sunday in September.

GRATTERI feast of the patron St James on 8–9 September.

ISNELLO feast of the patron St Nicholas on 5–7 September. Broad bean and boiled potato feast on 29 June. Pancake feast on 1 May.

COLLESANO Festa della Casazza in the Easter period when the life of Christ is re-enacted. **Paliu du Pipìu**, 1–3 August, a turkey race where people bet on the results.

CASTELBUONO Arruccata di li Ventimiglia in August (a historical pageant).

SCLAFANI BAGNI procession of the Ecce Homo on last Sunday in June.

POLIZZI GENEROSA Feast of St Gandulph, 3rd Sunday in September; hazelnut fair in August; and festivities on 26 December when a huge bonfire is lit in front of the ruined church of La Commenda.

Hill towns in the northern area of the Madonie

Gibilmanna

The sanctuary of Gibilmanna is in a beautiful position looking towards the sea, on the slopes of the Pizzo S. Angelo (1081m), with woods of olives, cork oaks, pines and chestnuts. Its name is derived from the Arab *gebel*, meaning mountain, and manna, which was extracted from the manna ash trees in the locality, and used for medicinal purposes. There was a sanctuary here founded by the Benedictines in the 6C; in 1535 it became a Capuchin convent: it is still a famous centre of pilgrimage on Sicily. The **sanctuary** (open daily 08.00–13.00, 15.00–17.30, ☎ 0921/421835), rebuilt in the 17C, has, however, been altered many times and its external appearance dates from the twentieth century. The interior preserves an 18C Baroque altar, a fresco of the *Madonna* and a *Crucifix* from an earlier church. The wooden tabernacle on the high altar is by Pietro Bencivinni (1700).

An interesting **museum of the Franciscan presence** in Sicily (open daily 11.00–13.00, 15.30–17.30, ☎ 0921/420883) preserves works of art from convents and churches in this area of the island. These include 16C–18C paintings, church vestments, statuettes (in wax and wood), ex votos, a rare early 18C wooden organ with cane pipes, and an ethnographical collection illustrating monastic life. It is possible to visit the Catacombs. An observatory (1952) stands on the nearby Cozzo Timpa Rossa (1006m).

Gratteri is a little hill town (657m) facing west with a fine distant view along the coast. The old churches are usually closed; the Nuova Matrice (19C) contains four thorns from the Crown of Jesus and a fragment of the True Cross, while the Matrice Vecchia, dedicated to the Archangel Michael, was built in the 14C and has a separate bell tower with seven bronze bells, one of them dated 1390. On the first Thursday after Corpus Domini (June) a very old ceremony takes place, with much beating of drums, going back to the time when the young men used to go hunting wolves on that day. Beautiful crochet is still made by the women.

Isnello

Isnello is a pleasant little town (600m) built along a long rock which gives the town its name, the Rocca dell'Asinello, with the ruins of the castle at one end.

The Chiesa Madre has 16C frescoes by Antonino Ferraro, 17C stuccoes by Giuseppe Li Volsi, and a carved wooden choir and organ loft dating from the early 17C. A marble ciborium is attributed to Domenico Gagini (1492). The *Deposition* is by Giuseppe Salerno Zoppo di Gangi. The little church of **S. Michele** has an important painted wooden ceiling, a wooden *Crucifix* by Fra' Umile da Petralia, a painting of *Martyrs* by Giuseppe Salerno Zoppo di Gangi, and a 15C fresco of *St Leonard*. The church of the Rosario (closed) contains a painting of the *Madonna of the Rosary* attributed to the Flemish school. The church of the **Annunziata** contains a *Nativity* by Giuseppe Salerno Zoppo di Gangi.

Steps lead up from the piazza by the Mother Church to the church of **S. Maria Maggiore** (key at no. 4 via Purgatorio) near the ruins of the castle and beneath a rock called the Grotta Grande. It has a pretty bell tower. The charming interior has a decorative organ loft at the west end, and a 15C–16C *Crucifix*, unusual in its iconography and painted on both sides, hangs from the centre of the nave ceiling. Off the north side, the Cappella del Crocifisso contains a processional Cross. Above the high altar is a *Madonna and Child* of the Gagini school (1547). There is also a charming little statue of the *Madonna* as a baby, lovingly preserved in a glass case.

The quality of the lace, crochet, embroidery and filet here is renowned; in fact a biennial course is organized by the local people to help keep the tradition alive.

The spectacular little medieval town of **Collesano** (population 4500) has several interesting churches including the Duomo (S. Maria la Nuova) which contains a painted *Crucifix* of 1555, a fine carved tabernacle of 1489 by Donatello Gagini, and a *Madonna with angels* by Giuseppe Salerno Zoppo di Gangi. The frescoes are the work (1624) of Gaspare Vazano, also known as Zoppo di Gangi, pupil of Giuseppe Salerno, again called Zoppo di Gangi. In S. Maria la Vecchia (1140) is a statue of the *Madonna* by Antonello Gagini. The pottery made here is unusual and interesting.

Castelbuono

An ancient town of warm rose-coloured stone and mellow old brick, whose rooftops are animated by jackdaws and swifts, Castelbuono (population 9000) basks at the foot of its spectacular castle, in a fold of hills covered with forests of manna ash and chestnuts. Of Byzantine origins, it became the seat of the Ventimiglia princes of Geraci in the 14C, and the medieval structure of the centre is still intact.

The road leads up past a 16C fountain with bas-reliefs and a statue of Venus to piazza Margherita, with another 16C fountain. Here the **Matrice Vecchia** (usually closed) of 1350 is preceded by a loggia. It contains a marble ciborium attributed to Giorgio da Milano (late 15C), a huge polyptych on the high altar attributed to Pietro Ruzzolone, and statues and frescoes of the 16C. The crypt has frescoes of the *Passion of Christ*.

Also in the piazza is a building owned by the Ventimiglia family in the 14C–16C and used as a prison from the 18C up to 1965. Exhibitions are now held here and it has a local tourist office. The ancient street continues uphill past the town hall to the **castle** (09.00–13.00, 15.00–19.00, ☎ 0921/671211) built by the Ventimiglia family in 1316, which has been exceptionally well restored. The castle is said to have both a ghost, that of Queen Constance Chiaramonte (14C), whose footsteps can be heard running through the rooms on the first Tuesday of every month, and a secret passage which unites the castle to the mausoleum of the Ventimiglias. Off the courtyard is the Chapel of St. Ann (c 1683) with white stuccoed cherubs on a gold ground by the school of Serpotta. The skull of the saint is preserved here in a 16C silver urn, and the chapel possesses a treasury. The castle houses the Civic Art Gallery (contemporary artists) and a small museum of country life and the manna extraction activity. Behind the castle the terrace has a view of the Madonie and the little hill town of Geraci Siculo.

From the Matrice Vecchia a road (signposted) leads up to a piazza with palm trees and a memorial surrounded by cannon used in World War I. Here is the **Matrice Nuova** begun at the beginning of the 17C (and rebuilt in 1830). It contains a painted *Crucifix* attributed to Pietro Ruzzolone, stucco altars, and a 16C triptych.

Another road leads up to the right of the Matrice Nuova to the church of **S. Francesco**, which has a pretty white and gold interior decorated in the 18C, with an organ and monks' choir above the entrance. It also has decorative chandeliers and charming little confessionals dating from 1910. Off the right side of the sanctuary, entered through a lovely late 15C doorway carved by the school of Laurana, is a pretty octagonal chapel with twisted columns. Here are tombs of the Ventimiglia family, including one dated 1543 and one 1687, and there should be somewhere here the secret passage to the castle. The two 15C frescoes were detached from the Franciscan convent. The attractive 18C cloister (under repair; delayed by new archaeological discoveries) of the convent is entered between two marble columns left of the church façade.

In via Roma the former Convent of S. Venera now houses the **Minà Palumbo Museum** (open daily 09.00–13.00, 15.00–19.00, summer 16.00–20.00, ☎ 0921/676596). It is named after the naturalist Francesco Minà Palumbo, a native of Castelbuono. His collections, which he carefully catalogued, provide a fascinating documentation of the Madonie. The exhibits include fossils, a botanical and natural history section, minerals, archaeological finds (including prehistoric material), examples of glass produced here from the late 16C to the end of the 18C, and examples of paper produced in the town between 1822 and 1846. There is also an interesting display illustrating the extraction of manna (used for medicinal purposes as a mild laxative, especially for babies, and also as a sweetener in cakes) from the trunks of manna ash trees in the area. Castelbuono and Pollina are the only places in the world where manna is still produced.

In the hill town of Pollina (730m) the church has works by Antonello Gagini. A theatre was built on the hillside here in 1979 (summer theatre festival).

Hill towns in the southern area of the Madonie

Sclafani Bagni

Sclafani Bagni, with 600 inhabitants, is a small remote fortress-village on a precipitous crag (813m) with superb views. Very ancient, it was a fortress from 734 BC, during the Greek colonization. The name derives from *Esculapiifanum*, that is Temple of Asclepios, a place of healing which stood by a thermal spring. The medieval **town gate** bears the coat of arms of the Sclafani (Matteo Sclafani, count of the town in 1330, constructed its defences). Higher up the **Chiesa Madre** contains a splendid Greek sarcophagus, in white Greek marble, with Bacchic scenes, two statues (the *Madonna* and *St Peter*) by the school of Gagini, an organ by Della Valle (1615), and a processional statue of the *Ecce Homo*, made of papier maché. Above, steps lead up to the scant remains of the Norman **castle**, with an excellent view.

In the lower part of the town is the church of **S. Giacomo** on the edge of the hillside, with charming stuccoes in the interior in very poor condition. The church of **S. Filippo** contains a tiled pavement, a 17C wooden processional Crucifix in a tabernacle, and two popular statues of waxed canvas (1901).

The famous *Regaleali* wine is produced by the Tasca d'Almerita family in the district of Sclafani Bagni, at Regaleali, many kilometres south of the town on the southern border of the province of Palermo (best reached from Vallelunga in the province of Caltanissetta). The cellars are open to the public (10.00–13.30, 15.00–18.00) and wine and local produce can be purchased (☒ www. tascadalmerita.it).

Caltavuturo is a 16C town with stepped streets. It lies in a superb position in cultivated uplands (635m) beneath outcrops of red rock and the ruined fortress taken from the Saracens by Count Roger. In 1980 a mysterious golden libation bowl of the 4C BC, known as the **mesomphalos phiale**, was found supposedly during excavations carried out by the telephone company on Mount Riparato. Sold on the clandestine antiquities market, it was bought by an unscrupulous American collector, but has now been recuperated, the first time ever that an art treasure has been returned to Sicily after legal proceedings. The bowl weighs about 1kg and has an embossed decoration of acorns and bees, with an inscription around the border referring to the magistrates of Sicily and giving the value of the object.

Polizzi Generosa

Polizzi Generosa (917m) is in a beautiful position at the head of the Imera valley. It is a delightful little town which received its name 'Generosa' from Frederick II in 1234. It once boasted 76 churches within its walls, and many of them now belong to local confraternities (who have the keys). The month of August is dedicated to a picturesque Hazelnut Festival. The speciality of the local pastry cooks is a pie made with fresh cheese, chocolate and cinnamon, called *sfoglio*.

From the small piazza Umberto, where all the main roads converge, via Cardinale Rampolla leads up to the **Chiesa Madre** with a charming 16C porch and two very worn statues of *St Peter* and *St Paul*. A Gothic portal has been exposed beside the Renaissance doorway. In the south aisle is a painting of the *Madonna of the Rosary* by Giuseppe Salerno Zoppo di Gangi. At the end of the aisle, a chapel on the right (closed by a grille) contains some particularly fine sculptures, including the sarcophagus of Beato Gandolfo da Binasco (recomposed) by Domenico Gagini; reliefs by the Berrettaro family, and a fragment of the *Last Supper* by Domenico Gagini and his workshop. In the sanctuary are two precious large triptychs: the one on the right with the *Madonna enthroned amidst angels* is attributed to the 'Maitre au feuillage en broderie'' (early 16C) and is one of the loveliest paintings in Sicily, and the one on the left (with the *Visitation*) dates from the 16C. In the Cappella Ventimiglia (left of the sanctuary) are interesting funerary monuments and in the left transept are 18C statues. The font (with a pagan base) at the west end dates from 1488. The decorative organ was made in the 18C.

Beside the Chiesa Madre is **S. Gandolfo la Povera** (1622) with a high altarpiece of *St Gandulph* by Giuseppe Salerno Zoppo di Gangi. The road continues up to the church of S. Francesco, founded in 1303, now used as an auditorium. On the left is piazza Castello with the ruins of the so-called castle of Queen Blanche of Navarre (11C). In the walled garden of Baron Casalpietro, two fir trees belonging to the endemic species *Abies nebrodensis* survive; there are only 27 of them left in the world. A little museum of the Madonie (visits by appointment, ☎ & 🖷 0921/551009, 🖂 www.abiesmam.it) in the piazza illustrates the local natural history. Below S. Francesco is the church of S. Nicolò de Franchis (locked) founded in 1167 by Peter of Toulouse, with a bellcote. Nearby is **S. Margherita** (or the Badia Vecchia), a 15C church. It has delicate white and gold stucco decoration. The barrel vault and sanctuary have 19C pictorial decorations, including a copy of Leonardo's *Last Supper*.

Another road from piazza Umberto leads up to the remains of the circular **Torre di Leo**, named after a family who purchased it in 1240, next to the church of **S. Pancrazio dei Greci**, which contains a painting by a Zoppo di Gangi. From the terrace there is an impressive view of the mountains.

The main street of the little town, corso Garibaldi, also starts in piazza Umberto. It leads past the centrally-planned church of **S. Girolamo** by Angelo Italia. Next to it is the former **Collegio dei Gesuiti**, a large building now occupied by the Town Hall and Civic Library, with 35,000 precious volumes. The fine interior courtyard has loggias on two levels and a single balcony on the top storey. In the morning visitors are allowed up to the top storey where an open balcony has a fine view over the roofs of the town (and the ruined church of the Commenda below). The corso continues past a flight of steps (right) which lead up to the large **Palazzo Carpinello** with a long, low façade. The corso ends at a terrace known as the belvedere which has a magnificent view: the motorway from Palermo to Catania is reduced to a winding stream in the distant valley below, while to the east rise the Madonie Mountains. The ancient church of **S. Maria Lo Piano** here, seat of the Teutonic Knights, contains 17C paintings. Via Malatacca leads down from the corso towards S. Antonio Abate, which has a red Arabic dome crowning its bell tower (once a minaret). Inside is another painting by a Zoppo di Gangi. It is worth taking a look at the one-storey houses in the Arab district here.

Petralia Sottana is a town (population 3800) on a hillside (1000m) enclosed by the mountains. The attractive corso Paolo Agliata passes S. Maria della Fontana (16–17C) and the 18C church of S. Francesco before reaching piazza Umberto I (with a view of the Imera valley). The **Chiesa Madre**, which has a lovely bell tower, was rebuilt in the 17C. It contains a fine sculpted altarpiece of 1501, and a 17C statue of the *Madonna and Child*. Above the town on the road for Petralia Soprana is the church and convent of the SS. Trinità with a marble ancona by Gian Domenico Gagini (1542). The women here still weave the brightly coloured rag rugs called *pezzane* or *frazzate*.

Petralia Soprana

In a beautiful position on a hillside (1147m) above pinewoods is Petralia Soprana, one of the most interesting and best preserved little towns in the interior of the island. *Petra* was important in the Roman era, and in 1062 it passed into the hands of Count Roger. During the 19C and early 20C rock-salt mines were in operation here, one of which is still in use. The exteriors of the attractive old stone houses have not been covered with plaster as in numerous other Sicilian towns.

In the central **piazza del Popolo** is a large war memorial by Antonio Ugo (1929) and the neo-Gothic town hall (1896). Via Generale Medici leads up past (left) the fine façade of S. Giovanni Evangelista (1770; closed) to piazza Fra Umile with a bust commemorating Fra Umile da Petralia (Pintorno: 1588–1639), the sculptor, famous for his Crucifixes which adorn many churches in Sicily, who was born here. On the right is the 18C Oratorio delle Anime del Purgatorio with a very worn portal. Further up is piazza dei Quattro Cannoli with a pretty 18C fountain and palace.

Beyond on the right a wide flight of steps leads down to the **Duomo**, consecrated in 1497, which has a delightful 18C portico. At one end is a squat tower and at the other is the 15C campanile with a two-light window in which two quaint statues of *St Peter and St Paul* have been placed. The gilded and white stucco decoration in the interior was carried out in 1859. On the north side the first altar has a fine painted statue of the *Madonna and Child*, and the fourth altar a marble statue of the *Madonna* (della Catena). The fifth altar has a high relief of the *Pietà* with symbols of the Passion. In the chapel to the left of the sanctuary is an 18C gilded wooden altarpiece. The realistic *Crucifix* in the sanctuary is the first work of Fra Umile da Petralia (c 1624). The polychrome statues of *St Peter and St Paul* are by the Neapolitan sculptor Gaetano Franzese (1764), and the large painting of their martyrdom is by Vincenzo Riolo. On the fifth altar on the south side is a beautiful *Deposition*, attributed since its recent restoration to Pietro Novelli or the school of Ribera. Above the duomo is the 18C domed circular church of S. Salvatore (closed), which was built on the site of a Norman church. It contains 17C–18C statues.

From the other side of piazza del Popolo (see above) via Loreto leads uphill past a pretty courtyard, several nice little palaces, and the 16C church of S. Michele. The street ends in the piazza (paved with cobblestones) in front of the attractive façade of **S. Maria di Loreto**. The façade of 1750 is by two local sculptors named Serpotta and the two little spires on either side are decorated with coloured stones. It is preceded by a wrought-iron gate of 1881. The beautiful interior has a carved high altarpiece attributed to Gian Domencio Gagini or Antonio Vanello (with a

Madonna attributed to Giacomo Mancini). It also contains paintings by Vincenzo Riolo, 18C–19C statues, and a fine sacristy of 1783. On the right a lane (via Belvedere) leads out under an arch to a terrace beside the apse of the church, with an excellent view which extends as far as Etna on a clear day.

On the edge of the hill, below corso Umberto, is the church of **S. Teodoro**, founded by Count Roger and rebuilt in 1759. An interesting sarcophagus decorated with animal carvings was discovered here in 1991.

Geraci Siculo (1077m) has a ruined castle (1072), which was the seat of the Ventimiglia before they moved to Castelbuono. The church of S. Maria della Porta contains a *Madonna and Child* by Domenico Gagini and his workshop (1475).

Gangi is a few kilometres east of the boundary of the Madonie park. It was the birthplace of Giuseppe Salerno, known as the 'Zoppo di Gangi' (the Cripple of Gangi), whose *Last Judgement* adorns the church, and of his student Gaspare Vazano, also known as the 'Zoppo di Gangi'. Attached to the castle is a Renaissance chapel attributed to the Gagini family (early 16C). The town was notorious as a stronghold of the Mafia until the late 1920s when one of their most infamous leaders, the 'Queen of Gangi' (who dressed as a man), was arrested by Cesare Mori, the police officer sent to Sicily by Mussolini to deal with the Mafia. At the same time some 100 inhabitants of the little town were convicted as members of the Mafia.

SOUTH AND WEST OF PALERMO PROVINCE

This section covers minor towns and villages widely scattered over the large province of Palermo. The most interesting town is **Piana degli Albanesi** which has been inhabited by Albanians since the 15C. The Bosco della Ficuzza is one of the best preserved forests on the island, and the Bagni di Cefalà a remarkable Arab bath house. Interesting excavations are in progress both on Mount Iato and near the remote village of Contessa Entellina.

Practical information

Getting there
By bus
Piana degli Albanesi is 24km south of Palermo. Buses (**Prestia e Comandè**) run several times a day from via Balsamo and piazza Stazione in Palermo.

By car
S. Giuseppe Iato, 25km from Palermo, is just off the new fast superstrada from Palermo to Sciacca. Partinico, 28km from Palermo, is on the main road to Trapani, and the places nearer the coast are in the vicinity of the Palermo–Trapani motorway. The southern part of the province is crossed by two roads to Agrigento, the main road via Lercara Friddi, and the secondary road via Corleone, which has some fine scenery and very little traffic.

Information office
APT Palermo, ☎ 091/583847.
Tourist Information Bureau, 8 piazza Garibaldi, Partinico, ☎ 091/8782032. Town Hall, via Matteotti, Piana degli

Albanesi, ☎ 091/8574144. ✉ www.
comunepianadeglialbanesi.it.
Tourist information Bureau, 5 via
Panzanella, San Cipirello, ✉ www.space.
tin.it/lettura/enania.
Tourist information Bureau, Town Hall,
corso Trieste, San Cipirello, ☎ 091/
8580111, ✉ www.millecose.it/sancipi/
home.htm.
Tourist information Bureau, Town Hall,
via Vittorio Emanuele, San Giuseppe
Iato, ☎ 091/8580211.

Where to stay
Hotels

There are a number of com-
fortable resort hotels on the coast at
Isola delle Femmine, Carini, Cinisi and
Terrasini.
MONTELEPRE ☆☆☆ *Il Castello di
Giuliano*, 1 via Magistrato Pietro
Merra, ☎ 091/8941013 or
091/8941006, ▤ 091/8941412.
Smart hotel on the outskirts of town.
The restaurant is particularly good as
are the local wines.

Farmhouse accommodation

NEAR SAN GIUSEPPE IATO
☆☆☆ *Casale del Principe*, SS 121
Palermo-Agrigento, exit San Giuseppe
Iato, ☎ 0918/579910. Set amid vine-
yards close to the excavations of Jetae,
this farm produces cereals and olive oil.
Mountain bikes, pottery courses and
horseriding on offer.
NEAR PARTINICO ☆☆☆☆
Arabesque, contrada Manostalla,
Balestrate, ☎ 091/8787755, ▤ 091/
8987663, ✉ www.agriturismoarabesque.
com. A few hundred yards away from
the sea at Balestrate. Citrus fruit and
olives are grown and thoroughbred
Arab horses are raised. Pool and many
activities are on offer.
☆☆☆ *Fattoria Manostalla*, località
Manostalla, Villa Chiarelli, Balestrate,
☎ 091/8787033, ▤ 0924/508742,
✉ www.wel.it. A lovely old farm in an

excellent position. Cattle and sheep are
raised, and there are vineyards producing *Bianco d'Alcamo*. Cookery courses,
deltaplaning, trekking and mountain
biking.
☆☆ *Il Pescheto*, 28 via Ecce Homo, contrada Pacino, ☎ 091/8783005 or
091/89906608, open summer only.
Small farm with peach orchards, close
to Partinico and the coast. Good simple
cooking.
**NEAR PIANA DEGLI
ALBANESI** ☆☆☆ *Argomesi*, contrada
Dingoli, ☎ 091/8561008, ▤ 091/
8561254. In a wildlife reserve.
Comfortable rooms; air conditioning.
Tennis; pool. Horseriding lessons; pony
trekking; mountain biking.
☆☆☆ *Masseria Rossella*, località
Rossella, ☎ 091/8460012, ✉ www.
masseria-rossella.com. 18C country
villa with frescoed ceilings and private
chapel, pleasant climate; close to the
Ficuzza woods and the Rocca Busambra;
just the place for nature lovers and birdwatchers; pool and mountain biking.

Alpine refuges

Both are in the Bosco della Ficuzza: ☆
Alpe Cucco, at Godrano (1080m), ☎ &
▤ 091/8208225; and ☆ *Val dei Conti*
at Bosco Ficuzza (710m), ☎ & ▤ 091/
8464114.

Eating out
Restaurants

**PIANA DEGLI
ALBANESI** €€ *Le Due Giare*, 26 viale
Otto Marzo, ☎ 091/8575589. Simple
and satisfying local dishes. Good wine
list. Closed Tues.
SAN CIPIRELLO € *Apud Iatum*, 49
via Trento, ☎ 091/8576188. Fantastic
antipasti and appetizing pasta dishes,
inexpensive. Closed Mon.
SAN GIUSEPPE IATO €€ *Da Totò*,
251 via Vittorio Emanuele, ☎
091/8573344. Also has rooms. Home-
made tagliatelle, delicious desserts.

Closed Fri evening.

VILLAFRATI (near Bagni di Cefalà)
€€€ *Mulinazzo*, contrada Mulinazzo, ☎
0918/724870, on the main Palermo-
Agrigento road (SS 121), 800m after
the turning for Bolognetta, on the right.
Many believe this to be the best restaurant in Sicily. Booking essential. Mouth-
watering dishes such as *mosaico di tonno
e verdurine con salsa alle olive* (tuna and
vegetables with olive sauce) or *seppia al
vapore con gelatina di pomodoro* (steamed
cuttlefish with tomato jelly). The wine
cellar is incredible. Attentive service,
expensive, but certainly worth a visit.
Closed Sun evening, all day Mon.

Cafés, pastry shops and ice cream parlours

San Pietro (ESSO) service station on the
Palermo-Agrigento road (SS 121)
shortly after the turning for Lercara
Friddi. Excellent Sicilian breakfasts and
snacks, home-made ice cream and sorbets. Clean too. A useful shop here sells
local cheeses, wines, olive oil and
durum wheat bread.

The *Moon Light Pub*, 82 viale della
Regione, Partinico ☎ 091/8781343 is
a delightful place to have a drink; pizzeria, fast food and live music in the
evenings.

Annual festivals

BISACQUINO On Good
Friday, the locals form a procession which slowly weaves its way
through the streets, singing the Passion
of Christ in Sicilian. The ceremony ends
when one of the young men of the town
is symbolically crucified. Like all religious feasts in Sicily, it is very moving
because everybody identifies with it,
even today; the unusual aspect of this
one is the recitation in the local tongue
(which almost disappeared as it was
practically outlawed by the first Italian
governments; it has only been taught in
schools since 2000).

MEZZOJUSO Il Mastro di Campo,
on the last Sunday afternoon of
Carnival (the last Sunday before Lent),
the town inhabitants perform the story
of a queen who had an affair with her
farmer. Cannons are fired, biscuits are
thrown into the crowd, Garibaldi's soldiers intervene, then the actors offer
wine and barbecued sausages to everybody. Information: ☎ 091/8203657.

PIANA DEGLI ALBANESI Easter
Sunday (and Good Friday) celebrations
are very special here. Women wear gorgeous traditional dress, Ancient
Albanian hymns are sung in the cathedral, there are readings from the Gospel
in seven languages, then a colourful
procession takes place, and the traditional red eggs are distributed.
Information from the Town Council,
☎ 091/8571787.

PRIZZI Il Ballo dei Diavoli, on
Easter Sunday, is really quite scary. In
the morning, Death, dressed in yellow
and the Devils dressed in red and wearing heavy tin masks, race through the
streets trying to capture souls to send to
Hell. In the afternoon the Madonna
meets her Son Jesus, and they and the
angels, who fight with swords, defeat
the devils and Good triumphs over Evil
once again. ✉ www.comune.prizzi.pa.it.

TERRASINI 'A festa di li Schietti,
although on Easter Saturday, is probably
of pagan origin and means 'the feast of
the Bachelors'. A young man who
wants to prove his strength has to lift an
orange tree weighing about 50kg with
one hand then parade it around the
town on his shoulders until he reaches
the home of the girl he admires, when
the orange tree is raised again. If she is
suitably impressed with his strength,
she may decide to marry him. It is great
fun, with the opportunity of sampling
the local delicacies and admiring
Sicilian folk music and dancing.
Information from the Town Council, ☎
091/ 8686733, ✉ www.terrasini.com.

The western part of the province

Piana degli Albanesi

Piana degli Albanesi, ◪ www.comunepianadeglialbanesi.it (720m) is the most interesting of the 15C Albanian colonies (population 6100) in Sicily. The inhabitants still use their native tongue, are Catholics of the Byzantine-Greek rite and wear traditional costume for weddings and important festivals; those taking place at Easter, the Epiphany, and St George's day (April 23) are the most characteristic. Garibaldi planned the tactics that led to the capture of Palermo from here. Piana is known for its excellent bread, cheeses and huge *cannoli di ricotta*.

In the pleasant main street, via Giorgio Kastriota, is the cathedral of S. Demetrio (usually open 10.00–12.30). On the west wall is a 19C painting of *St Nicholas* by Andrea D'Antoni (a pupil of Giuseppe Patania). On the north wall of the church is a small Byzantine *Madonna and Child*. The statues are attributed to Nicolò Bagnasco, and the damaged apse frescoes are by Pietro Novelli. The iconostasis was decorated with paintings in 1975.

The main street leads uphill to the piazza beside the church of the Madonna Odigitria (usually closed), on a design by Pietro Novelli. Just out of the square is the church of **S. Giorgio**, the oldest church in the town, built in 1495. On the south side is a mosaic by the local artist Tanina Cuccia (1984) and a painting of *St Philip Neri* by Giuseppe Patania. The iconostasis has 20C paintings. On the north side is a fresco of *St Anthony Abbot* by Antonio Novelli and a charming equestrian statue of St George, fully armed. Other churches of interest include **S. Vito** (18C, with statues) and **SS. Annunziata** (with a fresco by Pietro Novelli).

At the lower end of the main street, a stable block (no. 207) has been converted into a library, cultural centre and the delightful **Ethnographical Museum** (open 09.30–12.30; Sun & PH 10.00–13.00; Tues, Thurs, & Sat also 15.30–18.30; closed Mon) which has traditional costumes and 18C jewellery worn by the women of Piana on display.

A few kilometres south of the town is Portella della Ginestra, where there is a memorial to the peasants massacred here while celebrating a traditional May Day festival in 1947. Eleven people were killed and 59 wounded by outlaws led by Salvatore Giuliano from Montelepre (see below). This was later understood as an attempt by right-wing activists, in collusion with the Mafia, to combat Communism and advocate independence for the island (both the right wing and the separatists had just lost votes in the local elections).

Southeast of the town is the Lago di Piana degli Albanesi, a reservoir formed in 1923 by an impressive dam between Monte Kumeta (1200m) and Monte Maganoce (900m) across the Belice river.

Monte Iato

S. Giuseppe Iato, exposed by the media as a Mafia stronghold, is now fast becoming one of the most attractive destinations in Sicily, for adventurous visitors. Excavations on Monte Iato carried out over the past 25 years by the University of Zürich have unearthed remains of the ancient city of *Jetae* (the Roman *Iaitas*), which flourished from the 4C BC until it was destroyed by Frederick II in the 13C. The area now has 21 marked trails, of various levels of difficulty, for trekkers and ramblers, using for the most part ancient and medieval paths and bridle tracks, which had all but disappeared from sight and from memory. The trails offer unforgettable glimpses of historic remains, wildlife, and the lovely countryside of the area. Descriptions of the walks and maps are available from the *Azienda Provinciale Turismo* office in Palermo and from the local tourist offices.

Outside **S. Cipirello**, a road leads up through lovely countryside to the site on top of the hill. There is also a small museum (open daily 09.00–13.00; ☎ 091/8573083). The best preserved remains date from the Hellenistic period. From the entrance gate it is a walk of about 20 minutes to the top of the hill with the theatre (late 4C BC, reconstructed in the 1C AD), which could seat 4000, a temple of Aphrodite (c 550 BC), and a large villa on two floors with a peristyle and 25 rooms. The agora has also been partially uncovered. There are splendid views from this isolated spot. In the Civic Museum in S. Cipirello (open Mon–Sat 09.00–13.00, Sun 09.00–12.15, 16.00–18.15, PH closed) there are finds from the site, including the unusual statues found at the theatre.

Partinico

Partinico (population 29,500) is an agricultural town associated with the name of Danilo Dolci (1924–1997), a philanthropist from Trieste who dedicated his life to opposing the Mafia using non-violent methods.

In piazza Duomo is a fountain of 1716. The Biblioteca Comunale (Town Library) nearby has a museum (open Mon–Fri 08.00–14.00, ☎ 091/8578810) with finds from Monte Iato and Rocca d'Entella, and a local ethnographical collection, with an oil press and wine cellars. From the Duomo, corso dei Mille leads past a neo-classical bandstand (1875) to the 17C church of S. Leonardo with works by the school of Novelli. Opposite is the church of the Carmine (1634). Not far from Partinico is Borgetto, a small farming community where the women are famous for their very particular home-made macaroni.

In the hill town of **Montelepre**, the bandit Salvatore Giuliano reigned over a large part of the province, with the support of the Mafia, for seven years before he was murdered here in 1950 by his brother-in-law, Gaspare Pisciotta, at the age of 27. His body was shown to the press in a courtyard in Castelvetrano with the story that he had been tracked down and killed there by the authorities. He remained a mythical figure in the imagination of many Sicilians until 1960, when his connection with the Mafia and local police was revealed, as well as his part in the massacre of peasants at Portella della Ginestra (see above). A remarkable film by Francesco Rosi, *Salvatore Giuliano* (1961), tells his true story.

On the coast between Mondello, a suburb of Palermo, and the gulf of Castellammare there are a few holiday resorts. These include **Isola delle Femmine**, facing an island of the same name, which is now a wildlife reserve. To visit the island or for information about underwater exploration, call *LIPU*, the *Italian League for the Protection of Birds*, ☎ 091/8616167. The resort is surrounded by an industrial zone with a cement works which has somewhat hampered its development for tourism, but it has a nice harbour. **Carini** (population 20,500) gave its name to the gulf here. It has interesting stalactite caverns, and a fine 16C castle, remembered for the tragic story of the Baronissa di Carini, who in 1563 was murdered by her own father when he believed she had a lover. Called *Iccara* by the Greeks, it was the city of the legendary beauty Laide, thought to be the loveliest woman in the world, and carried off to Athens by General Nikias as a trophy of war in the late 5C BC. Beyond the airport at Punta Raisi and Mount Pecoraro (910m) is the lovely gulf of Castellammare which stretches away to Capo S. Vito (see p 179), the mountains behind providing a striking backdrop. It is a popular area for holiday homes, but the countryside is still beautiful, with olive and citrus groves.

Terrasini(⊠ www.terrasini.org; ⊠ www.tiscalinet.it/prolocoterrasini; ⊠ www.terrasini.com) is now a holiday resort. The town has a particularly good civic **museum**, with a natural history section, an archaeological display consisting of objects found on dives around shipwrecks, and a fine collection of painted Sicilian carts (Palazzo D'Aumale, lungomare Impastato, ☎ 091/8683178, open daily 10.00–13.00, 15.00–19.00).

The southern part of the province

Belmonte Mezzagno, founded in 1752, has a scenographic church built in 1776. The valley of the ancient River Eleutheros is now built on but some persimmon plantations survive. Above the plain is the ruined **castle** of Misilmeri. It takes its name from the Arab *Menzil el Emir* (village of the Emir). Here in 1068 Count Roger de Hauteville defeated the Saracens, paving the way for Norman domination of Sicily. The **castle** of Marineo (partly inhabited), at the foot of an oddly shaped rock, was reconstructed in 1559 by Matteo Carnelivari.

Ficuzza is a village dominated by the Palazzina Reale, a handsome building in sandstone with numerous chimneys and two clocks (now used by the Forestry Commission; for admission ☎ 091/8463655). It was built by Venanzio Marvuglia in 1803 as a hunting-lodge for the Bourbons, whose huge estate surrounded the lodge. Behind it extends the **Bosco della Ficuzza**, a splendid forest of oak, chestnut and ilex, which is the most extensive and interesting wooded area of its kind left on the island, noted for its fine trees, plants and wildlife. Although once much more extensive, it now covers some 4000 ha. Several rough roads and paths run through the woods, although much of it is fenced off for protection. Above the woods rises the the **Rocca Busambra** (1613m), a mountain wall of calcareous rock which dominates the plain for many kilometres around. Above the sheer rock face, its summit provides pastureland. Numerous birds nest here, including the golden eagle.

The Gorgo del Drago, the source of the River Frattina, is a lovely green oasis, with yellow and red rocks.

The town of **Cefalà Diana** has a remarkable bathhouse, the **Bagni di Cefalà**, which dates back to the 10C–11C and is considered the most interesting Arab building left on the island (open daily 09.00–13.00; Sun also 15.00–17.00; closed Mon). The baths have a splendid barrel vault and a pretty arch with two capitals and columns at one end. The water used to bubble up here at 38 degrees centigrade, but since 1989 the spring has been dry, and the baths, in use up until a few years ago, have lost much of their character after their recent restoration. The cufic inscription on a frieze of tufa ('Of our lord prince the Emir two admirable baths') which runs around the top of the outside wall has virtually disappeared. The 13C **castle** is very prominent on a rocky outcrop to the south (open weekdays 09.00–13.00; PH also 16.00–19.00, ☎ 091/8201184 or 091/8291546).

Baucina was founded in 1626. The church has a wooden *Crucifix* by the school of Salvatore Bagnasco. **Ciminna** has a number of interesting churches including the Chiesa Madre with 17C stuccoes by Scipione and Francesco Li Volsi and a painting of *St John the Baptist* by Paolo Amato.

The little hill town of **Mezzojuso** (534m) has Arab origins. Settled by Albanians in the 15C, several of its churches still have services according to the Greek rite. A monastery here has a restoration laboratory for antique books. **Vicari**, above the fertile valley of the S. Leonardo river, has a wonderfully romantic ruined castle, probably Saracen, with views of extraordinary beauty. Count Roger wintered here after the battles of 1077.

Lercara Friddi (660m), founded in 1605, with its attractive crumbling 18C churches, was once important for its sulphur mines. When the sulphur economy collapsed at the end of the 19C, a thousand families emigrated to Venezuela and the USA, practically depopulating the town. On the southern border of the province, in the hills above the Platani valley is **Castronuovo di Sicilia** where the churches contain 18C stuccoes by Antonio Messina, and the Chiesa Madre has works by the Gagini.

The medieval town of **Prizzi** stands near a lake, beneath curious outcrops of rock appropriately known as *Imbriaca* (or drunken). Excavations on the Montagna dei Cavalli in the vicinity have revealed 4C–3C BC remains thought to belong to the ancient city of Hippana. The little town of **Palazzo Adriano** is a late 15C Albanian colony, with its main monuments in piazza Umberto I.

Bisacquino, with stunning mountain views, was once an Arab citadel, then a medieval fortress town. 'Moth-soft Besacquino [sic]' wrote Lawrence Durrell in his *Sicilian Carousel*, an apt description of this gentle place where time stands still. Two inhabitants in particular know all about the passage of time: church clocks were made here until recently by two brothers, Rosario and Paolo Scibetta. Rosario passed away recently, but his brother, over ninety, is still fixing clocks. There is a **Museo dell'orologio da torre**, a museum of tower clocks in via Roma (information: *Pro Loco*, 22 via Bambino, ☎ 091/8351350 or 091/ 8352853). The bell tower of the Chiesa Matrice is unique in Sicily because of its triangular shape. The famous film director Frank Capra (1897–1991) was born here.

The outlying Olivetan abbey of S. Maria del Bosco has a church (1676–1757) attributed to Vanvitelli. It contains a terracotta of the Della Robbia school, two large cloisters (one of the 16C), and a fresco of the *Miracle of the Loaves* (in the refectory).

Contessa Entellina (524m; population 2100) is a charming mountain village that takes its first name from the Countess Caterina Cardona di Chiusa (who gave asylum to Albanian refugees in 1450) and its surname from *Entella* (a town of the Elymians which lies to the northwest on a high, isolated rock). On the extensive plateau, excavations of the ancient city which has been ravaged in the past by *tombaroli* (clandestine diggers) are in progress. So far the fortifications, part of the medieval fortress, and a building of 4C–3C BC have been identified. The necropoli lay at the foot of the hill. The archaeological area is always open; the museum is open daily (09.00–12.30, 16.00–19.30, Mon closed, ☎ 091/ 8355556, or 091/8355065).

At **Monte Adranone** (1000m), on the provincial border with Agrigento, excavations of the ancient city of *Adranon* were begun in 1968. This was an indigenous settlement occupied by a Greek city in the 6C BC, probably founded by Selinunte. It was destroyed at the end of the 5C by Carthage. The Carthaginian settlement was conquered by Rome in 263 BC and the site abandoned. Beside the small antiquarium is part of an Iron Age necropolis including the so-called 'Tomba della Regina' with an interesting entrance. Tombs of the 5C and 4C BC have also been found here. Other remains include walls and the south gate, a sanctuary, and part of the acropolis to the northeast.

Corleone

Corleone is a picturesque town of Saracen origin (population 11,400) nestled in the hillside, now surrounded by anonymous modern buildings. In recent years it has been notorious for its powerful Mafia gang, whose boss Totò Riina ruled Cosa Nostra for many years until his arrest in 1993, after more than 20 years 'in hiding' in Palermo.

A Lombard colony was established here by Frederick II in 1237. Traces of its importance as a medieval town can be seen in the old centre which preserves some fine palace doorways in its narrow streets. The **Chiesa Madre** (if closed, ring at the inconspicuous north door approached from the road on the left of the outside steps through a gate) contains some interesting wooden statues (16C–17C), wooden stalls by Giovanni Battista Li Volsi, and paintings (on the transept altars) by Fra Felice da Sambuca, and (first north chapel) Tommaso de Vigilia (*Adoration of the Magi*). The public gardens, laid out in 1820, are well kept. There is an archaeological collection in Palazzo Provenzano (open daily 09.00–13.00, 16.30–20.00; Sun mornings only, ☎ 091/8464907).

USTICA

Ustica (1188 inhabitants), a little over 50km from Palermo, is a small fertile island (just over 8.6 sq km), all that remains of an ancient volcano more than a million years old. The colours of Ustica are memorable; Gramsci, who was held here as a political prisoner, remembered the 'impressive rainbows, and the extraordinary colours of the sea and the sky'. Ustica's highest hills rise to c 240m above sea-level.

The island was once covered with trees but few woods remain, the landscape now dotted with cultivated wheatfields, vineyards, almond groves and orchards, with hedges of prickly pear. Capers and lentils are also produced on the island. Ustica has interesting migratory birdlife, including peregrine falcons, kestrels, storks, herons, razorbills and cormorants.

The rocky shoreline has numerous grottoes; it is particularly remarkable for its numerous fish—*cernia* (grouper) abound, as well as hake, red mullet, prawns, shrimps, lobsters and (in spring) swordfish—and for its seabed, hosting a great variety of seaweed, including the rare *laminaria*. In 1986 the first **marine reserve** in the Mediterranean was established around the island's coast, bringing renewed prosperity to the island. It is much visited by skin-divers and the marine reserve collaborates with the 30 local fishermen who live on the island to arrange boat trips for visitors (see above).

There is no source of water on Ustica apart from some of the caves, such as the Blue Grotto, but there is now a desalinization plant. The inhabitants love playing baseball and softball, and their teams are often in the top division.

The pleasant little village above the port of Cala S. Maria is well kept, and only crowded in the summer months. One road encircles the island, and mule tracks, ideal for trekking, go through the interior.

Practical information

Getting there
By sea
Car ferry from Palermo daily in 2 hrs 20 mins.
Hydrofoils from Palermo in 1 hr 15 mins. (more expensive, but several services a day) run by *Siremar*, 120 via Crispi, Palermo, ☎ 091/336631 or 091/8449002. **From Naples** From 1 June–30 Sept four times a week in 4 hrs, going on to Favignana and Trapani, *Ustica Lines*, ☎ 081/5800340 or 0923/27101.
✉ www.bookingitalia.it for up-to-date information on times, prices and connecting buses.

Information offices
Marine Reserve Visitors' Centre (*Centro Accoglienza*), piazza Umberto I, ☎ 091/8449456.
Comune di Ustica, ☎ 091/8449045.
Pro loco, piazza Vito Longo, ☎ 091/8449190.
Ustica on line: ✉ www.isoladiustica.it; ✉ www.isoladiustica.com.

Getting around
By bus
Mini-bus service every half hour from the port around the island. You can hire a donkey. Enquire at the Bar Centrale or the John Bar in Piazza Umberto.
Car and motor scooter hire
Giuseppe Picone, ☎ 091/8449210 or 091/8449318, rents cars, also with driver. Hotel Stella Marina rents motor scooters.
Boat hire
Ustica Mare, ☎ 091/8449270.

Boat trips
Local fishermen organise 2-hr trips (in summer) around the island 4–6 times a day. The trip includes visits to the grottoes and swimming time. Tickets from the marine reserve's *Centro Accoglienza*. The **glass-bottomed boat** belonging to the marine reserve also takes small groups of 20 around the coast (4 times a day). The trip lasts about 1 hr 30 mins.

Where to stay
Hotels
☆☆☆☆ *Grotta Azzurra*, contrada San Ferlicchio, ☎ 091/8449048, 🖷 091/8449396, ✉ www.framon-hotels.com. Very comfortable; built over the Grotta Azzurra, with garden and pool; panoramic views.

☆☆☆ *Punta Spalmatore*, località Spalmatore, ☎ 091/8449388, 🖷 091/8449482. In one of the most beautiful parts of the island, the hotel accommodation is in a series of little bungalows surrounded by a garden, for a comfortable holiday; there are many sports facilities and a fitness centre. Good restaurant.

☆☆ *Ariston*, 5 via della Vittoria, ☎ 091/8449042, 🖷 091/8449335. Elegant; small; central position with good restaurant called *Da Umberto*. Can help arrange dives and excursions.

☆☆ *Diana*, contrada S. Paolo, ☎ 091/8449109. Quiet hotel with a tiny private beach, garden and car park.

☆☆ *Patrice*, 23 via Refugio, ☎ 091/8449053, 🖷 091/8449663. Welcoming atmosphere and comfortable rooms.

☆☆ *Stella Marina*, 33 via Colombo, ☎ 091/8449014, 🖷 091/8449325. Handy for divers because it is close to the port. Good restaurant.

☆ *Clelia*, 33 via Magazzino, ☎ 091/8449039, 🖷 091/8449459, ✉ hotelclelia@tin.it. Welcoming, clean little hotel with good restaurant.

☆ *Locanda Castelli*, 16 via S. Francesco, ☎ 091/8449007. Simple, family-run establishment where you can be sure of a pleasant stay; excellent restaurant.

Farmhouse accommodation

☆☆☆ *Hibiscus*, località Tramontana, ☎ 091/8449543 or 091/8449179, ✉ www.usticaholidays.com/agriturismo. Charming farm offering self-catering accommodation in little cottages, there is a restaurant ten minutes' walk away; the farm produces wine and lentils. French and English spoken.

Eating out
Restaurants

€€€ *Mamma Lia*, 2 via S. Giacomo, ☎ 091/8449594. It is worth going to Ustica just to eat at Mamma Lia's! Her lentil soup is famous, so are the *totani all'agrodolce* (tattlers in sweet sour sauce).

€€ *Baia del Sole* at contrada Spalmatore, ☎ 091/8449175. Delicious stuffed baked squid, and pasta with capers, aubergines, shrimps, basil and tomato.

€€ *Giulia*, 16 via S. Francesco, ☎ 091/8449039. Booking essential. The restaurant is small and very famous! Chef Pina specializes in *cernia* (grouper), either marinated in lemon, or cooked with breadcrumbs, tomato, olive oil, lemon and garlic.

€€ *Mario*, 21 piazza Umberto I, ☎ 091/8449505. Spaghetti with sea urchins and other superb pasta dishes, including one made with cuttle fish ink.

€ *Le Terrazze*, 3 via Colombo. Pizzeria. Also serves other tasty dishes; from the terrace there are lovely views over the port.

Cafès, pastry shops and ice cream parlours

Bar Centrale, piazza Umberto I. A great meeting point, especially in the early morning and a good source of information about the island. Superb lemon sorbet.

John Bar, also in piazza Umberto, is another popular café.

Oasi Bar, piazza Vito Longo. Appetizing snacks and excellent espresso.

Wines

Albanella is a particularly good white wine, excellent with vegetable soups and fish, made with white Albanella grapes, which flourish on the island. A good cellar is that of *Girolamo Longo*, in contrada Tramontana, ☎ 091/8449179, who also produces a dessert wine called *Zabib*, from zibibbo grapes.

Sport and leisure
Diving centres and swimming

Ventotene, ☎ 091/8449014. Organizes dives or lessons; *Giuffrida*, at the port, ☎ 091/8449093, will also refill cylinders. Between June and September the *Rassegna internazionale delle attività subacquee* organizes various activities: a photography competition and a week dedicated to underwater archaeology. The coast provides excellent **swimming**, although in some areas of the marine reserve swimming is not allowed. Guides can be hired at the Visitors' Centre for **snorkelling** and skin-diving. Ustica is now considered to be the world centre for diving and underwater observation.

Walking

There are two pretty walks along well-kept paths. One leads up from the village above Cala S. Maria to the hill of

Culunnedda (with a radar station). It follows the side of the hill overlooking the cultivated plain of Tramontana. Above the macchia, where wild broom flowers in spring, there are woods of pines and eucalyptus. The other walk starts at the Torre S. Maria (archaeological museum) and skirts the south coast as far as the disused lighthouse at Punta Cavazzi, on the western tip of the island.

History

The name Ustica, from the Latin *ustum* (burnt), is derived from the colour of its black volcanic rock. Excavations have proved that it was inhabited in prehistoric times and in the Roman era. The Greeks called it *Osteodes*, (the place of bones), in reference to the 6000 mercenaries abandoned here by the Carthaginians when they rebelled after a pay dispute, at the time of the wars with Syracuse. Attacks of Barbary pirates defeated all attempts to colonise it in the Middle Ages. It remained deserted for many centuries until in 1762 it was repopulated from the Aeolian Islands and Naples by the Bourbons because of its strategic location on the trade route between Naples and Palermo. At the time three towers were constructed to defend the island.

The island was used as a place of exile and as a prison until 1961: Carlo and Nello Rosselli and Antonio Gramsci were held here as political prisoners under the Fascist regime. In September 1943 Italian and British officers met in secret on the island to discuss details of Italy's change of sides.

The little village above the port of **Cala S. Maria** was laid out on geometric lines by the Bourbons in the 18C. A road winds up to the pretty piazza (also reached by steps from the port). To the right of the church via Calvaria leads uphill to the via Crucis where on the left a path continues up to the **Rocca della Falconiera** (157m), a defensive tower, now used for exhibitions (the fort is also reached by car along a narrow road paved with pebbles). The tower is on the site of a 3C BC settlement, also inhabited in Roman times. It has been excavated on three levels; the most conspicuous remains include a staircase and some 30 cisterns used to collect the rainwater, and a number of tombs. There are fine views above the lighthouse which protects the eastern tip of the island and the rocky point known as the Punta Omo Morto, a nesting-place for numerous birds. To the southwest a necropolis of 5C–6C AD has been identified.

On the other side of the village the Torre S. Maria, another Bourbon tower once used as a prison, has been restored and is now the archaeological museum. The finds from the island, including Bronze Age objects from the village at Faraglioni and underwater finds, are well displayed. Near the tower are remains of a 16C Benedictine convent and interesting old houses known as the *centro storico*, with stables, built around courtyards, some of them carefully restored by the local inhabitants.

On the northern tip of the island, at **Faraglioni**, excavations begun in 1989 unearthed a large prehistoric village (14C–13C BC), probably settled from the Aeolian Islands, with some 300 houses built in stone. The defensive walls are among the best fortifications of this period known in Italy. The site is not yet open to visitors.

On the west coast, between Cala Sidoti and Caletta is the central zone of the **Riserva Naturale Marina** (☎ 091/8449040), a protected area marked by red buoys where fishing is prohibited and boats have to keep offshore. Swimming is allowed only at the extreme northern and southern ends of the reserve (limited access). The aquarium here has a fine display of Mediterranean sea plants and fish. Above the bay is the Bourbon **Torre dello Spalmatore** with fine vaulted rooms, owned by the marine reserve. There are plans to use it as a museum and cultural centre. Just to the south is the lighthouse at **Punta Cavazzi** which will become a scientific laboratory for marine research. A buoy in the sea here marks an **underwater archaeological itinerary** for skin-divers where a number of finds from various wrecks have been left in situ (☎ 091/8449456).

Trapani province

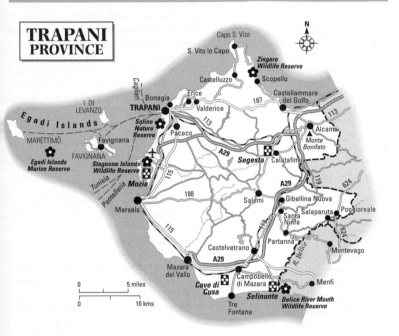

Trapani, the most important town on the west coast of the island, is the capital of a province which is different from the others in Sicily; wide, open landscapes and dazzling light, ever-changing colours of the sea and white straggling villages with flat roofs, give it a north African atmosphere. The province has many interesting archaeological sites, fascinating offshore islands, lovely countryside, and cities full of character, including, in the immediate environs, the beautiful little hilltown of **Erice**. There are some unique wildlife reserves, including the salt marshes south of Trapani and the coastal reserve of Zingaro. To the north is the promontory of Capo S. Vito, stretching beyond the splendid headland of Monte Cofano, and to the south, the lovely island of **Mozia** and the town of **Marsala**.

The classical sites of Segesta and Selinunte can easily be reached from Trapani and the town is also the port for the **Egadi Islands** and **Pantelleria**. The ancient industry of extracting salt from seawater evaporated in the ancient salt pans has recently been revived and is once more an important part of the local economy. Other local products include excellent olive oil, pickled olives and fine DOC wines, including those from Pantelleria, the various Marsalas and the famous *Bianco d'Alcamo*. In fact the province of Trapani produces more wine than any other in Italy, and has 42 per cent of the vineyards of Sicily.

TRAPANI

Trapani (population 70,000) lies below the headland of Mount Erice, with the Egadi Islands usually visible offshore. Its old quarter occupies a scimitar-shaped promontory between the open sea to the north and the port and salt marshes to the south, but from inland the town is approached through extensive modern suburbs laid out on a regular chessboard pattern. The elegant shops in the pedestrianised old town exude an air of opulence, the corso lined with interesting monumental buildings. Trapani has a number of unusual churches by the local architect Giovanni Biagio Amico (1684–1754). The collection of decorative arts in the Pepoli Museum is one of the best on the island, and attests to the traditional skill of the native sculptors, silversmiths and jewellers (particularly famous for their works in coral).

Practical information

 ### Getting there
By air

Vincenzo Florio Airport at Birgi, ☎ 0923/842502, ✉ www.airgest.com, 18km south. Daily services to Pantelleria, Rome, Milan Linate, Parma, Bergamo and Brescia by *Gandalf Air*, ☎ 0923/841777, and from 2003, also to Palermo and Catania. The connecting bus service for this airport is run by *AST* (☎ 0923/ 23222) from the bus station in piazza Malta.

By bus

Bus services run by *Autoservizi Segesta*, ☎ 0923/21754, from Palermo and from Falcone & Borsellino Airport at Punta Raisi terminate in piazza Garibaldi.

Around town. Town buses from the town centre to the Pepoli Museum (nos. 1, 10 and 11). The corso may be reached by buses from the station or Villa Margherita which terminate in piazza Generale Scio (near the Museum of Prehistory, at the end of the promontory).

Local buses are run by *AST* for Erice, Castellammare, San Vito lo Capo, Selinunte, Marsala, Mazara del Vallo and Nubia Salt Museum, and for Segesta by *Tarantola*, ☎ 0924/31020, all from piazza Malta.

By train

Railway station in piazza Umberto. Trains from Palermo, Marsala and Castelvetrano.

Car parking

On lungomare Dante Alighieri, in piazza Vittorio Veneto, or in via Mazzini (near the railway station).

Maritime services

Ferries to Pantelleria (daily June–Sept, exc. Sat Oct–May, in 4–5 hrs) and to the **Egadi Islands** (Favignana and Levanzo 4 daily, c 50 mins; Marettimo twice weekly, 2 hrs) from Molo della Sanità are run by *Siremar*, ☎ 0923/545455.

Hydrofoils for the Egadi Islands, run by *Siremar*, leave from Molo Dogana. Those run by *Ustica Lines*, 0923/22200, ✉ www.usticalines.it, leave from via Ammiraglio Staiti for the Egadi Islands, and in summer also for **Pantelleria**, **Naples** and **San Vito lo Capo**.

Ferries for Tunisia twice a week, one run by *Linea Alilauro*, ☎ 0923/24073, and the other by *Tirrenia*, ☎ 0923/21896, which also runs a service for Cagliari.

 Information offices

APT Trapani, 27 via S. Francesco d'Assisi, ☎ 0923/545511. Information office, piazza Saturno, ☎ 0923/29000.
Trapani on line: ✉ www.apt. trapani.it; ✉ www.cinet.it/apt; ✉ www. trapani-sicilia.it.

 Where to stay
Hotels

✫✫✫✫ *Crystal*, 17 via S. Giovanni Bosco, ☎ 0923/20000, ✉ 0923/25555, ✉ www.framon-hotels.it. New building in the modern city, luxurious rooms and good restaurant.
✫✫✫ *Nuovo Albergo Russo*, 4 via Tintori, ☎ 0923/22166, ✉ 0923/26623. Bright and comfortable, in front of the Cathedral in the atmospheric old town.
✫✫✫ *Vittoria*, 4 via Francesco Crispi, ☎ 0923/873044, ✉ 0923/29870, ✉ www.hotelvittoriatrapani.it. Pleasant situation, near bus and train stations.
✫✫ *Moderno*, 20 via Tenente Genovese, ☎ 0923/21247, ✉ 0923/23348. Good position in the old city.
✫ *Maccotta*, 4 via degli Argentieri, ☎ 0923/28418, ✉ 0923/437693, ✉ albergo-maccotta@comeg.it. In the old town. Comfortable rooms, friendly management.
S. CUSUMANO ✫✫✫ *Astoria Park*, lungomare Dante Alighieri, ☎ 0923/562400, ✉ 0923/567422, ✉ www.astoriaparkhotel.it. On the seafront not far from town. Fairly quiet; good restaurant, comfortable rooms; pool.

Farmhouse accommodation

✫✫✫✫ *Duca di Castelmonte*, contrada Xitta, 3 via Salvatore Motis, ☎ 0923/526139, ✉ 0923/883140, ✉ www.ducadicastelmonte.it. A comfortable old olive farm close to Trapani. Swimming pool, football and basketball; good restaurant.
✫✫✫ *Misiliscemi*, frazione Guarrato, Trapani, ☎ & ✉ 0923/864261, ✉ www.misiliscemi.it. Hilltop farm (summer only) between Erice and Marsala producing wine, olives, cereals and fruit; rabbits, chickens, pigs and sheep. Medieval castle nearby.

Campsite

BONAGIA ✫✫ *Lido Valderice*, just north of the town at Bonagia, 15 via del Dentice, ☎ 0923/573477, ✉ 0923/573086. On a shale beach, plenty of shade. Buses to Erice stop here.

 Eating out
Restaurants

€€€ *Da Peppe*, 50 via Spalti, ☎ 0923/28246; the home-made pasta is delicious. Closed Mon.
€€ *Cantina Siciliana*, 36 via Giudecca, ☎ 0923/28673. Excellent trattoria. Try chef Pino's *bruschette con uova di tonno* (croutons with tuna roe) as a starter, perhaps followed by fish couscous then

cassatelle di ricotta, an irrestistible dessert. Next door there is a well stocked wine shop run by the same management. **€€ *La Perla***, viale Motya contrada Marausa, ☎ 0923/841577. Outside the city to the south, by the salt pans where the flamingoes winter, is this simple restaurant indicated by the people of Trapani as being the very best place for seafood. Closed Mon.

€€ *Trattoria del Porto*, 45 via Ammiraglio Staiti, ☎ 0923/547822. Close to the dockside, a family-run restaurant preparing good simple food. Closed Mon.

€ *Trattoria Miramare*, 30 viale Regina Elena, ☎ 0923/20011. In front of the ferry terminal, a down-to-earth, family-run trattoria where tourists never come; excellent fish couscous and grilled squid, certainly one of the best restaurants in town.

Pizzerie

Calvino, 77 via Nunzio Nasi, ☎ 0923/21464. Simple, no frills. The best pizza in town. Closed Tues.

Pipitone, 8 via Fratelli Aiuto, Erice Casa Santa, ☎ 0923/531655. In the new town at the foot of Mount S. Giuliano, and well worth tracking down.

Cafés, pastry shops and ice cream parlours

Bar Novecento, 84 via Fardella, for authentic cassata siciliana.

Caffè Aiuto, 209 via Vespri.

Chupa-chupa, 108 via Bixio.

Colicchia, 6 via delle Arti, for Sicilian breakfast and cannoli di ricotta, also *granita di gelsomino*, sorbet made with jasmine flowers ('*scorsunera*')

La Voglia Matta, 160 via Manzoni, Erice Casa Santa district. Ice cream in Trapani is particularly good everywhere, but the locals say this is the best place, in the new part of town.

Picnics

A good place to picnic is in the gardens of Villa Margherita.

Handicrafts

Trapani has always been famous for its coral craftsmen. Today there is only one workshop remaining, ***Platimiro Fiorenza***, 36 via Osorio (behind Villa Margherita), ☎ 0923/20785. Platimiro makes exquisite jewellery using coral and silver. The coral comes mostly from Japan, since Trapani's coral reef is now protected by law. Using a secret procedure, ***Daniela Neri*** makes unique jewellery called *coralli di salina* which look exactly like antique pieces; they can be found at the *Ettore Infersa Salt Mill*, just outside Marsala, or in Trapani at *La Chiave*, 17 via San Pietro; at Erice, 2/B via De Stefano; in Palermo, 5 via Messina; in Rome, 13 via Vittoria and 4 via Toniolo, and in Genoa at 5 via Luccoli.

Internet point

Internet point, 31 via Carrara, ☎ 0923/593693; 09.00–13.00, 16.00–20.30, 21.30–24.00, open daily.

 ## Annual festivals

Procession on Good Friday of the **Misteri**, 20 groups of remarkable life-size figures in wood, linen and glue made in the 17C–18C, by local artists, including Andrea Tipa. Each group represents an episode in the Passion of Christ, and is carried by the representatives of the 20 corporations, or *mestieri*—hence the name. The procession starts at three in the afternoon, accompanied by a band playing sorrowful music, and continues all night long, and is so strangely hypnotizing, it is impossible to tear oneself away.

A music festival, the **Luglio Musicale Trapanese**, which usually includes opera, is held in the Villa Margherita in July.

History

Drepana or *Drepanon* (scythe), which occupied the promontory in ancient times and was once the port of Eryx (see p 170), but was raised to the status of a Phoenician city when Hamilcar Barca transferred part of the population of Eryx here in 260 BC. It was captured for the Romans by Catulus in 241. It acquired strategic importance as the maritime crossroads between Tunis, Anjou and Aragon in the 13C; King Theodore of Navarre died of typhoid here contracted near Tunis (1270), and here on the 'Scoglio del Malconsiglio', a rock at the extreme end of the cape, John of Procida is supposed to have plotted the Sicilian Vespers with his confederates. Edward I of England, who landed at Trapani on his return from the crusades in 1272, received the news of his accession to the throne here. The city was specially favoured by Peter of Aragon, who landed at Trapani as the saviour of Sicily in 1282, and by Charles V.

In 1940 and again in 1943 the city suffered many air raids and naval bombardments, the district of S. Pietro being razed to the ground.

From the large piazza Vittorio Emanuele (1869), with a monument to the king by Giovanni Duprè (1882), viale Regina Margherita skirts the north side of **Villa Margherita**, a lovely garden laid out in the late 19C, to **piazza Vittorio Veneto**, today's administrative centre. Here, early 20C buildings include the fine post office (1924). Close by is the old **Castello di Terra**, a castle which has been reconstructed during the centuries and which was converted into a barracks in the 19C. The outer walls have survived, but a modern building inside them now houses the police station. The streets to the north give access to the seafront, with a good view of the old city from its promontory.

Via Garibaldi leads towards the old centre past the 18C Palazzo Fardella Fontana, with an elaborate window above its portal, and the 18C Palazzo Riccio di Morana decorated with stuccoes. The 17C church of **S. Maria dell'Itria** has a façade completed in 1745. Inside is a sculptural group of the *Holy Family* by Andrea Tipa. Beyond is the 19C red-brick Palazzo Staiti opposite the 18C Palazzo Milo.

The salita S. Domenico (with steps and cobbled paving) leads up to the church of **S. Domenico**, with a blind 14C rose window. The interior contains a remarkable wooden *Crucifix* (thought to date from the 14C) in an 18C chapel by Giovanni Biagio Amico in the north aisle. Near the entrance is a 15C fresco fragment. The sanctuary preserves the sarcophagus of Manfred, son of Frederick III of Aragon. A chapel behind has some recently discovered fresco fragments of the 14C and 15C. The Baroque frames, pulpit and organ (in good condition), bear witness to the wealth of the city in the 18C, thanks to the importance of its salt and fishing industries.

Nearby, downhill to the south, is the church of **S. Nicolò Mirense**, which has a little garden. Inside is a 16C marble tabernacle on the east wall and in the left transept a striking sculptural group of *Christ between the two thieves*, a realistic 18C work in wood and papier mâché by a local sculptor. Via delle Arti and via della Badia lead back to via Garibaldi and the 17C façade of **S. Maria del Soccorso** (or the **Badia Nuova**), with a fine interior decorated in pink and grey marble and elaborate organ lofts. A short way back along via Garibaldi is the church of the **Carminello** (or S. Giuseppe), with an 18C portal with bizarre twisted columns. It was built in 1699 and the statue in the apse of *St Joseph and*

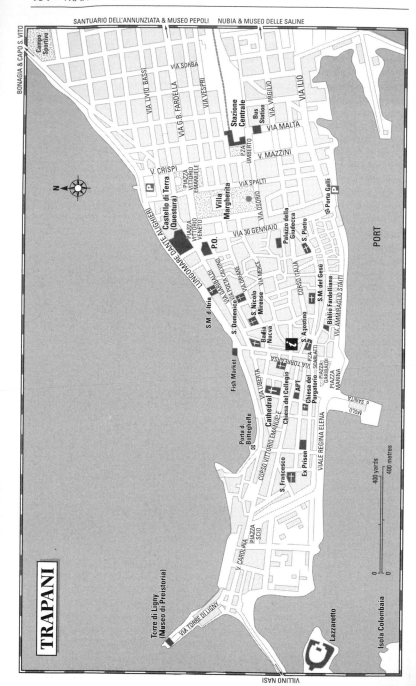

TRAPANI

SANTUARIO DELL'ANNUNZIATA & MUSEO PEPOLI   NUBIA & MUSEO DELLE SALINE

BONAGIA & CAPO S. VITO

Campo Sportivo

VIA LIVIO BASSI
VIA SORBA
VIA G.B. FARDELLA
VIA VESPRI
VIA VIRGILIO
VIA ILIO

Stazione Centrale
Bus Station
VIA MALTA
P.ZA UMBERTO
V. MAZZINI

V. CRISPI
PIAZZA VITTORIO EMANUELE
VIA SPALTI
Villa Margherita
VIA OSORIO

Castello di Terra (Questura)
PIAZZA VITTORIO VENETO
P.O.
VIA 30 GENNAIO

Porta Galli

LUNGOMARE DANTE ALIGHIERI

Palazzo della Giudecca
S. Pietro

S.M. d'Itria
VIA GARIBALDI
VIA PORTA CASINO
VIA ORDANE
VIA MERE
CORSO ITALIA

S. Domenico
S. Nicolo Mirense
Badia Nuova
S. Agostino
S.M. del Gesu
Biblio Fardelliana
VIA AMMIRAGLIO STAITI

Fish Market

VIA LIBERTA
VIA TORRE ARSA
PIAZZA GARIBALDI
PIAZZA MARINA
MOLO P. SANITA

Porta d'Botteghelle
CORSO VITTORIO EMANUELE
Cathedral
Chiesa del Collegio
APT
Chiesa del Purgatorio
PIAZZA SCARLATTI

S. Francesco
Ex Prison
VIALE REGINA ELENA

V. CAROLINA
PIAZZA SCIO

PORT

0   400 yards
0   400 metres

Torre di Ligny (Museo di Preistoria)
VIA TORRE DI LIGNY

Lazzaretto
Isola Colombaia

VILLINO NASI

the young Christ Child is a charming 18C sculpture by Antonio Nolfo (an earlier version of the statue, used for processions, is kept in the sacristy). A wooden *Crucifix* in the church is attributed to Giacomo Tartaglio.

From the Badia via Torrearsa leads right, past the 16C church of the **Carmine** with a fine exterior with tall pilasters and a high cornice, to the seafront passing an attractive market building (1874). Fish is sold under the portico and other produce is sold around a fountain with a statue of Venus in the piazza. Via Torrearsa leads in the other direction to **Palazzo Senatorio**, used as municipal offices, built in 1672, which has an eccentric theatrical façade with statues on the upper part.

From here the broad, handsome **corso Vittorio Emanuele** leads towards the end of the promontory. On the right is the **Chiesa del Collegio dei Gesuiti**, built c 1614–40 by Natale Masuccio, with a Baroque façade by Michelangelo Bonamici (1657). The interior, with stuccoes by Bartolomeo Sanseverino, has been closed for restoration for many years. Beyond the monumental former Collegio dei Gesuiti (now a school) is the **Cattedrale dl S. Lorenzo** (1635), built by Giovanni Biagio Amico in 1743, preceded by a portico. On the south side (fourth altar) is a *Crucifixion* attributed to the local 17C artist Giacomo Lo Verde, and on the north side (second altar) is a painting of *St George* by Andrea Carreca and (fourth altar) a fine painting of the *Deposition*, showing Flemish influence.

In front of the cathedral via Giglio leads to the **chiesa del Purgatorio** where the **figures of the Misteri** are kept in between the Good Friday processions (open daily 16.00–18.30, in the morning by arrangement, ☎ 0923/562882). The church has a fine tiled dome and elaborate façade by Giovanni Biagio Amico. Nearby in via S. Francesco is a 17C prison house, with four caryatids on its façade, and, further along, on the opposite side of via S. Francesco, the church of the **Immacolatella** with a delightful apse by Giovanni Biagio Amico (1732). At the end of via S. Francesco the church of **S. Francesco** (13C–17C) can be seen, with a green dome next to a fine doorway. Inside, on the left, is a curious 17C tombstone dedicated to the 'death of the nation of Armenia', with a bilingual inscription.

The corso continues past (left) the 18C Palazzo Berardo Ferro, which has an inviting courtyard, and then Palazzo Alessandro Ferro (1775), decorated with a clock and busts in medallions. Beyond on the right is the little Porta delle Botteghelle (13C), outside of which the defensive fortifications which protected the town from the sea can be seen. The corso, now at the narrowest part of the promontory (the sea can be seen at either end of the side streets), becomes less interesting. Some 800m further on (buses to piazza Generale Scio), via Torre di Ligny bears right and ends at the **Torre di Ligny**, a fortress built in 1671 by the Spanish Viceroy, on the tip of the promontory. It has been well restored to house the **Trapanese Museum of Prehistory** (closed for rearrangement).

From beside the Torre di Ligny there is a view across the bay to the **Isola Colombaia**, the base for the Romans' siege operations in 241 BC. An Aragonese castle here, the **Castello di Mare**, was restored in later centuries, and in 1714 the octagonal lantern was added by Giovanni Biagio Amico. It was used as a prison up until the 1960s. The boulevards which run alongside the harbour return to the town past (on the left) the so-called 'palazzo', a 14C building several times enlarged.

Near the south end of via Torrearsa (see above) is the restored Templars' church of **S. Agostino**, with its 14C rose window and portal (now used as a concert hall).

The Saturn fountain here is on the site of a 14C fountain. Nearby is the **Biblioteca Fardelliana**, the Civic Library, in the former church of S. Giacomo, with a fine Mannerist façade. Opened to the public in 1830, it contains some important manuscripts, and 90,000 volumes (open 10.00–13.00, 16.00–19.00; Sat 09.00–13.00, closed Sun & PH). In the rebuilt district of S. Pietro is **S. Maria del Gesù**, a church with a transitional 16C façade and a Renaissance south doorway bearing an *Annunciation* in Catalan-Gothic style. The fine simple interior, golden in colour, contains a decorative niche with a very beautiful *Madonna and Child* in enamelled terracotta by Andrea della Robbia under a marble baldachin by Antonello Gagini. Further east in the former Jewish district is the unusual **Palazzo della Giudecca**, usually called '*lo Spedaletto*', its embossed tower and 16C windows recalling the Plateresque style of Spain.

The Santuario dell'Annunziata

Inland, in the modern part of town (c 4km from the centre; bus nos 1, 10 and 11) is the Santuario dell'Annunziata (sanctuary of the Madonna of Trapani), founded in 1315 and rebuilt in 1760. Little remains of the 14C structure except the west front with a rose window which overlooks a garden. The bell tower dates from 1650. The entrance is through the north door on the main road. The unusual grey and white interior (open daily 07.00–12.00, 16.00–19.00, Sun & PH 07.00–13.00, 16.00–19.00; July and August late closing at 20.00) was redesigned in the 18C by Giovanni Biagio Amico. Off the right side is the beautiful **Cappella dei Pescatori** (the fishermen's chapel), built in 1481, perhaps an adaption of an earlier chapel. On the left of the presbytery is the **Cappella dei Marinai** (the seamen's chapel), another attractive chapel built in the 16C in a mixture of styles. From the sanctuary, which has a pretty apse, two fine 16C doorways lead into the **Cappella della Madonna**; here another arch, with sculptures by Antonino Gagini (1531–37) and a bronze gate of 1591 (by Giuliano Musarra), gives access to the inner sanctuary containing a highly venerated 14C statue of the *Madonna and Child*, known as the Madonna di Trapani, a very fine work by Nino Pisano or his workshop. Below it is a tiny silver model of Trapani by Vincenzo Bonaiuto, who also made the silver statue in the chapel of Saint Albert, to the right of this chapel.

Pepoli Regional Museum

In the former Carmelite convent, entered on the right of the façade of the church, is the Museo Regionale Pepoli (open 09.00–13.30, Sun & PH 09.00–12.30, Mon closed, ☎ 0923/553269 or 0923/531242). This includes a municipal collection formed in 1827, a group of paintings which belonged to General Giovanni Battista Fardella, and a large collection donated by Count Agostino Pepoli in 1906. The exhibits are beautifully arranged and well labelled. The entrance is through the paved 16C–17C cloisters, with palm trees. The rooms are not numbered but described below in their logical sequence.

Ground floor. Room I contains architectural fragments and Arab funerary inscriptions (10C–12C), and a wooden ceiling salvaged from a chapel. **Room II** contains a sculpted portal by Bartolomeo Berrettaro; a **stoup** of 1486 from the Santuario dell'Annunziata, and works by the Gaginis, notably a figure of *St James the Great*, by Antonello (1522). In the room on the left is a guillotine, complete with a basket for the head and a coffin.

The grand staircase (begun in 1639 and decorated in the 18C) leads up to the **first floor** where **rooms III–XI** are devoted to paintings of the Neapolitan and local schools. Room III, Master of the Trapani Polyptych, *Madonna and Child with saints* (from the church of S. Antonio Abate), Roberto di Oderisio, *Pietà* (c 1380). In **room IV** are three paintings by Il Pastura (Antonio del Massaro). **Room VI** contains *St Francis receiving the Stigmata*, attributed to Titian, and works by the local painters Andrea Carreca (1590–1677) and Giacomo Lo Verde. **Rooms VII–XI** display 17C Neapolitan works.

In the corridor there is a portrait of *Nunzio Nasi* by Giacomo Balla and cases of wooden figurines by Giovanni Matera (1653–1718) illustrating the *Massacre of the Innocents* in 16 tableaux. The bronze head of an old man is by Domenico Trentacoste. Also to be found here are 19C scenes of the *Adoration of the Magi* and *Nativity* by Andrea Tipa in wax, alabaster, and coral, a late 17C salt cellar; magnificent 18C–19C Sicilian coral jewellery and a 17C chalice.

In **rooms XII–XXI** is a superb collection of **decorative arts**, most of them made by local craftsmen in the 17C–19C, including silversmiths, jewellers and sculptors. Particularly important are the charming **crib figures**, the best by Giovanni Matera (1653–1718), and Nativity scenes.

At the end of the corridor there are some elaborate 17C objects in coral, a skill for which Trapani is particularly famous, notably a *Crucifixion* and a candelabra by Fra Matteo Bavera; 16C silver works from Nuremburg and exquisite jewellery made in Trapani. **Room XXI** contains locally made majolica, also pieces from Faenza and Montelupo. The archaeological collection in **rooms XXIII–XXIV** contains finds from Erice, Selinunte and Mozia, and coins of the 5C BC. At the top of the stairs, in the first corridor, are majolica tiled floors, including one with a splendid scene of tuna fishing (the *mattanza*). The small prints and drawings collection includes works by Stefano Della Bella and Jacopo Callot. The flag of *Il Lombardo*, the ship sailed by Garibaldi and the 'Thousand', is also owned by the museum.

The salt pans of Trapani

The *saline* or salt pans of Trapani can be seen from the secondary road which runs from the port to Marsala (to seaward of the railway line and the main road SS 115). A number of windmills survive, turning Archimedes' screws in order to raise the seawater from one pan to the next. Much of the area is now a WWF reserve, and flamingoes, great white herons, avocets and black-winged stilts are frequently seen (☎ and 📠 0923/867700).

At Nubia, on the coast c 5km south of Trapani, is the Salt Museum, the **Museo delle Saline** (open Mon–Sat 09.30–13.30, 15.30–18.30, sometimes open Sun & PH, ☎ 0923/867442 or 0923/867142). The old wooden mill is now used to illustrate the ancient salt extracting industry, started here by the Phoenicians and continuing in a number of salt pans between Trapani and Marsala. Thanks to the ever-increasing demand for natural, healthy foodstuffs, piles of salt, protected by tiles, are a common sight in the area, the salt

The salt pans of Trapani

being exported all over Europe. Trapani is the ideal place for making salt, because it is both windy and sunny, factors which favour evaporation, and the seawater has a naturally high level of salinity. From February to March seawater is pumped by the windmills from a canal into the salt pans. The water level is gradually decreased which encourages the evaporation process and the water assumes a reddish colour as the mineral content becomes stronger. The harvest begins in July, before total evaporation, to avoid the deposit of harmful minerals; the salt is raked from the pans to form the characteristic mounds visible on the banks, which are then covered with tiles for protection.

ERICE

· · · · · ·

Erice is a peaceful little medieval town (population 350) perched on top of an isolated limestone spur (751m), high above the sea. The resident population is diminishing rapidly, and many of its houses are now occupied only in the summer months by residents of Trapani or Palermo who come here on holiday to escape the heat: the number of inhabitants in August rises to about 5000. The locals call their town '*u Munti*', the mountain. It is often shrouded in a mist, known as '*il velo di Venere*' (Venus's veil), and it can be very chilly here, even snowy in winter, which contributes to its feeling of isolation. The perfect triangular shape of the town makes it difficult to find one's bearings, despite the fact that it is so small. The view to the north of Monte Cofano, one of the most beautiful promontories on the coast of Sicily, is unforgettable. To the southwest there is another remarkable view of Trapani and the Egadi Islands, and, on a clear day, Cape Bon in Tunisia can be seen, and looking east, even Mount Etna.

The grey stone houses of Erice (mostly dating from the 14C to 17C), hidden behind their high courtyard walls and the beautifully paved streets, usually deserted, give the town an austere aspect. But behind the walls are many charming courtyards, some of which have little gardens.

The pastries made here are unique in Sicily, beautiful to look at as well as good to eat, and were once made by the nuns of the many convents in the town. A number of churches in the town, including the Matrice, are now open regularly.

Practical information

Getting there
By bus

Buses from Trapani in c 40 mins (the cableway at the end of via Fardella at Raganzili has been out of action for more than 30 years but there are plans to rebuild it).

By car

Three roads ascend the hill from Trapani. The most spectacular leaves the east end of the town at Raganzili

(via Martogna) beside the disused cableway station and ascends in 14km. It passes beneath the cableway and begins to climb through pine woods, with fine views of Trapani and the Egadi Islands. Higher up it rounds the hill to reveal Monte Cofano and Capo S. Vito in the distance, then crosses an upland plain with a few vineyards and a picturesque group of abandoned farmhouses on a promontory. It then passes the turn for the S. Matteo Forest Museum (described

...he end of this chapter), joining the
...ad from Valderice and passing
...hrough dense woodland before entering Erice. Another road (constructed by
the Bourbons in 1850) forks left from
road SS187 outside Trapani and climbs
via the cemetery to the summit (10.5
km). The longest and the easiest road
(17km) forks off from road SS187 at
Valderice.

Parking

Outside Porta Trapani (in August a car
park is open near the youth hostel with
a minibus service to the centre).

Walking

Visitors to the town should remember to
wear suitable shoes with non-slip soles:
the streets are steep and paved with slippery stones.

Information office

Azienda Autonoma, 11 viale Conte
Pepoli, ☎ 0923/869388.

Where to stay
Hotels

✮✮✮ *Elimo*, 75 via Vittorio
Emanuele, ☎ 0923/869377, ▤ 0923/
869252, ✉ www.charmerelax.com,
www.elimohotel.com. Small and comfortable, on the main street, with a
rooftop terrace, garage and lovely little
courtyard garden.

✮✮✮ *La Pineta*, viale Nunzio Nasi,
☎ 0923/869783, ▤ 0923/869788.
1950s' building in the pinewoods below
the town.

✮✮✮ *Moderno*, 63 via Vittorio Emanuele,
☎ 0923/869300, ▤ 0923/869139,
✉ www.pippocatalano.it. Fascinating
old hotel with exceptionally good restaurant.

✮✮ *Edelweiss*, 5 cortile P. Vincenzo,
☎ 0923/869420, ▤ 0923/869158.
Very small; early booking is essential.

✮✮ *Ermione*, 43 via Pineta, ☎ 0923/
869138, ▤ 0923/869587, ✉ www.
ermionehotel.com. Built in the 1960s,
this hotel is a little bleak. In the
pinewoods a short walk from the town.

VALDERICE (at the foot of the mountain) ✮✮✮ *Baglio Santacroce*, SS187,
Valderice, ☎ 0923/891111, ▤ 0923/
891192, ✉ www.bagliosantacroce.it.
Elegant hotel, once a farmhouse (built
in 1627). Gardens, pool, delightful
views and a good restaurant.

✮✮✮ *Ericevalle*, 1 via del Cipresso,
Valderice, ☎ 0923/891133, ▤ 0923/
833178. Modern, comfortable hotel in
pleasant quiet position close to the town
of Valderice.

Bed and breakfast

ERICE ✮✮✮ *Agorà*, 111 via Vittorio
Emanuele, ☎ 0923/860133, ✉ www.
agoraerice.com. Lovely medieval house
within the ancient walls. Car space too.

✮✮✮ *Ashram*, 16 via Martogna, ☎ & ▤
0923/560606, ✉ www.ashram.it. The
former convent of S. Maria degli Angeli,
a short distance from town. Excursions
for guests, horseriding, handicrafts and
yoga. Very good cooking.

✮✮✮ *Maria Luisa*, 1 via Luigi Barberi,
☎ 347/7893651, ✉ luisaperaino@
libero.it; English spoken.

VALDERICE ✮✮✮ *Baglio Scuderi*, via
A. Fanara, ☎ 0923/833359,
✉ baglioscuderi@interfree.it.

Farmhouse accommodation

Belvedere San Nicola, contrada San
Nicola, Erice, ☎ 0923/860124,
▤ 0923/869139, ✉ www.pippo
catalano.it. Converted farmhouse.
Wonderful views. Really a small country
hotel under the same management as
Hotel Moderno. Excellent restaurant
and wine cellar. Horseriding, pool and
children's play area.

Youth hostels

Ostello della Gioventù G. Amodeo, contrada Raganzili, ☎ & ▤ 0923/552964.
At the foot of the hill on the Martogna
road. Well organized; excellent restaurant; disco.

Ostello della Gioventù, C.S.I., via delle

Pinete, ☎ & 🖶 0923/869144. Summer only.

Eating out
Restaurants

€€€ *La Pentolaccia*, 17 via Guarnotti, ☎ 0923/869362. The best couscous in Erice. Closed Tues.

€€€ *Moderno*, 63 via Vittorio Emanuele, ☎ 0923/869300. Exceptionally good, the restaurant is part of the *Buon Ricordo* chain.

€€ *Caffè San Rocco*, 23 via Guarnotti, ☎ 0923/869337. Welcoming bar and restaurant, crowded with scientists from the nearby Majorana centre. Tasty pasta. Closed Wed.

€€ *La Vetta da Mario*, 5 via Fontana, ☎ 0923/869404. Simple dishes and pizza in the evening. Closed Thurs.

Cafés and pastry shops

Caffè Maria, 4 via Vittorio Emanuele. In a beautifully furnished 19C house. Maria Grammatico, immortalized by Mary Taylor Simeti in *On Persephone's Island* and *Bitter Almonds*, is one of the most accomplished pastry-cooks in Sicily. Brought up by the nuns of S. Carlo in Erice, she was taught her craft in the tiniest detail. Her shop is called *Pasticceria Grammatico* at 14 via Vittorio Emanuele. Apart from the famous little cakes, Maria makes delectable *genovesi*, tiny shortcrust pastry pies filled with confectioners' custard, served warm. One of her Easter Lambs, made of marzipan and filled with candied citron, is on show at the American Craft Museum, New York.

There are two more excellent pastry shops near S. Domenico: *Antica Pasticceria del Convento* and *Silvestro*.

Picnics

At Villa Balio or in the pinewoods below the walls (off viale delle Pinete), or at the S. Matteo Museum.

Shopping
Rugs and tapestries

The women of Erice still weave the bright cotton rugs, once made of rags, which they call *frazzate*. Anna Angelo has a little shop at no. 9, via Vittorio Emanuele where she weaves them and sells them too. Signora Parisi, in via Pepoli, makes delightful rugs and tapestries.

Pottery

The pottery is unusual, with attractive floral ramages. A good address is *Ceramica Ericina*, 42 via Guarnotti.

Annual festivals
Procession of the Misteri on Good Friday. **Estate Ericina** festival in July and August, with music and art exhibitions. Last Wednesday in August is the **Feast of Our Lady of Custonaci**, the patron saint, with a magnificent procession organized by the women, who wear medieval dress. Coinciding with Christmas and New Year celebrations, is the unique bagpipe and folk music competition in which musicians from all over the world participate; the winner takes home the coveted *zampogna d'oro*, the golden bagpipes.

History

Eryx, an Elymian city of mythical origin, was famous all over the Mediterranean for the magnificent temple of the goddess of fertility, known to the Romans as Venus Erycina. This splendid site, naturally defended and visible for miles around, was a noted landmark for navigators from Africa. An altar to the goddess was first set up here by the Sicans and the sanctuary became famous during the Elymian and Phoenician period. The Carthaginians, who venerated her as Ashtarte, released every year from here hundreds of white doves and one red one to represent the goddess, which arrived nine days later at the temple of Sicca Veneria at Carthage. This ceremony took place in mid-August; by coincidence the feast of the patron saint of Erice, Our Lady of Custonaci, was always held on 16 August.

In 415 BC the inhabitants of nearby Segesta took the visiting Athenian ambassadors to see the rich treasury of the temple, which convinced Athens to take their side against Selinunte and Syracuse, a decision which led to the fatal attack on Syracuse in 413 BC and the consequent defeat of the Athenians. Captured by Pyrrhus in 278 BC it was destroyed in 260 by Hamilcar. The Roman consul L. Junius Pullus took the hill in 248 and was besieged by Hamilcar, who was himself blockaded by a Roman army, until the Carthaginians were defeated by the Romans, led by Catulus. The cult of Venus Erycina reached its maximum splendour under the Romans and the sanctuary was restored for the last time by Tiberius and Claudius. The Saracens called the place *Gebel Hamed*, which Count Roger—who had seen St Julian in a dream while besieging it—changed to Monte S. Giuliano, a name it kept until 1934. The city thrived in the 18C (population of around 12,000) and there were many religious communities. The town is now world famous for its Ettore Majorana Cultural Centre, founded by the local physicist Antonino Zichichi in 1963.

The entrance to the town is by **Porta Trapani**, beyond which via Vittorio Emanuele climbs steeply uphill. Just to the left is the **Matrice** (Assunta), which has a beautiful fortified Gothic exterior. The porch dates from 1426. The splendid detached **campanile** was built as an Aragonese look-out tower c 1315 by Frederic III, several years before the foundation of the church. The **interior** (open 09.30–12.00, 15.30–18.00, ☎ 0923/869123) received its impressive neo-Gothic form, with an elaborate cream-coloured vault, in 1852. The side chapels have pretty tiled floors. The apse is filled with a huge marble altarpiece by Giuliano Mancino (1513). In the sanctuary, through a small round opening on the left wall, a fresco fragment of an angel can be seen, the only part of the 15C decoration of the church to have survived. In a chapel on the left the 16C painting of the *Madonna of Custonaci* (the venerated patron of Erice) was replaced in 1892 by the present copy when the original was taken back to the sanctuary of Custonaci on the coast. The next chapel, with a beautiful dome, dates from 1568. Another chapel on this side has early 19C paintings. In a chapel on the right side is a *Madonna* by Domenico Gagini (1469), with a finely carved base. Outside, on the right wall, there are nine iron crosses, said to come from the temple of Venus.

Via Vittorio Emanuele continues steeply uphill past several old shop fronts and characteristic courtyards. At a fork via Vittorio Emanuele continues left past the old ruined Gothic church of S. Salvatore beside a lovely old narrow lane which leads downhill (and has a distant view of the sea). To the right via Bonaventura Provenzano ends at a house with a Baroque doorway and window near the church of **S. Martino** (open 15.00–18.00), with another Baroque portal, and an interesting 15C statue of the *Madonna* in the interior. Just before reaching piazza Umberto, beside a charming café in a 19C palace, a flight of steps leads down left to the monumental doorway with four columns of S. Rocco (closed).

The central piazza Umberto is the only large open space in the town. An elegant palazzo is now used by a bank, and a long 19C building houses the Town Hall and the **Cordici Library and Civic Museum** (open Mon–Fri 08.30–

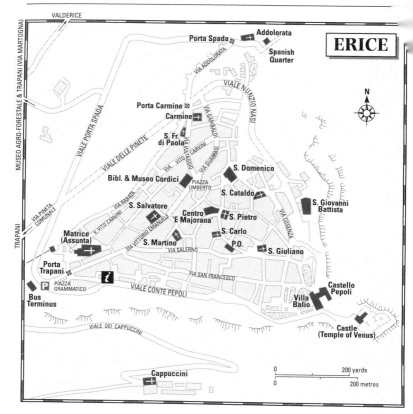

13.30, Mon and Thurs also 14.30–17.00; or on request), named after the local historian Antonino Cordici (1586–1666). The library was founded in 1867 with material from the suppressed convents of the city. It now has c 20,000 volumes. In the entrance hall is a beautiful relief of the **Annunciation** by Antonello Gagini, one of his finest works (1525), and a number of inscriptions. Upstairs in the small museum are interesting local archaeological finds (including a small Attic head of **Venus**, 5C BC); a 15C well-head; 16C–18C church vestments; a painting of **St Mary Magdalene and Martha** by the local 17C artist, Andrea Carreca; and a wooden **Crucifix** by Pietro Orlando (also 17C).

Via Guarrasi leads ahead out of the piazza and immediately on the left a stepped lane (via Argentieri) leads down across via Carvini into via Vultaggio which continues to wind down past the 17C church of **S. Francesco di Paola** (open 10.30–12.30) with a classical façade. The delightful interior was restored in 1954 by an American benefactor. It has white stucco decoration in very low relief on the walls and the barrel vault, a worn tiled floor in the sanctuary, fine woodwork, and popular votive statues.

Lower down on the right is the 14C Palazzo Militari with Gothic traces next to the Gothic church of the **Carmine** (closed). Porta Carmine stands nearby, with the worn headless statue of the Blessed Albert in a niche, on its outer face.

magnificent **walls** here, which stretch from Porta Spada to Porta Trapani, ~~p~~tected the only side of the hill which has no natural defences: on all the other ~~si~~des the sheer rock face made the town one of the most impregnable fortresses ~~o~~n the island. The walls are constructed on huge blocks of rough stone which probably date from the Elymian period (c 1200 BC), above which can be seen the square blocks added by the Carthaginians. The masonry in the upper parts, with stones of smaller dimension, date from the 6C BC. The defences were strengthened in the Roman era and in the Middle Ages, and six postern gates and 16 medieval towers survive. Inside the gate the stepped via Addolorata leads down past a well-preserved stretch of the walls, with a distant view ahead of Monte Cofano, to the church of the **Addolorata** (or S. Orsola; closed), surrounded by a little garden. It has an interesting 15C–16C plan. The 18C **Misteri sculptures** are kept here, which are taken in procession through the streets of Erice on Good Friday. In this remote and picturesque corner of the town is the Norman **Porta Spada**. Outside Porta Spada is the so-called **Quartiere Spagnolo**, a desolate group of buildings on a spur, intended by the Spanish to be the barracks for their troops in the 17C, and for some reason, never finished. Plans to complete the structure and transform it into a hostel will probably never materialize, because the local people say the place is haunted—particularly by *Birrittu Russu* or Red Cap, a mysterious phantom who has been spotted over the centuries in various parts of the city, but especially in the Spanish Quarter—and it is easy to believe it on damp foggy winter nights.

From Porta Carmine (see above) via Rabatà leads back to Porta Trapani following the walls where there are a number of postern gates. Tiny narrow alleyways, designed to avoid the wind, lead up left to via Carvini and piazza Umberto.

From piazza Umberto (see above), in front of the museum, via Antonio Cordici leads up out of the piazza past a few shops to piazza S. Domenico. The former church of **S. Domenico**, with a classical porch, has been restored as a lecture hall for the Centro Majorana (see below). From the right side of the church via S. Cataldo leads downhill (and right) past a neo-Gothic electricity tower to the bare façade of S. Cataldo (open for services only) on the edge of the old town. It was founded before 1339, and rebuilt in 1740–86. It contains a stoup of 1474 by the workshop of Domenico Gagini, and a painting by Andrea Carreca.

Further downhill and to the right is the church of S. Giovanni Battista (deconsecrated, opened on request by the religious community here) on the cliff edge, with a 15C dome whose shape recalls Arab architecture, and an ancient side doorway. It contains a statue of *St John the Evangelist* by Antonello Gagini, and of *St John the Baptist* by Antonino Gagini.

From piazza S. Domenico (see above), via Guarnotti leads up right to the church of S. Pietro (open for services) with an 18C portal. The beautiful white interior by Giovanni Biagio Amico (1745) has a worn tiled floor. Beside it is an arch over the road and on the right (at no. 26) a convent has been restored as the headquarters of the **Ettore Majorana International Centre for Scientific Culture**. Founded in 1963, this has become a famous centre of learning where courses and seminars are held for scientists from all over the world.

Via Guarnotti continues past the former convent and orphanage of **S. Carlo** next to the bare façade of the church of S. Carlo (open 10.30–12.30). It has a pretty majolica floor, and on a side altar there is a statue of the *Our Lady of Succour* with a tiny relief of St Michael Archangel on the base. The nuns' choirs are protected with carved wooden screens. On the right is the post office a downhill on the left is a pleasant raised piazza with the statue of a local saint, th *Blessed Albert*, in front of the church of **S. Giuliano** (deconsecrated, used by a religious community), with an elegant 18C campanile. The road continues down past two very old shop fronts and crosses via Porta Gervasi (with a view left of the church of S. Giovanni Battista with its dome, see above). A ramp leads up right to **Villa Balio**, delightful public **gardens** laid out in 1870 by Count Agostino Pepoli on the summit of the hill with wonderful views. It has a monumental entrance with a double staircase on via S. Francesco. Above is the **Castello Pepoli** (still privately owned by the Pepoli; no admission), a Norman castle reconstructed in 1875–85 by Count Pepoli, with a 15C tower restored in 1973. The excellent view from the terrace on the left encompasses Monte Cofano, the coast, and S. Giovanni Battista on the side of the hill. Below, among the trees you can see the abandoned neo-Gothic Torretta, also built by Count Pepoli.

A ramp leads down from the gardens beside the castle to viale Conte Pepoli, on the southern edge of the hill, which continues left to end beside the 17C steps up to the **Castello di Venere** (opened daily by volunteers 08.30–13.30, and sometimes in the afternoon), on the edge of the rock. Above the entrance to the castle is the coat of arms of Charles V and a Gothic window. In the disappointing interior, the ruined Norman walls surround the sacred area which was once the site of the famous Temple of Venus (see above), many fragments of which are embedded in the masonry of the castle. A few very worn Roman fluted column drums can be seen here and the so-called '*Pozzo di Venere*', once thought to be a ceremonial pool but more probably a silo or a water cistern. The view is breathtaking, extending to Mount Etna, Enna, and Caltabellotta.

Sacred prostitution at the temple of Venus

As in Corinth and at Sicca Veneria, sacred prostitution was carried out at the temple of Erice. Families could leave unwanted young girls, even babies, at the temple, where they would be brought up and instructed in the arts of lovemaking. The geographer Strabo tells us that anyone wishing to absolve a vow, man or woman, could leave girl slaves at the temple to become prostitutes. They started their career at the age of 12 or 13, and retired at 21, rich and much sought after as wives. Visitors to the temple to worship Venus, were expected to leave gifts for the girls in exchange for the act of love, during which it was believed that they assumed the guise of the goddess herself. The girls were fed on large quantities of milk and honey in order to make them pleasantly fat. They seldom conceived, perhaps because they were made to drink a potion prepared by the priests (parsley and hemlock? absinthe? sylphium? wild carrot juice?), about which we know very little.

On the hillside below the town is the interesting S. Matteo Forest Museum (open daily 08.00–14.00, ☎ 0923/869532). It is reached from the Raganzili road (described at the beginning of this chapter). About 3km below Erice a signposted turn leads in c 500m to the gates of the estate, run by the forestry commission. A rough road (c 1km) continues to the museum in the lovely old Baglio di S. Matteo, arranged in rooms around the courtyard. The exhibits include wine- and olive-presses, farm carts, saddle and tack, agricultural implements and household objects. There is also a natural history section. The beautifully kept farm of

500 ha may also be visited, where workhorses (a Sicilian breed known as 'San ratello') are raised. The site is spectacular with fine views towards Capo S. Vito, and the vegetation includes dwarf palm trees, cypresses, fruit trees and forest trees (experimental replanting is being carried out). A path leads past a small paleochristian oratory, below ground level. A smithy and carpentry shop operate on the estate.

S. VITO LO CAPO & CASTELLAMMARE DEL GOLFO

This chapter covers the coastal areas northeast of Trapani, including S. Vito lo Capo on the northernmost tip of the island and the town of Castellammare del Golfo. One part of this coast is now protected; the beautiful **wildlife reserve**, the Riserva Naturale dello Zingaro, can be explored on foot.

Practical information

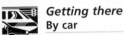

Getting there
By car

A road (38km) runs along the coast north from Trapani to Custonaci where it skirts Monte Cofano, and continues to S. Vito lo Capo, ending at the northern entrance to the Zingaro wildlife reserve just beyond the town. Castellammare del Golfo, 37km from Trapani, can only be reached by the road across the base of the peninsular via Valderice.

By bus

Buses from Palermo are run by *Autoservizi Russo*, ☎ 0924/31364, and from Trapani by *AST*, ☎ 0923/23222. The picturesque village of **Scopello** and its old tunny fishery are reached along a byroad (10km) from Castellammare. The buses from Castellammare are run by *Russo*.

Information offices
APT Trapani, ☎ 0923/545511.
Azienda Autonoma, via Savoia, San Vito lo Capo, ☎ 0923/972464.
Town Hall Tourist Office, 6 via de Gasperi, Castellammare del Golfo, ☎ 0924/592303-304, 📠 0924/30217.

Information Point, 1 viale Umberto, Castellammare del Golfo, ☎ 0924/31320.

Where to stay
Hotels

BONAGIA ☆☆☆☆ *La Tonnara di Bonagia*, piazza Tonnara, ☎ 0923/431111, 📠 0923/592177, ✉ www.framon-hotels.com. Beautifully restored tuna fishery on a tiny harbour, lovely rooms, some with private garden, apartments, internet, good restaurant, tennis, volleyball, seven-a-side football, bowls, pools, children's play area and diving centre.

☆☆☆ *Saverino*, via Lungomare, ☎ 0923/592727, 📠 0923/592388, ✉ hotelsav @libero.it. Family-run hotel, with an excellent restaurant.

CASTELLAMMARE DEL GOLFO
☆☆☆ *Al Madarig*, 7 piazza Petrolo, close to the castle and the old city, ☎ 0924/33533, 📠 0924/33790, ✉ www.almadarig.com.

☆☆☆ *Punta Nord Est*, 67 viale Leonardo da Vinci, ☎ 0924/30511, 📠 0924/30713, ✉ www.puntanordest.com. New hotel on the outskirts. Longish walk to the centre.

☆☆ *Belvedere*, SS187, ☎ & 📠 0924/

33330, ✉ www.hotelbelvedere.net. Spectacular position on the montain overlooking the bay, on the road to Scopello.

CUSTONACI ☆ *Cala Buguto*, 1 via D, contrada Scurati, ☎ 0923/973953, 📠 0923/973954, ✉ www.calabuguto. com. Tiny hotel recently opened in an old house not far from the Mangiapane Cave which encloses the hamlet of Scurati. Delicious meals on request.

☆ *Il Cortile*, 67 via Scurati, ☎ 0923/971750, 📠 0923/971029. Delightful little hotel in a *baglio* (fortified farmhouse) close to the Sanctuary, with restaurant serving excellent simple local dishes and good local wine. The owner, signor Andrea Oddo, is founder-member of the *Living Crib Association* (see below).

PIZZOLUNGO ☆☆☆ *L'Approdo*, 3 via Enea, ☎ 0923/571555, 📠 0923/571541, ✉ www.hotelapprodo.it. Small, simple hotel on the coast where Aeneas supposedly disembarked.

☆☆☆ *Tirreno*, 37 via Enea, ☎ 0923/571078, 📠 0923/571109, ✉ www.tirrenohotel.com. Just the place for people who love boats, and for scuba divers. This comfortable hotel has its own little harbour and organizes sailing and excursions.

S. VITO LO CAPO ☆☆☆☆ *Capo S. Vito*, 29 via Tommaso, ☎ 0923/972122, 📠 0923/972559, ✉ www.caposanvito.it. Right on the beach; garden, candlelight dinners on the terrace, well furnished rooms.

☆☆☆ *Egitarso*, 54 via Lungomare, ☎ 0923/972111; 📠 0923/972062, ✉ www.hotelegitarso.it. Pleasant location close to the beach. Welcoming rooms.

☆☆☆ *Mediterraneo*, 61 via Generale Arimondi, ☎ 0923/621062, 📠 0923/621061, ✉ www.hotelmediterraneo online.com. Small, elegant and comfortable.

☆☆ *Halimeda*, 100 via Generale Arimondi, ☎ & 📠 0923/972399, ✉ www.hotelhalimeda.com. Very sma... comfortable hotel. No restaurant.

☆☆ *Miraspiaggia*, 44 via lungomare, ☎ 0923/972355, 📠 0923/972263, ✉ www.miraspiaggia.it. Family hotel close to the beach, with good restaurant.

☆☆ *Pocho*, contrada Makari, ☎ & 📠 0923/972525, ✉ www.sicilian. net/pocho. Tiny hotel out of town, in a spectacular position, pool and good restaurant.

☆☆ *Riva del Sole*, 11 via Generale Arimondi, ☎ 0923/972629, 📠 0923/972621. Dependable little hotel, close to the beach.

☆ *Costa Gaia*, 123-125 via Savoia, ☎ 0923/972268, ✉ www.albergo costagaia.com. Small hotel with restaurant. Central; well run.

☆ *Locanda Lighea*, 1 via Immacolata, ☎ 0923/621023 or 349/2946032. Tiny inn about 600 yards from the beach.

☆ *Sabbia D'Oro*, 90 via Cavour, ☎ 0923/621405, 📠 0923/621163, ✉ www.hotelsabbiadoro.com. Close to the beach, ideal for families.

SCOPELLO There are several small, simple hotels with good restaurants in this charming village.

☆ *La Tavernetta*, 3 via Armando Diaz, ☎ & 📠 0924/541129.

☆ *Torre Bennistra*, 9 via Armando Diaz, and 19 via Natale di Roma, ☎ 0924/541128, 📠 0924/541128.

☆ *Tranchina*, 7 via Armando Diaz, ☎ & 📠 0924/541099.

Houses to rent

Rooms or apartments in the beautiful old 13C tuna fishery, Marfaraggio, at Scopello, close to the Zingaro wildlife reserve. Call Sig. Bargione, ☎ 091/328734 (only Italian spoken). A fascinating, expensive and exclusive experience.

Agenzia Viaggi Zingaro, ☎ 0924/31042, ✉ www.zingaroviaggi.it. Houses, villa and car hire.

SAN VITO LO CAPO *Maremonti*,

5 via Amodeo, ☎ 0923/972231, ⊟ 0923/621121, ✉ www.sanvito maremonti.com. Houses, apartments or rooms.

Farmhouse accommodation

CASTELLAMMARE DEL GOLFO
✩✩ *Camillo Finazzo*, contrada Badia Molinazzo. Small farm well placed for exploring the surrounding area. Self-catering or restaurant.

PIZZOLUNGO ✩✩✩ Adragna Pizzolungo, contrada San Cusumano, ☎ 0923/563710, ⊟ 0923/569780, ✉ www.pizzolungo.it. In a stunning position between Mt. San Giuliano and the sea, the farm produces wine, olives, vegetables and cereals; delightful rooms, good food and wine, or self-catering.

Bed and breakfast

SCOPELLO ✩✩✩ *Scopello*, 12 via Natale di Roma, ☎ & ⊟ 0924/541129. ✩✩✩ *The Best*, località Scopello, ☎ 0924/ 541031. ✩✩ *Angelo*, 4 via Marco Polo, ☎ 368/ 3654482, ✉ www.web.tiscali.it/case vacanze_angelo/.

Campsites

CASTELLAMMARE DEL GOLFO
✩✩✩ *Baia di Guidaloca*, ☎ 0924/ 541262, ⊟ 0924/35100.
✩✩✩ *Lu Baruni*, 27 località Barone, ☎ 0924/39133, ⊟ 0924/39133, ✉ www.elimi.it.
✩✩✩ *Nausicaa*, località Forgia, ☎ 0924/33030, ⊟ 0924/35173, ✉ www.nausica-camping.it.
✩✩ *Ciauli*, località Ciauli, ☎ 0924/ 39049.

S. VITO LO CAPO ✩✩✩✩ *El Bahira*, località Makari (Salinella), ☎ 0923/ 972577, ⊟ 0923/972552, ✉ www.elbahira.it. Lovely location, but long walk to the town.
✩✩✩ *La Fata*, via Mattarella, ☎ & ⊟ 0923/972133. Very central position.
✩✩✩ *La Pineta*, 88 via del Secco, ☎ 0923/972818, ⊟ 0923/974070, ✉ www.campinglapineta.it. Bar and

pizzeria on the premises.
✩✩ *Soleado*, 40 via del Secco, ☎ & ⊟ 0923/972166.

Eating out
Restaurants

CASTELLAMMARE DEL GOLFO €€ *La Cambusa*, 67 Cala Marina, ☎ 0924/30155, on the harbour. Excellent grilled fish. Closed Thurs. in winter.

€€ *Old Station*, 67 via Francesco Crispi, ☎ 0924/31414. On the main street in the new part of town. Relaxed atmosphere in this restaurant but the chef is a genius: wonderful *busiate alla Mondellana*, fresh home-made pasta served with a dressing of swordfish, aubergines and mint. Closed Mon.

€ *Kalos*, 4 piazza Petrolo, ☎ 0924/ 35210. An excellent pizzeria near the castle. Closed Tues.

€ *Lo Spiticchio*, piazza Petrolo, ☎ 0924/30889. Tasty snacks, sandwiches, couscous, spitroasted chicken, rabbit, excellent bread and olives. Closed Mon.

CUSTONACI €€€ *Stele d'Anchise*, piazza Riviera, contrada Cornino, ☎ 0923/971053. This little village is 20km from Trapani but it is well worth the journey. The shellfish are exceptionally good: oysters, clams, mussels, razorshells, shrimps and prawns, also lobster and sometimes crab. Closed Mon.

SAN VITO LO CAPO €€ *Gna Sara*, 6 via Abruzzi, ☎ 0923/972100. Welcoming trattoria, for the very best local cuisine. Closed Mon.

€€ *Tha'am*, 32 via Duca degli Abruzzi, ☎ 0923/972836. Delicious North African and Sicilian dishes, including kebabs, and Moroccan mint tea. Closed Wed. in winter.

SCOPELLO €€ *Torre Bennistra*, 9 via Armando Diaz, ☎ 0924/541128. The best restaurant in Scopello.

Cafés, pastry shops and ice cream parlours

SAN VITO LO CAPO *La Piazzetta*, 43 via Savoia. For the famous *caldofreddo*: ice cream and biscuits covered with hot chocolate sauce.
Bar Cusenza, via Savoia (next to the church of S.Vito), for Sicilian breakfast.
La Sirenetta, via Savoia (corner via Faro), for the best ice cream.
SCOPELLO *Bar Scopello*, 13 via A. Diaz. For Sicilian breakfast and the very best *cannoli di ricotta* or genoese pastries.

Sports

Scopello Cetaria Diving Centre, ☎ 0924/34222.

Beaches

San Vito lo Capo is renowned for its sandy beach, one of the loveliest in Italy. In the Zingaro Wildlife Reserve there are many little coves and small beaches, for memorable swimming. At Castellammare swimming is possible from Cala Marina, the old harbour, but most people prefer the magnificent sands of the Plaia, to the east of town. There is a small secluded beach just below the Hotel Madarig.

 ### Annual festivals

At S. Vito lo Capo in September, there is an international festival called **Cous Cous Fest**, with cooks from all around the Mediterranean competing for the trophy awarded for the best couscous. From 13–15 June the patron **Saint Vitus** is celebrated, culminating with firework displays and a competition among the fishermen who try to walk along a slippery pole suspended over the water to get a flag at the far end. People wear traditional dress during the festival. At Scurati (near Custonaci) the '**Living Crib**' takes place at Christmas. Local crafts and trades are on show in the houses of the now uninhabited village.

The road from Trapani to Capo San Vito

At the foot of Monte S. Giuliano is **San Cusumano** where a salt pan windmill can be seen, near a tuna fishery. Ships are alerted to the low-lying islands offshore here by a lighthouse. **Pizzolungo** is the spot where, according to Virgil, Aeneas came ashore, welcomed by King Acestes of Eryx. When they arrived, his father Anchises died, so he was obliged to bury him here (a white column commemorates this). During a subsequent visit his fleet caught fire, so on the whole Sicily could not have held happy memories for poor Aeneas. No wonder he went further afield to found his new kingdom. At **Bonagia** there is a picturesque tuna fishery which has been restored as a hotel (see *Where to stay*). Beside the little fishing port are hundreds of rusting anchors and a fine tall tower. **Custonaci** has a sanctuary with a venerated painting of the *Madonna*, and a number of marble quarries where the beautiful red stone called *perlato di Custonaci* is excavated. On the outskirts, a road (signposted Grotte Mangiapane) leads past an old quarry to the enormous Mangiapane Cave at the foot of Monte Cofano. The cave contains a little hamlet called **Scurati**, now no longer inhabited. On either side of the paved street are little houses with courtyards, bread ovens, and workshops, and high above, the vault of the cave serves as a second roof. The village comes to life at Christmas, in a very successful venture called *Presepe vivente*, or **Living Crib** when local people demonstrate the various trades and crafts of the area in the old houses. The initiative has been so popular that a similar event, the **Living**

useum, is held in summer (from mid-June to mid-September, Fri, Sat & Sun evenings from 20.00–24.00; entrance ticket can include dinner; information from the *Associazione Culturale Presepio Vivente*, ☎ 0923/973553 or 0923/971029, ✉ www.mcsystem.it/presepe) where sixty craftsmen and women demonstrate their skill.

Surrounded by barren hills is **Castelluzzo**, with one-storey houses and palm trees. It has a picturesque main street which leads downhill, and outside the town are groves of almonds and olive trees on the plain which descends to the seashore. There is a fine view of the beautiful headland of Monte Cofano, with Erice in the distance. On the main road is the interesting little 16C domed Cubola di S. Crescenzia, derived from Arab models.

San Vito lo Capo

San Vito lo Capo at the tip of the cape has been developed as a seaside resort (population 3500, which increases significantly in summer) with gorgeous beaches. Laid out on a regular plan in the 18C–19C, many of the houses are decorated with bright geraniums and bougainvilleas. The unusual church, a square fortress, was a 13C sanctuary which was fortified by order of Charles V in 1526 to defend it against pirate raids. On the eastern side of the beautiful promontory of Monte Monaco is a disused tuna fishery overlooking the Gulf of Castellammare. A deserted road (signposted Calampiso) continues high above the shore across bare hills through an African landscape, with dwarf palm trees and giant carobs, where broom and wild flowers blossom in spring. Beyond the holiday village of Calampiso (hidden below the road) the right fork continues to a road which ends at the northern entrance to the Riserva Naturale dello Zingaro (described below).

Castellammare del Golfo

Safe in the embrace of its surrounding mountains, Castellammare (population 13,500) lies on the bay, a jumble of little coloured houses; pink, cream, yellow and orange predominate. It is a place which makes no concession to modern frivolities. Here, the fishermen are still fishermen and the children still play in the road, streetwise and timeless; grandmas (and grandpas) still haggle over the price of lettuce with the wayside vendors, and there are few shops for tourists. It is absolutely authentic, and therefore not without its admirers, usually people from northern Italy, who are buying up the old fishermen's houses and transforming them into luxurious holiday hideaways. Perhaps the best time to experience the essence of Castellammare is when the sun drops behind the mountain and fishermen sit on the quay preparing the *conzu*, the bait for the night's fishing, while young blades cruise around on their vespas, studiously ignoring the pretty girls they are trying to impress, and wonderful cooking aromas waft from the open doorways.

The town was originally founded by the Elymians, as the harbour for the city of Segesta. The 18C Matrice houses an impressive life-size majolica statue of *Our Lady of Succour* in the act of threatening the enemies of the town with her distaff, Baby Jesus safely balanced on her left arm, and looking stern. The statue is thought to have been made in the 16C in Tuscany, probably by the Della Robbia workshop. The **Castle**, built by the Saracens in the 9C and then enlarged by the Normans and later again by the Swabians, is now the seat of the **Civic Museum** (open daily 09.00–13.00, ☎ 0924/30217), dedicated to life in the Mediterranean, with clothes, furniture, tools, pots and pans, and equipment for making wine and olive oil. The old warehouses on the seafront are very attractive; some of these, too, are being restored and turned into summer homes. They go back to the days when tuna fishing was big business here.

Scopello

A byroad follows the coast north of Castellammare for Scopello. Paths lead down to **Cala Bianca**, **Cala Rossa** and **Baia Guidaloca**, beautiful bays on the rocky coast, where the sea is particularly clear. It is said that Baia Guidaloca was the spot where Nausicaa found the shipwrecked Ulysses, and led him back to her father's court.

Scopello is a tiny picturesque village. From the little piazza (with a large drinking trough) an archway leads into the old paved courtyard with a few trees of an 18C baglio surrounded by one-storey houses, a number of them now used as cafés or restaurants.

Just beyond the village is the **Tonnara di Scopello**, usually called Marfaraggio, an important tuna fishery from the 13C up to the middle of the last century. It is easily visible on the sea below the road, beside fantastically shaped rocks on which ruined defence towers are situated. The buildings have been beautifully preserved (now private property, but accommodation can be rented, see above). A footpath leads down to the seafront where hundreds of anchors are piled up beside the picturesque old buildings. There is a little cove, where the sea is unbelievably clear, and feral cats teach their kittens the art of survival. The life of the fishermen who used to live here was vividly described by Gavin Maxwell in *The Ten Pains of Death* (1959).

Il Baglio

In western Sicily, *il baglio* is a fortified farmhouse or winery. The name derives from the Latin *balium* or *vallum*, both of which mean 'fortified place'. In Sicilian, the name becomes *'u bagghiu*. The structure is quite simple, a group of buildings forming a square or a rectangle around a central courtyard, with no openings to the outside, except for an entrance in the front wall, which can be quite lavish. In the centre of the courtyard there is often a wellhead, because underneath is the cistern for storing rainwater. On entering, the house right in front is that of the owner, usually with a private chapel on one side. Other buildings house the farmworkers, the wine or olive press, the stables, the warehouses, the wine cellars and the storerooms.

Zingaro wildlife reserve

The coast road soon ends at the southern entrance to the **Riserva Naturale dello Zingaro**, a beautiful wildlife reserve (open daily, Oct to Mar 08.00–16.00, Apr–Sept 07.00–21.00, ☎ 0924/35108, 🖷 0924/35752, ✉ www.riservazingaro. it), with 7km of unspoilt coastline that can be explored on foot along marked paths. There are also several beaches where you can swim. The well-preserved landscape is particularly beautiful and interesting for its ecology. No motorised transport of any kind is allowed inside the park, and the guardians and keepers use mules to carry out their work. The **museum**, about 500m from the Scopello entrance (open 09.00–16.00 in winter, and 08.00–21.00 in summer) illustrates the life of the peasants who lived in the area. The Grotta dell'Uzzo, also in the reserve (about 5km from the Scopello entrance), was inhabited in the Paleolithic

. There is another entrance to the park on its northern border, approached by
e road from S. Vito lo Capo (see above).

SEGESTA AND ALCAMO

Segesta, with its famous temple, is one of the most evocative Greek sites on the
island, in an isolated spot surrounded by beautiful countryside. The nearby town
of Alcamo has an unusually large number of interesting 18C churches and a
flourishing wine industry.

Practical information

Getting there
By bus

AST buses for Segesta run
from Trapani, piazza Montalto, ☎ 0923/
31020, or from Palermo (*Segesta*),
piazza Marina. For Alcamo, buses run
from Trapani (*AST*) and from Palermo
(*Segesta*).

By rail

There is a railway station (Segesta
Tempio) a 20-minute walk from the site
on the Palermo–Trapani line (but only
one train a day stops here from Palermo,
and one from Trapani). It is not practical
to take the train to Alcamo because the
station is 5km outside the town. See bus
services.

By car

The road (SS 113) and motorway
between Palermo and Trapani (exit at
Segesta, 29km from Trapani or 75km
from Palermo) run close to the Segesta site.

Information office

APT Trapani, ☎ 0923/
29000. Alcamo on line: ✉
www. alcamocheproduce.it, ✉ www.
alcamodoc.net.

Where to stay
Hotels

ALCAMO ☆ *Miramare*, 72
corso G. Medici, ☎ 0924/21197.
Uninspiring, but the only hotel in the
centre of Alcamo.

☆ *Terme Gorga*, contrada Gorga, ☎ &
📠 0924/23842. Simple little hotel at
the spa down by the railway station.
Open all year, it has a good restaurant.
CALATAFIMI ☆ *Mille Pini*, 4 piazza
Francesco Vivana, ☎ 0924/951260,
📠 0924/950223, ✉ millepini@tin.it.
Well organized small hotel, with good
restaurant.

Bed and breakfast

ALCAMO MARINA *Windsurf*,
contrada Calatubo, ☎ 0924/21420 or
339/8452508, ✉ www.
affittacamerewindsurf.it. Open all year,
this is a new place, close to the beach at
Alcamo Marina; there are restaurants,
pizzerie and coffee bars close by; all
rooms have private bathroom.
BUSETO PALIZZOLO ☆☆☆ *Baglio
Case Colomba*, open Apr–Oct, 185 via
Maggiore Toselli, ☎ 091/6841211 or
347/2116470, ✉ www.casecolomba.
com. Delightful old house in a village
ideally situated for touring the area,
close to Segesta, beautifully arranged
rooms with 19C furniture. Very kind
owners. B&B or apartment to rent.
English, French and Spanish spoken.

Farmhouse accommodation

CALATAFIMI ☆☆ *Villa del Bosco*,
contrada Mazurco, ☎ 330/849216,
✉ www.neomedia.it/personal/degaeta.
Small farm producing olive oil, wine and

honey, close to an ancient oak wood; English and French spoken; hilltop position, view of Segesta. Archery and excursions on foot or by 4WD vehicle.

Eating out
Restaurants, cafés and ice cream parlours

A L C A M O   €€ *Salsapariglia*, 1 via Libertà, ☎ 0924/508302. Good pasta dishes and grilled fish. Closed Mon.

€ *Trattoria dei Mille*, 10 via delle Rose, ☎ & 📠 0924/26232. Inexpensive robust meals. Closed Tues. Also pleasant rooms to rent.

Extra Bar, 29 viale Italia. Very good ice cream and pastries.

A L C A M O   M A R I N A   There are several very good pizzerie at this increasingly popular seaside resort.

S E G E S T A   Good café and restaurant by the entrance to the ancient site. (It also has a well-stocked book and gift shop.)

Handicrafts
Vita Coraci, 151 corso VI Aprile,

Alcamo, makes beautiful pottery, with very unusual patterns.

Wines
A good name for the famous *Bianco d'Alcamo* is *Rapitalà*. The Ceuso farm produces a successful red, using partly native vines and partly Cabernet and Merlot, which they call *Fastaia*; very nice with pasta, grilled steak or cheese.

Annual festivals
A classical **drama festival** is held in July at the theatre of Segesta. On Palm Sunday at Buseto Palizzolo the young people organize a pageant with *tableaux vivants* on floats drawn by tractors (unique in Sicily). Each float represents a moment in the Passion of Christ, with a group of characters who stay perfectly motionless for hours, accompanied by the music of local bands, as they go through the streets.

Segesta
The temple and theatre of Segesta are two of the most magnificently sited classical monuments in existence. From the old road, the view of the famous temple on a bare hill in deserted countryside backed by the rolling hills west of the Gaggera is unforgettable. It has been admired by travellers for centuries. The theatre is on a second, higher hill to the east.

History

Segesta, also originally known as *Egesta*, was the principal city of the Elymians, who are now thought to have come from the eastern Mediterranean, probably Anatolia; legend says they were the survivors of the Trojan war, and were led here by Aeneas; recent studies of their language would appear to confirm this. It was rapidly Hellenised, and was in continual warfare with Selinunte from 580 onwards. The city sought the alliance of Athens in 426. After the destruction of Selinunte in 409 Segesta became a subject-ally of Carthage, and was saved by Himilco (397) from the attacks of Dionysius of Syracuse. In 307, however, Agathocles sacked the city, and changed its name to *Dikeopolis*. It resumed its old name under the protection of Carthage, but treacherously murdered the Carthaginian garrison during the First Punic War, after which it became the first city in Sicily to announce allegiance to Rome. The city's fortunes declined during the Arab period and it was abandoned by the late 13C.

ιe ancient city which covered the slopes of Monte Barbaro is now being exten-
ιvely excavated, but the site of the necropolis has not yet been identified.
Sporadic excavations have in fact taken place since the end of the 18C, when the
temple was first restored. The theatre was brought to light in 1822. An important sanctuary at the foot of Monte Barbaro was discovered in 1950. The surrounding countryside is impressive, with its extensive vineyards, tiny olive trees
and lovely old farmhouses or *bagli*, and peaceful, in spite of the motorway.
Arriving by car from Palermo, the first thing that comes into view is the sustain-
ing wall of the theatre, standing out on the skyline of Monte Barbaro, and then
the temple.

Visiting the site and opening times
• The site has been enclosed, but is open daily 09.00–1 hour before sunset.
• The ticket office for the site is opposite the bar, below the car park. Tickets for
  the shuttle bus (every 30 mins) to the theatre (closed to cars) can be purchased
  at the bar.

The temple
From the car park a path and steps lead up through agaves to the temple. It is
beautifully situated on a low hill (304m) on the edge of a deep ravine formed by
the Pispisa river, across which is a hillside covered with pinewoods. It is one of the
grandest existing monuments of Doric architecture, practically without a
straight line anywhere in the structure, just a series of gentle curves, often of
only a few millimeters in depth, but sufficient to correct the optical illusion which
would let the temple appear as if deformed when seen from a distance. It almost
certainly represents an unfinished building, because there is no trace of a cella,
the columns have not been provided with the typical grooves, and the bosses
used for shifting the blocks of stone have not been removed. Although it may
have been constructed in a hurry, to impress the ambassadors from Athens
whom the Segestans were anxious to win over to help protect them from
Selinunte, it is certainly the work of a great Athenian master and probably dates
back to c 426–416 BC. It is peripteral and hexastyle with 36 unfluted columns (c
9m high, 2m wide at base) on a stylobate 58m by 23m. The high entablature and
the pediments are intact. The building is inhabited by a colony of garrulous jackdaws, but they do not disturb the magic of this wonderfully romantic spot, so
peaceful that it is hard to imagine the ferocious Agathocles, in 307 BC, catapult-
ing 8000 of the inhabitants into the ravine below, from the flat area behind the
temple, and taking three days to do so.

The theatre
A road climbs up Monte Barbaro to the theatre from the car
park. At the foot of the hill conspicuous excavations of part

of the walls (and gate) of
the ancient city can be
seen. Above a sheepfold,
yellow signs mark various
excavations including an
upper line of walls (2C BC)
and a cave dwelling (re-
used in Roman times; pro-
tected by a wooden roof

The temple of Segesta

Beside the car park near the top of the hill are two enclosures, the higher one ha remains of medieval houses built over public buildings from the Hellenistic era and the lower one has a monumental Hellenistic edifice, reconstructed in the Roman period. A path continues towards the theatre with a fine view of the temple below. On the right is an enclosure with a ruined church (12C–15C), on the summit of the hill are remains of a 12C–13C castle and, on the other side of the hill, a 12C mosque (destroyed by the owners of the castle in the 13C).

The theatre is in a spectacular position near the summit of Monte Barbaro (415m). It faces the gulf of Castellammare beyond Monte Inici (1064m) while more high mountain ranges rise to the east. It is one of the best preserved ancient theatres in existence, built in the mid-3C BC or possibly earlier. With a diameter of 63m it could hold 3200 spectators. The exterior of the cavea was supported by a high polygonal wall, which is particularly well preserved at the two sides. Beneath the cavea a grotto with late Bronze Age finds was discovered in 1927 by the archaeologist Pirro Marconi. Classical drama productions are performed here in summer; ✉ www.calatafimisegesta.it.

In contrada Mango at the foot of Monte Barbaro to the east near the Gaggera river is a large Archaic **sanctuary** (not fully excavated), of great importance, thought to date from the 7C BC. The temenos measures 83 x 47m. A huge deposit of pottery sherds dumped from the town on the hill above has also come to light here.

The nearest town to Segesta is **Calatafimi** (population 8400), a town frequently visited by the writer Samuel Butler between 1893 and 1900. He identified in this corner of Sicily all the places described in Homer's *Odyssey*, and in *The Authoress of the Odyssey* he reveals his belief that the epic was really written by a woman, Nausicaa. Southwest of the town (signposted Pianto Romano, off the SS 113) an obelisk commemorates Garibaldi's victory here on 15 May 1860. A cypress avenue leads to the monument by Ernesto Basile (1892) on which Garibaldi's words are inscribed, on reaching the hill after his disembarkation from Marsala ('*Qui si fa l'Italia o si muore*'; 'here we will create Italy or die'). There are fine views from the hilltop.

Alcamo

At the eastern extremity of the province of Trapani is the agricultural town of Alcamo (population 42,600), with numerous fine 18C churches. Founded at the end of the 10C, it derives its name from the Arabic *manzil al qamah*, perhaps meaning 'the farm of bitter cucumbers'. It was the birthplace of the 13C poet Cielo or Ciullo, short for Michele, one of the earliest exponents of the Sicilian School, forerunner of Italian literature. The town has a strongly Saracen flavour in its regular plan, with many beautifully cobbled streets.

In piazza Bagolino (car park) the terrace offers a fine panorama of the plain stretching towards the sea. Beyond the 16C Porta Palermo, corso VI Aprile leads into the town. On the left is the church of **S. Francesco d'Assisi**, founded in 1348 and rebuilt in 1716. It contains a beautiful marble altarpiece attributed to Giacomo Gagini (1568), statues of *St Mark* and *Mary Magdalene* by Antonello Gagini and a 17C painting of the *Immaculate Virgin* by Giuseppe Carrera. The corso continues past the former church of S. Tommaso (c 1450) with a carved Gothic portal, now the seat of the local Rotary Club. Opposite, next to a convent, s the church of **SS. Cosma e Damiano** (usually closed), a domed centrally planned building of c 1721 by Giuseppe Mariani. It contains two stucco statues by Giacomo Serpotta and two altarpieces by Guglielmo Borremans; the interior is among the finest examples of Baroque architecture in Sicily.

The corso crosses via Rossotti with a view left of the castle and right of S. Salvatore. The **Castello dei Conti di Modica** was built c 1350, on a rhomboid plan with four towers. For many years it was used as the local prison. Now it has been lovingly restored and is the seat of the **Civic Historical Library** and the **Oenological Museum** (open daily 09.00–13.00, 16.00–20.00, ☎ 0924/590270) dedicated to local wine production, the prize-winning *Bianco d'Alcamo*, one of Sicily's 18 wines guaranteed by the *Denominazione d'Origine Controllata (DOC)* label. Not far from the castle, tucked away in this part of town is **Torre De Ballis** (1495; private home, no entrance), one of the few surviving tower-houses in Sicily. **S. Salvatore** (closed) stands next to the monastery of the Badia Grande. It contains allegorical statues by Bartolomeo Sanseverino (1758), a follower of Serpotta. The vault fresco and high altarpiece are by Carlo Brunetti (1759–60). The statue of *St Benedict* is by Antonino Gagini (1545). Nearby is the church of the Annunziata, a Catalan-Gothic building in ruins (without a roof).

The corso continues past the former church of the Madonna del Soccorso (15C) with a portal attributed to Bartolomeo Berrettaro to the **Matrice**. Founded in 1332, it was rebuilt in 1669 by Angelo Italia and Giuseppe Diamante, with a fine dome. In the **interior** are columns of red marble quarried on Monte Bonifato. The frescoes in the vault, cupola and apse are by Guglielmo Borremans. **South side**: in the second chapel is a *Crucifix* by Antonello Gagini (1523); in the fourth chapel a late 16C sarcophagus with portraits of two members of the De Ballis family; in the fifth chapel there is a marble relief by Antonello Gagini. In the chapel to the right of the choir is the *Last Supper* by Giuseppe Carrera (1613). In the adjoining chapel (right) are two fine Gothic arches and a beautiful fresco fragment of the *Pentecost* (1430). In the chapel to the left of the choir is a wooden statue of the *Madonna* (1721) by Lorenzo Curti. On the altar of the north transept, the statue of *St Peter* is by Giacomo Gagini (1556).

The inner door of the sacristy (beyond the wooden door in the north aisle) is decorated with carvings of fruit attributed to Bartolomeo Berrettaro. **North side**: in the third chapel there is a high relief of the *Transition of the Virgin* by Antonello Gagini; in the first chapel there is a painting of the *Madonna* by Giuseppe Renda (late 18C). Opposite the Matrice is the former church of S. Nicolò di Bari with a fine portal of 1563.

The corso continues to the elegantly curved **piazza Ciullo**, at the centre of town and the market place in the Middle Ages. On the corner is the church of **S. Oliva**, built by Giovanni Biagio Amico in 1724. It was restored in 1990 after a fire in 1987 destroyed the 18C frescoes and stuccoes in the vault of the nave. The lovely interior has altars beautifully decorated with marble. On the fourth south altar is a statue of *St Olive* by Antonello Gagini (1511). The high altarpiece is by Pietro Novelli and on the left wall is a marble tabernacle by Luigi di Battista (1552). On the north side are 18C statues and a marble group of the *Annunciation* by Antonino and Giacomo Gagini (1545). Piazza Ciullo is dominated by the magnificent **Collegiate Church** (1684–1767) containing 18C stuccoes and altarpieces. On Sunday morning the whole population—the wine farmers and their families, the women elegantly dressed, the men wearing black serge jackets and cloth caps—tends to congregate in front of this church. Corso VI Aprile continues from piazza Ciullo past 18C and neo-classical palaces to the church of **SS. Paolo e Bartolomeo** (1689) with a splendid interior decorated by Vincenzo and Gabriele Messina and Antonino Grano. The oval *Madonna del Miele* (Our Lady of Honey), so-called because she is shown with a honeycomb symbolizing her sweetness, dates from the end of the 14C or beginning of the 15C.

In via Amendola, the road leading out of the square to the north, opposite the church of S. Oliva, is the **church of the Rosario** (**S. Domenico**) which contains a fresco attributed to Tommaso de Vigilia. Beyond the castle (see above) and the large piazza della Repubblica is the church of **S. Maria del Gesù** (1762). Beneath the portico is a portal attributed to Bartolomeo Berrettaro (1507). It contains a 16C altarpiece of the *Madonna and saints with the counts of Modica*, and a statue of the *Madonna and Child* attributed to Bartolomeo Berrettaro or Giuliano Mancino. The cloister of the adjoining convent is lovely. In via Caruso is the church of **S. Francesco di Paola**, rebuilt in 1699 by Giovanni Biagio Amico. The pretty interior has eight wonderfully modelled stucco statues by Giacomo Serpotta, commissioned in 1724, and an altarpiece of *St Benedict* by Pietro Novelli. The church is only open for services, but by ringing the bell of the Benedictine convent next door, sometimes one of the nuns will allow you to visit.

On **Monte Bonifato** (825m), south of the town, planted with conifers and pine trees, a ruined Norman castle of the Ventimiglia is situated, with the chapel of the Madonna dell'Alto (superb view). The medieval *Fontanazza* here is a huge reservoir or thermal edifice. To the north, between the town and the sea, the spectacular Saracen castle on a spur known as **Calatubo** adequately protected Alcamo on that vulnerable side. Close to the railway station is a **spa**, *Stabilimento termale Gorga*, ☎ 0924/23842, where water from hot springs flows into a pool; it is a lovely spot, prepared, says Diodorus Siculus, by the local nymphs for Hercules 'to refresh his body'. Certainly, the effect of a bathe is very pleasant and beneficial to the weary traveller; there is a small but comfortable hotel.

THE EGADI ISLANDS AND PANTELLERIA

The Egadi Islands, consisting of Favignana, Levanzo and Marettimo, lie 15km–30km off the west coast of Sicily. They are reached by boat and hydrofoil from Trapani or Marsala. The inhabitants (4300), once famed as skilled fishermen, are now turning to tourism to earn a living. The islands are very popular with divers. The sea between Favignana and Marsala is also of great interest to marine archaeologists because of the many sea battles fought here. The varied birdlife includes migratory species in the spring and in autumn and the islands now form a **marine wildlife reserve**, the largest in Italy.

Practical information

Getting to the Egadi islands
Maritime services from Trapani

Ferries daily (from Molo Sanità to **Favignana** (in 50 mins) and to **Levanzo** (in 1hr 20 mins). Once a week

(in 2hrs 40 mins) to **Marettimo**.
Hydrofoils (more expensive; several times a day) from via Ammiraglio Staiti (in 25 mins) to Favignana and Levanzo, and once a day (in 55 mins) to

Marettimo. Several companies operate the services including *Siremar*, ☎ 0923/921388 or 0923/540515; *Volaviamare*, ☎ 0923/872499 and *Ustica Lines*, ☎ 0923/21754. In bad weather the ferries are suspended as the moorings at the ports are poor but unless there are very high seas the hydrofoils usually operate.

Maritime services from Marsala, Naples and Ustica

Hydrofoils run from Molo Dogana, Marsala in summer. Also from Naples and Ustica, *Ustica Lines*, ☎ 081/5800340.

Maritime agencies on the islands

FAVIGNANA   *Siremar* (ferries) ☎ 0923/921368; *Ustica Lines* (hydrofoils) ☎ 0923/921277.

LEVANZO   *Siremar* (ferries) ☎ 0923/924128; *Ustica Lines* (hydrofoils) ☎ 348/08042681.

MARETTIMO   *Siremar* (ferries) ☎ 0923/923144; *Ustica Lines* (hydrofoils) ☎ 0923/923103.

Ferry and hydrofoil information website: ☒ www.bookingitalia.it gives up to date times, prices and bus connections for ferries and hydrofoils.

Bicycle hire

FAVIGNANA   Bicycles can be hired all year round from *Isidoro*, 40 via Mazzini, *Panzica*, via S. Leonardo/via Battisti, *Rita*, 11 piazza Europa.

Donkey hire

MARETTIMO   *Nino Anastasi*, ☎ 0923/923246. Riding donkeys is the best way to get around on the island.

Information offices

APT Trapani, ☎ 0923/29000.
Pro Loco, piazza Matrice, Favignana, ☎ 0923/921647.
Riserva Marina Egadi, Palazzo Florio, 1 via Florio, Favignana, ☎ & 🖷 0923/922585.
Egadi Islands on line: ☒ www.egadi.com, ☒ www.egadi.com/proloco.

Levanzo on line: ☒ www.tiscalinet.it/levanzo.

 ## Where to stay
Hotels

FAVIGNANA   ✶✶✶ *Aegusa*, 11 via Garibaldi (at the port), ☎ 0923/922430, 🖷 0923/922440, ☒ www.egadi.com/aegusa. A delightful little hotel, very welcoming.
✶✶✶ *Approdo di Ulisse*, località Calagrande, ☎ 0923/921380, 🖷 0923/921511, ☒ email: direttore favignana@club_vacanze.it. On the west of the island, this is a resort hotel with many amenities.
✶✶ *Bougainville*, 10 via Cimabue, ☎ 0923/922033, ☎ 0923/922649. Small but comfortable, family run, convenient situation in the town centre.
✶✶ *Egadi*, 17 via Colombo (at the port), ☎ & 🖷 0923/921232, ☒ www.egadi.com/egadi. Very small, usually fully booked because of the famous restaurant, which is probably one of the best in Sicily. Closed in winter.

LEVANZO   *Pensione dei Fenici*, 18 via Calvario, ☎ & 🖷 0923/924083. A well-run little hotel, the ideal choice for a restful holiday, good restaurant.
✶ *Paradiso*, via lungomare, ☎ & 🖷 0923/924080. Simple hotel with good restaurant, on the terrace in summer.

MARETTIMO   has no hotels, but rooms can be rented in private houses and there is a very good *residenza* on the island, with a selection of apartments in little cottages: ✶✶✶✶ *Marettimo Residence*, via Telegrafo, località Spatarello, ☎ 0923/923202 & 0923/923500, 🖷 0923/923386, ☒ www.marettimoresidence.it, ☒ www.marettimoresidence.com.

Rooms to rent

Rosa dei Venti, 4 via Punta S. Simone, contrada Crocilla, ☎ & 🖷 0923/923249, ☒ www.isoladimarettimo.it.
San Giuseppe Association. The fishermen of Marettimo have formed this

association so that they can offer tourists lodging in their homes and fishing trips on their boats, ☎ & ▤ 0923/923290, ✉ www.isoleegadi.it/S.Giuseppe.
Simmar, 1 piazza Scalo Nuovo, ☎ & ▤ 0923/923392, ✉ www.vacanze-marettimo.it. A group of young islanders can help you find and rent an authentic fisherman's house, or arrange boat trips.

Campsites

FAVIGNANA ✫✫✫✫ ***Miramare***, località Costicella, ☎ 0923/921330, ▤ 0923/922200, ✉ www.egadi.com/miramare.
✫✫✫ ***Egad***, località Arena, ☎ 0923/921555, ▤ 0923/539370, ✉ www.egadi.com/egad. Relaxed, happy atmosphere at this comfortable camp, constant fresh water from their own spring, diving centre.

Eating out
Restaurants

Prices are high on the Egadi Islands.
FAVIGNANA €€ ***Egadi***, 17 via Colombo, ☎ 0923/921232. Thought to be one of Sicily's finest restaurants; the fish is excellent and so fresh it can also be eaten raw as *carpaccio*; also spaghetti with lobster. Closed in winter.
€€ ***El Pescador***, 38 piazza Europa, ☎ 0923/921035. Popular with the locals. Try Donna Rosa's spaghetti with *ricci* (sea urchins). Closed Wed. and Feb.
€€ ***La Bettola***, 47 via Nicotera, ☎ 0923/921988. Quite elegant. There is a nice courtyard for eating al fresco; excellent octopus salad. Closed Nov.
€€ ***La Tavernetta***, 54 piazza Matrice, ☎ 0923/921639. Good meals with a pleasant area outside for al fresco dining.
LEVANZO €€ ***Paradiso***, 8 via Lungomare, ☎ 0923/924080. Simple little restaurant. Marvellous food, prepared with the freshest fish. Closed winter.

MARETTIMO €€ ***Il Pirata***, by the harbour, ☎ 0923/923027. Serves appetizing seafood risotto, lobster soup, and grilled fish. Also rooms to rent. Closed Jan.
€€ ***Il Timone***, via Garibaldi, ☎ 0923/923142. Signora Maria prepares homemade pasta and wonderful tuna dishes.
€€ ***Il Veliero***, also by the harbour, ☎ 0923/923195. Meals served on the terrace; try Peppe's legendary lobster soup in which he cooks spaghetti; the pasta dressing, *pesto di Trapani*, made with raw tomato is also memorable.
€ ***Al Carrubo***, above the town in contrada Pelosa, ☎ 0923/923132. Good pizzeria and trattoria, with a panoramic terrace.

Pizzerie and sandwich bars

FAVIGNANA ***Bar Cono***, 1 piazza Matrice. Tasty snacks and sandwiches.
Rais, 8 piazza Europa, ☎ 0923/921233. Pizza in the evenings.
MARETTIMO € ***La Hiera***, just off the main street, ☎ 0923/923017. Excellent pizza. Closed Wed.

Cafés, pastry shops and ice cream parlours

FAVIGNANA ***Giacomino***, off the corso and ***Albatros*** on the corso, are popular meeting places.
Bar del Corso, 40 via Vittorio Emanuele. The best place for Sicilian breakfast; unusual snacks.
Bar Due Colonne, 68 piazza Matrice. Fresh fruit juices and tasty snacks.
LEVANZO The *cannoli di ricotta* are excellent everywhere; they are freshly prepared every day with milk from the goats which roam the island. At the bakery in via Lungomare, Signora Olimpia makes delicious currant biscuits.
MARETTIMO ***Caffè La Scaletta***, at the main port. The best home-made ice cream, and fresh fruit juices.
Caffè Tramontana on the road above the port is the perfect place for relaxing and admiring the view.

Shopping
Fish
Casa del Tonno, 12 via Roma, Favignana, ☎ & ▤ 0923/922227, ✉ www.iltonno.com. For canned bluefin tuna in olive oil, smoked fish or roe, anchovies and sardines.
Handicrafts
LEVANZO Alberto Venza makes lovely souvenirs using stone, shells, and even swordfish swords. He is easy to find, just mention his name.

Foreign language newspapers
FAVIGNANA From Signora Rosaria Miceli in via Nicotera; she also stocks books and postcards.
MARETTIMO Order from the tobacconist in via Umberto.

Sport and leisure
Diving centres
FAVIGNANA *Progetto Atlantide*, Punta Lunga, ☎ 0923/922181, ✉ www.progettoatlantide.com. This is also a diving school.
Scubaduck Crociera Subacquea, ☎ 0923/593336, ✉ www. tiscalinet.it/scubaduck. Organizes cruises for dives.
MARETTIMO *Stella Marina*, ☎ 0923/923144.
Marettimo Diving Centre, ☎ 0923/923083.
Voglia di Mare, ☎ 339/4213845, ✉ www.vogliadimare.com.

History

These islands were the ancient *Aegades* or *Aegates*, off which Lutatius Catulus routed the fleet of Hanno in 241 BC in one of the most famous Roman victories over Carthage. In the middle of the 16C the islands were given to the Genoese Camillo Pallavicini, from whom they were purchased in 1874 by the Florio, a family from Calabria, who settled in Palermo, became important ship owners and were great entrepreneurs on the west coast of Sicily, especially in the period preceding World War I.

Favignana

Favignana, 17km from Trapani, is the biggest island of the group (19 sq km) and the seat of the council (population 3800). Shaped like a butterfly, the island is mostly flat, and the little town has a slightly run-down atmosphere, with a number of its cube-like houses half restored, half built, or for sale. The boats and hydrofoils dock at the little port, filled with numerous fishing boats.

The **Stabilimento Florio** is a huge old tuna fishery built in 1859 by Giulio Drago for the Pallavicini. The tuna fisheries here used to be the most important in the Mediterranean, and the bluefin tuna (*Thunnus thynnus*), renowned for its excellent quality, is still caught here. In a good year in the 19C a catch could sometimes exceed 10,000 fish; in 1865 14,020 were caught. Before the fishery was built the fish were salted: here, they were hung up by the tail then cut in pieces to be smoked, cooked or canned. Every piece of the fish was utilized; the skin was used as sandpaper, the tail and fins became brooms, some bones were used to make tools, and other parts either boiled to make glue or fishmeal. The industry thrived until 1874 when Drago ceded his contract to the Florio when they bought all three Egadi islands from the Pallavicini family.

The Florio family ran this factory until 1937. By 1977 it had closed down owing to competition from tuna fishing (yellowfin) in the Atlantic. The fine buildings are now owned by the region of Sicily and are undergoing restoration: they will house a restaurant, theatre, auditorium, artisans' workshops, a marine research centre, and the Archaeological Museum which will display a fascinating collection of many objects found under the sea here. A few years ago some fishermen discovered the wreck of an Arab ship dating from 1000, with its storage jars still intact, and in October 2000 four young divers found shards of pottery among the seaweed not far offshore, and an enormous octopus, jealously guarding a **pewter wine bottle**, still sealed with the wine inside (which they were able to wrest away from him with some difficulty). It is thought to be the oldest bottle of wine in the world, and goes back to the 14C. The bottle can be seen in the window at the Banca di Credito, 1 piazza Castello (☎ 0923/921788, open 08.30–13.30, Mon–Fri).

La Mattanza

In the deep channel between Levanzo and Favignana the traditional method of tuna fishing known as *la mattanza* has been practiced in spring since ancient times. A series of net traps form a corridor leading to a square pen called the *camera della morte* (death chamber), which is activated under the instructions of the head fisherman, called the *rais*. The wind called the *Favinio* which brings the fish here for spawning, starts to blow at the end of May or in early June; choosing the right moment for fishing is all important. The females, already fertilized by the males, escape the trap because they swim deep down, about 20m below the surface, while the males are much closer to the surface. When there are around 100 fish in the pen the area is encircled by boats, with the boat belonging to the rais in the centre, and the nets are slowly hauled in, accompanied by the ancient haunting chants of the fishermen, called *cialome*: 'aja mola, aja mola, aja mola e iamuninni... Gesù Cristu cu' li Santi...nianzò...nianzò...', to maintain the correct rhythm. It is very hard work, because the fish can be so big; one caught in 1974 weighed 600 kg. Tuna tend to dive when in danger so that during this operation they often collide with one another and hit their heads: by the time the net reaches the surface (the whole operation takes about an hour) many of them are wounded and stunned. They are then harpooned and pulled into the boats. The sea runs red with blood; it is a horrid but fascinating spectacle, and goes back at least to the Bronze Age.

The catch has drastically declined in recent years due in part to modern fishing techniques carried out by super-efficient Japanese and Korean boats, using huge nets (illegal for EU fishermen) and consequently quite indiscriminate in what they catch. The fish is frozen on board, taken to Malta and flown to the Far East. Sicily once had many tuna fisheries: they have nearly all closed now but there is strong local determination to save the Favignana fishery.

The little medieval town, where most of the inhabitants live, and where all its shops are situated, was refounded in 1637 by the Pallavicini family. Palazzo Florio, a large Art Nouveau palace near the port, was built in 1876 for Ignazio Florio by Giuseppe Damiani Almeyda. It is now used as a police headquarters. Nearby is a smaller 19C palace, now the Town Hall, with a statue of Ignazio Florio in front of it. The little church of S. Antonio da Padova is close by. Via Vittorio Emanuele, the main street, leads to piazza Matrice where there is a pleasant church with a green dome and the tourist office. The castle nearby has been

:ansformed into a modern prison. Numerous shops sell smoked tuna fish and *bottarga* (dried tuna roe).

The rest of the island is flat and has a rather bare landscape, mostly used as pastureland. The best **swimming** is at the rocky bay of Cala Rossa, on the north coast; there are more crowded sandy beaches on the south coast between Grotta Pergiata and Punta Longa. In the eastern part of the island are numerous disused tufa quarries (the white, sugary-looking tufa found here provides excellent building stone). The small quarries are now mostly used as orchards, although one quarry still operates, supplying the local market. Near the cemetery, several wells with huge wooden water wheels of Arab origin survive, once used for irrigation. At Punta Marsala there is a view of Marsala and (on the left) the low, green island of Mozia.

The prettiest part of the island is to the west beyond Monte S. Caterina (where a Norman castle is now used by the armed forces). On the south coast at Punta Longa is a tiny port and fishing village.

Levanzo

Levanzo (10 sq km), 15km from Trapani, has no natural springs and supports a population of just 200 (there are virtually no cars). It also has an austere, wind-beaten landscape and a few beaches. The island is particularly interesting for botanists; in fact, many of the plants are endemic species. It is famous for its prehistoric caves, notably the **Grotta del Genovese**, which has the most interesting prehistoric **wall paintings** in Italy, discovered by chance in 1950. The cave paintings date from the Neolithic period, and the incised drawings from the Upper Paleolithic period. A footpath leads across the island from the port to the cave, which can also be reached by boat; enquire for directions at the port, or ask the custodian, sig. Natale Castiglione, 11 via Calvario (☎ 0923/924032 or 339/7418800) who has the key and can arrange transport. Natale has a 4 wheel drive but he can also provide mules, for those who prefer it. The cave is now locked since vandals damaged some of the graffiti. A shipwreck was recently located close to the island, with its cargo of *garum* amphorae still intact.

Roman ketchup

In Roman times, Levanzo was noted for its production of *garum*, a fish sauce much appreciated by connoisseurs and extremely expensive. Garum was widely used in ancient times, for preparing dishes of meat, fish, or vegetables, and even in fruit recipes and in drinks. The flavour of the sauce varied according to the different kinds of fish used for making it, and gourmets could even distinguish from what part of the Mediterranean it had come. There were famous garum factories in Sardinia, Tunisia, Morocco, Lebanon, Spain and Sicily, but the garum produced on Levanzo was one of the most highly prized.

To make the sauce, small fish, or the intestines of big fish, or both, were placed in terracotta pots or stone vats, together with salt, sea water, and aromatic herbs. After a week in the sun, the mixture was stirred and again left to ferment. After 20 more days, the garum, or *liquamen*, was strained off into amphorae. The solids, called *allec*, left in the vats, were not thrown away, but sold in the markets, where the poor were only too glad to buy them to eat with their bread. The strong flavoured condiment was certainly useful to hide the bad taste of stale meat or fish, difficult to keep fresh in those days.

Between Favignano and Levanzo and Trapani are the little islands called **Le Formiche** (the Ants), one of which has a large old tuna fishery; they are an important part of the marine reserve.

Marettimo

Marettimo (12 sq km) is the most isolated of the Egadi Islands, 38km from Trapani. Breathtakingly beautiful, it is wild and mountainous, rich in natural springs and grottoes, and is the best preserved of the three islands, mainly because it was once a notorious pirate stronghold, which discouraged settlers. There are plenty of birds, especially during the migratory passage, and the nesting species include Bonelli's eagles, peregrine falcons, kestrels, lesser kestrels, buzzards, black wheatears and many interesting sea birds, including the storm petrel, gannet, and Cory's shearwater. In the interior of the island there are even boars and mouflons. The island is cared for by the Forestry Commission, and there are well signposted tracks to the various points of interest. With a little Moorish-looking village, it has a population of just 800 (and no cars). Samuel Butler suggested that this was the island described as Ithaca in Homer's *Odyssey*, the islets of Le Formiche being the rocks hurled by Polyphemus at Ulysses (see p 385). On the harbour there is a small **Museum of the Sea** (1 via Scalo Nuovo, ☎ 0923/923000).

A pleasant and spectacular trek leads to the ruins of an ancient castle at Punta Troia, and there are also some Roman ruins and a small paleochristian church. The beauty of Marettimo, however, is its wild and natural aspect, and this can best be appreciated by a boat trip around the island. At the end of the 19C many islanders from Marettimo found their way adventurously to Monterey in California, where they started up a flourishing canned fish enterprise, immortalized by John Steinbeck in his *Cannery Row*.

Pantelleria

Far away to the southwest, about 110km from the Sicilian mainland (and only 70km from Tunisia) lies Pantelleria (population 7500), the largest island (83 sq km) off the Sicilian coast. It has beautiful wild scenery and interesting volcanic phenomena including hot springs (the last eruption was in 1831). Its central conical peak rises to a height of 836m. The sea bathing and scuba diving is exceptionally good. It is also a sanctuary for migratory birds. Capers, thought to be the finest in the world, figs, and sweet raisin grapes called *zibibbo* are cultivated here despite the lack of spring water, and it is especially famous for its wines, *Moscato di Pantelleria* and *Moscato passito*. The cube-like white-washed cottages, called *dammusi*, with thick walls and domed roofs, are of Arab origin.

Practical information

Getting there
By air

Gandalf flies twice a day from Trapani (in 30 mins) and *Air Sicilia* once a day from Palermo (in 1hr 20 mins). In summer *Air One* and *Alitalia* fly from Rome, and *Alitalia* also flies from Milan, Venice and Bologna. Bus connection from the airport to the town of Pantelleria. Airport ☎ 0923/841222.

Maritime services from Trapani

Car ferries daily from Molo della Sanità (in c 5hrs) run by *Siremar*, ☎ 0923/540515, and *Traghetti delle Isole*, ☎ 0923/22467 or 0923/911502. **Hydrofoils** (in c 2hrs 30 mins) run by Ustica Lines, ☎ 0923/22200, ✉ www.bookingitalia.it. for up-to-date times, prices and connecting buses.

Car and moped hire

Hire these at the port or from *Autonoleggio Policardo*, 35 vicolo Messina, ☎ 0923/912844.

Information offices

Pro Loco, via S. Nicola, Pantelleria, ☎ 0923/911838.
APT Trapani, ☎ 0923/27273. Pantelleria on line: ✉ www.comune.pantelleria.it.

Where to stay
Hotels

☆☆☆☆ *Monastero*, contrada Kassà, Scauri Alta, ☎ (Milan) 02/58186229. Five ancient dammusi (stone cottages) have been restored to create this very unusual hotel. For peace and tranquillity. Pool; excellent meals. Extremely expensive.

☆☆☆ *Club Village Punta Fram*, località Punta Fram, ☎ 0923/918075, ▤ 0923/918244. Large, smart holiday village with rooms and apartments, lots of amenities: tennis courts, disco, a pool, and private sea access.

☆☆☆ *Cossyra*, località Cuddie Rosse, Mursia, ☎ 0923/911154, ▤ 0923/911026, ✉ www.cossyra.pantelleria.it. Close to a prehistoric settlement called *Sesi*. Comfortable hotel with pool, and a very good restaurant.

☆☆☆ *Khamma*, 24 lungomare Borgo Italia, ☎ 0923/912680, ▤ 0923/912570. Overlooking the harbour, with a pleasant open-air bar.

☆☆☆ *Mursia*, località Mursia, ☎ 0923/911217, ▤ 0923/911026, ✉ www.mursia.pantelleria.it. Very comfortable; under the same management as Cossyra. Famous restaurant. Pool and diving centre.

☆☆☆ *Port'Hotel*, 6 lungomare Borgo Italia, ☎ 0923/911299, ▤ 0923/912203, ✉ www.porthotel.pantelleria.it. Sauna, horseriding and other amenities.

☆☆ *Miryam*, 1 corso Umberto, ☎ 0923/911374, ☎ 0923/911777, ✉ www.miryamhotel.it, ✉ www.pantelleria.it/miryam.

☆☆ *Papuscia*, località Tracino, 28 contrada Sopra Portella, ☎ & ▤ 0923/915463, ✉ www.papuscia.com, ✉ www.papuscia.it. 300m above sea level, a family-run hotel with good restaurant serving simple meals.

☆ *Bue Marino*, contrada Bue Marino, ☎ 0923/911054, ▤ 0911680. Charming little hotel by the sea within walking distance of the harbour. Excellent restaurant; they also sell wine, capers, olive oil, tuna roe and other local products.

☆ *Club Levante*, 11 Cala Levante, ☎ 0923/915582, ▤ 0923/691023, ✉ studiopannoassociati@fastweb.net.

Apartments to rent

☆☆☆ *La Perla Rosa*, via Dante, contrada Itria, ☎ 0923/912181 or 0923/912188, ▤ 0923/912166, ✉ www.perlarosa.pantelleria.it. Good restaurant, riding school, pool, windsurfing and sailing.

☆☆ *Dammusi Sciuvechi*, località Sciuvechi, ☎ 0923/916174, ▤ 0923/916522, ✉ pantelleria.isola@tiscalinet.it. Self-catering in comfortable, typical *dammusi* (little stone cottages).

☆☆ *Agritour Abitare in Dammuso*, contrada Mursia, ☎ 0923/918298, ▤ 0923/918528, ✉ www.agritour.supereva.it. Offers carefully restored dammusi in a beautiful part of the island.

☆☆ *Zubeb Resort*, contrada Zubebi, ☎ 0923/913653, ✉ www.zubebi.it. On the mountain above the harbour, a new village with pool and comfortable accommodation in dammusi; shiatsu courses, internet centre.

Camping is prohibited on Pantelleria.

Eating out
Restaurants

Prices are higher here than they are on the mainland.

€€€ *I Mulini*, contrada Tracino, ☎ 0923/915398. The restaurant is famous for a delicious dessert called *baci*, crispy pastry layered with sweet creamy ricotta; the chef is from Milan, so he also prepares good risotto. Closed Jan, Feb.

€€€ *Castiglione*, 24 lungomare Borgo Italia, ☎ 0923/911448. Elegant restaurant serving excellent antipasti; the spaghetti with *ammogghiu*, the local raw pesto (ripe tomatoes, basil, mint, oregano, chilli and lots of garlic), is exceptional; chef Franco also prepares good fish soup.

€€€ *Le Lampare*, at the Hotel Mursia, ☎ 0923/911217. Try *ravioli amari* (the local ravioli, filled with ricotta cheese and mint), spicy couscous, *sciakisciuka*, a popular local dish made with vegetables and capers, and fresh sheep's milk cheese called *tumma*; good assortment of robust desserts.

€€ *Il Cappero*, 31 via Roma (at the port), ☎ 0923/912601. Among the best restaurants of Pantelleria, delicious tuna dishes; among the starters is *tagliatelle con totani e finocchietto selvatico*, fresh egg noodles with tattlers (a kind of cuttle fish) and wild fennel. Pizza in the evenings; crowded on Saturdays. Closed winter.

€€ *La Risacca*, 65 via Milano, ☎ 0923/ 912975. Open evenings only in summer, on a pretty terrace, serves excellent meals with good antipasti, also pizzas; very good spaghetti with lobster.

€€ *Trattoria di Bugeber*, contrada Bugeber, ☎ 0923/914009. Offers all the local specialities and has a panoramic veranda, on a high point of the island; ballroom dancing in the evenings in summer.

K A M M A : **€€** *Trattoria Favarotta*, ☎ 0923/915347. Serves very tasty rabbit. Closed Wed. and winter.

S C A U R I **€€** *Scauri*, ☎ 0923/ 916101. One of the oldest establishments of the island, with an excellent reputation for local ravioli, fresh fish and couscous.

€€ *La Nicchia*, ☎ 0923/916342. Restaurant and pizzeria in an Arab garden; very good food, including *focaccia al paté di capperi*, soft bread with caper paste. Closed Wed.

€€ *La Vela*, ☎ 0923/918368. Imaginative cuisine and excellent pizzas.

Cafés pastry shops and ice cream parlours

Goloso, on the harbour, is just right for an evening aperitif.

Cicci's Bar, piazza Cavour, prepares very good snacks.

Tikirriki, on the harbour, for splendid ice creams.

Sport and leisure
Diving centres

Green Divers, at Mursia, ☎ 0923/ 918209, ✉ www. greendivers.it. Can organize night dives or archaeological dips.

Dive-X, 16 via Milano, ☎ 0923/ 912403, ✉ www.pantelleriadiving. com.

Scauri Diving Centre, ☎ 0923/ 916066.

Yacht charter and rental

Quelli di Pantelleria, ☎ 0923/918306.

Shopping

German-born Ivan, contrada Rekhale, makes beautiful **candles** using beeswax. Rosa Pucci, also at Rekhale, makes distinctive straw **bags and hats**; while Antonia Rizzo sews bright **patchwork quilts** in the village of Tracino. Salvatore Gabriele makes **lobster-pots** (*nasse*) which can be turned into attractive lamps quite easily. In vicolo S. Nicolò, not far from the harbour, is *Il mirto e la rosa*, a shop offering a wide assortment of **dried herbs** and **flowers** growing on the island, and their byproducts.

Wines

The wines, thought to be among the finest available in the world, are made using a high proportion of white *zibibbo* grapes. They are mostly *DOC*, so the quality is guaranteed. Although they are usually considered to be dessert wines, they are surprisingly good as aperitifs, when drunk icy cold. The kinds to look out for are *Moscato di Pantelleria*, a sweet, strong wine, best drunk chilled, excellent with cheese; *Moscato passito di Pantelleria*, made with grapes which have been allowed to wither in the sun before harvesting, and becomes an exquisite nectar said to have aphrodisiac properties; *Tanit*, or *Nikà*, from the *Case di Pietra* cellars (✉ www.casedipietra.it) are good names, and *Ben Ryé*, from the *Donnafugata Rallo* estate (✉ www.donnafugata.it) has won no less than 12 gold medals and one silver medal in international competitions since 2000! The island also produces a light spumante called *Il Solimano*. A red wine from the island, strong and sociable, is *Martingana*, produced by *Salvo Murana*.

History

Legend says that the island was the home of Calypso, the lovely nymph who was able to keep Ulysses by her side for seven long years. Archaeological evidence has proved the island was inhabited in the Neolithic era, and later it housed a Phoenician settlement called *Hiranin*, meaning 'place of the birds'. The Greeks called it *Kossyra*, meaning 'the small one', a name it maintained under the Romans, who took it in 217 BC. The Arabs gave it the name it still bears, *Bint er-rhia*, or 'daughter of the wind'. After its conquest by Roger I in 1123 it remained a Sicilian possession. During World War II it was used as a base for harrying allied convoys; reduced by heavy bombardment during May 1943 it was taken from the sea on 11 June with 11,000 prisoners, allied casualties being reported as 'one soldier bitten by a mule'. It has been used as a place of exile for political prisoners.

The island is particularly attractive for sea lovers. There are no beaches, but swimming from the rocks is very pleasant, because the water is clean and clear. Dolphins are common, and the rare nun seal is once again occasionally spotted, after many years of absence from Italian waters. It is a good place for birdwatching too, especially during the migratory passage, when herons, cranes, flamingoes, geese and ducks can be seen. During the summer the hoopoe is resident, as is the cattle egret, the Tunisian chaffinch and the rock thrush. The inhabitants of the island are farmers rather than fishermen, and using incredible patience and fortitude to care for their plants in the difficult, windswept volcanic terrain, they produce superb wines, capers, olive oil and citrus.

Mussolini called the island 'the unsinkable aircraft carrier', but the Allies certainly did their best to sink it, unsuccessfully, of course, and the port of Pantelleria had to be completely rebuilt after World War II, so the little houses around the harbour are relatively new. The oldest building, in fact, is the forbidding Spanish **Castello Barbacane** (open daily 18.00–20.00, and for exhibitions). In località Mursia 58 prehistoric tombs known as *sesi*, were discovered by

Paolo Orsi in the 19C. These large domed tumuli were built in blocks of lava. Only 27 have survived, notably the **Sese Grande**, the others have either fallen into ruin or been engulfed by new buildings.

The beautiful inland crater lake of **Bagno dell'Acqua** (or the Lago di Venere) is about 6km from the port. It is fed by a hot water spring and is 500m in diameter and 2m above sea-level. The fine rocky coast is best seen from a boat (which can be hired at the port). Some of the best swimming on the island can be had at the Arco dell'Elefante.

MOZIA, MARSALA AND MAZARA DEL VALLO

This chapter covers the west coast of Sicily from Trapani to Mazara del Vallo and the islands in the lagoon, including San Pantaleo, ancient *Mozia* (or Motya). The **salt marshes** (saline) between Trapani and Marsala (now a protected area), have interesting birdlife. Many salt pans are still worked, and the landscape is characterised by piles of salt protected by tiles, and windmills used for raising water from one pan to the next by means of an Archimedes' screw. The coastal plain is reminiscent of North Africa, dotted with white cube-shaped houses, palms and Norfolk Island pines. The beautiful island of **S. Pantaleo** (reached by ferry, see 'Getting there') has interesting Phoenician remains, and **Marsala**, on the site of a Carthaginian city and famous for its wine, is well worth a visit. Between Marsala and Mazara del Vallo the plain is densely cultivated with olives, low vineyards, and gardens of tomatoes, melons and cantaloupes.

Practical information

 ### Getting there
From Trapani. Mozia, on the island of S. Pantaleo is 23km, Marsala 31km and Mazara del Vallo 53km.
By bus
AST (☎ 0923/23222) runs buses from Trapani to Marsala and Mazara del Vallo, *Lumia* (☎ 0922/20414) connects Marsala to Mazara del Vallo and Agrigento, while *Salemi* (☎ 0923/951676) runs buses to Trapani and Palermo.

The **quay** from where boats depart for Mozia (S. Pantaleo) is c 1km away from Ragattisi where the bus between Trapani and Marsala stops. Buses from Marsala (piazza del Popolo) run to Mozia, Trapani, Palermo, Mazara del Vallo, Castelvetrano and Agrigento.

By train
Trains run from Trapani to Marsala (in c 40 mins), to Mazara del Vallo (in c 1 hr) continuing to Castelvetrano. Trains stop at Ragattisi, the nearest station to the quay for the boat to Mozia (San Pantaleo; about a 1km walk from the station.
By car
The main road (SS 115) between Trapani and Marsala bears heavy traffic and has numerous traffic lights; it is worth taking the prettier secondary coastal road. This leaves Trapani on the seaward side of the railway, passing the salt marshes and the turning for Nubia and the Salt Museum (c 5km south of Trapani). It then passes close to the island of Mozia (S. Pantaleo); the turning is signposted for Mozia at

Ragattisi train station.

Parking

Car parking in Marsala, on lungomare Boeo, or outside Porta Nuova or Porta Garibaldi.

Maritime services

Ferry for **Mozia** (S. Pantaleo) from the lagoon edge 1km from Ragattisi station (signposted; see *By train*, above). From Marsala, Molo Dogana (July–Sept) for the **Egadi Islands** and **Pantelleria** on the *Sandokan*, ☎ 0923/953434.

Bicycle hire

Bicycles are available free of charge for visitors to the city of Marsala, at 32, via G. Anca Omodei, from Mon–Fri 09.00–13.00, 16.00–19.00, ☎ 0923/993332.

Information offices

APT Trapani, ☎ 0923/ 29000.
APT Marsala, 100 via XI Maggio, ☎ 0923/714097.
APT Mazara del Vallo, 2 piazza Santa Veneranda, ☎ & 📠 0923/941727.
Marsala on line: 🖂 www.liljbeo-marsala.com, 🖂 www.prolocomarsala.org, 🖂 www.comune.marsala.tp.it.
Mazara del Vallo on line: 🖂 www.comune.mazara-del-vallo.tp.it.

Where to stay
Hotels

MARSALA ✶✶✶✶ *New Hotel Palace*, Lungomare Mediterraneo, ☎ 0923/719492, 📠 0923/719496. Delightful 19C building, recently restored, lovely hall. Garden, good restaurant, excellent wine list.
✶✶✶ *Acos*, 14 via Mazara, ☎ 0923/ 999166, 📠 0923/999132, 🖂 www.acoshotel.com. Comfortable rooms but quite a distance from town centre.
✶✶✶ *Delfino Beach*, 672 lungomare Mediterraneo, contrada Berbaro, ☎ 0923/751076, 📠 0923/751303, 🖂 www.delfinobeach.com. 2km south

of the town, recently renovated, elegant hotel with renowned restaurant, nice beach.
✶✶✶ *President*, 1 via Nino Bixio, ☎ 0923/ 999333, 📠 0923/999115. Reliable, modern hotel, quite central, nice pool.
✶✶✶ *Villa Favorita*, 27 via Favorita, ☎ 0923/989100, 📠 0923/980264, 🖂 www.villafavorita.com. Beautiful old winery, excellent restaurant and wine list, comfortable accommodation, gardens, tennis court, bowls and pool.
✶✶ *Tenuta Volpara*, contrada Volpara Bartolotta, ☎ 0923/984588, 📠 0923/ 984667, 🖂 www.delfinobeach.com. Beautifully restored and furnished farmhouse; very good restaurant and pizzeria.
✶✶ *Garden*, 36 via Gambini, ☎ & 📠 0923/982320. Small, simple hotel behind the railway station.
MAZARA DEL VALLO ✶✶✶ *Hotel Hopps*, 29 via Hopps, ☎ 0923/946133, 📠 0923/946075, 🖂 hoppshotel@ tiscalinet.it. Friendly, comfortable hotel, recently restructured, pool, disco, garden, good restaurant, private beach.
PETROSINO ✶✶✶ *Baglio Basile*, contrada Triglia-Scaletta, ☎ & 📠 0923/ 741705, 🖂 www.delfinobeach.com; new hotel in a restructured *baglio* among the vineyards of Petrosino, between Marsala and Mazara del Vallo. Good restaurant with excellent local wines; garden.

Accommodation in a salt mill

✶ *La Finestra sul Sale*, Saline Ettore e Infersa, 55 contrada Ettore Infersa, Marsala, ☎ & 📠 0923/733142, 0923/733003, 🖂 www.cilastour.com. Air-conditioned accommodation in the Marsala Stagnone wildlife reserve, right in front of the island of Mozia. The setting is lovely, the rooms are very comfortable. Artists would particularly enjoy this spot. Canoes are available for excursions on the lagoon. The same management plans to open another mill for guests in 2003 on Isola Longa, in the lagoon. The ultimate in getting-away-from-it-all holidays, Isola Longa is a birdwatchers' paradise and is also ideal for artists.

Bed and breakfast

MARSALA ☆☆ *Andrea's*, 216 contrada Spagnola, ☎ 328/4849399, 🖳 0923/717391, ✉ archimedesistemi@tin.it. On the lagoon, very welcoming. ☆☆ *Figuccia*, 1 via F. Noto, ☎ 339/2052973 or 368/7455510, 🖳 0923/714035, ✉ peppefigo@hotmail.com, close to the animated piazza Pizzo.

Paese Albergo

Rooms or apartments in the historic centre of Marsala rented to visitors by the *Association of Young Tour Operators*, ☎ 0923/547889, 🖳 0923/551094.

Farmhouse accommodation

MARSALA ☆☆ *Baglio Vajarassa*, 176 contrada Spagnola, Marsala, ☎ & 🖳 0923/968628, ✉ www.bagliovajarassa.it. Beautiful old winery, lots of atmosphere; relaxing.

☆ *Samperi*, località Strasatti, 308 contrada Samperi-Fornara, ☎ & 🖳 0923/712202, ✉ samperigiuseppe@libero.it. Farm south of Marsala producing wine, olive oil, citrus and cereals. Guests are welcome to take part in the harvesting or other day-to-day activities. Good restaurant. Horse riding, minigolf, tennis.

MAZARA DEL VALLO ☆☆ *Poggio Gilletto*, contrada S. Nicola Sottano, 🖳 0923/717689, ✉ enopoliosavalla@libero.it. Peaceful farm producing wine and carobs, bordering on two WWF wildlife reserves, Gorghi Tondi and Preola. The beach can be reached by bicycle. Cookery, painting and pottery courses.

PETROSINO ☆☆ *Baglio Spanò*, contrada Triglia-Scaletta, ☎ 348/8822095, 🖳 0923/989840, ✉ www.bagliospano.com. Delightful old winery with garden; excellent restaurant reserved for guests, with good house wine.

Residenza

MAZARA DEL VALLO *Residence Mediterraneo*, 31 via G. Hopps, ☎ 0923/932688, ✉ www.residencemed.it. New structure with air-conditioned rooms and apartments; self-catering or restaurant nearby.

Youth hostel

MAZARA DEL VALLO *Foresteria monastica San Michele Arcangelo*, 6 piazza S. Michele Arcangelo, ☎ & 🖳 0923/906565. No restaurant.

Campsite

MAZARA DEL VALLO ☆☆☆ *Sporting Camping Club*, località Bocca Arena, ☎ & 🖳 0923/947230, ✉ www.campingbysicily.com. Also bungalows and caravans to rent, close to a sandy beach; disco, restaurant, minigolf, tennis, basketball and volleyball; shade.

 Eating out
Restaurants

MARSALA €€€ *Villa Favorita*, 27 via Favorita (on the southern outskirts), ☎ 0923/989100. This is the place for lunching or dining in style; the couscous is exceptional. Good wine list, lovely surroundings.

€€€ *'A Ciaramira*, 182 contrada Misilla, ☎ 0923/967767, closed Mon. 8km out of town on the road to Salemi (SS 188) is this extraordinary restaurant, where a fixed price menu covers everything. The menu varies daily. Couscous with snails, homemade macaroni, excellent local wines.

€€ *Delfino*, 672 lungomare Mediterraneo (1km south of the town), ☎ 0923/998188 or 0923/969565. Well-known restaurant and pizzeria. Closed Tues. in winter.

€€ *Trattoria Garibaldi*, 35 via Rubino, piazza Addolorata, ☎ 0923/953006. Popular with the locals. Excellent fish, good local wines. Closed Sat. midday, Sun. evening.

€€ *Capo Lilybeo*, 40 lungomare Boeo,

☎ 0923/712881. Close to the archaeological museum. Excellent pasta dishes, pizza is served in the evenings. Closed Mon.

€ *Nashville*, 24 piazza Pizzo, ☎ 0923/951826. Simple restaurant, tables in the square in the summer, for good pizza and pasta.

€ *Bizzy*, 143 corso Gramsci, ☎ 0923/711168. Appetizing, inexpensive and fast.

MAZARA DEL VALLO €€€ *Il Pescatore*, 191 via Castelvetrano, ☎ 0923/947580, on the outskirts of Mazara. Elegant restaurant which attracts gourmets coming from all over Italy, especially for the fish. Very good pasta dishes and couscous, delicious desserts, good wine cellar, impeccable service. Closed Mon. in winter.

€€ *Alla Kasbah*, 10 via Itria, ☎ 0923/906126. In the heart of the old city, intrigueing little restaurant offering Tunisian and Sicilian cuisine.

€€ *La Bettola*, 32 via Francesco Maccagnone, ☎ 0923/946422. Very good local fare and good local wines too. Closed Wed.

€€ *Al Pesciolino d'Oro*, 109 lungomare San Vito, ☎ 0923/909286. A favourite with the locals; the grilled and fried fish are superlative, so is the *zuppa di pesce* (fish soup). Delicious meat and local sausages also available. Closed Thurs.

€ *Lo Sciaittolo*, 9 via Tortorici, ☎ 0923/946313. Delicious pasta, couscous, and fish; exceptional antipasti; pizza in the evenings. Closed Thurs.

€ *Il Gambero*, 3 lungomare Mazzini, ☎ 0923/932932. Friendly, crowded restaurant on the seafront. Closed Tues.

Cafés, pastry shops and ice cream parlours

MARSALA *Bar Saviny*, 25/F piazza Piemonte e Lombardo. Fashionable tea room for unforgettable cakes and pastries, also snacks, sandwiches and lunches.

Aloha, 152 via Mazzini, excellent espresso and Sicilian breakfast.

Vito, 16 corso Gramsci, one of the best places in town for ice cream. If you don't have a sweet tooth, then here is a friendly tavern for you, *Osteria il mare colore del vino*, in via Caturca, a turning off via XI Maggio.

MAZARA DEL VALLO *Pasticceria Lamia*, 44 via Val di Mazara. Delicious local pastries; ask for the local biscuits: *muccunate* and *mazaresi al pistacchio*.

Picnics

The island of Mozia is a delightful place to picnic, so is the seafront near Capo Boeo.

Shopping

There are several good places in Marsala for buying **wines** or other local products. *Enoteca La Ruota* and *Enoteca Luminario* are close to each other on lungomare Boeo, near the Archaeological Museum. Another good shop in the old city centre is *Sombrero*, 30 via Garibaldi, with a very wide assortment of tempting goodies. If you have acquired a taste for Sicilian espresso, this is time to stock up on **coffee**; the beans are roasted on the premises. *Tradizioni di Sicilia*, at 35 piazza Caprera, ✉ www.tradizionidisicilia.com. is some way from the centre but you could order via their website, *Enoteca Fazio*, 99 via S. Bilardello, is a good example of how the younger generation is injecting new energy into long established industries; their wines and olive oil are surprisingly good.

Internet points

MARSALA The Biblioteca comunale (town library) during opening hours, at 100 via XI Maggio.

Internet Point Albacom, 110 via Mazzini.

MAZARA DEL VALLO *Net Phone*, 21 piazza Porta Palermo, ☎ 0923/909840.

Idea W, 2 via Santa Caterina, ☎ 0923/904001 or 0923/670795.

Annual festivals

MARSALA On Maundy Thursday there is a magnificent procession representing the Via Crucis, with many townsfolk taking part, wearing beautiful costumes. The little girls dressed as Veronica are particularly impressive, as traditionally they must wear all the family jewels!

MAZARA DEL VALLO The third Sunday in August is dedicated to '**U Fistinu di San Vitu**, celebrations for St Vitus, during which the fishermen pull a cart with his statue through the streets, many people wear 17C dress, there is a procession of *tableaux vivants*, and the partecipation of the townsfolk is total. For information, ☎ 0923/941777.

Mozia on the island of San Pantaleo and Lo Stagnone

The island of San Pantaleo, just 1km offshore (2.5km in circumference), famous as the site of the Phoenician town of *Motya* or *Mothia*, is one of three islands in the beautiful shallow lagoon, known as **Lo Stagnone**, protected from the sea by the Isola Longa. The lagoon (2000 ha) has an average depth of just over 1m, and is abundant in fish. Since Phoenician times salt has been extracted from the marshes and, after a period of decline, the industry is showing a promising revival. Pyramidal heaps of salt roofed with red tiles line the shore, and a few windmills survive.

Getting there

On the edge of the lagoon (signposted from the coastal road), in front of the island of S. Pantaleo, beside a hut there is a car park. Several boatmen are available to ferry visitors over to the island and back but the long-established boatman, who has been doing this for many years (quite alone until recently), is Michele Pace, easily spotted because he always takes his beautiful dog along for company (☎ 347/3430329); Franco Pace also runs a service (☎ 347/7790218).

There is a splendid view from the water's edge of the island of S. Pantaleo with its pine trees, just to the left of which can be seen the island of Favignana. Behind S. Pantaleo there is a view of the island of Levanzo, and to the left in the distance is the island of Marettimo. On the far right the mountain of Erice is prominent beyond salt pans, windmills and piles of salt.

S. Pantaleo is an oasis of luxuriant vegetation, a sanctuary for birds, with sweet-smelling plants, palm trees and pinewoods. The ruins of Phoenician Mozia are unenclosed (admission daily 09.00–17.00, 19.00 in summer, ☎ 0923/712598) and the views are delightful, with wonderful colours all around of the sky and the sea. Sandwiches and drinks are available at the custodian's house and it is a lovely place to picnic.

History

Motya was founded in the mid-8C BC by Phoenicians as a commercial base and industrial area (the word means 'mills'). By the mid-6C BC the island was entirely surrounded by defensive walls, 2400m long and over 2m thick. It became an important Carthaginian station, controlling a large part of the western Mediterranean. In his determination to wipe out the Carthaginians from Sicily, Dionysius I of Syracuse brought a huge army here in 398 BC. During the fierce battle which ensued, he used wooden towers so that his men could shoot over the walls, and also mount catapults. But the tyrant's fleet became trapped in the lagoon; Dionysius brilliantly solved the problem by dragging his ships over an isthmus 4 km wide, using logs, to the open sea where he finally defeated the enemy. By the following year the Carthaginians had moved their headquarters to *Lilybaeum*.

The island was owned by Joseph (Pip) Whitaker (1850–1936), a distinguished ornithologist and amateur archaeologist, and member of the famous family of Marsala wine merchants. He began excavations here around 1913, and since the death of his daughter Delia in 1971 the island has been the property of the *Joseph Whitaker Foundation* (167 via Dante, Palermo, ☎ 091/6820522). Excavations continued until around 1993. The low vineyards here still produce an excellent wine.

The boat crosses the lagoon with a view left of the island of Favignana and right of Monte Erice beyond the salt pans. It docks near a stretch of the fortifications of the Punic city. A path leads to a group of houses and, beside a bronze bust of Whitaker, the crenellated Whitaker villa. It is appropriately used as a **museum** (open daily 09.00–13.00, 15.00–18.30; in winter open mornings only, ☎ 0923/712598). It was founded in 1925, and some of the showcases brought at that time from Edinburgh and Belfast are still used. The material comes from excavations at Mozia, Lilybaeum and Birgi, carried out by Whitaker and (in the last few years) by the Italian State. It includes Phoenician ceramics, the earliest dating from the 8C BC, and Greek ware including proto-Corinthian and Corinthian vases and Attic black- and red-figure vases. Other finds from the island include Phoenician glass, alabaster and jewellery. Among the sculptural fragments is an extraordinarily vivid metope from the North Gate showing two lions attacking a bull, distinctly Mycenaean in style (end of 7C or beginning of 6C BC), and a marble krater with bas-reliefs (Augustan period). The very expressive statue of a young man (*Il Giovane di Mozia*) wearing a finely pleated linen tunic was found at Cappiddazzu on the northeast side of the island in 1979. He has rather a disdainful air, one hand on his hip, showing supreme self-confidence in his youth, beauty and power. This remarkable work, made of white marble, is thought to be by a Greek master and to date from c 440 BC. A recent theory is that the statue may represent Melqart (Hercules), the titular divinity of Tyre who was probably wearing a lion's skin made of bronze, which would have partially covered his head, and a bronze band around his chest. The statue was found buried under a thin layer of earth, face down in the road by the sanctuary. The face and the front are in fact abraded, and this could have happened when his bronze accoutrements were being torn from his body (during Dionysius's attack?). An explanation for the fact that he was not recovered and replaced in a temple, in spite of the enormous value, could be because the shocked survivors of the battle thought he had been profanated and preferred to bury him in the road where they found him.

Nearby is a small building used up until the 1970s for wine-making. During reconstruction work in 1995 remains of houses (called **Zona E**), dating from 7C–4C BC, were found beneath the pavement: the excavations can now be viewed from a walkway.

The excavations on the island are discreetly signposted along various paths which start from the museum. In front of the museum a path leads towards the lagoon to the **House of the Mosaics**, surrounded by a fence and rich vegetation,

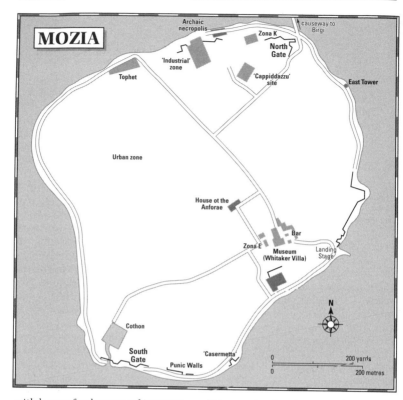

with bases of columns and interesting pebble mosaics showing a panther attacking a bull, a griffin chasing a deer, etc. (4C–3C BC). A longer path, flanked by bushes, leads from the custodian's house across the southern part of the island to the waterfront at the southeast corner, beside the **Cothon** and **South Gate**. This small basin (50 x 40m) within the walls is thought to have been an artificial dock used for repairing ships. A paved canal with ashlar walls of the 6C BC, thought to be its seaward entrance, has also been excavated. A path leads along the edge of the south shore past an enclosure near a clump of pine trees where excavations have unearthed a building, probably used for military purposes (and known as the Casermetta). There are fine views across the lagoon of the piles of salt on the mainland, and of the Egadi Islands.

The path continues along the water's edge past the jetty and the impressive fortifications (late 6C BC), the best preserved stretch on the island. The East Tower preserves its flight of steps. Beyond some recent excavations (protected by a roof) is the imposing North Gate, with a triple line of defences. It defended a submerged causeway (meant to be invisible from land, but perfectly practicable for a horse and cart), which was built in the late 6C BC to link the island to the mainland and a necropolis at Birgi. It is 7km long and just wide enough for two carts to pass each other. There is a fine view of Erice from here, beyond the low islands of the lagoon. A path leads inland through the north gate to **Cappiddazzu**, the site of an important sanctuary, perhaps dedicated to Melqart. The name means 'Big Hat' and refers to an enormous ghost which is said to haunt this part of the island, wearing a hat with a wide brim. The first sightings of the ghost go back to the early 19C. Above the level of the path is a building with mosaic remains. To the right is a field with low vines and two enclosed areas, the farthest of which, on the edge of the sea, is the Archaic necropolis with tombs dating from the 8C–6C BC. Nearby a fence surrounds an 'industrial area', known as **Zona K**, with interesting kilns, similar in design to some found in Syria and Palestine.

The largest enclosure is the Tophet, a Punic sacrificial burial ground dedicated to the goddess Tanith and to the god Baal Hammon, where children were sacrificed (replaced after the 5C BC by animal sacrifices). Excavations here produced cinerary urns, votive terracotta masks, and stelae (some with human figures). From the Tophet a path, marked by low olive trees, leads back through a vineyard in the centre of the island towards the museum. It passes (right) an enclosure with remains of the **Casa delle Anfore**, so-called because a huge deposit of amphorae was found here.

On the edge of the lagoon, near the jetty, is an old salt mill which is now a **museum** and a small hotel, *Saline Ettore e Infersa*. The various phases of obtaining salt from sea water (open daily in winter 09.30–13.30, 15.00–19.30, summer 09.00–20.00, contrada Ettore Infersa, ☎ 0923/966936) are explained. Boats or canoes can be hired (enquire on the island or at the Ettore Infersa Salt Mill) to visit the lovely **Stagnone lagoon**, with its three small islands, including the large Isola Longa (admission only with special permission), which has luxuriant vegetation and some abandoned salt works.

Marsala

Marsala (population 80,200) is a pleasant town with a 16C aspect, and an attractive open seafront on Capo Boeo, the site of the Carthaginian city of Lilybaeum. It gives its name to a famous dessert wine still produced here in large quantities from the vineyards along the coast, and stored in huge *bagli*. It is the most important wine producing centre on the island. The sunset over the lagoon is indescribably beautiful.

History

Lilybaeum, founded by the Carthaginians in 396 BC, near the headland of Capo Boeo, the western extremity of Sicily, and peopled from *Motya* (see above), was their strongest bulwark in Sicily, and succumbed to the Romans only after a siege of ten years (250–241). As the seat of the Roman governor of Sicily it reached its zenith. Cicero called it *civitas splendidissima*. In 47 BC Julius Caesar pitched camp here on his way to Africa. A *municipium* during the Augustan age, it was later raised to the status of *colonia*. It kept its importance as an avenue of communication with Africa during the Saracen dominion under the name *Marsa Alí*, the harbour of Ali, but declined after 1574 when Don Juan of Austria (illegitimate son of Charles V) almost completely blocked its port to protect it from Barbary pirates.

The **wine trade** was founded by John Woodhouse in 1773 when he made the first shipment of local white wine to Liverpool, conserving it on its month-long journey by adding alcohol. Marsala became popular in England as an alternative to madeira and port. In 1798, after the Battle of the Nile,

Nelson placed a large order of Marsala for his fleet. In 1806 Benjamin Ingham and his nephew Whitaker also took up trading in Marsala with great success; by 1812 they were exporting the wine to North America. Production on an even grander scale was undertaken by Vincenzo Florio (d. 1868), one of Sicily's most able businessmen. In 1929 the establishments of Woodhouse, Ingham Whitaker and Florio were taken over by *Cinzano*, and merged under the name of *Florio*. The house of *Florio* (open Mon–Thur 15.00–17.00, Fri 11.00–12.00, ☎ 0923/781111, 📠 0923/982380) continues to flourish along with many other companies, including *Pellegrino* (39 via del Fante, ☎ 0923/719911, 📠 0923/953542, ✉ www.carlopellegrino.it, visits from 09.00–12.00, 14.30–17.30 Mon–Fri, Sat mornings only), *Rallo* (2 via Vincenzo Florio, ☎ 0923/721633, ✉ www.donnafugata.it) and *Montalto*.

Garibaldi and the 'Thousand' landed here on 11 May 1860, being unobtrusively assisted by two British warships which were there to protect the wine merchants. In 1943, Marsala was heavily damaged by allied air attacks.

The town is entered by the monumental **Porta Garibaldi**, formerly the 'Porta di Mare', reconstructed in 1685. On the left is the church of the **Addolorata**, with a fine circular domed 18C interior, and a venerated popular statue of the *Madonna* wearing a black cloak. Municipal offices occupy a restored 16C military building, behind which is the market square. Via Garibaldi continues to the central piazza della Repubblica with the idiosyncratic **Palazzo Comunale** (Town Hall) which has original lamps on its upper storey. Opposite on via XI Maggio, is a wall and dome of the 17C church of **S. Giuseppe**, with a lovely interior and a fine organ.

The Cathedral

The Cathedral (S. Tommaso di Canterbury) has a Baroque front completed in 1957. The first church on this site was built in 1176–82 and dedicated to St Thomas Becket. A new building, begun in 1607 and completed in 1717 was ruined when the dome collapsed in 1893, and it was partly rebuilt in the 20C. The pleasant interior, with pretty tiled floors in the side chapels, has interesting 17C paintings and sculptures.

South side: in the first chapel there is an unusual statue of the *Assunta* and two reliefs on the side wall, all by Antonino Gagini. The delicately carved tomb slab dates from 1556. In the second chapel there is a 15C statue of the *Madonna*, and a tomb with the effigy of *Antonio Grignano* (d. 1475) attributed to Domenico Gagini. In the third chapel is an elaborate statue of the *Madonna dell'Itria*, and the tomb of Giulio Alazzaro with an amusing effigy, both by Antonino Gagini. The fifth chapel has a 15C Crucifix and an expressive popular statue of the *Virgin in mourning*. In the south transept is a good altarpiece of the *Presentation in the Temple* by Antonello or Mariano Riccio, and the tomb of Antonio Lombardo, who donated the tapestries to the cathedral (now in a museum, see below). In the chapel to the right of the sanctuary is an unusual statue of the *Madonna* (wielding a distaff), attributed to Giuliano Mancino, and a tomb with an effigy of *Antonio Liotta* (d. 1512), also attributed to Mancino. On either side of the sanctuary are two statues, one of *St Vincent Ferrer* attributed to Giacomo Gagini and one of *St Thomas the Apostle* by Antonello Gagini. In the apse is a 17C painting of the *Martyrdom of St Thomas* in the original frame. In the chapel to the left of the sanctuary is a beautiful gilded marble altarpiece of

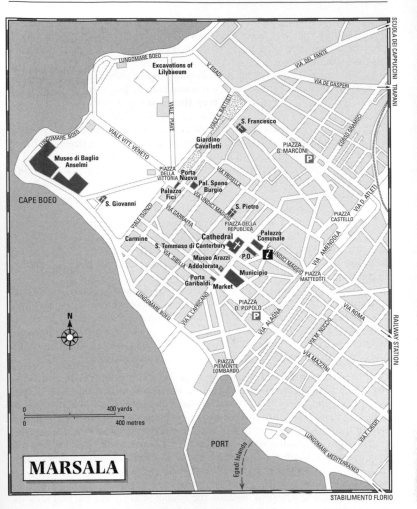

MARSALA

the *Passion* begun in 1518 by Bartolomeo Berrettaro and finished by Antonello Gagini (1532; four of the panels have been set into the walls).

North side: in the sixth chapel is a charming polychrome wooden statue of the *Our Lady of Carmel*, and in the second chapel is another wooden statue of the *Madonna* (1593), and two frescoed ex-votos with scenes of Marsala. A 17C silver statue of *St Thomas of Canterbury*, formerly outside the choir, has been removed for safety.

Behind the Cathedral, at no. 57 via Giuseppe Garraffa is the small **Museum of Tapestries** (open 09.00–13.00, 16.00–18.00, closed Mon, ☎ 0923/712903), opened in 1985 to display eight precious tapestries given to the cathedral in 1589 by Antonio Lombardo, archbishop of Messina (1523–95), born in Marsala and buried in the Cathedral. He became ambassador to Spain, and the very fine tapestries depicting the *Capture of Jerusalem* (made in Brussels between 1530 and 1550) are known to have come from the royal palace of Philip II in Madrid. They are displayed on three floors: since their careful restoration they have to be kept in darkened rooms.

Via XI Maggio runs off piazza della Repubblica (see above). The 15C **convent of S. Pietro**, in via Correale, with a massive pointed tower, is now used as the town library, cultural centre and **Civic Museum** (open every day except Mon 08.30–13.30, 15.00–20.00, Sun & PH 09.30–13.30, 16.00–20.00, ☎ 0923/716298). The museum has sections on Ancient History, the Risorgimento (the exploits of Giuseppe Garibaldi), and Popular Traditions. A street on the left leads towards the former church and convent of the **Carmine**, now used to house the municipal archives and an interesting art gallery (open daily 10.00–13.00, 17.00–19.00, closed Mon, ☎ 0923/711631). The pretty detached campanile was designed by Giovanni Battista Amico. The former convent was founded in the late 14C with an 18C cloister.

Nearby, in an attractive square with a Baroque fountain is the former church of **S. Cecilia**, which has a Baroque façade. Concerts are held here. In via XI Maggio, just before Porta Nuova, is the façade (left) of Palazzo Fici with a tall palm tree in its delightful Baroque courtyard. Opposite is the 19C–20C Palazzo Spanò Burgio (no. 15).

Outside the gate is the entrance (right) to the **Giardino Cavallotti**, lovely public gardens with huge ficus trees, magnolias and ornamental Norfolk Island pines. Between piazza della Vittoria and the seafront extends **Capo Boeo**, an open area with lawns and trees. Some picturesque old *bagli* on the seafront are still used as warehouses for wine, others have been converted into restaurants, and one of them houses the Archaeological Museum (see below).

Capo Boeo was the site of **Lilybaeum**, the excavations of which are reached by steps from viale Piave, or by a path from Porta Nuova (known as the Insula Romana (open 09.00–13.30, Wed, Fri, Sat & Sun also 16.00–18.30); visitors may find it closed for chronic shortage of custodians, (☎ 0923/952535). In a well-restored house are diagrams of the site, which includes a Roman villa (surrounded by a fence and covered for protection) dating from the 3C AD, which was built over in the Arab period. Around the impluvium are four mosaics of wild beasts attacking each other (thought to represent circus animals), probably the work of African craftsmen. There are remains of baths and other rooms with mosaics, including a head of *Medusa*, the symbol of Trinacria, the four seasons, etc. Nearby are more recent excavations including part of the walls, a necropolis, a Roman road, a Roman vomitorium, etc. A hypogeum with painted walls where Crispia Salvia was buried in the 2C AD has also been discovered.

On the tip of the promontory is the Baglio Anselmi, a former Marsala distillery and wine cellar, which has been restored as the **Baglio Anselmi Regional Archaeological Museum** (open daily 09.00–13.30; Wed, Fri, Sat & Sun, also 16.00–18.30; ☎ 0923/952535), with a very interesting collection. From the entrance hall the spacious courtyard is visible; the museum is arranged in two huge vaulted warehouses. The display begins in the hall on the left (and on the left wall), with **prehistoric material** from the Marsala area, in particular from Mozia. Beyond, two showcases have **Phoenician articles** from the *tophet* (sacrificial burial area) of Mozia. In the centre of the room are two cases of exquisite **Hellenistic gold**

jewellery found in Marsala. The finds from the Phoenician **necropolis of Lilybaeum** are displayed chronologically with explanatory diagrams and photographs, and include ceramics, funerary monuments, sculptures, terracottas, and Tanagra figurines (graceful, female dancing figures, so called because the first were found at Tanagra in Greece). On the end wall are fragments of funerary monuments, stele and edicole with carved inscriptions or paintings (3C–2C BC) from Mozia and Lilybaeum. Also here are fragments from a large mausoleum in local stone covered with a fine layer of white and polychrome stucco (its hypothetical form has been reconstructed in a drawing). A small room displays epigraphs. On the right wall of the hall are finds from **Roman Lilybaeum** (3C–4C AD), and in the centre of the room a model of the excavations on Capo Boeo. In show cases are fragments of wall paintings, a hoard of coins, lamps and a fragment of a female statuette of the 3C AD. In the centre, two mosaics (5C AD and 3C AD) and an *opus sectile* pavement from the 4C AD. The display ends with photographs of paleochristian finds, and a case of ceramics including Siculo-Norman ware. The last case illustrates the discovery of a Norman wreck offshore in 1983, with a few finds from the boat.

The other splendid hall on the right contains the **Punic ship**, discovered by Honor Frost in 1971 off the Isola Longa, in the Stagnone lagoon. The well-preserved poop was recovered from the seabed and the rest of the hulk, 35m long, was carefully reconstructed in 1980. Manned by 68 oarsmen, it is thought to have been sunk on its maiden voyage during the First Punic War. It is unique as the only warship of this period so far discovered; it is not known how the iron nails resisted the corrosion of the sea. The ship has been partly reconstructed around the original wood which is conserved beneath a huge tent, which makes viewing awkward. Drawings illustrate the original appearance of the ship. At the end of the room are two cases of objects found on board, including remains of ropes, a sailor's wooden button, a bone needle used for making nets, corks from the amphorae, a brush, some ceramic fragments, and cannabis leaves and stalks—possibly an aid to the oarsmen during battle. The underwater finds include numerous amphorae, of which the contents, place of origin and date offer an interesting insight on trade in the Mediterranean in ancient times.

Nearby is the little church of **S. Giovanni** (kept locked, enquire for the key at the tourist office), covering the so-called Grotto of the Sibyl, with a spring of water which later became an early Christian baptistery. There are still faint traces of ancient 5C AD frescoes.

The Sibyl of Lilybaeum

In the past people in the Mediterranean would often turn to prophetesses or sibyls when they wanted to know something about the future; it was believed that they could speak for the gods, especially Apollo, who was generous in this respect, and is often referred to as 'the far-seeing One'. There were several places where these oracles could be consulted such as at Delphi or Cuma, but the lilybean sibyl was considered to be quite reliable. The person requiring the information would enter the grotto where the priestess lived and put his question; she would then bathe his face and her own with water from the little pool. They would then take turns in sipping wine from a golden cup, after which the sibyl would enter a trance-like state and read the future in the dregs of wine remaining in the cup. The custom died out when Sicily became a province of Rome in the 3C BC.

On the road which continues along the seafront, lined with palms, is the former **Baglio Woodhouse** (the entrance is marked by two round towers in front of a jetty and next to a chapel built by the English). In the harbour only the base remains of the monument commemorating the Landing of the Thousand, by Ettore Ximenes. It was destroyed in World War II. The road passes a number of old *bagli*, and, beside two tall palm trees, is the **Stabilimento Florio** (see above for opening times). The monumental buildings were designed in 1833–35 by Ernesto Basile around an inner courtyard planted with trees. Visitors are shown the historic cellars and invited to taste the wine (free of charge). In the small museum a letter is preserved from Nelson, Duke of Bronte to John Woodhouse in 1800 with an order for Marsala for his fleet. The neo-classical villa built by Benjamin Ingham can be seen further along the waterfront.

North of the town, in the **Scuola dei Cappuccini** are remains of a Punic-Roman necropolis (open in summer). To the south, on SS115, the former Baglio Amodeo, one of the oldest Marsala wineries, is surrounded by a beautiful garden and is open as a hotel and restaurant (*Villa Favorita*).

Mazara del Vallo

Mazara del Vallo, at the mouth of the Mazaro, is the most important fishing town in Italy (population 47,800), of whom about 1000 are Tunisians who work on the farms and in the fishing fleet. It has a colourful waterfront and busy harbour. The town, built in golden tufa, has a distinctly Arab flavour. Animated and attractive, with elegant shops and graceful squares, Mazara is the most interesting town in western Sicily.

History

Mazara, once a Phoenician trading post, became an emporium of Selinunte and fell with it in 409 BC. It was held by the Carthaginians until 210 BC when it came under Roman rule. Here in 827 the Saracens, called in by the governor Euphemius to assist his pretensions to the Imperial purple, gained their first foothold on the island. There followed the most important period in the town's history, when it became the capital of the Val di Mazara, one of the three administrative districts into which the Arabs divided Sicily. It was finally captured by Count Roger in 1075; and it was here in 1097 that the first Sicilian parliament met, one of the oldest in the world.

The **Cathedral** was founded in 1093 and rebuilt in 1690–94. Above the west door which faces the sea, is a 16C sculpture of *Count Roger* on horseback. The interior contains a *Transfiguration* in the apse by Antonello Gagini (finished by his son Antonino, 1537). The two statues of *St Bartholomew* and *St Ignatius* are by Ignazio Marabitti. In the south aisle is a sculpted portal by Bartolomeo Berrettaro. In the vestibule of the chapter-house are two Roman sarcophaghi. Off the north side is a chapel with a 13C painted Cross, and in the chapel of the Madonna del Soccorso is a Byzantine fresco in a niche of *Christ Pantocrator*.

Between the Cathedral and the seafront is a **public garden** with fine trees on the the site of the Norman castle, a ruined wall of which faces the busy piazza Mokarta at the end of the main corso Umberto I. On the other side of the Cathedral is the 18C **piazza della Repubblica**, with a statue by Marabitti (1771) and the handsome **Seminario Vescovile** (1710) with a double portico. The **Diocesan Museum** (open Sat & Sun 10.00–12.00) contains the tomb of

Giovanni Montaperto (1495) by Domenico Gagini, paintings, vestments, etc. The precious cathedral **treasury** displayed here includes a processional Cross from Salemi dated 1386, by a Pisan artist, and another Cross attributed to Giovanni di Spagna (c 1448), as well as numerous 18C reliquaries and church silver.

Via S. Giuseppe leads to the church of **S. Caterina** decorated in 1797 by Giuseppe Testa, with a statue of the saint by Antonello Gagini (1524). On the other side of piazza della Repubblica via XX Settembre leads to piazza Plebiscito with the two 16C churches of the Carmine and **S. Egidio**, soon to become the **Museum of the Satyr** (due to open in 2003). In 1998 some local fishermen found a bronze statue of a satyr caught in their nets, while fishing in the Sicilian Channel. By returning to the same area a few weeks later they found the left leg of the statue and a bronze elephant's foot, perhaps from the same statuary group; they are still trying to find the missing arms and one leg. It is encouraging that the statue was not sold on the clandestine antiquarian market; those involved are extremely proud of their discovery. The Satyr could be Dionysos himself; he is shown with his body twisted in a dance of drunken ecstasy, head thrown back, hair wildly flying, pointed ears. He is a little larger than life size, the bronze is about 7mm thick, the weight, including the stand, is about 140 kg. Judging by other works of art on the same subject: statues, reliefs, cameos and so on, in various museums of Europe, the Satyr would have been carrying an empty wine cup in his left hand and a long rattle in his right. A panther skin would have been thrown over his left arm with its legs and tail flailing, and this, plus his donkey tail behind him, would have increased the effect of his frenzied whirling. Restoration and research on the statue is still being carried out, but a tentative date for it can be set between 404 and 280 BC, and one authority has even declared that it could be the work of Praxiteles himself. Close by is the church of S. Ignazio and the **Collegio dei Gesuiti** (1675–86), which now houses the municipal library and archives, and the **Civic Museum** (open weekdays 08.30–14.00) which has Roman finds from the area and two interesting sculpted elephants which once bore the columns outside the west porch of the Norman cathedral. A section dedicated to the history of the local fishing industry is also to be opened here.

The **harbour** lies at the mouth of the River Mazaro which is normally filled with the fishing fleet during the day, except on Saturdays. This is the most picturesque part of the city, together with the Tunisian district around via Porta Palermo and via Bagno. A short way upstream stands the little Norman-Byzantine church of **S. Nicolò Regale** with a crenellated top. The Lungomazaro continues along the river past the fish market to the bridge from which there is a splendid view of the boats. Further upstream are caves, once inhabited.

The church of the **Madonna dell'Alto**, erected in 1103 by Juliet, daughter of Count Roger, is 2km outside the town.

SELINUNTE AND THE BELICE VALLEY

Selinunte is one of the most impressive classical sites in Sicily because it was never subsequently built over: there are temples and the extensive remains of the acropolis. The nearest town, **Castelvetrano**, has a small archaeological museum. The quarries used for excavating the stone to build the temples of

Selinunte survive nearby at **Cave di Cusa** and are still an extraordinary sight in a lovely peaceful spot. At **Salemi** extraordinary loaves are baked by the local women twice a year, for the feasts of S. Biagio and S. Giuseppe.

Practical information

Getting there
By bus

Buses from Castelvetrano to Selinunte (the stop, near the disused railway station, is a 5 min walk from the entrance).

By train

From Trapani to Castelvetrano 121km in 2–3 hrs via Alcamo diramazione; a bus service has replaced the branch line from Castelvetrano to Selinunte, 14km in 25 mins.

By car

An interesting route by car from Trapani is along the coastal road via Mozia and Marsala (see p 196); there is also a motorway (longer but easier) all the way from Trapani via Segesta and Salemi to Castelvetrano, passing through really spectacular farmland.

Information offices

C/o Civic Museum, **Castelvetrano**, ☎ 0924/904932.
By the entrance to the archaeological park and car park, **Selinunte**, ☎ 0924/46251.
Poggioreale on line: ✉ www.poggioreale.com.it.
Salemi on line: ✉ www.comune.salemi.tp.it.

Where to stay
Hotels

SELINUNTE (MARINELLA) ☆☆☆ *Alceste*, 21 via Alceste, ☎ 0924/46184, ✉ 0924/46143, ✉ www.chshotels.com. Small, modern, family-run hotel with one of the best restaurants in Sicily; walking

distance from the archaeological park.
☆☆☆ *Paradise Beach*, contrada Belice di Mare, ☎ 0924/46333 ✉ 0924/46477, ✉ www.hotelparadisebeach.it. Large resort hotel in spectacular position, quite far from the site and the village (it is on the Menfi side of the valley), but many amenities including tennis, pool, sailing and horseriding.
☆ *Lido Azzurro*, 98 via Marco Polo, ☎ & ✉ 0924/46256, ✉ lazzurro@ freemail.it. Central position, good restaurant.
SELINUNTE (TRE FONTANE)
☆☆☆☆ *Hotel Club Ramuxara*, contrada Tonnara, Tre Fontane, Campobello di Mazara, ☎ 0924/945040, 0924/945050 ✉ 0924/945167, ✉ www.besthotels.travel.com. New resort hotel with plenty of facilities and good restaurant on a beautiful stretch of coast between the wildlife reserve at Capo Granitola and the (horrid) summer bungalow village of Triscina.

Bed and breakfast

CASTELVETRANO *Villa Mimosa*, run by Jacky Sirimanne, contrada La Rocchetta, Castelvetrano, ☎ 0924/44583 or 338/1387388, ✉ sirimanne @libero.it, about half-way between Castelvetrano and Selinunte, in the countryside. Jacky organizes painting holidays for her guests and can also provide meals on request; she is a sommelier and knows all about wine and olive oil.
SALEMI ☆☆☆ *Conte Umberto*, 172a via Giovanni Amendola, ☎ 0924/982062; faxes should be addressed to Giovanni Armata, ✉ 0924/981058. The arrangements are for self-catering, but signora Armata prepares breakfast and there is a restaurant

close by. The house is in the heart of the old city.

SELINUNTE (MARINELLA) *Il Pescatore*, 31 via Castore e Polluce, ☎ 0924/46303. Self-catering rooms but there is an excellent breakfast. *Selinon di Selinunte*, 8 via della Cittadella, ☎ & 🖷 0924/903744. Comfortable old farmhouse, all rooms with private bath; air conditioning; baby sitter available; credit cards accepted. Nice breakfasts, bicycles for hire, English, French & Spanish spoken. *The Holiday House*, 23 via Apollonio Rodio, ☎ 0924/46035. In the modern part of town and convenient for the archaeological site.

Farm accommodation

CASTELVETRANO (3km from Selinunte) ✫✫✫✫ *Masseria Anni Trenta*, contrada Latomie-Mortiluzzi, ☎ 368/591441, 🖷 0924/46542. Charming little farm, air-conditioned rooms with TV; small zoo; good food; ideal for children.
MENFI ✫✫✫✫ *Baglio San Vincenzo*, contrada San Vincenzo, Menfi, ☎ 0924/26103, ✉ www.baglio sanvincenzo.it. A 16C farm which produces excellent wine and olive oil; courses are arranged on wine tasting, also on Sicilian cookery; guests are invited to take part in the farm activities at harvest time; close by is the lovely, clean beach of Porto Palo. This is really in the province of Agrigento, but it is conveniently placed for Selinunte.
SALEMI ✫✫✫ *Settesoldi*, 111 contrada Settesoldi, Salemi, ☎ 0924/982011 or 0924/64025, 🖷 0924/64374, ✉ www.agrisettesoldi.it. Friendly farm within walking distance from Salemi. Vineyard and olive grove. Peaceful spot.

Rooms and apartments to rent

SANTA NINFA *Case Vacanze Santa Ninfa*, 45 via Scarlatti, ☎ 0924/62421, 🖷 0924/62584, ✉ www.casevacanza santaninfa.it.

Campsites

MARINELLA DI SELINUNTE ✫✫✫ *L'Oasi di Selinunte*, via Pitagora, Marinella, ☎ 0924/46885, 🖷 0924/941107. On a sandy beach; very comfortable. Also bungalows; pool; restaurant; disco; shade.
✫ *Athena* (SS115), località Marinella, ☎ & 🖷 0924/46132.
✫ *Il Maggiolino* (SS115) località Marinella di Selinunte, ☎ & 🖷 0924/46044, ✉ www.camping maggiolino.it.

 ## Eating out
Restaurants

MARINELLA DI SELINUNTE €€ *Hotel Alceste* (see above). This restaurant is the ideal place for grilled fish, local sourdough bread, perfect seafood risotto, spaghetti with clams or shrimps, *pasta cu' le sarde* (macaroni with fennel and sardines), all served with excellent local wines.
€ *Agorà*, 51 via Marco Polo, is an excellent pizzeria.

Picnics

Selinunte is a wonderful place to picnic (tables are also provided in the shady river valley off the road between the east group of temples and the acropolis).

Cafés pastry shops and ice cream parlours

SELINUNTE *Enoteca Siciliana*, 155 via Caboto. Right in front of the entrance to the ruins (archaeological park). Excellent espresso, Sicilian breakfast, or wine-tasting.

Local products
Olive oil

This area produces some of the finest olive oil in the world. A prize-winning farm is *Smeraldo del Belice*, 33 via Palestro, Castelvetrano-Selinunte, ☎ 0924/906729, ✉ www.oliodicastel vetrano.it, ✉ www.smeraldodelbelice.it.

Olives are gathered by hand from the tiny trees of the *nocellara del Belice* variety, and pressed the same day. Ancient millstones found on the farm prove that oil has been made here in the same way since the 5C BC.

Wines

In recent years attempts to produce Sicilian Chardonnay have yielded excellent results. The Belice Valley is ideal for viticulture; the Settesoli estate near Menfi (☎ 0925/77111), produces the prize-winning *Mandrarossa*, while *Fiano* vines on the Planeta estate (☎ 0925/80009, 🖳 www.planeta.it), produce a marvellous white wine called *Cometa*, a perfect accompaniment to rich fish dishes.

Beaches

A nice thing about the archaeological park of Selinunte is that you can leave the site and go back in again later, by showing your ticket. A very pleasant

way of passing the hot midday hours is to have a swim. Just below the Acropolis, at the far western end of Marinella, is a beautiful sandy beach. There is a path going down from the back of the upper car park, and a hole in the fence at the end of it. By walking back along the beach towards Marinella, the first place you find is the **Lido Zabbara** (☎ 0924/46194), a bathing establishment run by Jòjò (pronounced Yoyò), a popular figure around these parts. He rents out umbrellas and loungers and sells cold drinks and delicious snacks, salads, grilled fish and sausages. Showers are also available.

Festivals

On Easter Sunday morning in Castelvetrano, the **Aurora festival** is celebrated with a traditional procession and an encactment of the meeting of the Madonna with her arisen Son.

Selinunte

The extensive ruins (270 ha) of the ancient city of Selinunte (sometimes called Selinus) are on the edge of the sea, in a superb dominating position. On the coast the simple fishing village of **Marinella** has been developed as a little resort. The beautiful coast to the east, around the mouth of the Belice river (and as far as Porto Palo), with its sand dunes, has recently been preserved as a **nature reserve** (the Riserva Naturale Foce del Fiume Belice).

The ancient town with its acropolis occupied a terrace above the sea, between the River Selinon, or Modione, and the marshy depression now called Gorgo di Cottone or Galici, and possessed a harbour at the mouth of each valley. An important group of temples lay to the east of this site, and a necropolis to the north. The sandy soil is overgrown with wild celery, lentiscus, mandrake, acanthus and capers.

Visiting the site and opening times

• The site has been enclosed, and is now an archaeological park (the largest in Europe). Open daily 09.00–2 hrs before sunset, ☎ 0924/46277. The visit, best started early in the morning, takes at least 2–3 hours.

• The ticket office for the site is near the car park and the east group of temples (see plans). Re-entry with ticket is allowed.

History

Selinunte was colonised from Megara Hyblaea, probably as early as 651 BC. It takes its name *Selinus* from the wild celery, *Apium graveolens* (Greek, *selinon*),

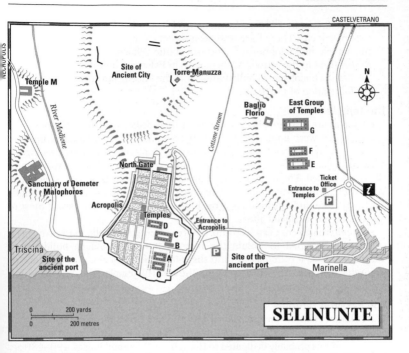

CASTELVETRANO

NECROPOLIS

Temple M

Site of
Ancient City

Torre-Manuzza

River Modione

Baglio
Florio

East Group
of Temples

G

Cottone Stream

F

E

North Gate

N

Sanctuary of Demeter
Malophoros

Ticket
Office

Acropolis

Entrance to
Temples

Temples

D

C

Entrance to
Acropolis

B

Triscina

A

O

Site of the
ancient port

Site of the
ancient port

Marinella

0   200 yards
0   200 metres

SELINUNTE

which still grows here in abundance, and which appears on its coins. Its most prosperous period was the 5C BC, when the great temples were built and the city was laid out on a rectangular plan. After the battle of Himera in 480 BC Selinunte allied herself with Syracuse against Carthage, and in 409 BC the Carthaginians, summoned to the help of Segesta, the mortal enemy of Selinunte, sent an army of 100,000 under Hannibal, son of Gisco, which took Selinunte before the allied troops of Agrigento and Syracuse could arrive. The city, which fell in only nine days, was sacked and destroyed, its inhabitants sold as slaves. A later settlement, led by Hermocrates, a Syracusan exile, was dispersed by Carthage in 250, and the population resettled at *Lilybaeum*. It is thought, however, that the utter destruction of every building, scarcely a single column being left upright, could also have been due to earthquakes. In fact, around and under the columns of Temple C are the ruins of a Byzantine settlement, and a later, Arab village called *Rahal al Asnaam*, or 'village of the columns', which must have been destroyed by an earthquake in the Middle Ages.

Excavations of the site

The site was rediscovered in the 16C; but systematic excavations were begun only in 1822–3 by the Englishmen William Harris and Samuel Angell, after a fruitless dig had been made in 1809–10 by Robert Fagan, British consul-general in Sicily. Harris and Angell found the famous metopes of Temples C and E, but Harris died of malaria, contracted while excavating here, and Angell was killed by bandits on a successive visit. In 1956–8 12 streets were excavated, and in 1973 excavations were begun to the north, on the site of the ancient city. There have also been recent excavations in the area around the Temple of Malophoros. A bronze statue (Phoenician, 12C–11C BC) of **Reshef** (kept in the Museo Archeologico in Palermo), found in the vicinity, is the first archaeological confirmation that the Phoenicians traded here before the foundation of Carthage.

The temples

The temples are distinguished by letters as their dedications are still under discussion. They were among the few temples in Sicily to have had sculptured metopes; many of these beautiful works are displayed in the archaeological museum in Palermo. All except Temples B and G are peripteral and hexastyle and all are orientated. The measurements given here refer to the temple stylobates. Many architectural fragments bear remains of *intonaco* (plaster), and throughout the site are underground cisterns, built to collect rainwater. Beside most of the temples are sacrificial altars.

The main road from Castelvetrano, before entering Marinella, passes (right) a large dyke, designed to isolate the temples from the modern buildings of Marinella, beside a roundabout (and the information office) at the entrance to the archaeological park, which includes the East Hill temples, the Acropolis, and the Temple of Malophoros.

The East Hill temples

The Collina Orientale, or East Hill, shows the ruins of three large temples (see plan). Beside the modern dyke and tunnel is **Temple E**, which measures 67.7 x 25.3m, and was probably dedicated to Hera. It is a Doric building of 490–480 BC; four of its metopes discovered in 1831 and now in the Palermo archaeological museum attest to the beauty and unique quality of its sculpture. Toppled by an earthquake, its colonnades were reconstructed in 1958. It is possible to visit the interior of the temple.

Metope from Temple E at Selinunte (Museo Archeologico, Palermo)

Temple F, the oldest on this hill (c 560–540 BC), totally ruined, had a double row of columns in front and 14 at the sides. It may have been dedicated to Aphrodite. Part of one column rises above others which are now only a few metres high.

The furthest north is **Temple G**, probably dedicated to Zeus; octastyle in form, it ranks second in size (110 x 50m), after the Olympieion at Agrigento, among Sicilian temples. Its columnar arrangement (8 x 17) is matched only by the Parthenon. It was laid out before the end of the 6C and left incomplete in 480. It is now an impressive pile of overgrown ruins with only one column alone still standing, called by the local people 'u fusu d'a vecchia, 'the old lady's distaff', which can with difficulty be encircled by eight people with their arms outstretched, but it is quite easy to 'enter' the temple and explore, and a path leads round the exterior. The columns, over 16m high with a base diameter of 3.4m, were built up of drums, each weighing c 100 tons, from the quarries at Cusa (see below). The fact that

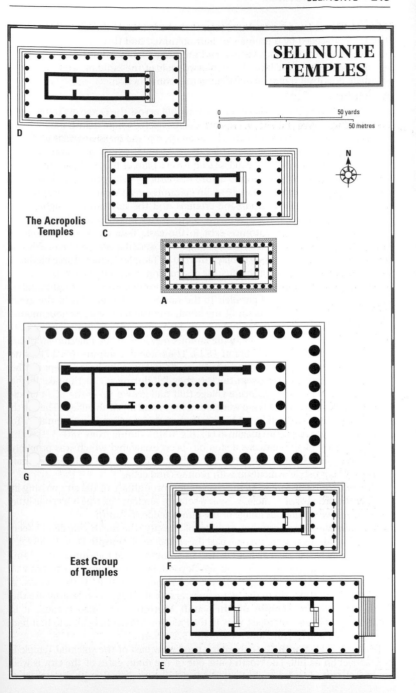

SELINUNTE TEMPLES

0 — 50 yards
0 — 50 metres

N

The Acropolis Temples

D

C

A

East Group of Temples

G

F

E

many of the columns are unfluted implies that the temple was never completed. The cella, preceded by a pronaos of four columns, had three aisles, the central aisle being open to the sky. At one end are huge blocks from the quarries; the fallen capitals give some idea of the colossal scale of the building. The enormous stylobate is in itself a marvel of monumental construction.

Acropolis

From the first car park a road continues downhill across the Gorgo di Cottone (site of one of the ancient harbours) and up to the Acropolis, where there is a second car park. From here a path continues up between the sea and massive double **walls**, in which five towers and four gates have been located, which date from around 307–306 BC. In front of the custodian's house is a plan of the site beside the stylobate of **Temple O**, whose superstructure has entirely disappeared, and, beyond, the stylobate of **Temple A** (40 x 16m; 36 columns), with some fluted drums. The cella was one step higher than the pronaos and the adytum one higher still. Between the cella and pronaos two spiral staircases led up to the roof. Fragmentary ruins of a monumental entrance exist to the east. Temples A and O, built in 490–480 BC, and identical in form and dimension, were the latest and probably the most perfect of the Selinuntine temples. In front of Temple O a sacred area has been excavated, thought to date from after the destruction of the city in 409 BC.

The ruins of the acropolis are crossed by two principal streets at right angles, with lesser streets running parallel. To the north are the remains of the great **Temple C**, on the highest point of the knoll, and the most conspicuous monument on the acropolis. It measured 63.7 x 24m, and dates from the early 6C. It was probably dedicated to Apollo; the famous metopes in the Palermo archaeological museum were found here in 1823. The colossal columns (6 x 17), some of which were monolithic, are nearly 2m in diameter at the base, except for the corner-columns which are even thicker; they fell during an earthquake in the Middle Ages, burying a Byzantine village that had grown up in the 5C (a crucifix and a Christian bronze lamp were found here) and an Arab village. The north colonnade was re-erected in 1925–27. Part of the sacrificial altar remains. To the south of the temple is a megaron (17.6 x 5.5m), dating from 580–570 BC. In the east corner of the temenos a stoa has been excavated which was probably built at the same time as the acropolis walls (late 6C). To the right is the small **Temple B**, a prostyle aediculum with pronaos and cella.

The path leads left, following the east–west thoroughfare of the city, passing in front of the pronaos of Temple A. Near a solitary ancient ilex tree is a crude little mosaic floor which has an image of the Punic goddess, Tanith.

The wide main northern thoroughfare of the city (the north gate can be seen at its end) leads away from the sea, past the stylobate of **Temple D** (570–554 BC) which stands beside the road: it carried 34 columns, and measures 56 x 24m. Some of its blocks still have their bosses. Beyond, by a small pine tree is a row of modest constructions, thought to have been shops, each with two rooms, a courtyard, and stairs up to the living quarters on the first floor. Nearby are the foundations of the **Temple of the small Metopes**, so-called because it is thought the six small metopes, now in the Palermo Museum, belong to it; it had a simple cella and adytum and measured 15.2 x 5.4m.

Just before the **North Gate** there is a good view east of the splendid Temple E (see above) on its hill. The North Gate, one of the main gates of the city, is well preserved. Outside it is a sophisticated defence system once thought to date from the time of Hermocrates, but probably constructed by Agathocles in 307–306 BC. The fortifications include three semicircular towers, and a second line of walls c 5m outside the earlier ones which were reinforced after their destruction by Hannibal in 409 BC using material from the acropolis, including capitals. The imposing remains are explained in a diagram at the site.

A sandy path continues through the low vegetation to the most recent area of excavations of the **ancient city** (not yet open to the public), near another well-restored farmhouse. The city was orientated north–south and recent research has suggested it may originally have extended beyond the (later) perimeter wall to the north, and into the valleys of the Cottone and Modione rivers. Another area of the city farther north, on the sand-covered hill of Manuzza, may have had a slightly different orientation. Farther north was a necropolis (probably on the site of a prehistoric burial-place).

Outside the North Gate (see above), to the west, can be seen the excavations on the right bank of the Modione. These can most easily be reached by the rough road (c 1km, used by the custodians) which branches off from the main crossroads near Temple C. Here the interesting **Sanctuary of Demeter Malophoros** (the Bearer of Fruits) consists of a sacred area enclosed by walls. It is now approached by a monumental entrance (late 5C) and portico. In the centre is a huge sacrificial altar, and beyond, the temple (a megaron), thought to have been built c 560, with a Doric cornice. Nearby are the scant remains of two other sacred precincts, one of them dedicated to Zeus Meilichios with two altars, where numerous stelae carved with a male and female head were discovered. More than 5000 terracotta figurines have been found in the vicinity. Another temple is being excavated to the south. Near a spring, some 200m north, a sacred edifice has recently been excavated and called **Temple M**. This may, in fact, be an altar or a monumental fountain of the 6C BC. The necropolis proper extends for some kilometres to the west: several tombs and heaps of bones are still visible, behind the modern village of Triscina, but at least another two burial grounds have been located.

The Quarries of Cusa

Off the road between Selinunte and Castelvetrano a country road (signposted) leads through extensive olive groves and vineyards to **Campobello di Mazara**, a wine-producing centre (population 11,800). A Crucifix in the church here is by Fra Umile da Petralia. From here a road (signposted) leads south towards Tre Fontane on the coast. At a crossroads by the ruins of the Baglio Ingham (a little beyond which, in a field on the left, lies a column drum abandoned on its way to Selinunte) a right turn continues past a sewage plant to end at the **Cave di Cusa**, the ancient quarries used for excavating the stone used for the construction of the temples of Selinunte. The entrance, guarded by a custodian, is open daily from 09.00 to 2hrs before sunset.

The quarries have not been worked since the destruction of Selinunte in 409 BC and no excavations have ever been carried out here. Ancient olive trees grow among the peaceful ruins, and the beautiful site, inhabited by birds, is surrounded by olive and orange groves and vineyards. The quarries (which are only about 120 m wide) extend for some 2km, and the fact that the site is not yet enclosed and there are no visible signs, make it one of the most romantic spots left in Sicily, especially on winter days when it is totally deserted. It is well worthwhile taking time to explore the site where the various processes of quarrying can be studied, from the first incisions in the rock to the empty spaces left by the removal of completed drums for columns. A block, still attached to the rock, seems to have been intended for a capital. Around each column carved out of the rock a space of c 50cm allowed room for the stonemason. Close together stand four drums which have been carved for the whole of their length and await only to be detached at their bases. The large cylindrical masses of stone (c 3 x 2m) were probably intended for Temple G. It is thought that wooden frames were constructed around the columns and that they were transported to Selinunte, about 18km away, on wheels of solid wood strengthened by iron bands and pulled by oxen.

Castelvetrano

Castelvetrano is a farming community (population 30,200) in the centre of a wine- and oil-producing area. The olive trees are very small, the fruits are gathered by hand for preserving or for making the oil, thought to be the finest in Sicily. To the south the view falls away across the cultivated plain towards the sea and the ruins of Selinunte. The simple architecture of many of the houses, with internal courtyards, is interesting, although the town was damaged in the Belice earthquake of 1968. The body of the bandit Salvatore Giuliano (see p 152) was 'found' here in 1950.

Piazza Garibaldi

In the centre of town is the cramped and oddly shaped piazza Garibaldi, which is planted with trees. The **Duomo** (usually entered by the side door in piazza Umberto I) is a 16C church with an unusual flowery portal. The central roof beam has preserved its painted decoration. Two triumphal arches are bedecked with white stuccoes of cherubs, garlands and angels, by Antonino Ferraro and Gaspare Serpotta (who also carved the four saints in the nave). In the presbytery there is gilded decoration by Antonino Ferraro and an *Assumption* by Orazio Ferraro (1619). The chapel to the right of the sanctuary has a 16C wooden Crucifix. The chapel to the left of the sanctuary has a marble Gaginesque statue, and, on the wall, a painting attributed to Pietro Novelli. Off the left aisle, the Cappella della Maddalena has fine decoration, especially in the dome, by Tommaso Ferraro. The detached campanile dates from the 16C. On the corner of piazza Umberto I is an elaborate fountain (1615) with a statue of a nymph by Orazio Nigrone. The church of the **Purgatorio**, which has a decorative 18C façade (now used as an auditorium), and the neo-classical **Teatro Selinus** (1870; by Giuseppe Patricolo) are also both in the piazza.

The Museo Civico

Via Garibaldi leads downhill past via Francesco la Croce, on the corner of which is the Biblioteca Comunale, housing the Civic Museum (open daily 09.00–13.00, 15.30–19.30; Dec–Mar 09.30–13.30, 14.30–18.30, ☎ 0924/904932 or 0924/909100) which displays objects excavated at Selinunte. On the ground floor is an unusual little room, well designed in an intimate arrangement to display the interesting bronze statuette known as the *Ephebus of Selinunte* (5C BC), which has finally been returned here after some travelling around. The statue was stolen from the Town Hall in 1962, presumably for the black market in antiquities, and subsequently recovered in 1968. After these adventures it was restored and displayed in the Archaeological Museum of Palermo, for security reasons, but now it is back home at last. Found by a nine-year-old boy at Selinunte in 1882, it is thought to be a locally produced work of c 480–460 BC. The small collection includes some other finds from Selinunte: a red-figure krater with four satyrs (470–460 BC); Corinthian ware; terracottas; coins; and a stele from the sanctuary of Malophorus. The statue of the *Madonna and Child* by Francesco Laurana and his workshop (c 1460) comes from the church of the Annunziata (the majestic head is especially fine). Upstairs is the quaint miscellaneous municipal collection, which includes bones from a Punic tomb discovered in 1929.

From the top of via Garibaldi, via Fra Pantaleo leads downhill southeast to piazza Regina Margherita, where there is a little public garden and two churches. **S. Domenico**, which has a plain façade, contains a riot of Baroque terracotta figures, coloured and stuccoed, by Antonino Ferraro (late 16C), and unusual funerary monuments.

On another side of the piazza is the church of **S. Giovanni Battista** with an elaborate façade and a green cupola. The interesting interior contains a remarkable statue of its patron by Antonello Gagini, 1522, and three 17C paintings, formerly attributed to Gherardo delle Notti.

About 3km west of the town is the church of the **SS. Trinità di Delia**. It is reached by taking the road downhill from piazza Umberto I and continuing straight ahead (signposted 'Trinità di Delia'), leaving the Trapani/Agrigento road on the left. After c 1km, at a fork, the road (unsignposted) continues left past a gravel works and straight on (signposted 'Lago di Trinità'). It passes a small eucalyptus wood and then follows the white wall of the farm, which incorporates the church. The key is kept at the modern house on the right. The chapel, dating from the 11C–12C, is a very fine building derived from Arab and Byzantine models. It was beautifully restored in 1880, and contains 19C family tombs. The crypt beneath is entered by an outside staircase. In the churchyard in a little wood is a romantic tombstone by Benedetto Civiletti, erected by the Saporito family. Beneath the hill is the beautiful, artificial Lago Trinità.

The Belice Valley

The Belice valley east of Castelvetrano, on the provincial border with Agrigento, was badly damaged in January 1968 by an earthquake in which 370 people died and 70,000 people were made homeless. Reconstruction was scandalously slow and many had to live in temporary shelters for years. The worst-hit place was the old town of Gibellina (400m), below a ridge of sulphur-bearing hills, which was abandoned after its total destruction. The new town, **Gibellina Nuova** (population 5200), was relocated some 20km to the west, on the plain, where it is unpleasantly hot in summer. The results of this questionable decision are not inspiring; the older inhabitants are nostalgic for their pretty little mountainside town, with its friendly, shady squares, its attractive churches and weatherworn rooftops, enlivened by countless swifts and jackdaws. Italy's most prominent artists and sculptors flocked to Gibellina in order to provide the new town with works of art, but some of these were so badly made that they are now rusting or crumbling away, even the paving along the streets is cracked and full of weeds. Frankly, it is all quite depressing. The new church collapsed without warning in 1994, before it had even been inaugurated. There are no balconies on the new houses, where the inhabitants can put a pot of basil or a geranium; there are no porticoes, no shady trees to linger for a chat with friends. The ruins of the old town were covered with cement as a work of 'Land Art' by the Tuscan sculptor Alberto Burri. During the summer, open-air theatrical performances called 'Orestiadi' are held here (for information, ☎ 0924/67536). The Elymian Museum has local Elymian and Greek archaeological material, and there is a local Ethnographical Museum.

On the eastern border of the province is the old town of **Poggioreale** (also destroyed in the earthquake and later rebuilt), to the east of which excavations in 1970 revealed part of a town and its necropolis (with 7C and 6C BC tombs). **Salaparuta**, famous for its vineyards belonging to the Corvo family, was abandoned after the earthquake and a new town partially reconstructed.

Partanna is an agricultural centre (population 12,000) which was also badly damaged in 1968. Its Norman castle (rebuilt in the 17C) survives and in its courtyard is a damaged coat of arms sculpted by Francesco Laurana who visited here in 1468. The Chiesa Matrice has been partially reconstructed after it was almost totally destroyed in the earthquake. It contains stuccoes by Vincenzo Messina, an organ by Paolo Amato, and a statue of the *Madonna* by the Laurana workshop.

Salemi

North of Castelvetrano is Salemi, probably the site of *Halicyae*, a town of the ancient Sicanians or Elymians, and later an important Arab city. The city structure is clearly Islamic in character, even today. When Philip of Spain signed the famous edict on 31 March 1492 banishing Muslims and Jews from Sicily, Salemi was one of the few places to offer them refuge. Garibaldi, three days after landing at Marsala, assumed the function of dictator in Sicily in the name of Victor Emmanuel II, and Salemi thus became the first capital of Italy, although only for three days. The town was badly damaged in the 1968 earthquake when a third of the population (about 4000 people) were housed in huts on the edge of the town. The Chiesa Madre and the Capuchin Monastery were destroyed.

The church of the Collegio (near the summit of the hill), with its twisted Baroque columns either side of the entrance, became the new Mother Church. The imposing castle of the mid-13C has fine vaulted rooms and a characteristic round tower. The Collegio dei Gesuiti in via D'Aguirre was restored to house the **Civic Museum** (open daily 09.00–13.00, 15.00–19.00; ☎ 0924/982376). Divided into four sections, it contains paintings and sculptures attributed to Domenico and Antonello Gagini and Francesco Laurana, brought here after the earthquake of 1968 damaged the churches; an archaeological section, with material excavated at Mokarta and Monte Polizzo; a section on the Risorgimento and memorabilia of Garibaldi's time in Sicily in 1860. On the outskirts of the town is the interesting early Christian basilica of **S. Miceli**, with mosaic floors.

Salemi is famous for its **decorative loaves** of bread, baked to celebrate the Feast of S. Biagio in February and for S. Giuseppe (19 March); they are also sold, and the proceeds go to charity. Prices are high, and can exceed 50 euros for one small, albeit very intricate, loaf. All the women of the town take part in the baking, which begins about ten days before the feasts.

Agrigento province and the Pelagian Islands

AGRIGENTO PROVINCE

AGRIGENTO

Agrigento (population 56,300), once one of the most prosperous of the ancient Greek cities on the island, preserves a remarkable series of Doric temples of the 5C BC, unequalled except in Greece itself. The medieval and modern city, on the site of the ancient acropolis, crowns a narrow ridge overlooking a valley which stretches towards the sea, in the midst of which, on a second lower ridge, stand the classical ruins. The temples have now been declared a world heritage site by UNESCO and the archaeological area is now a regional park. Haphazard, illegal building is no longer possible and some ugly structures close to the temples have already been demolished. Restoration work is being carried out in the medieval city centre and the ancient garden of Kolymbetra has been rescued.

Agrigento, until recently one of the poorest provinces in Italy, is now benefitting from tourism and its export of high quality agricultural produce; wines, oranges, olive oil and vegetables. It has also become an important international centre for the study of almond trees.

Practical information

Getting there
By train
Agrigento Centrale is the terminus for trains from Palermo, Caltanissetta, etc.

By bus
Around town. Small buses cross the upper town along via Atenea. Nos 1, 2 and 3 run from piazza Marconi to the Valle dei Templi (request stops at the museum and, lower down, for the temples at the Posto di Ristoro). Buses run from piazza Marconi to the birthplace of Pirandello, and Porto Empedocle. Bus no.1 to porto Empedocle and Kaos, bus no. 2 from piazza Marconi and the Valle dei Templi continues to San Leone on the coast.

Inter-city bus services *SAIS* and *Cuffaro* have frequent departures for Sciacca, Gela, Licata, Palermo, Catania, Caltanissetta, also Rome, Naples and many other mainland cities; from piazza Fratelli Rosselli. *Autolinea Licata* run 3 buses a day from Falcone Borsellino airport, Punta Raisi , ☎ 0922/401360.

By car
The coast road (SS 115) can be taken from Syracuse via Gela and Licata to Agrigento. It is a slow road however, and it is quicker from Syracuse to return to Catania and take the motorway A19 to Caltanissetta, then the SS 640 to Agrigento. The SS 115 is the best route from Mazara del Vallo and Sciacca. From Palermo there are two roads: the fast (and dangerous) SS 121 and SS 189, and the slow, winding road which goes through Piana degli Albanesi becoming the SS 118 at Ficuzza. For those in no particular hurry, there is also a long drive to Agrigento among spectacular scenery and many enticing little towns such as Corleone, Prizzi, S. Stefano Quisquina and Raffadali.

Parking
There are car parks near the archaeological museum, and at the Posto di Ristoro near the temples. In the upper town parking is extremely difficult, although space is sometimes available in piazza Fratelli Rosselli or viale della Vittoria. There is a multi-storey car park in via Empedocle.

Information offices
APT Agrigento, 255 viale della Vittoria, ☎ 0922/ 401352.
Azienda Autonoma Turismo, 15 via Cesare Battisti ,☎ 0922/20454, with its headquarters at 73 via Empedocle. Agrigento on line: ✉ www.agrigento sicilia.it.
✉ www.wel.it/Welcome/Sicilia/ ProvAgrigento.✉ www.egm.it/ comuni/agrigento.html.

Where to stay
Hotels
TOWN CENTRE ✩✩✩✩
Villa Athena, località Templi, ☎ 0922/596288, 🖷 0922/402180, ✉ www.athenahotels.com. This was once the finest hotel in Agrigento, it is a bit shabby now but the position, right in front of the Temple of Concord, is superb and there is a lovely garden and pool.
✩✩✩ *Pirandello*, 5 via Giovanni XXIII, ☎ 0922/595666, 🖷 0922/402497. In the modern city centre.
✩✩ *Belvedere*, 20 via S. Vito, ☎ & 🖷 0922/20051. Charming little hotel with garden and tennis court, no restaurant, close to the old city centre.
✩✩ *Concordia*, 11 piazza S. Francesco, ☎ 0922/596266. In the old part of the city.
ON THE OUTSKIRTS ✩✩✩✩
Colleverde, passeggiata Archeologica,

☎ 0922/29555, 🗐 0922/29012, ✉ colleverdehotel.it. Comfortable hotel close to the town and within walking distance of the temples. Beautiful garden and very good restaurant.

✮✮✮✮ *Jolly Hotel Della Valle*, via dei Templi, ☎ 0922/26966, 🗐 0922/ 22412. Good position, pool, within walking distance of the town.

ENVIRONS ✮✮✮✮ *Baglio della Luna*, contrada Maddalusa, ☎ 0922/511061, 🗐 0922/598802, ✉ bagliodl@oasi.it. A small converted castle with a very good restaurant (see Where to eat), the best in the area.

✮✮✮✮ *Domus Aurea*, contrada Maddalusa, ☎ 0922/511061, 🗐 0922/ 598802. Converted small country villa built in 1781, very luxurious accommodation, lovely sitting room, garden; close to the Baglio della Luna (same management).

✮✮✮✮ *Kaos*, contrada Pirandello, ☎ 0922/598622, 🗐 0922/598770. Near Pirandello's birthplace, comfortable hotel with large park and enormous pool.

SAN LEONE ✮✮✮✮ *Dioscuri Bay Palace*, 1 lungomare Falcone Borsellino, ☎ 0922/406111, 🗐 0922/411297, ✉ ricevimento.dio@framon-hotels.it. On the beach, pool, comfortable rooms.

✮✮✮ *Pirandello Mare*, 17 via de Chirico, ☎ 0922/412333, 🗐 0922/413693. Close to the sea at San Leone.

VILLAGGIO MOSE ✮✮✮✮ *Grand Hotel dei Templi*, via Leonardo Sciascia, villaggio Mosè, ☎ 0922/610175, 🗐 0922/606685. Garden with pool.

✮✮✮ *Akrabello*, contrada Angeli, villaggio Mosè, ☎ 0922/606277, 🗐 0922/ 606186. One of the Hollywood-style hotels built here in the 1970s; friendly staff and nice pool.

✮✮✮ *Grand Hotel Mosè*, contrada Angeli, villaggio Mosè, ☎ 0922/608388, 🗐 0922/608377, ✉ hotghm@tin.it. Similar to the Akrabello.

✮✮ *Villa Holiday*, 9 via Gabrici, ☎ 0922/606332. Pleasant, small hotel close to villaggio Mosè.

Bed and breakfast

Bed and Breakfast, 5 via Santo Spirito, Agrigento, ☎ 338/3945508. Modern building in the centre; French, English and German spoken; laundry service.

Rooms to rent

Camera con vista, contrada Bennici, Agrigento, ☎ 368/3111062 or 333/7158648. English, French and German spoken. Views over the temples.

Farmhouse accommodation

Fattoria Mosè, 4 via Pascal, villaggio Mosè, ☎ & 🗐 0922/606115, ✉ www. fattoriamose.com. Between the Valley of the Temples (about 2km from the Temple of Juno and the sea at San Leone), the farm produces almonds, oranges, wheat and olive oil.

Villa Capo, contrada Capo, Siculiana, ☎ 0922/817186. An 18C farmhouse in the hills above Siculiana; an ideal base for trekkers and birdwatchers. Organic vegetarian food.

Campsites

✮✮✮ *Internazionale San Leone*, near the sea at San Leone (7km), ☎ 0922/ 416121.

✮✮✮ *Nettuno*, San Leone, ☎ 0922/ 416268.

✮✮✮ *Marinella*, Porto Empedocle, contrada Ciuccaffa, 10 via delle Madonie, Porto Empedocle, ☎ 0922/535210.

Eating out
Restaurants

AGRIGENTO €€€ *Hotel Baglio della Luna* restaurant, contrada Maddalusa, ☎ 0922/511061, 🗐 0922/598802, ✉ bagliodl@oasi.it. Chef Damiano, a local man with years of experience in far-off cities prepares exquisite *mezze lune di pesce spada e aragosta in salsa vierge di pomodorini e bottarga* (swordfish and lobster with cherry tomato and tuna roe dressing);

for dessert try *fondente di cioccolato caldo e parfait di pistacchio alle 2 salse* (hot chocolate fondant with pistachio parfait and 2 sauces).
€€€ Kalos, 1 salita Filino, ☎ 0922/ 26389. Very high standard. Closed Sun.
€€€ Kokalos, 3 via Cavalieri Magazzini, ☎ 0922/606427. In the countryside near the town. Excellent antipasti and *cavatelli*, local home-made pasta, and pizza in the evenings; service can be slow.
€€€ Leon d'Oro, 102 viale Emporium, ☎ 0922/414400. The cuisine blends the flavours of land and sea: home-made pasta with swordfish, tomatoes and pistachio, or the delicious *bavette ai filetti di triglia e macco di fave* (fresh egg noodles with red mullet fillets and crushed broad beans). Closed Mon.
€€ L'Ambasciata di Sicilia, 2 via Giambertoni, ☎ 0922/20526. Local dishes; panorama from the terrace. Closed Sun.
€€ La Trizzera, contrada Kaos, near Pirandello's house, ☎ 0922/597427. Good grilled fish or mussel soup, inexpensive set menu. Pizzas in the evening. Closed Mon.
€€ Ruga Reali, 8 cortile Scribani, piazza Pirandello, ☎ 0922/20370. Subtle mix of country cooking and marine cuisine. Closed mid-day Sat. and all day Wed.
€ Black Horse, 8 via Celauro, ☎ 0922/ 23223, serves appetizing meals at very reasonable prices. Closed Sun.
€ La Forchetta, 9 piazza S. Francesco. A favourite with the local people, very good pasta. Closed Sun.
SAN LEONE 7km from the city on the coast. There are several excellent restaurants; all specializing in fish dishes, and pizzerie.

Cafés and pastry shops

Delicious sweets, made by nuns, can be purchased at the convent next to the church of S. Spirito, ☎ 0922/20664.
Caffè Concordia, 349 via Atenea. An old-fashioned café on the main street.
Infurna, 96 via Atenea. Another old-fashioned café on the main street.

Annual festivals

The **Sagra del mandorlo in fiore**, an international festival of folklore, is held at the temples around the first week in February when the almond trees are in blossom. For one week in July there is often a festival of plays by Pirandello at his birthplace near Porto Empedocle (see p 239). There are celebrations for **S. Calogero** (who is not the patron saint but that does not seem to matter, he is much loved in this part of Sicily), during the first week of July, with processions and fireworks; by tradition, when the procession goes along via Atenea, it is pelted with decorative loaves of bread (very small) from the people on the balconies.

Entertainment

Pirandello Theatre, Piazza Pirandello, ☎ 0922/20391. In the upper town. For drama performances in winter, especially from the Pirandello repertoire.

Handicrafts

In the old city, up via Bac Bac and then at no.8 via Saponara, is *Salvatore Zambuto* (☎ 0922/23924), a little shop run by the eponymous gifted artisan who makes perfect models of the temples of Agrigento and Selinunte out of pieces of cork (*templi di sughero*).

Sport

For **horseriding** in the Valley of the Temples contact Calogero Zambuto, ☎ 0922/411512, 0922/411512, 338/5614328 who speaks French.

Internet points

Libreria multimediale, via Atenea; Papua, piazzale Fratelli Rosselli.

Foreign language newspapers

There is a newsstand next to the bar at the *Posto di ristoro*.

History

Agrigento, the *Akragas* of the Greeks and the *Agrigentum* of the Romans, claims Daedalus as its legendary founder, but seems almost certainly to have originated in a colony from Gela (580 BC). From 570 to 555 the city suffered under the tyranny of Phalaris, though the bull-cult (of Moloch?) which he introduced was more likely Rhodian than Carthaginian, and the story (related by Pindar (who lived in the city) described Akragas as 'the fairest city of mortals'. Its population was then about 200,000. The local breed of horses was renowned, and the racing chariot found on many coins minted here may derive from their frequent successes at the Olympic games.

Conflict with Syracuse led to defeat in the field, after which Theron's dynasty gave place to a republican government. In 406 BC the Carthaginians, under Hannibal, son of Gisco, and Himilco, took the city and burned it after a siege of eight months. Timoleon conquered the Carthaginians (340 BC) and rebuilt the city, but it was taken by the Romans in 261 BC and again in 210 BC, and remained in their possession until the fall of the Empire. It fell into Saracen power in AD 827, and was delivered in 1087 by Count Roger, who founded the bishopric.

The present town occupies the acropolis of the Greek city. The name of Girgenti, abandoned in 1927, was derived from *Kerkent*, a Saracen corruption of Agrigentum.

Famous residents

The most famous native of Akragas was Empedocles (c 490–430), 'a poet, a physician, a patriot, and a philosopher'. His contemporary Acron, the physician, who invented fumigation and succeeded in stopping the plague which hit Athens in 430 BC. Luigi Pirandello (1867–1936), the Nobel prize-winning dramatist (see p 239) and Leonardo Sciascia (1921–89), the writer (see p 252), were born in the district.

The medieval and modern city

The old part of the town occupies the summit of Monte Camico (326m); its modern suburbs extend along the ridge to the east below the Rupe Atenea, and the city is expanding down the hillsides to the north and south. Three connected squares effectively divide the centre of the town; the area to the west contains the old city. To the north is **piazza Fratelli Rosselli** (250m) where the roads from Palermo and Enna enter the city; the circular post office is also here. To the south is **piazzale Aldo Moro**, with a garden, and farther south still, and at a lower level, lies piazza Marconi with the central railway station; opposite, at a confused intersection, the straight tree-lined viale della Vittoria runs for over 1km along the edge of the ridge below modern buildings while via Crispi descends to the Valley of the Temples.

Via Atenea, the long main street of the old town leads west from piazzale Aldo Moro. Via Porcello (right) and the stepped Salita S. Spirito lead steeply up to the abbey church of **S. Spirito** (if locked, ring for the custodian at no. 2 or 11 salita S. Spirito, offering expected, or at the convent), founded c 1290 for Cistercian nuns. The nuns still make exquisite sweets (*frutti di martorana*, marzipan fruits, *cous cous dolce*, with pistachio and cocoa, marzipan shells filled with pistachio, etc.) which may be purchased here. A Gothic portal survives and inside are good stuccoes (c 1693–95), by Serpotta and his school. The statue of the **Madonna enthroned** is by the workshop of Domenico Gagini.

Part of the convent was restored in 1990 to house part of the **Civic Museum** (open 09.00–13.00, 15.00–18.00; Sat am only; closed Sun & PH, ☎ 0922/590371), formerly in piazza Luigi Pirandello (see below), with a miscellany of objects, poorly labelled. It is approached through an over-restored cloister, and up a modern flight of stairs. The two rooms on the top floor contain a local ethnographical collection (agricultural implements, domestic ware, etc.).

On the floor below archaeological material and remains of frescoes are displayed. Steps lead down to the **Stanza della Badessa** in a tower with a Gothic vault and a painted 15C Crucifix. Another room has architectural fragments including a carved marble doorway and a Crucifix. The fine dormitory has good vaulting and an exhibition of international folk costumes, as well as a collection of butterflies and shells. On the ground floor a chapel with a Gothic vault has a crib, with charming domestic scenes, made by a local craftsman (1991). The chapter-house (now used for weddings) is also shown. The paintings include works by Pietro Novelli, Luca Giordano and Fra Felice da Sambuca.

Further along via Atenea is the unfinished façade of S. Rosalia beside the church of the **Purgatorio** or S. Lorenzo (containing elegant statues by Giacomo Serpotta). The lion to the left of the church sleeps above the locked entrance to a huge labyrinth of underground water channels and reservoirs, built by the Greek architect Phaiax in the 5C BC. Beyond the neo-Gothic exchange building the street widens at the undistinguished piazza Nicola Gallo, once the centre of the old city. Beyond the church of S. Giuseppe, at the top of the rise, via Atenea descends to piazza Luigi Pirandello (formerly piazza del Municipio). On the right is the Baroque façade of S. Domenico; occupying the former convent (mid-17C) are the Town Hall and the fine **Pirandello Theatre**.

To the right of S. Giuseppe (see above) via Bac Bac leads to the stepped via Saponara (signposted for S. Maria dei Greci). From here it is a steep climb up the salita Eubernatis and salita S. Maria dei Greci to (right; inconspicuous entrance) **S. Maria dei Greci** (usually open 08.00–12.00, 15.00–dusk except on Sun & PH afternoons), preceded by a charming little courtyard with a palm tree and a cypress. The custodians live at no. 1 salita S. Maria dei Greci (opposite the church; donation expected). This small basilica was built with antique materials, on the site of a Doric temple, perhaps that of Athena, begun by Theron in the 5C BC. The interior preserves fragments of charming 14C frescoes. Parts of the temple may be seen here, and in a passage (entered from the churchyard; unlocked on request by the custodian) below the north aisle are the stumps of six fluted columns on the stylobate.

Via del Duomo

The alleys on the north side of the church join via del Duomo. The **duomo** (S. Gerlando), though altered at the east end in the 17C is basically a 14C building with an unfinished campanile (to the southwest) that shows in its Gothic windows a mixture of Arab-Norman and Catalan influences.

interior. A single round arch divides the nave into two parts; to the west the
polygonal piers support an open painted roof of 1518, to the east a coffered
ceiling of 1603. At the end of the south aisle is the chapel of the Norman St
Gerland (who refounded the see after the Saracen defeat), with a silver reliquary
by Michele Ricca (1639). Opposite, in the north aisle is the tomb of Gaspare de
Marino, by Andrea Mancino and Giovanni Gagini (1492), and other Baroque
funerary monuments, and fragments of 15C frescoes. A curious acoustical phenomenon (*il portavoce*) permits a person standing beneath the cornice of the apse
to hear every word spoken even in a low voice near the main doorway, though
this does not work in reverse.

The Seminary (17C–18C) has an arcaded courtyard, off which (shown on request)
is a Gothic hall with a double vault, remains of the Chiaramonte Steri (14C).

The extensive façade of the **Biblioteca Lucchesiana** lines via del Duomo.
This fine building was founded here in 1765 as a public library by the bishop of
Agrigento. Its treasures number 40,000 volumes (including Arab MSS. still
housed in the original presses of 1765).

The Valley of the Temples and the ancient city

The ancient city of Agrigento, encircled by a wall, occupied the angle between
the rivers *Hypsas* and *Akragas* (now the rivers S. Anna and S. Biagio) which meet
near the coast to flow into the sea. The temples should, if possible, be seen at several different times of the day, especially in the early morning and at sunset; and
at night when floodlit. In early spring, when the almond trees are in bloom, they
are particularly beautiful. Butterflies are in the valley in abundance.

Visiting the site and opening times
The museum and all the main ruins are linked by road. At least a whole day
should be allowed if on foot as the site covers a large area (ancient Akragas and
its temples measured 4.5 x 3km). Buses run from piazza Marconi (next to the railway station) along viale Crispi, past the Hellenistic and Roman districts and the
museum to the car park and the Posto di Ristoro (probably the site of the Agora)
where there is a café. Those with less time should not miss the **museum**, the
temples on the Via Sacra and the **Temple of Zeus**.

• The temples and the Hellenistic and Roman District are open daily
08.30–17.00 (there are plans to keep the temples open until midnight from
summer 2003), ☎ 0922/497341. Tickets are available at the entrance to the
Temple of Zeus (near the car park) or at the other end of the via Sacra, by the
Temple of Hera. You can buy one ticket which allows entry to all of the temples or a combined ticket for temples, museum and Pirandello's birthplace.

• The museum is open daily 09.00–13.00; and (usually) additionally on Wed,
Thurs, Fri & Sat 14.30–17.30; Sun & PH 09.00–13.00.

Temples of Herakles, Concord and Hera
The Via Sacra (closed to cars) crosses the ridge on which the temples of Herakles,
Concord and Hera are built. Beyond the Temple of Concord it leads through
delightful countryside, here undisturbed, with beautiful groves of almonds and
ancient olive trees.

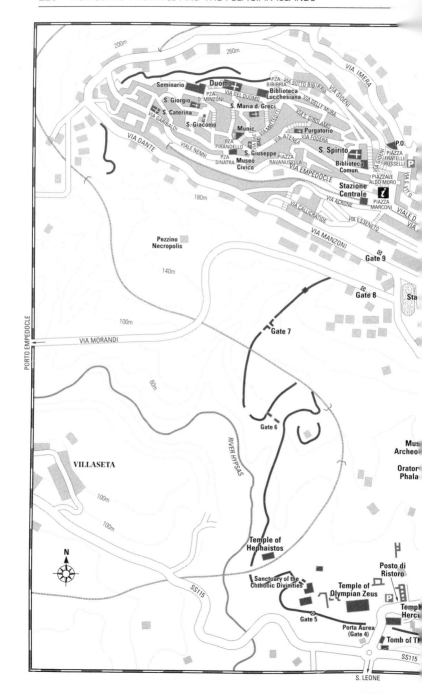

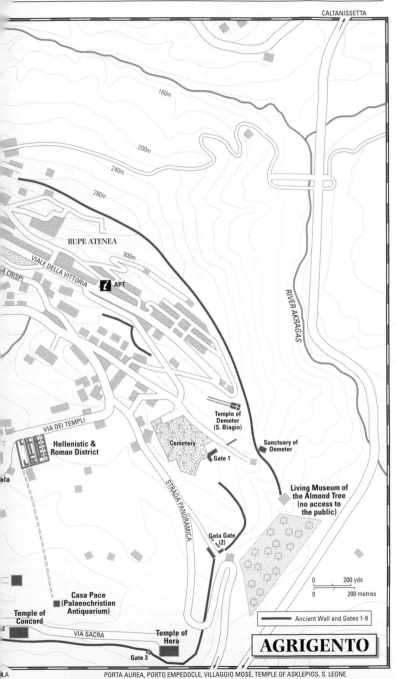

CALTANISSETTA

160m

200m

240m

280m

RUPE ATENEA

VIALE DELLA VITTORIA

A CRISPI

300m

APT

RIVER AKRAGAS

VIA DEI TEMPLI

Hellenistic & Roman District

Temple of Demeter (S. Biagio)

Cemetery

Sanctuary of Demeter

Gate 1

Living Museum of the Almond Tree (no access to the public)

STRADA PANORAMICA

Gela Gate (2)

Casa Pace (Palaeochristian Antiquarium)

Temple of Concord

VIA SACRA

Temple of Hera

Gate 3

0   200 yds
0   200 metres

— Ancient Wall and Gates 1-9

AGRIGENTO

At the beginning on the right is a footbridge above a deep street of tombs carved into the rock which leads to the **Temple of Herakles**, a heap of ruins showing traces of fire, with nine upright columns, eight of them re-erected in 1922–3 by the munificence of Captain Alexander Hardcastle. This is probably the oldest visible temple of Akragas (built c 500 BC). It was peripteral and hexastyle (67 x 25m) and had 38 columns (6 x 15), 9.9m high and 2m in diameter, and a cella (perhaps roofless) with pronaos and opisthodomus in antis. In ancient times it was famed for its statue of Herakles, which Verres attempted to steal, and for a painting of the infant *Herakles strangling the Serpents*, by Zeuxis.

Verres, the corrupt administrator

In 73 BC Caius Verres, influential in Rome, was given the plum job of Governor of Sicily. Without wasting time, he ensconced himself in the royal palace once belonging to Hieron ll in Syracuse, and proceeded to systematically pillage the island's works of art. At first, he requisitioned beautiful objects from private homes but later he stole cult statues and paintings from the temples. Catania lost her statue of *Ceres*, Syracuse lost the gold and ivory doors of the Temple of Athena together with the paintings and the statue of the goddess, said to have a gold face and hands. But no city was spared. The magnificent bronze statue of *Apollo*, signed by Myron, was once again stolen from the Temple of Asklepios at Agrigento, having been carried away by the Carthaginians in 406 BC (it had been returned by Scipio in 146 BC). Not content with this, Verres sent a group of soldiers to steal the statue of *Hercules* from his temple at dawn one day, but word of his plans had spread and the soldiers were overpowered by furious citizens, including tiny children and the infirm, who attacked them with stones. Cicero, who had been called by the Sicilians in 71 BC to plead their cause in front of the senate, described the statue as the most beautiful work of art he had ever seen, and the effect of Verres on the island as more devastating than a war. He won his case, but Verres was only nominally punished: he went into voluntary exile to Marseilles, where he died in 43BC. The stolen art works were never recovered.

Beyond, on the via Sacra is the **Villa Aurea** (now used as offices, admission only with special permission) surrounded by a luxuriant and beautifully kept garden. In the forecourt is a memorial bust of Captain Alexander Hardcastle set up in 1984. This eccentric Englishman repaired the villa in 1921 and lived here with his brother Henry until his death in 1933. The Captain provided substantial funds to restore and excavate the ancient city, supporting the work of Pirro Marconi. He also took an interest in the modern city, and provided an aqueduct from there to the temple valley. In gratitude, the Italian government awarded him the important honorary title of *commendatore della Corona d'Italia* and the Home Office allowed him to wear the insignia. The villa now contains an antiquarium (material from the Pezzino Necropolis, and excavations in contrada Mosè), and in the garden are tombs and underground cisterns.

Further up on the left is a **Palaeochristian necropolis**. Here there are Christian tombs cut in the surface of the rock, as well as extensive **catacombs** with subterranean passages extending below the road. In the field here are two tholos tombs thought to date from the 5C BC.

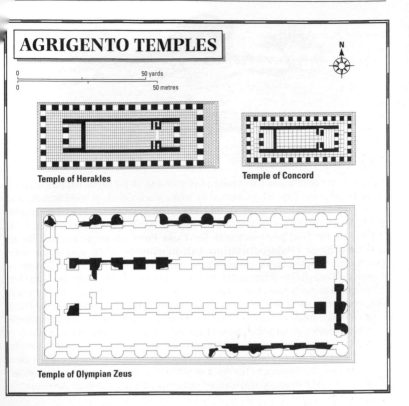

AGRIGENTO TEMPLES

N

0   50 yards
0   50 metres

Temple of Herakles

Temple of Concord

Temple of Olympian Zeus

Temple of Concord

The road continues up to the so-called **Tempio della Concordia**, the best preserved of all Greek temples except the Theseion at Athens, which it recalls in its
majestic symmetry and rich colour. For preservation reasons, it is sadly no longer
possible to enter the building. The name occurs in a Latin inscription found here,
but has no real connection with the temple (although there is a tradition among
the inhabitants of Agrigento that the temple should be visited by a husband and
wife on their wedding day).

The building, which probably dates from about 430 and was only slightly
harmed by the Carthaginians, stands on a stylobate of four steps (39.3 x 16.9m)
and is peripteral and hexastyle with 34 Doric columns (6 x 13), 6.8m high
including the capitals, with a diameter of 1.4m at the base. The intercolumnia-
tions of the façades become narrower towards the sides (to accommodate the
corner metopes); this is one of the earliest instances in Sicily of this refinement
in temple design. The cella has a pronaos and an opisthodomus, both in antis.
From the east end of the cella two spiral staircases mount to the architrave. The
complete entablature survives at both ends.

The excellent state of preservation of the temple is explained by the fact that it
was converted into a church by S. Gregorio delle Rape (i.e. of the turnips), bishop
of Agrigento, in the 6C AD. It was restored in the 18C, but the arches of the nave

Temple of Concord, Agrigento

remain in the cella walls. The material of this and of the other temples is easily eroded sandstone, formerly protected by white stucco made of marble dust, and brightly painted above the capitals, and now burnt by the sun to a rich tawny gold. From the temple the pretty building of the Villa Athena hotel can be seen. A little gate on the road gives access to the **Casa Pace**, an attractive little house restored to house a **Palaeochristian Antiquarium** (officially open at the same time as the temples, but if closed ask at the custodian's hut by the Temple of Concord). The exhibits illustrate the history of the three early Christian churches so far found in Agrigento (one outside the walls at the eastern edge of the temple ridge, one built inside the Temple of Concord and one excavated beside the Hotel Villa Athena). Finds include a finely carved sarcophagus (5C AD), left unfinished. Upstairs are photographs and plans of the necropoli excavated in the area.

The Via Sacra, now more peaceful, continues parallel to the ancient city walls, the inner face of which contains many Byzantine tomb recesses. There is a view on the left of the cemetery, to the right of which S. Biagio can be seen (see below) beside a clump of trees. On the skyline, radio masts mark the Rupe Ateneo.

Temple of Hera

About 1km farther east, stands the much ruined but picturesque Temple of Hera, called the Temple of Juno Lacinia, from a confusion with a temple dedicated to Hera on the Lacinian promontory at Croton, in Calabria. It resembles the Temple of Concord in form, but is slightly smaller and older (c 450 BC). Since a landslide in 1976 threatened its stability the entrance has been fenced off. The stylobate, on a massive artificial platform, measures 38 x 16.8m. Of its 34 columns (6 x 13), 6.4m high with a base-diameter of 1.3m, nine have fallen. Traces of a fire (which probably occurred in 406) are still visible, and the work of the Roman restorers was ruined by an earthquake. To the east is the sacrificial altar; to the west an ancient cistern.

Looking west there is a good view of the outer face of the wall, in some places carved out of the natural rock, clinging to the brow of the hill. Nearby are the scant remains of Gate Three (one of the ancient city gates), and outside the city walls, an ancient roadway with deep wheel ruts can still be seen.

Temple of Olympian Zeus

The entrance to the Temple of Olympian Zeus is next to the Posto di Ristoro (see above). Excavations here extend to the westernmost edge of the temple ridge, and the Garden of Kolymbetra. The custodians of the ancient monuments of Agrigento whose offices are here are helpful and informed. Enquire here for mission to areas found closed or for the key to sites normally kept locked.

Beside the entrance is the vast, complicated heap of ruins of the Temple of Olympian Zeus, or **Olympieion**, thought to have been begun by the Carthaginian prisoners taken at Himera, and left unfinished in 406: its destruction, due in part to the Edict of Olympia (6C AD), in part to earthquakes, was completed by quarrying in the 18C, much of the stone going into the foundations of Porto Empedocle.

This huge Doric temple (110.1 x 52.7m, virtually a double square), is the largest Doric temple known, and is unique in form among Greek temples. It was built of comparatively small stones (each capital was composed of three blocks) and then covered in stucco. It is heptastyle and pseudoperipteral, i.e. the seven columns at each end and the 14 on each side were engaged in the walls, being rounded externally and presenting a square face towards the interior. In between the semi-columns, 16.7m high and 4m thick at the base, were 38 colossal telamons set on the outer wall; their exact arrangement is still under discussion (see below). In the east pediment a *Gigantomachia* was represented, and in the west pediment the *Capture of Troy*. The cella was divided into three aisles, separated by square pillars (to support the vast roof).

Little remains in position except the stereobate, but this alone is sufficient to convey an impression of the immensity of the monument. Part of the north wall survives (note the outer face), and the foundations of the aisle pillars. To the east, beyond the wall which (curiously) 'blocked' what is thought to have been the entrance, are the foundations of the altar platform. All around the temple is a heap of ruins, amid which lies a copy of a **giant** (7.6m high), one of the telamons; the original 19C reconstruction is displayed in the Archaeological Museum. The U-shaped incision visible on many stones is believed to have facilitated their being raised by ropes. Near the southeastern corner, below one of the colossal fallen capitals, is a small temple of archaic date with a cella divided by piers. The agora of the ancient city is thought to have been to the east (under the car park).

Sanctuary of Chthonic Divinities

To the west is a complicated area of excavations including remains of houses, and traces of an L-shaped portico which enclosed a sanctuary and a tholos on a spur beside **Gate Five**. The carriageway is obstructed by masonry which apparently fell in Greek times. It was probably a double gate defended by a tower. On the other side of the gate are various shrines that together formed the Sanctuary of the Chthonic Divinities (the gods of the earth–Dionysus, Demeter and Persephone or Kore). The shrines were entirely enclosed by a precinct wall, a portion of which is visible on the west side. The misnamed **Temple of Castor and Pollux** is here. The four columns bearing a portion of the architrave, which have been used as the picturesque symbol of Classical Sicily, are a reconstruction of 1836 now known to incorporate elements from more than one building on this site.

Superimposed ruins show the existence of shrines dedicated to the cult of the earth goddesses as early as the 7C BC. The structures on the north side, notably the pairs of altars, one circular and one square, date from this period. To the south of these are the remains of two unfinished 6C temples; the third is that formerly misascribed to Castor and Pollux, which was probably to the same plan as the Temple of Concord. A fourth temple was built just to the south, in Hellenistic or Roman times. Many of the fallen column drums belong to the last temple and the well preserved altar east of the platform.

Beyond the custodians' house is an Archaic Sanctuary, recently excavated on the edge of the hill. From here two columns of the Temple of Hephaistos (or Vulcan) can be seen on the hill across a delightful fertile little valley where there are orange trees. This is the Kolymbetra Garden, recently restored and opened to the public by the *FAI*, the Italian National Trust. The garden was originally an artificial lake, dug by the Carthaginian prisoners taken by the tyrant Theron after the Greek victory at Himera in 480 BC. It was intended for use as a reservoir and a source of freshwater fish for the king's table. Historians describe it as a place of great beauty with swans, ducks and many other birds. After a relatively short time, probably little more than a century, the lake was filled in, perhaps because of malaria, and it became a flourishing garden where the Arabs cultivated oranges. Abandoned for centuries, it will be cared for by the FAI for 25 years. From the garden it is easy to cross the railway line to reach the remains of the Temple of Hephaistos.

Beneath the viaduct of the via Morandi the Pezzino necropolis (admission from via Dante) has been excavated.

Regional Archaeological Museum

On the main road (Via dei Templi), about 1km uphill from the Posto di Ristoro (see the plan), is the Museo Regionale Archeologico (☎ 0922/401565, open daily, see *Visiting the site* p 227), one of the finest museums in Sicily, spaciously arranged in a 1960s' building. It is approached through a garden and the 15C cloisters of the convent attached to the church of S. Nicola (see below). In the cloisters is a long bench carrying an inscription to Herakles and Hermes found in the Agora zone of the city.

Room I contains Early and Late Bronze Age material from sites near Agrigento, including a small Mycenaean amphora (probably found at Porto Empedocle), and painted vases. Also, prehistoric objects found in Agrigento beneath the classical area.

Room II contains objects from nearby Gela (6C–7C BC), including Corinthian and Rhodian ware (note the head of a bull), as well as locally made vases; votive statuettes from Licata (late 4C BC).

Room III displays a superb collection of vases, including a group of outstanding **Attic vases**, from the mid-6C BC to the early 3C BC. The following description follows the cases in sequence from the top of the steps left in a clockwise direction around the four halls (see p 457 for the nomenclature of vases). On the walls are photos of some of the most famous vases found in Agrigento and now in other museums. **Case 1:** Attic black-figured vases, including a fine amphora; **case 2:** red-figured kraters; **case 3:** Attic red-figured vases including a lekythos with Nike sacrificing (460–450 BC), and a krater with Dionysiac scenes (c 440 BC); **case 4:** krater showing Perseus and Andromeda in polychrome on a white ground, a rare example of c 430 BC, and a stamnos (440–430 BC) showing a sacrifice to Apollo (stamnos means 'it can stand alone'; these pots were provided with lids, and were just the right size for storing small objects, rather like a beauty case; they have often been found in tombs with cosmetic necessities inside); **case 5:** a small red-figured krater with a bull being led to sacrifice, and several kraters and stamni with banqueting scenes (some by the 'Painter of Lugano', c 400 BC); **case 6:** Hellenistic vases. At the end of the hall, fine marble statue of a warrior (damaged); belonging to the Early Classical period, this may ave adorned part of the pediment of the Temple of Herakles (c 480 BC). **Case 7** contain vases (4C BC) from Campania. **Cases 8 and 9**: vases from Apulia (4C BC); **case 10**: Attic red-figured vase of the first half of the 5C BC, including two kraters by the 'Harrow Painter', and a krater showing the burial of a warrior; **cases 11 and 12**: black-figured Attic vases of the end of the 6C BC, including a lekythos with Herakles and the hydra; and a large amphora with four gods and a quadriga by the 'Painter of Dikaios'.

Room IV contains architectonic fragments including a remarkable variety of lion-head water spouts from various buildings (including the Temple of Herakles and the Temple of Demeter). **Room V**: statuettes and heads in terracotta, notably, female votive statues; (**case 45**) askos, the mule of Dionysos (late 6C BC, found in an offering pit), and the mask of a black African of the same date; two cases of moulds; (**case 51**) head of Athena with a helmet (c 490 BC); (**case 55**) head of a kouros (500 BC). On the end wall are delicate bas-relief friezes, including some showing the telamons. Beyond the steps which descend to **room VI**, **case 59** on the balcony displays the head of a kouros (?) of c 540 BC, and a female bust of the end of the 6C BC. Other cases here contain finds from the area near the Temple of Herakles, including architectonic fragments in terracotta.

Steps descend to **room VI**, devoted to the Temple of Zeus. Here the remarkable **giant** (7.6m high) is displayed, one of the telamons from the temple, which was recomposed from fragments in the 19C; along the wall are three colossal telamon heads illustrating three different ethnic types. The blocks of stone were originally covered with plaster. Plans and models suggest possible reconstructions of the temple, and the controversial position of the telamons. The discovery of a leg attached to a block of stone of one of the statues has shown that their feet must have been further apart than is indicated here. **Room VII** contains fragments of wall paintings (recomposed) and mosaics (including three in small tesserae of animals) from the Roman District. **Room VIII** (inscriptions) and **room IX** (coins) are opened only on special request.

Room X is reached from the balcony (room V). In the first part three statuettes are displayed: the *Ephebus of Agrigento*, a statuette of Apollo, or the river-god Akragas (c 480 BC), a fragment of a female kneeling statue of Aphrodite (2C–1C BC) and a fragment of a male torso. In the second part material found in the bouleuterion is displayed, including coins. A corridor, overlooking a little garden with two Roman statues, has panels illustrating the political history of Akragas. **Room XI**, has finds from various necropoli, notably that at contrada Pezzino. It is the oldest necropolis in Agrigento and the one that has produced the richest finds (early 6C–3C BC). The miniature vases were found in children's tombs. At the end of the room, the fine alabaster sarcophagus of a child, with poignant childhood scenes (ended by illness and death), a Hellenistic work of the 2C BC, was found near Agrigento. Nearby is another Roman sarcophagus. From the window here recent excavations can be seen.

Room XII has an introductory display of prehistoric material, and finds from Sciacca; in **room XIII** there are objects from the province of Agrigento, including finds from the Grotto dell'Acqua Fitusa and from S. Angelo Muxaro. The fragments of ochre are thought to have been used to colour vases. Material from Eraclea Minoa is displayed in **room XIV**, and Greek and Roman helmets; busts from Licata; bronze cooking utensils, etc. **Room XV** contains a single magnificent red-figured krater from Gela (5C BC). In perfect condition, it displays an episode from the Trojan War: the battle with the Amazons on one side, an Achilles falling in love with Pentesilea queen of the Amazons as he strikes her to death, on the other. It could be the work of Polignotus of Athens. Photographs on the walls show other vases, now in the Gela museum. **Room XVII** has finds from Caltanissetta (notably a fine red-figured krater showing horsemen of 450–440 BC).

The museum exit is left past room XVIII (opened only on special request), which houses the contents of the cathedral treasury: especially noteworthy are two reli-quaries of Limoges-enamelled copper, a portable altar-stone with Byzantine enamels (13C), an ivory crozier, and a *Madonna* attributed to Guido Reni.

Outside the museum is the entrance to an area of **excavations**. The **bouleu-terion** (or ekklesiasterion) was built in the 4C–3C BC and transformed into an odeon in the Imperial era. It was used for the meetings of the *boulé*, a political rul-ing body. It could hold some 300 people: the participants are thought to have stood. The narrow divisional rows are carved into the rock. In one corner is the so-called **Oratory of Phalaris**, a prostyle building in antis, probably a late-Hellenistic shrine, which was transformed into a Gothic chapel. A footbridge crosses an area with remains of late-Hellenistic houses, and Imperial Roman buildings (mosaics).

The early 13C church of **S. Nicola** (closed between 13.00 and 15.00) has a curious façade made up of a Gothic doorway in strong relief between antae with a Doric cornice (the material probably came from a Roman edifice nearby). The architecture of the interior, reconstructed in 1322, and altered in 1426, is inter-esting. In the second chapel (right; a contribution is requested for the lighting) there is a magnificent **sarcophagus** of white Parian marble. With great delicacy and purity of style it portrays four episodes in the story of Hippolytus and Phaedra; it could be a Greek work of about 450 BC, or a later Roman copy of the original. The front panel shows Hippolytus with his male companions and numerous horses and dogs, and the side panel illustrates Phaedra with female companions. The angle figures are particularly skilful, as well as the delicate frieze at the top and bottom of the scenes. The last two sides do not appear to have been completed, possibly because the sarcophagus was placed in the corner of a building. In 1787, when it was in the Duomo, it was much admired by Goethe as the best preserved Classical relief carving he had seen. The church also contains a venerated wooden Crucifix, a statue of the *Madonna and Child* by the Gagini school, and an unusual stoup supported by a grey marble hand, bearing two dates (1529 and 1685). From the terrace there is a fine view of the Valley of the Temples.

The Hellenistic and Roman district

On the opposite side of the Via dei Templi is the entrance to the enclosure (behind a green fence) with the conspicuous remains of the Hellenistic and Roman District of the city (for admission see above). Here an area of c 120 sq m has been excavated, exposing four cardines, running north and south, with their complex of buildings sloping downwards from east to west in a series of terraces. The dis-trict was first developed towards the end of the 2C BC and its civic life lasted probably to the 4C or 5C BC. The drainage system is elaborate and traces of stairs show that buildings were of more than one storey. Houses, of sandstone blocks, are built around a peristyle, or with an atrium; many of their rooms have good floors (the best, which include the **Casa della Gazzella** and the **Casa del Maestro Astrattista**, are covered for protection).

Rock Sanctuary of Demeter and San Biagio

From via Crispi opposite the Jolly Hotel Della Valle, a road to the left crosses a main road and continues to the **cemetery**. Captain Alexander Hardcastle who was responsible for excavating the ancient walls here, was buried in this cemetery beside a 'window' in the wall. A gate on the left (signposted) is officially open at the same time as the temples but it is often locked. Beyond it an unsurfaced road (c 200m) leads (on foot) to the edge of the cliff.

On the hillside above is **S. Biagio**. This Norman church was built on the cella of a small temple begun after the victory at Himera in 480, and dedicated to Demeter and Persephone. The pronaos and stylobate of the temple protrude beyond the apse of the church. To the north are two large round altars. The temple was approached by the ancient track with deep wheel ruts, still clearly visible, mounting the side of the hill. On the rock face a marble plaque records Captain Hardcastle's (see p 230) excavations here.

On the edge of the cliff the line of the ancient city **walls** can clearly be seen running from the Rupe Atenea (see below), above S. Biagio, to the Temple of Hera; beyond, the view extends along the temple ridge and to the sea. Just outside the walls and below the cliff edge is the entrance gate to the **Rock Sanctuary of Demeter**, reached by a long, steep flight of steps (20C) built into the rock face which lead down through a delightful garden. Beside two natural caverns in the rock (in which numerous votive busts and statues dating from the 5C–4C BC were found) is a tunnel which carries a terracotta aqueduct from a spring far inside the hill. In front is a complex series of cisterns on different levels and remains of what may have been a monumental fountain. The sanctuary was formerly thought to antedate the foundation of the city by some two centuries, but some scholars now believe it was constructed in the 5C BC.

Another unsurfaced road (signposted) leads along the wall of the cemetery to (200m) an interesting wedge-shaped **Bastion** built to guard this vulnerable spot where a valley interrupts the natural defence line. To the north is **Gate One**.

The **Rupe Atenea** (351m), a rocky hill, the highest part of the town, was part of the acropolis of Akragas. It is reached by a road (not signposted) which runs beyond the hospital but as it is now military property the ruins of a large ancient building found here are inaccessible.

Viale Crispi continues downhill from the Hotel Della Valle (see above), and the Strada Panoramica forks left, passing near the **Porta Gela** (**Gate Two**) and continues to the Temple of Hera (described above).

Just below the Posto di Ristoro the main road (the ancient road to the sea) descends through the rock on the site of the **Porta Aurea** (Gate Four). This was the main gate of Akragas built over in Byzantine times. Just before the roundabout on the high ground to the left is a Roman funerary monument, miscalled the **Tomb of Theron**, a two storeyed edifice with a Doric entablature and Ionic corner columns. It stands on the edge of a huge Roman cemetery (1C BC–5C AD) which extends eastwards below the line of the walls.

Temples of Asklepios and Hephaistos

The Gela road (SS 115) runs east from the roundabout beneath the temple ridge and walls, past a park of 4 ha which has recently been designated to protect some 300 varieties of almond trees growing here. This **Living Museum of the Almond Tree** (no public access) is run jointly by the province and the university.

Temple of Asklepios

The first unsurfaced road on the right (signposted) leads through another almond orchard to a farm beside the little Temple of Asklepios on the bank of the S. Biagio river (near a medicinal spring). Excavations are in progress here and the site has recently been enclosed (it is closed for restoration but is usually unlocked on request at the custodian's office, at the entrance to the Temple of Olympian Zeus, see above). This is a small Doric temple in antis with a pronaos, cella and false opisthodomus. In spite of its size, it shows the advanced techniques of construction (including convex lines) associated with the (contemporary) Parthenon. The stairway is preserved between the cella and pronaos. This is the temple mentioned by Polybius in his account of the Roman siege of 262 and it once contained the statue of *Apollo* by Myron (stolen by Verres in 72 BC) whose adventures are chronicled by Cicero.

Temple of Hephaistos

In the other direction, the Porto Empedocle road (SS 115) leads (c 500m) westwards from the roundabout (see above) to the bottom of a little valley where, just before a bridge, an unsurfaced road (not signposted) forks right. Follow it as far as the high railway viaduct. Here, steps (signposted) lead up past agave and aloe plants to the Temple of Hephaistos (or Vulcan), beyond an orchard of graceful almond trees and beside a primitive farmhouse. The temple, hexastyle and peripteral, was built c 430 BC and two columns remain upright. The cella was partly built over a small archaic temple of the early 6C. A marble stone beneath the stylobate on the south side records excavations here in 1930 by Alexander Hardcastle. From here the irregular line of walls is pierced by **Gates Six, Seven, Eight and Nine**.

PORTO EMPEDOCLE AND THE ISOLE PELAGIE

Porto Empedocle, an industrial town (population 17,700) with cement works and a fishing port (in decline), is also the port for the remote Pelagian Islands which lie nearer to Tunisia than Sicily. Playwright and novelist Luigi Pirandello was born in the countryside called Kaos, near Porto Empedocle.

Practical information

Getting there
By air to the Pelagian Islands

Information on flights to the islands is on p 240.

By sea to the Pelagian Islands

Information on ferry and hydrofoil services are on p 240.

By bus to Porto Empedocle

SAIS and *Cuffaro* buses from Sciacca sometimes stop at Porto Empedocle. From Agrigento, buses leave from the railway station until 20.30 (10 mins).

Parking

It is not advisable to leave cars unattended in the port area when visiting the islands. Alfonso Stagno (☎ 0922/636029) has two garages near the port and will take care of your car: call him a few days beforehand to be sure of a place.

ourist information

Porto Empedocle on line: ✉ www.por-
toempedocle.tk (there is no tourist office).

Where to stay

Visitors to the islands are advised to stay
in nearby Agrigento or its environs (see
listing on p 222). Ferry services run late
into the evening.

Eating out
Restaurants

€€ *San Calogero*, via Roma
32, ☎ 0922/ 637255; this is the little
restaurant immortalized by a very popular Italian author, Andrea Camilleri (✉
www. andreacamilleri.net), in his series of
stories about a police superintendent
called Montalbano, who likes his food:
spaghetti al nero di seppia (spaghetti with
squid ink) delightfully spicy, or baby octopus; or perhaps fresh red mullet '*da
arricriari lo stommaco*' ('to make your
stomach feel good').

Café and pastry shop

Albanese, 35 via Roma, is where
Camilleri (and of course Montalbano)
come for espresso and *cannoli*.

On the inner quay, built between 1749 and 1763, partly of stone from the temples of Agrigento, is a massive tower. On the western outskirts a Roman villa, the
Villa Romana di Durrueli, dating from the 1C AD, has been excavated. Nearby
at Punta Grande is the **Scala dei Turchi** , remarkable white rocks of limestone
and sandy clay which have been eroded by the sea into fantastic shapes.

Just outside Porto Empedocle is **Kaos**, Luigi Pirandello's birthplace (1867–
1936), now a delightful small **museum** (admission daily from 08.00–20.00, ☎
0922/511102).

> ### Luigi Pirandello
> Luigi Pirandello became famous as a playwright after World War I, making
> his name in 1921 with the first performance of *Sei personaggi in cerca d'au-
> tore* (*Six characters in search of an Author*). He was a theatre director in Rome
> from 1925 to 1934, the year in which he was awarded the Nobel prize for
> literature. In his writings he conveys an idea of man suffering from solitude,
> disillusioned by his ideals. With a strong element of irony he suggests that
> his characters frequently reveal the necessity of 'wearing a mask'.
>
> Pirandello was a prolific writer, and was widely acclaimed in his lifetime:
> one of his most famous novels is *Il Fu Mattia Pascal*, (*The Late Mattia Pascal*),
> published in 1904, but it is as a playwright and short story writer that his
> genius fully emerges.

Under a wind-blown pine, the ashes of the dramatist and novelist are buried
according to his wishes, beneath a 'rough rock in the countryside of Girgenti'.
There is usually an open-air festival of his plays here in July.

The Isole Pelagie

The Isole Pelagie (Pelagian Islands; from the Greek pelagos, meaning sea) lie
about 205km southwest of the Sicilian mainland (and 113km from
Tunisia). Matisse would have loved these hauntingly beautiful islands where the
sea varies in hue from pale green through to turquoise and deep cobalt.

There are three islands, **Lampedusa**, **Linosa** and **Lampione**, all quite differ-ent in character. They fell to the allies without resistance in June 1943: Lampedusa surrendered to an English airman who landed by accident, having run out of petrol. The **Isolotto dei Conigli**, just offshore of Lampedusa, is now a wildlife reserve, protecting turtles (*Caretta caretta*) which stilll lay their eggs on the beach here. Whale watchers should come in March when the rorqual whale passes along the south coast of Lampedusa and mates off the east coast.

Practical information

Getting there and around
By air

There are daily flights from Palermo to Lampedusa Airport (☎ 0922/970006) run by *Air Sicilia* (☎ 091/6250566) and from 1 June to 31 October daily direct flights from Turin, Milan, Bologna, Venice and Rome, run by *Air Sicilia* and *Air One*.

By bus

Autolinea Licata (☎ 0922/401360) run 3 buses a day to Porto Empedocle (and Agrigento) from Falcone Borsellino Airport, Punta Raisi connecting with ferries to Lampedusa.

By sea

Car ferries from Porto Empedocle to Linosa and Lampedusa are run by *Siremar* every day except Sunday (☎ 0922/636777, 0922/636683). However, the service is not very effi-cient; the ferry boat *Paolo Veronese* is old and sometimes breaks down causing considerable inconvenience. Visitors are not allowed to bring cars to the islands in summer.

Hydrofoils from Porto Empedocle are run by *Ustica Lines* twice daily (☎ 0923/22200 ▤ 0923/23289 ✉ www.usticalines.it) to Linosa (4 hrs) continu-ing on to Lampedusa, ☎ 0922/970003.

Ferry and hydrofoil ticket offices on the islands L A M P E D U S A *Siremar*, lungomare Rizzo, ☎ 0922/971964; *Ustica Lines*, c/o Strazzera, lungomare Rizzo, ☎ 0922/970003.

L I N O S A *Siremar* and *Ustica lines*, c/o Cavallaro, 46 via Re Umberto, ☎ 0922/972062.

For up-to-date information on shipping lines, timetables, tariffs and bus connec-tions, consult ✉ www.bookingitalia.it.

Inter-island communications

Hydrofoil connections twice a day between Lampedusa and Linosa in summer, once a day the rest of the year.

Car and bicycle hire

Licciardi, via Siracusa, ☎ 0922/970768. Rents out the popular old cars with the roof cut off, also motorcycles and bicycles.

Information offices
APT Agrigento, ☎ 0922/401352.

Pro loco, on Lampedusa, 3 via Anfossi, ☎ 0922/971390.

Sogni nel Blu, via G.Bonfiglio, Lampedusa, ☎ 0922/973566 ▤ 0922/973682, ✉ www.sogninelblu.it. The agency will supply timetables for flights, ferries and hydrofoils; assist in finding accommodation in hotels, apartments, rooms or local cottages (*dammusi*); organise car, moped, bicycle or boat rental, diving excursions (also noctur-nal); or even devise the whole trip from start to finish.

Lampedusa on line:
✉ www.isoladilampedusa.it.
✉ www.lampedusa.to.

Where to stay
Hotels

Accommodation on the islands is considerably more expensive than in similar establishments on the mainland. The hotels usually demand a minimum stay of three nights.

LAMPEDUSA ✰✰✰✰ *Medusa*, via Rialto Medusa, ☎ 0922/970126, 📠 0922/970023. Elegant hotel on Guitgia Bay, good central position, all rooms with seaview, tennis court, private catamaran, *Il Condor* for excursions to Lampione and Linosa.

✰✰✰ *Alba d'Amore*, 1 via Favarolo, ☎ 0922/970272, 📠 0922/970786. Pleasant and bright.

✰✰✰ *Cupola Bianca*, contrada Madonna, ☎ 0922/971274. The rooms are in *dammusi* (stone cottages); peaceful position with a lovely garden and palm trees; open-air dining, tennis court.

✰✰✰ *Guitgia Tomasino*, via Lido Azzurro, ☎ 0922/970879, 📠 0922/970316.

✰✰✰ *Le Pelagie*, 11 via G. Bonfiglio, ☎ 0922/970211, 📠 0922/971045. Central position in the village.

✰✰✰ *Piddu Club*, 10 via Madonna, ☎ 0922/971050. Charming little hotel close to the harbour with lovely terrace and patio; private motor boat for excursions with lunch on board.

✰✰✰ *Sirio*, 8 via Antonello da Messina, ☎ 0922/970401. Simple little hotel recently completely refurbished; family-run, very good food; situated between Guitgia Bay and the harbour.

LINOSA ✰✰✰ *Algusa*, via Alfieri, ☎ 0922/972052. Modern, brightly coloured, comfortable building.

✰✰✰ *Linosa Club*, ☎ 0922/972060. Bungalows on the sea, pool.

Rooms to rent

On these islands everyone has rooms to rent; they are extremely friendly people, the accommodation is spotlessly clean, meals taken with the families are a delightful experience.

Campsites

LAMPEDUSA ✰✰ *La Roccia*, ☎ 0922/970055.

 ## Eating out
Restaurants

The restaurants are all extremely expensive by Sicilian standards. A popular dish served by most of them is *siluri di Gheddafi* (Gheddafi's missiles), very tasty and filling stuffed squid. The dishes are quite spicy and couscous is frequently on the menu. Most restaurants are closed in winter.

LAMPEDUSA €€€ *Gemelli*, 2 via Cala Pisana, ☎ 0922/970699, for the best couscous, also bouillabaisse and paella.

€€€ *Tomasino*, via Lido Azzurro, cala Guitgia, ☎ 0922/970879. The hotel (Guitgia Tomasino) restaurant; fish is prepared in a thousand different ways.

€€ *Al Gallo D'Oro*, 45 via Vittorio Emanuele. Very friendly atmosphere and inexpensive set menu.

€€ *Trattoria Pugliese*, 3 via Cala Pisana, ☎ 0922/970531. A cosy and quiet trattoria. The chef is from Apulia; this guarantees excellent pasta dishes.

€ *Magica Napoli*, 6 via delle Grotte, ☎ 0922/971938. A characteristic Neapolitan pizzeria.

LINOSA €€ *Trattoria da Anna*, ☎ 0922/972048. Her lentil soup is famous, or try the *pasta con gli sgombri* (pasta with mackerel). Anna also has **rooms** to rent.

€€ *Trattoria Savoca*, ☎ 0922/973080. Unforgettable grilled fish.

Cafés, pastry shops and ice cream parlours

There are many of these, especially along the busy via Roma (Lampedusa). The *cannoli di ricotta* are renowned. One of the most popular cafés is the *Bar Roma*, in via Ulisse Maccaferri (off via Roma), where the pastries are delicious.

Irish pub

Glenadin, 50 via Roma.

Handicrafts

The fishermen often devote their spare time to diving for sponges, which they then clean and sell to the tourists. They also sell seashells.

Diving centres

Lo Verde Diving 118 via Roma, ☎ 0922/971986.
Mediterranee Immersioni, on the harbour, ☎ 0922/971526.

Lampedusa

Lampedusa is the largest of the three islands with an area of 20 sq km and 5700 inhabitants. On the African continental shelf, it is a flat limestone rock, similar to the Tunisian coast behind it, with crystal clear waters and lovely sandy beaches, but it is impossibly crowded in July and August with holidaymakers from northern Italy, attracted by the clean sea and the memorable seafood. Italians really love crowded beaches.

The **Isolotto dei Conigli**, just offshore, is now a wildlife reserve run by the *Legambiente* to protect the turtles (*Caretta caretta*) which still lay their eggs on the beach. They have a small museum and library at 28 via Maccaferri, ☎ 0922/971611.

Lampedusa has important US and Italian military installations; the Libyans made an unsuccessful attack in 1986 when two missiles fell 2.5km short of the island. In April 2002 an unfinished illegal village called Villaggio Sindona, built in the wildlife reserve of Cala Creta, was demolished.

Linosa

Linosa, 42km north of Lampedusa, has an area of 5.3 sq km and 170 inhabitants. Volcanic in origin, it is quite hilly and the most fertile of the islands. In summer there are thousands of little blue butterflies (*Lycaenidae* family) everywhere. The houses are colourful, the atmosphere very peaceful; it is just the place for a restful holiday. The small beaches are of black volcanic sand; there are lovely secluded rocky coves for memorable swims. Although visitors are not permitted to bring cars to the island in summer they are not necessary, the island is so small. Some people think this could be part of Atlantis; offshore to the east there are great rectangular blocks of basalt on the seabed, and what appears to be a primitive divinity carved in stone, now covered with seaweed. The *Caretta caretta* turtle also lays her eggs on one of the beaches here (no access).

Lampione

Lampione, with an area of just 1.2 sq km, is uninhabited; white limestone like Lampedusa, its waters are frequented by divers in the summer. Practically inaccessible, it is home to an important colony of Cory's shearwaters.

SCIACCA AND ERACLEA MINOA

Sciacca, although surrounded by new buildings, has an interesting and picturesque old centre and a local ceramic industry. It is also a spa centre. Eraclea Minoa is an ancient site in a wonderful position on the sea.

Practical information

Getting there
By bus
Frequent services to Sciacca from Agrigento and Palermo. There is no direct public transport to Eraclea Minoa but *Lumia* (☎ 0922/20414) runs a service from Agrigento (Piazzale Fratelli Rosselli) for Cattolica Eraclea, and from there (June–Sept only), *Cacciatore* (☎ 0922/39016) runs buses the rest of the way, about a 15 min. bus ride. Alternatively, *Cuffaro* or *SAIS* buses run to Sciacca; ask to get off at the crossroad for Eraclea, where you can pick up the *Cacciatore* bus from Cattolica (check the timetable the day before as times change frequently) but waiting around in Cattolica is definitely more interesting than passing time in the middle of nowhere.

Information offices
Azienda Autonoma, 84 Corso Vittorio Emanuele, Sciacca, ☎ 0925/21182.
Azienda Autonoma delle Terme, 2 via Agatocle, ☎ 0925/961111, Sciacca (information on both spas: the new spa in town and the ancient one in the caves of S. Calogero).
Tourism Information Bureau, ☎ 0925/20478, Sciacca.
APT Agrigento, ☎ 0922/401352. Sciacca on line ✉ www.azienda turismosciacca.it. ✉ www.terme disciacca.it (not only information on spas). ✉ www.carnevaledisciacca.com.

Where to stay
Hotels
SCIACCA ✵✵✵✵ *Grande Albergo delle Terme*, via delle Nuove Terme, ☎ 0925/23133, 🗏 0925/87002, ✉ www.grandhoteldelleterme.com. Pleasant 1950s building next to the spa, good restaurant
✵✵✵✵ *Villa Palocla*, contrada Raganella, ☎ 0925/902812, ✉ www. villapalocla.it. Panoramic position over the city; excellent restaurant.
✵✵✵ *Garden*, via Valverde, ☎ 0925/26299, 🗏 0925/26299. In the modern city.
CONTRADA SOVERETO ✵✵✵ *Alicudi*, ☎ 0925/994000, 🗏 0925/994016. ✵✵✵ *Lipari*, ☎ 0925/994024, 🗏 0925/994030. West of the town, these are two large and comfortable hotels built a few years ago when everybody believed Sciacca could become a big tourist destination; there are lots of facilities, including sailing, windsurfing, horseriding, waterskiing, tennis, minigolf and fitness centres.
RIBERA ✵✵✵ *Miravalle*, 2 via Circonvallazione, Ribera, ☎ 0925/61383, 🗏 0925/61863. Comfortable, well kept establishment east of the town. No restaurant.
SICULIANA ✵✵✵ *Villa Sikania Park*, 300 via SS 115 Km 169, Siculiana, ☎ 0922/817818, 🗏 0922/815751, ✉ villasikania@villasikania.com. Lovely new hotel with pool, close to the town.

Bed and breakfast
SCIACCA *Cortese Scaduto*, via Aranci, ☎ 0925/992347.
Villa Rosa, contrada Capo S. Marco, ☎ 091/335300. House on the sea, open summer only, breakfast is served on the terrace.

Farmhouse accommodation
Augello, 11 via Tripoli, Bruca, Sciacca, ☎ 0925/23146, ✉ paolo.augello@ tin.it. The farm, 8km from town and 7km from the sea, produces wine, olive oil, oranges and vegetables, the owner also raises ostriches and horses.
Montalbano, contrada Scrunchipani, ☎ & 🗏 0925/80154. Farm producing fruit and olive oil; about 7km from

Sciacca and the sea.Two-room flats to rent. Pool, archery, swings.

Surriano, 153 via Cappuccini, about 7 km along the road to Menfi from Sciacca, ☎ & ▯ 0925/80101. Olive and orange groves, panoramic position, campers are also welcome.

Monastery accommodation

CALTABELLOTTA *Badia*, 16 via Colonnello Vita, Caltabellotta, ☎ & ▯ 0925/951121. A beautiful convent in the old centre of the little town with a lovely garden, run by nuns who use the proceeds to help young people. Stunning views; comfortable rooms, each with private bath. The nuns organize excursions from time to time.

Campsites

NEAR SCIACCA ☆☆ *Baia Makauda*, ☎ 0925/997001. Near the sea.

☆ *Gioventù*, ☎ 0925/991167. By the sea.

☆ *Tre Sirene*, contrada San Giorgio, ☎ & ▯ 0925/997242. Little round huts on the beach.

Apartments to rent

BAIA RENELLA, contrada Renella San Marco, ☎ & ▯ 0925/991640, ▧ www.futuralink.it/baiarenella. On the beach.

SICULIANA MARINA ☆☆ *Canne*, ☎ 0922/815255.

☆☆ *Herbesso*, ☎ 0922/ 817221.

ERACLEA MINOA *Eraclea Minoa Camping*, ☎ 0922/846023, in a pine wood near the beach, with restaurant and discotheque.

NEAR MENFI ☆☆☆ *Geser Club*, contrada Torrenova, ☎ 0925/74666.

☆ *La Palma* in contrada Fiori, ☎ 0925/ 77232.

 ## Eating out
Restaurants

SCIACCA €€€ *Hostaria del Vicolo*, 10 vicolo Samaritano, ☎ 0925/ 23071. Well cooked fresh fish, with some very special dishes: *spaghetti frutti di mare e finocchietto* (spaghetti with shellfish and wild fennel), *merluzzo ai fichi secchi* (cod with dried figs), or swordfish ravioli. Closed Mon.

€€ *La Lampara*, 33 vicolo Caricatore, lungomare Cristoforo Colombo, ☎ 0925/ 85085. Very fresh fish. Closed Mon.

€€ *Vecchia Conza*, 37 via Conzo, ☎ 0925/25385. Picturesque little restaurant much liked by the local people. Closed Mon.

€ *Trattoria del Camionista*, via Salerno, ☎ 0925/21984. Inexpensive, simple delicious food. Closed Sun in winter only.

Self service restaurants and pizzerie

Self Service La Giara, via Pietro Gerardi, ☎ 0925/26926. For a quick meal, snacks or sandwiches. Closed Mon.

Steripinto, corso Vittorio Emanuele. Pizzeria.

Pizza Libera, via A. De Gasperi. Pizzeria.

La Grotta, 174 via Incisa.

Ice cream parlour

Punto e virgola, via Aldo Moro, for the finest ice cream in town.

Irish pub

Murphy, via Inveges.

Picnics

Eraclea Minoa is a beautiful place to picnic.

Boat hire

Nautica Gerardi, Porto di Ponente, next to the Capitaneria del Porto (Port Authority), ☎ 0925/22002. Fishing boats or sailing boats available.

 ## Annual festival
Carnival procession in Sciacca with allegorical floats, thought to be the oldest in Sicily (February).

Sciacca

Sciacca (population 40,000) is a spa town known since Greek times, when it was the thermae of Selinunte. It is thought to be the oldest spa in existence. It took the name of Sciacca after the Arab domination (9C–11C AD); as the town rises in front of a white limestone cliff, that looks rather like an iceberg when seen from the sea, the name probably derives from the Arabic *as-saqqah*, meaning 'ice'. It has an important fishing harbour, where every day about 5000 tons of fish are disembarked, most of it for processing. The people here build their own boats. Along the tiny streets of the old centre, both men and women clean sardines and anchovies ready for salting. A local ceramic industry flourished here in the 16C and 17C, and there are several artisans' workshops in the town; the colours and the patterns are quite different from those seen elsewhere in Sicily.

In the centre of the town beside part of its old fortifications is the unusual **Porta S. Salvatore** (1581), a fine work by local stonemasons. Beside it is the eccentric façade of the **Carmine** with a half finished neo-classical lower part and an asymmetrical 13C rose window. The dome, with green tiles, dates from 1807. The church contains a good painting of the *Transition of the Virgin*, the last work of Vincenzo da Pavia, completed by Giampaolo Fondulo in 1572.

A short way up via Geradi (left) is the **Steripinto**, a small fortified palace in the Gothic Catalan style. It has an interesting façade, with diamond-shaped stone facing, erected in 1501 by Antonio Noceto. Opposite the Carmine, on the other side of via Incisa, is the north portal of the church of **S. Margherita**, sculpted in 1468 by Francesco Laurana and his workshop, deconsecrated many years ago, and now used for concerts and exhibitions. It contains polychrome stuccoes by Orazio Ferraro. Beyond is the Gothic portal of the former church of S. Gerlando and the abandoned Ospedale di S. Margherita. Opposite are the late-Gothic Palazzo Perollo-Arone and the 15C Torre di Pardo.

Corso Vittorio Emanuele continues into the central **piazza Angelo Scandaliato** planted with trees. From here there is a view of the old houses rising in terraces above the fishing harbour. The former **Collegio dei Gesuiti** (now the Town Hall), begun in 1613, has a fine courtyard.

The corso continues to the dilapidated **piazza Duomo** where the Duomo, called the Basilica and dedicated to Mary Magdalene, has statues by Antonino and Gian Domenico Gagini on its façade. It was rebuilt in 1656 by Michele Blasco, and the vault fresco is by the local artist Tommaso Rossi (1829). It has some good sculptures including a statue of the *Madonna* (1457), a marble ancona with reliefs by Antonino Gagini, and (on the high altar) the *Madonna del Soccorso* by Giuliano Mancino and Bartolomeo Berrettaro.

The corso continues to **piazza Friscia** which has pretty 19C public gardens with tropical plants, in a pleasanter part of the town. Via Agatocle leads past the new theatre to the edge of the cliff. Here, the **Nuovo Stabilimento Termale**, a pink spa building in Art Nouveau style (1928–38) offers thermal swimming pools (32° C, open June–October) and mud baths. The Grand Hotel was built next door in 1952.

From piazza Friscia via Valverde leads up to the gardens in front of the church of S. Maria delle Giummarre (or Valverde), its façade tucked in between two castellated Norman towers; the restored chapel in the left tower has an interesting interior. The elaborate 18C rococo decoration in the main church is the work of Ferraiolo. The vault was frescoed by Mariano Rossi (1768). Also in the upper town is **S. Nicolò La Latina**, a simple 12C church. Above is the ruined **castle** of the Spanish Luna family. Their feud with the Perollo clan in 15C–16C became notorious under the name of *caso di Sciacca* (the Sciacca affair); it was resolved only after the population of the town had been reduced to almost half its size.

Three churches are situated in piazza Noceto, with the 16C Porta S. Calogero, including **S. Michele** (1614–20), which contains an 18C cantoria, a Gothic wooden Crucifix, and a 16C marble bas-relief. In piazza Don Minzoni next to the duomo, there is the **Scaglione Museum** (☎ 0925/83089), the private collection of Francesco Scaglione, a local aristocrat who lived in the 19C, consisting of paintings, ceramics and objets d'art, lovingly displayed.

The island that disappeared

Not far off the coast of Sciacca, in July 1831, a volcanic island formed, rising through the water with fountains of volcanic mud and clouds of ash; by 17 July the island was 9 metres high, and on 11 August it was 25 metres high with a circumference of nearly 2 km. Then it appeared to have stopped growing, and adventurous people started organizing boat trips and picnics on it. An enterprising captain, commander Senhouse, passing with his ship close by the island at the beginning of August, had planted the Union Jack on it and announced the island to be British territory. Obviously this was contested by Ferdinand II of Bourbon, who even sent warships to the spot. On 17 August the island was named Isola Ferdinandea and annexed by the Kingdom of the Two Sicilies; but it did not last long. By November the island was seen to be gradually sinking, and it disappeared completely on the 8 December. Experts have announced that Isola Ferdinandea is rising again, and is not far below the surface.

The environs of Sciacca

Northeast of Sciacca is **Menfi** (population 13,000), a town laid out on a regular plan in 1698, with the houses arranged around courtyards off the main streets, many of which were made uninhabitable by the Belice earthquake in 1968. A new town has been built on the higher ground above. On the coast, beyond woods, is the fishing village of **Porto Palo**. There are good beaches on the unspoilt coast here which adjoins the nature reserve around the mouth of the Belice river in the province of Trapani (which extends to Marinella and Selinunte).

North of Menfi is **S. Margherita Belice** where the country house described by Lampedusa in *Il Gattopardo*, called Donnafugata, was destroyed together with most of the town in the 1968 earthquake but has now been completely restored. To the east of Menfi, **Sambuca di Sicilia** (population 7000) has an old centre which preserves its Islamic layout (near piazza Navarro). The church of the Concezione has a 14C portal and the church of the Carmine contains 19C stuccoes and a statue of the *Madonna* attributed to Antonello Gagini. In Palazzo Panitteri there is a museum of 19C wax models. The Chiesa del Collegio and Cappuccini have works by Fra Felice da Sambuca (1734–1805). To the north, on the provincial border with Palermo, are the excavations of Adranone and Contessa Entellina, described on p 154.

Caltabellotta, northeast of Sciacca, is a little town (population 5200) in a beautiful location in a commanding position (849m). Here the peace treaty ending the war of the Sicilian Vespers (see p 42) was signed in 1302. The Norman church (usually locked) has statues by the Gagini. In 1194 the castle sheltered Sibylla of Acerra, widow of King Tancred, and her infant son who reigned for a few months as William III, shortly before they were imprisoned by the new king of Sicily, Henry VI. The church of the Salvatore, below the rock face, has a late Gothic portal. On the outskirts is the hermitage of S. Pellegrino (17C–18C; now derelict). Below Caltabellotta is the little town of **S. Anna**, founded in 1622.

East of Caltabellotta, **Villafranca Sicula**, founded in 1499, was also damaged in the Belice earthquake. **Burgio** is an agricultural town with a local ceramics industry founded in the 16C and one of the last two bell foundries of Sicily. A Saracen castle survives here (just about) and in the Mother Church there is a *Madonna* by Vincenzo Gagini, and a 13C wooden Crucifix which is much revered and carried in procession every year to the sanctuary 8km away of **S. Maria di Rifesi**, built in the 12C by Ansaldo, steward of the royal household of Palermo. The 17C Convent of the Capuchins has recently been restored and opened to the public; during the works a painting by Zoppo di Gangi was discovered, complete with the original early 17C frame, considerably the worse for wear after having been exposed to the elements for several years. A small **museum**, called *La dimora delle Anime* (the Dwelling-place of the Souls) has been created and displays a poignant collection of bodies, once carefully preserved by the monks, then allowed to decay after the convent was abandoned, and now refreshed and rearranged. Mummification was once a privilege of the members of the Church and wealthy citizens, and the art of preserving bodies was almost exclusively confined to the Capuchins in Sicily. This was something that people planned and paid for whilst still in good health, even stipulating the fine clothes in which they should be dressed on their death. The best examples of preserved bodies can be seen at the Capuchin Convent of Palermo, but there are plenty more elsewhere in Sicily, for example at Savoca near Taormina.

From Burgio, return to Sciacca via Caltabellotta, a narrow mountain road, or take the SS 386 to Ribera, then the SS 115 to Sciacca. Behind the town (signposted) is **Monte Kronio** (or Monte S. Calogero; 388m) which has caves (closed Dec–Mar) with steam vapours, known since Roman times, and now a little spa. The sanctuary of S. Calogero (1530–1644) has a statue of the saint by Giacomo Gagini. There is a small museum, **Antiquarium Kronio**, ☎ 0925/28989, with a collection of vases and fragments found in the grottoes and dating from the Neolithic to the Copper Age.

On the Agrigento road (SS 115) east of Sciacca is the '**Castello incantato**' (enchanted castle), ☎ 0925/993044 (well signposted), a park with olive and almond trees where thousands of heads were sculpted in wood and stone by a local farmer, Filippo Bentivegna (d. 1967), who after being hit on the head during a robbery in the USA (where he had emigrated), carved heads wherever he could find space in his garden. The city of Lausanne has dedicated a room to him in the Museum of Art Brut. Heading back to the coast and south of Burgio is **Ribera** (population 18,000), lying in an agricultural area of olive groves, vineyards, strawberries and orange groves. The town was founded in 1627 by Luigi, Prince of Paternò, and named in honour of his Spanish wife, Maria de Ribera. It was the birthplace of the politician Francesco Crispi (1818–1901), Garibaldi's Secretary of State, who supported his landing in Sicily in 1860. He was a deputy in the first national parliament and twice prime minister of Italy (in 1887 and 1893).

The beautiful coastline to the south of Ribera, which includes Torre Salsa, has interesting flora and fauna and parts of it are protected by the WWF. Further information on the nature reserve is available from 156/D via Roma, Siculiana, ☎ 0922/818220 🗐 0922/817995, ✉ wwftorresalsa@tin.it.

Eraclea Minoa

The excavations of Eraclea Minoa are in a magnificent, isolated position on the sea at the mouth of the ancient *Halykos* river (now the Platani). The road follows the lovely meandering river valley as it climbs the hill, passing vineyards. Beyond the turning for the seaside village an unsurfaced road continues for the last 500m. Here part of the town **defences** can be seen, which were improved in the 4C (when the length of the walls was increased to c 6km). Above the dirt road on the left are the foundation of a circular Greek tower and a section of well preserved wall (ending in a square Roman tower). The continuation of the walls has been lost in landslides. A splendid view extends along the wooded shore and white limestone cliffs to Capo Bianco, beyond the river.

Visiting the site and opening times

• The main entrance to the excavations of Eraclea Minoa is beside the ruins of Hellenistic houses. Admission daily, 09.00 to 1hr before sunset. No refreshments are available, but it is a beautiful place to picnic.

History of Eraclea Minoa

The name Eraclea Minoa suggests that it was originally a Minoan colony; a legend that Minos pursued Daedalus from Crete and founded a city here was reiterated by Diodorus who records that Theron of Akragas found the bones of Minos at Minoa. A colony was founded here by the inhabitants of Selinunte in the 6C BC, and the name *Heracleia* was probably added later in the century by Spartan emigrés. The Halykos formed the boundary between the Greek and Carthaginian territories in Sicily. The town thrived during the 4C BC when it was resettled by Timoleon, but it seems to have been uninhabited by the end of the 1C BC. The first excavations took place in 1907 (and were resumed in 1950–61).

A small **Antiquarium** (open 09.00–15.00 or 16.00) houses finds from Eraclea Minoa, and has informative plans of the area so far excavated. A path leads on through the beautifully kept site where the visible remains (excavations in progress) date mainly from the 4C. The well preserved **theatre** was built at the end of the 4C. The soft sandstone is now protected by a perspex cover. The site of the **city** is on the hillside in front of the theatre. Under cover is the so-called **governor's house**: part of the wall decoration and mosaic floor survives. Also here is a little altar for sacrifices (under glass). Outside excavations have revealed three levels of destruction; the level of the archaic city is at present being uncovered. The second line of the walls (built when the eastern part of the town was abandoned) is visible nearby. A path (or steps) lead up to the top of the hill above the theatre and a paved path leads over the hillside to the line of walls to the north east, with square towers, built in the 4C BC.

Near Eraclea is the little town of **Montallegro**, rebuilt in the 18C below its abandoned predecessor on the hill (a grotto here has produced finds from the Early Bronze Age to the Copper Age). To the north is Cattolica Eraclea, founded in 1610.

Siculiana, on a low hill between Eraclea Minoa and Agrigento, has a prominent domed church (1750–1813). The castle dates from 1350. A byroad leads down to the pretty coast (with good beaches) beside the **Torre di Monterosso** where there is a also a WWF reserve open to the public.

THE NORTHERN PART OF AGRIGENTO PROVINCE

There are a number of small towns well worth a visit which are scattered over the province of Agrigento. In the northern part of the province the River Platani flows through remote country. Sulphur was mined in the hills here up until the middle of the nineteenth century.

Practical information

Information office
APT Agrigento, ☎ 0922/401352.

Where to stay
Hotels

CAMMARATA ☆☆ *Falco Azzurro*, 66 via Venezia, ☎ 0922/900784.
☆☆ *Rio Platani*, via Scalo Ferroviario, ☎ & ▨ 0922/909051. Two small hotels, both with excellent restaurants.

Annual festivals
SAN BIAGIO PLATANI **Easter festival** which goes back to the early 17C, where special bread is baked and streets are decorated with flower arches, and branches of palm leaves, fruit, bread and dates. CASTELTERMINI The **Tataratà** is held in May.

Aragona, about 12km from Agrigento (population 10,000), founded in 1606, has an interesting street plan: straight, regular streets delimitating blocks of houses, which reveal a host of tiny alleys and little courtyards, Saracen style. Almonds and pistachios are cultivated in the surrounding fields. Nearby are the **Vulcanelli di Macalube**, tiny conical volcanoes, only 0.5–1m high, filled with salty bubbling mud.

Raffadali to the west, is a town of 14,200 inhabitants, where the church contains a Roman sarcophagus depicting the *Rape of Proserpine* in bas relief. A prehistoric necropolis on the hill of **Busone** has yielded finds including a number of statuettes of a female divinity made from pebbles. **Joppolo Giancaxio** to the south of Raffadali, is a pretty village in a fine position with an 18C castle and church.

S. Angelo Muxaro, north of Raffadali, surrounded by rugged farming country, is possibly the site of the ancient *Kamikos*. Prehistoric tombs pepper the hillside. Those near the foot of the road which mounts to the village date from the 11C–9C BC; the higher domed tombs were used in the 8C–5C BC. Across the Platani river is **S. Biagio Platani** where an unusual festival takes place at Easter; hundreds of decorative loaves of bread are baked, and the streets are covered with arches made of canes and branches, dates, palm leaves, flowers, fruit, and the loaves.

To the east, above the narrow Platani valley with its odd-looking sulphurous hills is **Casteltermini**, once a sulphur mining town, which has an interesting festival on the last Sunday in May known as the Tataratà.

The Feast of Tataratà and sulphur mining in Sicily

The name 'Tatarata' refers to the sound of the drums accompanying the colourful processions which take place during this celebration, commemorating the miraculous discovery of an ancient crucifix in the 17C. The cross, carbon dated to the first century AD, is thought to be the oldest in the world. It is kept in a little church 3km from the village, and this is where the processions go on the Friday and the Sunday of the first week in May. The participants wear magnificent costumes, and even the horses are richly arrayed. The last procession, on Sunday evening, is a frenetic dance of hordes of 'Moors' accompanied by the drums. It is said that the Muslims in this area were miraculously converted when the Cross was discovered.

The sulphur mines in central Sicily (in the provinces of Agrigento and Caltanissetta), which were worked throughout the 19C, gave Italy a world monopoly of sulphur by 1900. Some 16,000 miners were employed by 1860, and in the 300 or so mines in operation, steam engines were used in only four of them, and horses in only ten. In all the other mines sulphur was extracted manually from an average depth of 60m, and many of the workers, known as *carusi*, were children under 14. Working conditions were shocking: little children were used because they were small enough to crawl through the galleries; many of them only saw the light of day once a week.

By the end of the century American sulphur was dominating the market, being much cheaper; the consequent collapse of this part of the economy is one of the reasons for the mass emigration at the end of the nineteenth century.

It was not until 1934 that legislation was introduced forbidding employers to use women and boys under 16 as miners. The appalling working conditions endured by these people influenced many native writers, including Pirandello and Sciascia (see below). The last mines in the province of Agrigento were closed down in 1988, and those at Cozzo Disi and Ciavolotta may become museums. The mines in the province of Caltanissetta were abandoned in the 1970s. You can see models of the mines in the Museum of Mineralogy in Caltanissetta (see p 257).

If you visit **Casteltermini** it is worth crossing the provincial boundary to visit Sutera and Mussomeli, both in Caltanissetta province. **Sutera** rises above the left of the road at the foot of the gypseous outcrop of Monte S. Paolino (819m) surmounted by a chapel. The ruined Chiaramonte castle of **Mussomeli** also in the province of Caltanissetta, stands on an impregnable crag. In 1976, at the age of 83, Genco Russo died here; he was one of the most powerful Mafia bosses of his time.

Cammarata is a little medieval town with three unusual feasts, held for the crucifixes of the three main churches; the first Sunday in May, for the Cross of St Anthony, the last Sunday in May for the Cross of the Angels, and the first Sunday in September for the Cross of the Rain. **S. Stefano Quisquina** (population 5800) is another pleasant little town where the Chiesa Madre has an altarpiece of the *Resurrection of Lazarus* by the Carracci school. The Santuario di S. Rosalia on a hill to the east, has frescoes by the Manno family.

Bivona (population 5000), where peaches are cultivated, also has a number of fine churches. **Cianciana** is a little town founded in 1640.

THE EASTERN PART OF AGRIGENTO PROVINCE

There are many small towns in the eastern part of the province which have some 17C–18C churches of interest, but which are now surrounded by untidy outskirts. Racalmuto was the birthplace of Leonardo Sciascia.

Practical information

Information office
APT Agrigento, ☎
0922/401352.

Eating out
Restaurants
CANICATTÌ €€ *Zaliclò,* 170 viale della Vittoria, ☎ 0922/ 85354. Friendly restaurant, famous around these parts for its delicious home-made pasta.

On the edge of remote countryside, planted with almond trees, olives and vineyards, is **Palma di Montechiaro** (population 25,000), founded in 1637 by the prince of Lampedusa, ancestor of novelist Giuseppe Tomasi di Lampedusa.

> ### Giuseppe Tomasi di Lampedusa
> Tomasi di Lampedusa (1896–1957) wrote his famous novel *Il Gattopardo* (*The Leopard,* translated into English in 1960) at the end of his life and it was published posthumously. The book recounts the life of his great-grandfather Giulio Tomasi (1815–1885), renamed Don Fabrizio Salina in the novel, who reacted with instinctive resignation to the turmoil produced by the landing of Garibaldi on the island in 1860. It had enormous success and was made into a film by Visconti in 1963.
>
> Lampedusa was born in Palma di Montechiaro, however, the palace of Donnafugata he describes in *Il Gattopardo* is not that of Palma di Montechiaro but a palace in S. Margherita Belice, which was destroyed in the earthquake of 1968. His family were princes of Lampedusa and dukes of Palma di Montechiaro. Another villa (built in 1770), which was bought by his great-grandfather around 1845 (also described in the book) survives on the Piana dei Colli outside Palermo. Lampedusa also wrote *I Racconti,* translated in 1962 as *Two Stories and a Memory.*

The town is surrounded by hundreds of half-constructed houses (now abandoned concrete shells), begun by emigrants in the 1960s. The conspicuous Chiesa Madre is a fine building (1666–1703) by Angelo Italia which is approached by a scenic flight of steps. The 17C Lampedusa palace, now owned by the town council, has been partially restored and is sometimes open in summer at weekends.

A plain surrounds **Licata**, an unattractive town (population 41,200), suffering from economic decline; it was once a busy port for the shipping of Sicilian sulphur, but became isolated after the sulphur industry collapsed, cut off from world trade routes. It occupies the site of *Phintias*, the Greek city founded by the eponymous tyrant from Gela (see below). On 3–5 May a very picturesque series of celebrations are held for the patron saint Angelo, who was martyred in the 13C.

In years following a good crop, the farmers take a mule into the church with an offering of money, fruit and flowers, as a thanksgiving to Sant'Angelo, while if the season is very dry, the statue of the saint is taken out to sea on a boat and threatened with being thrown in the water, unless he sends rain.

In the **Palazzo del Municipio** (1935), designed by Ernesto Basile, are antique reliefs, a 15C triptych and a *Madonna* by Domenico Gagini (1470).

The corso leads past Palazzo Canarelli, which is decorated with grotesque heads. Beyond (left) is **S. Francesco**; its fine convent (now a school) was reconstructed in the 17C and the marble façade added in 1750 by Giovanni Biagio Amico. Behind, piazza S. Angelo is surrounded by pretty 18C buildings.

The 17C church of S. Angelo has a façade and cupola attributed to Angelo Italia. The corso ends at the Duomo. A chapel in the south transept, elaborately decorated in 1600–1705, has a wooden Crucifix which narrowly escaped destruction at the hands of the raiding Turks in 1553. The church of **S. Domenico** in corso Roma has two paintings by Filippo Paladino.

The 16C Badia del Soccorso houses the important **Archaeological Museum** (open Mon–Sat 09.00–13.00, closed Sun and PH; ☎ 0922/772602) which contains local archaeological material from the prehistoric and Greek periods, including Hellenistic votive statuettes, ceramics and red-figure vases from a necropolis of the 5C BC; a lovely 5C BC statue of a female divinity, probably Hera, in Greek marble, and a curious boat-shaped oil lamp.

Off the mouth of the River Salso (the ancient *Himera*), Attilius Regulus defeated the Carthaginian fleet in 256 BC, but in 249 a convoy of Roman merchant ships for Africa was driven ashore by the Carthaginians during a tempest. Landings were effected here by the 7th Army in 1943, under General Patton.

Ravanusa, a small town not far from Licata, was founded in 1621. Nearby on **Monte Saracino**, excavations have revealed a prehistoric site, Hellenised at the end of the 7C BC. **Campobello di Licata** was founded in 1681.

There is a castle of the Chiaramonte family (1275; enlarged in 1488) in **Favara** (not far from Agrigento on the old SS 122 to Canicattì), which has been damaged and 'restored'.

Leonardo Sciascia

Sciascia (1921–89), one of the greatest Italian writers of the last century, was born in Racalmuto. He left his library to the town, where he lived for most of his life, and a foundation was inaugurated here in his memory in 1994. He is also fittingly commemorated, by a life-size bronze statue (1997), on the pavement in the main street near the Chiesa Madre, by a local artist. His simple white marble tomb slab surrounded by jasmine is in the little cemetery nearby. He is famous for his novels, including *Il giorno della civetta* (1961) (*The day of the owl*), *A ciascuno il suo* (1966) (*To each his own*), *Il Consiglio d'Egitto* (*The council of Egypt*) and *Todo modo* (1974) (*One way or another*), written in a particularly simple and direct style. In some perceptive articles and essays he also wrote about the problems which afflict the island, and exposed the insidious power of the Mafia and corruption in politics long before these two evils of Italian society were generally recognised in public. Sciascia was extremely reserved and often pessimistic, but had a particularly high moral standing in Italy in the 1970s as an intellectual figurehead.

The little town of **Racalmuto** (from the Arabic *Rahal-maut*), in lovely countryside, was the birthplace of Leonardo Sciascia. Another inhabitant was Pietro d'Asaro (1597–1647), called *'il Monocolo'* ('one eye'), whose paintings can be seen in the churches of the town. In the town centre is the beautiful little 19C opera house (a miniature version of the one in Palermo), which has recently been restored and will be used for concerts and plays. The theatre is called Regina Margherita and was designed by Dionisio Sciascia.

Canicattì (population 34,500) is a market town of some importance and a railway junction. It is surrounded by vineyards which produce a table grape called *Italia*, which can be marketed during the winter months thanks to the technique of covering the vines with thick plastic in August, when the grapes are just beginning to ripen. This blocks the ripening process indefinitely. When the farmer wants to sell his grapes, he takes off the plastic three or four days before picking. In this way enormous bunches of tasty, crunchy white grapes, can decorate the dining tables of northern Europe for Christmas and the New Year. When covered with the plastic sheeting, the vineyards look like an endless silver sea. They also grow peaches, nectarines and plums. The little town of **Naro** stands on a hilltop (520m), once defended by battlemented walls (1263). It has early 17C churches and a Chiaramonte castle (13C–14C). The simple restaurants are well worth a lunch break, while the coffee bars serve exquisite almond biscuits. In the town centre is the ancient Palazzo Malfitano which houses in two enormous wings Sicily's only **Graphics Museum** (Museo della Grafica, 54 via Piave, ☎ 0922/953403, open Mon–Fri 09.00–13.00) with a collection of 250 works by artists ranging from Bruno Caruso to Guttuso and Goya.

Serradifalco gave a ducal title to Domenico Pietrasanta (1773–1863), author of an important work on Sicilian antiquities.

Caltanissetta province

CALTANISSETTA

Caltanissetta is a prosperous provincial capital (population 62,000), with 17C and 18C works in its churches and an interesting local archaeological museum. Its brightly coloured churches make it unique among the Sicilian cities. The economy is based on the production of wheat and fruit, especially table grapes, peaches and plums, but once it was the centre of the most important sulphur industry in the world. The province has some of the most important wildlife reserves of Sicily, dramatic castles, beautiful beaches, and some of the most fascinating and intriguing archaeological excavations.

Practical information

Getting there
By train

Centrale station, piazza
Roma, Caltanissetta, with services via
Canicattì to Agrigento, Gela, Ragusa
and Syracuse. There are not many
trains because *Trenitalia* would like to
close this line (the local people are
opposing it). The station of
Caltanissetta Xirbi, 7km north, is on
another line between Palermo, Enna
and Catania.

By bus

Frequent services (usually faster than
the trains) from piazza della Repubblica
for Palermo, Catania and Agrigento
(*SAIS*); for Piazza Armerina (*ASTRA*)
and for towns in the province.

Parking

Parking is difficult, there is a 1hr limit
in corso Umberto. Space sometimes
available in via Francesco Crispi and via
Kennedy.

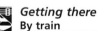

Information offices
APT Caltanissetta, 109 corso
Vittorio Emanuele ☎ 0934/
530411.
Information office, 20 viale Conte
Testasecca ☎ 0934/21089.
Caltanissetta on line: ✉ www.aapit.cl.it.
✉ www.caltanissetta-sicilia.it.

Where to stay
Hotels

☆☆☆☆ *San Michele*, via Fasci Siciliani, ☎ 0934/553750, 📠 0934/598791, 🖳 www.hotelsanmiche lesicilia.it. The town's most elegant hotel. Reliable service, good restaurant, out of the centre.

☆☆☆ *Plaza*, 5 via B. Gaetani, ☎ & 📠 0934/583877, 🖳 www.hotelplaza caltanissetta.it. Central position, modern and comfortable, with restaurant.

☆☆☆ *Ventura*, contrada Gurra Pinzelli on road (SS 640) to Agrigento, ☎ 0935/53780 📠 0934/553785. The hotel is out of town, but is a good choice for an overnight stop.

☆☆ *Hotel Giulia*, 85 corso Umberto, ☎ 0934/542927, 📠 0934/543237, 🖳 www.albergogiulia.it. Charming small hotel, friendly service, central and comfortable.

Farmhouse accommodation

Bioagri Palladio, contrada Palladio, Riesi, ☎ & 📠 0934/921305. Large wine farm with plenty of facilities, lake for fishing, sauna, riding, trekking.

Il Castello, contrada Castello, Resuttano, ☎ & 📠 0934/673815. In the north of the province, by an old castle, close to the Madonie Park and the Himera Valley Wildlife Reserve, carefully prepared food.

Campsites

Eurocamping 2 Rocche, contrada Faino, Butera, ☎ 0934/349006. Close to the sea, lots of trees, good facilities for guests. **Motorcaravans** can park in via Guastaferro, headquarters of the local caravan lovers' association, they give assistance and information, ☎ 0934/596911.

Eating out
Restaurants

€€ *Ristorante Archetto*, the restaurant used by Hotel Giulia (see above), ☎ 0934/542927.

Small and friendly.

€€ *Vicolo Duomo*, 3 piazza Garibaldi, entrance from 1 vicolo Neviera, ☎ 0934/582331. Local dishes in romantic old building in tiny alley, menu includes the authentic *farsumagru*. Closed all day Sun and mid-day Mon.

Cafés, pastry-shops and ice cream parlours

Fiorino, viale S.Caldura, is the place for the traditional Caltanissetta crunchy nougat covered with plain chocolate. *Romano*, 147 corso Umberto, also has excellent nougat, almond biscuits, home-made ice cream.

Picnics

Villa Cordova is a pleasant place to picnic.

Annual festivals

Holy Week, with a series of manifestations, including the procession of **I Misteri**, impressive scenes describing the Passion of Jesus, each one sponsored by one of the corporations of the city—the *mestieri*, or trades. The rest of the year they are kept in the church of S. Pio X in via Napoleone Colajanni, but are not usually on show to the public.

Entertainment

The Margherita Opera House. Baufremont Theatre, salita Matteotti, for concerts and prose.

Handicrafts

CALTANISSETTA *Salvatore Amorelli*, 424 via Xiboli, ☎ 0934/566886, 🖳 www.amorelli-italy.com. There is a shop on site. Beautiful pipes, made exclusively from briar from the Peloritan Mountains and Calabria, which is seasoned for 5 years. With his ten workers, Salvatore produces 3000 pipes a year, not enough to satisfy the demand, especially from Britain, North America, Japan and Germany.

SANTA CATERINA VILLARMOSA, not far from the city. The embroidery is famous.
VALLELUNGA PRATAMENO In the northern part of the province, along the SS 121 Caltanissetta-Palermo, is the workshop of Carmelo Amenta (77 via Verdi, ☎ 0934/814166) who makes fine saddles.

Internet points

Exenya, 106 corso Sicilia.
Net Point Service, 27 via Don Minzoni, ☎ 0934/555151.

History

The name of the town was for many years thought to have been derived from that of the ancient Sicel city of *Nissa*, with the Arabic prefix *Kal'at* (castle); but the name could derive from *Kal'at el nissaat*, that is, castle of the young women. Excavations in 1989 on Monte S. Giuliano (or del Redentore) yielded 7C–6C BC finds. The site was then abandoned until the Roman period. After its conquest by Count Roger in 1086 it was given as an apanage to his son Jourdain, and passed subsequently into the hands of Corrado Lancia (1296) and the Moncada family (1406).

The province was an extremely important centre of sulphur mining from the 18C up until the early 20C (the last mines were closed down in the 1970s), and potassium salt was also extracted in the area. In 1834 there were 196 sulphur mines in Sicily, of which 88 were around Caltanissetta.

In the central **piazza Garibaldi** is an amusing fountain with two monsters spraying a hippogryph by Michele Tripisciano (1860–1913), a talented local sculptor, whose statues also decorate corso Umberto I, the town hall and the public gardens. Here is the façade of the **Duomo** (1570–1622), which was damaged in the last war. In the pretty interior, decorated with white and gold stuccoes, the vault painting is thought to be Guglielmo Borremans' masterpiece (1720). In the second south chapel is a wooden statue (covered with silver) of the *Immacolata* (1760). In the chapel to the right of the sanctuary is a charming wooden statue of the archangel *Michael* by Stefano Li Volsi, and two marble statues of archangels by Vincenzo Vitaliano (1753). The high altarpiece is by Borremans, and the organ dates from after 1653. In the north transept is a painting by Filippo Paladino, and in the second north chapel is a Crucifix attributed to Fra' Umile da Petralia.

The church of **S. Sebastiano**, opposite, has an unusual façade (1891), painted bright red, and a blue campanile. At the east end is a fine 17C wooden statue of the titular saint. The last side of the piazza is closed by a large former convent which now houses the

The Duomo of Caltanissetta

Town Hall (with statues by Tripisciano) and the Margherita Opera House.

Beside the Town Hall, corso Umberto I leads up to a statue of Umberto I (wearing a flamboyant hat) by Tripisciano, outside the church of **S. Agata**, also painted red, and preceded by an outside staircase. It was built on a Greek cross plan in 1605. In the interior is fine marble *intarsia* decoration, especially on the two side altars. The north altar (with a delightful frontal with birds) is surmounted by a relief of *St Ignatius* by Ignazio Marabitti. The little chapel in the northwest corner has frescoes by Luigi Borremans. The high altarpiece, the *Martyrdom of St Agatha*, is a good work by Agostino Scilla (1654). Statues by Salvatore Marino (1753) stand beside the altar with cherubs by Marabitti above. The first north chapel has frescoes by Borremans (including an *Assumption* in the vault, and a *Nativity* on a side wall).

Off the right side of corso Umberto is the grand Palazzo Moncada (1635–38), left unfinished. A street on the left side of the Duomo leads downhill to via S. Domenico which continues to the church of **S. Domenico** with a delightfully shaped Baroque façade fitting an awkward site. The stuccoes inside have recently been repainted in bright blue (the pastel shades in the nave instead date from 1961). The fine painting of the *Madonna of the Rosary* is by Filippo Paladino (1614). The painting of *St Vincent Ferrer* by Guglielmo Borremans (1722) has been removed to the Museum of Sacred Art (see below).

From here the 14C church of S. Maria degli Angeli (closed) can be reached in ten minutes. Sadly ruined, its west door survives. Beyond a warehouse, on a fantastic rock, stand the shattered ruins of the **Castello di Pietrarossa**, residence of Frederick III of Aragon.

To the south, near the station, in via Napoleone Colajanni, is the **Civic Archaeological Museum** (09.00–13.00, 15.30–19.00, closed last Mon every month). The museo civico has a particularly interesting archaeological collection from sites in the province. **Room 1**. Objects from tombs at Gibil Gabib, including fine kraters (many with animal illustrations), and black- and red-figure vases; figurines found recently on Monte S. Giuliano (on the northern outskirts of Caltanissetta), the earliest portrayal of the human figure so far discovered in Sicily, after the paleolithic graffiti in the Addaura caves near Palermo. Dating from the Early Bronze Age, they are thought to have been used in a prehistoric sanctuary. The Arab period finds date from 996 AD to 1020 AD.

Room 2 displays material from Sabucina (see below), dating from 1270 BC to 1000 BC; red-figure kraters and a lekythos on a white ground (c 500 BC); a child's doll and shell necklace; a unique votive model of a Greek temple in terracotta (6C BC) from Sabucina. **Rooms 3** and **4** display finds from Capodarso and Mimiani, including a bronze helmet of the 6C BC. On the floor below is a sculpture gallery, with notable works by Michele Tripisciano (see above).

Near the public gardens the Seminary (51 viale Regina Margherita, open 09.30–12.30, 16.00–18.00, except Wed, Sun & PH; ☎ 0934/23014), houses a small **Museum of Sacred Art** with 17C and 18C vestments and two paintings by Guglielmo Borremans. At no. 73 viale della Regione is a **Museum of Mineralogy** (open 09.00–13.00, except Sun & PH), with a collection of some 3000 minerals, and scale models of many of the sulphur mines once operating in the provinces of Caltanissetta and Agrigento (see p 250).

Environs of Caltanissetta

South of Caltanissetta is the site of the ancient city of **Gibil Gabib** (closed). The name is derived from the Arabic *Gebel Habib* (pleasant hill), and it was discovered in the 19C. A necropolis here has yielded finds from three periods of occupation: 7C BC, 6C BC and the 4C BC.

The **Abbazia di S. Spirito**, also outside Caltanissetta, is a basilica founded by Roger and his wife Adelaide (probably between 1086 and 1093), and consecrated in 1153. It was attached to a fortified building, parts of which now form the sacristy. The church has a fine treble apse, recently restored. The charming small interior (ring at the door on the right marked *Abbazia*, 11.00–12.00 17.00–18.00) contains a large font below an interesting painted *Crucifix* dating from the 15C. On the walls are three detached 15C frescoes which have been restored. The striking 17C fresco of **Christ in benediction** was repainted in 1974. On the arch of the apse is the dedication stone (1153), and nearby is a little Roman cinerary urn (1C AD), with rams' heads, birds and a festoon. A 17C sedan chair, with its original fittings, which used to be used as a confessional, has been removed to the priest's house (shown on request).

Off the Enna road, beneath Monte Sabucina, is the site of **Sabucina** (open Mon–Sat 09.00–14.00, PH closed, ☎ 0934/554964). The approach road climbs up past several disused mines, and there is a view up to the right above an overgrown mine of the line of walls of Sabucina, just below the summit of the hill. After 2km the asphalted road ends beside recent excavations of a necropolis and the new circular museum building (still closed). An unsurfaced road continues downhill for another 500m to a gate by a modern house at the entrance to the site, in a fine position with wide views. Monte Sabucina was first occupied in the Bronze Age. A thriving Iron Age village was then settled by the Greeks in the 6C BC. The city declined after the revolt of Ducetius in 450 BC. The long line of Greek fortifications with towers and gates were built directly onto the rock. Sacred edifices can also be seen here. Some of the rich material from the necropolis is displayed in the Civic Museum at Caltanissetta (see above).

East of Caltanissetta is the forbidding **Terra Pilata**, a sterile upland of white clay offering a fine retrospective view of Caltanissetta. The River Salso is crossed by Ponte Capodarso, a graceful bridge built in 1553 by Venetian engineers. A legend says that once a year the devils hold a market on the bridge; anyone lucky enough to see it, may purchase just one fruit, which next day will turn into solid gold. Nearby is the archaeological zone of **Capodarso**, an ancient city which had disappeared by the beginning of the 3C BC. Part of the walls and necropolis survive. Finds from the site are kept in the museum in Caltanissetta (see above), and the area is now part of a large nature reserve. At **Villarosa**, between Caltanissetta and Enna, is an intriguing **Museum of Mining and Country Life** (09.30–12.00, 16.30–20.00, closed Mon, ☎ 0935/31126), on a train parked in the local station, where there is also a nice little restaurant. One carriage is dedicated to the history of steam trains in Sicily. At Villarosa it is possible to visit the local baron's house, Villa Lucrezia, where another small museum has recently opened (☎ 0935/567095).

GELA

Gela is an important port and now the fifth largest town in Sicily (population 78,000). Its superb **Greek fortifications** at Capo Soprano testify to its ancient importance, and it has one of the best archaeological museums on the island. The petro-chemical plant which has dominated the east side of the town since the 1960s has been accused of causing pollution, and it now runs the risk of being completely dismantled; its loss would cause mass unemployment in the area.

Unregulated new building in the 1960s and 1970s, in the wake of the false prosperity brought to the city by the refinery, has rendered Gela perhaps the ugliest city on the island, certainly the untidiest and the least comfortable both for its inhabitants and its visitors. Many of these houses, left half-finished, have now been abandoned, some were demolished.

Mafia, here called *'a stidda*, is still very powerful and business is controlled by a racket, forcing honest tradesmen into bankruptcy and resulting in numerous murders between rival clans every year. In 1983, 5000 inhabitants occupied the town hall destroying documents in protest against the chaotic local administration. In January 2002 the mayor resigned, declaring his city to be quite ungovernable without further intervention from the state. Do not let this put you off your visit; the inhabitants of Gela are charming, and extremely helpful, the museum alone is worth the journey to Sicily and the Greek fortifications are unique in the world and in splendid condition. Recent excavations at **Bosco Littorio**, site of the tradesmen's quarters and the harbour of the old city, has brought to light some warehouses buried under 6m of sand, untouched since the 5C BC. Among the material recovered are three unique terracotta altars which can be seen in the museum.

Practical information

Getting there
By train
The station is on the Syracuse, Ragusa, Canicattì, Agrigento line.
By bus
Yellow **city buses** leave from the station to Capo Soprano and the Archaeological Museum; information and tickets from the booth opposite the station.
Local buses. *Etna trasporti*, ☎ 095/ 532716 to and from Catania; *SAIS*, ☎ 0922/595260 to and from Agrigento and Licata.
Parking
It is easy to park near the Archaeological Museum and at Capo Soprano, but extremely difficult to park in the town centre.

Information office
APT information office, via Palazzi (corner of via Francia), ☎ 0933/911509.

Where to stay
Hotels
☆☆☆ *Sileno*, ☎ 0933/911144, ▤ 0933/ 907236. In the suburbs at Giardinelli, not far from museum.
☆☆ *Sole* 32 via Mare, ☎ 0933925292.
Farmhouse accommodation
BUTERA *Farm*, contrada Strada, Butera, ☎ & ▤ 0934/346600, ✉ www. farm-ospitalitàdicampagna.it. One of the finest examples of farmhouse accommodation in Sicily. Set in spectacular countryside, where Bonelli's eagle flies, its position is ideal for exploring the

towns of Caltagirone, Gela, Piazza Armerina, Niscemi, Butera and Mazzarino, all only a few minutes' drive away. The style is truly Mediterranean—Andrea, the owner, is Sicilian, Nabil, the manager, is Moroccan and the excellent cook, Mohamed, is Egyptian. Beautiful suites, comfortable bathrooms, good food. The farm produces DOC wine, wheat, olive oil and almonds; children are welcome; there is a large lake on the estate. Expensive and exclusive.

Eating out
Restaurants

€€ *Il Delfino*, 12 via Siracusa, ☎ 0933/924513. By general agreement, the finest restaurant in Gela, good menu and wine list. Closed Mon.
€€ *Aurora*, 1 piazza Vittorio Veneto, ☎ 0933/917711. Excellent fish dishes.
€€ *Gelone 2*, 39 via Generale Cascino, ☎ 0933/917314. A reliable restaurant specializing in fish. Closed Sun.
€ *Eschilo*. A good pizzeria close to the museum. There are several others on the seafront, open only in the evening.

Picnics

Capo Soprano, by the famous Greek fortifications is a lovely place to picnic.

History of Gela

The modern city, known until 1927 as Terranova, was founded by Frederick II in 1230, on the site of Gela, a colony of Rhodians and Cretans established in 689 BC. Gela soon rose to importance, sending out a colony to Akragas in 580 and influencing the Hellenization of local settlements in the interior of the island. The ancient site of the city corresponds roughly to the area of the medieval town and the present historical centre.

Under Hippocrates (498–491) the city reached its greatest prosperity, but Gelon, his cavalry commander and successor, transferred the seat of government and half the population to Syracuse in 485. The dramatist Aeschylus was killed at Gela in 456, apparently by an eagle which dropped a tortoise on to his bald head, mistaking it for a stone. In 405 the town was destroyed by the Carthaginians, but Timoleon refounded it in 339. The new city was larger than the earlier one and received a new circle of walls. Phintias, tyrant of Akragas, transferred its inhabitants in 282 to his new city at the mouth of the Himera (see Licata, p 251), and Gela disappeared from history. Hieron I of Syracuse and the ancient comic poet Apollodorus were among the distinguished natives of Gela.

Regional Archaeological Museum

At the east end of the town, on corso Vittorio Emanuele is the sumptuous Regional Archaeological Museum (open daily 09.00–13.00, 15.00–19.00, closed the last Mon of the month, ☎ 0933/912626), with a beautifully displayed collection. It contains some of the painted vases for which Gela is best known and which are exhibited in most of the archaeological museums in Europe and the USA, the three famous terracotta altars recently excavated in the emporium area of the city, and a superb coin collection.

Ground floor Near the entrance, displayed in a case on its own, is the foot of a black-figure Attic kylix with an inscription to Antifemo, one of the founders of the Greek colony. **Section I** is dedicated to the **acropolis area** (east of the modern city) which was inhabited from prehistoric times up to the 5C BC. Finds from a sacred area dedicated to Athena (with two Doric temples built in the 6C–5C BC) include terracottas, bronzes, architectural fragments, votive statues, the head of a horse, a charming little statuette in stone of a girl holding a wreath (6C BC), and a lovely marble basin dating from 338 BC. **Section II** displays later material from the acropolis (4C–3C bc) when it was an artisans' district. There is also material salvaged from an Archaic Greek ship found off the coast of Gela in 1988, finds from a warehouse, and from an urban sanctuary dedicated to Hera.

Section III is devoted to **Capo Soprano**, now at the western extremity of the modern city, where there was a residential area and public edifices were erected in the late 4C BC, including (in case 22) a small altar of the 6C BC, showing Hercules slaying Alkyoneus. The last section has an exhibition illustrating the production of various potteries, some with dedicatory inscriptions on their bases.

Upstairs On the balcony, is **Section IV** where more than 50 amphorae (7C–4C BC) attest to the importance of Gela's commerce with other centres in the Mediterranean. **Section V** is dedicated to sanctuaries found outside Gela, most of them dedicated to Demeter and Kore, with numerous votive statuettes and Corinthian ware. **Section VI** displays material from the prehistoric to Hellenistic era from the surrounding territory. Roman and medieval material found during the restoration of the Castelluccio (see below) is displayed in **Section VII**. Also on display here is the exceptional **numismatic collection** of more than 2000 pieces, including a magnificent hoard of c 600 silver coins, minted in Agrigento, Gela, Syracuse, Messina and Athens, between 515 BC and 485 BC, and one of the most important collections in existence. Discovered in Gela in 1956, the coins were stolen in 1973, but most of them were subsequently recovered. All the coins on display were found in or around Gela, although some of them were minted in other cities. In front of the coin room are the three **terracotta altars**, with images on the front in relief, found recently in the emporium part of the ancient city. Dating from the beginning of the 5C BC, the two larger ones are unique for their size, artistic quality, subject matter, and state of conservation. The one on the left represents a magnificent **Gorgon Medusa**, running with her babies Pegasus the winged horse and the warrior Chrysaor in her arms, and tightening her snake belt as she goes; the smaller central one shows a graceful lioness attacking a bull in the top part, and underneath the goddess of dawn Eos making away with the shepherd Kephalos; the altar on the right shows **three goddesses**, probably Hera, Demeter and Aphrodite; Demeter is smoothing her braids complacently.

Downstairs **Section VIII** contains the 19C **Navarra collection**, one of the most important private collections of ancient vases in Sicily (with a fine group of Attic black-and-red figure vases, and Corinthian ware from the 8C–6C BC). Also here is the smaller Nocera collection and two cases of finds from the necropolis. In Case F no. 3 is an Attic lekythos on a white ground showing Aeneas and Anchises (460–450 BC) and Case G has an exquisite Attic red-figure lekythos, by the Nikon painter.

Outside the museum is the entrance to the **Molino a Vento Acropolis** (09.00–19.00, closed last Mon every month; same ticket as museum), which now overlooks the oil refinery. This was part of Timoleon's city on a terraced grid plan with shops and houses (c 339–310 BC), above the ruins of a small sacred enclosure. In the garden on the site of the acropolis of the earliest city, stands a single (re-erected) column of a temple probably dedicated to Athena (6C BC), and the basement of a second earlier temple also dedicated to Athena. This area had been abandoned by 282 BC. Excavations in the area have been suspended.

Greek fortifications at Capo Soprano

Corso Vittorio Emanuele crosses the long, untidy town but the most pleasant way of reaching Capo Soprano and the Greek fortifications (which are over 3km from the museum) is along the seafront. The remarkable Greek fortifications (open 09.00–1hr before sunset every day; same ticket as museum) of Capo Soprano have been excellently preserved after centuries beneath the sand: they extend for several hundred metres, and reach a height of nearly 13m. They were first excavated in 1948. The walls were begun by Timoleon in 333 BC and completed under Agathocles. Their height was regularly increased to keep ahead of the encroaching sand, a danger today removed by the planting of trees. In the lovely peaceful site close to the sea, with eucalyptus and acacia trees, a path (right) leads past excavations of battlements to a circular medieval kiln (under cover). From here there is a view of the coast.

The path follows walls (partly under cover) and foundations of the brick angle towers to the west gate, and then descends to the best stretch of walls: the lower course is built of sandstone, while the top is finished with plain mud bricks (being restored). A little postern gate in the walls can be seen here, dating from the time of Agathocles (filled in with mud bricks soon after it was built), as well as a well-preserved drain. Steps lead up past a little house which contains photographs of the site and then another path leads back past the abutment wall to the entrance.

About 500m from the fortifications (signposted Bagni Greci), now engulfed by modern apartment blocks, are remains of **Greek baths** (4C). The baths, including hip baths (with seats) are protected by a roof, but are always open, surrounded by a little garden behind a railing.

Environs of Gela

On the coast west of Gela is **Falconara** with its spectacular 15C castle in an oasis of palm trees around a large fountain (a custodian lives near by). Beyond are vegetable and melon fields (protected from the wind by cane fences). The sandy beaches are particularly inviting.

Inland from Gela is **Butera**, perched on a flat rock, with fine views towards the sea. Important archaeological excavations of the prehistoric settlement have been carried out nearby; the finds are in the archaeological museum in Gela. One of the largest cities in Arab Sicily, it became a Lombard centre under the Normans, and later the seat of the Santapau family, Catalans, who became the first feudal lords on the island to receive the title of prince in 1563 from Philip II of Spain. The 11C castle is romantic and imposing.

Mazzarino was the ancient city of *Maktorion*, which in the 14C became the seat of the Branciforte family from Piacenza. Always renowned for their culture and learning, in 1507 King Ferdinand the Catholic invested Niccolò Branciforte with the title of count of Mazzarino, a privilege which induced him to embellish and enlarge the town, and to build his magnificent residence, which still survives, looking like a miniature royal palace, with its own theatre and printing shop. The churches of the town preserve notable works of art, including Branciforte funerary monuments and paintings by Filippo Paladino. Mazzarino also has two spectacular medieval castles close by. At **Riesi**, where sulphur miners and farm workers have always led a hard existence, a kind of trade union uniting them all became strong enough for the town to declare itself a Socialist Republic in 1893; it was however short-lived. The inhabitants are very proud of their history.

On the Caltagirone road is the 13C **Castelluccio**, a castle said to be haunted by the ghost of a mysterious lady who sometimes entices travellers inside; when this happens they are never seen again (open at the same times as the archaeological museum in Gela, it is accessible with the same ticket). It occupies a good site dominating the surrounding plain, now cultivated with artichokes.

On the approach road there is a little war memorial to the battle of 1943 which followed the landings of the American assault forces on the beaches in the Gulf of Gela. It is appropriately sited beside two 'pill-box' defences. There is a prehistoric necropolis on Monte Disueri (7,4km along the SS190 to Mazzarino from the junction with the SS170 bis to Gela; on the left-hand side) with more than 2000 tombs carved into the rock. It is the most important Sicel necropolis after Pantalica (see chapter on Syracuse), and dates from the 11C–9C BC, but the paths have all but disappeared; wear trekking boots for exploring.

Enna province

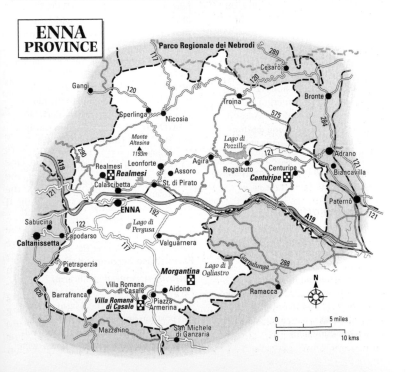

ENNA

Enna, known as the *Belvedere della Sicilia* because of its wonderful position on the top of a precipitous hill (931m) that dominates the whole of Sicily, is one of the most interesting inland towns (population 28,500) on the island. Its vast castle was an almost impregnable stronghold for centuries. The view of the medieval hill town of Calascibetta from Enna is exceptional. Much new building has taken place in recent years on the southern edge of the hill and in the valleys beneath, and the old centre is fast losing its population. The province is the most important in Sicily for the production of cereals, and provides a large proportion of the durum wheat used by the Italian pasta industries. Enna is a good centre for visiting the famous mosaics in the Roman villa near **Piazza Armerina**, and the excavations of **Morgantina** (see p 283). The secondary roads in the province often traverse spectacular countryside, and small towns of interest include Leonforte, Sperlinga and Nicosia (see below).

Practical information

Getting there
By train
The **railway station** is in the valley, 5km from the town centre, on the Palermo–Catania line.
By bus
The **bus station** is in viale Diaz. Services run by *SAIS* to Catania (via the motorway in 1hr 20mins), Palermo, Messina, Caltanissetta and Agrigento, Caltagirone, Piazza Armerina (in 45mins), Nicosia, Leonforte, Adrano, and Paternò; also mainland destinations, Rome, Naples, Bologna etc.
Parking
Parking in piazza Prefettura and piazza Umberto I.

Information offices
APT Enna, 411 via Roma, ☎ 0935/528188, 0935/528228.
Azienda Soggiorno, 6 piazza Colajanni, Enna, ☎ 0935/26119.
Tourist Information Bureau, c/o Municipio (town hall), 1 piazza Coppola, Enna, ☎ 0935/40436 or 0935/40356. Enna on line: ✉ www.enna-sicilia.it; ✉ www.apt-enna.com.

Where to stay
Hotels
☆☆☆ *Grande Albergo Sicilia*, 7 piazza Colajanni, ☎ 0935/500850. One of the best hotels in town, with restaurant and terrace, comfortable and well furnished rooms.
☆☆☆ *Demetra*, contrada Misericordia, SS 121, ☎ 0935/502300, ▤ 0935/502166. In a panoramic position close to the railway station and to the motorway exit. Simple but very comfortable.
LAGO DI PERGUSA (9km south of Enna) ☆☆☆ *La Giara Park*, 125 via Nazionale, ☎ 0935/541687, ▤ 0935/541521. Small hotel with air conditioning and pool, in a quiet position; good restaurant.
☆☆☆ *Riviera*, via Autodromo, ☎ 0935/541267, ▤ 0935/541260. Air conditioning, pool, garden; welcoming and comfortable; view over the lake.
Farmhouse accommodation
Pollicarini, contrada Pollicarini, Pergusa, Enna, ☎ 0935/541800, ▤ 0935/542163. Wheat farm in central position for Enna, Pergusa and Calascibetta, renowned for the marvellous food; the bread and the house wine

are exceptional; horseriding, mountain biking, friendly welcome.

Campsite

Agricampeggio Gerace, contrada Gerace, Enna, ☎ 0935/501770, 339/5771014. Open summer only, places also for motorcaravans.

Eating out
Restaurants

ENNA **€€** *Centrale*, 9 piazza VI Dicembre, ☎ 0935/500963. Sicilian cuisine; long-established family-run restaurant; terrace for summer lunches. Closed Sat. in winter.

€€ *Liolà*, 2 via Duca d'Aosta, ☎ 0935/37706. Cosy restaurant with frescoes on the walls inspired by the works of Pirandello; good Sicilian cooking, also *pizze* in the evening. Closed Tues.

€ *Fontana*, 6 via Volturo, ☎ 0935/25465. Family-run establishment, very tasty Sicilian dishes; open-air lunches in summer, with panoramic views.

€ *Da Marino*, 62 viale Savoca, ☎ 0935/25878. Simple restaurant and pizzeria close to the castle. Closed Wed.

PERGUSA **€** *Da Carlo*, 34 via Nazionale, ☎ 0935/541030. Excellent grilled meat or vegetables; pasta and good local wine. Closed Tues.

Picnics

Places to picnic at the Castello di Lombardia.

Cafés, pastry shops and ice cream parlours

ENNA *Caffè Roma*, 312 via Roma, opened in 1921. It has a good reputation. *Caprice*, 17 via Firenze.

BIVIO S. ANNA On the way down to Pergusa, is the famous *Bar Di Maggio*, known throughout Italy, for cakes and biscuits, snacks and excellent ice cream.

Annual festivals

The religious ceremonies in Holy Week culminate with a procession of the Confraternities on Good Friday. On 2 July, festivities in honour of the **Madonna della Visitazione**, which almost certainly go back to the ancient rites in honour of Demeter and Persephone, who were particularly venerated here. The celebrations begin a month before, culminating on the evening of 2 July, when 124 bearers chosen among the farmers carry the statue of the Madonna in procession, on a magnificent float called the *nave d'oro*, the golden ship, made by Scipione di Guido in 1590.

Entertainment

Garibaldi Theatre for concerts and prose.
Open-air performances in summer at the **Castello di Lombardia**.

History

The city occupies the site of *Henna*, a Sicel stronghold subjected to Greek influences, perhaps from Gela, as early as the 7C BC. The legendary scene of the rape of Proserpine (see below), and the centre of the cult of Ceres or Demeter, her mother, to whom Gelon erected a temple in 480 BC, it fell by treachery to Dionysius I of Syracuse in 397. In 135 BC the First Servile War broke out here under the slave Eunus, and the town was taken in 132 by the Roman army only after two years' siege. The Saracens, who took it in 859 by crawling in one by one through a sewer, named it *Kasr Janni* (Castrum Ennae); and it was not captured by the Normans until 1087. From then on the town was known as Castrogiovanni until in 1927 it became the chief town of a new province.

The short via S. Agata leads into **piazza Vittorio Emanuele**, at the centre of

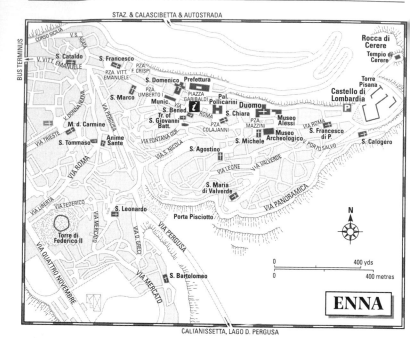

STAZ. & CALASCIBETTA & AUTOSTRADA

CALTANISSETTA, LAGO D. PERGUSA

the city. On the north side is the church of **S. Francesco**, with its fine 16C tower. On the left is piazza Crispi which has an excellent view across the valley to Calascibetta, and, on a clear day, to Etna. The bronze statue on the fountain is a copy of Bernini's *Rape of Proserpine*. Via Roma, the principal street, continues uphill traversing a series of piazze. In piazza Umberto I is the neo-classical *municipio* (Town Hall), which incorporates the Garibaldi Theatre. The Baroque façade of S. Benedetto (or S. Giuseppe) decorates piazza Coppola, off which is the 15C tower of S. Giovanni Battista with Gothic arches, and crowned by a Saracen cupola.

On the north side of via Roma the Prefecture tower (1939) rises from piazza Garibaldi. **S. Chiara**, in piazza Colajanni, is a war memorial and burial chapel. Two majolica pictures (1852) decorate the tiled pavement, one celebrating the advent of steam navigation, and the other the triumph of Christianity over Islam. The bronze statue of Napoleone Colajanni (1847–1921), in the piazza outside, is by Ettore Ximenes.

The view to the southwest takes in the Torre di Federico II (see below) surrounded by new apartment blocks. Here **Palazzo Pollicarini** retains one or two Catalan-Gothic features. Via Roma continues up towards the Duomo past several narrow side streets on the left which lead to the edge of the hill.

The Duomo

The Duomo, founded in 1307 by Eleonora, wife of Frederick II of Aragon, and damaged by fire in 1446, was slowly restored in the 16C. The strange front with a 17C bell-tower, covers its Gothic predecessor. The transepts and the polygonal apses survive in their original form (they can be seen from the courtyard of the Alessi Museum, see below). The south door is also partly original.

The **interior** has dark grey basalt columns with splendid bases, carved with grotesques, and Corinthian capitals (1550–60; the work of various artists including Gian Domenico Gagini who carved the symbols of the Evangelists on the first two at the west end). The nave ceiling is by Scipione di Guido, who probably carved the stalls as well. On either side of the west door are 16C statues of the *Annunciation*. The two stoups in the nave date from the 16C, and at the east end of the nave are richly carved 16C organ lofts. The altarpieces on the south side are by Guglielmo Borremans (the painting of *Saints Lucille and Hyacinth* on the second altar is particularly good). In the presbytery are five paintings of New Testament scenes by Filippo Paladino (1613). The late 15C painted Crucifix was restored in 1990. In the chapel to the right of the sanctuary is 18C marble decoration and a painting of the *Visitation* attributed to Filippo Paladino. There are more works by Borremans in the north transept and on the fourth north altar. The Renaissance font is preceded by an interesting screen.

Alessi Museum

The very fine Alessi Museum (open daily 09.00–20.00, ☎ 0935/503165) is in a building behind the east end of the Duomo. It is named after Canon Giuseppe Alessi (1774–1837), a native of Enna, who left his remarkable collection to his brother intending that he should donate it to the church. The church instead had to buy it in 1860 and it was first opened to the public in 1862. In the **basement** are church vestments of the 17C and 18C. On the **ground floor**: the *Sala Alessi* has interesting small paintings collected by Alessi, together with his portrait. The other room has paintings from various provenances, including a *Pietà with symbols of the Passion* (late 15C), *St John the Baptist and St John the Evangelist*, attributed to Antonello Crescenzio (Il Panormita); the *Mystical Marriage of St Catherine* by Antonio Spatafora (1584); a striking 16C *Madonna and Child*, and *St Peter the fisherman* by the school of Ribera. In the corridor are works by 19C local painters.

On the **first floor** the **Treasury of the Duomo** is exhibited, with splendid 16C and 17C works, one of the richest on the island. In the large room the 16C pieces include a monstrance by Paolo Gili (1536), and four reliquaries by Scipione di Blasi (1573). The room at the other side of the stairs contains 18C and 19C silver and two large paintings by Zoppo di Gangi. In the little adjoining room is a precious gold crown, encrusted with jewels and enamels, made for a statue of the *Madonna* in 1653 by Leonardo and Giuseppe Montalbano and Michele Castellani, and a beautiful 16C jewel in the form of a pelican.

The **gallery** has the **numismatic collection** made by Alessi, one of the most important in Sicily. The Greek, Roman and Byzantine coins are arranged topographically and include many in bronze used in everyday transactions. A section of Roman coins is arranged chronologically. Alessi's charming archaeological collection (with some of his original labels) is also displayed here. It includes missiles (*glandes*) used in the Servile war, bronzes, pottery, etc. In the last room the Egyptian *ushabti* figurines (664–525 BC), which also formed part of the Alessi collection and were presumably found in Sicily, are of the greatest interest.

Across piazza Mazzini the attractive 15C **Palazzo Varisano** houses the **Archaeological Museum** (or **Museo Varisano**; open daily 09.00–18.30, ☎ 0935/24720). The collection is well displayed and includes finds from Calascibetta and Capodarso (7C BC local products), including the prehistoric rock tombs of Realmese; Enna (Greek, Roman, and medieval ceramics, including an Attic red-figure krater); Cozza Matrice (where the necropolis was in use from the Bronze Age up to the 5C BC) and prehistoric material from the lake of Pergusa. There is also a collection of coins, interesting Hellenistic objects from Rossomanno (and an unusual bronze belt or necklace of the 6C BC), and material from Assoro, Agira, Cerami and Pietraperzia.

Via Roma continues up to the **Castello di Lombardia** (or Cittadella; open daily 08.00–18.30), built by the Swabians and adapted as his residence by Frederick III of Aragon. One of the best preserved medieval castles on the island, six of the 20 towers remain. Outside is a World War I memorial by Ernesto Basile (1927). On the left, steps lead up to the entrance to the castle. The first courtyard is filled with a permanent open-air theatre used in summer. Beyond the second court, planted with trees, the third has remains of a church, and (beneath a roof) tombs carved in the rock. Here is the entrance to the **Torre Pisana**, which can be climbed by a modern flight of stairs. The view from the top encompasses Etna, Centuripe on its hill and Lake Pozzillo. In the other direction, the edge of the lake of Pergusa and Calascibetta can be seen. At the edge of the hill, beyond the castle, are the unenclosed remains of the **Rocca Cerere**, where traces of antique masonry mark the site of the Temple of Demeter. Steps lead up to the summit with a view of Etna straight ahead. To the left you can see Lake Pozzillo and Centuripe, and Calascibetta.

The **lower town** is reached by following the other branch of via Roma, which takes a sharp turn to the south below piazza Vittorio Emanuele. On the right are the churches of **S. Tommaso**, with a 15C tower and a marble altarpiece by Giuliano Mancino (1515), and the **Carmine** (behind S. Tommaso), with another 15C campanile and a curious stair-tower. On the left, near the southwest end of via Roma, rises the octagonal **Torre di Federico II**, surrounded by a public garden, a Swabian work recalling the towers of Castel del Monte (it can sometimes be climbed on request).

Lake Pergusa, 9km south of Enna, is apparently disappearing, perhaps because building activity nearby has damaged its supply channels. The sheet of brackish water (182 ha), now polluted and drying up, has no visible inlet or outlet. The vegetation on the shores, as well as the birdlife, have been virtually destroyed since the 1950s, when it was decided to build a motor racing track around it, which also makes access to the water practically impossible. According to legend the lake occupies the chasm through which Pluto carried Proserpine off to Hades:

> ... *Not that faire field*
> *of Enna, where Proserpin gathring flours*
> *Her self a fairer Floure by gloomie Dis*
> *was gatherd, which cost Ceres all that pain*
> *To seek her through the World;*
>> Milton, *Paradise Lost*

On a hill above the lake (signposted) excavations (not open to the public) were begun in 1878 of the necropolis, city and walls of **Cozzo Matrice**. About 10km southwest of the lake in località **Gerace**, a Roman villa with polychrome mosaics was discovered in 1994; the excavations have since been covered over.

CALASCIBETTA, LEONFORTE AND CENTURIPE

These small hill towns are situated in beautiful countryside with panoramic views, in the province of Enna. They have interesting works of art and Leonforte is particularly charming.

Practical information

Getting there
By bus
Calascibetta can be reached by bus from Enna (central bus terminal). **Leonforte** and **Agira** can be reached from Catania by *INTERBUS* and from Enna (*SAIS*). Nicosia can be reached from Enna (*SAIS*). **Centuripe** has poor connections: a bus runs from Catania and Enna (*Romano*, ☎ 0935/73114) on weekday afternoons but the only morning bus is on Sunday (leaves 09.00 from Catania).

Information offices
APT Enna, ☎ 0935/528228. *Tourist Information Bureau*, 10 via Conte Ruggero, Calascibetta, ☎ 0935/569111.
Tourist Information Bureau, 28 piazza Vittorio Emanuele, Centuripe, ☎ 0935/919411.
Pro Loco Centuripe, 35 piazza Duomo, Centuripe, ☎ 0935/74616.
Tourist Information Bureau, 231 corso Umberto, Leonforte, ☎ 0935/665111.
Pro Loco Leonforte, 265 corso Umberto, Leonforte, ☎ 0935/901681.
Pro Loco Assoro, 280 Via Crisa, ☎ 0935/667204.

Where to stay
Hotels
☆☆☆☆ *Costellazioni*, contrada S. Michele, Troina, ☎ 0935/653966, 0935/653660. Modern and comfortable structure with congress hall, fitness centre, garden, indoor swimming pool.
Bed and breakfast
Da Pietro, between Enna and Calascibetta, contrada Longobardi, ☎ 0935/33647.
Farmhouse accommodation
Le Querce di Cota, contrada Cota, Troina, ☎ 095/356266, 339/8430536. Ancient farm for the production of oil, almonds and wheat, completely restored with comfortable rooms; panoramic position; horseriding, trekking, relaxation courses.

Eating out
Restaurants
CENTURIPE € *Tre Archi*, 13 via C. Battisti, ☎ 0935/74393. Traditional central Sicilian gastronomy. Closed Mon.
LEONFORTE € *La Piramide*, 26 via Pirandello, ☎ 0935/902121. Homely atmosphere, simple food; excellent grilled meat, vegetables, also pizza. Closed Mon.
Cafés, pastry shops and ice cream parlours
CALASCIBETTA *Caffè Centrale*, 2 piazza Umberto. Authentic country-town coffee bar; very good biscuits.
CENTURIPE *Pasticceria Centrale*, 11 piazza Sciacca. Very special confectionery, unique to the town.

Calascibetta

Calascibetta is a town perched on a flat-topped hill (691m) opposite Enna. It is particularly picturesque when seen from a distance (and provides one of the most delightful views from Enna). The narrow main street (keep left) leads up to the **Matrice**. Its 16C column bases are similar to those in the Duomo at Enna. There is a good view from the terrace.

A one-way street leads back down to piazza Umberto where the signposted road to Enna leads downhill past the church of the **Cappuccini**, on the edge of the hill. It contains a splendid large altarpiece of the *Epiphany* by Filippo Paladino, in a huge wooden frame. In Calascibetta they make special biscuits for Christmas called *sgrinfiati*, different shapes but all made with nuts, and the crunchy almond nougat is made year round.

The **Realmese necropolis** (unenclosed), northwest of Calascibetta, is well signposted. Here some 300 rock tombs (850–730 BC) have been found.

The road between Calascibetta and Leonfonte undulates through farming country where there are some orange groves.

Leonforte

Leonforte (603m) is a delightful little town founded in 1610 by Nicolò Placido Branciforti, which bases its economy on the production of lentils, broad beans, and late-ripening peaches. Via Porta Palermo leads to corso Umberto, just before which, below the road to the left, is the **Chiesa Madre** (17C–18C), with a striking façade in a mixture of styles. It contains numerous interesting wooden statues.

A very short steep road can be followed on foot downhill past the church of S. Stefano to the church of the Carmelo beside the delightful **Granfonte** (built in 1651 by Nicolò Branciforte) an abundant fountain of 24 jets (it can also be reached by car from via Porta Palermo). The water is collected in a stream which follows a picturesque lane downhill. Beside it is the gate of an overgrown botanical garden, with palms and orange trees. From here the defensive walls and turret in front of the Palazzo Baronale can be seen.

Just beyond the Chiesa Madre is piazza Branciforte with the impressive façade of the 17C **Palazzo Baronale**, and, at the end, a stable block built in 1641 (the town used to be famous for horse-breeding). The well-proportioned corso leads gently up through a pretty circular piazza. Beyond, a side street (left) leads to the church of the **Cappuccini**. It contains a huge high altarpiece of the *Calling of St Matthew* by Pietro Novelli. On either side are niches with Gaginesque statues. A finely carved arch (1647) precedes the Branciforte funerary chapel, with the sumptuous black marble sarcophagus (1634) of Caterina di Branciforte, supported on four lions.

15km to the west of Leonforte is **Mount Altesina**, 1193m, thought by the Arabs to be exactly in the centre of the island. Now a wildlife refuge run by the forestry commission, it is a pleasant trek through the woods to the top, where the remains of a Sicel village are to be found.

Assoro

To the east of Leonforte is Assoro, another interesting little town. Occupied in the Greek and Roman period, it was taken by the Arabs in 939, and by the Normans in 1061. The road leads up past the campanile of the former church of S. Caterina to piazza Umberto I, with a view from its terrace. The side façade of Palazzo Valguarnera (see below) is connected by an arch to the porch of the **Chiesa Madre** (S. Leone), which has a square bell-tower. It is entered by a

Catalan doorway and has an unusual interior with twisted columns and a carved and painted wooden roof, and early 18C stucco decoration. In the raised and vaulted presbytery is a fine marble ancona (1515) with statues and reliefs, and two early 16C Valguarnera funerary monuments on the side walls. Over the nave hangs a painted Crucifix (late 15C). The high altar has three Gothic statues. To the left of the presbytery is a double chapel, the first with Gothic vaulting and bosses, and the second with Baroque decoration. Here is a carved processional Crucifix attributed to Gian Domenico Gagini, and two 17C sarcophagi. In the nave are some particularly interesting 16C polychrome gilded wooden statues.

The main façade of the Chiesa Madre faces piazza Marconi, and the front of **Palazzo Valguarnera**, situated here, has a balcony with grotesque heads. The Baroque portal of an oratory is also in the square.

Agira

The little town of Agira is perched on a conical hill (670m). The ancient *Agyrion* was a Sicel city colonised with Greeks by Timoleon (339 BC). Traces have been found here of Roman houses with mosaic pavements, a temple on what must have been the acropolis and necropoli of the 4C–3C BC. Diodorus Siculus, the historian (90–70 BC), was born here: in his description of Timoleon's city he declares the theatre was the most beautiful in Sicily after that of Syracuse. Diodorus was the first historian to use the chronology of the Olympic Games to date historical events. The town was the scene of the miracles of the apocryphal St Philip of Argirò, possibly a Christianised form of Herakles, the tutelary deity of the town, who is said by the local people to have imprisoned the devil in a nearby cave; sometimes on stormy nights, he can be heard wailing. The churches in the town are usually kept closed (the largest of which is S. Antonio da Padova, with a dome, built in 1549, in the lower town). On the road to Regalbuto, outside Agira (left; well signposted) is a Canadian Military Cemetery (490 graves) beautifully kept in a clump of pine trees on a small hill.

The partly wooded shores of the pretty lake **Pozzillo**, the largest artificial lake in Sicily, are used as pastureland. The lovely countryside has almond trees, prickly pear and agave. There are plans to create a vast recreational park here, with hotels and a golf course.

North of Agira is **Troina**, on a steep ridge, the highest town (1120m) in Sicily. Its early capture by the Normans in 1062 (Count Roger and his young bride Adelaide spent a very cold winter that year in the castle, with little food, sharing one blanket between them, when they were besieged by Greeks and Arabs who had improvised an alliance, according to the historian John Julius Norwich) is recalled by Norman work (1078–80) in the Chiesa Matrice, which has a good 16C campanile. The Normans also instituted the first of their Basilian monasteries here. Parts of the Greek walls remain, and the Belvedere has a fine view.

At **Regalbuto** the church has a campanile crowned by a spire. The little town has some fine 18C buildings and a public garden. Beyond red and ochre hills on the left there is a splendid view ahead of Etna. The plain is filled with bright green citrus groves, many of them protected by 'walls' of olive trees, and Centuripe can be seen on its hill to the right.

Centuripe

Parking

The streets are so narrow that driving through them requires considerable skill. It is advisable to park on the outskirts.

Handicrafts

Salvatore Stancanelli, of *Ken Arte*, 79 via Roma, ☎ 0935/73359, and *Sebo Ceramiche d'Epoca*, via M. Rapisarda, ☎ 0935/73649, make perfect replicas of antique pottery.

History

Centuripe was founded by the Sicels, who called it *Kentoripa*. It occupies a superb commanding position facing Etna, at a height of 719m; when Garibaldi saw it in 1862 he aptly named it '*il balcone della Sicilia*'. With the advent of Greek colonization, the city maintained good relations with these newcomers, but later it discovered that its true sympathies lay with Rome, and this alliance brought prosperity, wealth, power and the gratitude of Augustus, who rebuilt the town after the destruction wreaked by Pompey during the Civil War in the 1C BC. In the early Middle Ages decadence set in, although it remained an important strategic stronghold. The people made the mistake of rebelling against Frederick II of Hohenstaufen in 1232, who forcibly removed the entire population to the southeast coast, founding the city of Augusta, after razing Centuripe and its castle to the ground. Some trickled back, however, and started rebuilding; but it was a forlorn effort. Crushed once more in 1268 by Charles I of Anjou, it was not until 1548 that it was refounded by Francesco Moncada. Its capture by the Allies in 1943 caused the Germans to abandon Sicily. It was the birthplace of the physician Celsus (fl. AD 14–37).

Lonely and remote, a cascade of coloured houses surrounded by harsh countryside; hills dappled with light, an occasional prickly pear, a few almond trees. The city has grown out in five directions on the top of its ridge, like a starfish. The town centre is the piazza near the 17C pink and white Chiesa Madre. On the edge of the cliff a pine avenue leads to the remains of a monument possibly of Roman (2C AD) origin (locally known as *Il Corradino* in allusion to the Swabian, Corrado Capace, who is supposed to have built a castle here). There are impressive views.

A new **Archaeological Museum** close by in via Giulio Cesare (open 09.00–19.00, closed Mon, ☎ 0935/73079; on request the custodians will show you around the town) houses an enlightening display of 3000 objects discovered in the area, including a few of the famous **Centuripe vases**, unique in Sicily for their shape and decoration. The terracotta itself has a particularly rich hazelnut colour, and the ceramists used to decorate the articles further by adding details in relief before firing, and brightly coloured painted motifs afterwards. In the 4C and 3C BC this pottery was prized all around the Mediterranean, and more recently, in post-war years, its particular beauty has given rise to a flourishing activity of clandestine excavations to supply the black market of unscrupulous collectors; unfortunately, a large part of the collection was stolen while the museum was being built. Several craftsmen of Centuripe proved expert at faking antiquities, some of which apparently even now hold pride of place in important museums of the world. Today, however, the craftsmen are limiting their activities to making souvenirs for the tourists, and the *tombaroli* (clandestine diggers) seem to have found more honest occupations.

The museum is conveniently situated in the archaeological area and the remains are all within walking distance. The local people are extremely friendly, proud of their town, and more than willing to show visitors around. In the valley (Vallone Difesa), east of the town, excavations beneath and near the church of the Crocifisso have revealed an important Augustan edifice, known as the *Sede degli Augustali*. On Monte Calvario (contrada Panneria) is a Hellenistic house, and to the northwest in Vallone dei Bagni, is a large Roman thermal edifice with five niches. Close by in via Genova in what used to be the slaughterhouse, is the **Anthropological Collection**, a well arranged collection of tools, furniture, and equipment used by farmers, artisans and labourers until quite recently (open daily 09.00–13.00, Sun 10.00–13.00, 15.30–17.30, ☎ 0935/919093).

On the road to Adrano, near the Ponte del Maccarone, a large aqueduct (31 arches) constructed in 1761–6 can be seen. Adrano is described, together with Etna on pp 376–381.

NICOSIA AND SPERLINGA

These remote small towns in the province of Enna are in particularly spectacular countryside. Nicosia has interesting churches and the lovely little town of Sperlinga has a splendid castle.

Practical information

Getting there
By bus
Nicosia can be reached by bus from Catania (*INTERBUS*) or from Enna (*SAIS*). **Sperlinga**, **Cerami** and **Gangi** can be reached from Nicosia, and there is also a bus to/from Palermo (*SAIS*).

Information offices
APT Enna, ☎ 0935/528228.
Tourist Information Bureau, c/o Town Hall, piazza Garibaldi, Nicosia, ☎ 0935/638139.
Pro Loco Nicosia, via IV Novembre (under the portico next to the Tribunal).
Tourist Information Bureau, c/o Town Hall, via Umberto I, Sperlinga, ☎ 0935/643177.

Where to stay
Hotel
NEAR NICOSIA ☆☆☆ *Pineta*, 35/A via S. Paolo, ☎ 0935/647002, 🖷 0935/646927. Pleasant hotel with garden.
Farm accommodation
NEAR NICOSIA *Mercadante*, contrada Mercadante, ☎ & 🖷 0935/640771, 0935/646092, ✉ agrimerc@tin.it. Beautiful farmhouse belonging to an aristocratic family; good restaurant for simple local dishes; archery, minigolf, obstacle course, library, bowls, darts, play area for children; sheep are raised on the farm.
CERAMI *Pancallo*, contrada Pancallo, ☎ & 🖷 0935/931666. A farm producing organic food and olive oil. It is close to the little town of Cerami in the north of the province and the

Nebrodi Regional Park and belongs to the aristocratic Cutrona family. A large part of the land is covered with oak forest. Thoroughbred Arab horses are raised here. Pleasant restaurant.

NEAR SPERLINGA *Santa Venera*, contrada S. Venera, Sperlinga, ☎ 0921/564028. In a good position for exploring Nicosia, Sperlinga and Gangi. Ancient monastery transformed into a sheep farm. There is a *SAIS* bus stop right outside the gate. Excellent food and home made pasta.

 Eating out
Restaurants

NICOSIA *Vigneta*, contrada S. Basile, ☎ 0935/638940. Just outside the town, Spacious, nice veranda, Sicilian dishes; also have rooms to let. Closed midday Tues.
La Cirata, on SS117, ☎ 0935/640561. South of town. An enormous restaurant, very good food. Closed Mon.

Cafés, pastry shops and ice cream parlours

NICOSIA There are many really excellent places for Sicilian breakfast, *cannoli di ricotta*, snacks or ice cream, including *Bar Diana*, 5 piazza Garibaldi and *Antica Gelateria*, 9 piazza Garibaldi.

SPERLINGA A special cake is made here called *tortone*, with durum wheat flour, olive oil, cinnamon and sugar. Try it at *Bar Li Calzi*, 1 piazza Marconi.

Internet point
Tourist Information Bureau in the Town Hall of Nicosia.

Nicosia

Nicosia (700m) was a place of some importance in the Middle Ages. The local dialect betrays the Lombard and Piedmontese origins of its early colonists. It was damaged by a landslide in 1757, by an earthquake in 1968 and a flood in 1972. Known locally as the town with two Cathedrals and two Christs, because for a time the churches of S. Maria Maggiore and S. Niccolò took turns in being the Mother Church, there were two processions for Good Friday, with two crucifixes, and considerable rivalry between the two groups.

Piazza Garibaldi is at the centre of the town. On the square are the Palazzo di Città (Town Hall) by Salvatore Attinelli (early 19C), and the elegant portico of the Duomo (S. Niccolò). The decorative 14C west door is in extremely poor repair; the entrance is by the south door. The imposing campanile, struck by lightning some years ago, has been partially rebuilt.

In the **interior** the vault was decorated by the Manno brothers in the early 19C. On the west wall is the organ by Raffaele La Valle. On the south side, in the second bay is a **Martyrdom of St Placid** by Giacinto Platania, and in the third and fifth bays, the **Immaculate Virgin** and **Holy Family** both by Filippo Randazzo. The pulpit is attributed to Gian Domenico Gagini. In the south transept is a Gaginesque statue of the **Madonna della Vittoria (Our Lady of Victory)**. Over the crossing, in the octagonal vault, surrounded by 17C paintings by Antonio Filingelli, is a large statue of *St Nicholas* by Giovanni Battista Li Volsi, a very unusual sight. In the chapel to the right of the high altar, is a venerated wooden Crucifix by Fra Umile di Petralia, one of the two carried in procession through the town on Good Friday. In the presbytery the carved stalls are by Stefano and Giovanni Battista Li Volsi (c 1622; with a relief showing the old town of Nicosia). In the chapel to the left of the high altar is delightful polychrome marble decoration, and in the north transept, a statue of *St Nicholas* by Filippo Quattrocchi, and the funerary monument of Alessandro Testa by

Ignazio Marabitti. On the north side are statues by Giovanni Battista Li Volsi (fifth and second bays), and a font by Antonello Gagini. Above the nave vault (access difficult) the original 15C painted wooden ceiling is preserved.

Opposite the south door of the Duomo is the fine 18C **Bishop's Palace**. From behind the east end of the Duomo via Francesco Salomone leads up past **Palazzo La Motta Salinella** (right) which has an amusing façade, and the ruined convent of S. Domenico. Ahead is an isolated carved portal in front of a modern building, and on the right (behind two palm trees) the 18C portal of S. Giuseppe (in poor repair and closed) with two statues.

Via Ansaldi continues up to the former convent of S. Vincenzo Ferreri (1555), with an interesting closed balcony at the top of its façade for the nuns. It contains frescoes by Guglielmo Borremans.

Further uphill to the left is **S. Maria Maggiore** built in 1767. The campanile crashed to the ground in 1968 and in 1978 the bells were rehung on a low iron bracket beside the façade. Next to the interesting west door several houses built into the rock face can be seen. The interior contains a huge marble ancona at the east end, finished by Antonello Gagini in 1512, a statue of the *Madonna* in the north transept, and two statues by Li Volsi. There is a view from the terrace of the modern buildings of the town, and the church of S. Salvatore perched on a rock. Via Carlo V and via del Castello climb up behind S. Maria Maggiore to the ruins of the Norman **castle**; views from here are splendid and it is well worth the climb.

From piazza Garibaldi (see above) via Fratelli Testa leads down past the closed churches of **S. Calogero** (with a good ceiling and works by Filippo Randazzo) and S. Antonio Abate. On a rocky outcrop at the top of the hill the portico and campanile of **S. Salvatore** can be seen, rebuilt in the 17C. Via Testa ends at via Li Volsi with (left) the church of the **Carmine** which contains two statues of the Annunciation attributed to Antonello Gagini. At the top of via Li Volsi, which is lined with trees, the Baroque façade of Palazzo Speciale can be seen, propped up by concrete pillars.

In the church of **S. Michele** (just east of the town) is a 16C font and two wooden statues by Giovanni Battista Li Volsi.

The landscape is particularly beautiful east of Nicosia, with frequent glimpses of Etna in the distance. In the rugged countryside at the foot of the Nebrodi mountains (described on p 444) the fields are dotted with *pagliari*, conical huts of straw and mud, used by the shepherds as temporary refuges.

Sperlinga

To the west of Nicosia is Sperlinga, the only Sicilian town which took no part in the 'Vespers' (see p 42). It is a delightful little place laid out beneath the conspicuous castle rock. The road enters the town past the 17C church of S. Anna and on the right yellow signs indicate grottoes, inhabited up until a few years ago. They are preserved as a little museum (approached by steps up the salita del Municipio beside a very tall palm tree; the key is with Signora Siracusa at no. 15).

The castle of Sperlinga

Further along the main road, a road (signposted right) leads up past the large 17C chiesa madre to a car park just below the entrance to the medieval castle (open daily 09.00–12.30, 14.30–18.00; if closed apply at the Town Hall), built on the sheer rock face. Two grottoes are used as local ethnographical museums with agricultural implements. Steps lead up across a small bridge (on the site of the drawbridge) through the double entrance. Stables, carved out of the rock in the Middle Ages, were later used as prisons. In one room are old photographs of Sperlinga, some taken during the occupation in 1943 by Robert Capa (1913–53). From a terrace a flight of high steps hewn out of the rock leads up to the battlements from which there are wonderful views covering 360 degrees.

PIAZZA ARMERINA AND MORGANTINA

Piazza Armerina, a pleasant little town, has given its name to the Roman Villa nearby which has some of the most extensive and most beautiful Romans mosaics known. The excavations of the ancient city of Morgantina are surrounded by wonderful countryside with superb views, and the deserted and peaceful site is one of the most memorable places on the island.

Practical information

Getting there
By bus
Piazza Armerina. *SAIS* bus from Enna (in 45mins), *AST* or *Etna Trasporti* buses from Catania. **Aidone**. *SAIS* bus from Enna (in 1hr) or *Etna Trasporti* bus from Catania.

Information offices
APT Enna, ☎ 0935/528228. *APT Piazza Armerina*, 12 via Floresta, ☎ 0935/85200. *Azienda Autonoma*, 15 via Cavour, ☎ 0935/680201. *Tourist Information Bureau* Aidone, c/o Town Hall, 286 via Vittorio Emanuele, ☎ 0935/691677. *Pro Loco Aidone*, 1 via Mazzini, ☎ 0935/86557.

Where to stay
Hotels
PIAZZA ARMERINA ✩✩✩ *Park Hotel Paradiso*, contrada Ramaldo, ☎ 0935/680841, ▤ 0935/683391.

Comfortable hotel with many facilities, pool.
✩✩✩ *Villa Romana*, 18 via De Gasperi, ☎ 0935/682911, ▤ 0935/682911. The only hotel in the town centre.
✩✩ *Mosaici da Battiato*, 11 contrada Casale Paratore, ☎ & ▤ 0935/685453. Within walking distance of the Roman Villa. The restaurant is very good.
S. MICHELE DI GANZARIA (not far away from Piazza Armerina, S. Michele is a charming little hilltop town) ✩✩✩ *Hotel Pomara*, 84 via Vittorio Veneto, ☎ 0933/978143, ▤ 0933/977090. A modern, family-run establishment with one of the best restaurants in Sicily.
Youth hostel
Ostello del Borgo, 6 largo S. Giovanni, ☎ 0935/687019, ▤ 0935/686943, ✉ www.ostellodelborgo.it. An old monastery in the heart of the city, restored, with comfortable rooms.
Farmhouse accommodation
S. MICHELE DI GANZARIA

Gigliotto, contrada Gigliotto, ☎ & 📠 0933/970898, ✉ www.agrisavoca.it. A very large farm, stunningly beautiful with olive groves and vineyards, cereals and prickly pears. The farm buildings comprise the original 14C farmhouse and an ancient monastery. All the food comes from the farm and is strictly organic; even the wine is produced from grapes which are not treated with pesticides. Guests can help with the farm activities; preparation of jams and preserves; honey and home-made liqueurs. Horseriding, fishing in the lake, cycling; swimming pool.

PIAZZA ARMERINA *Savoca*, contrada Polleri, Piazza Armerina, ☎ & 📠 0935/683078, ✉ www.agrisavoca. com; 3km from Piazza Armerina. A 19C farm surrounded with poplars. Comfortable rooms and private chapel, swimming pool; cookery courses, horseriding, bicycle trekking, archery, bowls; all the food is organic.

Agricasale, contrada Ciavarini, Piazza Armerina, ☎ 0935/686034, ✉ www. paginegialle.it/agricasale. Close to Piazza Armerina, a large and well organized farm with tennis court, pool, good restaurant, horseriding, miniature football pitch; places for campers and motorcaravans.

Grottacalda, contrada Grottacalda, Piazza Armerina, ☎ & 📠 0935/958533. The farm is inside the Floristella Grottacalda Regional Minerary Park, designed to protect this sulphur mining area as an example of industrial archaeology. Horseriding, organic food, live music, archery; places for campers and motorcaravans.

Isola Felice, contrada Favara, Nissoria, ☎ 0935/640390. Large farm producing cereals, olive oil and wine, and raising pigs, goats, sheep and chickens; tennis, archery, bowls.

 Eating out
Restaurants
PIAZZA ARMERINA CENTRE € *Pepito*, 140 Via Roma ☎ 0935/685737. Close to Public Gardens; inexpensive tourist menu.

PIAZZA ARMERINA ENVIRONS €€ *Bellia*, contrada Bellia, ☎ 0935/680622. Excellent mushroom risotto and grilled meat. Closed Thurs.

€€ *Coccinella*, 2 via Renato Guttuso, ☎ 0935/682374. Just outside the city to the north. Simple, tasty dishes that are typical of this area. Closed Mon.

NEAR CASALE €€ *La Ruota*, contrada Paratore Casale, ☎ 0935/680542. Shortly before reaching the Roman Villa, this place will be seen on the left; one of the best restaurants in central Sicily, the special dish of the house is *coniglio alla stemperata* (rabbit with tomatoes, olives and capers).

AIDONE €€ *Morgantina*, 42 via Adelasia, ☎ 0935/88088. Comfortable and quite elegant. Traditional dishes; also rooms to rent.

S. MICHELE DI GANZARIA €€ The restaurant of the *Hotel Pomara* is exceptionally good; people come from miles around for the marvellous food: home-made macaroni with tomato and fennel; vegetable fritters; grilled meat, home-made sausages and many dishes featuring ricotta and other cheeses.

Picnics
Picnic places at Villa Garibaldi. Morgantina is a lovely place for picnics and there is also a good bar-restaurant on the site.

Cafés, pastry shops and ice cream parlours
Break Coffee, 14 via Generale Ciancio, for Sicilian breakfast (this is the place that makes the best morning pastries).

Diana, 34 piazza Generale Cascino, for *tiramisù*, *cannoli di ricotta*, and almond biscuits.

Pasticceria Zingale, 8 via Generale

Muscarà, for the local nougat, made with hazelnuts and covered with chocolate.

Internet point

SELCA, 30 piazza Generale Cascino, ☎ 0935/680043, open daily 09.00–21.00.

 ### Annual festivals

In Piazza Armerina: *San Giuseppe*, 19 March, with the traditional banquets and ornamental loaves of bread; the *Palio dei Normanni* on 13–14 August; Our Lady of the Victories, 15 August.

Piazza Armerina

Piazza Armerina is a pleasant well kept little town with dark cobbled streets and interesting Baroque monuments. It was little known to travellers before the discovery of the Roman villa nearby at Casale, but, with 22,600 inhabitants, it now rivals Enna as the most important centre of the province. Here in 1295 Frederick of Aragon summoned the council that decided to contest his brother's attempt to cede Sicily to Charles II of Anjou. To the north of the town are dense woods of pine, eucalyptus, cypress and poplar trees. The Parco Ronza has picnic areas and a little wildlife enclosure.

A number of streets converge on the central **piazza Garibaldi**, with its palm trees. Here is the 18C Palazzo di Città next to the church of the Fundrò (or S. Rocco), with a carved tufa doorway. Between them via Cavour leads up past the former seat of the electricity board, restored as the Law Courts. Further uphill is the former convent of S. Francesco with an elaborate balcony by a Gagini high up on the corner.

The road continues past the 17C Palazzo del Vescovado to piazza del Duomo, at the top of the hill, with a pretty view from its terrace. Here is a statue to Baron Marco Trigona (1905), who was responsible for financing the rebuilding of the **Duomo** in 1627. The fine brick façade of the large 18C Palazzo Trigona is also in the piazza. The façade was added in 1719 and the dome in 1768. The fine campanile (c 1490) survives from an earlier church.

The entrance to the Duomo is by one of the side doors. In the **interior** the crossing and transepts decorated in white and blue are unusually light and spacious. On the high altar is a copy of a venerated Byzantine painting, the *Madonna of the Victories*; the original is preserved behind in a 17C silver tabernacle. It is said to have been given by Pope Nicolas II to Count Roger. Three of the 17C paintings in the sanctuary are by Zoppo di Gangi. In the little chapel on the left of the sanctuary (above the door of which is a painting of the *Martyrdom of St Agatha* by Iacopo Ligozzi) is a Cross, painted on wood, attributed to a Provençal artist (1485).

The altarpiece in the north transept of the *Assumption of the Virgin* is by Filippo Paladino. The organ is by Donato del Piano (1760). The font is surrounded by a Gaginesque portal in mottled beige marble, decorated with monsters' heads, which survives from the earlier church. An equestrian statuette of Roger and a reliquary by Paolo d'Aversa (1392–1405) are among the cathedral's treasures, which may one day be exhibited in a museum.

The picturesque via Monte leads downhill through an interesting part of the town, while via Floresta leads down past the back of Palazzo Trigona with its Renaissance loggia and ends in piazza Castello. Here is the overgrown 14C **castle** and four small 17C palaces. The road continues down past the Jesuit College, the charming façade of **S. Anna** (18C), and the 17C façade of **S. Ignazio di Loyola** (preceded by an outside double staircase) to end in piazza Garibaldi.

To the east of the centre, in piazza Umberto I, is **S. Giovanni dei Rodi** (now used by a youth club; enquire locally for the key). This plain 13C chapel of the Knights of St John is lit by lancet windows. Nearby are the eccentric façades of S. Stefano and the Garibaldi Theatre (1905). Downhill are the fine public gardens in Villa Garibaldi near the 16C church of S. Pietro. On the rise to the south the **Chiesa del Carmine** preserves a campanile and cloister of the 14C–15C.

To the north of the town, is the Norman church of **S. Andrea** (open on Sun; at other times enquire locally for the key). Dating from 1096 the austere interior contains 13C–15C frescoes, including one of the *Crucifixion* of the titular saint.

West of the town, reached from the road to Casale, a rough track climbs the Piano Marino (or Armerino) to the little church of **S. Maria di Platea** where the Byzantine *Madonna delle Vittorie* (see above) was found. Nearby are the ruins of a castle, traditionally thought to have been founded by Count Roger. The views are delightful.

At **Montagna di Marzo**, northwest of Piazza Armerina, recent excavations have revealed a sanctuary of Demeter and Kore, in use from the 6C–3C BC. Votive statuettes and coins have been found here.

The Roman villa at Casale

The famous Villa Romana lies 5.5km southwest of Piazza Armerina, in the contrada of Casale, off SS 191. The road from Piazza Armerina (signposted) leads under a high road viaduct and then along a pretty valley. The villa has been declared a World Heritage Site by UNESCO.

• Admission daily 08.00–19.30, ☎ 0935/680036, 0935/683000. The villa receives thousands of visitors a day and is beginning to show signs of strain, especially in spring when the school groups go through, showering plastic cups and bottles, drink cans, crisp packets and chewing gum all over the mosaics. Officially, no food or drinks can be brought into the site.

History

This luxurious country mansion must have belonged to one of the wealthiest men in the Roman Empire, possibly Diocletian's co-Emperor Maximian (Maximianus Herculeus). It lay in a wooded and secluded site at the foot of Monte Mangone; the nearest Roman settlement was Philosophiana (Soffiana), 5km south, a station on the route to *Agrigentum*. In richness and extent the villa is comparable to Hadrian's Villa at Tivoli or Diocletian's Palace at Split (Spalato), but while enough remains of the walls to give an idea of the elevation, it is the extent of the **polychrome mosaics** covering the floors that makes the building unique.

The **villa**, which consists of four distinct though connected groups of buildings on different levels, appears to date in its entirety from the early 4C, and to have succeeded a more modest 2C dwelling. The mosaics are of the Roman-African school (probably 4C AD). The buildings seem to have been kept in a habitable state up to the Arab invasion. From c 1000 they were occupied until their destruction by William the Bad (c 1160), when they were abandoned to a few cottagers, and soon obliterated by a landslide. The buried ruins remained unnoticed until 1761 and it was not until 1881 that any but spasmodic excavations were put in hand; in 1929 and again in 1935–39 the work was continued, and finally, from 1950, with official assistance, the main structure of the building was exposed, under the direction of Vinicio Gentili; the slaves' quarters and the outbuildings still remain to be explored. The mosaics have had to be extensively restored after flood damage in 1991.

Most of the site has been protected against the weather by a plastic shelter, its shape designed to give an idea of the original villa. This description follows the order in which it is possible to view the rooms from platforms and elevated walkways; the plan is numbered in the same order. The plan shows the layout of the villa without the protective structure; for clarity, however, the parts enclosed have been shaded.

From the ticket office a path leads to a courtyard and the main **entrance** (1) of the villa, recalling in its massive form the Roman triumphal arch. It had two fountains on each face, probably fed from a reservoir. The **atrium** (2) is a huge polygonal court surrounded by a portico of marble columns. To the right is the villa proper, with the **tablinum** (3) leading to steps which descend into the **peristyle**, a quadriporticus of ten columns by eight, interrupted on the east side by an arch. It has been laid out as a garden, and in the centre is a large fountain. Immediately opposite the entrance is an **aediculum** (4), the shrine of the patron deity of the house, decorated with a mosaic showing an ivy motif. The peristyle walks are paved with mosaic, divided by geometrical borders into panels, in which animal heads are framed in laurel wreaths, with birds native to Sicily in the corners.

Off the west walk opened a small court giving access to the **small latrine** (5), a sumptuous construction whose brick drain, marble hand-basin, and pictorial decoration attest the standards of imperial Roman comfort. From here it is possible to look down into the **Salone del Circo** (35; this was the narthex of the thermae, described below), so called from the scenes of the Roman circus depicted in its mosaic floor, the most extensive of their kind known. The obelisk has been identified as the obelisk of Constantius II in the Circus Maximus in Rome which received this form in AD 357. Steps lead up past a vestibule (6; this was formerly another entrance to the thermae). Its coloured mosaic, showing a mother with a boy and girl and two slave-girls carrying bathing necessities and clean clothing, is doubly interesting because it reveals the style of dress, and because it probably represents the imperial household in a family scene.

The majority of the **rooms on the north side of the peristyle** have geometrical mosaics, several of them damaged by Norman structural alterations. Representations of the Seasons figure in one (7); another (8) shows fishing scenes with cupids. Of most interest is one called the *Piccola Caccia* (9), where a number of hunting scenes are depicted in great detail.

From the east walk steps ascend to the **ambulacrum** (10), a corridor (64m long) running the width of the building to isolate the private apartments and closed at either end by an exedra. An arcade would have overlooked the peristyle. The corridor (reached from the walkway by a little curving stair) is paved throughout with a wonderful series of **hunting scenes** (*venationes*), one of the finest Roman mosaics known. By the stair is a dignified figure robed in Byzantine splendour, protected by two 'bodyguards' holding shields, perhaps a portrait of Maximian himself. In the exedrae are personifications of two Provinces, flanked by wild beasts, representing perhaps two opposing points of the Mediterranean,

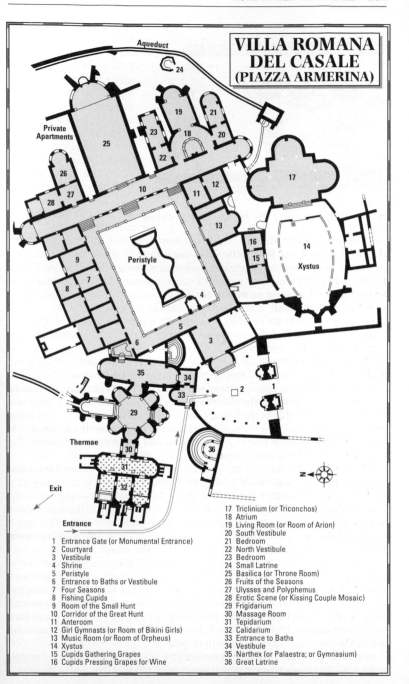

VILLA ROMANA DEL CASALE (PIAZZA ARMERINA)

Aqueduct

Private Apartments

24
19
21
23
18
20
25
22
26
27
28
10
11
12
13
17
16
15
14
Xystus
9
Peristyle
7
8
4
5
6
3
35
34
2
33
1
29
Thermae
30
36
31
32
Exit
Entrance

1 Entrance Gate (or Monumental Entrance)
2 Courtyard
3 Vestibule
4 Shrine
5 Peristyle
6 Entrance to Baths or Vestibule
7 Four Seasons
8 Fishing Cupids
9 Room of the Small Hunt
10 Corridor of the Great Hunt
11 Anteroom
12 Girl Gymnasts (or Room of Bikini Girls)
13 Music Room (or Room of Orpheus)
14 Xystus
15 Cupids Gathering Grapes
16 Cupids Pressing Grapes for Wine
17 Triclinium (or Triconchos)
18 Atrium
19 Living Room (or Room of Arion)
20 South Vestibule
21 Bedroom
22 North Vestibule
23 Bedroom
24 Small Latrine
25 Basilica (or Throne Room)
26 Fruits of the Seasons
27 Ulysses and Polyphemus
28 Erotic Scene (or Kissing Couple Mosaic)
29 Frigidarium
30 Massage Room
31 Tepidarium
32 Calidarium
33 Entrance to Baths
34 Vestibule
35 Narthex (or Palaestra; or Gymnasium)
36 Great Latrine

Detail of 4C mosaics at the Roman villa at Casale

since the landscape between them is divided in the centre by a sea full of fish on which large galleys sail, which are transporting exotic animals. The hunting scenes are remarkable for the number of species of wild animals and for the accuracy with which they are depicted in action (the mosaics of the leopard on the antelope's back, and the tigress rescuing her cub are particularly skilful).

At the southeast corner of the peristyle steps lead back up to an ante-room (11), and, beyond, the **Sala delle dieci ragazze** (12), whose late mosaic (4C) shows ten girls performing gymnastic exercises, wearing 'bikinis'. In one corner is part of an earlier geometric pavement which was ruined by damp. Adjacent is a **summer living-room or music room** (13) with a damaged mosaic representing the Orphic myth; again the animals are lovingly depicted.

Steps descend from the building, and, outside, a path skirts the apse of the triclinium (see below) to enter the **xystus** (14; uncovered), a large elliptical court surrounded on three sides by a portico and closed at the west end by a wide exedra. **Rooms 15 and 16** (to the north) are adorned with mosaics of vintage and fishing scenes. From the east end, steps lead up to the **triclinium** (17), a room 12m square with deep apses on three sides. The theme of the central pavement is the *Labours of Hercules*, the violent episodes being combined into a single turbulent composition. Ten of the labours can be distinguished, those missing being the Stymphalian Birds and the Girdle of Hippolyte. In the apses the *Glorification of Hercules*, *Conquered Giants* and *Lycurgus and Ambrosia* are depicted. The tonal shading of the figures is remarkable.

A path (signposted for the exit) leads round the outside of the triclinium and back towards the main building following the line of the aqueduct and past a small latrine (24) to enter the private apartments. The original approach was through the semi-circular **atrium** (18; with a mosaic of cupids fishing), divided by a tetrastyle portico into a nymphaeum and an ambulatory. On either side a vestibule leads into a bed-chamber, while the centre opens into a **living-room** (19), whose walls were decorated with marble; the mosaic shows Arion surrounded by Naiads and marine creatures and is the best known representation of this myth. The **south vestibule** (20), decorated with nursery scenes leads into a **bed-chamber** (21) in which the mosaic shows scenes of drama; the musical instruments and the indication by Greek letters of musical modes are of unusual interest. Off the **north vestibule** (22), with its stylised tableau of Eros and Pan, is a **bed-chamber** (23) with scenes of inexperienced young hunters, those in the centre already amusingly routed by their quarry.

Steps lead down past the large **basilica** (25; covered and seen only through windows), the throne room in which guests were received. The apse is decorated with marble *intarsia*. Steps lead up on the right to the northern group of **private apartments** which consists of a chamber (**26**) with a decorative mosaic depicting a variety of fruit, and an antechamber (**27**) with a large mosaic of Ulysses and Polyphemus. The adjoining chamber (**28**) has a perfectly preserved floor in *opus musivum* with a faintly erotic scene in its 12-sided centre panel.

Return down the same steps and follow the path which leads round the outside of the buildings to a group of pine and cedar trees. Here can be seen remains of the **Thermae** (partly covered). The **frigidarium** (**29**), an octagon with radiating apses of which two served as vestibules, four as apodyteria, and two, larger than the rest, as plunge baths, was covered with a dome. The mosaics show robing scenes and in the centre, marine myths. Those in the adjoining room (**30**), depicting the massage of bathers by slaves, suggest its use as an aleipterion, a function consistent with its position between the cold baths and the **tepidarium** (**31**) and **calidaria** (**32**) which lie beyond.

The aediculum (**33**), designed for a statue of *Venus*, was the original entrance to the baths. The vestibule (**34**) was the entrance to the long narthex (**35**). In both these the partial disappearance of the floor has exposed the hypocaust beneath.

Near the atrium (**2**) of the villa are the remains of the **great latrine** (**36**), the marble seats of which are lost.

Aidone

The little town of Aidone (889m) lies 10km north east of Piazza Armerina surrounded by lovely woods of pine and eucalyptus trees. It is built of local red stone.

In the upper part of the town, in a restored 17C Capuchin convent, is an Archaeological Museum (open daily 09.00–18.30, ☎ 0935/87307), with a well-displayed collection of finds from Morgantina (see below). The entrance is through a charming little church with wooden statues. On the ground floor **room 1** contains Bronze and Iron Age finds from the Cittadella, the area of Morgantina occupied before the Greek era. This includes material from huts inhabited by the Morgetic colony. An elaborate spiral staircase leads up to **room 2** which continues the display from Cittadella, with Corinthian and Attic ceramics, antefixes with gorgons' heads (6C BC), a large red-figure krater by the Euthymides painter, an Attic Corinthian krater with birds and lekythoi. **Room 3** contains a fine collection of ceramics from the agora zone of Serra Orlando (including a plate with three fish), and from the houses excavated on the west and east hills (including statues). There are also numerous votive statuettes and very fine large busts of Persephone (3C BC) from the three sanctuaries of Demeter and Kore so far found in the district. Another room on two levels has a delightful display of household objects, cooking utensils, agricultural implements, toys, masks, etc. found at Morgantina.

Morgantina

The extensive and extremely interesting remains of the ancient city of *Morgantina* (open every day, 09.00–17.00, in summer closes one hour before sunset, ☎ 0935/87955) lie some 4km beyond Aidone and its lovely eucalyptus woods, in beautiful deserted countryside, dotted with farms, with pastureland for cattle and sheep.

The approach road forks left from the main road before entering Aidone and continues east for 2km. A paved road (1km) curves left at a fork (signposted) where there are spectacular views. On the right, behind a green fence and under a plastic roof, is a **sanctuary of Demeter and Kore** (4C BC), still being excavated by Princeton University. Beyond is a car park beside olive trees, just below which is an attractively restored old house now used as a ticket office.

History

The huge site (c 20ha) occupies the long tufa ridge of **Serra Orlando** to the west and the conical hill of **Cittadella** (578m) to the east; they are separated by a deep valley. The city was built in the centre of a rich agricultural plain near the source of the River Gornalunga. A colony of Sicels called *Morgetians* was founded c 850 BC on the Cittadella, on the site of an Early Bronze Age settlement. Signs of Greek occupation here date from the 6C BC, but the Cittadella was abandoned after its sack by Ducetius in 459 BC. The new city was built on Serra Orlando, and it probably reached its zenith in the reign of Hieron II (269–215 BC). Having sided wrongly in the Second Punic War, it was given in 211 by the victorious Romans to the Spanish mercenary Moericus. By the time Augustus was in power it had lost its importance. The site was identified in 1955 by Princeton University, and excavations by them continue here every year.

The main excavations consist of the area of the agora laid out in the 3C BC and the houses on the two low hills to the east and west of the agora. The entrance, by a group of cypresses, to the **agora** is through the **north stoa**, with remains of the **gymnasium**. A number of Hellenistic lava millstones have been placed here. This area of the **upper agora** was also enclosed on the west and east side by a stoa. At the extreme right-hand corner, at the foot of the hill, are remains of shops and a paved street near the **bouleuterion**, where the Senate met. In the centre of the upper agora, surrounded by grass, is the large rectangular **macellum**, added in 125 BC, a covered market with shops, around a tholos. The long **east stoa** (87m) consisted of a narrow portico. A monumental fountain (under cover) with two basins has been excavated at its north end, and at its extreme south end is the so-called **prytaneion**, a kind of hotel for prestigious visitors such as ambassadors. In the centre of the piazza is a monumental three-sided flight of steps, 55m wide, which descends to the lower polygonal **agora**. These are thought to have served as an **ekklesiasterion** for public assemblies; nowadays during the summer months classical drama is presented here. Beside the steps is a **sanctuary of Demeter and Kore** with two round altars (under cover). Behind this, built into the hillside, is the **theatre**. To the right, beyond a long terracotta conduit, are shops in the hillside, part of the west stoa (see above).

In front of a conspicuous ruined house in the centre of the site, a rough lane leads up along the fence (with fine views) in c 15 minutes to the **west hill**, with a residential district. It passes the large so-called **Casa del Magistrato** with 24 rooms, on the slope of the hill near the walls (well preserved here outside the fence). It follows the outer wall of the house and continues to the top of the hill where a number of houses have been excavated, separated by roads on a regular grid plan. Here the **Casa del Capitello Tuscanico** has some good floors; across the street, near a large olive tree, is the **Casa Pappalardo**, a luxurious house with more mosaics. To the north, partly covered by a building for protection, is the **Casa della Cisterna ad Arco**, with a cistern beneath a low arch,

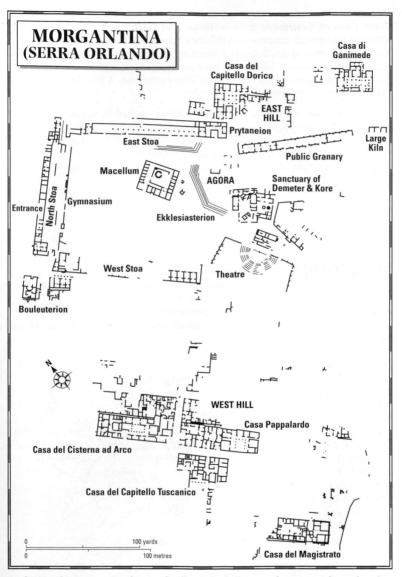

**MORGANTINA
(SERRA ORLANDO)**

Casa di Ganimede

Casa del Capitello Dorico

EAST HILL

Prytaneion

East Stoa

Large Kiln

Public Granary

Macellum

AGORA

Sanctuary of Demeter & Kore

North Stoa

Gymnasium

Entrance

Ekklesiasterion

West Stoa

Theatre

Bouleuterion

WEST HILL

Casa Pappalardo

Casa del Cisterna ad Arco

Casa del Capitello Tuscanico

Casa del Magistrato

| 0 | 100 yards |
| 0 | 100 metres |

and several mosaics. On the north side of the hill (near the approach road to the site) new excavations are in progress of another house (covered for protection).

On the other side of the sanctuary of Demeter and Kore (see above), at the foot of the east hill is the large oblong **public granary**, with a small pottery kiln (under cover), and at the other end (by the fence), a larger kiln for tiles and bricks with elaborate ovens (under cover). From the ekklesiasterion a stepped street zig-zags up the **east hill** to the **Casa del Capitello Dorico**, just below the summit.

Beyond an old farmhouse on the extreme right, in a little group of almond trees, is the **Casa di Ganimede** built c 260 BC, and destroyed in 211 BC, with two columns and mosaic fragments in two little huts (seen through glass doors). The Ganymede mosaic is particularly interesting as one of the earliest known cut-stone tesserae mosaics, which also incorporates natural pebbles. There is a fine view of the agora and, on a clear day, of Etna to the east. A lane leads back past the farmhouse and down towards the exit.

To the east of the site the hill of the **Cittadella** (reached from here by a rough road in c 3km) can be seen, which was separately fortified. On the summit is a long narrow temple of the 4C BC. Here a hut village of the Morgetians (850–750 BC) was excavated, and rock hewn tombs of Siceliot type yielded considerable finds of pottery. Parts of the **walls** (7km in circumference) of Serra Orlando and the west gate can be seen near the approach road to the site.

Ragusa province

This province now has a high average annual income per person in Sicily, thanks to rich agricultural land, light industry and off-shore oil wells that provide a large proportion of the national requirement.

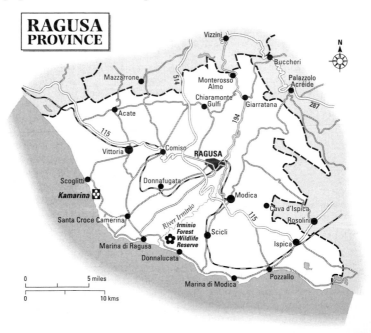

RAGUSA

The **upper town** of Ragusa (population 70,000) is an elegant provincial capital (Ragusa is the smallest of the Sicilian provinces) laid out after the earthquake of 1693. It occupies a ridge (502m) that runs from west to east between two deep gorges, and has expanded across the river gorge to the south, where high bridges now connect it to the modern town. On another hill just below it to the east is **Ragusa Ibla**, a beautiful quiet old town, one of the best preserved in Sicily. It is connected to the upper town by a steep winding road (and steps), and has exceptionally fine Baroque palaces and churches.

Practical information

 ### Getting there
By train
Railway station Piazza del Popolo, in the newest part of the upper town; subsidiary station of Ragusa Ibla at the bottom of the hill of Ibla on SS 194. Between Gela, Modica, Noto and Syracuse, it has services to Syracuse in c 2hrs, but *Trenitalia* is trying to close this line down.

By bus

Bus no. 3 runs every half hour from the upper town (corso Italia) to Ibla (piazza della Repubblica and piazza Pola), no. 1 from the main railway station to Ibla. Country buses from piazza del Popolo run by *AST* and *Etna Trasporti* to Catania, Syracuse, Enna and Agrigento (via Gela). Services in summer to Kamarina and resorts on the coast.

Parking

In the upper town: via Natalelli, or piazza Libertà; in Ragusa Ibla, piazza Duomo.

 ### Information offices
APT Ragusa, 33 via Capitano Bocchieri, Ragusa Ibla, ☎ 0932/221511, 📠 0932/623476. Ragusa on line: ✉ www.ragusa turismo.com, ✉ www.ragusaonline.com.

 ### Where to stay
Hotels

UPPER TOWN ☆☆☆☆
Mediterraneo Palace, 189 via Roma, close to the archaeological museum, ☎ 0932/621944, 📠 0932/623799, ✉ www.mediterraneopalace.it.
☆☆☆☆ *Rafael*, 40 corso Italia, small modern and comfortable. ☎ 0932/654080, 📠 0932/653418.
☆☆☆ *Hotel S. Giovanni*, 3 via Trasportino, ☎ 0932/621013.
☆☆☆ *Kroma*, 60 via Gabriele D'Annunzio, ☎ 0932/622800, 📠 0932/622680. Pleasant small hotel, central position, with restaurant.
☆☆☆ *Montreal*, 8 via S. Giuseppe, ☎ 0932/621133, 📠 0932/621026, ✉ hotelmontreal@sprintnet.it.
SOUTH OF RAGUSA ☆☆☆☆☆ *Eremo della Giubiliana*, 8km south of Ragusa, ☎ 0932/669119, 📠 0932/623891, ✉ www.eremodellagiubiliana.it. Hard to classify according to Italian standards; it is really a *relais*. A restored villa with authentic antique furniture, once a convent and then a fortified farmhouse. Excursions (on request) by private plane to Malta, Lampedusa, Aeolian Islands and Etna, or by private boat. Very good restaurant, excellent wine list.

Bed and breakfast

IBLA ☆☆☆ *Giardino di Pietra*, 13 via Chiasso Guerra, ☎ 0932/621809, grgtum@tin.it.

✿✿ *Villa Carcara*, contrada Carcara, ☎ 0932/623506, www.villacarcara.com. Between Ragusa and the sea. Meals on request. Sleeps six.

Farmhouse accommodation

✿✿✿ *Girlando*, contrada Girlando Ragusa, Frigintini, very simple and friendly farm (cattle and olives), pool, open fireplaces, English spoken, beautiful surroundings. ☎ & 📠 0932/774109, www.agriturismo-girlando.it.

 Eating out
Restaurants

RAGUSA IBLA €€€

Locanda di Don Serafino, 39 via Orfanotrofio, ☎ 0932/248778. New restaurant in the converted stables of an aristocratic mansion. Attentive service, excellent local dishes, such as *coniglio farcito con pistacchi di Bronte e pancetta iblea* (rabbit stuffed with Bronte pistachios and bacon from the Hyblean mountains); good wine cellar. The *locanda* is also a wine bar and a pizzeria in the evenings. Closed Tues.

€€€ *Ristorante Duomo*, 31 via Bocchieri, ☎ 0932/651265. very refined restaurant with excellent wine cellar. Ideal for dinner. Closed Mon, Sun evenings in winter.

€€ *Antica Macina*, 129 via Giusti, ☎ 0932/248096. Specializes in fish; the appetizers might include whitebait patties, oysters, shrimps and mussels, while *spaghetti alla Sortino*, with crayfish,

shrimps and borage is a good starter. Closed Mon.

€€ *Iblantica*, 36 corso 25 aprile, ☎ 0932/683223; old-fashioned rural atmosphere, country food, including the local ravioli. Closed Mon.

€€ *La Rusticana*, 68 corso 25 Aprile, ☎ 0932/227981. Pleasant atmosphere in this restaurant which specializes in pasta dishes, including the celebrated local ravioli. Closed Tues.

€€ *'U Saracino*, 9 via del Convento, ☎ 0932/246976. A favourite with the locals. Excellent ravioli, delicious soups in winter; inexpensive set menu. Closed Wed.

Picnics

The public gardens (Giardino Ibleo) at Ibla.

Cafés, ice cream parlours and pastry shops

Di Pasquale, 104 corso Vittorio Veneto, on the main street of the upper city. One of the finest confectioners in Italy, Di Pasquale has won many prizes. Try *testa di turco* (Turk's head), a creamy confection typical of Castelbuono in the Madonie Mountains (see p 139).

Olimpia, 12 via SS. Salvatore, close to the *Hotel Mediterraneo* and museum. Dazzling array of nougat and cakes.

 Annual festivals
Festa di S. Giorgio on the last Sunday in May in Ibla; **Festa di S. Giovanni** in the upper town on 29 August.

History

Ragusa Ibla occupies the site of the Sicel *Hybla Heraea*. The county of Ragusa, created in 1091 by Roger for his son Godfrey, was united in 1296 by Manfredi Chiaramonte with that of Modica.

After the earthquake of 1693 a new town arose to the west, and the two became separate communities from 1865 to 1926 when they were reunited as a new provincial capital.

The area is known for its asphalt mines. Oil was found here in 1953, and there used to be oil wells scattered about the upper town. Drilling now takes place offshore, and the oil is piped from Marina di Ragusa to Augusta.

The upper town

The monumental cathedral of **S. Giovanni** dominates piazza S. Giovanni, at the centre of the well-kept upper town (Ragusa Superiore). Fronting the cathedral's wide façade is a scenographic terrace (with cafés beneath), surrounded by a small garden. Built after 1694 by Mario Spada of Ragusa and Rosario Boscarino of Modica, it has a pretty campanile. Just beyond the east end of the cathedral is the elegant 18C **Casa Canonica**. Across corso Italia is the **Collegio di Maria Addolorata**, with a handsome façade of 1801 next to its convent.

Cathedral of S. Giovanni, Ragusa

Corso Italia, the handsome, long main street, lined with trees, descends very steeply to the edge of the hill above Ibla (see below). Uphill, above the cathedral, it crosses via Roma (which to the right ends in a rotonda with a view of Ibla). Via Roma leads south of the cathedral towards Ponte Nuovo (1937), which crosses the torrente S. Domenica high above the public gardens of Villa Margherita. From the bridge, there is a good view (left) of Ponte dei Cappuccini (1835) and Ponte Papa Giovanni XXIII (1964) beyond. Across the bridge is piazza Libertà, with buildings erected in the Fascist era.

Museo Archeologico Ibleo

Just before the bridge on the right (below an *Iviesse* department store) steps lead down to a building beneath the road viaduct which houses the **Hyblean Archaeological Museum** (open daily 09.00–13.30, ☎ 0932/622963). The collection, poorly labelled, has finds from the province, from prehistoric to Roman times. The first section is devoted to prehistory. The Bronze Age civilisation of *Castelluccio* is particularly well documented. Here also material belonging to the Thapsos culture (1400–1270 BC) is displayed. Pride of place in the museum is given to a unique sculpture known as the ***Warrior of Castiglione***, discovered by a farmer in 1999 while ploughing his field north of Ragusa. Made to fit over a door, the sculpture probably stood over the entrance to the warrior's tomb. Castiglione would have been a Sicel centre when this warrior was buried at the end of the 7C BC. The sculpture, carved from a magnificent block of local limestone, shows the warrior on horseback with his shield in front, at one side a bull and at the other a sphinx, probably symbolizing his nobility (horse), strength (bull) and wisdom (sphinx). The carving bears an inscription with the name of the warrior, Pyrrinos son of Pyttikas, and is also proudly signed by the sculptor, Skyllos, very unusual for the times.

The **second section** (cases 5–14) displays objects dating from the Archaic to the Classical period found at Kamarina. Case 6: Two black-figured amphorae, one with a scene of wild boars and lions, and one showing Hercules and the lion; reconstructed necropolis of Passo Marinaro; finds from the necropolis (cases 9 and 10) include small red-figured vases of the 5C BC and a lekythos

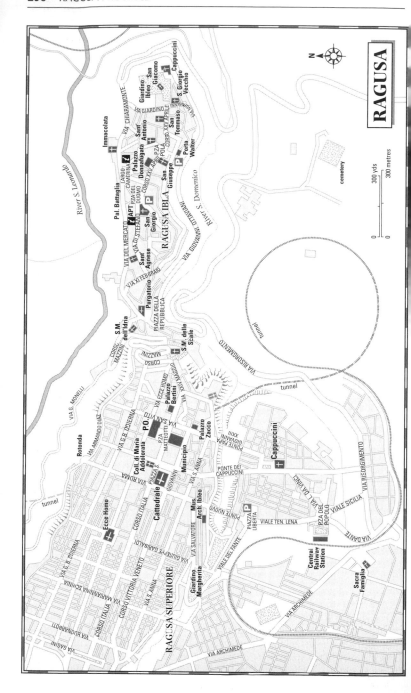

with a white ground. A statue of a kore was found in the Temple of Athena. Three levels of excavations have been reconstructed here. **Case 13** contains terracotta statuettes of Demeter found in a deposit near a pottery workshop (active from the end of the 5C to the beginning of the 3C BC).

Third section, dedicated to indigenous centres inhabited by the Sicels (Archaic to Classical period). **Cases 14–18** contain finds from Monte Casasia and Licodia Eubea ware; in **case 15** is a rare Ionic kylix with an inscription in the native language. **Cases 17–18** display finds from the necropolis of Castiglione, north of Ragusa. **Case 20** displays finds from the necropolis of Rito, including an Attic kylix with animals outside and a running warrior inside attributed to the circle of the 'Griffin bird painter' (c 550 BC).

Fourth section (Hellenistic centres). A potter's workshop from Scornavacche has been reconstructed, and the terracotta figurines (**cases 22–24**) are particularly noteworthy. **Fifth section** (Roman and late Roman cities). Finds from Kaukana, and mosaics from S. Croce Camerina (with Christian motifs) are displayed here. **Case 26** contains Roman glass. The **sixth section** displays various material acquired from private collections, and police confiscations.

From piazza S. Giovanni (see above) corso Italia descends steeply past (right; no. 90) the fine 18C **Palazzo Lupis** to piazza Matteotti. Here is the **Town Hall** (*municipio*), (1880; enlarged 1929) opposite the monumental post office (1930), with colossal statues on the top. Corso Italia next crosses via S. Vito in which, on the right, is the fine Baroque **Palazzo Zacco** (in poor repair). Further down corso Italia is the late 18C **Palazzo Bertini** (no. 35) with three huge grotesque heads.

The corso ends at via XXIV Maggio, with two palaces well sited at the corner, which narrows and becomes steeper as it begins the descent to Ragusa Ibla, now seen in its magnificent position on a separate spur. At the foot of an elegant little Baroque palace, a small tabernacle recalls a cholera epidemic here in 1838; in front, wide steps descend to an interesting group of houses with courtyards, overlooking the valley. The road continues down past (left) the pretty via Pezza, which runs along the hillside, and via Ecce Homo which climbs uphill to the left, past a handsome little Baroque palace.

Via XXIV Maggio ends at the balcony beside the campanile of S. Maria delle Scale where there is a superb bird's-eye view of Ragusa Ibla, with its beautifully coloured roof tiles which have been carefully preserved. Many fragments of the 15C structure of the church of **S. Maria delle Scale** survived the rebuilding of 1693. Outside, beneath the campanile is part of a Gothic doorway and the remains of an outside pulpit. Inside (usually closed) is an elaborate Gothic arch decorated with sculptures and (over a side altar) a relief (very ruined) of the *Dormition of the Virgin* in coloured terracotta, by the Gagini school (1538).

Ragusa Ibla

A beautifully preserved little town, with peaceful streets, Ragusa Ibla lends itself to exploration on foot. It is, however, suffering from depopulation and many of the old houses have been abandoned. Ibla can be reached from here by the zigzag corso Mazzini or on foot by various flights of steps, described below. The Discesa S. Maria continues down straight ahead. On the road is a relief of the *Flight into Egypt* (15C–16C), probably once part of a votive tabernacle. Across the road another flight of steps continues under the road, and then a walkway leads left in front of some houses. Just after rejoining the road, steps immediately to the left continue downhill and pass under the road twice before reaching the delightful **Palazzo Nicastro** (or Vecchia Cancelleria), erected in 1760 with tall pilasters, a decorative doorway, and windows with large balconies. To the left is the bell-tower and little dome decorated with majolica tiles of the 18C church of **S. Maria dell'Idria**. The salita Commendatore continues down past (left) the 18C **Palazzo Cosentini**, with splendid Baroque pilasters, capitals, and more fantastic balconies. Its main façade is on corso Mazzini which now continues right to **piazza della Repubblica** at the foot of the hill of **Ragusa Ibla**.

To the left of the closed 17C church of the **Purgatorio** via del Mercato leads up round the left side of the hill with a view of Palazzo Sortino Trono above the road. Further on it continues left past the old abandoned market building and has splendid views over the unspoilt valley. Via XI Febbraio, which is more peaceful and nicely paved, forks right off Via del Mercato for the centre of Ibla. On a bend there is a view (left) of the hillside covered with characteristic dry-stone walls. Via S. Agnese continues left, and then steps lead up to the wide via Tenente Di Stefano near the church of S. Agnese beside a low 19C palace in a pretty group of houses. It continues uphill and soon narrows with a good view ahead of the cathedral's 19C dome. On the left are the seven delightful balconies of **Palazzo La Rocca**, beautifully restored as the seat of the *APT* of Ragusa. It has an interesting double staircase in black asphalt stone, and a little garden with citrus trees overlooking the unspoilt hillside.

Via Di Stefano continues round the side of the Duomo into **piazza del Duomo**, planted with a row of palm trees. It slopes up to the magnificent three-tiered golden **façade** of the cathedral of **S. Giorgio** which stands above a flight of steps surrounded by a 19C balustrade. The church was built by Rosario Gagliardi in 1744. The neo-classical dome (hidden by the façade but visible from the road behind or from the extreme left side of the piazza) dates from 1820.

The contemporary **interior** (entered by one of the side doors) is lit by the delightful **dome** which rises above its high drum with windows between the coupled columns. The stained glass dates from 1926. In the south aisle, above the side door (and behind glass), is an equestrian statue of *St George*; in the third altar is Vito D'Anna's *Immaculate Virgin* and in the fourth altar, *Rest on the Flight into Egypt* by Dario Guerci. In the north transept is *St George and the dragon*, also by Dario Guerci. In the sacristy is a lovely stone tabernacle with the equestrian statue of *St George* between saints *Ippolito* and *Mercurio*, with ruined reliefs below. Above the side door in the north aisle is a silver reliquary urn. By the west door is a stone statue of *St George* by the school of Gagini. The organ in the nave is by the Serassi brothers.

Palazzo Arezzi, in the piazza, has a delightful balcony over a side road. At the lower end of the piazza is a charming little fountain and the handsome Palazzo Veninata (early 20C). The fine neo-classical **Circolo di Conversazione** (c 1850), which preserves an interesting interior, houses an exclusive club recently opened to women members. Next to it is **Palazzo Donnafugata** with its delightful little wooden balcony, from which it was possible to watch the passers-by in the road below without being seen. The palace contains a private art collection formed in the mid-19C by Corrado Arezzo de Spuches (admission only with special permission) and a little theatre built in the late 19C (150 seats; recently restored) where public performances are sometimes held.

The wide corso XXV Aprile continues to piazza Pola, with the splendid tall Baroque façade of the church of **S. Giuseppe** (1590, probably by Gagliardi). In the oval domed interior there are pretty galleries once used by the nuns. The interesting floor is made with black asphalt, mined locally. The altars are made of shiny painted glass.

In the centre of the dome is a painting of the *Glory of St Benedict* by Sebastiano Lo Monaco (1793). Above the high altar, in an elaborate frame, is the *Holy Family* by Matteo Battaglia. The side altarpieces, including a *Holy Trinity* by Giuseppe Cristadoro, are in poor condition.

Corso XXV Aprile continues to wind downhill past the closed church of the Maddalena and the high wall of **S. Tommaso** which has a pretty bell-tower. In the interior is an interesting font in black asphalt (1545). Just beyond, beside the church of St Vincent Ferrer is the entrance to the **Giardino Ibleo** (open 08.00–20.00), delightful public gardens laid out in 1858, with a splendid palm avenue and beds of lilies. It contains several small churches.

Beyond the colourful campanile of St Vincent Ferrer is the locked church of S. Giacomo, founded in the 16C with a façade of 1902. At the end is the church of the **Cappuccini**, now the seat of a restoration laboratory and of the Diocesan Museum (closed). It contains a very fine altarpiece with three paintings by Pietro Novelli. The beautifully kept gardens have fountains and views of the hills, and, beyond the War Memorial, the church of S. Giorgio can be seen on the skyline, with the large church of the Immacolata on the right.

In an orchard below the balustrade ancient tombs can be seen carved out of the rock. Outside the entrance to the gardens, in via Normanni, is the 15C Gothic side portal of the church of **S. Giorgio Vecchio** (in very bad condition), with a relief of *St George*, behind a little garden. The church was destroyed in the earthquake of 1693.

From piazza Pola (see above), with a view of the top of the façade of S. Giorgio and its dome, via Orfanotrofio leads past the church of S. Antonio (closed) with remains of a Gothic portal next to a little Baroque side doorway. Just beyond is the 18C **Palazzo di Quattro** with a balcony along the whole length of its façade.

A road descends on the right past S. Teresa to reach the Immacolata (closed), with a fine campanile. It contains interesting works in asphalt stone. Its Gothic portal stands in piazza Chiaramonte, in a little garden of orange trees. The narrow via Chiaramonte leads up past the campanile to the back façade of **Palazzo Battaglia** (no. 40), a very original building. Beyond the arch on the left the main façade can be seen on via Orfanotrofio, beside the church of the Annunziata. Just uphill from Largo Camerina, via Conte Cabrera leads back past more interesting palaces, to piazza del Duomo.

A road leads out of the other side of the piazza, under the arch of Palazzo Arezzi, to (left) the salita Ventimiglia (steps) which lead down to the closed church of the Gesù. The interior has stuccoes and frescoes by Matteo Battaglia (1750). Behind the church is the **Porta Walter**, the only one of Ibla's five medieval gates to have survived.

MODICA

Modica (population 53,100) is an unusual town divided into two parts, **Modica Bassa** (lower town) and **Modica Alta** (upper town), with decorative palm trees and elegant Baroque buildings, which bases its economy on the rich agriculture of its hinterland. At the end of the 19C Modica was the fourth largest town in Sicily. Like many towns in this corner of Sicily it had to be rebuilt after the earthquake of 1693. The lower town occupies a valley at the confluence of two torrents, which were channelled and covered over in 1902 after a disastrous flood. On the steep spur between them the upper town rises in terraces above the dramatic church of S. Giorgio. For many centuries Modica was known as the 'Venice of Sicily', for its rivers which were waterways, and for the intellectual fervour of its inhabitants.

Practical information

 ### Getting there
By train

The **railway station** is beyond via Vittorio Veneto, 600m west of corso Umberto I. On the line from Gela via Ragusa, Modica and Noto to Syracuse. Services to Syracuse in c 1hr 30min.

By bus

Services run by *AST* to Ragusa, Syracuse, Catania, etc.

Parking

Parking is very difficult in the upper town; in the lower town on corso Umberto I or viale Medaglie d'Oro.

 ### Information offices
APT Ragusa, 33 via Capitano Bocchieri, Ragusa Ibla, ☎ 0932/621421.
Pro Loco Modica, ☎ 0932/762626; in summer ☎ 0932/905803.
Tourist Information Bureau, 1 Corso Umberto, Modica, ☎ 0932/759204.
Pro Loco Ispica, 21 via Bellini.
Pro Loco Scicli, 4 via Castellana.
Modica on line: ✉ www.modicaonline.it; ✉ www.turismodica.com.

 ### Where to stay
Hotels

✭✭✭ *Bristol*, 8/b via Risorgimento, ☎ 0932/762890, 📠 0932/763330.
✭✭✭ *Motel Modica*, 1 corso Umberto I, ☎ 0932/941022, 📠 0932/941077.
✭✭ *I Tetti di Siciliando*, 24 Via Cannata, ☎ & 📠 0932/942843, ✉ www.siciliando.it. Tucked away, close to the Cathedral, tiny hotel offering handicraft and photography courses and excursions on horseback or bicycles.

Bed and breakfast

✭✭✭ *Deiruta*, in a tiny alley near St. George's, ☎ 0932/755600, ✉ www.deiruta.it.
✭✭ *San Giorgio*, 25 via Raccomandata (old city), ☎ & 📠 0932/751170, ✉ www.drypoint.it.
MARINA DI MODICA ✭✭✭ *Graziella*, 100 lungomare Bisani, ☎ 0932/239681 & 333/3819163. Mini apartments, air conditioning, nice garden, right on a lovely sandy beach, good cooking.

Holiday village

MARINA DI MODICA ✭✭✭ *Conte di Cabrera*, contrada Maganuco, ☎ 0932/777070, 📠 0932/777050. Pleasant holiday village by the sea.

Farmhouse accommodation

☆☆☆☆ *Agrihotel*, contrada Pantano Secco, Ispica, ☎ 0932/951172 🖨 0932/951343, ✉ www.agriturismo.com/agrihotel. An 18C Spanish-style farmhouse, all rooms with TV, air conditioning, bathroom, organic food, not far from the sea and the town of Ispica; the farm raises cattle and horses.

☆☆☆☆ *Nacalino*, contrada Nacalino, ☎ & 🖨 0932/904989, ✉ nacalinoagriturismo@tin.it. Quiet farm producing organic products; dairy cattle; carobs. 19C farmhouse.

☆☆☆ *Il Granaio*, 2/c contrada Palazzella, Modica, ☎ & 🖨 0932/909081, ✉ www.ilgranaio.com. On the hills near Modica, very comfortable farmhouse.

Villa Teresa, contrada Bugilfezza, close to Cava d'Ispica, ☎ 0932/771690.

Eating out
Restaurants

Modica is famous for its excellent cuisine.

€€€ *Fattoria delle Torri*, 14 vico Napoletano, ☎ 0932/751286. Local ingredients prepared with a twist, such as *ravioli di fave verdi con ricotta montata ed erba cipollina* (ravioli of tender broad beans with whipped ricotta and chives), excellent wines. Closed Mon & Sun evening.

€€ *L'Arco*, 11 piazza Corrado Rizzone, ☎ 0932/942727. Good home-made pasta. Closed Mon.

€€ *Le Magnolie*, 179 via Gianforma, ☎ 0932/908136. Innovative cuisine using high quality, local ingredients. Closed Mon.

€ *Rosticceria Blandino*, 9 via Sacro Cuore, ☎ 0932/905064. Tasty simple dishes. Closed Sun.

Cafés and pastry shops

Bonaiuto, 159 corso Umberto, sells delicious local sweets including '*mpanatigghi* (light pastry filled with mincemeat, chocolate, and spices), *cedrata* (honey and citron rind), *cobaita* (honey and sesame seeds), and Modica chocolate. *Caffè Adamo*, 15/17 via M. Tedeschi, offers superb chocolate cake, homemade ice cream and sorbets, including *gelato caldo* (warm ice cream).

Old-fashioned grocery stores

Rizza, 128 corso Umberto, for olive oil, fresh roasted coffee, herbs, pepper, and Modica chocolate, including *cioccolato al peperoncino* (chilli flavoured chocolate). *Casa del Formaggio*, 3 via M. Tedeschi, for typical cheeses, hams and salami, Modica chocolate, carob products and liqueurs. This shop is famous in Germany!

Irish pub

Tullamore Dew, 10 via M. Tedeschi (old centre).

Annual festivals

Traditional processions during Easter week. The **Festa di S. Giorgio** in April, and the **Festa di S. Pietro** at the end of June, with a fair.

Internet point

At 43 via M. Tedeschi.

History

The site of Modica was occupied by the Sicels, then by the Greeks and the Romans; it was an important centre in Byzantine times. Under the Normans it became a county, one of the most powerful fiefs of the Middle Ages, and passed from the Chiaramonte in 1392 to the Spanish Cabrera family. In the 15C it ruled over Ragusa, Vittoria, Comiso and the whole of the present-day province of Ragusa. After 1704 it came through Spanish connections to the seventh Duke of Berwick and Alba.

The poet Salvatore Quasimodo (1901–68), who won the Nobel prize for literature in 1959, was born in Modica. His father worked as a railwayman here.

Modica Bassa

Modica Bassa (300m), is crossed by **corso Umberto I**. The corso is unusually wide since it occupies the bed of a river torrent, covered over in 1902. It is lined with handsome 18C and 19C palaces, and there is a splendid view of the monumental church of S. Giorgio (described below) half-way up the hillside between the lower and upper town. On the extreme right, on top of a bare rock face, a round tower surmounted by a clock can be seen, which is all that remains of the castle of the counts of Modica.

A monumental flight of steps, decorated with statues of the apostles, leads up to the church of **S. Pietro**, rebuilt after the earthquake of 1693. Nearby, off via Clemente Grimaldi, is the inconspicuous entrance to a grotto used until recently as a storeroom. Here three layers of frescoes were discovered in 1989, the earliest of which may date from the 11C. They decorated an ancient church which has been given the name of **S. Nicolò Inferiore**.

Chocolate and the Aztecs

During the 16C, cocoa beans imported from Mexico by the Cabreras were made into chocolate by the confectioners of Modica, using the ancient Aztec method of grinding the beans between two stones and then adding maize. Elsewhere in Europe the method of manufacture evolved rapidly in order to industrialize the product, improve the flavour and lower the cost. In Modica, however, the method is still basically the same, the only difference being that sugar instead of maize is added towards the end of the grinding operation, giving a typical grainy consistency to the finished product. Natural flavourings are also added, such as cinnamon, vanilla, orange essence or chilli pepper.

In the centre of the town, at the former confluence of the two rivers, the corso forms a fork with the unusually broad via Marchesa Tedeschi, also on the site of a riverbed. Here is the Town Hall, next to the church of **S. Domenico** which contains a 16C painting of the *Madonna of the Rosary*. On the other side of the corso, in via De Leva, is a fine Arab Norman doorway in a little garden, probably once part of a 13C palace. In via Marchesa Tedeschi is the church of **S. Maria di Betlem** which incorporates a beautiful chapel built in the 15C by the Cabrera. The elaborate crib in the north aisle, with 60 terracotta statuettes, was made in Caltagirone in 1882.

On the other side of the Town Hall (see above) corso Umberto I continues past piazza Matteotti where there are decorative palm trees. Here the 15C church of the **Carmine** contains a marble group of the *Annunciation* by the Gagini school.

The corso ends at viale Medaglie d'Oro above which in via Mercè is the church of S. Maria delle Grazie next to its huge former convent, the **Palazzo dei Mercedari**, restored as the seat of the Civic Museum and the Museum of Traditional Arts and Crafts. On the ground floor the **Civic Museum** (open daily 09.00–13.00, except Sun & PH, ☎ 0932/945081) has an archaeological collection formed at the end of the last century. It was catalogued and opened in 1960 by the local scholar Franco Libero Belgiorno (1906–71). The display is chronological, from the Neolithic era onwards, with finds from Cava d'Ispica and Modica.

On the top floor, in lovely vaulted rooms of the old convent, is the **Hyblean Museum of Arts and Crafts and Popular Traditions**, a private museum opened on request (☎ 0932/757747). This fascinating local ethnological collection of artisans' tools and utensils is displayed in reconstructed workshops (a smithy, shoemaker's shop, basketworker's store, a laboratory for making chocolate, a cartwright's shop, a saddlery, a carpenter's workshop, etc.) Local artisans will give demonstrations of their skills by appointment. A local farmhouse has also been faithfully reconstructed and there is a collection of Sicilian carts.

The imposing church of **S. Giorgio** is reached from corso Garibaldi which runs parallel to corso Umberto I. Some 250 steps (completed in 1818) ascend to the church which was rebuilt in 1643 and again after 1693. The **façade** is one of the most remarkable Baroque works in Italy. It has five original doorways and a very tall, central bell-tower. It is attributed by most scholars to Rosario Gagliardi (1702–38); the upper storey was added in the 19C.

In the **interior**, with double side aisles, the apse is filled with a huge polyptych attributed to the local painter Bernardino Niger (1573). The silver high altar was made in 1705. In the south aisle is a 16C painting of the *Nativity* and (on the second altar) an *Assumption* by Filippo Paladino (1610). At the end of the south side is a 14C silver reliquary urn. In the chapel to the right of the presbytery is a popular equestrian statue of *St George*, while in that to the left of the presbytery is a statue of the *Madonna* by Giuliano Mancino and Bartolomeo Berrettaro. The fine Serassi organ dates from 1886–88.

On the left side of S. Giorgio is the 18C **Palazzo Polara** from which there is a fine view of the lower town and the hillside beyond. Uphill behind S. Giorgio, on corso Francesco Crispi, is the Baroque **Palazzo Tomasi-Rossi**, which has pretty balconies.

Modica Alta

Roads and lanes continue steeply uphill to Modica Alta which is well worth exploring. Its main street, the corso Regina Margherita, has handsome 18C and 19C palaces. At the highest point of the hill another monumental flight of steps leads up to its most important church, **S. Giovanni**. Its façade was erected in the Baroque style in 1839. In another part of the upper town, within a prison enclosure (but visible from the outside), is the elaborate doorway of 1478 of the ruined church of **S. Maria di Gesù**.

Environs of Modica

The Cava d'Ispica

The Cava d'Ispica lies 11km east of Modica (signposted). It is a deep gorge 13km long which follows a river (now usually dry) with luxuriant vegetation. The sides of the canyon are honeycombed with prehistoric tombs and medieval cave-dwellings; here the presence of man can be traced from the earliest times to the most recent, although the valley was greatly damaged in the earthquake of 1693. Beside the entrance is a hut used as an office by the Superintendence for Antiquities of the region (☎ 0932/826004), and the site is currently being enclosed (open daily 09.00–13.30, 15.00–18.30; mornings only in winter). Just below the entrance are extensive Christian **catacombs** known as *Larderia* (4C–5C AD). They extend for some 36m inside the rock.

Across the main road is the little church of **S. Nicola** (unlocked on request) which contains very damaged traces of late Byzantine frescoes. A path near here leads along the dry riverbed to the prehistoric tomb of **Baravitalla**, dating from the Castelluccio period (1800 BC), and a Sicel tomb with a design of pilasters on its façade. Nearby traces of a hut village have been uncovered. From the entrance (see above) a gravel road (c 400m) leads past numerous **caves**, including some on more than one storey, ruined by the earthquake. Outside the enclosure an overgrown path continues along the splendid valley, with luxuriant vegetation, for some 13km. It passes numerous **rock tombs** and dwellings, including the so-called '*castello*' on four floors. At the far end is the Parco della Forza, best approached from Ispica (see below).

Ispica

Southeast of Modica, in pretty countryside typical of this region of the island, with low dry-stone walls between fields of pastureland and crops, and small farmhouses built of the local grey stone, is the little town of Ispica (population 14,800). It was rebuilt on its present site after the earthquake of 1693 destroyed the former town on the floor of the valley, and it has fine 18C and 19C buildings. It was known in the Middle Ages as Spaccaforno, but re-adopted its old name in 1935. The chalk eminence on which it stands is pierced with tombs and cliff dwellings. These can be seen in the **Parco della Forza** (open daily 09.00–18.45, mornings only in winter, ☎ 0932/951133, 🖳 www.ispicaweb.it) at the south end of the Cava d'Ispica (see above). It has interesting vegetation, various cisterns, catacombs, etc., and a remarkable tunnel known as the *Centoscale*, 60m long, formerly used by those carrying water from the river to the town centre.

In the little town, the church of **S. Maria Maggiore** is an attractive building by Vincenzo Sinatra with 19C stuccoes and frescoes by Olivio Sozzi (1763–65), who is buried here. **Palazzo Bruno di Belmonte**, an Art Nouveau building by Ernesto Basile (1910) has been restored as the Town Hall. The church of the **Annunziata** is filled with stuccoes carried out in the mid-18C, attributed to Giuseppe Gianforma.

Scicli

A pretty byroad leads from Modica across an upland plain with low stone walls and carob trees. Before descending to Scicli, it passes the site of the old medieval town marked by the ruined church of **S. Matteo**, once its Mother Church. Remains survive of its façade of 1762.

Scicli (population 26,000) has occupied the floor of the valley, surrounded by rocky cliffs, since the 14C. Prosperous under Saracen and Norman rule, and prosperous again today thanks to its vegetables, especially cherry tomatoes, it is another charming Baroque town rebuilt after the 1693 earthquake, with numerous churches. Here the annual festival of the **Madonna of the Militia** is celebrated in May, which commemorates the battle between the Normans and Saracens. In piazza Italia, planted with trees and surrounded by some neo-classical buildings, is the 18C **Duomo**. It contains a papier mâché *Madonna dei Milici* which is carried in procession in May. Opposite is the Baroque **Palazzo Fava** which has attractive balconies, on the corner of via S. Bartolomeo, which opens out in front of the well-sited church of **S. Bartolomeo**, in front of a rock face. The pleasantly coloured façade, crowned with a cupola, was built at the beginning of the 19C by Salvatore D'Alì. It contains a crib with very large statues by Pietro Padula (1773–75) the only one of its kind in Sicily; it comes in fact from Naples and the figures are carved in lime wood.

Via Nazionale leads uphill and on the right, at the end of a short street, is the corner of **Palazzo Beneventano**, with remarkably eccentric Baroque details. Off the other side of via Nazionale is the prettily paved via Mormino Penna. The Town Hall (1906) stands next to the elegant church of **S. Giovanni**, with a fine façade. Via Penna winds on past **S. Michele** with a well-designed side door, past Palazzo Spadaro and the church of S. Teresa.

Via Nazionale continues to piazza Busacca, planted with palm trees, with a 19C statue by Benedetto Civiletti, of the philanthropist Pietro Di Lorenzo (d. 1567). Here is the church of the **Carmine** (1751–69), beside its convent with a decorative balcony. Beyond, to the right, is the elegant church of **S. Maria della Consolazione**. Still further on, surrounded by a rocky cliff, in an interesting part of the old town, is the church of **S. Maria la Nova**. The neo-classical façade dates from 1816. In the interior, decorated with stuccoes, is a high altarpiece of the *Birth of the Virgin* by Sebastiano Conca. The presbytery was designed by Venanzio Marvuglia. A silver statue of the *Immaculate Virgin* dates from 1844, and there is a Gaginesque statue of the *Madonna*. On the second altar to the left is a very highly venerated statue of *Our Lady of Pity*, made of cypress wood and thought to be Byzantine.

For **drawn thread work** (*sfilato siciliano*) and **embroidery**, visit *Giovanna Massari* (32 piazza Italia, Scicli, ☎ 0932/779009) for some of the most beautiful linens in Sicily.

COMISO AND VITTORIA

These small towns west of Ragusa have fine Baroque buildings and the surrounding countryside is beautiful. Industrious and hard working, these people still enjoy the traditional way of life.

Practical information

Getting there
By train

Comiso and Vittoria are both on the Syracuse–Ragusa–Gela line.

By bus

Giamporcaro (☎ 095/536201) runs services between Catania and Comiso. *AST* (☎ 091/6882783) has a service from Palermo to Comiso. *AST* (0932/942445) also runs a bus to/from Ragusa/Comiso. Chiaramonte Gulfi can be reached by bus from Ragusa.

By car

The SS 115 runs from Syracuse and Ragusa. From Catania the SS 194–514 leads straight to Comiso.

Information offices
APT Ragusa, ☎ 0932/621421.
Pro Loco, 6 Via Di Vita, Comiso, ☎ 0932/961586.
Pro Loco, 53 via Cavour, Vittoria, ☎ 0932/510260.

Where to stay
Hotels

COMISO ✰✰✰ *Cordial*, 284 corso Deserto, ☎ & ▯ 0932/967866. No restaurant but there are some nearby.
VITTORIA ✰✰✰✰ *Vittoria Residence*, 17 via Castelfidardo, ☎ & ▯ 0932/992990, ✉ www.vittoriaresidence.com. Modern hotel in the centre,

also has apartments.

✹✹✹ *Grand Hotel*, 53 via Vico II Carlo Pisacane, ☎ & 🖷 0932/863888.

✹✹✹ *Villa Orchidea*, contrada Bosco Rotondo, close to Vittoria and Comiso, ☎ 0932/879107, 🖷 0932/879034, 🖾 www.villaorchidea.it. Tennis courts, pool and large garden. A frequent conference venue.

✹✹ *Sicilia*, 62 via Cernaia, ☎ 0932/981087, 🖷 0932/981150.

CHIARAMENTE GULFI ✹✹ *Villa Nobile*, 168 corso Umberto, ☎ 0932/928537. Friendly service. Good restaurant.

Bed and breakfast

ACATE ✹✹ *Villa Mogghi*, ☎ & 🖷 0932/988711, 2km from the sea. Old fortified farmhouse surrounded by an Arab garden and pines. Guests can help prepare jam, sun-dried tomatoes and sauces.

Farmhouse accommodation

ACATE *Il Carrubo*, contrada Bosco Grande Canalotti, ☎ and 🖷 0932/989038. Hillside position 13km from the sea and 4km from Acate. A fascinating ancient farm producing citrus, olives and forage; places for campers. Good, simple restaurant, organic food.

COMISO *Torre di Canicarao*, contrada Canicarao, Comiso, ☎ 0932/731167, 🖷 0932/683309, 🖾 www.canicarao.it. 15C farmhouse with its own Buddhist temple. Stunning countryside; quiet peaceful atmosphere. Excellent wine and organic food.

CHIARAMONTE GULFI ✹✹✹ *Villa Zottopera*, contrada Roccazzo, ☎ 0932/244018, 🖷 0932/621442.

🖾 www.agrobiologica-rosso.it. An old fortified farmhouse with swimming pool and tennis court, surrounded by olive groves. The farm won first prize at an international competition for its olive oil in 2002. Some self-catering apartments in outbuildings; meals are available on request.

Eating out
Restaurants

CHIARAMONTE GULFI €€ *Majore*, 12 via Martiri Ungheresi, ☎ 0932/928019. Excellent local dishes, using the best ingredients in Sicily. Closed Mon.

€ *Pizzeria D'Amato*, 52 via Vittorio Emanuele, ☎ 0932/928500. Open in the evening for delicious pizzas. Closed Mon.

VITTORIA €€ *Opera*, 133 via Carlo Alberto, ☎ 0932/869129. Traditionally high standards. Closed Sun. evening.

Feasts and festivals

In February at **Chiaramonte Gulfi** there is a spectacular carnival called **Carnevale della Contea**. At **Acate**, the third Sunday after Easter is the feast of the patron saint Vincent the Martyr, with the colourful **Cavalcata di S. Vincenzo**. **Vittoria** is famous for the **Tavolata di S. Giuseppe** (18 March) when a banquet is prepared by the people of the town who have reason to be grateful to the saint; ornamental loaves, fruit, flowers decorate the lavish meal which is then donated to the poor.

Comiso

The pretty Baroque town of Comiso (population 29,000) is dominated by the domes of the Chiesa Madre and the SS. Annunziata. The handsome paving on the streets around the old centre is made from the local stone, which has the appearance of marble. Comiso has a strong economy, based on the quarrying of the stone, the year-round vegetable crops, and several small but flourishing industries. There is an airport, now no longer used by the American military, which is being transformed for civil use. The author Gesualdo Bufalino

(1920–96), one of Italy's most important contemporary writers, was born here. so was the artist Salvatore Fiume (1915–1997).

Three palm trees stand outside the church of **SS. Annunziata**, which has a lovely blue dome, rebuilt in 1772–93. The luminous interior has stucco decoration in blue, grey and white. It contains a wooden 15C statue of *St Nicholas* on the first south altar, and a *Crucifix* attributed to Fra Umile da Petralia in the south transept. On the second north altar is a painting of the *Transition of the Virgin* by Narciso Cidonio (1605). The font is a fine work by Mario Rutelli (1913). The organ is by the Polizzi brothers of Modica.

Via Papa Giovanni XXIII leads downhill in front of the church, and via degli Studi leads right to piazza del Municipio with its amusing fountain (1937). The waters of the **Fonte di Diana** were said to refuse to mix with wine when poured by unchaste hands; in Roman days they supplied a bath-house, with a mosaic of Neptune, the remains of which are visible beneath the Town Hall. Just out of the piazza rises the Chiesa Madre, **S. Maria delle Stelle**, also with a dome. The fine façade is attributed to Rosario Gagliardi. The interior has a vault painted in the 17C attributed to Antonio Barbalunga. Below its terrace is piazza delle Erbe, with a fountain, on to which faces the handsome **market** building, with a raised portico, built in 1867. It has been restored as the seat of the Civic Library and Picture Gallery, entered from the delightful courtyard which has a fountain. The collection of paintings includes 19C portraits. The library is now officially known as the **Biblioteca Bufalino** (☎ 0932/962617), because it houses his private collection of more than 6000 books, together with newspaper articles written by him or about him, photographs and other memorabilia. Close by is the **Civic Museum of Natural History** (☎ 0932/722521), with a good collection of fossils and an interesting exhibit on rare creatures washed up on the beaches of Sicily and Calabria.

From via Giovanni XXIII a road leads shortly (right) to the church of **S. Francesco** (if locked, ring at the convent), founded in the early 14C. The present church was built in 1478, and the very interesting **Cappella Naselli** (1517–55) was added at the east end by Gaspare Poidomani, using a fascinating pastiche of architectural styles. Arab-Norman squinches support the dome, and classical details are incorporated in the decoration. It contains the funerary monument of Gaspare Naselli, attributed to Antonello Gagini. At the west end is a 15C wooden choir loft. The 15C **Castello Feudale** owned by the Naselli family, at the entrance to the town, was altered in 1575 (closed).

Chiaramonte Gulfi

Chiaramonte Gulfi (population 8300; ✉ www.comune.chiaramonte-gulfi.rg.it) was founded by Manfredi Chiaramonte for the survivors of Gulfi, an Arab town destroyed in 1299 by the Angevins, who killed most of the inhabitants, including the women and children, in a massacre still remembered for its horror. Called the **City of Museums**, of which it has eight, it is also famous for its top quality olive oil officially recognized by the *DOP* (*Denominazione d'origine protetta*) seal, excellent bread, pasta, pork, salami and cured hams. It is a delightful little town in an excellent strategic position, dominating the ancient routes of southeastern Sicily. Chiaramonte Gulfi is twinned with Clermont de l'Oise in Picardy. At the foot of the hill, at Scornavacche, remains have been found of the Greek colony of *Acrillae*, founded 70 years after Syracuse, and destroyed in the 9C by the Arabs.

City museums

The efficient civic administration has led to the opening of eight museums, some of which have been set up in the historic Baroque Palazzo Montesano, the others close by in the town centre. They are all open from 17.00–20.00 Sat, 10.00–13.00, 15.00–19.00 Sun, but on request they can be visited on any day of the week, ☎ 0932/928049 (Town Hall) or ☎ 0932/711239 (Tourist Information Bureau).

• **Giovanni De Vita Art Gallery** houses about 60 paintings of this local Impressionist artist, the ones he wanted to keep with him during his life, and donated by his family when he died.
• **Olive Oil Museum** information about the town's most precious product, with a complete collection of presses and tools used by the craftsmen through the ages. Things have not changed very much; even today the excellence of this oil is due to the fact that the olives are gathered by hand and processed the same day, using only stone presses.
• **Ornithological Collection** shows about 500 stuffed birds of Sicily and Italy (some now extinct), prepared by the Azzara brothers, expert taxidermists.
• **Ethnic Musical Instruments Museum** is a beautiful arrangement in seven rooms of more than 600 rare musical instruments from all over the world.
• **F. Gulino Collection of Historic Military Relics** contains about 1000 interesting mementoes, most of them relating to the two World Wars.
• **Museum of Sacred Art** is considered to be one of the finest museums of its kind in Italy. Among the rare and precious objects from the churches of the town there is a crib of 40 terracotta figures about 30cm high, dressed in the traditional 19C County of Modica costumes.
• **Museum of Embroidery and Sicilian Drawn-thread Work** (*Sfilato Siciliano*), in one of the tiny alleys off the magnificent stairway to the church of S. Giovanni, is a display of beautiful embroidery and lace made by the local women, together with the tools used in their craft through the years. Its success has led to the creation of the first Town School for Embroidery in Sicily, where more than 60 experts teach whoever wants to learn, so that this precious skill is not lost. Many of the traditional designs can be traced back to the pottery of the Middle Ages or even further back to prehistoric art, showing fishing nets, honeycombs, flowers, leaves, ears of wheat and birds.
• **Museum of Liberty or Art Nouveau**, at Palazzo Montesano, is the latest museum and illustrates with photographs, paintings and furniture the fervid period between 1895 and 1913 when this style was fashionable in Sicily.

East of Chiaramonte Gulfi is the little town of **Giarratana**, with 3400 inhabitants it is the smallest town in the province. Rebuilt on lower ground after the earthquake of 1693, its three Baroque churches stand close together. Nearby is **Monterosso Almo** (691m), the highest and northernmost town of the province of Ragusa, and very ancient; it was a centre of the Sicels. In the large central piazza are the church of S. Giovanni Battista, attributed to Vincenzo Sinatra, and neo-classical palaces. Via Roma leads down to the Chiesa Madre, which has a neo-Gothic façade and inside a 12C stoup. Opposite is the church of S. Antonio Abate which has 16C paintings.

Vittoria

Vittoria (population 60,000) is a prosperous agricultural town (market garden produce and flowers), and centre of the wine trade, especially the famous *Cerasuolo di Vittoria*. It was named after the daughter of the viceroy Marcantonio Colonna in 1607. It is built to a rigid grid-style street plan on a plain overlooking the Ippari, a small river bordered by pine forests.

In the main square the elegant neo-classical **Opera House** (1869–77) stands next to the church of the **Madonna delle Grazie**, which has an attractive façade of 1754. The **Chiesa Madre**, with an unusual façade (18C–19C), contains paintings by the school of Pietro Novelli. There are a number of Art Nouveau palaces in the town, and Palazzo Traina is in the Venetian Gothic style.

Northwest of Vittoria is Acate (population 8400), known as Biscari up until 1938, surrounded by olive groves and vineyards, some of which produce excellent Chardonnay. In the central piazza Libertà, is the impressive 18C Castello dei Principi di Biscari and the Chiesa Madre, rebuilt in 1859. The Palio di S. Vincenzo is celebrated here after Easter.

DONNAFUGATA AND KAMARINA

In the southern part of the province of Ragusa is the elaborate 19C castle and garden of Donnafugata and the excavations of the **Greek city of Kamarina**. The southern part of the province also encompasses the southeastern coast of the island where there are many small coastal towns.

Practical information

 Getting there
By bus

Etna Trasporti (☎ 0932/623440) and *Tumino* (☎ 0932/623184) both have services from Ragusa railway station to **S. Croce Camerina**, and in summer to Kamarina. Donnafugata can only be reached by car.

By car

From Ragusa a provincial road leads south to S. Croce Camerina and Punta Secca. About 10km from Ragusa a sign-posted road leads to Donnafugata.

 Information office
APT Ragusa, ☎ 0932/221511.

 Where to stay
Hotels

SCOGLITTI (Vittoria): ☆☆☆ *Agathae*, 33 via Eugenio Montale, ☎ 0932/980730, 📠 0932/871500. ☆☆☆ *Mida*, lungomare riviera Gela, ☎ 0932/871430, 📠 0932/871589.
MARINA DI RAGUSA ☆☆☆ *Baia del Sole*, lungomare A. Doria, ☎ 0932/239844, 🖂 www.baiadelsole.it. ☆☆ *Miramare*, lungomare A. Doria, ☎ & 📠 0932/615966, 🖂 mirarg@tin.it. ☆☆☆ *Terracqua*, 35 via delle Sirene, ☎ 0932/61560, 📠 0932/615580, 🖂 www.framon-hotels.com.
MARINA DI ISPICA ☆☆☆ *Marispica*, via Zecchino, contrada S. Maria del Focallo, ☎ 0932/791111, 📠 0932/791106, 🖂 www.marispica.it. Well-organized holiday village near Pozzallo.

Farmhouse accommodation

SANTA CROCE CAMERINA *Al Casale*, contrada Cavalusi, ☎ 0932/664079, 664009, ✉ casale@ltsnet.it. Old-fashioned farm producing olive oil; very good food. Cattle and horses are raised. Close to Kamarina and to Santa Croce.

Campsites

SANTA CROCE CAMERINA ☆☆☆ *Baia dei Coralli*, punta Braccetto, ☎ 0932/918192, 🗐 0932/918282, ✉ www.baiadeicoralli.it. A holiday village by the sea; restaurants, shops and a pool.

☆☆ *Rocca dei Tramonti*, punta Braccetto, ☎ 0932/918054. By the sea.

☆ *Scarabeo*, punta Braccetto, ☎ 0932/918096, ✉ www.scarabeocamping.it.

Very pleasant, quite small, completely refurbished.

MARINA DI RAGUSA ☆☆☆ *Baia del Sole*, lungomare A.Doria, ☎ 0932/239844, 🗐 0932/230341.

POZZALLO ☆ *The King Reef*, contrada Scaro, ☎ 0932/957611.

Eating out

Restaurants

€€ *Ristorante Castello di Donnafugata*, ☎ 0932/619313. Next to the castle. Closed Tues.

€€ *Sakalleo*, 12 piazza Cavour, Scoglitti (Vittoria), ☎ 0932/871688. In the centre of the village. Fresh fish and good wine; the appetizers are very special. Closed Wed. in winter.

Castello di Donnafugata

A pretty byroad leads southwest from Ragusa through lovely countryside with numerous farms to the Castello di Donnafugata, acquired by the town council of Ragusa in 1982, restored by them and now open to the public daily (09.00–12.00, 15.00–18.00, closed Mon, ☎ 0932/619333).

On the site of a 17C building, the present castle was constructed by the politician Baron Corrado Arezzo De Spuches (1824–95). It is a large country villa, built in an eclectic style, with a Venetian Gothic loggia. Its delightful setting survives, with its farm surrounded by beautiful countryside. In the exotic **gardens** with splendid old ficus trees, are a stone maze entered over a miniature drawbridge guarded by a stone soldier, a coffee-house, a little neo-classical temple

Castello di Donnafugata

above a grotto and an amusing little chapel.

Many of the 122 rooms of the **castle** have been magnificently restored, the most interesting of which is the **Salone degli Specchi**, the contents of which include some paintings of the Neapolitan school and a spinet. The Donnafugata described in Lampedusa's book *Il Gattopardo* was near S. Margherita di Belice (see p 251).

Kamarina

The excavations of Kamarina are signposted from the little town of S. Croce Camerina, which has some Art Nouveau palaces. There are splendid celebrations for St Joseph on 19 March, with elaborate banquets and beautifully made loaves of ornamental bread prepared for the poor in the name of the saint. Near the sea are market gardens (many covered with plastic greenhouses) and ancient carob trees. The road passes several enclosures with excavations (if closed, usually unlocked on request at the museum) before reaching the **Regional Archaeological Museum** (open 09.00–14.00, 15.00–18.00, ☎ 0932/ 826002).

Kamarina was a Syracusan colony, founded c 598 BC, which suffered alternate sacking and repopulation by Gela, Syracuse and Carthage. It was finally destroyed by the Romans in 258 BC, but there are signs of occupation in the Republican and Imperial eras and of a late Arab Norman settlement.

The **museum** is housed in a restored 19C farmhouse built above the remains of a Temple of Athena. A room displays underwater finds made offshore where six shipwrecks have so far been identified. These include a Greek bronze helmet (4C BC), and objects from Punic and medieval boats. In 1991 a hoard of some 1000 bronze coins was found from the treasure chest of a Roman cargo ship which sank offshore in AD 275.

Outside in the courtyard, beneath a porch are sandstone sarcophagi and a circular stone tomb. Beyond, part of the temple's cella wall can be seen. Another building contains a plan of the site and explanatory diagrams, and Bronze Age finds from the area. Material from the 6C BC includes a beautiful Corinthian black-figure vase with a hunting scene. In another building the foundations of the temple, dating from the early 5C BC, have been exposed (it was re-used as a church in the Byzantine era). A room on two floors has a splendid display of amphorae (mostly Corinthian and Carthaginian), c 1000 of which were found in the oldest necropolis of Kamarina known as Rifriscolaro. The various excavated areas, overlooking the sea, include fragments of the walls, part of the street layout and houses with three or four rooms opening on to a courtyard (built after 405 BC) and part of the agora. A necropolis has yielded a great number of tombs (mostly dating from the early 6C). Traces of the port have been found on the River Hipparis. There are plans to unite the entire area of excavations in one enclosure.

The south coast between Kamarina and Pozzallo

On the coast to the north of Kamarina is Scoglitti, the resort of Vittoria (see p 303). It overlooks the Gulf of Gela, a long shallow bay whose beaches provided the chief landing-place for the American assault forces on 10 July 1943. The land, watered by several rivers, is now intensively cultivated with vegetables under frames in the winter, and also strawberries, olives, oranges, and vineyards.

Kaukana, a large harbour town mentioned by Procopius, where the fleet of Belisarius put in on the way to Africa, has been excavated (signposted) and is now an archaeological park near Punta Secca, a simple little resort on Capo Scalambri.

Marina di Ragusa is a resort which grew up in the 1950s, with palm trees along the seafront. A fast superstrada connects it to Ragusa. Oil is drilled offshore and piped from here to Augusta (see p 350). There are good views ahead of the coastline. The reedy sand-dunes around the mouth of the Irminio river near Playa Grande are now part of a nature reserve, where black-winged stilts and avocets nest.

Donnalucata is a pretty little resort (with an open fish market on the beach). Near Cava d'Aliga there is an unspoilt sandy bay. Inland the landscape is dotted with dark shady carob trees and hedges of prickly pear. Market garden produce is grown here together with olives and almonds. Among the characteristic low stone walls are some handsome country houses built of golden stone.

Marina di Modica is a little resort known for its fish restaurants.

Pozzallo (population 18,000) is a busy little port with a prominent square tower built in the 15C by the Cabreras to protect it from pirate raids (reconstructed after 1693). It was used as the loading point for shipping to various destinations the enormous quantities of wheat grown in the county. Now the area is acquiring importance for the production of carobs, while the harbour is increasingly used both for trade and tourism, and catamarans arrive from Malta daily, the year round (*Virtu Ferries*, 80, Via Studi, ☎ 0932/954062, ✉ www.virtuferries.com). The beaches here are hidden behind tree-covered dunes where cane fences control the sand. Some marshy areas have survived the drainage operations of the 1930s, and now form a wildlife reserve for the protection of migrating birds, known as the Pantani Longarini. It is usually possible to spot flamingoes, or black-winged stilts and avocets. To the east is Pachino on the southeastern tip of the island in the province of Syracuse, described on p 340.

Syracuse province

SYRACUSE

Siracusa, usually known as Syracuse in English, is the successor (population 140,000), of the once magnificent *Syracusae*, which rivalled Athens as the largest and most beautiful city of the Greek world. It was one of the most delightful cities of Europe when its centre was based on the lovely island of **Ortygia**, but after World War II the modern town expanded in a disorderly way onto the mainland, becoming increasingly more detached from the Ortygia district. At the same time the coastline was ruined by industrial plants and new buildings which polluted the sea to the north and south.

Although Ortygia suffered from depopulation up until a few years ago, there are at last signs that this beautiful and peaceful area of the town, which has many monuments of great interest, is again becoming the heart of the city, and it now has numerous good restaurants and a lively atmosphere in the evenings.

SIRACUSA PROVINCE

The principal ruins of the Greek city, including the famous theatre and splendid archaeological collection, survive in **Neapolis**, somewhat protected from the modern city by a park. Cicero noted that Syracuse knew no day without sun, and it has a mild marine climate throughout the year.

Practical information

Getting there
By train

Railway station (**map 2; 6**). Services operate via Catania and

Taormina to Messina (with some through trains to Rome, Milan or Turin); to Gela via Noto, Modica and Ragusa (a line which may be closed)

☎ 0931/69722, 0931/60980, 0931/69735.

By bus

The **city buses** tend to be infrequent but a few are useful to visitors.
No. **1 For the main archaeological zone of Neapolis**. Riva della Posta (Ortygia) • via corso Umberto • corso Gelone • viale Teracati. No. **4 For S. Giovanni and the Archaeological Museum**. Riva della Posta (Ortygia) • via corso Umberto • viale Cadorna • viale Teocrito. No. **2 For S. Lucia**. Riva della Posta (Ortygia) • via corso Umberto • via Agatocle • via Montegrappa. No. **11 For Castello Eurialo and Belvedere**. Every 40 minutes from Riva della Posta (Ortygia) • via corso Gelone.

Inter city buses run by *Interbus* from piazza della Posta (**map 1;1**), ☎ 0931/66710, daily to Catania, Palermo (in 3hrs 15mins), and to Palazzolo Acreide. Services run by *SAIS/Interbus* from piazza Marconi to Catania (in c 1hr), Catania airport, Palermo and Enna; to Noto (in c 1hr) and Pachino. Daily express service run by *SAIS/Interbus* (terminal at 28 via Trieste, ☎ 0931/66710) for Rome and many other mainland destinations, via Catania and Messina.

Parking

For the Neapolis archaeological zone, there is limited parking in viale Augusto (**map 2; 2**). For Ortygia, there are several places to park: there is a small car park in the middle of Ponte Umbertino (**map 1;1**), on the passeggio Adorno above the Foro Vittorio Emanuele II (**map 1; 3**), in the car park in front of the Grand Hotel, or on the lungomare di Levante (**map 1; 4**).

Car hire

Avis, 9 via dei Mille, ☎ 0931/22420; *Tirreno*, 75 via Tisia, ☎ 0931/442087.

Maritime services

Capitaneria di Porto, piazzale 4 Novembre. The main quay is at Molo Zanagora (**map 1; 3**) where trips round the harbour are organised.

Information offices

APT Siracusa, 45 via S. Sebastiano (**map 2; 2**; ☎ 0931/ 67710.
Azienda Autonoma (**map 1; 4**), 33 via Maestranza, Ortygia, ☎ 0931/65201.
Tourist Information Point in the old Market building on Ortygia, near Temple of Apollo, 2 via Trento (**map 1;1**), ☎ 0931/449201; there is also a good restaurant and pizzeria, bancomat, book shop, and bicycles to rent. **Syrako Tourist Point**, under Porta Marina (**map 1; 3**), has lots of information and can arrange walks on the old walls, ☎ 0931/24133.
Syracuse online:
✉ www.siracusa-sicilia.it.
✉ www.apt-siracusa.it.

Where to stay
Hotels

✫✫✫✫ *Grand Hotel*, 12 viale Mazzini (**map 1; 3**), first of the glorious historical hotels to be restored, ☎ 0931/464600, ▤ 0931/464611.
✫✫✫✫ *Holiday Inn* (**map 2; 2**), 30 viale Teracati, modern, near the Archaeological Park, ☎ 0931/440440 ▤ 0931/67115, ✉ www.holiday-inn.com/siracusaitaly.
✫✫✫✫ *Jolly* (**map 2; 6**), 45 corso Gelone, dependable, good restaurant, a little démodé, ☎ 0931/461111 ▤ 0931/461126.
✫✫✫✫ *Roma* (**map 1; 6**), 10 via Minerva, delightful, on Ortygia right next to the Cathedral, ☎ 0931/465626 ▤ 0931/465535.
✫✫✫✫ *Villa Politi* (**map 2 ; 4**), 2 via Politi, on the Latomy of the Capuchins, this was Winston Churchill's favourite, ☎ 0931/412121, ▤ 0931/36061.
✫✫✫ *Domus Mariae* (**map 1; 4**), 76 via Vittorio Veneto, the nuns who run it have turned part of their 15C convent

to good use, ☎ 0931/24854, 📠 0931/465565.

✧✧✧ *Gran Bretagna* (map 1; 3), 21 via Savoia; charming little hotel on Ortygia, beautifully restored, some rooms with 19C frescoes, plate glass floor in lounge reveals 16C Spanish bastions, ☎ 0931/68765.

✧✧✧ *Gutkowski* (map 1; 4), 26 lungomare di Levante, medieval palazzo on seaward side of Ortygia, a hotel for travellers of taste, ☎ 0931/465861 📠 0931/ 480505.

✧✧✧ *Posta* (map 1; 1), 33 via Trieste, in a pleasant quiet part of Ortygia near central Post Office, ☎ 0931/21819 📠 0931/61862, 🖳 www. hotelpostasiracusa.com.

✧✧ *Archimede* (map 2; 6), 67 via Francesco Crispi, close to railway station, ☎ 0931/462458.

✧ *Milano* (map 2; 7), 10 corso Umberto, basic accommodation close to Ortygia, ☎ 0931/66981.

Hotels outside the city

✧✧✧✧ *Caiammari* (in the countryside to the south), contrada Fanusa. Beautiful, restored villa, huge pool with waterfall, good restaurant, but considering the price category some bathrooms are a bit small, ☎ 0931/721217 📠 0931/722104.

✧ *Relax*, 159 viale Epipoli, ☎ 0931/740122, comfortable hotel with restaurant, pool and garden, outside the city on the road to the Castello Eurialo at Belvedere.

Bed and breakfast

Minerva (map 1; 6), 56/60 via Roma, ☎ 0931/22606. Excellent rooms; central position; English spoken.

Viaggiatori Viandanti e Sognatori (map 1; 6), 156 via Roma, ☎ & 📠 0931/24781 🖳 www.bebsicilia.it. Gorgeous view from rooftop terrace,

Artemide (map 1; 4), 9 via Vittorio Veneto, ☎ 0931/69005.

Abaco Home, ☎ 0931/61982,

0931/946657, 🖳 www. siracusahomecoming.it. Various apartments and rooms with breakfast on Ortygia.

Belvedere San Giacomo (map 1; 4), 111 via Maestranza, also cottages and flats, ☎ & 📠 0931/69005, 🖳 www. bedandbreakfastsicily.com.

Eurialo, 251 viale Epipoli, ☎ 0931/711459, 3398635931. Close to Belvedere and the Castello Eurialo.

Dolce Casa, 4 via Lido Sacramento, ☎ & 📠 0931/721135, 🖳 www.iblea2000. com/dolcecasa. Not far from town, a very comfortable villa with lovely garden.

Apartments to rent

Alla Giudecca, 52 via Alagona, ☎ & 📠 0931/22255, 🖳 www. siracusarentalhomes.com. A whole group of medieval houses, part of the Giudecca or Jewish Quarter, beautifully restored and transformed into little flats for short term rentals. During the restoration, a *miqva*, a spring for ceremonial ablutions, came to light; it is the oldest one in Europe and in perfect condition.

Farmhouse accommodation

Terrauzza sul Mare, contrada Terrauzza, ☎ & 📠 0931/66395, 🖳 www.terramar.it. Wheat farm, on Plemmyrion peninsula 10km from centre, apartments for self-catering, private rocky beach (very clean sea), courses in ceramics.

Il Limoneto (Adele Norcia), ☎ 0931/717352 (with restaurant), 9km from the centre, strada provinciale 14 maremonti.

Villa Lucia (Lucia Palermo), contrada Isola, walking distance from sea, ☎ 0931/721007 📠 0931/721587.

Campsites

The nearest site is the *Agriturist Rinaura*, 5km south of the town on SS 115, contrada Rinaura, ☎ 0931/721224. In summer sites are open on the coast to the south: *Fontane Bianche*, ☎ 0931/790333 and at Avola, *Sabbiadoro*, ☎ 0931/822415.

Eating out
Restaurants

€€€ *Le Terrazze del Grand Hotel*, 12 viale Mazzini ☎ 0931/464600. After a period of decline, this is once again the finest restaurant in the city, beautiful rooftop setting.

€€€ *Archimede*, 8 via Gemellaro, ☎ 0931/69701. Excellent fish dishes.

€€€ *Don Camillo*, 96 via Maestranza, ☎ 0931/67133. Superb pasta dishes.

€€ *La Foglia*, 39 via Capodieci, ☎ 0931/66233. Very unusual restaurant, principally vegetarian; the experience is rather like eating in someone's front parlour, hospitable owners but nothing matches—all odd crockery, tablecloths and cutlery; it should not be missed; superb grilled vegetables.

€€ *Le Baronie*, 24 via Gargallo, ☎ 0931/68884. Beautiful old Catalan building with courtyard, excellent cuisine; live music in the evenings.

€€ *Darsena da Jannuzzo*, 6 Riva Garibaldi, ☎ 0931/66104. On the harbour front; very good fish.

€€ *Il Cenacolo*, 9/10 via del Consiglio Reginale, ☎ 0931/65099. In one of Ortygia's most beautiful squares; Syracuse fish soup (unique); pizza is served also at lunchtime; Sicilian folk music in the evenings.

€€ *Minerva*, 20 piazza Duomo, ☎ 0931/69404. Lovely position, outside tables. Pizza available at lunchtime.

€ *Stop and Go* self service, close to catacombs and Paolo Orsi Museum, 3 via Mons. Baranzini, ☎ 0931/62245.

€ *Pasta e basta*, 37/41 via Costanza Bruno, ☎ 0931/30930; near Archimedes' tomb. Self-service and take away, inexpensive menu.

Cafés, pastry shops and ice cream parlours

Caffè La Piazza, and *Caffé del Duomo*, piazza Duomo, fashionable place for aperitifs, brunch on Sunday.

Marciante, 9 via Landolina, excellent pastries.

Caffè Minerva, 15 via Minerva, good coffee and snacks.

Bel Bon, 142 viale Zecchino, for an incredible assortment of ice cream, also served in crêpes or waffles.

Il Gelatiere, 66 corso Matteotti, lots of different flavours of ice cream and sorbet.

Bianca, 43 via Roma. Old-fashioned **bakery** for delicious bread, biscuits and snacks.

Picnics

On the sea front in Ortygia. In the environs, on the River Ciane or at Castello Eurialo. An old fashioned **grocers** at 123/A viale Teocrito, near catacombs, has good picnic food, and good wines.

Annual festivals

S. Lucia, 13 December, procession from the Cathedral to the church of S. Lucia; S. Lucia 'delle Quaglie' is celebrated on the first and second Sundays in May (commemorating a miracle of the saint which took place here in 1642). A traditional procession takes place on 8 December (**Immacolata**).

Entertainment

Classical drama festival in the Greek Theatre every May and June. The **Opera House** has been closed for restoration for many years. Concerts are held in the auditorium of S. Pietro al Carmine. The **puppet theatre** *Mauceri* is at 19, via Giudecca, ☎ & 🖷 0931/465540.

Handicrafts and souvenirs

There are many places in this city where craftsmen make paper by hand, using **papyrus** grown in the Ciane river, then local artists paint or draw on the paper, turning each piece into a work of art.

Il Bazar delle cose vecchie, 7 via

Consiglio Reginale, has beautiful and unusual curios, antiques, and authentic puppets. A little further along, at no.30, is *La Regina dei Quadri*, for paintings by local artists, oils and watercolours, also on papyrus.

Markets

La Fiera, a large general market is held on the outskirts of the town in via Algeri (north of **map 2; 4**, near the sea) on Wednesdays. A daily market (exc Sun) is held in the morning in Ortygia on the streets near the Temple of Apollo, around the former market building (**map 1; 3**). Fresh fish is sold here. There is another daily market (except Wed) at S. Panagia (north of **map 2; 2**).

Internet points

Adda Internet Centre, 12 via Garigliano, ☎ 0931/465311.
Internet Point, 22 via Maniace, ☎ 0931/30027.
Photografikamente, 7 viale Regina Margherita.

Proteus Computer, 12 via Ierone II, ☎ 0931/483078.
Planet Web Café, 5 via Cairoli, (10.00–02.00), ☎ 0931/60691.

Foreign language newspapers, phone cards and stamps

At the newsagent in piazza Duomo, the tobacconist at 45 via Roma, or by the Arethusa Fountain.

Sport and leisure
Beaches

Lido Maniace is on Ortygia, close to Castello Maniace, for sunbathing and swimming. Diving centre, salad bar, open day and night. There are plenty of lidos at Fontane Bianche, south of the city; bus nos 21 and 22 from the post office.

Diving centres

Pianeta Blu, 12 via Menfi, ☎ 0931/756236; *Siracusa Diving*, 13/15 strada Torre Milocca, ☎ 0931/490621.

History

At the height of its power ancient Syracuse was composed of five districts: **Ortygia**, an island linked to the mainland by a causeway c 550 BC, now occupied by the older part of modern Syracuse, which lies between the Great Harbour (640ha in area), extending south to the headland of Plemmyrion, and the Small Harbour to the north; **Achradina**, covering the area adjacent to the mainland; **Tyche**, named after a Temple of Fortune to the northeast of Achradina; **Neapolis** (new town), to the northwest of Achradina; and **Epipolae** (upper district), stretching to the outer defences, inland on the north and west. Ortygia was a fortified citadel; Achradina represented the commercial, maritime and administrative centre, and Neapolis the social centre; Tyche was a residential area, while Epipolae was sparsely populated. The ancient buildings were built of an oolitic limestone from the stone quarries (*latomiae*), now covered with luxuriant gardens.

This part of the Sicilian coast had a number of important Bronze Age sites. The Corinthian colony under Archias (734 BC), which drove out the Sicel (or perhaps Phoenician) inhabitants of Ortygia, increased so rapidly in power and wealth that, within a century of its foundation, it was able to found four sub-colonies at Akrai, Kasmenai, Eloro and Kamarina. Internal dissensions were put down by the firm government of Gelon, tyrant of Gela (c 485–478) who in 480, in alliance with Theron of Akragas, defeated the Carthaginians at Himera. Hieron I (478–c 467) helped the Cumaeans to overcome the

Etruscan fleet (474) and welcomed the poets Aeschylus, Pindar, Simonides and Bacchylides to his court; but Thrasybulus brought about his own downfall through misrule and a republic was established (466).

The increasing power of the republic aroused the jealousy of Athens, which despatched a hostile expedition (415) under Alcibiades and Nicias. Alcibiades was soon returned to Athens under political arrest, but escaped and deserted to Sparta. The Athenian operations were almost successful, as they tried to enclose the city within a double wall and blockade it by sea. But a reinforcement from Sparta led by Gylippus (despatched by the renegade Alcibiades), together with the courage of the Syracusans under Hermocrates and Athenagoras, saved the city. Athenian reinforcements under Demosthenes were themselves blockaded and their fleet destroyed in the Great Harbour. A frantic attempt to escape led in 413 to the final defeat of the Athenian army on the Assinaros, and those who survived were left to languish in the stone quarries unless, it is reported, they could recite Euripides.

In 405, Syracuse, again threatened by Carthage, was led by Dionysius the Elder, who built the Castello Eurialo, defeated Himilco (397), and made Syracuse the most powerful city of Sicily and sovereign of the Western Mediterranean. Under his less successful son Dionysius II (367–343) the Carthaginians again threatened the city, but it was saved from both tyrants and its enemies by the successful hero Timoleon of Corinth, who briefly re-established a democracy and died an ordinary citizen (336). Agathocles, a man of humble birth but strong personality, took power in 317, carried the war against Carthage into Africa (310), and left Syracuse once more in a position of hegemony. Pyrrhus, king of Epirus, liberated the city from a Carthaginian siege and on his departure from Sicily, left the whole island clear for Hieron II (276–215), who wisely allied himself with Rome. His successor, Hieronymus, reversed this policy, and the city fell to Marcellus after a two-year siege (c 214–212). The besiegers' task of sacking the town was aggravated by the ingenious inventions of Archimedes, who was killed while quietly pursuing his studies. The Roman booty included innumerable works of art which initiated the appreciation of classical art in Rome, and, according to Cato, were the earliest factors in the decline of the true Roman spirit. Under Roman occupation, Syracuse was governed both by the infamous Verres, who further despoiled it, and Cicero, the orator, assumed by the Sicilians to take their defence against him. St Paul stayed at Syracuse for three days on his way from Malta to Rhegium in the Alexandrian ship *Castor and Pollux* (Acts xxviii, 11–12).

After the Roman period, Syracuse's power declined rapidly, though the Emperor Constans II resided here in 662–68. It was destroyed by the Saracens in 878, and freed for a time by George Maniakes (1038–40), Basil II of Byzantium's general. The temporary importance Syracuse regained between 1361 and 1536 by holding the quasi-independent seat of the *Camera Reginale* or Queen's Chamber, a kind of miniature Parliament, did not last and in 1837, having rebelled unsuccessfully against the Bourbons, it even ceded its rights as a provincial capital to Noto for a time. After the conquest of Libya the port expanded again, and during World War II it was a target first for the Allied air forces, and, after its capture on 10 July 1943, for German aircraft.

Famous residents

The most famous Syracusans of ancient times, besides Archimedes (287–212), are Theocritus (fl. 270 BC), the father of idyllic poetry, and Moschus (fl. 200 BC), another pastoral poet. Plato visited the city in c 397, and probably returned several years later on the invitation of Dionysius II to advise him on how to rule his kingdom. Corax of Syracuse and his pupil Tisias founded the Greek art of rhetoric in the 5C. Elio Vittorini (1908–66), the writer, was born in Syracuse.

Ortygia

The beautiful island of Ortygia is joined to the mainland by two bridges. This charming old town, best explored on foot, has delightful streets of Baroque houses with pretty balconies and numerous trees. When the modern centre of Syracuse moved to the mainland, Ortygia faced serious problems of depopulation, but there have been signs in the last few years of a return here, and it is once more becoming a fashionable place to live. Numerous buildings are being restored and there are a great many characteristic restaurants, pubs and open-air cafés. Several hotels have also been reopened here in the last few years and it is certainly the nicest place to stay in Syracuse.

From **Ponte Umbertino** numerous small boats can be seen and part of the fishing fleet moored in the channel. The monumental Post Office by Francesco Fichera (1934) has an interesting interior with neo-classical and Art Nouveau decorations. Piazza Pancali with ficus trees leads to **largo XXV Luglio** (map 1; 3). The old covered **market place**, a fine building of 1889–1900, is now a Tourist Information Centre and a venue for exhibitions, and a daily market, where fresh fish is also sold, is held in the surrounding streets every morning. Nearby is a small area of interesting narrow streets, once the old *casbah* district, centred on **largo della Graziella**.

The remains of the **Temple of Apollo** (map 1; 3) are in largo XXV Luglio, surrounded by lawns, papyrus plants and palm trees. It is the earliest peripteral Doric temple in Sicily, built of local limestone in the late 7C BC and attributed to the architects Kleomenes, responsible for the project, and Epicleos, who designed the columns. Some scholars have identified it with the Artemision recorded by Cicero, but the inscription to Apollo cut in the steps of the stereobate seems conclusive. It was freed in 1938 from overlying structures, and two monolithic columns and part of the cella walls remain intact. Fragments of its polychrome terracotta cornice are preserved in the Regional Archaeological Museum.

Via Savoia leads to the waterfront overlooking the Porto Grande, near the elaborate Chamber of Commerce building. Here is the **Porta Marina** (map 1;3), a plain 15C gateway to the Great Harbour with a plaque in the Spanish Gothic style. The long promenade by the water's edge, planted with splendid ficus trees, called the **Foro Vittorio Emanuele II**, is known locally as the *Marina*. There is a lovely view across the harbour to the wooded shore on the headland of the ancient Plemmyrion. Within the gate to the left (in the street of the same name) is the attractive little church of **S. Maria dei Miracoli** (map 1;3; open evenings), with a fine doorway resting on little lions, with a sculptured lunette, and a worn tabernacle in the Gothic-Catalan style. The interior has a pretty 14C chancel,

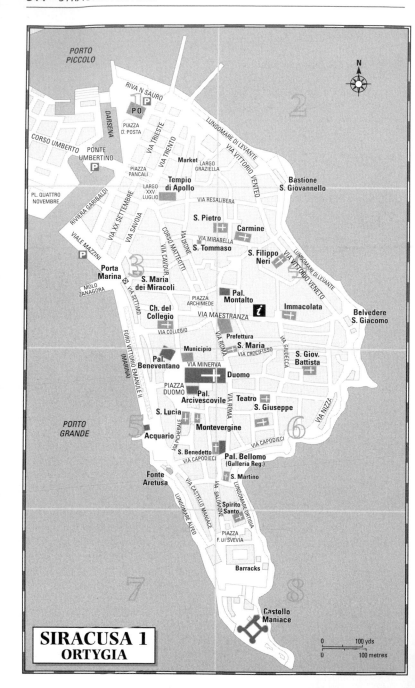

PORTO
PICCOLO

N

RIVA N SAURO

P.O.

DARSENA

PIAZZA
D. POSTA

VIA TRIESTE

LUNGOMARE DI LEVANTE

VIA VITTORIO VENETO

2

CORSO UMBERTO

PONTE
UMBERTINO

VIA TRENTO

Market

Largo
GRAZIELLA

Bastione
S. Giovannello

PIAZZA
PANCALI

PL. QUATTRO
NOVEMBRE

RIVIERA GARIBALDI

Largo
XXV
LUGLIO

Tempio
di Apollo

VIA RESALIBERA

VIALE MAZZINI

VIA XX SETTEMBRE

VIA SAVOIA

S. Pietro

Carmine

VIA MIRABELLA

S. Tommaso

S. Filippo
Neri

VIA VITTORIO VENETO

LUNGOMARE DI LEVANTE

Porta
Marina

MOLO
ZANAGORA

VIA SETTIMO

CORSO MATTEOTTI

VIA CAVOUR

VIA DIONE

S. Maria
dei Miracoli

PIAZZA
ARCHIMEDE

Pal.
Montalto

Immacolata

Belvedere
S. Giacomo

Ch. del
Collegio

VIA COLLEGIO

VIA MAESTRANZA

i

3

Prefettura

FORO VITTORIO EMANUELE II
(MARINA)

Municipio

VIA ROMA

S. Maria

VIA CROCIFISSO

S. Giov.
Battista

VIA GIUDECCA

PORTO
GRANDE

Pal.
Beneventano

VIA MINERVA

Duomo

PIAZZA
DUOMO

Pal.
Arcivescovile

Teatro

S. Giuseppe

VIA NIZZA

5

S. Lucia

Acquario

VIA PICHERALE

Montevergine

VIA CAPODIECI

6

VIA ROMA

S. Benedetto

VIA CAPODIECI

Pal. Bellomo
(Galleria Reg.)

Fonte
Aretusa

S. Martino

LUNGOMARE ORTIGIA

VIA CASTELLO MANIACE

VIA SALOMONE

Spirito
Santo

LUNGOMARE ALFEO

PIAZZA
F. DI SVEVIA

Barracks

7

8

Castello
Maniace

**SIRACUSA 1
ORTYGIA**

0   100 yds

0   100 metres

and a painting of *St Conrad the Hermit* attributed to Giovanni Maria Trevisano.

Ahead, via Ruggero Settimo emerges on a terrace above the trees of the marina, and via del Collegio leads away from the sea skirting the high walls of the **Chiesa del Collegio** with its Corinthian pilasters and overhanging cornice (1635–87), whose incomplete façade recalls that of the Gesù in Rome. The interior (closed for repairs) contains altars from the former Jesuit college in Palermo, moved here in 1927–31. The church faces via Cavour, off which parallel streets run down towards the sea.

To the right is **piazza del Duomo** (map 1;5), where there are some fine Baroque buildings: to the left the **Town Hall** occupies the former Seminary (begun in 1628 by Giovanni Vermexio). Under the building lie the remains of an Ionic temple which was probably never finished, and probably dedicated to Artemis, found in 1963. An ancient Sicel necropolis, with tombs hewn in the rock, was discovered a few years ago whilst the square was being repaved.

The Duomo

Across via Minerva is the Duomo (**map 1; 5,6**), S. Maria del Piliero or delle Colonne (closed 12.45–16.00)

> The Duomo was reconstructed by Bishop Zosimus in the 7C from the ruins of the Doric **Temple of Athene**, erected by Gelon in 480 BC to celebrate the victory of Himera. Work probably continued for 10 years, although some scholars think it took only two years to complete. The magnificence of the building and its works of art were famous throughout the Mediterranean, and the golden shield on the front which reflected the rays of the sun, was a landmark for sailors. The treasures were despoiled under Roman rule by the terrible proconsul Verres (see p 230).
>
> Under Byzantium it became a Christian church and the arches were cut in the wall of the Greek sanctuary. The Normans raised the height of the roof and added the side chapels, but it was damaged by the earthquake of 1542 and was again rebuilt after the earthquake of 1693 when the Norman façade fell. In via Minerva 12 columns of the splendid temple, with their architrave and triglyphs, punctuate the medieval north wall of the church, their cornice replaced by islamic battlements. Excavations beneath the cathedral carried out by Paolo Orsi in 1912–17 revealed details of an archaic temple, demolished to make way for the later temple, and, at a lower level, pre-Greek huts of the 8C BC.
>
> The present façade of the cathedral, a graceful Baroque composition erected between 1728 and 1754, was designed by Andrea Palma. The marble statues of **Sts Peter and Paul** flanking the steps are the earliest known works of Ignazio Marabitti; he also sculpted the statues (1754) on the façade. The entrance is through an elaborate vestibule.

The **interior** was stripped of its Baroque decoration between 1909 and 1927, reducing the **nave** arcades to the plain massive piers formed by opening eight arches in the side walls of the cella. The ceiling dates from 1518. The stained glass is by Eugenio Cisterna (1862–1933). The stoups are by Gaetano Puglisi (1802). On the west wall two columns from the opisthodomos of the cella are preserved, and 19 columns of the peristyle are incorporated in the aisles, those on the north side being engaged.

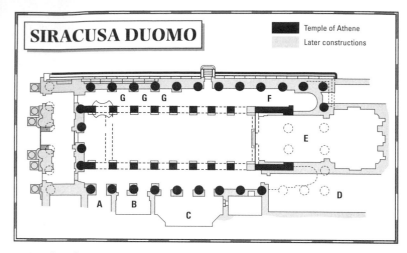

SIRACUSA DUOMO

■ Temple of Athene

Later constructions

G G G   F

E

A   B

C

D

South aisle. First chapel (**A**): is now used as a font. A 5C BC krater, carved from Paros marble, with a Greek inscription (found in the catacombs of S. Giovanni where it had been used as a burial urn), rests on seven miniature bronze lions (13C); on the wall are fragments of mosaics which survive from the earlier church. In the second chapel (**B**; 1711), closed by bronze gates, the work of Pietro Spagnuolo (1605), is a statue of *St Lucy* by Pietro Rizzo (1599; shown only on certain religious festivals and carried in procession on 13 December) and supported on a coffer attributed to Nibilio and Giuseppe Gagini, all of silver. The two marble medallions are attributed to Ignazio Marabitti. The third chapel (**C**), closed by wrought iron gates (1811), was designed in 1650–53, probably by Giovanni Vermexio. The frescoes in the vault are by Agostino Scilla (1657). The altar frontal bears a beautiful relief of the *Last Supper* by Filippo della Valle (1762). Above is a ciborium by Luigi Vanvitelli (1752).

At the end of the aisle, in the **Cappella del Crocifisso** (**D**), is a painting of *St Zosimus* attributed to Antonello da Messina, and a fine painting of the seated *St Marcian*, by an early 16C painter. In the sanctuary is a Byzantine Cross and 13 panels from a polyptych by the school of Antonello. Other works of art which are to be exhibited here include two paintings by Marco di Costanzo (*St Jerome and the Annunciation*).

The bronze candelabra in the chancel (**E**) date from 1513, while the splendid **High Altar** is the work of Giovanni Vermexio (1659). It incorporates a monolith originating from the temple of Athene. The two paintings over the choir, of *St Paul preaching to the Christians of Syracuse* and *St Peter sending Marcian to be Bishop of Syracuse*, are fairly recent, the work of Silvio Galimberti. In the Byzantine apse (**F**) of the north aisle is a *Madonna of the Snow* by Antonello Gagini.

The end of the pronaos wall of the temple with its column can be seen here. The noticeable irregularity of the pillars is due to the earthquake of 1542. In the north aisle (**G**) are three statues with fine bases: *St Lucy* by Antonello Gagini; *Madonna and Child* by Domenico Gagini; and *St Catherine of Alexandria* by the Gagini school.

Forming part of the **Archbishop's Palace** (Palazzo Arcivescovile) is the **Biblioteca Alagoniana**(Alagonian Library, not open regularly to the public; 13C Greek, Latin and Arabic manuscripts, ☎ 0931/67968, 0931/60248), which has a pretty hanging garden with palm trees. Archbishop Alagona who founded the library in 1780, loved books so much that he excommunicated anyone caught stealing them.

On the other side of the piazza, opposite the town hall, is **Palazzo Beneventano del Bosco**, a fine building by the local architect Luciano Alì (1778–88). It has a particularly attractive courtyard. Next to it is the curved, pink façade of Palazzo Gaetani e Arezzo, and, beyond, the building of the *Soprintendenza ai Beni Culturali e Ambientali* which used to house the Archaeological Museum (see below), and now contains one of the finest coin collections in the world (to see the collection call at least the day before for security reasons, ☎ 0931/481111, open Mon–Fri 09.30–13.00, Wed also 15.30–17.30). At the end of the piazza, with a balcony on the corner, is Palazzo Impellizzeri and the church of **S. Lucia alla Badia**, which has a lovely façade begun c 1695, probably by Luciano Caracciolo (the upper storey was added in the mid-18C). Just out of the piazza is the church of Montevergine (closed) with a façade by Andrea Vermexio.

From the piazza via Picherale, passing the former Hotel des Etrangers (soon to reopen), which incorporates part of the medieval Casa Migliaccio, leads down to a charming terrace in a quiet spot on the waterfront surrounding the **Fonte Aretusa**(Arethusa Fountain, **map 1; 5**), which was one of the most famous fountains of the Hellenic world. The spring of the water nymph Arethusa was celebrated by Pindar and Virgil. It now flows into a pond (built in 1843), planted with papyrus, abounding in fish and inhabited by ducks, under a splendid old ficus tree.

Myth relates that when Arethusa was bathing in the River Alpheus near Olympia the river god fell in love with her. To escape from him she plunged into the Ionian sea and is supposed to have reappeared here. Although the goddess Artemis transformed her into a spring, Alpheus pursued her and mingled his river water with that of the spring (in ancient times it was believed that the river in the Peloponnesus was connected, via the sea, to the fountain of Arethusa). A freshwater spring, called the *Occhio della Zillica*, still wells up in the harbour.

The spring of Arethusa diminished after the erection of the Spanish fortifications, and was mixed with salt water after an earthquake. Nelson claimed to have watered his fleet here before the battle of the Nile. The attractive seafront with its magnificent shady *Ficus benjamin* trees, is the favourite spot for the *passeggiata*.

The end of the promontory, beyond piazza Federico di Svevia with its barracks, has been closed to the public. **Castello Maniace (map 1; 6)** now belongs to the town council and is in need of restoration. Visitors are only admitted with special permission at present (ask at the Syraka Information Centre at Porta Marina), although it is planned to open it to the public soon. The castle was built c 1232 by Frederick II but named after George Maniakes, supposed (in error) to be its founder. The keep, c 51 sq m, with cylindrical corner towers, has probably lost a third of its original height. On either side of the imposing Swabian doorway are two consoles, formerly bearing splendid bronze rams, one of which is now in the Regional

Archaeological Museum in Palermo. Overlooking the harbour are the remains of a large three-light window. Beneath the castle is the so-called Bagno della Regina (unlit staircase), an underground chamber which was probably a reservoir.

Via Salomone and via S. Martino return past (right) the church of **S. Martino**, founded in the 6C, with a doorway of 1338. The interior, dating from Byzantine times, contains a fine triptych by a local 15C master.

3C bronze ram from Castello Maniace, now in the Museo Archeologico, Palermo

At the end of the street (left) stands the church of **S. Benedetto** (under repair), with a huge canvas of the *Ecstasy of St Benedict* by Mario Minniti, a local painter. Adjacent is Palazzo Bellomo (**map 1;6**), and the Regional Gallery.

The Regional Gallery

The Galleria Regionale is appropriately housed in a building combining elements of its Swabian construction (c 1234) with alterations of the 15C. The collection is well displayed and labelled (open daily 09.00–13.30, Sat also 15.00–19.00, Mon closed, ☎ 0931/69511). The **vestibule**, now used for exhibitions, has a crossed vault with keystones bearing the eagle, symbol of Frederick II. A polychrome marble and glass inlaid panel with two lions and a palm tree dating from the 12C is displayed here. The staircase in the courtyard is a good example of the Catalan style; a second court with two palm trees, to the north, containing offices, formed part of the Benedictine monastery and dates from 1365. The walls are covered with 15C–18C coats of arms. The collection of **sculpture** is displayed on the **ground floor**. Room 1 (right) contains sculptural fragments including Byzantine fragments (7C–9C). **Room 2** (right; sometimes closed), contains a fragment of a portal (11C–12C); a charming 14C altarpiece of the *Annunciation*, *Adoration of the Magi* and the *Crucifixion*, and an 11C stoup. In **room 3** (off the left side of the courtyard), is the tomb of Giovanni Cardinas, perhaps by Antonello Gagini; a monument to Eleonora Branciforte (1525) by Giovanni Battista Mazzola; the *Madonna of the Goldfinch*, attributed to Domenico Gagini; a carved tomb slab of Giovanni Cabastida (d. 1472) and other interesting sculptures. In the loggia behind are two carriages (17C and 18C).

An attractive outside staircase leads up to the **first floor** and the **Picture Gallery**. Room 5 (to the right) contains a beautiful *Annunciation* (1474) by Antonello da Messina, brought from Palazzolo Acreide, and transferred to canvas; Pedro Serra (attrib.; 14C), *Madonna and Child enthroned with saints*. In **room 6** (left) is the *Burial of St Lucy*, a superb work by Caravaggio (1608), from S. Lucia (see below); *Madonna* and three panels by Lazzaro Bastiani; Master of the Retable of St Lawrence (early 15C), *St Lawrence and stories of his life*. **Room 7** incorporates a pretty window of the palace, and displays 16C works including Marco di Costanzo's *Trinity and saints* (attributed; c 1496), and a tiny illuminated *Book of Hours* by the Flemish school. **Rooms 8** and **9** display more 16C works, including an album of drawings by Filippo Paladino (c 1544–1614) and an *Immacolata* by Guglielmo Borremans.

A charming collection of **Sicilian decorative arts** is displayed in **rooms 10–17**. This includes 18C statuettes, marble intarsia panels and ecclesiastical objects. In **room 10** is a silver reliquary in the form of a ship (*navicella*) of St Orsola (1785). The other rooms contain Sicilian *presepio* (crib) figures including a crib by Emanuele Moscuzza (1806–58), church vestments, 18C costumes, furniture and 19C terracotta figurines by Bongiovanni Vaccaro. Old plans of Syracuse are displayed in the last room.

Via Roma (**map 1;6**), with delightful overhanging balconies, leads away from the sea front (there is a pretty palace on the corner) north past the Opera House (which is being restored). On the corner of via Crocifisso is the church of **S. Maria della Concezione** (1651) which has a fine interior with a tiled floor. On the vault is a fresco by Sebastiano Lo Monaco, and the altarpieces on the north side and on the first south altar are by Onofrio Gabrielli. Its former monastery is being restored.

Piazza Archimede (**map 1; 3**) was laid out between 1872 and 1878 in the centre of Ortygia, where there is a fountain by Giulio Moschetti. Palazzo Lanza is on the south side and the courtyard of the Banca d'Italia on the west side preserves medieval elements. Off the square, reached by via Montalto, is the façade of **Palazzo Montalto** (**map 1;4**) in the Gothic Chiaramonte style of 1397; it has been propped up with concrete bastions. From the car park behind, the shell of the building is visible, with a fine loggia.

The interesting via Maestranza leads east from the square towards the sea, past several Baroque palaces and the church of the **Immaculate Virgin** (or S. Francesco; **map 1;4**) with an attractive little convex façade. It has a fine late 18C interior, with 12 small paintings of the apostles in the apse. On either side of the pretty Baroque east end two Gothic portals have been exposed. A narrow street called **Giudecca** recalls the Jewish district of the city. At no. 110 via Maestranza is the 18C Palazzo Rizza. Last turning on the right is Via Alagona, where at no. 41 you will find Palazzo Cordaci which houses Sicily's only Museum of Cinema. Besides a vast library of books about cinema and theatre, there is a collection of more than 2600 films. Cameras and posters going back to the early days of cinema are also on view. Visits can be booked online through ■ www.cinemuseum.it. Via Vittorio Veneto, lined with smaller 17C–18C Spanish palaces continues left. It emerges on the sea by the church of **S. Filippo Neri** (**map 1;4**) which bears the lizard symbol and signature of the architect Vermexio next to the fine restored Gothic **Palazzo Interlandi**, a convent. Ring here and the nuns will open the church for viewing. You can see the Bastione S. Giovannello from here.

Via Mirabella (with Palazzo Bongiovanni on the corner) leads away from the seafront past the Carmine which preserves part of its 14C structure. Opposite the former church of the **Ritiro**, with a façade attributed to Pompeo Picherali (c 1720), is being restored. Nearby is the church of **S. Pietro** (open only for concerts), a small aisled basilica founded in the 4C–5C, and altered in Byzantine times. It preserves a fine Gothic doorway. Via Vittorio Veneto ends near the post office and the bridges which lead back to the mainland.

The mainland: Achradina and Tyche

The buildings of interest described below are widely scattered around the uninspiring modern town; to cover the distances between them a bus is recommended where possible (listed above).

The area on the mainland adjoining Ortygia corresponds to the ancient **Achradina**. Northeast of Achradina is **Tyche** where the Regional Archaeological Museum is situated (described below).

From piazza Pancali buses run across the bridge along corso Umberto to the **Foro Siracusano** (map 2; 6), a large and busy square with a Pantheon war memorial (1936), and fine trees. Here are some remains of the ancient **Agora**; recent excavations have revealed other parts of the Agora near corso Umberto and corso Gelone where dwellings of the late 8C BC have also come to light, the earliest of the Greek period so far found in Syracuse.

From piazza Marconi, via Crispi forks right to the station, while via Elorina (left) leads to the so-called **Ginnasio Romano** (map 2; 6: usually closed), a complex ruin surrounded by lawns and palm trees. A portico surrounded on three sides, an altar, a temple and a small theatre. The portico on the north side, and part of the high temple podium remain. The theatre's orchestra is now under water, but a few of the lower steps of the cavea are visible. The buildings, all of Imperial date, probably formed part of a *serapeum*, a Roman temple dedicated to Serapis.

On the opposite side of piazza Marconi is the Foro Siracusano; the viale Diaz leads off it towards borgo S. Lucia. On the left are two excavated sites, the first (straddled by a brown modern block of flats) includes a small bath house of Roman origin, possibly the **Baths of Daphne** in which the Emperor Constans II was assassinated in 668. The second, just beyond, behind railings, marks the **Arsenale Antico**, where the foundations can be seen of the mechanism used by the Greeks to drag their ships into dry dock. In a simple house at no. 11 in via degli Orti di S. Giorgio, a figure of the Virgin is supposed to have wept in 1953 (plaque in piazza Euripide; the sanctuary of the Madonna delle Lacrime is described below). The long, narrow riviera Dionisio il Grande continues north, seaward of the railway, through the district of S. Lucia.

A long way northeast (bus no. 2) is the large piazza, surrounded by an avenue of ficus trees, in front of the church of **S. Lucia** (map 2; 3). The façade, which collapsed without warning in the 20C, has been faithfully reconstructed. It was begun in 1629 on a plan by Giovanni Vermexio, and completed in the 18C (perhaps by Rosario Gagliardi), on the spot where St Lucy (?281–304), patron saint of Syracuse, was buried. The portal, the apses and the base of the campanile are Norman work and the rose window is of the 14C. Outside is the chapel of S. Sepolcro (see below), which has a pretty exterior.

Inside the church, in a chapel off the left side, are two ancient *Crucifixes* (one T-shaped). A superb painting of the *Burial of St Lucy* by Caravaggio, which belongs to the church, is displayed in the Regional Gallery (see above).

A tunnel from the church leads past the entrance to the **catacombs**, which are closed indefinitely. These are the oldest in Sicily and the most extensive in existence, after those in Rome. Caverns in the limestone existed here before the Christian era; there are Christian remains of the 2C and fragmentary Byzantine paintings. The tunnel emerges in **S. Sepolcro**, a domed octagonal chapel by

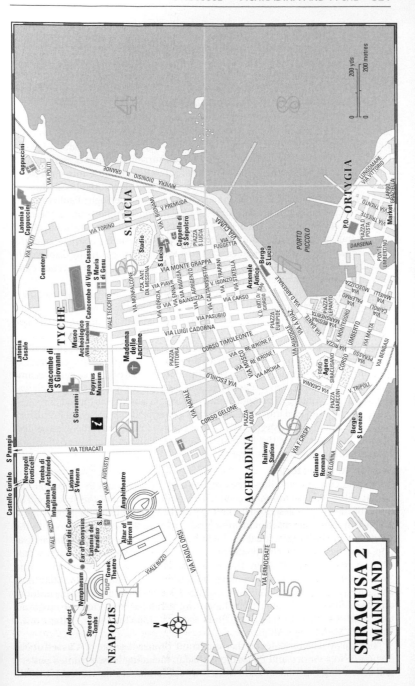

SIRACUSA 2
MAINLAND

200 yds
200 metres

NEAPOLIS

Aqueduct
Street of Tombs
Nymphaeum
Greek Theatre
Grotta dei Cordari
Ear of Dionysius
Latomia del Paradise
Altar of Hieron II
Amphitheatre
S. Nicolò

Castello Eurialo
S Panagia
Necropoli Grotticelli
Tomba di Archimede
Latomia Intagliatella
Latomia S Venera

Catacombe di S Giovanni
S Giovanni
Papyrus Museum
Museo Archeologico (Villa Landolina)
Catacombe di Vigna Cassia
S Maria di Gesù
Madonna delle Lacrime

TYCHE

Latomia Casale
Latomia d Cappuccini
Cappuccini
Cemetery

S. LUCIA

Stadio
S Lucia
Cappella di S Sepolcro
Borgo S Lucia
Arsenale Antico

ACHRADINA

Railway Station
Gimnasio Romano
Foro
Agora
Borgo S Lorenzo

ORTYGIA
PO.
Market
DARSENA
PORTO PICCOLO

VIALE RIZZO
VIALE AUGUSTO
VIA TERACATI
VIA TEOCRITO
VIA PAOLO ORSI
VIALE RIZZO
VIA RIZZO
VIA POLITI
VIA POLITI
VIA TORINO
VIA MONFALCONE
VIA MONTE GRAPPA
VIA PIAVE
VIA ENNA
VIA GORIZIA
VIA RAGUSA
VIA BAINSIZZA
VIA CALTANISSETTA
VIA ISONZO
VIA TRAPANI
VIA STATELLA
VIA CARSO
VIA PASUBIO
VIA LUIGI CADORNA
CORSO TIMOLEONTE
V.D. ORTI DI S.GIORGIO
PIAZZA EURIPIDE
VIA MISCO
VIA RE IERONE II
VIA RE IERONE I
VIA ARCHIA
PIAZZA VITTORIA
VIA ESCHILO
VIA NATALE
CORSO GELONE
PIAZZA ADDA
VIA F CRISPI
VIA AGATOCLE
VIA F. ELORINA
VIA ERMOCRATE
VIA CATANIA
VIA DANTE
CORSO UMBERTO
PIAZZA MARCONI
V. TRIPOLI
PIAZZA SIRACUSANO
VIA PICIZZA
PTE MONTEDORO
VIA MALTA
VIA REGINA MARGHERITA
VIA BENGASI
VIA PERASSO
VIA TASSO
VIA MOSCUZZA
VIA MAIELLI
VIA PALERMO
VIA CAIROLI
VIA MESSINA
PZA ANT DI MESSINA
V. BIGNAMI
V PREMUDA
VIA LUCIA
VIA FUGGETTA
PIAZZA S LUCIA
VIA D ARSENALE
RIVIERA DIONISIO IL GRANDE
VIA VITTORIO
LUNGOMARE
LARGO GRAZIELLA
VIA TRENTO
VIA TRIESTE
PIAZZA D. POSTA
PONTE UMBERTINO
CASTELLO MANIACE

N

Giovanni Vermexio, partly below ground. This was the burial place of St Lucy and from here her body was taken to Constantinople in 1038 (the empty tomb remains behind the altar). The 17C statue of the saint is by Tedeschi; a 16C silver statue by Pietro Rizzo is kept locked in the Duomo (but displayed here for eight days in December).

Paolo Orsi Regional Archaeological Museum

The area of the city immediately to the north of Achradina corresponds to ancient **Tyche**. About 500m northwest of the church of S. Lucia, on viale Teocrito (bus no. 4 from Ortygia via corso Gelone), is the park of **Villa Landolina**, set in a small stone quarry which surrounds the modern building (opened in 1988). Here the **Museo Archeologico Regionale Paolo Orsi** (open Tues–Sat 09.00–14.00, 15.00–17.00, Sun & PH 09.00–14.00, closed Mon, ☎ 0931/464022; **map 2;2,3**) is dedicated to the great archaeologist Paolo Orsi, the director of the collection from 1895–1934. The museum has one of the most interesting archaeological collections in Italy, especially representative of the eastern half of Sicily, and is among the finest museums in Europe. The material from excavations made by Paolo Orsi is outstanding. It is beautifully displayed in a handsome functional building designed by Franco Minissi in 1967. When complete, the displays will occupy two floors and 9000 sq metres.

The garden, with splendid trees and some antique remains, was used as a Protestant cemetery. Among the 19C British and American tombstones (reached by the upper path which encircles the garden) is that of August von Platen (1796–1835), the German poet.

Beyond the entrance hall the centre of the building has a display illustrating the history of the museum. The Civic Museum of Syracuse, which opened in 1811 under the supervision of the wealthy aristocrat Saverio Landolina, became a national museum in 1878. Paolo Orsi was director of the collection which was displayed in a building in piazza Duomo on Ortygia until it was moved here.

The display is divided into three sections: Geology, Paleontology and Prehistory (A), Greek colonies in Eastern Sicily (B), and sub-colonies and Hellenized centres (C). On the upper floor the Hellenistic, Roman, Paleochristian, Christian and Medieval material is to be displayed.

Section A: prehistory

An introductory display illustrates the geology of Sicily, and in particular the region of the Hyblean Mountains which form the backbone of the province. The fauna of the island is described including dwarf elephants (with their fossil bones and two models). The strictly chronological display in this section begins with the **neolithic period**, represented by the **Stentinello** culture, an agrarian civilisation, characterised by fortified villages and the use of impressed pottery. It is particularly well represented on the east side of the island around Etna and Syracuse. Four moated villages have been identified at Stentinello, Matrensa, Megara Hyblaea and Ognina. Plain, unglazed pottery with impressed decoration, and tools made of obsidian from Lipari are exhibited from **case 14** onwards. **Cases 38–44** have Bronze Age finds from S. Ippolito (near Caltagirone), Valsavoia, Messina and Milazzo.

The display which relates to the important Bronze Age site of **Castelluccio** (between Noto Antica and Palazzolo Acreide), including brown painted pottery and interesting carved door slabs from rock-cut tombs, begins with **case 45**. The pottery reveals trading links with Egypt and the Aegean, and shows Minoan-Mycenaean influences.

A ramp leads up to **cases 61–81** with Middle Bronze Age material from **Thapsos** on the Magnisi peninsula. The necropolis was excavated by Paolo Orsi, but the inhabited area (1500–900 BC) has only recently been excavated. Finds include imported pottery (from Mycenae, Cyprus and Malta) and a splendid display of large storage jars. There are also some fascinating *lebetes*, water bowls with a pedestal underneath and a strange upright back, perhaps recalling a divinity who protected water? They had handles behind, so they could be carried from one place to another. Material from other coastal settlements of the Thapsos culture are also exhibited.

Cases 82–89 Material from **Pantalica**, the most important Late Bronze Age site in Sicily, which was naturally defended. This seems to have been inhabited by the Sicels who are thought to have migrated here from the Italian peninsula c 1700 BC, and whose culture remained virtually unchanged until the arrival of the Greeks. There is a splendid display of the characteristic red vases, made this time by using a potter's wheel, and some of them (the heart-shaped jugs for carrying water) reminiscent of Mycenaean ware, with shiny glaze, and numerous bronze artefacts.

Other centres of this date are illustrated, including material from the necropolis of Madonna del Piano at Grammichele (the tombs have been reconstructed), and (**cases 112–125**) bronzes from Mendolito near Adrano. The finds from the Marcellino valley near Villasmundo (**cases 131–135**) include interesting pottery; the examples of imported Greek ware represent the earliest known examples (8C BC) so far found on the island. The last cases (**136** and **137**) in this section contain finds from Polizzello and **S. Angelo Muxaro**, with local and imported pottery.

Section B: Greek colonisation

This period begins in the mid-8C when colonists from Corinth, Rhodes, Crete and the Chalcides arrive on the island. With the defeat of Carthage at Himera in 480 BC Greek supremacy in the Mediterranean was established, and the great victory over Athens at Syracuse in 413 BC symbolised the importance Sicily attained in the Greek world. Finds are displayed from the earliest Greek colonies on the island: **Naxos**, founded c 734 BC (**cases 138–140**), Mylai, Zancle and Katane. The finds from **Lentini** include a fine *kouros* (late 6C BC), the head of which is probably in the Civic Museum of Catania. A large section is dedicated to **Megara Hyblaea**. The pottery includes imported Greek ware and local products. The highly interesting archaic sculpture includes a Greek marble statue (c 560–550 BC), thought to be a funerary monument, with an inscription on the leg naming the physician Sambrotidas, son of Mandrokles, and a headless statue made from local limestone of a mother goddess suckling twins (mid-6C BC), smashed into more than 900 pieces by workers building the oil refineries for fear of having the work stopped and their hopes of employment dashed. The head was lost in antiquity.

It is now necessary to go out into the central rotonda and re-enter the pavilion (still Section B) beside the splendid headless statue of *Venus Anadyomene*. This is an Imperial Roman adaption of a Hellenistic original of the 2C BC, remarkable for its anatomical perfection. It was found in Syracuse in 1804 by the aristocrat Saverio Landolina, and greatly admired by Guy de Maupassant when he visited Syracuse in 1885 (he left a vivid description of it). The section dedicated to

Syracuse begins here. Finds from **Ortygia** are arranged topographically, and include material from recent excavations in piazza della Vittoria (**case 226**), where a sanctuary of Demeter and Kore of the late 5C and early 4C BC has been found. There are hundreds of votive statuettes and a polychrome bust in terracotta (**case 185**). Numerous pottery types are displayed. Finds from necropoli near Syracuse include those from the Fusco district, with proto-Corinthian ware (725–700 BC) and a fine bronze statuette of a horse, in the geometric style (**case 188**; late 8C BC). Models of the Temples of Apollo and Athena have been reconstructed and terracotta fragments from them are exhibited. The frieze of seven lion-faced gargoyles comes from the Temple of Athena. The stunning marble relief of the running Gorgon was part of its acroterion. The display of finds from sanctuaries outside the urban area include an archaic limestone head from Laganello (near the Ciane spring).

Section C: sub-colonies and Hellenised centres

To enter section C, go out into the central rotonda and back towards the entrance. The display begins with material from **Eloro** (**case 226**), including votive terracottas. Finds from **Akrai** include statues, one of a female deity, and another of a male figure enthroned (7C–6C BC). **Kasmenai** is represented by a high-relief in limestone of Kore holding a dove (570–560 BC), and ex-votos. The finds from **Kamarina** include a horse and rider (6C BC), used as part of the roof decoration of a temple. A marble torso by a Greek artist (c 500 BC) and a terracotta goddess enthroned (late 6C BC) come from **Grammichele**. There are numerous examples of local pottery and imported Greek ware. A votive deposit found recently at **Francavilla di Sicilia** includes a remarkable series of recently discovered *pinakes*, reliefs in terracotta (470–460 BC), which previously had only been found at the sanctuary of Persephone at Locri, in Calabria. A lovely little clay miniature altar bears a relief of the 6C BC showing a lion attacking a bull (**case 280**) from **Centuripe**. The bronze statuette (**case 281**) known as the *Ephebus of Mendolito* from Adrano dates from c 460 BC.

The last section is devoted to Gela and Agrigento. Finds from **Gela** include architectural terracottas, cinerary urns and sarcophagi. The vases from Gela, include (**case 297**) a wine jar signed by Polygnotus (440 BC); part of a cup signed by Chachyrylion (520–510 BC); lekythoi depicting the struggle of Thetis and Peleus and of Aeneas with Anchises (black-figured; 6C); lekythos with a Nike, signed by Douris (470–460 BC); a bronze dish with relief of horses (from the necropolis at Gela, 7C BC). Also, a fragment by the 'Painter of Panaitos', and fine bronze kraters. The finds from **Agrigento** (mostly made by Paolo Orsi) include votive terracottas and busts of Demeter and Kore. Three rare wooden statuettes of archaic type dating from the late 7C BC, were found by a sacred spring at Palma di Montechiaro (**case 309**).

To the south is the vast circular sanctuary of the **Madonnina delle Lacrime** (Our Lady of Tears), begun in 1970 to enshrine a miraculous little mass-produced plaster image of the Madonna, and inaugurated in 1994. This figure is supposed to have wept for four days in 1953 in a house in Achradina (see above). The church (by Michael Andrault and Pierre Parat), where the miraculous image is preserved, incorporates some remains of Greek dwellings. The huge conical spire (98m high, including the statue) towers above the buildings of the city. The irreverent say it looks rather like a lemon squeezer with an egg beater on the top. In the crypt below, typical of pilgrimage shrines, are numerous ex-votos.

Adjoining it to the south, in **piazza della Vittoria**, extensive excavations begun in 1973 during the construction of the church of the Madonnina delle Lacrime have revealed a group of Hellenistic and Roman houses, a Sanctuary of Demeter and Kore (late 5C BC or early 4C BC), and a monumental fountain of the 5C BC. These are visible from outside the fence. Five thousand votive statuettes of terracotta were found here, some of them are now exhibited in the Regional Archaeological Museum (see above).

Church and Catacombs of San Giovanni

Off viale Teocrito, just to the northwest of the Archaeological Museum, via S. Giovanni leads right. Here, amidst modern buildings, are the ruined church and catacombs of S. Giovanni (**map 2; 2**; open 09.00–12.30, 14.30–16.30 or 17.30 in summer, closed Mon, ☎ 0931/36456, ✉ www.kalosnet.it). The façade is preceded by three arches constructed of medieval fragments. To the right is the entrance and ticket office, beyond which is the entrance (right) to the **catacombs** and (left) to the ruined church and crypt. The catacombs were probably in use from the 3C to the end of the 6C. They are among the most interesting and extensive in Italy outside Rome: there are thousands of loculi. From the *decumanus maximus*, or principal gallery, adapted from a disused Greek aqueduct, smaller passages lead to five domed circular chapels, one with the rock-cut tombs of seven nuns, members of one of the first religious houses established after the persecutions in Syracuse, and one containing a sarcophagus bearing a Greek inscription.

On the left of the entrance, a little garden with palms and cacti and flowering shrubs now occupies the ruins of the roofless **church** which was built into the western portion of an old basilica. It was reconstructed by the Normans in 1200, and reduced to ruins in 1693 by an earthquake. A fine 14C rose window survives, as well as its 7C apse.

Steps lead down to the **crypt**, in the form of a Greek cross, with three apses, the site of the martyrdom of St Marcian (c 254 AD): the sanctuary was transformed into a basilica at the end of the 6C or the beginning of the 7C and was probably destroyed by the Arabs in 878. The visible remains (which include faded frescoes) date from a Norman reconstruction. The fine Byzantine capitals, with symbols of the Evangelists, are thought to have been reused from the earlier basilica. In one apse are traces of 4C and 5C frescoes from a hypogeum. The column against which the saint was martyred (he was flogged to death), and his tomb, surrounded by some of the earliest catacombs, can be seen. An altar is said to mark the site of St Paul's preaching in Syracuse.

The **Latomia Casale** (no admission), a few minutes north of S. Giovanni, has luxuriant vegetation. To the east of Villa Landolina (**map 2;3**) is the **Vigna Cassia** with 3C catacombs, which may be visited with permission (for information ☎ 0931/36456).

To the northeast, near the sea (bus no. 4 from corso Umberto) is the **Latomia dei Cappuccini** (**map 2; 3**), to the right of the former Capuchin convent. This quarry has been closed indefinitely because of landslides, but can be seen in part from the road outside. One of the most extensive of the ancient quarries (see below), it is now overgrown by plants and trees. Adjacent is the Villa Politi, the hotel where Churchill stayed on his holidays in Syracuse. From piazza dei Cappuccini, in front of the 17C church, is a view of Ortygia.

Viale Teocrito crosses via Teracati Neapolis. At the end of viale Augusto (500m) is the entrance to the archaeological zone.

Neapolis: the archaeological zone

Visiting the site and opening times
- Take **bus no. 1** from the town centre. A single entrance gives access to the Latomia del Paradiso, the Greek Theatre and the Roman Amphitheatre (**map 1; 1**. The site is open daily 09.00–two hours before sunset.

Off viale Augusto the **Casa del Quartiere Ellenistica**, surrounded by a piece of wasteland (**map 2;2**), is used by the council for small exhibitions. Beside a splendid giant magnolia tree and a group of ficus trees is the little church of **S. Nicolò** (**map 2; 1**). The funeral service of Jourdain de Hauteville, son of Count Roger, was held here in 1093. The church has been restored but is kept locked. Below it, part of an aisled piscina can be seen, a reservoir used for flushing the amphitheatre (see below), to which it is connected by a channel.

A short road (closed to cars), overlooking the Latomia del Paradiso on the right and the Altar of Hieron on the left, continues to the ticket office and entrance to the **archaeological area** (**map 1; 1**), enclosed in a park. The monuments were pillaged in 1526 to provide stone for the Spanish defence works.

A path leads through the beautiful garden with lemons and pomegranates of the **Latomia del Paradiso**, the largest and most famous of the several deep quarries excavated in ancient times, and since then one of the great sights of the city. Their size testifies to the colossal amount of building stone used for the Greek city, for export throughout the Mediterranean, and for the fortifications of Dionysius. Following the northern limit of Achradina from here to the Cappuccini near the sea, they also served as a defensive barrier. They were used as prisons and according to Thucydides some 7000 Athenians were incarcerated here. Part of the rock face is now protected with scaffolding; this is the only latomy at present open to the public.

The right-hand path reached by steps from the ticket office ends at the **Orecchio di Dionisio** (Dionysius' ear), a curved artificial cavern, 65m long, 5–11m wide, and 23m high, in section like a rough Gothic arch. Its name was given to it by Caravaggio in 1608. Because of the strange acoustic properties of the cavern, it has given rise to the legend that Dionysius used the place as a prison and, from a small fissure in the roof at the upper end, heard quite clearly the whispers of the captives at the lower end. Before Caravaggio, local people called the cave the 'grotto of the noises'. It amplifies every sound and has an interesting echo, which only repeats each sound once. Now it is filled with the strange echoes of noises made by the pigeons which nest here. Once your eyes get accustomed to the dark you can walk to the far wall. The entire surface bears the marks of the chisels.

In the northwest wall of the latomy is the **Grotta dei Cordari**, named after the rope makers who used to work here. It is a picturesque cavern supported by huge pillars and covered with maidenhair ferns and coloured lichens. Access has been prohibited since 1984 because of its perilous state.

The Greek Theatre

Another path leads to the Greek Theatre (**map 1; 1**), the most celebrated of all the ruins of Syracuse, and one of the largest Greek theatres known (138m in diameter). Archaeological evidence confirms the existence on this spot of a wooden theatre as early as the 6C BC, and here it was that Epicharmus (c 540–450 BC) worked as a comic poet. In c 478 BC Gelon excavated a small stone theatre, engaging the architect Demokopos. This was inaugurated by Aeschylus in 476 BC with the first production of *Women of Etna*; his *Persian Women* was performed shortly afterwards. The theatre was enlarged in the 4C BC, under Timoleon by excavating deeper into the hillside; it was again enlarged under Hieron II (c 230 BC) by extending the cavea upward, using blocks of stone. It could hold an audience of 15,000. Under the Romans the scena was altered several times, eventually to make it suitable for gladiator battles and the circus. The Romans probably also cut the trapezoidal lines around the orchestra, when creating a kolymbetra, an ornamental garden with fish pool, but it was abandoned in the 1C AD in favour of the elegant new Amphitheatre (see below).

The existing cavea, with 42 rows of seats in nine wedges, is almost entirely hewn out of the rock. This is now believed to represent Hieron II's auditorium of 59 rows, less the upward extension which has been quarried. The extent of Timoleon's theatre before Hieron's excavations is marked by the drainage trench at the sixth row, above the larger gangway. Around the gangway runs a very worn frieze bearing, in large Greek characters, the names of Hieron (II), Philistis (his queen), Nereis (his daughter-in-law, wife of Gelon II), and Zeus Olympius, which served to distinguish the blocks of seats. The foundations of the scena remain, successive alterations making it difficult to identify their function, except for the deep recess for the curtain. The view from the upper seats was especially good in the early morning (the hour at which Greek drama was performed). Above the theatre were two porticoes (to provide shelter from the weather). The little house which dominates the cavea is a medieval watch tower for pirates.

Steps at the far end of the Greek theatre, or a path near the entrance (which passes behind the medieval watch tower perched on a rock) lead up to the rock wall behind the theatre. Here there are recesses for votive tablets and a grotto (or nymphaeum) in which the abundant Galermi aqueduct, which traverses Epipolae bringing water from the Bottigliera river near Pantalica, 33km away, ends. The view of the port is spoilt by the spire of the Madonna delle Lacrime. At the left hand end of the wall the **Street of Tombs** (via dei Sepolcri) begins, rising in a curve 146m long. The wheel ruts in the limestone were made by carts in the 16C serving the mills which used to occupy the cavea of the theatre. The Byzantine tombs and Hellenistic niches in its rock walls have all been rifled. Its upper end (no admission) crosses the rock-hewn **Acquedotto Galermi**.

Immediately to the west of the theatre a **Sanctuary of Apollo Temenites** has been discovered. A smaller, and probably older theatre lies to the southwest.

Across the road from the ticket office (see above) is a good view of the foundations of the huge **Altar of Hieron II**, hewn out of the rock (no entry, for preservation reasons). The altar, built between 241 and 217 BC, was used for public sacrifices to Zeus, when as many as 450 bulls could be killed in one day. It was 198m long and 22.8m wide (the largest altar known), and was destroyed by the Spaniards in the 16C to obtain stone for harbour fortifications (1526).

The Roman Amphitheatre

Near S. Nicolò (see above) is the entrance (somewhat hidden by souvenir stalls) to the Amphitheatre (**map 2; 1,2**) approached past stone sarcophagi from cemeteries in Syracuse and Megara Hyblaea. An imposing Roman building probably of the 1C AD, partly hollowed out of the hillside, in external dimensions (140 x 119m) the amphitheatre is only a little inferior to the one in Verona. The perfection of the masonry is probably attributable to a Syracusan architect. Beneath the high parapet encircling the arena runs a corridor with entrances for the gladiators and wild beasts; the marble blocks on the parapet have inscriptions (3C AD) recording the ownership of the seats. In the centre is a rectangular depression, probably for the machinery used in the spectacles. The original entrance was at the south end, outside which a large area has been exposed, including an enclosure thought to have been for the animals, and a large fountain. Excavations have revealed an earlier roadway and the base of an Augustan arch here.

There is a good view of the archaeological park from **viale Rizzo** (**map 2; 1**) above: in the foreground is the theatre and the Latomy of Paradise, beyond, the Altar of Hieron and the amphitheatre, and in the distance the Great Harbour and Ortygia (obscured by modern apartment blocks, and disfigured by the Sanctuary of the Madonna of Tears).

A short way to the north of the church of S. Nicolò (see above) is the beautiful garden of the **Latomia di S. Venera** (closed indefinitely after landslides), in whose walls are niches for votive tablets. Above it is the **Necropoli Grotticelli**, a group of Hellenistic and Byzantine tombs, one of which, with a Doric pediment, is arbitrarily known as the 'Tomb of Archimedes'. The recent excavations here can be seen from the fence along the main road, via Teracati.

ENVIRONS OF SYRACUSE

Castello Eurialo is one of the most important Greek military sites known and is still a very impressive sight. The romantic little Ciane spring where papyrus grows is a lovely peaceful spot.

Practical information

Getting there
By bus

For the **Castello Eurialo**, take bus **no. 11** (every 40mins) for Belvedere from Ortygia (riva della Posta) via corso Gelone. For the **Olympieion and River Ciane** take bus **no. 24** (in summer) or buses **22** or **23** from corso Gelone via via Elorina for the Olympieion.

By car

The road (8km) leaves Syracuse north of the archaeological zone of Neapolis: at first, signposted to Catania, it leads through the modern city. In the suburbs the road (signposted for Belvedere) forks left. The Olympieion (c 3km) is reached from the Noto road which crosses first the Anapo and then the Ciane rivers. The Ciane is reached by a (signposted) road off the main road to Canicattini Bagni.

Information office
APT Siracusa, ☎ 0931/67710.

 ### Eating out
Café and pastry shop at Belvedere

Bar Ciccio, 1 via de Gasperi, astonishing array of cakes and pastries, memorable *cannoli* and *tiramisu*, also snacks and light lunches.

Picnics

Both Castello Eurialo and the source of the River Ciane are lovely places to picnic.

Boat trips

Boat trips up river, leave from the bridge over the Ciane on the main road (SS 115) organised by Signor Vella (☎ 0931/69076 or 368/3168199). It is no longer possible to reach the source because the Ciane is now a wildlife reserve.

Castello Eurialo

Castello Eurialo is at the western limit of the ancient city on the open, barren plateau of Epipolae. The approach road crosses the great **Walls of Dionysius** which defended the Epipolae ridge. Begun by Dionysius the Elder in 402 BC, they were finished by 387 and were 30km long. Just before the main Belvedere road crosses the walls, a path (50m) leads right (near a house and water deposit) to the **Latomia del Filosofo** (or Bufalaro), so-called from the legend that Philoxenus of Cythera was confined here for expressing too candid an opinion of the verses of Dionysius. The quarry was used for the construction of the walls and the castle.

The main road winds up towards **Belvedere**; just after the signpost for the town, a narrow road (signposted) leads right for the **Castello Eurialo** (or Euryelos, meaning broad-based; open every day 09.00–one hour before sunset).

History

Built on the highest point (172m) of the plateau of Epipolae, the castle commanded the western extremity of ancient Syracuse (as the view shows), at the most delicate point in the walls of Dionysius. These impressive ruins are the most complete and important Greek military work extant. The castle was begun by Dionysius the Elder in 402–397, and probably altered by Agathocles in 317 BC. Archimedes is thought to have strengthened the defences in the late 3C, but his work was left unfinished because of the sack of the city in 212.

Three ditches precede the west front; the outermost is near the custodian's house. Between the second and the third are the ruins of an outwork, whose walls have partly collapsed into the second ditch. On the left, steps lead down into the **innermost ditch**, the principal defence of the fortress which gave access to a labyrinth of casemates and passages to all parts of the fort. On the right the three piers of the drawbridge are prominent. There are 11 entrances from this main ditch to the gallery parallel with it; from here three passages lead east; the longest, on the north (174m long; closed since 1983) connects with the Epipolae Gateway (see below). Prominent in this part of the castle are the remains of five towers, originally 15m high, and surmounted by catapults invented by Dionysius.

The dark corridor to the south leads to a ditch outside the south wall of the

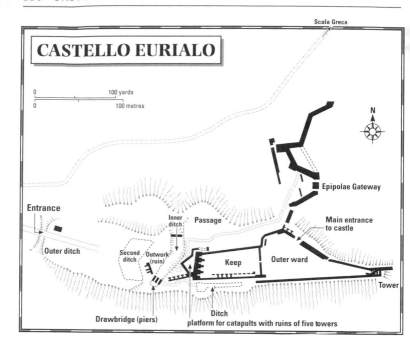

CASTELLO EURIALO

Scala Greca

0 — 100 yards
0 — 100 metres

N

Epipolae Gateway

Entrance

Main entrance to castle

Inner ditch

Passage

Outer ditch

Second ditch

Outwork (ruin)

Keep

Outer ward

Tower

Drawbridge (piers)

Ditch

platform for catapults with ruins of five towers

castle. At the end, steps (which were concealed from the enemy) lead up to the outer ward of the **castle** proper, which consisted of a keep with an irregular outer ward on the east. In these parts of the castle the barracks and cisterns were located. On the northeast side of the outer ward was the main entrance from the town; on the southeast rose a tower connected with the south wall of Dionysius.

From here there is a good view of the **Epipolae gateway** below, a 'pincer' type defence work on the spur of the north **wall of Dionysius** (described above), which can be seen, broken at intervals by towers and posterns, stretching towards the sea. It was united to the keep by a complicated system of underground works, notable for their ingenious provisions for shelter and defence.

An arch leads back towards the entrance into the **keep**. On the left a few steps lead down to a path which follows the edge of the site back to the entrance.

The Olympieion and the River Ciane

The Olympieion or **Temple of Zeus** is on the right bank of the Ciane. On the approach its two columns can be seen among trees on the skyline of a low hill, the **Polichne**, a point of great strategic importance, invariably occupied by the besiegers of Syracuse. About 1km after the bridge over the Ciane, at the top of the rise, a road (right; signposted) leads in less than 1km (keep right) to the temple in a cypress grove. Built in the 6C, just after the Temple of Apollo (see p 313, Ortygia), it is the second oldest Doric peripteral temple in Sicily. It was hexastyle and peripteral with 42 monolithic columns, two of which remain standing on part of the stylobate. There is a view of the island of Ortygia.

The source of the **River Ciane** is reached by a turning off the Canicattini Bagni road SP14. After crossing the Anapo, a byroad (left; signposted) leads for 3km through a fertile valley with orange and lemon groves and magnificent old olive trees (and some 'pill-box' defences left over from World War II). Beyond a tributary of the Ciane, a road (signposted) continues left to end in a grove of eucalyptus and cypress trees beside the romantic spring (the ancient 'Cyane'), overgrown with reeds and thick clumps of papyrus. This plant grows only here and along the River Fiumefreddo in Sicily, and in no other part of Europe. The name of the spring (in Greek, blue) describes the azure colour of its waters, but a myth relates how the nymph Cyane, who tried to prevent Hades from carrying off Persephone, was changed into a spring and condemned to weep forever.

Beyond the bridge a path follows a fence along the reeds to the large pool, inhabited by numerous waterfowl. Both springs, the **Testa della Pisma**, and the smaller **Pismotta** have pools planted with papyrus.

Plemmyrium and the coast to the south

The ancient district of *Plemmyrium*, now sometimes known as the peninsula of the Maddalena, was on the headland opposite Ortygia on Syracuse's Great Harbour. The headquarters of Nicias were established here after his defeat on Epipolae by Gylippus, in the famous battle between Athens and Syracuse in 415 BC.

Neolithic settlements have been found further south on the offshore islet of **Ognina** where Neolithic and Early Bronze Age pottery finds suggest that it may have been a Maltese trading outpost. There is a pretty little port here and sea bathing at Capo Sparano, just to the north.

The bay to the south, **Fontane Bianche**, used to be one of the best bathing beaches on the island; it has now been spoilt by illegal building. Nearby is **Cassibile**, where a huge Bronze Age necropolis and hut village yielded extremely interesting finds, now in the archaeological museum in Syracuse. In an olive grove near here on the afternoon of 3 September 1943, Generals Bedell Smith and Castellano signed the military terms of surrender of the Italian army to the Allies. Several 'pill-boxes' survive along the road and on the bed of the river. At the mouth of the Cassibile, the ancient *Kakyparis*, the Athenian general Demosthenes, covering the rear of Nicias' forces during the retreat from Syracuse, was cut off and forced to surrender (see above). There are wonderful old olive trees, carobs, almonds and citrus fruit plantations in this area.

NOTO
• • • • • •

The inhabitants call their city '*il giardino di pietra*', or the garden of stone. It is no exaggeration. Noto (population 21,700) is the most charming and best preserved of the 18C Baroque cities of Sicily. It was built after the earthquake of 1693 when the former town of Noto (now known as *Noto Antica*, see below, 14km away) was abandoned. It is known that Giuseppe Lanza (Duke of Camastra), Giuseppe Asmundo, Giovanni Battista Landolina, and the Jesuit Angelo Italia, all played a part in planning the new city. It is an excellent example of 18C town planning, and its architecture is exceptionally homogeneous. Many of the fine buildings, with theatrical exteriors, including numerous churches and convents, were built between 1715 and 1780 by Rosario Gagliardi, his pupil Vincenzo Sinatra and Paolo Labisi. The fragile local white tufa has been burnt honey gold by the sun. After years of oblivion its beautiful buildings have now been restored.

The vineyards around the city produce a rare and exquisite dessert wine, *Moscato di Noto*, a rich gold colour, like the nearby Baroque monuments. Made from white Muscat grapes, the wine comes in three varieties: *naturale*, *spumante* and *liquoroso*, all DOC.

Practical information

Getting there
By train

Railway station, 1.5km south of the public gardens, on the Syracuse–Gela line (trains from Syracuse in c 35mins).

By bus

Buses (*AST* and *SAIS*) from Syracuse to largo Pantheon c every hour in 45 mins. Services run by *Caruso* from Noto to Noto Marina on the coast.

Parking

The easiest place to park is outside Porta Reale. Noto is bad news for motorists and lends itself to exploration on foot; there are lots of stairs.

Information office
APT Noto, piazza XVI Maggio
(☎ 0931/ 573779).
Noto on line: ✉ www.comune.noto.sr.it.

Where to stay
Hotels

NOTO MARINA ✮✮✮
Eloro, località Eloro Pizzuta, ☎ 0931/ 812244, 🖷 0931/812200.
✮✮✮ *Helios*, località Pizzuta, ☎ 0931/ 812366, 🖷 0931/812378.
INLAND ✮✮✮ *Fattoria Don Bosco*, contrada Arco Farina Pianette, in a hillside position, ☎ & 🖷 0931/946275.
BETWEEN THE CITY AND THE SEA ✮✮✮ *President*, contrada Falconara, ☎ 0931/812543, 🖷 0931/ 812578.
✮✮✮ *Villa Favorita*, contrada Falconara, ☎ 0931/812912, 🖷 0931/812896,

✉ www.hotelvillafavorita.it.

Bed and breakfast

✮✮✮ *Centro storico*, 64 corso Vittorio Emanuele, ☎ 0931/573967, ✉ www. chrislibra@jumpy.it.
✮✮ *Noto B&B*, 70 via Cavarra, ☎ 349/ 4943546.
✮✮ *The Central Stay*, 4 via Cavalieri di Vittorio Veneto, ☎ 0931/835534.
✮✮ *Vicoli stretti*, 22 vico Ombrone, ☎ & 🖷 0931/835816. Offers various rooms in the alleys of the centre.
OUT OF TOWN *Sierra Vento*, contrada Serra del Vento, Belvedere, ☎ 0931/573722, ✉ www.sierravento.it.

Rooms or apartments to rent

Belvedere, 1 piazza Perelli Cippo, ☎ & 🖷 0931/573820, ✉ www. camerebelvedere.com. In the upper part of the city.
Carmine, in a tiny alley in the heart of the city, 5 vico Curtatone, ☎ 338/ 1713573.
L'Arca, 14 via Rocco Pirri, ☎ 0931/ 838656, 🖷 0931/573360.
La Pietra d'Oro, 80 via Duca Giordano, ☎ 0931/574788, 🖷 0931/838878.
OUT OF TOWN *Ambra*, 14 via Giantommaso, ☎ & 🖷 0931/835554.
Villa Teresa Residence, contrada Baronazzo, San Corrado di Fuori, ☎ 0931/813065. Pool.

Youth hostel

Il Castello, 1 via Fratelli Bandiera, ☎ & 🖷 0931/571534.

Farmhouse accommodation

Il Carrubo, contrada Castelluccio, ☎ 0931/810114. Dairy farm.

Organic food.
Monte Alveria, Noto Antica, ☎ 0931/
810183 and 0931/838132, 📠 www.
agriturismo.com/fattoriamontealveria.
Old farm at Noto Antica, self-catering
facilities and restaurant. Bicycle
trekking and horseriding. The farm
raises horses and donkeys. Very peaceful.
Terra di Pace, contrada Zisola, ☎ &
📠 0931/838472, 📠 www.agriturismo-
sicilia.com/terradipace. Close to the city;
organic food; pool.
Villa Rosa, contrada Falconara, ☎ &
📠 0931/812909, 📠 www.
fattoriavillarosa.it. Beautiful old farmhouse. Pool, beach nearby, horseriding,
excellent food.

Campsites

☆☆☆ *Il Forte*, località Spinazza,
Marzamemi, ☎ 0931/841011. On the
coast, lots of facilities.
☆☆☆ *Capo Passero*, località Vigne
Vecchie, Portopalo, ☎ 0931/842333.
☆☆ *Captain*, Isola delle Correnti,
Portopalo, ☎ 0931/842595.

Eating out
Restaurants

€€ *Il Barocco*, via Cavour,
☎ 0931/835999. In the old stables of
Palazzo Astuto-Barresi with a lovely
patio. Try chef Graziella's prize-winning
spaghetti ca pateddi d'a roccia (spaghetti
with limpets).
€ *Trattoria del Carmine*, via Ducezio,
☎ 0931/838705. Serves pizza in the
evenings, and sandwiches during the
day. Closed Mon.
€ *Trattoria Il Buco*, via Zanardelli,
☎ 0931/838142, close to S.Francesco.
Excellent *caponata* (mixed vegetable
starter) and *ravioli di ricotta*. Closed midday Sat.
€ *Al Terrazzo*, strada Alfredo Baccarini,
☎ 0931/839710. Close to town hall,
tables outside, surrounded with flowers.

Cafés, pastry shops and ice cream parlours

Corrado Costanzo, 7/9 via Silvio
Spaventa.
Mandolfiore, 2 via Ducezio. The best
place in town for cakes, biscuits and ice
cream; try tangerine sorbet or *dessert di
carruba* made only with carobs. *Cubbaita*
nougat (sesame seeds and honey) is
available all year round.
Caffè Sicilia, corso Vittorio Emanuele.
Unusual home-made jams.
La Vecchia Fontana, piazza Immacolata.
Good coffee, and prickly pear ice cream.
Rosso e Nero, largo Porta Nazionale.
Delicious ice creams, biscuits and
cannoli di ricotta.
Piero e Figlio, via Matteo Raeli, under
the cathedral. Tasty snacks, sandwiches
and ice cream.

Picnics

In the public gardens outside Porta
Reale. **Snacks** (*focacce*) can be bought at
the *Trattoria del Carmine* in via
Ducezio (see above) and *Trattoria Piero*
in piazza XVI Maggio.

Opening times

Most of the churches are open every
day, all with the same timetable:
09.00–12.30, 16.00–19.00.

Annual festivals

Festivities in honour of **S.
Corrado** on 19 February, the
last Sunday in August, and the first
Sunday in September. The procession of
the **S. Spina** takes place on Good Friday,
and other religious ceremonies during
Easter week. The **Infiorata** is held on
the third Sunday in May, when via
Nicolaci is carpeted with fresh flowers.
La notte di Giufà, at the end of July, is
a whole night dedicated to music and
story-telling, from sunset till dawn; the
musicians come from all over the world.

Entertainment
Concerts
Concerts are given in several churches in the town, including the courtyard of the convent of S. Domenico. The **International Classical Music Festival** is held here in July and August.

Theatre
Theatre and concert seasons at the Victor Emanuel III Opera House (Jan–June).

Internet point
Archè, 1 via Mauceri (close to S.Francesco), ☎ 0931/574790.

History

After the earthquake of 1693, which severely damaged *Noto Antica*, this new site was chosen in 1702 by a majority of the inhabitants. In 1837–65 Noto displaced Syracuse as the provincial capital. In 1986 many buildings in the town had to be propped up by scaffolding, and closed; a serious earthquake in 1990 did further damage, and in 1996 the dome of the cathedral collapsed. The city appeared to be doomed, but now it is shrugging off its scaffolding and the palaces, churches and convents are dazzling again, like fantastic golden jewels still warm from the crucible. Repairs are now almost complete. The funds allotted to the city by the government, the Region and UNESCO (the town was declared a World Heritage Site by UNESCO in 1996), have (amazingly) really been used to repair the easily eroded tufa and to carry out urgent restoration work.

At the east end of the town are the **public gardens** where the thick evergreen ficus trees form an impenetrable roof over the road. **Porta Reale**, erected by Orazio Angelini, for Ferdinand II's visit in 1838, leads into **corso** Vittorio Emanuele from which the town rises to the right and falls away to the left. By skilful use of open spaces and monumental flights of steps a straight and level street, 1km long, has been given a lively skyline and a succession of glimpses of the countryside. The main streets are paved with blocks of stone, the side streets are cobbled. On the right a grandiose flight of steps leads up to **S. Francesco all' Immacolata** (1704–48) by Vincenzo Sinatra, which has a good façade and a

S. Francesco all'Immacolata

pretty white stucco interior. The convent of **S. Salvatore** (now a seminary) faces via Zanardelli with a fine long 18C façade and attractive tower (possibly designed by Rosario Gagliardi).

Opposite S. Salvatore is the **church of S. Chiara** (usually open on Sunday morning) with an oval interior by Gagliardi (1730–48), and a *Madonna* by Antonello Gagini. The **Civic Museum**, which has been closed for many years, is to be arranged in part of the convent.

Beyond, at the heart of the city, the immense façade of the **cathedral**, rising above fine steps, looks down on **piazza Municipio** with its symmetrical horseshoe hedges of ficus. The cathedral (S. Nicolò) was built in several stages

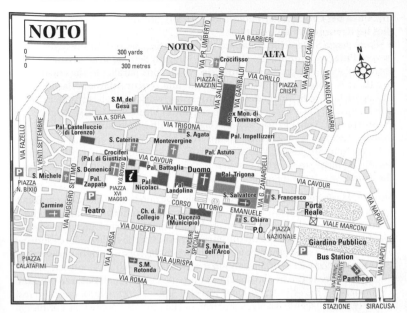

throughout the 18C, probably with the intervention of Gagliardi and Vincenzo Sinatra. Part of the dome, which was rebuilt in the 19C, collapsed in 1996 (repairs should be complete in 2004) but it is possible to view the works.

Beside the Duomo is the Bishop's Palace and **Palazzo Landolina**, once the residence of this important local family. Beyond the Bishop's Palace is the basilica of **S. Salvatore**. The façade was designed by Andrea Gigante of Trapani and probably built by Antonio Mazza (1791). The pretty polychrome interior, with a vault painting by Mazza, contains 18C paintings by Giuseppe Velasquez and an organ of 1778 by Donato del Piano.

On the south side of the piazza, facing the Duomo, is **Palazzo Ducezio** (the Town Hall), a splendid building begun in 1742 by Vincenzo Sinatra. The upper floor was added in 1951. Inside is a vault painting by Antonio Mazza. On the other side of the corso there is a good view up via Corrado Nicolaci of the façade of the church of Montevergine (described below). In the corso is the **Chiesa del Collegio** (S. Carlo al Corso), with a curved façade probably by Gagliardi (1730; restored by Vincenzo Sinatra in 1776). It has a luminous interior, with frescoes on the vault. It is possible to climb up the bell tower, for a view over the rooftops of Noto (open daily 10.00–13.00, 15.30–19.00).

Beyond, the long façade of the former **Collegio dei Gesuiti** (now a school) stretches as far as piazza S. Domenico (or piazza XVI Maggio), with the **Victor Emanuel III Opera House** (1861, inaugurated in 1870; open daily 08.30–13.30, 15.00–20.00), a perfectly preserved gem, with a lovely interior and 330 seats. In front of the building, in a delightful little garden is an 18C fountain from Noto Antica with a statue of *Hercules* that is thought to be Roman. In the pavilion behind is the *APT* information office. Above to the left is the glorious soaring, golden façade of **S. Domenico** (1737–56) by Gagliardi, perhaps his most successful building in the town. In via Bovio above is the former convent of the **Casa dei Crociferi** by Paolo Labisi (1750), finished by Vincenzo Sinatra. It has been restored as law courts.

From piazza S. Domenico (piazza XVI Maggio) the corso continues to the rather severe **Palazzo Zappata**. To the left via Ruggero Settimo leads past an aristocratic palace to the pretty **via Ducezio** which runs parallel to the corso to the south. It is closed at the west end by the fine concave Baroque façade (with Rococo details) of **S. Maria del Carmine**, a late work by Gagliardi with a charming interior. At the other end of the street, on via Vicerè Speciale, is the church of **S. Maria dell'Arco** (1730), also by Gagliardi with an elegant portal, and a decorative stucco interior with two stoups from Noto Antica. Nearby is an interesting Art Nouveau house. Via Aurispa, parallel to via Ducezio on the south, is another pretty street with simpler buildings and the church of **S. Maria Rotonda**, which has a Baroque façade.

From S. Maria dell'Arco, via Vicerè Speciale leads up to the splendid rear façade of the town hall (see above). To the left is **Palazzo Rau della Ferla**, which has a graceful façade and a courtyard covered with jasmine. Part of the palace houses *pasticceria Costanzo*. At the end the impressive wall of the Collegio dei Gesuiti can be seen, which a road now follows uphill back to the corso, straight across which via Corrado Nicolaci continues uphill towards the church of Montevergine. Via Nicolaci is overlooked by the delightful Baroque balconies of **Palazzo Nicolaci** (Villadorata; 1737–65), open daily 10.00–13.00, 15.00–19.00, once the residence of Don Giacomo Nicolaci, a patron of the arts. He donated part of his collection of books to the important City Library, which has been housed in the palace since 1982.

The façade of **Montevergine** is attributed to Vincenzo Sinatra. Deconsecrated, it has a magnificent 18C floor of majolica tiles from Caltagirone, and paintings by Costantino Carasi. The church is on the handsome **via Cavour**, another 18C street, with views of the countryside at either end. It leads west past **Palazzo Battaglia** (1735), on the corner of via Rocco Pirri, in which a charming little market-place, with a loggia supported on iron pillars surrounding a fountain, has been restored. Via Cavour continues west past the former **Oratorio di S. Filippo Neri** (1750) and the **church of S. Caterina** (right; attached to the oratory, on via Fratelli Ragusa). Beyond, near the end of via Cavour, is the large neo-classical **Palazzo di Lorenzo** (**Castelluccio**) owned by the Knights of Malta. Opposite is a basket maker's workshop.

Walking back down Via Cavour, to the right of Montevergine, is the beautiful **Palazzo Astuto** (late 18C; possibly the work of Vincenzo Sinatra or Paolo Labisi). Further on, on the right, is the fine **Palazzo Trigona** (1781; restored by Bernardo Labisi), part of it renovated as a congress centre. The Sala Gagliardi here has been restored as an exhibition room and auditorium. At the far end of the the the palazzo wall you can see the side of the church of S. Salvatore.

Via Mariannina Coffa (partly stepped) leads uphill to the upper part of the town known as **Noto Alta**. This simpler district was laid out on a different plan and orientation from the lower monumental district with its four long, straight, parallel streets running from east to west. There is a view of the battlemented former Convento di S. Antonio di Padova on the top of the hill. The road continues left past **Palazzo Impellizzeri S. Giacomo** (1752) with a balcony along the whole length of the first floor. Part of the palace is now used to house the city archives (open to the public Mon–Fri 09.00–13.00, 15.00–19.00, Sat morning only), often used for exhibitions, and in one room there is a splendid 18C crystal chandelier. The corner and bell tower of the former **Ospedale Trigona** are visible here. Via Trigona leads past the former convent to the deconsecrated church of **S. Agata** (closed), attributed to Gagliardi and finished by Paolo Labisi. It contains stuccoes by Labisi and paintings by Costantino Carasi. Opposite is **S. Annunziata e Badia**, another church dating from 1720. Just beyond, approached by a double stairway, is **S. Maria del Gesù**, next to its convent.

Via Trigona leads back to the impressive former **Monastero di S. Tommaso** (1720), with an attractive façade and double stairway. It is now used as a prison, which extends as far as piazza Mazzini. On the summit of the hill, at the centre of Noto Alta is the church of the **Crocifisso**, by Gagliardi (1715), which contains a number of works of art from Noto Antica, including (in the right transept) a beautiful statue of the *Madonna della Neve* (*Our Lady of the Snows*) signed by Francesco Laurana (1471), and two Romanesque lions. The **Cappella Landolina** contains paintings by the school of Costantino Carasi. On the high altar is an 18C reliquary designed by Gagliardi which contains part of a venerated Crucifix from Noto Antica. A relic of the Holy Thorn also belongs to the church (only shown on Good Friday).

The lower town is reached from here by returning down the street to via Cavour and taking the stepped via Gioberti down past S. Salvatore to the corso.

ENVIRONS OF NOTO

The little ruined town of Noto Antica, destroyed by earthquake in 1693, is a very unusual sight in lovely countryside. The **nature reserve** of Vendicari is one of the most beautiful areas left on the coast of the island. The Cava Grande del Cassibile is a well preserved river gorge with lovely vegetation. Eloro is an interesting Greek site in a fine position on the sea. The beaches of Noto Marina are exceptionally beautiful, and the sea water has been declared among the cleanest in Italy.

Practical information

 Getting around
There is no public transport to most of the places described below, and the railway line from Noto to Pachino has been substituted by a bus service (operated by *SAIS*).

 Information offices
APT Siracusa, ☎ 0931/ 67710 and *APT* information office in Noto, ☎ 0931/ 573779.

Noto Antica
The road from Noto to Noto Antica (12km, signposted for Palazzolo Acreide) leads uphill to the left from the public gardens. It crosses Noto Alta, a pleasant area of low-lying Art Nouveau houses.

The little town of **S. Corrado di Fuori** has more attractive early 20C houses. Outside the town, in the Valle dei Miracoli, amid fertile vegetation, is the hermitage of S. Corrado Confalonieri (not open), who lived here in the 14C. The 18C sanctuary contains a painting of the saint by Sebastiano Conca. The road continues across a fine upland plain with old olive trees. It then descends to cross a bridge decorated with four obelisks.

The byroad (left) for Noto Antica is lined with early 20C Stations of the Cross on the approach to the large sanctuary of **S. Maria della Scala** (open 09.30–12.30, 15.00 or 16.00–18.00 or 19.00), next to a seminary, which has a pleasant façade (1708) with three statues and a balcony.

The road now descends to cross another bridge over a ravine before reaching **Noto Antica**, abandoned since the earthquake of 1693 and now utterly deserted. The scant ruins, mostly reduced to rubble, are almost totally overgrown and provide an eery romantic sight.

History of Noto Antica

This was a settlement that long antedates its legendary foundation by the Sicel chief Ducetius in 448 BC, and was the only Sicilian town to resist the depredations of Verres. The last stronghold of Muslim Sicily, it gave its name to the Val di Noto, one of the three areas into which the Arabs divided up the island. It fell to the Normans in 1091. A flourishing medieval city, it was the birthplace of architect Matteo Carnelivari. After the terrible earthquake of 1693 the inhabitants decided to move their city to its present site (see p 331).

The entrance is through the monumental **Porta della Montagna** (restored) with remains of the high walls on either side. A rough road leads up past a round tower and along the ridge of the hill. The conspicuous wall on the left (the highest one to survive) belonged to the Chiesa Madre. After 1km, beside a little monument, the right fork continues (and the road deteriorates) to end beside the **Eremo della Madonna**, a small deserted chapel, with a good view of the surrounding countryside. There are usually custodians who act as guides here in the morning. Some distance to the west is the remote prehistoric village of **Castelluccio** (c 18C–14C BC), which has given its name to the most important Early Bronze Age culture of southeast Sicily. The rock tombs had carved portal slabs (now in the archaeological museum at Syracuse).

Cava Grande del Cassibile

The Cava Grande, on the banks of the River Cassibile, where centuries-old plane trees grow, is a **nature reserve**. There is spectacular scenery in this gorge some 250m deep and nearly 10km long; it is the deepest canyon in Europe. Thousands of **tombs** (11C–9C BC) have been identified here (finds in the archaeological museum in Syracuse). The easiest approach to the gorge is via Villa Vela, a pleasant little village with some Art Nouveau villas on the road between Noto and Palazzolo Acreide. You can go into the cava from here, and then walk as far as you like or start from the belvedere at the end of the very winding road to **Avola Antica**, (destroyed, like Noto Antica, in 1693). However, the path here is steep and overgrown with plants.

Avola

Avola (population 32,100) is a prosperous agricultural town and the most important centre of almond cultivation in Italy. It has expanded in a disorderly way around its interesting centre which retains the hexagonal plan on which it was built after 1693 by Angelo Italia. In the centre is piazza Umberto I where the **Mother Church** (S. Nicolò) is situated, which contains an 18C organ by Donato del Piano. Four smaller squares open off the outer edge of the hexagon, one of which, piazza Vittorio Veneto, has a fountain with three amusing 20C lions by Gaetano Vinci. The 18C churches include **S. Antonio Abate** and **S. Annunziata** (with a façade by Giuseppe Alessi) and there are a number of Art Nouveau buildings. The church of the **Cappuccini**, outside the hexagonal centre, in piazza Francesco Crispi, has a lovely 17C altarpiece.

The coast from Noto Marina to Porto Palo

Noto Marina (or **Lido di Noto**) is a little resort on the sea, which with **Calabernardo** has some of the best beaches on the east coast of the island. The beautiful landscape here has huge old olive, carob, almond and citrus fruit trees. The Asinaro river, which reaches the sea near Calabernardo, is the ancient *Assinaros*, where Nicias' retreating Greeks, trying to reach Heloros, were overtaken while drinking at the river and killed after the great battle between Syracuse and Athens in 413 BC.

Eloro
Near the mouth of the Tellaro river, on a low hill, in lovely countryside, are the remains of Eloro (*Heloros*); open daily 08.00–14.00), the first sub-colony to be founded by Syracuse, probably at the beginning of the 7C BC. The excavations are in a lovely deserted position by the sea and there is a good view inland of the Pizzuta column (see below), with Noto beyond green rolling hills. The view along the unspoilt coastline extends to the southern tip of the island.

The road passes the basement of a temple dedicated to Asklepios. To the right of the road, in a large fenced enclosure sloping down to the canal, is a sanctuary of Demeter consisting of a larger temple and a monumental stoa. A theatre has been partially excavated nearby. To the left, beyond the custodian's house, is another enclosure of recent excavations. An ancient road continues to the walls and north gate. Outside the walls has been found another later (Hellenistic) temple of Demeter and Persephone; it has been reconstructed in the museum of Noto.

The so-called **Pizzuta**, a column over 10m high, can be reached by returning to the approach road beyond the railway bridge. This was once thought to be a monument to the Syracusan victory (see above), but it is in fact a funerary memorial of the 3C BC. From the road for the tourist village of Eloro, a rough road leads right through an almond and olive grove past the column.

Villa del Tellaro
From the main road, just by the bridge across the Tellaro river, a road leads inland towards a farmhouse (conspicuous to the right of the road) in the locality of Caddeddi, less than 1km from the main road. Beneath the farmhouse a Roman villa of the second half of the 4C AD, known as the Villa del Tellaro, was discovered in 1972, open 08.00–19.30, ☎ 0931/573883. Some of the splendid polychrome mosaics, reminiscent of those at Piazza Armerina, can be seen, but the best ones have been removed for restoration and will probably not return here but will be exhibited in the museum in Noto.

Vendicari

The stretch of coast south of the River Tellaro was one of the first coastal areas on the island to become a reserve (open daily 09.00–dusk; for information ☎ 0931/ 462452; further information is at the entrance and guides are available). This beautiful marshy area of the coast (1500ha; closed to cars) of the greatest interest for its wildlife (an oasis for migratory birds), has been protected since 1984 after opposition led by the *Ente Fauna Siciliana* succeeded in halting the construction of a vast tourist village here. It is an excellent place to picnic.

From the main road, beyond the railway, a poorly surfaced road continues for c 1km past lemon groves to the entrance. At the south end is the 18C farmhouse of **S. Lorenzo Lo Vecchio**, with remains of a Hellenistic temple transformed into a Byzantine church. On the edge of the shore are ruins of a Norman tower, and a tunny fishery (closed).

The landscape from here to the southern tip of the island is less striking. In the shallow bay by the fishing village of **Marzamemi**, excavations begun in 1959, have brought to light 14 ancient shipwrecks (four Greek, five Roman and five Byzantine ships). There is a diving and sailing school here, *Opi Tour Sea Service*, 12 via Marzamemi, Marzamemi, 🖥 0931/61200, ✉ scubaclub@tin.it; sailplay@ hotmail.com.

Pachino (population 21,000) is a wine producing centre. Beyond almond and olive trees near the sea and an inland lagoon is the untidy fishing port of **Portopalo**. There is a disused tunny fishery on the sea front next to an 18C palace. The lighthouse stands on **Capo Passero**, the ancient *Pachynus*, the southeast horn of Sicily. A Roman necropolis has been excavated here, and the island of Capo Passero is of great interest for its naturalistic value. The southernmost point is the little **Isolotto delle Correnti**, 6km southwest of the cape. Sea turtles and pelicans are still frequently spotted on the shore here.

Rosolini, an inland town (population 17,400) between Pachino and Noto, was founded in 1713. A rock-hewn basilica of early Christian date lies beneath the Castello del Principe (1668) amid extensive catacombs (now used as a garage).

PALAZZOLO ACREIDE

Palazzolo Acreide is the successor (population 9200) to the Greek city of *Akrai*. A pleasant little town, its finest buildings were built after the earthquake in 1693. It also has some interesting 19C and early 20C palaces. The important Greek remains are on the outskirts of the town.

Practical information

 ### Getting there
By bus

Buses run by *AST* from Syracuse to Palazzolo Acreide (piazza del Popolo) about every hour in 40mins.

 ### Information offices
APT Siracusa, ☎ 0931/ 67710.
Tourist Information Bureau Palazzolo, ☎ 0931/8820000.
Pro Loco, 2 Corso Vittorio Emanuele,

☎ 0931/881354.
Palazzolo on line: www.palazzolo-acreide.it.

 ### Where to stay
Hotels

✰✰✰ *Senatore*, largo Senatore Italia. Modern hotel with restaurant, garden and bar, ☎ 0931/883443, ▤ 0931/ 883444.
✰ *Santoro*, 21 via S. Sebastiano, ☎ 0931/883855 ▤ 0931/883692. Friendly service, panoramic terrace.
BUCCHERI ✰✰✰ *Monte Lauro*, 62 via Cappello, ☎ 0931/873174. Good service, nice rooms, with garage and restaurant,

Camping and farmhouse accommodation

Fattoria Giannavì, contrada Giannavì, Palazzolo, ☎ & ▤ 0931/881776; www.fattoriagiannavì.it. Facilities for campers, also accommodation in the farmhouse. Wonderful isolated position in the Hyblean Mountains not far from the town. Music. The farm raises sheep for milk.
BUSCEMI *Casmene*, contrada Guffari, ☎ 0931/880055. 3km from Buccheri, very well organized farm (organically raised cattle), restaurant, pool, mountain bikes.

Pastry shops

Corsino, 2 via Nazionale, has been open since 1889 and is famous throughout Italy for excellent sweets, especially the nougat (*torrone*).
Caprice, 1 via Iudica. Traditional *pignuccata* and *giuggiulena* made with local honey.
BUCCHERI *Bar Mazzacana*, 55 piazza Roma, excellent *cannoli* and pastries made with ricotta.

 ### Eating out
Restaurants

€€ *Il Portico*, largo Senatore Italia. Hyblean mountain dishes, ☎ 0931/881532. Closed Tues.
€ *Il Camino*, 13 via Martiri di via Fani, ☎ 0931/881860. Cosy. Delicious pasta, local sausage. Closed Tues.
€ *Valentino*, via Galeno, corner of 30 ronco Pisacane, ☎ 0931/881840. Extensive menu, including fish. Closed Wed.
IN THE ENVIRONS €€ *La Trota*, 7km outside the town on the SS 287, contrada Pianette, ☎ 0931/883433. Beautiful park and pools where the trout are raised (smoked trout for sale). The restaurant is in an ancient cave. Closed Mon.
BUCCHERI €€ *'U Lucale*, 14 via Dusmet, ☎ 0931/873923. Very good food, boar meat (*cinghiale*). Closed Tues.

Foreign language newspapers

Available at the newsstand next to Hotel Santoro in via S.Sebastiano.

 ### Annual festivals

Carnival (February) is unique for the particular papier mâché floats; great fun. The **Feast of S. Paolo** on 29 June is an emotional experience, wonderful fireworks. The ancient theatre is used for plays in summer, especially for students in classical studies, from all over Europe. On the first weekend in October at Sortino there is a **Puppet Festival** and a celebration of the area's famous thyme honey.

History

Akrai was a sub-colony founded by Syracuse in 663 BC. In a treaty between Rome and Hieron II in 263 BC, Akrai was assigned to Syracuse. Its period of greatest splendour followed, and its main monuments, including the theatre, were built at this time. It had a conspicuous Christian community, and was destroyed in the 9C by the Arabs. The name 'Palazzolo' was probably added some time in the 12C. It was governed from 1374 for two centuries by the Alagona family. It was damaged by earthquake in 1693 and bombed by the Allies in 1943 (with 700 casualties).

Just outside the town is the **Cimitero Monumentale**, an unexpected site, with elaborate funerary monuments erected in the mid-19C. The **Duomo** is in the lower town near **S. Paolo**, with a good façade perhaps by Vincenzo Sinatra. Inside there are two late 19C carved thrones used for transporting a 16C statue of the saint in procession. The charming sacristy with a pretty vault dates from 1778 and retains its original furniture.

In piazza Umberto I, nearby, is the red 18C Palazzo Zocco, which has a decorative long balcony. Via Annunziata leads downhill from the piazza towards the edge of the town and the church of the **Annunziata**, with a lovely 18C portal decorated with four twisted columns and vines and festoons of fruit. In the white interior, covered with stuccoes, is a fine high altar in *pietre dure*. The *Annunciation* by Antonello da Messina, now in Palazzo Bellomo in Syracuse, was commissioned for this church in 1474. From Piazza Moro via Garibaldi leads uphill past Palazzo Caruso (no. 127), with monsters' heads beneath its balcony. Further uphill, after a flight of steps, is Palazzo Ferla with four graceful balconies. The Museo Archeologico in via Gaetano Italia has been closed for many years.

The centre of the busier and more attractive **upper town** is piazza del Popolo. Here is the 18C church of **S. Sebastiano**, which has a theatrical façade and a portal by Paolo Labisi. In the interior is a painting of *St Margaret of Cortona* by Vito D'Anna (fourth north altar). The town hall dates from 1808. In corso Vittorio Emanuele the 19C Palazzo Judica has an eccentric façade with vases on its roof.

Just off the piazza at 19 via Macchiavelli, entered through a courtyard, is the **Casa-Museo** (open daily 09.00–13.00; ring the bell, ☎ 0931/881499), a delightful local ethnographical museum created by the late Antonino Uccello and displayed in his 17C house. It was acquired by the region of Sicily in 1983. The interesting material from the provinces of Syracuse and Ragusa includes farming utensils and tools, household objects, puppets, terracotta statuettes, etc., beautifully displayed. An oil press and a press used for making honey are also preserved here.

At the top of the road is S. Michele, propped up with scaffolding. Via Acre continues uphill to Piano Acre and the church of the **Immacolata**. Its convex façade is difficult to see as the church is now entered through the courtyard at the east end (ring at the central door, at the house of the custodian of a school). It contains a very fine statue of the *Madonna* by Francesco Laurana.

The ruins of Akrai

Beyond the Immacolata a road continues westwards up to the entrance to the Greek remains of Akrai (open daily 09.00–1 hour and a half before sunset, ☎ 0931/881499), the first colony founded by Syracuse (663 BC). It is a beautifully kept site, although part of it is at present inaccessible. A *strada panoramica* (above the entrance gate) circles the top of the Acropolis, with traces of its fortification walls. It gives a splendid idea of the site, and has panoramic views. Excavations began here in 1824, and were continued in the last century.

The small **theatre**, built in the late 3C BC, is well preserved. The *scena* was altered in Roman times, and in 600 AD a mill with round silos was built over the ruins. Nearby is an altar for sacrifices. Behind the theatre is the **bouleuterion**, a tiny council chamber (connected to the theatre by a passageway). From here (through a locked double gate) there is a good view of the recent excavations of the ancient city. There is a long stretch of the decumanus, the main street, constructed in lava (altered by the Romans), and parts of another road at right-angles which passes close to a circular **temple**. Probably dedicated to Persephone, it is thought to date from the 3C BC. It was covered by a cupola with a circular opening in the centre, supported on girders of terracotta (no longer *in situ*, but preserved); the holes for them are visible in the circular walls, and the pavement survives. Excavations continue here in the area thought to have been the Agora.

The rest of the enclosure consists of a depression between two **latomies**, or stone quarries, showing traces of a Heroic cult and of later Christian occupation. On the face of the smaller latomy, nearest to the path, niches can be seen (formerly closed with commemorative plaques carved with reliefs and inscriptions) and an interesting funerary bas-relief of c 200 BC, showing two scenes, one Roman, with a warrior sacrificing, and one Greek, with a banquet scene. Further on (at present kept locked) are extensive Byzantine **catacombs** carved into the rock (some of them adapted by the Arabs as dwellings). The larger family chapels are decorated with unusual lattice-work *transennae*. From the other path the larger latomy can be seen, and near the theatre a monumental gateway. Beyond a locked gate is the basement of a Temple of Aphrodite (6C BC).

On request, at the entrance gate, a custodian will accompany you (in your car) to visit the so-called **Santoni**, interesting statues of Cybele, carved in a rock face. The road goes down the hill to the Ragusa road, off which a paved byroad (left) ends beside a gate (unlocked by the custodian). Steps continue down past 12 remarkable life-size statues dating from around the 3C BC representing the goddess Cybele, hewn out of the rock (protected by wooden huts). The goddess is shown between the two dioscuri on horseback; with Marsyas, Hermes and other divinities; with her daughter Persephone; seated and flanked by two little lions; etc. They are extremely worn, and were vandalised in the 20th century. There was a sanctuary here near a spring on the road to the necropolis across the valley from the city. It was reached via the **Templi Ferali**, on the east side of the hill, in a vertical cliff. These temples of the dead, containing Greek inscriptions and votive niches survive, but it is not at present possible to visit them.

Environs of Palazzolo Acreide

East of Palazzolo Acreide, on the fast road to Syracuse is **Canicattini Bagni** now surrounded by new buildings. Founded in 1678 it has interesting early 20C houses decorated in the local stone in Art Nouveau style. Nearby the **Grotta Perciata** is the largest cave so far discovered in Sicily, where prehistoric artefacts have been found.

Across the Anapo valley north of Palazzolo Acreide is the attractive little hill town of **Buscemi** (⊠ www.museobuscemi.org), rebuilt after 1693. The main road runs uphill past its four impressive churches. S. Antonio di Padova has an 18C façade which incorporates ten splendid large columns on its curving front (with three bells hung across the top). Higher up is S. Sebastiano, and then the neo-classical 19C church of S. Giacomo. At the top of the town is the well sited 18C Chiesa Madre. A number of artisans' workshops in the town can be visited (signposted), forming a collective museum.

On the barren **Piana di Buccheri** (820m), with views to Monte Lauro (986m), the highest point of the Hyblean Mountains, and of Etna to the north, some pinewoods have recently been planted. **Buccheri** (www.comune.buccheri.sr.it), at 820m over sea level, is another 18C town. The road passes S. Maria Maddalena, built in the 18C, which contains a statue of *Mary Magdalen* by Antonello Gagini (1508). From piazza Toselli a steep flight of steps rises to the towering façade of S. Antonio.

THE ANAPO VALLEY & PANTALICA

The Anapo Valley is a beautiful unspoilt valley. Above it, in spectacular deserted countryside is the most important prehistoric site in Sicily, the necropolis of Pantalica, where thousands of tombs carved in the rock can still be seen. Sortino is famous for its thyme honey gathered from the Hyblean mountains. It also has a strong tradition of puppet theatre.

Practical information

Getting there

The Anapo Valley is 36km from Syracuse and Pantalica is 56km from Syracuse but it is extremely difficult to reach Pantalica using public transport.

By bus

From Syracuse there is a bus to Sortino but the town is at least 5km from Pantalica. Another bus runs twice daily from Catania (14.15 and 18.30, weekdays only).

By car

Take SS 124 via Floridia, then turn right onto the byroad for Ferla.

Information offices

APT Siracusa, ☎ 0931/67710.
The Forestry Commission in Buccheri, ☎ 0931/873093; in Syracuse, ☎ 0931/462452; and in Sortino, ☎ 0931/953695.
Pro Loco Pantalica Sortino, 146 via Pietro Gaetani, ☎ 0931/953359. Anapo Valley on line: www.galvaldanapo.it.

Where to stay
Farmhouse accommodation

Pantalica Ranch, contrada Chianazzo, Sortino, ideally situated for trekking and horseriding in the Pantalica Wildlife Reserve, country food, also camping, courses in pottery, painting and drawing, basket weaving and Italian classes, ☎ & 📠 0931/942069; www.pantalicaranch.it.

Paese Albergo

Many homes in Sortino have been transformed into accommodation for tourists. Information from *Pro Loco Pantalica Sortino*, ☎ 0931/953359 📠 0931/952900.

Eating out
Restaurants

€ *Anaktoron*, 88 via Libertà, ☎ 0931/953676. Hyblean mountain food. Closed Tues.
€ *Osteria da Vincenzo*, 35 via Libertà, ☎ 0931/954545. Simple and satisfying. Closed Mon.

Picnics

Both the Valle dell'Anapo and Pantalica are wonderful places to picnic (food should be bought in Ferla). Picnic places with tables are provided in the Valle dell'Anapo.

closed PH. ☎ 0931/952079, 0931/917433. ✉ www.comune. sortino.sr.it.

 Museums and galleries
Puppet Museum
9 piazza S. Francesco, Sortino, open daily 10.00–12.00, 15.30–17.30,

 Shopping
Buy local products on line from ✉ www.protilo.it.

The Anapo Valley

The plateau above the Anapo valley to the south has pretty countryside with some attractive farmhouses and low dry-stone walls. Here and there are dark carob trees providing welcome shade, and olive groves renowned for the high quality oil which they yield. Shepherds pasture their flocks and small herds of cattle wander around apparently untended; the sound of the bells they wear around their necks lingers after their passage. In the area are Byzantine tombs and caves showing evidence of Neolithic and Bronze Age occupation.

Near Cassaro is a car park and a hut owned by the Forestry Commission, at the entrance (signposted) to the Valle dell'Anapo (open every day 07.00–one hour before sunset, ☎ 0931/462452). This beautiful deep limestone gorge, a protected area since 1988, is run by the Forestry Commission. A map of the paths in the area is available at the hut. No private cars are allowed but a van takes visitors for 8km along the rough road on the site of the old narrow-gauge railway track (and its tunnels) which used to run along the floor of the valley (on the Syracuse–Vizzini line).

The interesting vegetation includes ilexes, pines, figs, olives, citrus fruit trees and poplars. The only buildings to be seen are those once used by the railway company. Horses are bred here, and may one day be used to transport visitors by carriage along the road. Picnic places, with tables, are provided. The van stops in the centre of the valley from where there is a good view of the tombs of the necropolis of Pantalica (see below) high up at the top of the rock face. There is another entrance to the valley from the Sortino road (approached from Solarino), where another van takes visitors along the valley for some 4km before joining this road.

On the Ferla road is the site of the little town of **Cassaro** which was moved after the earthquake of 1693 up to the top of the cliff face (seen above the road). On the approach to Ferla are terraces planted with orange trees, prickly pear and pomegranate, some of which have been allowed to grow wild. **Ferla** is a pretty little town traversed by one long main street which slopes steeply uphill past its four Baroque churches and interesting early 20C houses. Half-way up the main street is the turning (right; signposted) for Pantalica.

Pantalica

The lonely road leads from Ferla for 12km along a ridge through beautiful remote farming country and pine woods to the remarkable prehistoric **necropolis of Pantalica** (marked by a yellow sign), in totally deserted countryside. All around can be seen rock tombs carved in the cliffs (see plan). The road runs through this huge unenclosed site and ends here. Footpaths are signposted from the road.

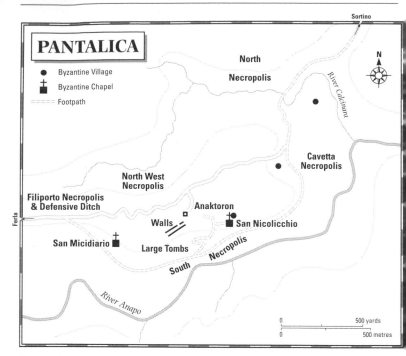

The deep limestone gorges of the Anapo and Cava Grande rivers almost encircle the plateau of Pantalica, occupied from the 13C BC to the 8C BC. In this naturally defended site Sicels from the Italian mainland settled c 1270 BC. Their way of life remained virtually unchanged up until the arrival of the Greeks in the second half of the 8C BC. The cliffs of the vast necropolis, the largest and most important in Sicily, are honeycombed with 5000 tombs of varying shapes and sizes. Each cell held a family tomb, and there appears to have been an arrangement of the cells in groups. The objects discovered in them, including fine pottery, are displayed in the archaeological museum in Syracuse.

The city disappeared after the foundation of the Greek colony of Akrai (see p 342) in 663 BC, and some of the tombs were converted into cave dwellings during the barbarian invasions, and later inhabited by Christians.

An easy footpath (signposted Villaggio Bizantino) at the beginning of the road leads to a tiny Byzantine oratory carved in the rock (with traces of fresco) known as **S. Micidiario**, and the southern necropolis. Off the road, further on, a track leads up to the top of the hill and the so-called '**Anactoron**', or Palace of the Prince, a megalithic building dating from the late Bronze Age, the foundations of which survive (35 x 11m). Nearby are short sections of wall and a defensive ditch, the only remains of the city, recently identified with the legendary *Hybla* whose king allowed the Megarese colonists to found Megara Hyblaea (see p 348).

Far below, the Anapo valley (described above) can be seen, with a white track following the line of the old railway. Further on, downhill, near the end of the road a signpost indicates the **Cavetta** cemetery (9C–7C BC), and another Byzantine village.

A path leads towards the **northern necropolis** (beyond the stream in the valley). The road ends abruptly here and the road from Sortino (see above), which now will never be completed, can be seen across the valley. There is a view of Sortino in the distance. Sometimes in January or February, flocks of ravens can be seen in the area, performing a mysterious mating flight, almost like a dance, during which they fly upside down and link feet for a moment, apparently enjoying it immensely.

On the main road (SS124) between Ferla and Syracuse is **Solarino**, founded in 1759 with a handsome neo-classical palace. From here **Sortino** can be reached, which was rebuilt after the earthquake of 1693, and has some interesting 18C churches and palaces. This byroad, 6km before reaching Sortino, passes an entrance to the Valle dell'Anapo (see above). Near Solarino is **Floridia** (population 19,400), founded in 1628, with more 18C churches. The Madonna delle Grazie was built by the Spaniards to celebrate the victory over the Austrians in 1720.

MEGARA HYBLAEA AND LENTINI

Megara Hyblaea is an important Greek coastal site north of Syracuse. In the 1950s it was surrounded by oil refineries and other industries, the site was chosen for its proximity to Libya, the main source of its crude oil. Inland is Lentini, another important site which is now a bustling agricultural centre, famous for its oranges, among the finest in the world.

Practical information

 ### Getting there
By car
Megara Hyblaea is 16km from Syracuse and can only be reached by car.
By train
Lentini is on the railway line between Syracuse and Catania.

Information office
APT Siracusa, ☎ 0931/67710.

 ### Where to stay
Hotels
☆☆☆☆ *Venus Sea Garden*, Monte Amara Brucoli, ☎ 0931/998946 📠 0931/998950. Beautiful, restored villa close to sea. Activities; good restaurant.

Holiday village
☆☆☆ *Brucoli Village*, Gisira Brucoli, ☎ 0931/994401 📠 0931/994446. On a lovely stretch of coast.
Farm accommodation
Casa dello Scirocco, contrada Piscitello, Carlentini (close to Lentini), ☎ 095/7836120, 095/447709 📠 095/7139257; ✉ www.casadelloscirocco.it. This is an ancient complex of caves, entirely carved out by hand thousands of years ago. Most of the rooms are arranged in these prehistoric caves, Moorish style décor. Very high standard. The farm produces oranges, and raises ostriches. Excursions are arranged, also cookery courses with an aphrodisiacal slant—'*La cucina dell'Eros*'.

History of the Gulf of Augusta

Capo S. Panagia, the headland north of Syracuse, has been identified with ancient *Trogilus*. Fossils exist in the limestone caves and in the over-lying clays are remains of Neolithic habitation. The flat **Magnisi peninsula**, a little further north along the coast, was the ancient *Thapsos*, under whose northern shore the Athenian fleet anchored before the siege of Syracuse. It is almost an island (2km long and 700m wide), since its only connection with the mainland is a sandy isthmus 2.5km long and little more than 100m wide at one point. The fleet of Marcellus also moored near here during the Roman siege of Syracuse. Finds from its vast necropolis have given name to a Bronze Age culture (see the archaeological museum in Syracuse) and interesting domed rock tombs line the shore west of the lighthouse. Two Mycenaean vases were found here in 1974.

The shores of the Gulf of Augusta, once lined by the ancient cities of Syracuse, Thapsos and Megara Hyblaea, are now a jungle of oil refineries, and oil tankers are anchored offshore. The industrial zone extends from here to Priolo and Augusta, and has the largest concentration of chemical plants in Europe. Nowadays about 40 percent of the crude oil comes from Sicily; there are offshore oil wells at Ragusa. The industries here are going through a bad period at the moment and many workers have been laid off. After years of pollution problems, and criticism from many quarters, what was intended to be the once-and-for-all solution to the woes of southeastern Sicily is beginning to reveal its shortcomings. For the starving peasants who were trying to pull themselves together after the horrors of World War II, the industrial area really did seem a dream, and the population of Syracuse rocketed from 44,000 to 135,000 people, attracted by the prospect of finding work in their region, without having to emigrate.

The inhabited area of Thapsos, where the most recent excavations have taken place, shows three periods of occupation: c 1500–1400 BC, characterised by round huts; c 1300–1200 BC, where the square houses are of the Mycenean type (a bronze bar with figures of a dog and fox, unique in prehistoric Sicily, and thought to be of Aegean origin, was found here); and a final period c 1100–900 BC, with finds of remarkable pottery (now in the archaeological museum in Syracuse).

Megara Hyblaea

Near the large port of **Priolo**, a fast road, signposted *Zona industriale* and *Catania via Litorale* (coast road to Catania) branches off towards the sea through a jungle of industrial plants. Yellow signposts indicate the way to the excavations of the ancient city of **Megara Hyblaea** (open daily 09.00–one and a half hours before sunset, ☎ 0931/512364).

History

Founded by the Megarese of Greece towards the end of the 8C BC, the city was destroyed by Gelon in 483. A second city was founded by Timoleon in 340 BC, which in its turn was obliterated by the Romans in 214. In c 630 BC Pammilus was invited from Megara in Greece by the settlers to 'found' their sub colony at Selinunte. Excavations of the site were begun by the French School in Rome in 1949, and they still supervise digs here most years. The site is enchanting in spring, when wild chrysanthemums (*fiori di maggio*) carpet the surrounding countryside with gold.

The excavations are approached by a byroad which runs alongside a citrus grove behind a line of cypresses. The road continues right (signposted *scavi*) and here in a group of pines is a stretch of **Archaic walls** (6C BC) with four semicircular towers (a fifth has been destroyed). The walls can be followed on foot for some 250m as far as the **Archaic west gate**. A number of tombs have been placed near the walls, salvaged from excavations of the two necropoli which are now

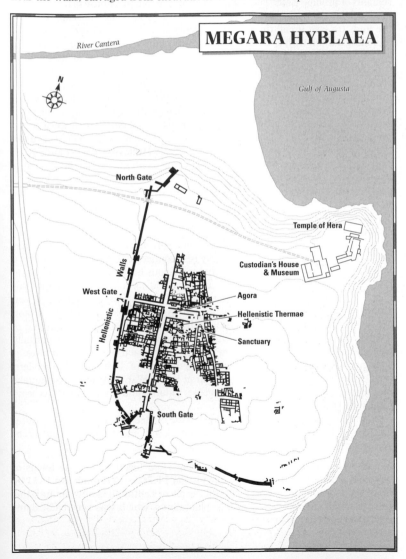

covered by industrial plants. The third necropolis was located in the vicinity of these walls. Further on, below ground level, is an oblong construction with seven bases for columns. Excavated in 1880, it is of uncertain significance. Just before the little bridge over the railway is a car park; cars can continue over the narrow bridge along a rough road past some abandoned farmhouses.

The road passes over the second line of **Hellenistic walls** built around the Hellenistic town (they follow a line of cypresses, see below). To the left of the road here the **Hellenistic north gate** of the city has been identified near the remains of archaic walls. The road ends at the custodian's house in a pretty little garden.The well restored farmhouse here is used as a small museum to house the finds (to visit it call the Superintendency in Syracuse, ☎ 0931/481111), including a tomb with a decorative frieze, although the most important archaic sculptures excavated here are now in the Syracuse archaeological museum.

A path leads across a field to the main area of excavations: the complicated remains include buildings from both the Archaic and Hellenistic periods (the red iron posts indicate the Archaic areas, and the green posts the Hellenistic buildings). At the intersection of the two main roads is the Agora, near which are a sanctuary, interesting **Hellenistic thermae** with good pavements, and a poorly preserved small **Doric temple** of the 4C (protected by a roof). The main east–west road leads from the Agora to the narrow **Hellenistic west gate** in the walls (with two square towers) along the line of cypresses. Near the gate, on a lower level to the south, are ovens and houses of the Archaic period. The main north–south road ends at the **Hellenistic south gate**, a 'pincer' type defence work.

Augusta

Augusta, the most important oil and military port in Italy (see above), now has 34,700 inhabitants. It stands on a rocky islet connected with the mainland by a long bridge. To the east and west are two capacious harbours, the Porto Xifonio and the Porto Megarese, the latter with two old forts (1595). Augusta was founded by Frederick II in 1232 as a refuge for the inhabitants of Centuripe and Montalbano, which he himself had destroyed. In 1269 it was sacked by Philip and Guy de Montfort. It was taken by the French in 1676 after the defeat in the bay of a Dutch fleet under De Ruyter by Admiral Duquesne. De Ruyter was mortally wounded in the action and died a few days later at Syracuse, where he still lies.

Augusta was totally destroyed by the earthquake of 1693, and the modern town suffered severe damage from the air in World War II. Another earthquake hit the town and the provinces of Syracuse, Catania and Ragusa in 1990, leaving 13,000 people homeless.

On the coast to the north is the ruined castle of **Brucoli**, erected by Giovanni Bastida in 1468. *Trotilon*, one of the oldest Greek settlements on the island, probably stood on the bay of Brucoli which now has a large holiday village.

Inland between Augusta and Catania, lying close together, are the towns of Carlentini and Lentini. **Carlentini** (population 11,700) was founded in 1551 by Charles V as a summer residence for the people of Lentini. It is now an undistinguished town, surrounded by orange plantations, which was very badly damaged in an earthquake in 1990.

Leontinoi

A poorly signposted road leads to the site of the Greek city of Leontinoi (open daily 09.00–13.00, ☎ 0931/481111).

History

Founded by the Chalcidians of Naxos in 730–728 BC, on the site of an earlier Sicel settlement. In the 6C BC Panaetius set himself up as tyrant of Leontinoi, the first such ruler in Sicily. In the early 5C it was taken by Hippocrates of Gela, and soon afterwards succumbed to the Syracusans. In 427 BC it despatched the orator Gorgias (480–c 380) to invoke the assistance of Athens against her tyrants. Hieronymus, the last native tyrant of Syracuse, grandson of Hieron II and barely fourteen years old, was assassinated at Leontinoi in 215 BC, a month or so after coming to power.

The excavations are in a nicely planted and well kept site. A path leads down from the entrance to the elaborate **south gate**. Across the valley steps lead up to a path which follows the walls to the top of the hill, from which there is a fine view of the site and the surrounding hills. The site of the prehistoric settlement, with a **necropolis** (6C–4C BC), and hut village, are not at present open to the public.

Lentini is a busy agricultural centre (population 31,700). The medieval town was destroyed in the earthquake of 1693, and the modern town was again badly shaken in 1990. The Chiesa Madre preserves an icon thought to date from the 9C. The churches of S. Luca and S. Trinità have interesting 16C paintings. In piazza Studi, at the far end of Via Piave, a street leading from close to the Cathedral, is the **Archaeological Museum** (closed for repairs until 2004, ☎ 095/7832962) with a well arranged collection of local finds including three fine calyx kraters, and a reconstruction of the south gate of the ancient city.

Southwest of Lentini is the hill town of **Francofonte** (population 14,200), also damaged in 1990, whose town hall occupies the 18C Palazzo Palagonia adjoining the medieval castle. The orange groves produce the *tarocco di Francofonte*, voted by an international jury recently as the finest orange in the world. Quite large, it peels easily and the flesh is tinged with red. The flavour is reminiscent of strawberries. Opera lovers will remember that in *Cavalleria Rusticana* this is the place where *compare* Alfio came to get his wine.

Catania province

CATANIA

Catania, with a population of 348,000, is the second city on the island after Palermo, but it is certainly the livelier of the two. It has been destroyed nine times in the course of its history, by earthquakes, bombardments, and lava, yet it has been rebuilt every time, exactly where it stood before. The city enjoys a love-hate relationship with the volcano at whose foot it stands; the people never call Etna by its name, preferring instead to refer to it affectionately as 'a muntagna, the mountain. The spacious homogeneous appearance of the centre, recently declared a World Heritage site by UNESCO, with long straight streets of imposing Baroque churches and palaces, dates from the reconstruction which followed the earthquake of 1693. The colour scheme of the city centre is black and dark grey, relieved with white limestone details around the doors and the windows. The dark colour is provided by the lava sand used in the plaster on the exterior walls. The effect is rarely sombre; Catania is one of the sunniest cities in Europe and can well afford to use the glittering black 'azzolu on the house fronts, the result is an extremely elegant town centre. Blocks of basalt have also been used for paving the streets. The most prosperous city on the island, Catania was known in the 1960s as the 'Milan of the South', but the life of the city deteriorated drastically in the 1970s and 1980s due to chaotic local administration, when all enterprise was stifled. Things have been changing fast, however, in recent years. New factories have been opened for the manufacture of microelectronic components and the University has opened a special school for microelectronics, the first in Italy. There are now thousands of people employed in this sector. Catania is the place where large quantities of fruit, vegetables, wheat, wine and raw materials for export are brought to be sorted, graded, packed and shipped to various destinations. Noisy, untidy, it is at the same time generous and fun; a city of enormous cultural fervour; a city of many theatres and occasions to listen to music.

Practical information

Getting there
By air
International and national airport at **Fontanarossa**, 5km south. For flight information ☎ 095/304505, 🖳 www.aeroporto.catania.it. The **airport bus** *Alibus* runs every 20mins (05.00–24.00) from the Stazione Centrale (**map 8**) stopping at via Libertà • piazza Verga • piazza Trento • via Etnea • the port and airport. *Giuntabus* run a direct service from the airport to Messina and Milazzo (Aeolian Islands), summer only. *Sais-Interbus* run to the

airport for Enna, Syracuse, Agrigento, Ragusa and Palermo.
By sea
Year-round **ferries** for Malta, Venice and Ravenna, Livorno, Genoa and Naples. In summer *Virtu Ferries* run a **catamaran** service to Malta.
By bus
Buses nos **129** and **136** cross the city from the station via via Etnea. For the **airport bus**, see above. No. **241** for Ognina; no. **27** for the Playa beach. **Local buses**. An excellent network of buses (nearly all of which terminate at

CATANIA PROVINCE

Parco Regionale dei Nebrodi

Parco Regionale dell'Etna

MT ETNA ▲ 3323m

VAL D. BOVE

Mti. Rossi ▲

Randazzo
Moio Alcantara
Francavilla di Sicilia
Maniace
Passopisciaro
Castiglione di Sicilia
Taormina
Linguaglossa
Calatabiano
Giardini Naxos
Bronte
Maletto
S. Alfio
Fiumefreddo di Sicilia
Montagnola
Milo
Riposto
Rifugio Sapienza
Giarre
C. Cantoniera
Zafferana Etnea
Adrano
Biancavilla
Trecastagni
Acireale
Ragalna
Nicolosi
Acitrezza
Cyclops Riviera
Paternò
S-Giovanni La Punta
Aci Castello
Motta
Misterbianco
CATANIA
GOLFO DI CATANIA
Fontanarossa
Oasi del Simeto Wildlife Reserve

Lago di Ogliastro
R. Gornalunga
Ramacca
Lago di Lentini
Palagonia
San Michele di Ganzaria
Militello in Val di Catania
Mineo
Caltagirone
Grammichele
Vizzini
Buccheri
Mazzarrone

0 ___ 5 miles
0 ___ 10 kms

the railway station) serve the surrounding areas. For **buses to Mount Etna** and environs, see p 371.

Long-distance coaches around Sicily. *Sais-Interbus* from 181 via d'Amico (**map 8**) run buses about every hour via the motorway for Palermo (2hrs 40mins) and Messina (1hr 30mins); less frequently via the motorway for Enna (1hr 30mins) and Caltanissetta (1hr 35mins); for Syracuse (c 1hr); Taormina (45 mins–1hr); Agrigento (2hrs 30mins) and Noto (2hrs 30mins). Some of these also stop at the airport. *AST* run a bus from piazza Giovanni XXIII outside the station (**map 8**) to Gela, Caltagirone, and the province of Ragusa. Buses run by *Etna Trasporti* (185 via d'Amico) to Piazza Armerina (2hrs 30mins) and Aidone.

Long-distance coaches to the rest of Italy. Daily coaches from 181 via d'Amico to Rome, Naples, Salerno, Amalfi, Siena, Florence, Pisa, Bologna, Perugia, Bari, Brindisi etc.

By rail

Stazione Centrale (map: **8**), for all services, on the line to Palermo via Enna and on the coastal line between Syracuse and Messina (with some through trains to Rome, Turin and Milan). **Circumetnea station** (☎ 095/541246, ✉ www.circumetnea.it) is at the top of *via* Caronda (off map), for the line which runs around the foot of Etna.

Car hire

Hertz, Fontanarossa airport, ☎ 095/341595 or at 16/c via Toselli (Catania), ☎ 095/322560, ✉ www.hertz.it. *Holiday Car Rental*, Fontanarossa airport, ☎ 095/346769, ✉ www.holidaycarrental.it). *Sicily By Car*, Fontanarossa airport, ☎ 095/349900 or 095/349888 ✉ www.autoeuropa.it. *Maggiore*, Fontanarossa airport, ☎ 095/340594 or at 48 Piazza Verga (Catania), ☎ 095/536927, ✉ www.maggiore.it.

Car parking

There is a multi-storey car park in piazza Grenoble (map: **7**). Garages in the centre charge reasonable tariffs.

Information offices

APT Catania (map: **6**), 10 via Cimarosa, ☎ 095/7306211, ✉ www.apt.catania.it. Open daily 09.00–18.00. Other APT offices also at the railway station and airport (and at the port in summer). The APT offers free guided tours on different themes and days. Ask at the offices for programmes. They also distribute the **tourist card**, offering a range of services, discounts on shopping, museum entrances, and transport.

Where to stay
Hotels

☆☆☆☆☆ *Excelsior* (map: **4**), 39

piazza Giovanni Verga, ☎ 0957/476111, ✉ 095/537015, ✉ www. thi.it. Catania's best hotel; fitness centre.
☆☆☆☆ *Jolly Bellini* (map: **3**), 13 piazza Trento, ☎ 095/316933, ✉ 095/316832, ✉ www.jollyhotels.it. Comfortable and central.
☆☆☆☆ *Jolly Ognina*, 626 via Messina, ☎ 0957/528111, ✉ 0957/121856, ✉ www.jollyhotels.it. Practical position on northern outskirts.
☆☆☆☆ *Katane Palace* (map: **3**), 110 via F. Aprile, ☎ 095/7470702, ✉ 095/747 0172, ✉ www.katanepalace.it. Recently converted 19C building is now one of the most comfortable hotels; good restaurant, garage parking.
☆☆☆☆ *Nettuno*, 121 viale Ruggero di Lauria, ☎ 0957/125252, ✉ 095/498 066, ✉ www.hotel-nettuno.it. On the seafront between city centre and Ognina; pool, private lava rock beach.
☆☆☆☆ *Villa del Bosco* (off map) 62 via del Bosco, ☎ 0957/335100, ✉ 0957/335103, ✉ www.hotelvilladelbosco.it. Turn of the 20C elegance, good restaurant called *Il Canile* (the Dog Kennel!).
☆☆☆ *Duomo* (map: **11**), 28 via Etnea, ☎ 095/2503177, ✉ 095/7152790, ✉ www.hoteldelduomo.it. Delightful hotel tucked away between the Cathedral and the University.
☆☆☆ *Etnea 316* (map: **2**), 316 via Etnea, ☎ 095/2503076. All rooms have private bathroom, air conditioning, TV and personal computer access; room service.
☆☆☆ *La Ville* (map: **8**), 15 via Monteverdi, ☎ 095/7465230, ✉ 095/7465169, ✉ www.rhlaville.it. Small but luxurious, a hotel which also has apartments.
☆☆☆ *Moderno* (map: **10**), 9 via Alessi, ☎ 095/326250, ✉ 095/326674. In the old city centre.
☆☆☆ *Poggio Ducale* (off map), 5 via Gaifami, ☎ 095/330016, ✉ 095/580103, ✉ www.poggioducale.it. Excellent restaurant.

☆☆☆ *Savona* (**map: 11**), 210 via Vittorio Emanuele, ☎ 095/326982, 📠 0957/158169.

☆☆ *Gresi* (**map; 7**) 28 via Pacini, ☎ 095/322709, 📠 0957/153045, ✉ gresihotel@hotmail.com. Welcoming atmosphere.

☆ *Centrale Europa* (**map: 11**), 167 via Vittorio Emanuele, ☎ 095/311309, 📠 095/317531. Air conditioning.

☆ *Hotel Rubens* (**map: 7**), 196, via Etnea, ☎ 095/317073, 📠 095/7151713. Large comfortable rooms with private bath, TV and air conditioning. Courteous management.

PLAYA BEACH ☆☆☆☆ *Parco degli Aragonesi*, 2 lungomare Kennedy, ☎ 095/7234073, 📠 095/349826. South of the city in front of the long sandy beach. Spacious and modern. Pool; large park; good restaurant.

S.GREGORIO (close to the motorway exit) ☆☆☆☆ *Garden*, 12 via Madonna delle Lagrime, Trappeto, ☎ 0957/177767, 📠 0957/177991. Comfortable with good restaurant, pool.

☆☆☆☆ and ☆☆☆ hotels also at Aci Castello and Acireale (see p 382).

Youth hostel

Agorà Hostel, 6 piazza Currò, ☎ 095/7233010, 📠 095/349029, ✉ www.agorahostel.hypermart.net. Central position. Innovative; internet.

Bed and breakfast

☆☆ *Like at home*, 66 via Verdi, ☎ 095/7158576, ✉ www.bedandbreakfast.it/likeathome. University professor's home, bilingual babysitter, internet, library, English and German spoken.

Casamia, 48 via D'Annunzio, ☎ & 📠 095/445682, ✉ casamia48@tin.it. Garage; internet.

Sicilianhome, 66 via Vittorio Emanuele, ☎ 095/316557, ✉ www.sicilianhome.com. Also evening meals.

Campsites

OGNINA ☆☆ *Jonio*, 2 via Villini a Mare, ☎ 095/491139, 📠 095/ 492277, ✉ www.camping.it/sicilia/jonio.

PLAYA BEACH ☆☆ *Europeo*, 91 viale Kennedy, ☎ 095/591026. On the southern outskirts of the city.

☆ *Internazionale Playa*, 47 viale Kennedy, ☎ 095/340880.

Farmhouse accommodation

☆☆☆☆ *Alcalà*, near Misterbianco, ☎ 095/7130029, ✉ www.omnia.it/alcala. Peaceful location in an orange grove, *Ruvitello*, contrada Cuba, nr Misterbianco, ☎ 095/451405 & 095/7470104, 📠 095/533150, ✉ www.ruvitello.it. Orange farm with pleasant atmosphere, pool, delicious food. Open May–Oct.

Eating out
Restaurants

€€€ *Da Rinaldo*, 59 via Simili, ☎ 095/532312. Excellent. Closed Aug.

€€€ *I tre bicchieri*, 31 via S. Giuseppe al Duomo, ☎ 0957/153540. Superb food and good wine cellar. Cookery courses on arrangement. Closed midday Sun and Mon.

€€ *La Lampara*, 49 via Pasubio, ☎ 095/383237. Excellent fish, Closed Sun evening and Wed.

€€ *Osteria Antica Marina*, 29 via Pardo, ☎ 095/348197. Tiny restaurant tucked away inside the fish market. Booking is essential. *Alici marinati* (raw anchovy salad) or *spaghetti coi ricci* (spaghetti with sea urchins) are both very tasty dishes. Closed Wed.

€€ *Sicilia in bocca*, 33–35 via Dusmet, ☎ 095/2500208. Medieval atmosphere within the bastions, good pizzeria next door. Closed Mon.

€ *Break Selfservice,* 24 via Puccini, ☎ & 📠 095/310209.

€ *Pierrot*, via Di Sangiuliano, ☎ 095/7150555. Spaghetti, pizza, sandwiches, salads. Popular after-theatre rendezvous.

€ *I Pitagorici*, 59 via Archimede, ☎ 095/532626. Vegetarian restaurant.

€ *Taverna dei Conti*, 41 via Oberdan,

☎ 095/310035. Homely and friendly.
€ *Trattoria Posillipo di Turi La Paglia*,
27 via Pardo. Next door to the *Antica
Marina*; also specializes in fish.
CATANIA OUTSKIRTS €€€ *La
Siciliana*, 52 viale Marco Polo, ☎
095/376400. One of the *Buon Ricordo*
chain. Closed Mon and PH evenings.
OGNINA €€€ *Costa Azzurra*, 2 via de
Cristoforo, ☎ 095/494920. Stylish.
Closed Mon.
S. GIOVANNI LI CUTI €€
Cutilisci, 67/69 via S. Giovanni Li Cuti,
☎ 095/372558. Innovative organic
dishes and excellent pizza on the
seafront.

Pizzerie

Coppola, 39 via Coppola, ☎ 095/
312909. Catania's favourite pizzeria,
also famous for salads, *carpaccio di
pescespada* (raw swordfish) and *panna-
cotta* for dessert.
I Viceré, 97 via Grotte Bianche,
☎ 095/320188.
Vico S. Filomena, 35 via S.Filomena,
☎ 095/316761. Offers 7 types of
Sicilian pizza: from Syracuse, Rosolini,
Enna, Gela, Catania, Vittoria and S.
Giuseppe Iato.

Cafés, pastry shops and ice cream parlours

Caprice, 32 via Etnea. Also light
lunches and snacks.
Comis, 7 piazza Vittorio Emanuele. Very
popular with local people for snacks, ice
cream and light lunches.
Ernesto, 91 viale Ruggero di Lauria. Ice
cream.
Europa, 302 corso Italia. Excellent pistachio sorbet.
Mantegna, 350 via Etnea. Cakes and
pastries.
St Moritz, 206 & 198 via Etnea. Ice
cream.
Savia and *Spinella*, via Etnea (opposite
Villa Bellini). Two bars offering breakfast.
Scardaci, 84 via S.Maddalena, also at
158 via Etnea. About midnight the

insomniacs and nightowls line up here
for fresh breakfast pastries, the famous
cornetti.

Picnics

Villa Bellini and Villa Pacini are pleasant
places to picnic.

Pubs

St Patrick, 35 via S. Orsola, behind
Opera House; Irish, also restaurant.
The Stag's Head, 7 via Michele
Rapisardi; English.
Il Tulipano Nero, 62 via Coppola; Dutch.
Waxy O'Connor's, 1 piazza Spirito
Santo; Irish.

Annual festivals

The *Feast of Saint Agatha* (S.
Agata) is celebrated on 3–5
February and 17 August with traditional
processions and magnificent fireworks.
A music, dance and theatre festival is
held in summer at **Le Ciminiere**
(Centro Culturale Fieristico) near the
station (beyond **map: 8**). A popular out-
door music festival is held in the city in
July.

Entertainment
Theatre

Massimo Bellini Opera House
(**map: 11**), piazza Bellini, for opera and
concerts. *Teatro Stabile Verga*, 35 via
dello Stadio, for plays.
Other theatres include the *Musco*, the
Metropolitan and the *Ambasciatori*.

Concerts

Concerts are also held at the
Metropolitan. From October–May the
Associazione Musicale Etnea perform
here. In summer concerts are given in
many of the Baroque churches in the
city, and (open-air) at Villa Bellini and at
the Playa Beach amphitheatre.

Puppet shows

Puppet shows by *Fratelli Napoli*, via
Madonna di Fatima, ☎ 095/416787.

Internet points

Nievski, 15 scalinata Alessi
(13.00–18.00, 20.00–02.00, closed Mon).
RAS, 1b via Corridoni (09.00–19.00).
Tertulia, 1 via Michele Rapisardi
(10.30–02.00; Sun 17.00–02.00).

Shopping
Markets

A large daily food market is
held in piazza Carlo Alberto (**map: 7**)
and a general market in the surrounding streets (including via S. Gaetano alle
Grotte). On Sunday morning this
becomes an **antiques market**. In the
streets to the south of piazza Duomo
and via Garibaldi (including via Gisira;
map: 14) there is another daily food
market called **La Pescheria**, where
fresh fish, meat and other foodstuffs are
sold.

Foreign language newspapers

Foreign language newspapers and periodicals are available at the railway station and the airport, sometimes at the
newsagents in piazza Stesicoro (**map:7**).
USA Today is sometimes available in
front of the University (**map: 10**).

History

Catania was perhaps a Sicel trading post when the first Greek colony
(Chalcidians from Naxos) established itself here in 729 BC, and, as *Katane*, it
soon rose to importance. Charondas (7C or early 6C) drew up a written code
of laws here which was eventually adopted by all the Ionian colonies of
Sicily and Magna Graecia; the poet Tisias of Himera, called Stesichorus,
died here (c 540); and Xenophanes, the pantheistic philosopher, adopted
Catanian citizenship (c 530). Hieron of Syracuse took the city in 476 and
exiled the inhabitants to Leontinoi (now an excavated site, see p 351),
refounding the town with celebrations for which Aeschylus wrote his
Women of Aetna; the exiles returned and drove out his Doric colonists in 461.
In 415 it was the base of the Athenian operations against Syracuse, but it
fell to Dionysius in 403, when the citizens were sold as slaves. After the
defeat of the Syracusan fleet by Magus the Carthaginian it was occupied by
Himilco. Catania opened its gates to Timoleon in 339 and to Pyrrhus in 278,
and was one of the first Sicilian towns to fall to the Romans (263). Its greatest prosperity dated from the time of Augustus who rewarded it for taking
his part against Pompey.

In early Christian days Catania was the scene of the martyrdom of St
Agatha (238–251), the patroness of the city. In the Middle Ages it was
wrecked by an earthquake (1169), sacked by Henry VI (1194), and again by
Frederick II (1232), who built the castle to hold his rebellious subjects in
check. Constance of Aragon, his empress, died here on 23 June 1222. The
17C saw the calamities of 1669 and 1693, the former the most terrible eruption of Etna in history, the latter a violent earthquake. The lava flows which
reached the town in 1669 can still be seen from the ring road. In 1943
Catania was bombarded from the air and from the sea.

Famous residents

The composer Vincenzo Bellini (1801–35); the poet Mario Rapisardi
(1844–1912); the composer Giovanni Pacini (1796–1867). The writer
Federico de Roberto (1866–1917) lived most of his life in Catania, and died
here. Frederick III of Aragon died in Catania in 1377. The sculptor Emilio

Greco (1913–1995) was also born in the city. Giovanni Verga (1840–1922), one of Sicily's most influential writers, was born in Vizzini but lived and worked all his life in Catania.

Piazza del Duomo

The old centre of the city is the well-proportioned piazza del Duomo (**map: 11**). In the middle of it stands a fountain with an antique lava elephant (which has since become the symbol of Catania) and an Egyptian obelisk that was once perhaps a turning-post in the Roman circus, set up here in 1736 by Giovanni Battista Vaccarini, a native of Palermo, who became the official municipal architect in 1730. It is modelled on the monument by Bernini in piazza Minerva in Rome. The people call the elephant *Liotru*, after Heliodorus, a Byzantine negromancer who used it as a 'Jumbo Jet' to fly between Catania and Constantinople in the 6C AD. The square is surrounded by 18C buildings, mostly by Vaccarini.

The 18C elephant fountain

The **Duomo** (**map: 11**; closed 12.30–17.00), dedicated to St Agatha, was founded by Count Roger in 1094 and rebuilt after the earthquakes of 1169 and 1693. The granite columns on the lower storey of its Baroque **façade** (by Vaccarini, 1736–58) come from the Roman theatre. The **cupola**, by Battaglia, dates from 1804. The **north door**, with three statuettes, is attributed to Gian Domenico Mazzola (1577). The structure of the mighty 11C black lava **apses** can be seen from no. 159 via Vittorio Emanuele.

In the **interior** during restoration work in the 1950s, the foundations of the 11C–12C basilica were revealed beneath the nave. The fine antique columns (of late Imperial and Byzantine date) in the transepts and three apses have also been uncovered. **South side**. Against the second pier is the tomb of Vincenzo Bellini (see below), by Giovanni Battista Tassara. The second and third altarpieces are by Borremans.

South transept. A doorway by Giovanni Battista Mazzola (1545) leads into the Norman **Cappella della Madonna** which preserves a Roman sarcophagus, with the figures (very worn) finely carved in the round, thought to come from Izmir. It contains the ashes of Frederick II (d. 1337), Louis (d. 1355), Frederick III (d. 1377) and other illustrious members of the House of Aragon. Opposite is the beautiful tomb of Queen Constance of Aragon (d. 1363), wife of Frederick III, with contemporary scenes of Catania. The sculptured fragment above the door dates from the 15C. The other chapel in the south transept is the **Cappella di S. Agata** (seen through a magnificent wrought iron gate, about which the people wryly comment that the gate was erected only after the body of the saint had been stolen) which contains a marble altarpiece (*Coronation of the saint*); the tomb (right) of the Viceroy Fernandez d'Acuña (d. 1494), a kneeling figure attended by a page, by Antonello Freri of Messina; and (left) the treasury, with a rich collection of relics of St Agatha, including her reliquary bust by Giovanni di Bartolo (1376). These are exposed only for the saint's feast days (3–5 February, 17 August, and, in procession, on 4 and 5 February).

The stalls in the **choir**, finely sculpted by Scipione di Guido of Naples (1588), represent the life of St Agatha and the adventures of her corpse.

North transept. The Norman **Cappella del Crocifisso** is approached through an arch designed by Gian Domenico Mazzola (1563). In the **sacristy** is a fresco painted in 1675 showing the destruction of Catania by the lava flow from Etna in 1669. To the right of the Cathedral is the sumptuous **Diocese Museum** open 09.00–12.30, 16.00–19.30, closed Mon, ☒ www.museo diocesicatania.it), which splendidly displays the cathedral treasure, fine art works and objects pertaining to the cult of S. Agata. From the terrace there is an interesting view over the old city centre.

The **Municipio** (Town Hall), begun in 1695, was finished by Vaccarini in 1741. Two state carriages are on view in the courtyard. The vista on the south side of piazza Duomo is closed by the fine **Porta Uzeda** (1696) which leads to the little public garden called Villa Pacini and beyond to the harbour. The streets behind the marble **Amenano Fountain** (1867), an underground river which emerges at this point, are lined with a colourful daily market, where meat, fish and vegetables are sold.

Saint Agatha

Pagan pageant or Christian ritual? Both of these and much more! The Feast of St Agatha (S. Agata) galvanizes the whole population of the city during the first week of February, and again on 17 August. An early Christian martyr, Agatha was only thirteen years old when she was arrested for her religious beliefs. In spite of blandishments and then threats, she would not recant her faith. On 4 February 251 she underwent terrible tortures including the mutilation of her breasts. She miraculously recovered during the night, so the following day her tormentor, Quinziano, Roman governor of Catania, decided to burn her on a grill set up in the amphitheatre in front of the populace. The flames would not touch her, and a sudden earthquake caused the Romans to flee from the town leaving Agatha unscathed. She asked to be taken to her prison cell, where she died, but even after death she could not rest in peace. Her body, still intact, was carried off to Constantinople by the Byzantine general George Maniakes as a gift for the emperor in 1040, but on 17 August 1126 she was brought back to Catania by two soldiers of the imperial guard, who had cut her body into pieces in order to smuggle her back home.

St. Agatha is the patron saint both of women who have undergone mastectomy, and also of firemen. The processions in her honour are impressive and richly Baroque. The huge float, carrying boxes containing parts of her body and the 14C **reliquary**, glittering with jewels, which holds her torso and head, is dragged through the streets by thousands of *divoti* wearing traditional white robes and black caps, preceded by the *candelore*, enormous highly decorated candlesticks representing the corporations of the city. The celebrations are concluded with spectacular fireworks. To witness the feast is an unforgettable experience, in itself worth the visit to Sicily, but best avoided if you do not like crowds; in 2002 about 300,000 people attended.

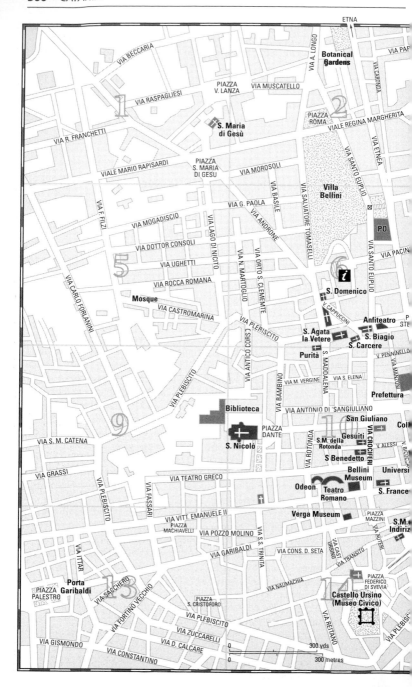

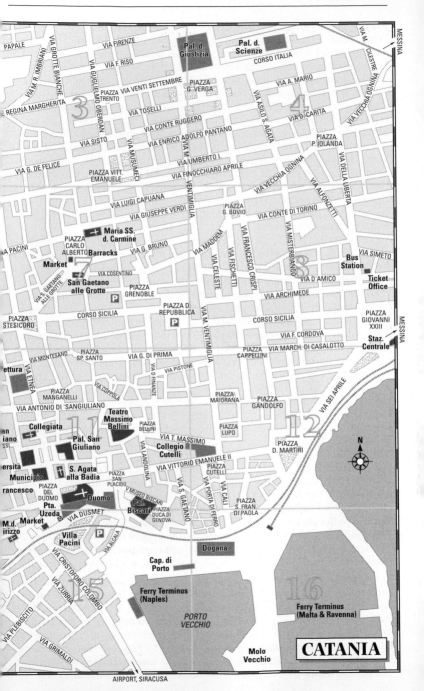

CATANIA

Piazza San Francesco, Via Crociferi and San Nicolò

From piazza del Duomo the handsome, long, straight via Vittorio Emanuele II which contains a number of Baroque church façades, leads west. In **piazza S. Francesco** (map: 10) a large votive deposit of 6C BC pottery came to light in 1959. Dominating the little square, which in the Middle Ages was the vegetable market, is the monument to the cardinal and archbishop Giovanni Benedetto Dusmet (1935), who died in 1894, already considered a saint by his flock. People of Catania have a pithy sense of humour. They say that his posture: his hands held out in front of him, palms up, and his downcast gaze, conveys his thoughts: 'I know this is a horrible monument, don't blame me! I didn't ask to be put up here!' His body, uncorrupted, can be seen inside the Cathedral, under the last altar on the south side. The church houses some of the *candelore*, the impressive candlesticks representing the city corporations used during the processions for St Agatha, so it is possible to take a close look at them, and appreciate the skill of the bearers. Each one weighs about a ton, and is borne by eight stalwarts chosen from the category represented.

Facing the Baroque façade of **S. Francesco**, is a palace containing a small flat (across the courtyard to the left and up an old flight of steps) which houses the **Bellini Museum** (open 09.00–13.00; Tues & Thurs also 15.00–18.00). This delightful little museum commemorates the great composer Vincenzo Bellini (1801–35), who was born here and lived here for 16 years. The charming rooms have retained their character and are crowded with mementoes, including his harpsichord (in the alcove where he is thought to have been born), several pianos and his death mask. The **music library** (open to students) preserves the original scores of *Adelson e Salvini, I Capuleti ed i Montecchi*, and *I Puritani*, besides fragments of all the remaining operas. On the opposite side of the same palace there is a museum (opening times as for Bellini Museum) dedicated to the graphic works of the sculptor **Emilio Greco**, who was born in Catania.

From piazza S. Francesco, beyond the arch of S. Benedetto (1704) begins **via Crociferi** (map: 10), the prettiest 18C street in Catania (totally closed to traffic), lined with Baroque churches, convents and palaces, many of them approached by a short flight of steps. Recent excavations here have revealed remains of the Roman city.

S. Benedetto (left) has a graceful façade and vestibule of 1762. The softly coloured interior (entrance in via S. Benedetto; open Thurs 06.30–12.00, 15.30–18.00; Sun & PH 09.00–10.00 and 17.00–18.00) has an elaborate nuns' choir, a frescoed barrel vault by Giovanni Tuccari (1725), and a beautiful floor. **S. Francesco Borgia** (closed) has a dome frescoed by Olivio Sozzi: the church and the large Jesuit college (with four courtyards) are the work of Angelo Italia (1754). On the right **S. Giuliano** was begun in 1739 and continued by Vaccarini (who is responsible for the façade). In the fine elliptical interior is a 14C painted *Crucifix*.

Via Antonio di Sangiuliano (map: 10), a handsome street lined with oleanders, with splendid views of the sea, leads uphill to the highest part of the city, once the acropolis of ancient *Katane*, and the church of **S. Nicolò** (map: 10). It faces a little crescent of houses which may have been designed by Stefano Ittar. This is the largest church in Sicily (105m long, transepts, 42m), begun in 1687 by Giovanni Battista Contini, and rebuilt in 1735 by Francesco Battaglia, probably to the design of Antonino Amato. The dome was designed by Stefano Ittar. The striking façade with its gigantic columns was left incomplete in 1796.

The simplicity of the **interior** (open 09.00–13.30; Wed also 15.00–17.30) emphasises its good proportions. The meridian line on the floor of the transept dates from 1841. The choir stalls are by Gaetano Franzese and Nicolò Bagnasco. Only the beautiful case remains of the huge organ (2916 pipes) which is being restored. Its builder, Donato del Piano (d. 1775), lies buried beneath. Goethe alluded to its wonderful sound when he heard it here in 1787. The chapels at the east end have been made into war memorials. The roof is accessible and there is a breathtaking view.

Next door is the remarkable **convent**, the largest in Europe after that of Mafra in Portugal. When Patrick Brydone saw it in 1770 he thought it was a royal palace, only to discover it 'was nothing else than a convent of fat Benedictine monks, who wanted to assure themselves a paradise in this world, if not in the other'! (It is now used by two university faculties, but is sometimes shown on request by the porter, Monday–Friday.) It was almost entirely rebuilt after 1693 to the design of Antonino Amato and his son Andrea; the rich detail of its Baroque ornamentation combines well with its simplicity of line.

The first court is overlooked by the splendid façade with delightful windows and balconies. Excavations here have found prehistoric fragments as well as Greek and Roman remains, including a lava road. In one of the cloisters there is a beautiful (enclosed) garden with a majolica neo-Gothic tabernacle, and another has a graceful arcade. The monumental neo-classical staircase (1794) was designed by Antonino Battaglia. The impressive long corridors have fine vaults.

The remainder of the conventual complex (entered to the right of the church), is occupied by the municipal **library**, one of the most valuable in Sicily, and the Ursino Recupero Library. The monastic library, with its original bookcases and majolica floor of 1700 also survives. Outside the convent wall, to the left of the church façade (surrounded by railings), some remains of Roman baths can be seen, well below ground level.

Via Gesuiti (**map: 10**), with herringbone paving in large blocks of lava (typical of the side streets of the city), descends from S. Nicolò past modest houses. Via Rotonda branches off to the right. Remains of Roman baths are visible here under the primitive domed church of **S. Maria della Rotonda**. Many of the adjacent houses have been converted from another bath-house. Via S. Agostino continues back down to via Vittorio Emanuele II past the Odeon (described below).

The Archaeological Park

The old city centre of Catania, corresponding approximately to the area occupied by the Greek *Katane*, is now an archaeological park.

Visiting the site and opening times

- The site is open daily, 09.00–13.00; Roman Theatre also 15.00–17.00, but a chronic shortage of custodians may mean that one or more of the monuments are closed. Ask at the ticket office; all efforts will be made to allow interested visitors access to the various sites.
- The ticket office is at the entrance to the Roman Theatre. Tickets also allow entry to the Roman Amphitheatre, the Rotonda and Indirizzo bath complexes.

At no. 266 via Vittorio Emanuele is the inconspicuous entrance to the **Roman Theatre**, Teatro Romano (**map 10**), now overlooked by houses. This is a Roman building on the site of the theatre where Alkibiades harangued the men of

Catania to win them to the cause of Athens (415 BC). The building is of lava, practically all of the marble facing having disappeared. The underground passageways which gave access to the cavea are very well preserved. The cavea has nine wedges of seats in two main tiers; the diameter was 86m, the depth of the orchestra 29m. The orchestra is sometimes flooded since the underground River Amenano comes to the surface here at certain times of the year. From the top of the cavea a path leads round to the small **Odeon**, a semicircular building used for rehearsals and for competitions. Concerts are now given here in the summer. One colonnade of the **Foro Romano** (no admission) remains near piazza S. Pantaleone, to the southwest.

Not far from the Cathedral, at 201 via Vittorio Emanuele, is Catania's new **Toy Museum** (10.00–23.00 Tues–Sun, Mon closed; café and gift shop), housed in the lovely Baroque Palazzo Bruca. A fascinating collection of toys has been carefully arranged: old dolls and teddy bears, tea sets and dolls' prams, card games and puppets. One room provides space for temporary exhibits and impromptu creativity, with a little puppet theatre.

On the other side of via Vittorio Emanuele at no. 8 via S. Anna (**map: 10**) is the **Verga Museum** (open 09.00–13.30; Wed also 15.00–17.30; closed Sun & PH). On the second floor, upstairs on the left is the spartan (restored) apartment which belonged to the parents of the writer Giovanni Verga who lived and died here. Some of the original furnishings have been preserved in his study, library and bedroom. The library is open to students and there are photocopies of the autograph works which belong to the museum (now kept at the university for conservation reasons). These include the manuscripts of his most famous works.

Giovanni Verga

Verga is considered by many critics to be the greatest Italian writer after Manzoni. He is famous for his naturalistic fiction, which gives a dramatic picture of the tragic social conditions of everyday Sicilian life using a simple and direct language and style. His first great success was *Storia di una Capinera* (published in 1871). His masterpieces include *Vita dei campi* (a collection of short stories, including *Cavalleria Rusticana*), *I Malavoglia* and *Mastro-don Gesualdo*. By 1884 he was acclaimed as the greatest living Italian writer. He made contact with Emile Zola and remained a life-long friend of the writer Luigi Capuana, also born in the province of Catania. Although his fame diminished towards the end of his life, his eightieth birthday was publicly celebrated in Catania with Luigi Pirandello as orator, and he was nominated senator in the same year.

Castello Ursino

Via S. Anna leads to the busy via Garibaldi. The Baroque **Porta Garibaldi** (1768) can be seen at the west end, 1km away. In the other direction is **piazza Mazzini**, charmingly arcaded with 32 columns from the Roman basilica (beneath S. Agostino).

Via Auteri, in a dilapidated poor district of the city, with a daily street market, leads south to piazza Federico di Svevia, where low houses surround the Castello Ursino (**map: 14**) built by Frederick II, Riccardo da Lentini directed the works. It was partly destroyed by the lava of 1669, which completely surrounded it.

The castle was restored after 1837 and for many years has housed the **Museo**

Civico (☎ 095/345830, open daily 09.00–13.00, 15.00–18.00, Sun and PH morning only). Material from the monastery of S. Nicolò was augmented by the archaeological treasures collected by the Prince of Biscari (see below) in the 18C. Although exhibitions are held here, and extensive repairs are now complete, the arrangement of the collections is still in progress at the time of writing. There are

Castello Ursino

plans to house the archaeological collections in a new museum inside the old Bourbon Prison in piazza Majorana (**map: 12**). A fine courtyard contains sculptural fragments and sarcophagi. New archaeological excavations around the castle have revealed long sections of the Norman fortifications.

Near the submerged railway line just out of the piazza is the simple little church of **S. Maria dell'Indirizzo** (**map: 14**). Behind it, in the courtyard of a school are the remains of Roman baths called Terme dell'Indirizzo and a tiny domed Greek-cross building in black lava. Via Zappalà Gemelli, with a Baroque palace, leads back through the market to piazza Duomo.

East of the Duomo

Via Vittorio Emanuele II leads east out of piazza del Duomo (**map 11**) between the north side of the Cathedral and the Baroque church of **S. Agata alla Badia** (open 08.00–13.00), another work by Vaccarini (1748–67; the Rococo interior was completed after his death). Beyond in a little piazza on the right is the church of **S. Placido** (usually closed) with a façade of 1769, attributed to Stefano Ittar, and a pretty interior.

Via Museo Biscari is named after the **Palazzo Biscari**, the most impressive private palace in Catania. The best view of the exterior is from via Dusmet. Here in the 18C the Prince of Biscari, Ignazio Paternò Castello collected for his famous museum, part of which is preserved in the Museo Civico (see above). Concerts are occasionally held in the lovely Rococo Salone della Musica.

On the other side of via Vittorio Emanuele II via Landolina leads to the splendid Opera House, **Teatro Massimo Bellini** (1873–90). The narrow streets in this area, once a run-down part of the city, are now full of life; many pubs and open-air cafés open in the evening, giving rise to the so-called '*movida*' of Catania: live music for all tastes, jazz, pop or classical, especially in the summer.

Via Vittorio Emanuele II continues towards the sea passing on the right via Bonaiuto, where a **Byzantine chapel**, built between the 6C and the 9C is open to the public (Tues to Sat, 08.30–16.00, Sun 09.00–13.00, Mon closed), there is a nice little café too. Further along is the **Collegio Cutelli** (left), with a remarkable round courtyard designed by Vaccarini (1779). Piazza dei Martiri has a statue of S. Agata on top of a column removed from the ancient theatre. Here a wide terrace overlooks the harbour.

Via Etnea

On the north side of piazza del Duomo (**map: 11**) is the handsome via Etnea, nearly 3km long, the city's main street. It has the most elegant shops (especially clothes and books) and some cafés and its wide lava pavements are always crowded. It rises to a splendid view of the peak of Mount Etna in the distance.

Beyond the Town Hall is the distinguished **piazza dell'Università**, laid out by Vaccarini. The **university** (**map: 11**) was founded in 1434 by Alfonso V of Aragon as the first university in Sicily, and rebuilt after the earthquake of 1693; the courtyard was begun by Andrea Amato and finished in 1752 by Giovanni Battista Vaccarini. Just beyond is the **Collegiata**, a royal chapel of c 1768 by Stefano Ittar.

Some way further on via Etnea runs through **piazza Stesicoro** (map 6,7), the heart of modern Catania, with a monument to Bellini by Giulio Monteverde (1882). Overlooking the piazza is the 18C church of S. Biagio. In the centre are the scant ruins of the **Roman amphitheatre** in black lava, thought to date from the 2C AD. The external circumference was 389m, and the arena was one of the largest after the Colosseum in Rome. There were 56 entrance arches. The visible remains include a corridor, part of the exterior wall, and fragments of the cavea supported on vaults; the rest of the structure still exists in part beneath the surrounding buildings. Its destruction had already begun under Theodoric when it was used as a quarry; Totila made use of the stone in building the city walls in 530, and Count Roger stole its decorative elements to embellish his cathedral in 1091. In 1693 the area was used as a dump for the rubble of the earthquake.

Nearby, in piazza della Borsa are remains of the 18C church of **S. Euplio** covering a 3C Roman hypogeum. It was partially restored in 1978 after its destruction in 1943 (for admission to the crypt apply at the Town Hall).

Via Manzoni (**map: 10**), which leads out of the south side of the square parallel to via Etnea is interesting for its numerous well-stocked haberdashery shops and old-fashioned children's clothes shops. Beyond the top end of the square behind S. Biagio is the church of the **S. Carcere**, flanked by a strong defence wall. Incorporated into the Baroque façade is a doorway with grotesque animal heads, which dates from 1236; it was formerly in the façade of the Duomo. In the interior (open Thurs & Sat 16.00–19.00; Sun & PH 09.30–12.00) St Agatha's prison, with a Roman barrel vault, is shown by the custodian.

Via Cappuccini continues uphill to via Maddalena where the church of **S. Agata la Vetere** (**map: 6**), probably built only a few years after the martyrdom of the saint in the 3C stands opposite the church of the **Purità** (or the **Visitazione**), with a curving façade by **Battaglia** (1775) next to its handsome convent. S. Agata la Vetere was once Catania's cathedral.

A little to the north is the church of **S. Domenico** (**map: 6**; open before 09.30 and 17.00–18.30; ring at the convent next door). It contains a beautiful *Madonna* by Antonello Gagini (1526), and a painting of *St Vincent Ferrer* by Olivio Sozzi (1757).

From piazza Stesicoro on via Etnea, with its monument to Vincenzo Bellini, via S. Gaetano alle Grotte with its daily market leads to the little church of **S. Gaetano alle Grotte** which dates from 1700. The former church, built into a volcanic cavern beneath in 1262, is now usually closed but is sometimes open for Mass. The cave itself probably represents the oldest Christian place of worship in the city, and perhaps the first burial place of St. Agatha.

The main market for produce and textiles occupies **piazza Carlo Alberto** (map: 7). The piazza is overlooked by a fine palace occupied by the Lucchesi-Palli barracks (in the courtyard of which is an ancient tomb traditionally held to be that of Stesichorus) next to the church of the Carmine.

Via Etnea continues north past the post office. Steps lead up to the charming **Villa Bellini** (map: 2, 6), a fine public garden laid out c 1870. It contains busts of famous citizens and a monument to Giovanni Pacini (1796–1867), another local composer. At the north end of the garden a gate leads out to viale Regina Margherita, part of the modern east–west artery of the city, c 5km long.

Further north is a fine **Botanical Garden** (map; 2; open weekdays 09.00–13.00). The main entrance is on via Etnea, but the usual entrance is on via Longo. It is particularly famous for its cactus plants. Via Etnea ends at Parco Gioeni, on a lava flow, an attractive and unusual public park.

About 500m west of the Botanical Garden, surrounded by tall, modern apartment blocks, is the church of **S. Maria di Gesù** (map: 1), founded in 1442 and built in 1465. To the left is the pretty exterior of the Cappella Paternò which survived the earthquake of 1693. It is entered from the north aisle of the church through a doorway by Antonello Gagini (1519) with a *Pietà* in the lunette above. Inside is a fresco (transferred to wood) of the *Madonna with St Agatha and St Catherine*, by Angelo di Chirico (signed 1525). Above the main altar of the church is a *Crucifix* by Fra Umile di Petralia, and in the second north chapel, a *Madonna with two angels in adoration* by Antonello Gagini.

In the other direction viale Regina Margherita and its continuation viale XX Settembre, run east beyond via Etnea into piazza Giovanni Verga, a large square dominated by the **Palazzo di Giustizia** (map: 3; 1952) and the focus of a new and fashionable district. The fountain in the centre by Carmelo Mendola (1975) is a monument to Giovanni Verga and represents the moment of tragedy in his masterpiece *The House by the Medlar Tree*, when the Malavoglia family lose their fishing boat. Further east, in corso Italia, the **Palazzo delle Scienze** (map; 4; 1942) houses the geological and volcanological collections of the university. The corso terminates at the sea in piazza Europa, with a watchtower on top of a mound of lava. Viale Ruggero di Lauria leads from here to the Ognina and **Museo del mare** or Sea Museum (14–17 piazza Ognina and 18 via dei Conzari, ☎ 095/7128989, open daily 09.00–13.00). Many of Catania's fishermen live in this part of town and the museum is a way of honouring the fishing community. Mementoes of fishing from the past, anchors and boats are on display, and traditional fishing methods are explained. In the other direction viale Africa leads south towards the main railway station past **Le Ciminiere** (the Chimney Stacks), with its tall chimneys, which was built in the 19C as a sulphur refinery. It has been restored as a cultural centre with exhibition halls and space for theatrical performances and concerts, and will house the Puppet Theatre and some new museums, including the **Museo Storico Sbarco in Sicilia 1943**, the Museum of the Allied Landing in Sicily 1943 (☎ 095/533540; Tues–Sun 10.00–13.00, 16.00–20.00, closed Mon; last tickets one hour before closing). A collection of uniforms, weapons, photographs and films, reconstructions of a bunker and an air-raid shelter, together with wax models of the protagonists of 'Operation Husky' as it was called; documents on a crucial moment in the history of World War II.

MOUNT ETNA

Mount Etna, to the northwest of Catania is the highest volcano (c 3350m) in Europe and one of the largest in the world. The fertile territory on the lower slopes of the mountain, and the lava-built towns at its foot, including **Adrano** and **Randazzo** are well worth a visit. Other places of particular interest are **Castello Maniace** near Bronte, and **Acireale** on the coast.

Etna

In 1987, the volcano was at last declared a regional park, protecting 59,000ha of unique geology, flora and fauna, the particular villages and farms and the traditional methods of forestry.

The ascent of Etna, although now easy and commonplace, is an experience which should not be missed, not only for its volcanic phenomena but also the superb view. The extent of a visit is always subject to current volcanic activity, and the visibility determined by cloud conditions and the direction of the smoke from the main craters. There are splendid views of the lava fields on the approach roads to **Rifugio Sapienza** and **Piano Provenzana**: the two starting points for the ascent to the top of Etna. Higher up it is usually possible to see smoking and gaseous fissures, and explosions from the main craters. There is often a strong smell of sulphur and much of the mountainside is covered by yellow sulphur patches. The view, beyond the mountain's hundreds of subsidiary cones and craters, can extend across the whole of Sicily, the Aeolian Islands and Calabria. The spectacle is unique owing to the enormous difference in height between Etna and the surrounding hills. Etna online: ✉ www.etnaonline.it

Statistics

Etna's circular cone is nearly 40km in diameter at the base. From a distance it appears almost perfectly regular in shape and the great width of its base detracts from its height. But the terminal cone, with its four open summit craters, rises from a truncated cone 2801m high on whose sides are about 300 side craters. The smaller craters are nearly always arranged along a regular line of fracture, called 'button formations'.

On the northeast side is the Valle del Bove, an immense chasm, 19km in circumference, bounded on three sides by sheer walls of tufa and lava, in places 900m high. During the eruptions of 1978–79, 1986 and 1992 the lava flowed into this huge natural reservoir, avoiding the towns on the southeast slopes.

Vegetation and wildlife

The soil at the foot of Etna is extraordinarily fertile because the volcanic ash is rich in nutrients. In the cultivated zone (*pedemontana*) oranges, lemons and tangerines are grown behind low black lava dry-stone walls. The higher slopes of the mountain were forested up until the 19C, but now they are planted with groves of olives, apples, pears, pistachios, hazelnuts and vineyards. The endemic Etna broom flourishes on many of the lava flows. At 1300m forest trees grow, especially oaks, chestnuts, pines and beeches. This is the southernmost point in Europe where the beech tree can be found, and this is also where it reaches its highest altitude, growing up to 2250m. It is also the extreme southern limit for the silver birch, which is found in its endemic form, *Betula aetnensis*. From 2000 to 3000m the black lava is colonised by tough little plants, most of them found only on this volcano, such as the holy thorn of Etna (*Astragalus aetnensis*), or the Etna violet (*Viola aetnensis*), creating a wonderful carpet of flowers in the spring and early summer. Botanists should not miss the **Nuova Gussonea Alpine Garden**, run by the University of Catania. It is not far from the Grande Albergo, and can be reached from the Nicolosi-Rifugio Sapienza road (for information ☎ 095/502218, ▤ 095/553273).

Since the creation of the park the golden eagle has returned after an absence of more than a hundred years, and nests regularly and Etna is the only place in Sicily where the long-eared owl can be found. Wolves and boars no longer roam through the forests, and there are no squirrels and badgers in Sicily, but to compensate there are plenty of foxes and rabbits, hares, porcupines, wildcats, hedgehogs, the garden and the common dormouse, many species of bats, five snakes (of which only the viper is venomous), tortoises and two kinds of toad. There are plans to reduce access to the area of maximum protection (*zona A*) to allow nature to take over again, and to reintroduce some long-absent species, such as the roe deer and the griffon vulture.

Pot-holers or speleologists will find the numerous lava tunnels on Mount Etna fascinating but exploration should not be attempted without expert help. Those interested should call the *CUTGANA* group at the University of Catania (☎ 095/317097, ▤ 095/7306052, ▨ www.cutgana.it), for these or other caves in Sicily. The heat of the rocks and the hot vapours from the terminal cones cause the snow to melt partly even in winter, but in certain depressions with a northern aspect the snow used to be preserved for refrigeration purposes throughout the summer by covering it with volcanic ash, and it was transported on mule-back down to the towns.

History

Etna, called *Aetna* in ancient times and *Mongibello* (from *Monte* and *Jebel*, the Arabic word for mountain) by the Sicilians (often simply '*a Muntagna*), probably originated from a submarine eruption which took place 500,000 years ago in the gulf which is now occupied by the plain of Catania. Some 130 eruptions took place in historical times. In ancient Greece the volcano was held to be the forge of Vulcan or of the Cyclopes, or the mountain from beneath which the imprisoned Titan, Enceladus, forever struggled to free himself. Empedocles, the philosopher, scientist and statesman from Agrigento who lived in the 5C BC, was said to have thrown himself into the crater to obtain complete knowledge.

Among early eruptions that of 475 BC was described by Pindar and Aeschylus, while that of 396, whose lava reached the sea, is said to have prevented the Carthaginian general Himilco from marching on Syracuse in the 4C BC. Hadrian climbed Etna to see the sunrise and the conical shape of the mountain reflected on the island. The eruption of 140 BC covered the city of Catania and the surrounding countryside under a thick layer of sand, so much so that the senate in Rome exempted the inhabitants from paying taxes for ten years! In 1169, 1329 and 1381 the lava again reached the sea, twice near Acireale, the third time (1381) at Catania.

The largest eruption ever recorded took place in 1669 when an open cleft extended from the summit to Nicolosi and part of Catania was overwhelmed by an enormous river of rock 14km long. The Monti Rossi were formed at this date. Since 1800 there have been over 35 eruptions, the one in 1928 being the most destructive in the 20th century because the lava covered the town of Mascali. The British statesman William Ewart Gladstone ascended the volcano in 1838 and left a graphic account in his journal. In 1847 Edward Lear wrote: 'From Catania we saw Etna and went up it; a task, but now it is done I am glad I did it; such extremes of heat and cold at once I never thought it possible to feel.'

In 1908 a huge pit of lava opened in the Valle del Bove. In 1911 there were two eruptions on the north side, creating a cleft 5km long and about 170 temporary craters. The eruption of 1947 threatened Passopisciaro, and that of 1950–51 menaced Rinazzo and Fornazzo before the lava halted. The 1971 eruption destroyed the observatory and the second stage of the cableway on the summit, as well as vineyards and some houses near Fornazzo. The lava stream cut several roads, and stopped just above S. Alfio. Eruptions on the western slopes at a height of 1600m and 2850m took place in 1974–75. In 1978–79 four new cones erupted and the lava flowed into the Valle del Bove; the town of Fornazzo was again threatened. Nine people were killed by an explosion on the edge of the main crater itself in 1979. An eruption in 1981 caused considerable damage around Randazzo, crossing the main road for Linguaglossa. In the spring of 1983 activity started up on the opposite side of the mountain above Nicolosi and Belpasso, forming the southeast crater, which has since been the most active of the summit cones. The main road up the southern slopes from Nicolosi was damaged and so was the cableway above Rifugio Sapienza. After several months dynamite was exploded in an unsuccessful attempt to divert the lava stream.

In 1984 an earthquake damaged the little town of Fleri and in 1986 eruptions took place on the east side above Milo, but no damage was caused as the lava flowed into the Valle del Bove. In 1987 two people were killed by an explosion on the edge of the main crater. In 1991–92 eruptions took place for four months and threatened the town of Zafferana Etnea again. Dynamite was exploded and huge blocks of concrete dropped from helicopters in an attempt to arrest the flow and divert it into the Valle del Bove. Although the concrete blocks had no effect, the lava halted within one kilometre of Zafferana Etnea.

The eruption of summer 2001 started just below the Montagnola at 2800m, on 18 July, but within a few days 18 temporary craters had opened up all over the top of the volcano, providing spectacular firework displays at night. The lava was successfully prevented from doing too much damage, but the following year, in October 2002, another very strong active phase began, accompanied by eruptions, earthquakes, showers of volcanic sand and the formation of several new craters.

This list of destruction sounds simply terrifying, but the inhabitants of the area are devoted to their 'muntagna' and would hate to live anywhere else. Immensely proud of the strength and power of Etna, they accept the moments of destruction, often followed by long periods of fruitful benevolence, with patience and fortitude.

The ascent of Etna

- The volcano can be visited from the southern side or the northern side. There are **organized excursions** from **Rifugio Sapienza** on the southern slopes (Etna sud) and from **Piano Provenzana** on the northern slopes (Etna nord), both of which can be reached easily by car or bus (see below).

- The upper part of the volcano can also be explored **on foot** from both these points, and there are some spectacular **walks** which are signposted on the lower slopes of the mountain (see below). Near the top there is almost always a very strong wind and the temperature can be many degrees below freezing: a warm jacket, sturdy shoes and a hat are in order (shoes and jackets can be hired at the cableway station near Rifugio Sapienza).

- The four summit craters are strictly off limits.

The southern approach ~ Etna Sud

Practical information

Getting to the Rifugio Sapienza
By bus

AST runs a daily bus (in c 2 hrs) to the Rifugio Sapienza, departing at 08.00 from the railway station's square (piazza Giovanni XXIII) in Catania. An extra service runs in July and August, leaving piazza Giovanni XXIII at 11.15 for Nicolosi where a connecting bus continues to the Rifugio Sapienza. A bus returns to Catania from the Rifugio Sapienza daily at 16.00.

By car

The journey (34km) from Catania to the Rifugio Sapienza (1920m) and back may be made easily in a day. The visibility is usually best in the early morning, as the summit is often shrouded in clouds later on in the day.

Walks

There are a number of walks along marked footpaths which start from the road up to the Rifugio Sapienza, including the nature trail to Monte Nero degli Zappini. There are also walks from the town of Zafferana Etnea towards the Valle del Bove.

Information offices
Parco Regionale dell'Etna, via Etnea 107, Nicolosi, ☎ 095/ 821111, ▤ 094/914738, ✉ www.parcoetna.ct.it. *SITAS* information offices, 45 piazza Vittorio Emanuele, Nicolosi, ☎ 095/911158; also at the cableway station, ☎ 095/ 916356. **Mountain guides**, ☎ 095/ 7914755.

Getting to the summit

The organised excursion to the summit leaves from the Rifugio Sapienza and takes about 2hrs. Tickets are purchased at the cableway station near the Rifugio Sapienza. The cableway itself was severely damaged during the eruptions of July 2001 and November 2002 but will hopefully be repaired. If weather conditions are adverse, 4WD vehicles are used to reach a height of about 2800m, where the guides take people on foot to the interesting areas. From the Rifugio Sapienza guides also take people walking to the 2001 crater, close by. It is absolutely forbidden to approach the rim of the summit craters.

Ascent on foot

Before undertaking the climb alone advice must be obtained about weather conditions, etc. at the *SITAS* offices at the cableway station, or at Nicolosi (where guides are available to accompany walkers). The easiest and most usual approach from Sapienza follows the track used by the small buses. About 4hrs should be allowed for the return trip from the refuge. The most spectacular time for the ascent is before dawn.

Where to stay
Hotels

NICOLOSI ☆☆☆☆ *Holiday Palace*, 39 via Leopardi, ☎ 0957/918004. New; fitness centre and sauna.
☆☆☆ *Biancaneve*, 163 via Etnea, ☎ 095/911176, 🖷 095/911194, 🖾 www. hotel.biancaneve.com. With swimming pool.
☆☆☆ *Gemellaro*, 160 via Etnea, ☎ 095/911373, 🖷 095/ 911071.

Bed and Breakfast

Casa Vinciguerra, 70 via Guglielmino, Tremestieri Etneo, ☎ & 🖷 095/71251723. In a small town on the lower slopes of Etna, the modern home of a university professor and a tour guide (who is a wonderful cook, when she is available), French and English spoken.

Campsite

NICOLOSI ☆☆ *Etna*, via Goethe, Pineta Monti Rossi, ☎ 095/914309, 🖷 095/7915186.

Mountain refuge

Rifugio Sapienza (1,920m) ☎ 095/916107. This legendary refuge has been completely refurbished. Very comfortable, good restaurant.

Youth hostel

NICOLOSI *Etna*, 7 via della Quercia, ☎ 095/7914686. Open all year.

Eating out
Restaurants

NICOLOSI €€ *Antico orto dei limoni*, 4 via Grotte, ☎ 095/910808. Old wine press, wonderful atmosphere, delicious food. Closed Tues.
€ *Etna*, 93 via Etnea, ☎ & 🖷 095/ 911937.

Cafés

NICOLOSI *Café Esagonal.* Right in front of the cableway station. Delicious coffee, hot chocolate and snacks or pasta, and all the latest information on the volcano's activity. Gift shop too.

Olive oil

The *nocellara etnea* olive is grown on the slopes around Ragalna, and produces some of the world's finest olive oil, stone-ground, and processed on the day of harvesting. The Barbagallo farm uses no artificial fertilizers or pesticides; *G. Barbagallo azienda agricola*, Ragalna, c/o 5 via Simili, Catania, ☎ & 🖷 095/ 532817, 🖾 studiobarbagallo@ interfree.it.

The **Strada dell'Etna** was opened in 1934 by Vittorio Emanuele III from Catania. It is well signposted beyond Nicolosi. **Nicolosi** (990m; population 5400) is one of the best centres for visiting Etna. To the west are the craters of the **Monti Rossi** (949m), which represent one of the most important subsidiary groups of craters (over 3km round), formed in 1669.

Beyond Nicolosi the road climbs through lava fields and some woods, crossing the lava flows of 1886 and 1910; the names of the craters on either side of the road are indicated. **Walks** off this road are also signposted. A loop road (left) leads to the winter sports fields of **Serra La Nave** (1750m). Several ski lifts were destroyed in the eruptions of 1983. From here there is one of the closest and best views of the summit, the line of the cableway, and some of the more recent lava streams.

The astronomical observatory here can sometimes be visited. The main road continues to the **Casa Cantoniera** at 1910m and ends at the 2001 lava stream beside the **Rifugio Sapienza**. There are souvenir shops, an information office, cafés and restaurants, and honey vendors here. In the desert of hardened volcanic lava nearby several extinct craters can be explored easily on foot, and the 400 metres wide 2001 lava flow is impressive, with the 2002 lava on top of it.

A cableway (currently under repair) ascends from here up the slopes of the **Montagnola** (2507m), a crater of 1763, through a desert of lapilli with splendid views of the sea and port of Catania. It takes about 15 minutes to reach the site of the Piccolo Rifugio, destroyed during the 2001 eruption. Although at present you are not allowed any nearer to the main crater, from this distance you can usually see (and hear) volcanic activity. A road has been cut through the 2001 lava stream, making it possible to reach the Silvestri Craters, formed during the eruption of 1892, and continue down the thickly wooded eastern slopes of the mountain and across the 1892 lava to Zafferana Etnea (see below).

The northern approach ~ Etna Nord

Linguaglossa (550m; population 5600) is the best centre for excursions on the northern slopes of Etna. The pleasant little town has a number of late 19C and early 20C houses. The 18C church has its doorways and windows decorated with lava and elaborate lamps on its façade.

The mountain road, known as the Mareneve, which climbs towards the summit of Etna, begins here. It leads up through the **Pineta di Linguaglossa**, ancient pinewoods of great interest to naturalists, to the ski-fields of **Piano Provenzana** (1800m), the main ski resort on Etna, with a refuge, and five ski-lifts (1800m and 2300m) completely destroyed by the earthquakes and lava during the 2002 eruption, and under repair (refuge, hotels, ski lifts, ski runs etc). From here excursions by 4 wheel-drive vans are organised to below the summit. It is also possible to walk up the cone from here in c 3hrs (the easiest way is to follow the track used by the excursion vans).

Another mountain road descends from Piano Provenzana following the eastern slope of the mountain passing beneath the Citelli refuge at 1741m, to Fornazzo.

Practical information

Getting to Piano Provenzana
By rail and bus

Excursions run in summer by *Circumetnea* (from Catania Borgo station) by train and bus to Linguaglossa. In January–April a **ski-bus** run by *FCE* (*Ferrovia Circumetnea*), leaves Catania for Piano Provenzana on Sun and PH at 07.00 (1hr 30mins), returning at 15.30.

Getting to the summit
From May–October excursions are organised in 4WD vehicles from Piano Provenzana by *STAR*, 233 via Roma, Linguaglossa, ☎ 095/643180.

Information office
Pro Loco, piazza Annunziata, Linguaglossa, ☎ 095/ 643094.

Where to stay
Hotels

LINGUAGLOSSA ☆☆
Happy Day, 9 via Mareneve,
☎ & 📠 095/643484.
Mountain refuge
Rifugio Citelli (1,740m), ☎ 095/
930000.

Eating out
Pastry shops

LINGUAGLOSSA *Pino
Azzurro*, 10 piazza Matrice (in the
church square).
PIEDIMONTE ETNEO *Caffé Calì*,
19 via Vittorio Emanuele, for a very
special almond cake.

THE FOOTHILLS OF ETNA

Practical information

Getting there
By rail

The *Circumetnea*, opened in
1898, provides a classic rail trip (but
you need to take two trains to circum-
navigate Etna by train). From Catania
(Borgo station; off map at the top of via
Caronda) to Randazzo (in c 2hrs), continuing less frequently to Giarre (in c
1hr); from there the direct return (poor
connections) may be made by the mainline train on the Messina–Syracuse line.

By bus

Frequent bus service from Catania to
Paternò, Adrano and all the villages on
the slopes of Etna.

By car

The road which encircles the foot of
Etna passes through spectacular countryside with rich vegetation. The fertile
land is densely cultivated and there are
numerous plantations of pistachio trees,
prickly pear and vineyards. The journey
offers lovely, ever-changing views of
Etna and its volcanic outcrops
(although the summit is often hidden by
cloud in the afternoon).

Information offices
APT Catania, ☎ 0957/
306211.
Pro Loco Bronte, ☎ 095/691035,

📧 www.comune.bronte.ct.it.
Pro Loco S.Alfio, ☎ 095/968772.
Pro Loco Milo, ☎ 095/955437.
Pro Loco Linguaglossa, ☎ 095/643094,
📧 www.prolocolinguaglossa.it.
Pro Loco Zafferana Etnea, ☎ 0957/
082825.
Information Bureau Randazzo, ☎ 800/
880013-800/261310, 095/444101.
Randazzo on line, 📧 www.comune.
randazzo.ct.it.

Where to stay
Hotels

PATERNÒ ☆☆ *Sicilia*, 391
via Vittorio Emanuele, ☎ 095/853604,
📠 095/854742.
RANDAZZO ☆☆☆ *Scrivano*, via
Bonaventura, ☎ & 📠 095/921126,
📧 www.hotelscrivano.it. Very comfortable modern hotel. Good restaurant.
S.GIOVANNI LA PUNTA ☆☆☆☆
Paradiso dell'Etna, 37 via Viagrande,
☎ 095/7512409, 📠 095/7413861,
📧 www.paradisoetna.it. A beautiful little
1920s' hotel, with excellent restaurant.
ZAFFERANA ETNEA ☆☆☆ *Airone*,
67 via Cassone, ☎ 095/7081819,
📠 095/7082142.
☆☆☆ *Primavera dell'Etna*, 86 via
Cassone, ☎ 095/7082348, 📠 095/
7081695, 📧 www.hotel-primavera.it.

Bed and breakfast

CASTIGLIONE DI SICILIA *Le Chevalier* (Vincenzo Fallone), 12 piazza Lauria, ☎ 0942/984679. In the main square, a café and pastry shop with lovely rooms.

La Dispensa dell'Etna, 2 piazza Sant'Antonio, ☎ 0942/984258, 📠 0942/984402, 🖥 www.ladispensadelletna.com. Comfortable rooms over the wine shop, delicious meals served on request.

VIAGRANDE *Casa Consoli*, 11 via Conte Mare, Viagrande, ☎ & 📠 095/7890116. Eleonora Consoli is a well known expert on Sicilian cuisine; in her beautiful home in the old town of Viagrande, she offers bed and breakfast and cookery courses on request; French and English spoken.

Casali dell'Etna (Fabio Bonaccorsi), 387 via Giuseppe Garibaldi, ☎ & 📠 095/7890656, 🖥 casadelletna.it. Accommodation in the old farmhouses of Etna. Fabio is a naturalist, local rep of the *LIPU* (Italian Society for the Protection of Birds) and can advise on birdwatching and excursions.

Farm accommodation

RANDAZZO ✩✩ *L'Antica Vigna*, contrada Montelaguardia, ☎ 095/924003, 📠 095/923324. Quiet farm not far from the town, producing olive oil and wine; tennis court.

S.ALFIO ✩✩✩ *La Cirasella*, 13 via Trisciala, ☎ & 📠 095/968000. Old winery in village within Etna Park. Ancient Roman wine press and vats, home cooking, vegetarian meals on request, yoga courses.

S. VENERINA ✩✩✩✩ *Tenuta San Michele*, 13 via Zafferana, ☎ 095/950520, 📠 095/954713, 🖥 www.murgo.it. Working wine farm producing the DOC Etna Rosso, Bianco and Rosato, offering very comfortable rooms with private bath and TV. English spoken, meals on request.

ZAFFERANA ETNEA *Casale Mongibello*, 1 via Matteotti, ☎ 348/7704126 (Valeria Privitera), 🖥 www.casalemongibello.com. Old winery in convenient position. Good management.

Campsite

MILO ✩✩✩ *Mareneve*, 30 via del Bosco, ☎ 095/7082163.

Eating out
Restaurants

BRONTE € *Don Ciccio*. ☎ 095/7722916. Delightful, simple restaurant near Nelson's Castle (Castello Maniace).

Fiorentino, ☎ 095/691800. Delightful restaurant not far from Nelson's Castle (Castello Maniace).

MILO € *Azienda Agricola Perrotta*, 2 via Andronico, ☎ 095/968928. Now this well-known farm also has rooms to rent. Restaurant closed Tues in winter.

RANDAZZO €€ *Hotel Scrivano*, via Bonaventura, ☎ 095/921126.

€€ *Ristorante Veneziano*, 8 via Romano, ☎ 0957/ 991353. Closed Mon and Sun evening.

€ *Pizzeria la Fontana*, piazza Bixio, ☎ 095/923621.

€ *San Giorgio e il Drago*, 28 piazza S. Giorgio, ☎ 095/923972, closed Tues. Good value for money; delicious local dishes.

S.GIOVANNI LA PUNTA €€ *Il Giardino di Bacco*, 3 via Piave, ☎ 0957/512727. Good wine list.

TRECASTAGNI €€ *Villa Taverna*,42 via Cristoforo Colombo, ☎ 0957/ 806458. Typical Catania fare. Closed Mon and Sun evening.

€ *Osteria I Saponari*, 201 via Francesco Crispi, ☎ 0957/809907. Delicious Etna dishes and homemade yoghurt. Closed Mon.

ZAFFERANA ETNEA €€ *Parco dei Principi*, 1 via delle Ginestre, ☎ 0957/082335, 📠 0957/081990. Very elegant. Closed Tues.

Picnics

The castle grounds of Castello Maniace are a lovely place for picnics.

Cafés and pastry shops

BRONTE *Caffetteria Luca*, 273 via Messina, for pistachio ice-cream and confectionery.

RANDAZZO *Chiamatemi Pure Maestà* (Alberto) 73 via Umberto. Superb confectionery and snacks and a stunning Art Nouveau interior.

Musumeci, 5 piazza S. Maria. *Biscotti della nonna* (grandma's biscuits), *croccantini alla nocciola* (hazelnut crunchies), *paste di mandorla aromatizzate* (almond biscuits flavoured with lemon, orange or tangerine). Excellent pistachio cakes.

SANT'ALFIO *Bar Papotto*, 12 piazza Duomo. Vittorio Papotto supplies the Italian prime minister with his exquisite confectionery.

SANTA VENERINA *Russo*, 105 via Vittorio Emanuele. Excellent Sicilian breakfast: *granita, cornetti al miele* (honey pastries), and hot chocolate in winter. They make various biscuits which are packed in practical tins.

TRECASTAGNI *Bar Sport*, 46 Piazza Marconi. Delicious arancini, pastries and ice cream.

ZAFFERANA ETNEA *Ristorante Corsaro* and *La Capannina* are both situated close to the Silvestri craters and serve hot or cold drinks, snacks and lunches, and also sell souvenirs, honey and local liqueurs.

Salemi, 6 piazza della Regione. Delicious biscuits called *foglie da tè* (tea leaves).

Newspapers

At Zafferana Etnea foreign language newspapers and magazines are readily available at the two newsagents near the main square.

 ## Annual festivals

BRONTE pistachio festival in early October.

RANDAZZO: festival of the Madonna on 15 August.

S. ALFIO feast of the patron saint on 10 May.

TRECASTAGNI feast in early May for the three patron saints—*i tre casti agni*—Alfio, Cirino and Filadelfo, culminating on 10 May with parades, Sicilian carts and fireworks, and Siciliy's largest garlic market.

ZAFFERANA ETNEA autumn festival known as the *Ottobrata*, held on October Sundays with local specialities sold in the square, and craftsmen (carpenters, stonemasons and beekeepers) demonstrating their skills along the main street.

Handicrafts

The shepherds of Maletto make their own bagpipes. *Vincenzo Bonina* is one of them, 17 via Martire della Libertà, Maletto, ☎ 095/699066.

The eastern and southern foothills

Zafferana Etnea (600m) is the main town on the east side of Etna. It is one of the most important honey-producing areas of Italy, renowned for its *miele di zagara* or citrus-blossom honey. The area was damaged by an earthquake in 1984, and a lava flow in 1992 reached the outskirts of the town (this can now be visited: it is at the end of a signposted road, where a statue was set up as an offering to the Madonna). Climbs towards the Valle del Bove can be made from here.

To the north is **S. Alfio** near which is a famous giant chestnut tree known as the *Castagno dei Cento Cavalli*, because its branches were reputed to be able to shelter 100 horses with their riders. It is one of the largest trees to survive on the island, with a circumference of over 60m and it is over 2000 years old. The area was once a forest of chestnuts, and some large trees still survive, but nowadays most of them are coppiced for the valuable timber of the saplings. The numerous lovely old farmhouses in the district, built of lava, have now almost all been abandoned. The fruit from the orchards in the district is sold on the streets in the autumn, together with chestnuts and wild fungi.

To the south at **Trecastagni**, ⊠ www.trecastagni.it, the Chiesa Madre is perhaps the purest Renaissance building in Sicily, thought to be the work of Antonello Gagini. The Chiesa del Bianco has a good 15C campanile. The town is renowned for its good quality wine, called *Etna Rosso*. Nicolosi, the most important centre for exploring the southern slopes of Etna, is described above.

At **Paternò** (population 48,500), important centre for the production of oranges, the town sprawls at the base of an 11C castle (open Tues–Fri 09.15–18.30, Sat, Sun 09.15–12.30, closed Mon, ☎ 095/621109). The austere tower built of volcanic rock commands the wide Simeto valley. It was restored in 1900, with a fine hall and frescoed chapel. From the terrace there is a good view. Frederick II of Aragon died near Paternò while journeying to Enna. The churches of S. Francesco and S. Maria della Valle di Giosafat retain Gothic elements.

East of Paternò is the village of **Motta S. Anastasia** perched on an extremely interesting rock formation, a 'neck' of lava, with a fine 12C Norman castle which preserves its crenellations. The unusual name of **Misterbianco**, a town now surrounded by industrial suburbs, comes from a Benedictine monastery, the *monastero bianco* which was destroyed along with the town, in 1669.

North of Paternò is **Biancavilla** where excellent oranges and clementines are grown: beside the extensive orange plantations are olive groves and hedges of prickly pear.

Adrano

Adrano (560m), ⊠ www.comune.adrano.ct.it, with 36,000 inhabitants, represents the ancient *Adranon* founded by Dionysius the Elder close to the site of a Sicel temple dedicated to the god Hadranon, said to have been guarded by hundreds of dogs called *cirnechi* (from Cyrenaica) originally purchased from Phoenician merchants, and still today raised in the area. Of medium size, with upright ears, a long, thin straight tail, ginger in colour with a pinkish nose, they are extremely intelligent. Overlooking the public gardens, Giardino della Vittoria (with superb trees) is the former monastery of **S. Lucia**, rebuilt in the 15C–16C, and now a school, flanked by the towering façade of its church (1775), with a pretty oval interior.

The imposing black lava **castle**, was built in 1070 by Count Roger. The interior houses a delightful local museum (☎ 0957/692660, open 09.00–13.00, 15.00–19.00; Sun only morning, Mon closed). The archaeological section includes prehistoric material from Stentinello and Castelluccio (ground and first floors). On the second floor the later finds from Mendolito (see below) include a hanging *Ascos* and 6C BC bronze figurine, *Il Banchettante*. In a little Norman chapel, with an apse fresco, is a collection of coins from ancient Adrano. On the third floor are paintings, most of them in very poor condition.

Next to the castle is the **Chiesa Madre**, of Norman origin. The interior incorporates 16 basalt columns, possibly from the ancient temple of Hadranon. High up above the west door is a fine polyptych by the 16C Messina school in a good frame. The painted 15C *Crucifix* was damaged by restoration work in 1924. In the transepts are four panels (two saints and the *Annunciation*) by Girolamo Alibrandi. In the pretty sacristy is a fine painting of the *Last Supper* by Pier Paolo Vasta.

Off a byroad below the town (signposted *Strada per il Ponte dei Saraceni*) a poorly surfaced road between low lava walls leads (in c 1.5km) past citrus plantations and lovely small, old farmhouses to the Simeto river spanned by the impressive 14C **Ponte dei Saraceni**, an extremely well-preserved bridge. It has four unequal arches decorated with black lava and the path over the top is still passable. In this beautiful peaceful spot there is a view of Etna and a waterfall on the rocky bed of the Simeto. Nearby (not signposted) are a few remains of the walls and south gate of the ancient Sicel town of **Mendolito**.

Ponte dei Saraceni near Adrano

Remains of Greek **walls** can be seen in fields outside Adrano to the east (in contrada Cartalemi).

The western foothills

Bronte (760m), a town of 19,800 inhabitants, is an important centre for the cultivation of pistachio trees (90 per cent of the pistachios produced in Italy are grown here). The fruit is harvested every two years at the end of August and beginning of September. Pistachios are used in local cuisine for pasta dishes, sweets and ice creams.

Castello Maniace

To the north, in a little wooded valley on the Saraceno, a tributary of the Simeto, is Castello Maniace or **Abbazia di Maniace** (open every day in winter 09.00–13.00, 14.30–17.00; summer 09.00–13.30, 15.00–19.00. ☎ 095/690018).

History of the abbey and castle

A convent was founded here in 1173 by Margaret of Navarre, mother of William II, on the spot where the Byzantine general George Maniakes defeated the Saracens in 1040, with the help of the Russian Varangian Guard and Norman mercenaries, among whom may have been the Scandinavian hero Harold Hardrada.

The house and estate were presented to Admiral Horatio **Nelson** in 1799 by Ferdinand IV (later King Ferdinand I of the Two Sicilies). Nelson was bestowed with the dukedom of Bronte in gratitude for his help the year before when the king had fled from Naples on Nelson's flagship during the Napoleonic invasion. A country parson from Yorkshire, a great admirer of Nelson, changed his name from Patrick Brunty to Patrick Brontë to celebrate his hero's success: he was the father of the Brontë sisters. Nelson apparently never managed to visit Maniace, but the title and estate passed, by the marriage of Nelson's niece, to the family of Viscount Bridport who sold the property in 1981 to the Bronte town council.

In the courtyard is a stone cross memorial to Nelson. The original 13C **chapel**, with the original portal, has a Byzantine *Madonna and Child*, two charming primitive reliefs of the *Annunciation*, and two 15C paintings. In the **barn**, where the roof has been restored, there are walkways above excavations of an older church. The house retains its appearance from the days when it was the residence of Alexander Hood who lived here from 1873 until just before World War II: it has lovely tiled floors and English wallpaper.

The delightful **gardens**, also designed by Hood (with palm trees, planted in 1912, magnolias, cypresses and box hedges), can also be visited. The Scottish writer William Sharp (who also published under the pseudonym Fiona Macleod) died here in 1905 and is buried beneath an Iona cross in the **cemetery** (shown on request).

The northern foothills

Between Bronte and Randazzo the landscape is barren, with numerous volcanic deposits. The countryside, studded with little farmhouses built of black lava, is used for grazing and the cultivation of vineyards. There is a large lava stream of 1832 near **Maletto**, whose sandstone cliff called Pizzo Filicia (1140m) is the highest sedimentary rock on Etna (views). The vineyards in this region produce excellent red and white wines (*Etna rosso* and *Etna bianco*); the vines are grown close to the ground (known as the *alberello* method) for climatic reasons.

Randazzo

Randazzo (765m), above the Alcantara valley, is a lava-built town of great antiquity (population 11,700), which has never in historic times suffered volcanic destruction. Its medieval history resolves itself into a rivalry between the three churches of S. Maria, S. Nicolò, and S. Martino, each of which served as the Cathedral for alternate periods of three years. The parishioners of each church (of Greek, Latin and Lombard origin) spoke different dialects until the 16C. The town was damaged from allied bombs when, in August 1943, the Germans made it the strong-point of their last resistance in the island.

S. Maria, the present cathedral, is a 13C church (attributed without foundation to Leone Cumier), with fine black lava apses and a three-storeyed south portal (approached by two flights of steps) in the Catalan-Gothic style of the 15C. The dome is attributed to Venanzio Marvuglia and the black and white tower was badly restored in 1863. The terrace, with another fine doorway and the sacristy with 16C portico, looks out over the Alcantara valley.

The **interior** (1594) has fine black columns and capitals, one of which serves as an altar. Over the south door is a small painting with a view of the town attributed to Girolamo Alibrandi (15C); over the north door is a fragment of a fresco of the *Madonna and Child* (13C). The church contains six paintings by Giuseppe Velasquez (on the first north altar, the fourth and fifth altars in the north and south aisles, and on the right wall of the sanctuary). The *Crucifix* in the chapel to the right of the sanctuary is by Fra' Umile da Petralia. The second north and second south altarpieces are by Onofrio Gabrieli. The third south altar is by Jean van Houbraken, of the 17C Messina school. The treasury (closed) contains a chalice given to the church by Peter I of Aragon. Outside, the south side shows beautiful windows of the original structure and a magnificent Gothic Catalan doorway with a tiny marble relief of the *Madonna* over it, probably from Pisa.

Via Umberto I leads past the southern flank of S. Maria past a little natural history museum (with an ornithological section and a collection of shells) to piazza Municipio where the **Town Hall** (Palazzo Comunale) occupies a 14C convent reconstructed in 1610. The lovely cloister has columns of lava. From here the narrow, pretty **via degli Archi** leads beneath four arches to the church of **S. Nicoló** which dates mainly from the 16C–17C (damaged in 1943). The apse, however, is original (13C). In the north transept is a seated statue of *St Nicholas* (with two small reliefs below) by Antonello Gagini signed and dated 1523. In the south transept is a 16C painted *Crucifix* and four delicately carved bas-reliefs of the *Passion* by Giacomo Gagini. Outside, there is an 18C copy of a curious antique statue of a man, thought to symbolise the union of the three parishes (see above). Called '*Old Randazzo*' or '*Piracmone*' by the local people, the eagle represents the regality of the Latins, the snake the wisdom of the Greeks, and the lion the strength of the Lombards. Nearby is Palazzo Clarentano (1509) and a medieval arch tunnels beneath houses back towards the corso.

Via Umberto I continues to the district of S. Martino, with evident signs of shell fire from the last war. At no. 51 the **information bureau** has brochures about Randazzo and its museums, and maps of the surrounding regional parks and wildlife reserves (09.00–13.00, 15.00–19.30, mornings only on Sun).

The damaged church of **S. Martino** still has its fine 14C campanile. On the top is a charming old-fashioned iron weathervane, in the form of a cherub. The façade has 15C reliefs of saints and martyrs. In the **interior** are black lava columns and in the south transept a statue of the *Madonna and Child* by the Gagini school (which retains part of its polychrome decoration). In the north aisle is a triptych by a local painter influenced by Antonello da Messina. There is a story about the **Crucifix** in this part of the church, made of papier maché and recently restored. The work of Giovannello Matinati, it is signed and dated 1540. The people of Randazzo call it the 'Crucifix of the water', because when Matinati was transporting it from Messina, where he lived, to an unknown destination, he was surprised by a deluge in Randazzo, so he took refuge in the church of S. Martino to prevent the delicate work of art from getting wet. But every time he tried to leave, it started raining again, and in the end he left the Crucifix in the church where it apparently wanted to stay. The marble font is by Angelo Riccio da Messina (1447).

In front of the church is the 13C **castle** which was rebuilt in 1645 and used as a prison up until 1973. It has now been restored as the **Vagliasindi Museum**, ☎ 0957/991611, open daily 09.00–13.00, 15.00–19.00, summer closing at 21.00. The collection includes some fine vases from a neighbouring Greek necropolis (5C–2C BC), including a 5C red-figure oinochoe, as well as coins and jewellery. A collection of puppets is also displayed here. There is a lovely view of the church of S. Martino from the uppermost tower. Just beyond is Porta S. Martino (1753) in the walls.

To the east of **Passopisciaro**, near a massive lava flow (1981), oaks and chestnuts are now being replaced by vineyards and olive trees. Some of the prettiest scenery in the Etna foothills can be seen here, with numerous handsome old russet-coloured houses (many of them now abandoned), excellent views of the volcano and, to the north, the wooded mountains beyond the Alcantara.

An attractive Byzantine Arab building locally called **La Cuba** can be seen to the north in the beautiful valley of the Alcantara. It is reached by taking the Malvagna road from the little horticultural centre of **Moio Alcantara**. After the cemetery the first turning on the right (unsignposted) leads to the tiny ruined chapel which survives in a field just to the right of the road amidst olive trees (before the road reaches the local stadium).

Castiglione di Sicilia is a quiet little town of 4700 inhabitants, in a stunning position perched on a crag (621m). Founded by the survivors of the destruction of Naxos (wreaked by Dionysius of Syracuse in 396 BC) it was once a stronghold of Roger of Lauria (see below). Its many churches are all closed most of the time, which is a great pity because they contain remarkable works of art. The **Chiesa Madre** (S. Pietro), however, whose magnificent 1105 apse is visible from outside, opens at 08.00 every day and 11.00 on Sunday for Mass. Inside is an interesting meridian line traced by Temistocle Zona in 1882. Below it is the church of **S. Antonio** (key at wine shop in front), with an ingenious façade and campanile, in a charming little piazza. Inside it preserves delightful marble inlay work (1700) and four octagonal paintings by Giovanni Tuccari. In the sanctuary is an elaborate wooden confessional supporting a pulpit and a simple painted organ loft. It is worth climbing up to the **Castle of the Lion** which gives its name to the town. Extremely interesting and of great antiquity, it is said to have been constructed in 750 BC by a Greek commander called Lion, even before the creation of the first colony at Naxos. The old stones are haunted by jackdaws and the views are peerless, over the rooftops to Mount Etna, the Alcantara Valley and the Peloritan Mountains. Castiglione is magical, especially on certain winter mornings when the air is crisp and clear, Etna is covered with snow, and the scent of woodsmoke lingers in the air; or on hot summer evenings, when the sky is like a bowl of deep blue Murano glass, and swifts screech and whirl untiringly among the steeples. Castiglione is twinned with Killarney in Ireland.

Below the town, off the Randazzo road (well signposted for the *Cuba Bizantino*) is another abandoned Byzantine Arab building surrounded by vineyards, usually called the **church of Santa Domenica**. It is approached along a narrow country road beyond a railway line. Built of lava, probably in the late 8C, it has an interesting plan and although very ruined the vault survives.

There are pinewoods and hazelnut groves near **Linguaglossa**, an important centre for excursions on Etna (described above). At **Rovittello** there is an 18-hole golf course. **Piedimonte Etneo** is another pleasant little town surrounded by fine citrus groves, with views of Taormina and Castelmola. Nearer the sea is **Fiumefreddo di Sicilia** (population 9200) amid plantations of lemons. For the coastal reserve at the mouth of the River Fiumefreddo, see below.

ACIREALE AND ITS COASTAL ENVIRONS

Famous for exquisite almond confectionery, the sound of church bells, and stubborn people, **Acireale** (population 47,100) is a beautiful little city with lots of atmosphere, perched at 161m between Etna and the sea on a cliff of lava called the **Timpa**. Time stands still in the maze of tiny jasmine-scented streets of the centre, in fact it is often used as a film set. The surroundings are intensely cultivated with lemon trees, and rich in mineral-water springs which have been exploited since Roman times for health cures. It is interesting for its Baroque buildings, some of which date from the 17C; others were erected after the earthquake of 1693. In 1642, Philip IV of Spain decreed it to be a royal city; thanks to this status, Acireale gained considerable prestige. Acireale and eight other neighbouring towns and villages derive their name from the Aci, the mythical river which came into being on the death of Acis, the shepherd beloved by Galatea and killed by Polyphemus.

Practical information

 ### Getting there
By rail and bus

Trains and buses to many destinations. All trains stop at Acireale, even the expresses.

Car parking

Piazza Cappuccini at Acireale has ample space.

 ### Information offices

Azienda Autonoma Soggiorno e Turismo, 15 via Oreste Scionti, ☎ 095/ 892129, 🖷 095/ 893134.

Acireale Terme, 47 via delle Terme, ☎ 0957/634597.

Acireale on line, 🖳 www.comune. acireale.com.

Acitrezza on line, 🖳 www. acitrezzaonline.it.

 ### Where to stay
Hotels

ACIREALE ✫✫✫ *Maugeri*, 27 piazza Garibaldi, ☎ 095/608666, 🖷 095/608728, 🖳 www.hotel-maugeri.it. Very central.

✫✫✫ *Orizzonte*, viale Cristoforo Colombo, ☎ 095/886006, 🖷 0957/ 651607, 🖳 orizzontehotel@ tiscalinet.it. Panoramic position, but out of town.

✫✫✫ *Santa Tecla*, 100 via Balestrate S. Tecla, ☎ 0957/634015, 🖷 095/ 607705, 🖳 www.hotelsanteclapalace.com. Down by the sea under the Timpa.

✫✫✫ *Aloha d'Oro*, 10 viale Alcide De

Gasperi, ☎ 095/604126. Set in a park on the Timpa, dilapidated but good restaurant.

✫✫✫ *Excelsior Palace Terme*, 103 via delle Terme, ☎ 095/604444. A converted pasta factory, comfortable and close to the centre.

✫✫✫ *Perla Ionica*, 10 via Unni Capomulini, ☎ 095/7661111, 🖳 www.tau.it/laperlaionica. Large holiday village. Nice lunches in summer in the garden.

ACI CASTELLO & ACITREZZA
✫✫✫✫ *Galatea Sea Palace*, 146 via Livorno, ☎ 0957/116902, 🖷 095/ 277320, 🖳 www.videobank.it/ egacom/galatea. Modern hotel squeezed in between a beautiful stretch of rocky coast and a busy highway.

✫✫✫✫ *President Park*, 88 via Litteri, ☎ 0957/116111, 🖷 095/27756, 🖳 www.italiaabc.it/az/ presidentparkhotel. Panoramic position over Acitrezza.

✫✫✫ *Park Hotel Capomulini*, between Acitrezza and Acireale, ☎ 095/ 877511, 🖷 095/877445, 🖳 www.gte.it/hpc. On the sea, recently restored, pool.

✫✫ *Acitrezza Inn*, via Livorno 97, ☎ 095/7117828, 339/6008581, 🖳 www.acitrezzainn.it. Well-run hotel, all rooms with shower, TV and air conditioning; they also have apartments to rent.

✫✫ *I Malavoglia*,1 via provinciale Acitrezza, ☎ 095/276711. In a little fishing village.

CANNIZZARO ✮✮✮✮ *Baia Verde*, 10 via Angelo Musco, ☎ 095/491522, 🖨 095/494464, ✉ www.baiaverde.it. Excellent.

✮✮✮✮ *Sheraton*, 45 via Antonello da Messina, ☎ 095/ 271557, ✉ www.sheratoncatania.com. A little *demodé* but still comfortable.

Bed and breakfast

ACIREALE *Aci e Galatea*, 22 via S.Carlo, ☎ 095/ 604088, ✉ danielagrasso@libero.it.

Akis, 11 via Grassi Bertazzi, ☎ 095/ 7111101, ✉ rosettanicolosi @Virgilio.it.

San Domenico, 3 via Lilibeo, ☎ 339/ 6561096.

Villa Terra di Aci, 6 via del Santuario Loreto, ☎ & 🖨 095/7633011, 328/ 2224441, ✉ www. villaterradiaci.it. Beautiful and quite luxurious, lovely terrace and sumptuous Sicilian breakfasts, next to the famous Sanctuary. Longish walk into town.

SCILLICHENTI *Casa Giulia*, 39 via D'Amico, ☎ 349/6169925 & 348/ 4776402, ✉ casa_giulia@yahoo.it. Close to the sea; old winery surrounded by lemon groves, organic food.

Farmhouse accommodation

SCILLICHENTI *Il Limoneto*, 41 via D'Amico, ☎ & 🖨 095/886568. Working lemon farm in wonderful position under the Timpa.

Campsites

ACIREALE ✮✮ *La Timpa*, 23 via Floristella, ☎ 095/7648155. By the sea.

✮✮ *Panorama*, 55 via S. Caterina, ☎ 095/634124. By the sea.

NEAR GIARRE *Almoetia*, località San Marco, Calatabiano, ☎ 095/ 641936.

 Eating out
Restaurants

ACIREALE €€€ *I Ruderi*, 104/106 via S. M. delle Grazie, ☎ 095/ 7635631. An old converted cottage a short distance from the centre of town. Very high standard of Sicilian cuisine, excellent wine list. Closed Mon.

€€ *Al Molino*, 104 via Molino, ☎ 0957/648116. Fish dishes in the tiny village of S. Maria La Scala under the Timpa. Closed Wed.

€€ *L'Oste Scuro*, 5 piazza Vigo, ☎ 0957/634001. Cook your own food on a hot stone. Lovely setting in front of St. Sebastian's. Closed Wed.

€€ *Sotto il Convento*, 29 via P. Vasta, ☎ 095/608243. Unusual and delightful restaurant situated in an old convent garden. No meat is served; antipasti include excellent grilled vegetables; delicious pasta, many salads; good wine list. Closed Tues.

€ *La Taverna*, 4 via Ercole, ☎ 095/ 601261. In the heart of the old fish market, a simple, friendly restaurant much favoured by the locals.

Pizzerie

Dietro L'Angolo, 23 piazza S. Domenico, ☎ 095/7631776. Extensive choice.

Il Tocco, 38 viale dello Ionio, ☎ 095/7648819. This is just off the busy main road between the city and the Timpa and a little hard to find, but it is worth the effort.

Jungle Pub, via Provinciale per Riposto, Santa Tecla, ☎ 339/8140144. Down by the sea under the Timpa; live music three or four times a week, Salvo prepares memorable pizzas, also good salads.

ACITREZZA €€ *da Federico*, 115 piazza Verga, ☎ 095/276364. Closed Mon.

€€ *da Gaetano*, 119 piazza Verga, ☎ 095/276342. Closed Wed.

€€ *Pellegrino*, 40 via Nazionale, ☎ 095/274902. Closed Mon. These three restaurants are renowned for excellent fish so they are crowded at weekends, booking necessary.

CANNIZZARO €€€ *Alioto* (ex *Selene*), 24 via Mollica, ☎ 095/494444. A restaurant that is almost legendary for the people of Catania. Closed Mon.

Cafés, pastry shops and ice cream parlours

ACIREALE *Bar Duomo*, 36 piazza Duomo. Authentic pistachio ice cream.
Condorelli, 26 via Scionti. The best *granita* ice cream and home-made nougat; their unique breakfast pastry is called *senzanome alla ricotta* (nameless one with ricotta).
Sotto il Convento, 29 via P. Vasta. A restaurant, but also a delightful place for afternoon tea in the garden, with all the trimmings, and you can taste different kinds of chocolate from all over the world.
SANTA MARIA LA SCALA This tiny village of at the foot of the cliff is also a good place for *granita*: almond, fresh fig, or pistachio.

Annual festivals

The *carnival of Acireale* (February) is one of the most famous in Italy. Colourful processions and fireworks for *St. Sebastian* (20 January).

Entertainment
Puppet theatres

Turi Grasso, ☎ 095/7652440, near Perla Ionica Hotel; Acireale. *Opra dei Pupi*, vico Alessi, Acireale, ☎ 095/7652440. *'I Paladini'* (Orazio Scalia), ☎ 339/4103951, summer performances in via Romeo.

Internet points

Computermania, 86 corso Savoia, Acireale, ☎ 095/604429. Tiny, friendly, crowded.
Internet www.sicilia, 130 via Galatea, Acireale.

Newspapers

Coco, 1 corso Umberto, Acireale. Foreign language publications, stamps and phone cards.

Handicrafts

Cartera Aetna, 9 via Pappalardo, Piano d'Api, Acireale. Here the artist-artisan Franco Conti and his son make paper using cotton fibres, a technique introduced by the Arabs (the oldest documents in Europe on paper are Sicilian); they supply artists all over the world, and the London stationers which supplies the Royal household; paper is made to order only and not sold on the premises. ☎ 095/7651290.
Sadisapone, 85 via Nazionale Cannizzaro Acicastello, ☎ 095/274072, is where Sabrina Delfino and her friends make high quality soap, using ingredients from Sicily such as honey, olive oil, flowers and fruits, nuts and seeds, lava from Etna, and also spices from the East. Each bar of soap is a work of art, and may look like a cake, cheese, or even a pudding. There is no shop on the premises, but the soap can be found in many retail outlets of Sicily.

Sport and leisure
Diving centre

Isole dei Ciclopi Diver, 28 via Gondar, Acitrezza, ☎ & 🖷 095/276156, ✉ www.isoledeiciclopidiver. com. Boat trips, snorkelling, etc.
Sailing lessons

Etnasail, 130 via Re Martino, Catania, ☎ 095/7126952, ✉ www. etnasail. com, Acitrezza.

The **sulphur baths** of S. Venera are at the south end of town in a park; water and volcanic mud are used for treating various ailments. The spa building of 1873 is under repair.

The main corso Vittorio Emanuele leads up to piazza Vigo, where the church of S. Sebastiano has a fine 17C façade in the Spanish Baroque style with numerous statues and a delightful frieze of cherubs with garlands. The balustrade and statues are by Giovanni Battista Marino (1754). On the other side of the piazza with fine palm trees and two charming little kiosks, is the large classical **Palazzo Pennisi di Floristella**. Beyond, the main streets of the town meet at the long piazza Duomo. Here is the 17C **Town Hall** which has splendid balconies supported by grotesque figures, and the basilica of **SS. Pietro e Paolo**, with a fine early 18C façade and campanile. The 17C **Cathedral** has a neo-Gothic façade which was added at the beginning of this century by Giovanni Battista Basile, and an interesting early 19C meridian line in the transept. At the east end are 18C frescoes by the painter **Pier Paolo Vasta**, but the best place to admire the work of this much-loved local artist is at the church of **S. Maria del Suffragio** in via Romeo, where a dazzling series of frescoes carried out in 1750 can be seen, or at the **S. Camillo** church in via Galatea, a little gem, called the 'church of the women' by the local people, because the theme chosen by Vasta for the frescoes was women of the Old Testament, such as Bathsheba, Judith, Abigail, and Rebekah. Vasta is noted for his lovely soft pastel colours; his tender pinky-reds and mauves are unmistakable, as are the graceful dancing movements of his subjects.

Opposite the Cathedral, via Cavour leads to the church of **S. Domenico**, which succeeds in being graceful and dramatic at the same time, close to the large 17C **Palazzo Musmeci** with an unusual curving façade and pretty windows. At no. 15 via Marchese di S. Giuliano is the Library and Art Gallery of the Zelantea Academy, in a fine building of 1915. The Academy was founded in 1671, and the **library** (open Mon to Fri 10.00–13.00, 15.30–18.30, Sat 10.00–13.00), in 1716. It now has some 150,000 volumes and is one of the most important on the island. The art gallery and museum are under reconstruction.

At the north end of the town is the **Villa Belvedere**, a public garden laid out in 1848. Nearby is the little neo-classical church of **S. Maria dell'Indirizzo**, by Stefano Ittar.

A pleasant walk follows via Romeo from the Cathedral and the picturesque *strada delle Chiazzette* through the Timpa reserve to **S. Maria la Scala**, a little fishing village.

Environs of Acireale

To the south of Acireale is **Acitrezza** which was described by Giovanni Verga in his masterpiece, *I Malavoglia (The House by the Medlar Tree)*.

Aci Castello (population 18,600), is a little dormitory town close to Catania, but it has a pretty little quay with colourful fishing boats beneath its castle (☎ 095/737414, 095/271026; open daily 09.00–13.00, 15.30–18.00) on a splendid basalt rock which sticks sharply out of the sea. The town was covered with lava in the eruption of 1169. It was rebuilt by Roger of Lauria, the rebel admiral of Frederick II (1297). Frederick succeeded in taking it by building a wooden tower of equal height alongside. A long flight of steps built in the lava leads up to a little cactus garden. Here is the entrance to the small **museum**, with interesting mineralogical, palaeontological and archaeological material, including underwater finds (well labelled). From here there is a fine view of the **Isole dei Ciclopi** (or **Faraglioni**), remarkable basalt rocks of volcanic origin. These were said to be the rocks which the blinded Polyphemus hurled at the ships of Ulysses, the largest of which is the **Isola Lachea**. Further south, on a little bay, is Ognina, now a suburb of Catania, perhaps the Portus Ulixis of Virgil's *Aeneid*, half-filled with lava in the 14C.

To the north of Acireale the coastline is known as the **Riviera dei Limoni**; lemon groves continue along the coast all the way to Taormina. Outside Mangano is the fertile lava stream of 1329.

The wide main road runs through **Giarre** (population 27,300), still paved in lava, where ceramics and Sicilian folk art are sold. The town has unexpectedly grand eclectic buildings and a huge 18C church. In the northeast corner of the province, near Marina di Cottone, is a wildlife reserve at the mouth of the **River Fiumefreddo**, a protected area since 1984. Papyrus and other aquatic plants grow at the source of the river.

Away from the coast, **Calatabiano** is dominated by a medieval castle, which is not built on lava, despite the legend that Himilco was diverted here by a lava stream from his direct march on Syracuse (396 BC).

CALTAGIRONE AND ENVIRONS

Caltagirone, in the province of Catania, is one of the most important inland towns of the island (population 38,500). The old town, with pleasant Baroque and Art Nouveau buildings, is built on three hills (608m), to which it owes its irregular plan and narrow streets and its medieval name '*Regina dei Monti*', or Queen of the Mountains. It has always been renowned for its ceramic ware because there is an enormous vein of high quality clay in the area—the Arabs opened many potteries, introducing new techniques, colours and designs—and today there are numerous artisans' workshops here, and a prestigious School of Ceramics. The use of majolica tiles and terracotta finials is a characteristic of the local architecture. The old centre of Caltagirone, with its Baroque architecture, has recently been declared a World Heritage Site by UNESCO.

Practical information

 ### Getting there
By bus

Buses from the railway station to Catania and Piazza Armerina (*AST*); to Palermo and Gela (*SAIS*), to Catania (*Etna Trasporti*) and to Ragusa and its province (*Ditta Pitrelli*).

By rail

The railway station is in Piazza della Repubblica, built in 1975 about 500m from the public gardens. On the Catania–Gela line, it has services to Catania in c 2hrs.

Car parking

In via Roma (some free spaces; others with an hourly limit).

 ### Information offices
Azienda Autonoma del Turismo, 3 via Volta Libertini (off via Emanuele Taranto), Caltagirone, ☎ 0933/53809, ✉ www.comune.caltagirone.ct.it.
Pro Loco, 1 cortile Alemanna, Militello, ☎ 095/7941111, 095/655155.
Pro Loco, 34 via Umberto, Mineo, ☎ 0933/981676, 0933/981475.
Pro Loco, 8 via Lombarda, Vizzini, ☎ 0933/965905.

 ### Where to stay
Hotels

CALTAGIRONE ✯✯✯✯ *Villa S. Mauro*. 10 Porto Salvo, ☎ 0933/

26500, 📠 0933/31661, 🖰 www.
framon-hotels.com. Modern hotel with
good restaurant, breathtaking views of
the city.
☆☆ *Monteverde*, 11 via delle Industrie,
☎ 0933/53682, 📠 0933/53533.
GRAMMICHELE ☆☆☆ *Hotel
L'esagono*, ☎ 0933/946700, 🖰 www.
enexa.com/esagono. Just outside the
town, with restaurant, pizzeria and
pool.

Farm accommodation

☆☆☆☆ *Il Casale delle Rose*, contrada
S.Stefano, ☎ 0933/25064,
🖰 ilcasaledellerose@ agriturismo.it.
Hard to reach but worth it; marvellous
food.
☆☆☆ *Casa degli Angeli*, contrada Angeli,
SP39 Caltagirone-Niscemi, ☎ &
📠 0933/25317. Beautiful old farmhouse, vineyards, olive grove, excursions
on horseback or mountain bike.
☆☆ *Valle dei Margi*, contrada Margi,
☎ 0933/940464, 📠 0933/977281,
🖰 www.valledeimargi.com. Citrus farm,
handicraft and cookery courses, music,
pool, tennis, minigolf, lovely food.
VIZZINI ☆☆ *'A Cunziria*, Contrada
Masera, ☎ & 📠 0933/965507. In the
old tannery and surrounding caves,
with horseriding, archery and bowls.
NEAR LICODIA EUBEA ☆☆☆☆
Dain, contrada Tana Calda,
☎ 0933/965682, 📠 0933/970652,
🖰 www.informasicilia.it/dain.
Vineyards and olive groves, riding
school, pony trekking, bowls, excursions.

Eating out
Restaurants

CALTAGIRONE €€
Floriano, 29 via Pirandello,
☎ 0933/54001. Also a pizzeria. Good
wine list. Try the *tagliolini al profumo di
limone*, fresh egg noodles with lemon.
Closed Mon.
€€ *La piazzetta*, 20/a via Vespri,
☎ 0933/24178. Besides the meat, wonderful vegetarian dishes. Closed Thurs.

€ *La Scala*, 8 scala S. Maria del Monte,
☎ 0933/57781. Lots of atmosphere.
Closed Tues. Also rooms to rent.
€ *La vecchia locanda*, 26 via
Infermeria, ☎ 0933/27150. Also
sandwich bar, delicious *antipasti* and
grilled vegetables.
€ *Non solo vino*, 1 via Vittorio
Emanuele, ☎ 0933/31068. Good wine
list and representative local dishes.
Closed Mon. Also rooms to rent.
€ *S. Giorgio*, via S.Luigi Altobasso,
☎ 0933/55228. Self-service and pizzeria, local cheeses and pickled fungi, the
spaghetti with basil and aubergines are
good. Open midday only, Sat and Sun
also evenings.
BOSCO S. PIETRO € *La Quercia*,
contrada Corvaccio, ☎ 0933/60381.
Outside the town. Home-made pasta
and delicious grills. Closed Mon.
MILITELLO *'U Trappito*, 125 via
Principe Branciforte, ☎ 095/811447.
Delicious recipes typical of the interior
of Sicily, served in a transformed oil
press. Closed Mon.

Pastry shops

CALTAGIRONE *Rubonello*, 84 via
Don Luigi Sturzo.
MILITELLO *Snack Poker Bar*, via
Umberto I. For Militello's specialities: the
cassatelline, *infasciatelli*, *totò* and
inzulli.

Picnics

The public gardens in Caltagirone,
Vizzini and Militello.

Annual festivals

The majolica decorated stairway, the **Scala S. Maria del
Monte**, is illuminated with oil lamps on
24–25 July, when there is a also a
ceramics fair, and the procession of S.
Giacomo. During Easter week, there are
processions and events, including an
exhibition of terracotta whistles. There
are also various events at Christmas.
Every third Sunday of the month,
throughout the winter, *'a Truvatura* (the

treasure hunt) takes place, with puppet shows, concerts, and antique fairs. In the last week of May the feast of the *Madonna of Conadomini* takes place which culminates with a procession of Sicilian carts and decorated tractors, to assure a good harvest, called *'a Russedda*. The Santa Maria del Monte stairway is completely decorated with vases of flowers, forming a design.

Handicrafts

There are some 120 ceramic workshops in the town which sell their products. Many of them are around piazza Umberto and on the Scala.

History

Traces of one or more Bronze Age and Iron Age settlements have been found in the area. The Greek city, together with other centres in central and southern Sicily, came under the influence of Gela. The present name is of Arabic origin (*kalat*, castle and *gerun*, caves). The town was conquered by the Genoese in 1030 and destroyed by the earthquake of 1693. A bombardment of July 1943 caused more than 700 casualties.

Famous residents

The sculptor Antonuzzo Gagini (c 1576–1627) died at Caltagirone, where his son Gian Domenico was probably born. The politician and priest Don Luigi Sturzo (1871–1959) is a much honoured native of the town. He advocated local autonomy and he improved social conditions here while he was mayor. He was a founder of the national Partito Popolare in 1919, and remained secretary of the party until 1923. This was the first Catholic political party, a forerunner of the Christian Democrat Party which came into being in 1942 and was to remain at the centre of Italian political life for most of the 20th century.

In the central piazza Umberto I a bank occupies a building by Natale Bonaiuto (1783). The **Cathedral** was completely transformed in 1920. In the south aisle are altarpieces by the Vaccaro, a 19C family of local painters, and in the south transept an unusual carved wooden (or papier mâché?) *Crucifix* attributed to Giovannello Matinati (1500). Beyond is the **Corte Capitaniale**, a delightful one-storey building decorated in the 16C–17C by Antonuzzo and Gian Domenico Gagini. In piazza del Municipio is the neo-classical façade of the former Opera House, which serves as an entrance to the **Galleria Luigi Sturzo**, an unusual monumental building inaugurated in 1959. The **Town Hall** has a fine façade of 1895.

Adjacent to the piazza rises the impressive long flight of 142 steps known as the **Scala S. Maria del Monte**. It has colourful majolica risers, predominantly yellow, green and blue, on a white ground. They were designed by Giuseppe Giacolone in 1606, and altered in the 19C. It is a climb (past numerous little ceramic workshops) up to **S. Maria del Monte**, once the Mother Church. The Baroque façade is by Francesco Battaglia and Natale Bonaiuto. The campanile, by Venanzio Marvuglia, is one of the very few bell-towers which can be climbed in Sicily. A little spiral staircase, which gets narrower and lower as it reaches the top, leads to the bell-chamber, from which there is a fine view. The church owns a *Madonna* attributed to the workshop of Domenico Gagini. Further up the hill is the former church of S. Nicola; there are also interesting medieval streets in this area.

From near the foot of the steps via Luigi Sturzo leads past the church of **S. Maria degli Angeli** with a 19C façade, behind which the façade of **S. Chiara** can be seen, by Rosario Gagliardi (1743–48), which contains majolica decorations. Further uphill is **Palazzo della Magnolia** (no. 76), an elaborate Art Nouveau house. Just beyond, the 19C façade of **S. Domenico** faces that of **S. Salvatore** by Natale Bonaiuto (1794). It has a pretty white and gold octagonal interior with a Gaginesque *Madonna*. A modern chapel contains the tomb of Luigi Sturzo (1871–1959; see above). Via Sturzo continues uphill past the former **Ospedale delle Donne**, an interesting building, recently well restored and now used for exhibitions of contemporary art. The road ends at **S. Giorgio**, rebuilt in 1699, which contains a beautiful little *Trinity*, attributed to Roger van der Weyden (a fragile painting in poor condition). From the terrace (left) there is a fine view of the countryside.

From piazza del Municipio (see above) the pleasant corso Vittorio Emanuele passes several fine palaces, and the Art Nouveau post office (still in use) on the way to the basilica of **S. Giacomo**, rebuilt in 1694–1708; at the side a pretty flight of steps ascends through the base of the campanile. In the interior, above the west door, the marble coat of arms of the city is by Gian Domenico Gagini. In the north aisle is a blue-and-brown portal (formerly belonging to the baptistery), and a blue and gold arch in the Cappella del Sacramento by Antonuzzo Gagini. In the north transept is the charming little *Portale delle Reliquie*, also by Antonuzzo, with bronze doors by Agostino Sarzana.

In the chapel to the left of the sanctuary (behind glass doors) is a silver urn (illuminated on request), the masterpiece of Nibilio Gagini (signed 1604). In the sanctuary is a processional statue of *St. James* by Vincenzo Archifel (1518) protected by a bronze canopy of 1964 (the original gilded throne is kept in the museum). This and the urn are carried through the streets of the town in a procession on 25 July.

From piazza del Municipio via Principe Amedeo returns to piazza Umberto I past (left) the **Chiesa del Collegio**, with a good façade decorated with statues, well seen below the road. It was built at the end of the 16C. It contains a painting of the *Annunciation* by Antonio Catalano, and a *Pietà* by Filippo Paladino.

Below piazza Umberto I is the **Civic Museum** (open 09.30–13.30 daily ex. Mon; Sun 09.30–12.30, Tue, Wed, Sat, Sun also 16.00–19.00) housed in a massive building built as a prison (Carcere Borbonico) in 1782 by Natale Bonaiuto with an interior court and double columns. On the stairs are architectural fragments and on the landing, four 19C terracotta vases by Bongiovanni Vaccaro. Beyond a room with modern local ceramics, another room contains the gilded *Throne of St James* (16C, by Scipione di Guido; the statue is kept in the church of S. Giacomo), a bishop's 19C sedan chair, and a crib by Benedetto Papale (19C). There is a room dedicated to the works (paintings and ceramics) by the local artists Giuseppe, Francesco and Mario Vaccaro. There are also some 16C–17C paintings (including *Christ in the Garden* by Epifano Rossi), and two cherubs by Bongiovanni Vaccaro. On the top floor are modern works. The archaeological section is not yet open. Beside the museum is the fine façade, also by Bonaiuto, of S. Agata (closed).

Via Roma leads to **Ponte S. Francesco**, an 18C viaduct, which has pretty majolica decoration and a good view of Palazzo S. Elia below the bridge. The road continues past the piazza in front of the church of **S. Francesco d'Assisi**, founded in 1226 but rebuilt after 1693. It contains paintings by Francesco and Giuseppe Vaccaro and a Gothic sacristy. Behind the church (reached by via S. Antonio and via Mure Antiche) is **S. Pietro** with a 19C neo-Gothic majolica façade.

Via Roma continues past the **Tondo Vecchio**, an exedra built by Francesco Battaglia in 1766. Beside the church of S. Francesco di Paola a road leads up past the **Teatro Politeama Ingrassia**, with interesting Art Nouveau details, to the entrance gate of the delightful **public gardens** laid out in 1846 by Giovanni Battista Basile. The exotic trees include palms, cedars, ficus and huge pines. There is a long balustrade on via Roma decorated with pretty ceramics from the workshop of Enrico Vella, and throughout the gardens are copies of terracotta vases and figures by Giuseppe Vaccaro and Giacomo Bongiovanni. There is also a fountain by Camillo Camilliani and a decorative bandstand. The palace of Benedetto Ventimiglia, also on via Roma, is preceded by a colourful ceramic terrace.

The Regional Ceramics Museum

The museum (open daily 09.00–18.30, ☎ 0933/26972 or 0933/21680) is situated in the gardens, entered through the elaborate **Teatrino** (1792) by Natale Bonaiuto. From the top of the steps there is a good view beyond a war memorial by Antonio Ugo and some palm trees to the hills (with the town on the left). The museum contains a fine collection of Sicilian ceramics from the prehistoric era to the 19C. In the corridor to the right are 17C and 19C ceramics from Caltagirone. Beyond a room with 18C and 19C works, the archaeological material is displayed, including Hellenistic and Roman terracotta heads and figurines. Cases 19 and 20 contain fragments from Caltagirone (5C–4C BC). Nearby is a bas-relief in stone with sphinxes (6C BC). Prehistoric pottery from S. Mauro and Castelluccio is exhibited in cases 21 and 22. In case 26 is a krater depicting a potter at his wheel protected by Athena (5C BC). Case 27 contains the Russo Perez collection, including 5C BC red- and black-figure vases.

In the courtyard bases used in various potteries from the 11C to 13C are exhibited. In the large room on the left are Arab-Norman stuccoes from S. Giuliano, 10C–12C Arab-Norman pottery, and medieval works (Case 48 onwards). In the room by the entrance are 17C and 18C works from Caltagirone including tiles, and in a little room beyond part of a 17C tiled floor is exhibited, along with elaborate 17C–18C ecclesiastical works.

On a lower level is a large hall with 17C–19C ceramics from Palermo, Trapani, Caltagirone and Sciacca, including blue enamelled vases and pharmacy jars. The fine collection of terracotta figures includes works by Giuseppe Bongiovanni (1809–89) and Giacomo Vaccaro (1847–1931). The hall is also used for exhibitions.

Via S. Maria di Gesù leads south from the public gardens to (10 minutes) the church of **S. Maria di Gesù** (1422), with a charming *Madonna* by Antonello Gagini.

Outside the town, on the Grammichele road is the remarkable neo-Gothic **cemetery**, built in 1867 by Giovanni Battista Nicastro, with terracotta decorations by Enrico Vella.

Environs of Caltagirone

Grammichele (🖳 www.grammichelect.it), 15km east of Caltagirone, was founded by Carlo Maria Carafa Branciforte, Prince of Butera, to house the people of Occhiolà, destroyed in 1693. The ruins of the old town, about a mile away, are now a very interesting archaeological park (open 09.00–17.00 daily, until dusk in summer; ☎ 0933/944855, 🖳 www.parcoocchiola.it). Its remarkable concentric hexagonal plan is preserved around **piazza Carafa** with palm trees and a medley of houses between the six roads. Here the well-sited **Chiesa Madre** begun in 1723 by Andrea Amato stands next to the **Town Hall** (1896, by Carlo Sada). The **Civic Museum** (☎ 0933/859229; open 09.00–13.00, 16.00–18.00) has a small collection which is very well arranged and contains finds from excavations in the district, begun in 1891 by Paolo Orsi who identified a pre-Greek settlement at Terravecchia. Exhibits include prehistoric bronzes and Bronze Age ceramics, vases found in tombs (6C BC), terracotta votive statuettes and 15C–16C majolica from Occhiolà.

Vizzini, further east, nestles among the Hyblean Mountains at a height of 619m. It occupies the ancient site of Bidis, recorded by Cicero. In the central piazza is a stairway decorated with majolica tiles like the one in Caltagirone, and an 18C palace which used to be owned by Giovanni Verga's family: the great writer was born here and many of his works are set here or in the vicinity, such as *Cavalleria Rusticana*, *La Lupa* (the she-wolf), and *Mastro-don Gesualdo*. It is a prosperous farming community, renowned for its excellent sheep's milk cheese, olive oil, prickly pears and durum wheat. In the past leather was tanned at Vizzini, along a little river just outside the town. Now the workshops and the vats, many carved out of the rock, and the homes of the workers, all long since abandoned, are being repaired and transformed into a cultural centre called '*a Cunziria* (the tannery). The mountains around Vizzini are ancient volcanoes, now rich pastures or wheat fields, where flocks of ravens still fly. If at all possible, there are several other nearby hilltop towns which are worth a visit, such as Licodia Eubea, Monterosso Almo, or Buccheri.

Militello in Val di Catania is a splendid little town with remarkable Baroque buildings, well worth a visit, and recently declared a World Heritage Site by UNESCO. The churches contain paintings by Vito D'Anna, Olivio Sozzi, Pietro Ruzzolone (attributed; *St Peter enthroned*) and others. The main square, piazza Municipio, houses the great **Abbey and church of St Benedict**, now the Town Hall, modelled on the Benedictine Monastery of St Nicholas, Catania. Inside the church, the choir stalls carved in walnut in 1735 are of particular interest. Beside the Chiesa Madre, in via Umberto I, is the **Museum of S. Nicola** (open 09.00–13.00, 16.00–19.00, Tues closed, ☎ 095/811251) with 17C and 18C works, including vestments, church silver, sculpture and paintings. In the church of **S. Maria della Stella** there is an altarpiece in enamelled terracotta by Andrea Della Robbia (1487) with the *Nativity, Annunciation to the Shepherds*, and (in the predella) a *Pietà* and the *Twelve Apostles*. The half-ruined **S. Maria la Vetere**, outside the town to the east, has a porch supported on lions and a magnificent doorway of 1506. There is a prickly pear festival here on the second Sunday in October, and the last week in August is dedicated to Baroque art (*Settimana del Barocco*).

Mineo is a small town on an ancient settlement founded by Ducetius, king of the Sicels, in the 5C BC and later occupied by the Greeks and Romans. High quality olive oil is produced here. The church of the Collegio and S. Agrippina have 18C stuccoes. This is the birthplace of **Luigi Capuana** (1835–1915), who wrote various works both in Italian and Sicilian, including lovely tales for children. In piazza Buglio is the **Biblioteca-museo Luigi Capuana** (open daily 09.00 –14.00, ☎ 0933/981856), the public library is dedicated to the writer, and there are plays and exhibitions during the first week of October.

Palagonia is in a district well known for its oranges. Outside the town is the 7C shrine of S. Febronia. This was the ancient Sicel town of *Palica*, close to a sacred lake which was a sanctuary for runaway slaves. The town is on the edge of the fertile **Plain of Catania**, known to the Greeks as the Laestrygonian Fields, the home of the cannibal Laestrygones. Its vast citrus groves are watered by the Simeto and its tributaries, the Dittaino and the Gornalunga.

The Oasi del Simeto, at the mouth of the River Simeto, is a wildlife reserve for birds (usually open 09.00–18.00). Although numerous holiday villas were built here from the 1960s onwards, it was first protected in 1975 and became a nature reserve in 1984, thanks mainly to the strenuous efforts of Wendy Hennessy Mazza, a British resident and birdwatcher, local representative of the LIPU, the Italian society for bird protection. In 1989, 54 of the numerous houses erected within the area without building permission were demolished. The marshes and brackish lakes offer protection to numerous birds, both nesting and migratory, including rare ducks, great white heron, flamingo, black-winged stilt, godwit, cattle egret, glossy ibis, avocet and spoonbill. The purple gallinule has recently been successfully reintroduced. Amber can sometimes be found on the shore here. The entrance to the reserve is on the left bank of the river near Ponte Primosole on the main road (SS 114). On the left bank of the Simeto stood the ancient town of *Symaethus*, whose necropolis survives on the Turrazza estate.

Messina province and the Aeolian Islands

MESSINA

Messina, on the western shore of the Straits bearing its name, extends along the lowest slopes of the Peloritan Mountains (Monti Peloritani) above the splendid harbour, one of the deepest and safest in the Mediterranean. With its fine port and ideal position between Europe and Africa, the Straits of Gibraltar and the Bosphorus, Messina was the centre of the world, an important trading post from the Bronze Age until the discovery of America, and for some time afterwards.

Today the port is always busy with ferries and hydrofoils travelling to and from the mainland. The third largest city (population 270,000) in Sicily, it was completely wrecked by an earthquake in 1908, when 84,000 people died of a population of 120,000. It was soon rebuilt with broad streets planted with trees and low buildings to minimise the danger from future earthquakes. The centre of Messina now combines sea, sky and hills in a pleasant, open townscape. It is particularly subject to the *maestrale*, which blows from the northwest.

Practical information

Getting there
By air
Aeroporto dello Stretto-Reggio Calabria is the nearest airport on the mainland, a few kms north of Reggio (internal flights and summer charter flights only), ☎ 0965/640517 ▨ 0965/642722; *Alitalia* (information) ☎ 0965/643095-0965/644394; *Air One* (information) ☎ 0965/644394, ▨ www.flyairone.it.
Aeroporto di Catania see Catania.

By sea from the mainland

Car ferries (*traghetti*) cross the Straits of Messina from **Villa San Giovanni**, in Calabria. These are run by:
Trenitalia, the Italian state railways (*FS*), ☎ 090/661674, ▨ www.FS-on-line.it, every 20–30 mins, taking 40 mins.
Caronte, ☎ 090/3718324, ▨ www.carontespa.it/caronte, c every 10 mins, taking 20 mins, from viale della Libertà.
Tourist Ferry Boat, ☎ 090/3718510, ▨ www.paginegialle.it/touristfb, c every 10 mins, taking 20 mins, from viale della Libertà.
Fast boats (*navi veloci*). Trenitalia run a frequent service (in 20 mins) for Reggio Calabria or for Reggio Calabria Airport (Aeroporto dello Stretto). The pier is next to the Stazione Marittima, the 'fast boats' are either large motorboats or hydrofoils.

By sea to the other islands

Hydrofoils (*aliscafi*) in 90 mins from Messina to Vulcano or Lipari (Aeolian Islands) run by *SNAV*, via Cortina del Porto, ☎ 090/364045, ▨ www.snavali.com.

By bus

Around town. Buses no. 79 from the station, via Primo Settembre, Duomo, Corso Cavour and via Garibaldi to the Regional Museum (continuing to Ganzirri and Punta Faro) or no. 28 (*velocittà*) from piazza Cairoli and via Garibaldi. No. 29 from piazza Cairoli to the cemetery.
Inter-city bus services run by *SAIS-INTERBUS* (terminal in piazza della Repubblica) to Catania (direct via the motorway) in 90 mins (continuing to Catania airport); to Taormina (via SS 114) in 90 mins; to Rome in 9hrs 30 mins, and many other mainland cities. Information: *SAIS-INTERBUS*, 6 piazza della Repubblica (by the railway station), ☎ 090/661754-090/6415199.
Airport bus run by *Cavalieri* (terminal Cavallotti in via Primo Settembre and piazza Duomo) connecting with domestic flights from Reggio Calabria Airport.
Coach service by *Giuntabus* from 8 via Terranova (at the junction with viale San Martino) to Milazzo in 50 mins (connecting with hydrofoils to the Aeolian Islands; see p 431). Information: *Giuntabus*: ☎ 090/673782, ▨ 090/679677.

Car hire

Avis, 109 via Garibaldi, ☎ 090/679150-661866.
Hertz, 113 via Vittorio Emanuele II, ☎ 090/363740.
Maggiore-Budget, 75 via Vittorio Emanuele II, ☎ 090/675476.
Sicilcar, 187 via Garibaldi, ☎ 090/46942.

Parking

Parking is difficult in the centre of the town. There is a car park, Cavallotti, in via Primo Settembre.

Information offices
APT Messina, 301 via Calabria (corner of via Capria), ☎ 090/674271, 090/674236; ▨ www.aapitme.it.
Azienda Autonoma Turismo, 45 piazza Cairoli, ☎ 090/694780.

Messina on line: www.
messinacitymap.com

Where to stay
Hotels

✩✩✩✩ *Grand Hotel Liberty*, 15
via Primo Settembre, ☎ 090/6409436,
📠 090/6409340, ✉ ricevimento.
liberty@framonhotels.com. One of the
oldest and most prestigious hotels,
beautifully restored, special facilities for
ladies.

✩✩✩✩ *Jolly Hotel*, 126 via Garibaldi,
☎ 090/325575, 📠 090/325577,
✉ messina@jollyhotels.it. Jolly Hotels
are an institution in Italy, the restaurants are always excellent. Good views
over the harbour to Calabria.

✩✩✩✩ *Royal Palace Hotel*, 224 via T.
Cannizzaro, ☎ 090/6503, 📠 090/
2921075, ✉ ricevimento.royal@
framon-hotels.it. Good location in the
town centre.

✩✩✩ *Excelsior*, 32 via Maddalena,
☎ 090/2931431. Good location in the
town centre. No restaurant.

✩✩✩ *Villa Morgana*, 237 via C. Pompea,
north of the town at Ganzirri, ☎ 090/
325575, 📠 090/325577.

✩✩ *Cairoli*, 63 viale San Martino, ☎ &
📠 090/673755. Excellent position; no
restaurant.

✩ *Locanda Donato*, 8 via Caratozzolo,
☎ & 📠 090/393150; charming hotel at
Ganzirri, close to sea and lake, garden.

Rooms to rent

Residence Principe Umberto, 40 via
Principe Umberto, ☎ 090/6671,
📠 090/667622.

Campsites

Camping Il Peloritano, Contrada
Tarantonio Rodia, ☎ 090/348496 or
348526.

Eating out
Restaurants

€€ *Il Gattopardo*, 184 via S.
Cecilia, ☎ 090/673076. A favourite

with local people; also serves pizza.
Closed Mon.
€€ *Le Due Sorelle*, 4 piazza Municipio,
☎ 090/44720. Vegetarian food, also
sushi, couscous and other unusual
dishes. Closed Sat and Sun midday.
€€ *Piero*, 121 via Ghibellina, ☎
090/718365. Marvellous fish. Closed
Sun.
€ *Al Padrino*, 54 via S. Cecilia, ☎ 090/
2921000. Good pasta, simple style.
€ *Il Veliero*, 301 via Valori, close to
maritime station, ☎ 090/771626.
Grungy seamen's bar, excellent local
food, ice cream, and the best espresso in
Messina. The warm seafood salad
(*insalata di mare*) and the spicy spaghetti
with clams (*spaghetti alle vongole*) are
particularly good.

There are numerous restaurants and
trattorie near the **Lago di Ganzirri**,
10km north of the town, including €€
Anselmo, 29 via Lago Grande, ☎ 090/
393225 and €€ *La Napoletana-
Salvatore*, 18 via Lago Grande,
☎ 090/391032.

Pizzerie and sandwich bars

Pizzeria Fusco, 70 via dei Mille, corner
of via Fabrizi, ☎ 090/711267. Just
right for a quick meal, self-service
counter, good pizza, delicious sandwiches and snacks. *Paninoteka*, 63 via
G. Bruno. Good sandwiches.

Cafés and pastry shops

Cardullo, 7 via U. Bassi. Excellent ice
cream and snacks.
De Pasquale, 39 via C. Battisti, close to
the Duomo.
Irrera, 12 piazza Cairoli. One of the
most famous pastry shops, especially
renowned for its *pignolata messinese* and
cassata siciliana.
Ritrovo Dolce Vita, 14 piazza Duomo,
next to the Duomo. Good coffee.

Annual festivals

The **Fiera di Messina**, a
trade fair held during the first

15 days of August, coincides with the traditional processions of the **Giganti** (Giants) on 13 and 14 August and the **Vara** (float with tableau) for the feast of the Assumption (15 August). Other processions take place on 3 June (**Madonna della Lettera**, protectress of the city), on Good Friday (**Varette**) and on Corpus Domini (**Vascelluzzo**).

Entertainment
Theatres

Vittorio Emanuele Opera House (for opera and concerts) and *Sala Laudamo* (for theatre and music), information: ☎ 090/ 5722111 (daily 09.00–13.00, 16.00–18.40; Mon and PH closed).

Internet points
Ap@ Web, via L. Manara, ☎ 090/670229.

Internetwork, 20 via Dogali, ☎ 090/ 6512030.
Internet point, 200 via dei Mille, ☎ 090/6783289.
Internet Provider Eniware, 116 via Industriale, ☎ 090/693958.
Internet Sicilia on Line, 44 via della Zecca, ☎ 090/710204.

Consulate
British Consulate, 14 via Cadorna, ☎ 090/662227.

Foreign language newspapers and periodicals
On sale in piazza Cairoli (kiosk on the west side) or at the Stazione Marittima (tobacconist).

History

Zancle, as Messina was called by the Greeks in allusion to the sickle-shaped peninsula enclosing its harbour, was probably a settlement of the Sicels before its occupation by the Euboeans (from the island of Euboea east of Athens) and later by a colony from Chalcis. In 493 BC it was captured by Anaxilas, tyrant of Rhegium, and renamed Messana, in honour of his native country of Messenia in the Peloponnese. It took part in local wars against Syracuse and then against Athens, and was destroyed by the Punic general Himilco. Rebuilt by Syracuse, it was occupied by the Campanian mercenaries of Agathocles, who called themselves Mamertines. These obtained the alliance of Rome against the Carthaginians and Messina prospered with the fortunes of Rome. Under Byzantium and later under the Arabs the surrounding hills were planted with groves of mulberry trees to support the burgeoning silk industry, which brought fame and fortune until the 19C when it came to a standstill, due to a minute parasite which attacked the silkworms.

Under the Normans it was renowned for monastic learning and was important as a Crusader port. In September 1190 Richard Coeur de Lion and Philip Augustus of France arrived to spend the winter here before leaving for their Crusade in March 1191. Philip behaved like a gentleman, but the people of Messina had little cause to love Richard, who after ensconcing himself and his troops in the revered Basilian monastery of S. Salvatore, ransacked and looted the city in order to redress the offences he thought his sister Joanna, widow of William II, had suffered. The cruel Emperor Henry VI died of dysentery at Messina in 1197. After a heroic and successful resistance to Charles of Anjou in 1282, the city flourished until it lost its privileges by rebelling against Spanish misrule in 1674.

From Messina Cervantes sailed in the *Marquesa* to Lepanto (1571) and in the hospital of Messina recovered from the wound received in the battle. Shakespeare's *Much Ado About Nothing* is set in Messina. The French geologist Dolomieu (1750–1801), returning from Napoleon's Egyptian expedition, was captured and imprisoned for two years (1799–1801) in Messina.

From then on its story is one disaster after another: the plague in 1743, an earthquake in 1783, naval bombardment in 1848, cholera in 1854, another earthquake in 1894, culminating in the catastrophe of 1908. Experts believe it to be one of the worst earthquakes ever recorded anywhere. The first shock, at 05.20 in the morning of 28 December, only lasted about 20 seconds but destroyed the entire city, and caused the shore to sink over half a metre. The subsidence caused a violent tsunami which swept the coast, rising to a height of 8m; its effects were felt in Malta 24 hours later. This was the cause of the enormous deathtoll: most of the victims were in fact drowned by the huge wave when they were escaping from their ruined homes. A series of lesser shocks continued almost daily for two months. More than 120,000 people were killed on both sides of the Straits. Reconstruction, though assisted by liberal contributions from all over the world, was by no means complete when the city was again devastated in 1943 by aerial bombardment (when 5000 people lost their lives). In 1955 a preliminary agreement was signed by the 'six' in Messina to found the European Union (EU).

Was Shakespeare Sicilian?

Over the last few years, some literary researchers in Sicily have been studying a rather far-fetched theory, that William Shakespeare was in fact born in Messina, where he was known as Guglielmo Crollalanza. When still a boy, he went to Verona, where his family had relatives, and from there on to England, where he arrived a few years later, translating his name to William Shakespeare to facilitate his acceptance into new surroundings. His rich vocabulary would in fact indicate a good knowledge of Italian, and he used many Sicilian proverbs in his works. 'Much ado about nothing', for example, translates to the old Sicilian proverb *tantu schifiu ppi nenti*, and 'All's well that ends well' becomes *si chiuriu 'na porta e s'apriu un purticatu*.

Piazza del Duomo, in the centre of the city, was spaciously laid out in the 18C. Beside the cathedral the 1933 bell tower stands harmoniously next to the **Orion Fountain**, the masterpiece of Giovanni Angelo Montorsoli (1553), and thought by some to be the loveliest Renaissance fountain in Italy. It was commissioned to celebrate the construction of an acqueduct from the nearby River Camaro, which brought running water to most households in the city—quite a breakthrough for the times. Although the people wanted Michelangelo to design their fountain, they had to settle for his pupil, Montorsoli. Montorsoli apparently enjoyed his stay in Messina, only returning to Tuscany more than 10 years later. The male figures around the fountain represent the Nile, Tiber, Ebro and Camaro, and they are shown looking in the direction of their respective rivers. On the top is Orion, founder of the city, with his faithful dog Sirius.

The beautiful fountain caused quite a stir in Sicily, especially in Palermo (see p 77). There had always been intense rivalry between the two cities, both of which considered themselves to be the true capital of the island.

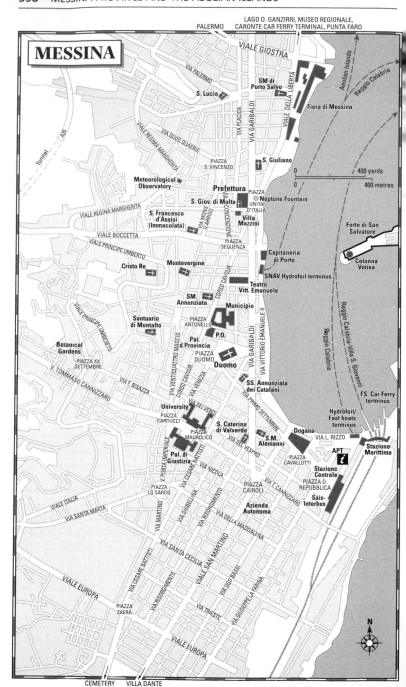

MESSINA

LAGO D. GANZIRRI, MUSEO REGIONALE,
CARONTE CAR FERRY TERMINAL, PUNTA FARO

PALERMO

VIALE GIOSTRA

VIA PALERMO

Aeolian Islands

Reggio Calabria

S. Lucia

SM di
Porto Salvo

VIA PLACIDA

VIA GARIBALDI

VIALE DELLA LIBERTÀ

Fiera di Messina

VIA QUOD QUAERIS

VIALE REGINA MARGHERITA

tunnel A20

PIAZZA
S. VINCENZO

S. Giuliano

0   400 yards
0   400 metres

Meteorological
Observatory

Prefettura

PIAZZA
UNITÀ
D'ITALIA

Neptune Fountain

Forte di San
Salvatore

VIALE REGINA MARGHERITA

S. Giov. di Malta

S. Francesco
d'Assisi
(Immacolata)

VIA MONS. D'ARRIGO

VIA DELLA CONCEZIONE

Villa
Mazzini

Colonna
Votiva

VIALE BOCCETTA

VIALE PRINCIPE UMBERTO

PIAZZA
SEQUENZA

Capitaneria
di Porto

Cristo Re

Montevergine

CORSO CAVOUR

SNAV Hydrofoil terminus

Teatro
Vitt. Emanuele

SM.
Annunziata

Municipio

VIALE PRINCIPE UMBERTO

Santuario
di Montalto

PIAZZA
ANTONELLO

P.O.

VIA VENTIQUATTRO MAGGIO

Pal.
d Provincia

PIAZZA
DUOMO

Duomo

Botanical
Gardens

PIAZZA XX
SETTEMBRE

CORSO CAVOUR

VIA VENEZIA

V. TOMMASO CANNIZZARO

VIA F. BISAZZA

SS. Annunziata
dei Catalani

VIA PRIMO SETTEMBRE

VIA VITTORIO EMANUELE II

VIA GARIBALDI

Reggio Calabria-Villa S. Giovanni

Reggio Calabria

FS. Car Ferry
terminus

VIA DEI VERDI

University

PIAZZA
CARDUCCI

PIAZZA
MAUROLICO

S. Caterina
di Valverde

VIA DEL VESPRO

Dogana

Hydrofoil/
Fast boats
terminus

V. PORTA IMPERIALE

Pal. di
Giustizia

S.M.
Alemanni

VIA L. RIZZO

APT

Stazione
Marittima

VIA CESARE BATTISTI

VIA NICOLA

PIAZZA
CAVALLOTTI

Stazione
Centrale

PIAZZA
LO SARDO

VIALE ITALIA

VIA SANTA MARTA

VIA MARTINO

VIA GHIBELLINA

PIAZZA
CAIROLI

VIA T. CANNIZZARO

PIAZZA D.
REPUBBLICA

Sais-
Interbus

Azienda
Autonoma

VIALE EUROPA

VIA CESARE BATTISTI

VIA SANTA CECILIA

VIA RISORGIMENTO

VIALE SAN MARTINO

VIA DELLA MADDALENA

VIA UGO BASSI

PIAZZA
ZAERA

VIA TRIESTE

VIA GIUSEPPE LA FARINA

VIALE EUROPA

N

CEMETERY   VILLA DANTE

The **Duomo** (08.00–19.00), despite successive reconstructions, retains much of the appearance of the original medieval church.

Originally built by Count Roger, the Duomo was one of the greatest Norman churches in Sicily. The church was consecrated in 1197 in the presence of Emperor Henry VI. It was first destroyed in 1254 by a fire which broke out during the funeral service for Conrad IV, son of Frederick II, because the mourners had lit too many candles. After rebuilding, the cathedral was shattered in 1783 and 1908 by two terrible earthquakes. In 1943 it was hit by an incendiary bomb aimed at the port. The fire raged for three days, and many of its treasures were completely destroyed, including the mosaics and the frescoes, the royal tombs and choir stalls. But everything that could be salvaged was carefully replaced in the reconstructed church. A surviving column can be seen outside the building on the north side, with a carved fragment from the church on top, erected as a monument in 1958 to record the 50th anniversary of the disaster.

The lower part of the façade preserves much of the original sculptured decoration including panels in relief with delightful farming scenes, and three fine doorways, by 14C, 15C and 16C artists. The beautiful central doorway has a tympanum by Pietro da Bonitate (1468). On the south side is a doorway by Polidoro Caldara da Caravaggio and a wall, still intact, with fine Gothic Catalan windows.

The majestic basilican **interior**, in pink and grey tones, was remarkably well restored after the fire. The side altars (copies of originals by Montorsoli), the columns, the marble pavement and the painted wooden roof were all replaced. In the south aisle on the first altar is a statue of *St John the Baptist* by Antonello Gagini (1525). At the end of the aisle is the so-called tomb of five archbishops (14C), with five Gothic trilobed arches. On the nave pillar in the transept is the fragmented tomb slab of Archbishop Palmer (d. 1195) carved in 1195 in Byzantine style.

From the south aisle is the entrance to the **Treasury** (winter: 09.00–13.00, Sun & PH 10.00–13.00, 16.00–18.30; summer: daily 09.00–13.00, 15.30–18.30). Arranged in four rooms and on two floors, it is particularly rich in 17C and 18C objects, including church silver made in Messina. Among the most important pieces are: a lamp in rock crystal dating from 969, altered in 1250; a 12C silver reliquary of an arm; a 15C silver reliquary of the arm of St Nicholas; an octagonal bronze reliquary of the *Madonna della Lettera* (14C); a 17C vase with silver and gilded bronze flowers; a 17C embroidered chasuble and two gilded silver chalices decorated with enamels (14C). The very fine **reliquary** of the arm of S. Marziano was commissioned by Richard Palmer (as the inscription states) when he was bishop of Syracuse; he brought it here when he became Archbishop of Messina around 1182. It shows the influence of Islamic and Byzantine goldsmiths' art. The most precious piece in the treasury collection is the golden *Manta*, used only on important occasions to cover the portrait of the *Madonna della Lettera*. It was made by a Florentine goldsmith, Innocenzo Mangani (17C). Other works of particular interest include: a 13C processional *Cross* attributed to Perrone Malamorte (1194–1250); a large, brightly coloured 17C silk embroidery, and a pair of silver candlesticks made in 1701 by Giuseppe d'Angelo and Filippo and Sebastiano Juvarra.

Outside the right apse chapel, elaborately decorated in marble, is the charming (but damaged) **tomb** of Archbishop De Tabiatis by Goro di Gregorio (1333). The sumptuous high altar bears a copy of the venerated Byzantine *Madonna della Lettera* (destroyed in 1943). The canopy, the stalls (designed by Giorgio Veneziano in 1540), and the bishop's throne have all been reconstructed. In front of the high altar is a lower altar which encloses a silver frontal attributed to the Messinese silversmith Francesco Juvarra (late 17C or early 18C), depicting the Madonna in the act of consigning a letter to the ambassadors of Messina. The mosaic in the central apse has been recomposed. In the left apse chapel is the only original mosaic to have survived in the church from the 14C. The **monument** to Bishop Angelo Paino (1870–1967), who rebuilt the cathedral after the last war, to the left of the apse, was sculpted by M. Lucerna.

In the two transepts part of the organ can be seen, manufactured by Tamburini of Crema in 1948; with its 16,000 pipes and 127 registers it is the largest in Italy and one of the biggest in Europe. In the north transept the **tomb effigy** of Bishop Antonio La Lignamine is surrounded by 12 fine small panels of the Passion sculpted by the Gagini school. Nearby is a 17C bust of Archbishop Proto, and part of the tomb of Archbishop Bellorado by Giovanni Battista Mazzola (1513). In the north aisle, beside the doorway, is a 16C relief of St Jerome (the exterior of the 15C north doorway can be seen here). At the end of the aisle, the baptistery, with a reconstructed font, contains a striking wooden Crucifix.

The **campanile** was designed by Francesco Valenti to house a remarkable **astronomical clock**, the largest of its kind in the world, built by the Strasbourg firm of Josef Ungerer in 1933. At 12 noon the chimes herald an elaborate and very noisy movement of mechanical figures, representing episodes in the city's history, religious festivals, the phases of life and the days of the week, accompanied by the music of *Ave Maria*. On the right side of the tower are the quadrants showing the planetarium, the phases of the moon, and the perpetual calendar.

A short way north of the cathedral is the circular **piazza Antonello**, dedicated to the famous local painter Antonello da Messina (see box p 403), laid out in 1914–29 with a group of monumental buildings: the post office (1915), the seat of the Province (1918), the Town Hall (1924; its façade faces corso Garibaldi), and an arcade (1929) with a café, offices and shops. In via Cavour is the circular domed church of S. Maria Annunziata dei Teatini (1930), better known as the church of S. Antonio Abate. In via XXIV Maggio, a street parallel to corso Cavour, are the remains of the 18C Monte di Pietà (pawnshop), with a beautiful flight of steps, and the church of **Montevergine** with a lovely Baroque interior. Just south of corso Cavour the University (1927), whose library dates from the university's foundation in 1548, faces the Law Courts, a monumental neo-classical building in ochre stone by Marcello Piacentini (1928), surmounted by a Roman chariot representing the victorious course of justice.

From piazza Duomo, **via I Settembre** (the stone on the corner records the outbreak of the Sicilian revolution in 1847) leads towards the railway station. It passes two Baroque corner fountains, which survived the earthquake, near (left) the church of **SS. Annunziata dei Catalani** (open for special services only), a 12C Norman church, shortened under the Swabians. The exterior is remarkably fine. The apse, transepts and cupola, with beautiful arcading, date from the 12C, while the three doors at the west end were added in the 13C. The interior has a brick apse and dome in yellow and white stone, and tall dark grey columns with

Corinthian capitals. The windows and nave arches are decorated with red and white stone. The large stoup is made up of two capitals. This church has always withstood the earthquakes remarkably well; perhaps because it was built on the Greek temple of Poseidon, god of earthquakes. In the piazza is a statue of *Don John of Austria*, by Andrea Calamech (1572), which was erected to celebrate his victory over the Turks at Lepanto in 1571.

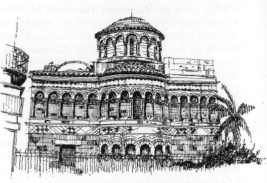

SS. Annunziata dei Catalani

Just off corso Garibaldi, a long broad thoroughfare, which crosses via I Settembre are the ruins of **S. Maria degli Alemanni** (c 1220), founded by the Teutonic order of knights, damaged by the 1783 earthquake and recently restored, interesting as the one of the few Gothic churches in Sicily, and thought to have been built by German craftsmen, hence the name 'Alemanni'. On the opposite side of the corso, the church of **S. Caterina di Valverde** contains a painting of the *Madonna dell' Itria between Sts Peter and Paul* by the local artist Antonello Riccio.

Corso Garibaldi ends in the huge **piazza Cairoli**, the centre of the town and the most popular meeting place for those engaged in the *passeggiata*. Thanks to its magnificent ficus trees, it is always cool and shady.

Further south, **viale S. Martino**, one of the main shopping streets, traverses an area of attractive Art Nouveau-style houses. The avenue itself is now the most beautiful in Messina, with recently planted date palms (acquired fully grown in Egypt). It ends at the public gardens of **Villa Dante** beside the monumental **cemetery**, designed in 1872 by Leone Savoia. The luxuriant garden, built in terraces on the slopes of the hill, has a lovely view of Calabria. The *Famedio*, or Pantheon, was damaged by the 1908 earthquake, but almost all the smaller family tombs were left intact. The temple of Christ the King, which dominates the city with its huge dome, was designed to be a collective memorial for the victims of the earthquake and for all those killed in war. In 1940 the British cemetery, founded during the Napoleonic wars, was transferred here (reached by a path on the extreme left side of the cemetery) by the Italian authorities when its original site near the harbour was needed for defence works.

From piazza Cairoli (see above), corso Garibaldi runs north, parallel to corso Vittorio Emanuele and the waterfront, with a view of the busy harbour, and the sickle-shaped tongue of land which protects it ending at the Forte di S. Salvatore, erected by the Spaniards in 1546. Right on the point of the sickle, at the entrance to the port, is the golden statue of the *Madonna*, patron of Messina, on a white pillar 60m high. The **Victor Emmanuel Opera House** (1842; by Pietro Valente), on corso Garibaldi, was re-opened in 1985 after repairs; strangely, the earthquake had spared the perimeter walls and only the interior was ruined.

The two parallel streets passing a statue of Ferdinand II, end in piazza Unità d'Italia, with the **Neptune Fountain** by Montorsoli (1557; the figures of Neptune and Scylla are 19C copies; the originals are kept in the Museo Regionale, see below). Behind it is the huge Prefecture designed by Cesare Bazzani in 1920. Nearby is the little church of **S. Giovanni di Malta** (c 1590; by Camillo Camilliani and Jacopo del Duca) where a Church Treasury has been arranged. It displays vestments, church silvers and paintings (09.00–13.00, 15.30–19.00; closed Mon). Also facing the piazza is Palazzo Carrozza built in the 1930s in an eclectic style. There is a garden with pines and ficus trees facing the waterfront, and, behind, the public gardens of Villa Mazzini, where there is an aquarium.

Viale Boccetta, which was a water course before the earthquake, leads inland to the church of S. Francesco d'Assisi, better known by the inhabitants as the **Immacolata**. Built in 1252 with a large convent in Gothic Sicilian style, it stood outside the city walls. The church can be identified in some of Antonello da Messina's works but then so can the Straits of Messina, which often appear in the background.

Viale della Libertà (bus, see above), which follows the shore in full view of the Calabrian coastline, passes the *passeggiata a mare*, opposite which is the church of S. Giuliano with red domes in eclectic style, and the Messina Fair. The road runs along the coast passing the church of **Gesù e Maria del Buonviaggio**, known as the church of Ringo, an old fishing village close by. Built in 1598 and dedicated to seamen, its façade is adorned with a fine portal, Corinthian capitals and two niches with statues of Christ and Mary—both statues have one hand pierced to hold oil lamps to guide passing boats. From here, viale della Libertà leads to the Museo Regionale (c 3km from the Duomo).

Regional Museum

Housed in an old silk mill since the 1908 earthquake, the important Museo Regionale (open daily 09.00–13.30, except Sun & PH 09.00–12.30; Tues, Thurs and Sat also 15.00–17.30 or 16.00–18.30 in summer; closed Mon; ☎ 090/ 361292) is still awaiting its definitive arrangement. This remarkable collection of local art is particularly interesting for its fine examples of 15C and early 16C paintings (many of them recently restored), including works by Antonello da Messina and Caravaggio.

The entrance to the museum is along a wide path lined by flower beds containing architectural fragments from the old city. The inner court has more fragments, including capitals from the cathedral, three church doorways (from S. Domenico, S. Maria della Scala and S. Maria di Basicò) and a 16C tomb.

Room 1 contains works of the **Byzantine and Norman periods**. It also contains 12C sculptural fragments; two fonts; the sarcophagus of the archimandrite Luke; an exquisite mosaic niche of the Madonna and Child, called *La Ciambretta* (13C); a painted *Madonna and Child* of the Byzantine type; fragments of the medieval painted wooden ceiling salvaged from the cathedral, and a mosaic *Head of an Apostle*. The marble bas-relief of the *Praying Virgin* (13C) was made in Constantinople, and comes from the church of S. Francesco d'Assisi. Also here is a fine capital from the Duomo, a painting of *St Placid* and a damaged mosaic of the *Madonna and Child*.

Room 2 Gothic period This room contains a fragment of a 14C painting of the *Madonna and Child*, a triptych of the *Madonna and Child between Sts Agatha and Bartholomew* attributed to the Master of the Sterbini Diptych; a strangely twisted statue from the cathedral by Goro di Gregorio, known as the *Madonna degli Storpi* (1333), or the Madonna of the Cripples; and from the 14C–15C Veneto-Marchigiana school, a polyptych of the *Madonna and Child with four saints* (tempera on panel).

Antonello da Messina

Antonello da Messina, born around 1430 in Messina, was one of the masters of the Italian Renaissance and the greatest southern Italian painter. Antonello made a number of journeys from Sicily including several to Naples, where he studied with Colantonio, and Venice (in 1475, four years before his death). His work shows the influence of the Flemish school, particularly Jan van Eyck, in its attention to detail and particular sense of light. He was one of the earliest Italian painters to perfect the technique of painting in oil, and he had an important influence on Giovanni Bellini. His son, Jacobello, and his nephew Antonello de Saliba, were also painters.

Some of his most beautiful works are still in Sicily (including the *Virgin Annunciate* in the Regional Art Gallery in Palermo, and the *Portrait of a Man* in the Mandralisca Museum in Cefalù), while other masterpieces are now in the National Gallery of London, the Metropolitan Museum in New York, the Louvre in Paris, and other museums in Berlin, Dresden and Venice.

Room 3 Early 15C This room contains a very fine painted wooden *Crucifix*. After the earthquake it was found on a donkey cart, where it had been abandoned by looters, and the church from which it came remains a mystery. It may be the work of a Catalan artist. There are also architectural fragments from the cathedral; a Della Robbian tondo of the *Madonna and Child*; bas-reliefs including *St George and the Dragon* (attributed to Domenico Gagini) and the *Madonna and Child* (attributed to Desiderio da Settignano), a polyptych of the *Madonna and Child with four Saints* (tempera on panel), an example of florid Gothic, and a marble statue of the *Madonna and Child* from the central doorway of the cathedral.

Room 4 contains works by **Antonello da Messina**, his school, and Flemish and Spanish works. Displayed on its own is the beautiful polyptych of the *Madonna with Sts Gregory and Benedict* (oil on panel), an ideal synthesis of Flemish and Italian Renaissance styles, painted by Antonello da Messina in 1473 and bearing his signature. Painted for the monastery of St Gregory, it was much damaged in the earthquake but has since been restored. On the other wall, an *Ecce Homo* is attributed to the school of Antonello. Also in room 4 are a polychrome marble statue of the *Madonna and Child* attributed to the sculptor Francesco Laurana; a lovely painting of the *Madonna and Child* (oil on panel) attributed to a follower of Petrus Christus; *Pietà and symbols of the Passion* (oil on panel), by an unknown Flemish painter, perhaps the Master of the St Lucy Legend; a *Madonna of the Rosary* (1489), oil on canvas, by an unknown painter of the school of Antonello; a *Madonna and Child between Sts John the Baptist and Peter* (oil on panel), attributed to Salvo d'Antonio, a disciple of Antonello; *St Clare and Stories from her Life and St Thomas of Canterbury* (oil on panels) by Giovannello da Itala; *Madonna and Child* (oil on panel), attributed to Antonello de Saliba, nephew and disciple of Antonello; two fragments of a triptych (oil on panel) of *St Gregory, the Princess and the Dragon and Magdalen, St Martin and the Beggar*; and another *Madonna and Child* (oil on panel) of the school of

Antonello. On the other side, two Flemish triptychs by unknown artists; a triptych from the church of St Francis of Assisi, by Jacob Cornelisz van Costzanen, the funerary monument of Admiral Angelo Balsamo by Antonello Freri; *St John the Baptist and stories from his life*, attributed to Henri Met de Bles, and a *Deposition* by Colijn de Coter (oil on panel).

Room 5 Girolamo Alibrandi and the early 16C This room is dedicated to Girolamo Alibrandi, a local artist who admired the work of Leonardo and Raphael; the influence of these great painters is visible in the two panel paintings of the *Circumcision* and the *Presentation in the temple* (1519), this latter work is thought to be his finest. It was recovered after the earthquake in more than 300 fragments and patiently restored in 1922, but since then many more of the missing parts have been discovered, and it has recently been restored again. Alibrandi is well represented with other paintings such as *St Peter*, *St Paul*, *The Last Judgement*, *St Catherine of Alexandria*. Also in room 5 is a fine painting by Vincenzo Catena of the *Holy Family and St George*; a statue of *St Anthony of Padua* (1534) attributed to the school of Gagini; the head of *Archbishop Pietro Bellorado* (from his funerary monument, 1513) by Giovanni Battista Mazzolo; a marble statue of the *Madonna and Child* by Antonello Gagini; a polychrome marble statue of *St Catherine of Alexandria* with stories of her life, of the school of Laurana; a ciborium by Antonello Gagini, from the cathedral, and a bronze lectern in the form of a pelican, from the church of St Francis of Assisi.

Rooms 6–7 contain works of the 16C–17C, in the **Sicilian Mannerist style**. Room 6. Stefano Giordano, *St Benedict between Sts Mauro and Placido* (1541); Polidoro Caldara da Caravaggio, *Adoration of the Shepherds* (1533). The influence of Raphael, with whom Polidoro studied, is visible in this work. Montorsoli, *Scylla* (the original from the Neptune fountain); Deodato Guinaccia, *Resurrection*, and works by Mariano Riccio and Stefano Giordano. Room 7. Deodato Guinaccia, *Adoration of the Shepherds* (oil on panel); a high relief in marble of the *Trinity* by Montorsoli; a 16C painting of *Christ carrying the Cross* by Jacopo Vignerio (oil on panel); a relief by Rinaldo Bonanno of the *Adoration of the Shepherds*; fragments of funerary monuments; examples of silversmiths' craft of the 16C–17C.

Room 8 contains the funerary monument of *Francesca Lanza Cibo* (1618, gilded copper); and paintings by Alessandro Allori, *Madonna of Itria* (1590); Antonio Biondo, *Marriage of St Catherine* (oil on canvas); and a collection of majolica pharmacy vases (mostly from the Casteldurante and Venetian workshops).

Room 9 Paintings by Antonio Catalano il Vecchio, *Madonna appearing to Sts Francis and Clare* (1604); Giovan Simone Comandè, *Miraculous catch of fish*; Filippo Paladini, *St Francis receiving the stigmata*; Antonio Catalano il Giovane, *Madonna of the Letter* (1629).

Room 10 contains two masterpieces by **Caravaggio**, both very dramatic late works painted during his stay in Messina in 1608–09: *Nativity* (commissioned by the Senate of Messina for the church of the Capuchins) and *Raising of Lazarus*, commissioned by the De Lazzari family for their private chapel in the church of St Camillo.

Works by Sicilian artists of his school displayed here include: Alonzo Rodriquez *Meeting between Sts Peter and Paul*; Mario Minniti, *Miracle of the widow of Naim*; and a work by Matteo Stomer, *Muzio Scevola before Porsenna*, and a hauntingly beautiful painting by Carlo Sellito, *St Lucy*.

Caravaggio

Outrageous, gifted, unhappy: one of Italy's most extraordinary artists, Michelangelo Merisi was born in 1573 at Caravaggio, a village close to Milan. When still very young, his genius was recognised, and it was not long before he was much in demand in Rome. His vigorous, realistic style was quite in contrast with the Mannerist art which was still popular at the time. However, for every week he spent painting, he needed another week to recover by frequenting low taverns and ball games, where he invariably ended up in a brawl. He seldom washed, and never changed his clothes; he liked rich brocades and fine velvets, but he wore them until they fell off in rags. In 1606 he killed a man in a fight; forced to leave Rome, he eventually reached Malta, where he was enthusiastically received and awarded the Grand Cross of the Knights of Malta. Involved in another fight, he was arrested and beaten, but he escaped from his prison tower by night, using the classic method of strips of sheet. From Malta he arrived in Sicily at Syracuse.

Again enthusiastically received by local art lovers, in Sicily he painted four of his finest works—the works of his maturity—the large dark canvases where subtle rays of light allow the figures to emerge, the story to unfold. Restless as ever, he tried to return to Rome after receiving his pardon; due to a misunderstanding, he was arrested and imprisoned at Civitavecchia while his ship sailed away with his painting materials and his pardon on board. Released, he ran after the ship, trying in vain to reach it, and walked all the way from Civitavecchia to Porto Ercole. The strain was too much, and he died, either from heat stroke or malaria; it was summer 1610.

In Syracuse his painting of the *Burial of St Lucy* (1608) can be seen at the Palazzo Bellomo Gallery, while his *Resurrection of Lazarus* and *Adoration of the Shepherds* (1609) are in Messina. Another *Nativity*, painted in 1609 for the Franciscans of Palermo, was stolen in 1968.

Room 11 The **17C works** here include marble intarsia panels, items of silverware, embroidery, two marble statues (*Faith* and *Hope*) from the church of the Annunziata dei Catalani, and paintings by Domenico Marolì, *Lot and his daughters*, Giovanni Battista Quagliata, Mattia Preti, who was a Calabrian disciple of Caravaggio (tondo of the *Dead Christ*), Giovanni Fulco, and Agostino Scilla.

Room 12 contains **18C works** including paintings by Giovanni Tuccari (*Marriage at Cana*); Filippo Tancredi; Sebastiano Conca; and an impressive state coach by Domenico Biondo.

From room 12 stairs lead up to a mezzanine floor to the **Treasury**. It includes vestments, altar frontals, church silver (16C–18C), a 17C ivory and ebony cabinet; an 18C silver altar frontal and ceramics. The rest of the collection, which will be displayed when the new exhibition space is available, includes the archaeological and numismatic sections.

On the slopes of the hillside above the town is **Cristo Re** (Christ the King, 1939), a centrally planned church with a cupola, at the side of which stands an old tower called the Torre Guelfonia with a great bell (diameter 3m) made from the melted down enemy guns of World War One. The church is a memorial to the dead of the two world wars. The interior is richly decorated with fine marbles and stuccoes; in the crypt is a sarcophagus on which lies the marble image of a soldier.

From here viale Principe Umberto runs north, passing Torre Vittoria and the ruins of the 16C Spanish walls, and the Sanctuary of Montalto (rebuilt in 1930) to the Botanical Gardens.

Punta Faro

Punta Faro (14km north; bus no. 79), at the extreme north eastern tip of the island and the nearest point to Calabria, can be reached by the old road lined with a modest row of houses facing the sea front, which traverses the ambitiously named suburbs of Paradiso, Contemplazione, Pace, and S. Agata.

Punta Faro is at the mouth of the Straits of Messina, the *Fretum Siculum* of the Romans. This is the site of the legendary whirlpools called Scylla and Charybdis, greatly feared by sailors in ancient times. The name of Cape Peloro recalls Pelorus, Hannibal's navigator, who was unjustly condemned to be thrown into the sea for misleading the fleet. Further south the Calabrian coast is sometimes, in hot weather, strangely magnified and distorted by a mirage called *Fata Morgana*.

The new fast road (Panoramica dello Stretto), which starts from viale Regina Elena and runs along the hillside above, provides a good view of the Calabrian coast; it is to be extended as far as Mortelle.

Just short of the cape is the fishing village of **Ganzirri**, now a resort on two little lagoons (the **Pantano Grande** and the **Pantano Piccolo**), separated from the sea by a dune barrier and fed by artesian water, once famous for mussels, but now polluted. There are still mussel and oyster beds in the smaller lagoon, but no fishing takes place in the prettier Pantano Grande, one side of which is lined with palm trees.

Reaching Punta Faro, or Cape Peloro, you will see a lighthouse and a pylon which once carried the huge cable, now on the sea bed, bringing electricity from the power station at Milazzo to Calabria. The twin pylons, over 150m high, are quite a landmark, and stand where the bridge between Sicily and the mainland might one day be built.

Discussions have been going on for many years about the long-term project to connect Messina and Calabria by bridge: the latest plan, proposed in 1986, and re-examined in 1997, involves a single-span suspension bridge for road and railway 3300m long, carried on two pylons 376m high. This would be the longest bridge of its kind in the world. Work on the bridge should begin in 2005.

Swordfishing has taken place off the coast here since ancient times; it was for many years considered one of the sights of Messina. The traditional method of harpooning the fish from characteristic small boats (*luntri*) with tall look-out masts, is still carried out, but most fishermen nowadays use modern equipment and motor boats called *felucche*. Modern fishing methods, and above all, modern fishing fleets coming from the Far East, have decimated the quantity of fish found in this area.

TAORMINA

Taormina is renowned for its magnificent position above the sea on a spur of Mount Taurus (206m), covered with luxuriant vegetation, commanding a celebrated view of Etna. With a delightful winter climate, it became a fashionable international resort at the end of the 19C, and during the 20C it became the most famous holiday place on the island. The small town (population 11,000; with some 60 hotels), with one main street and many side lanes, is now virtually given over to tourism and can be very crowded from Easter to September. Many of the villas and hotels, built in mock Gothic or eclectic styles at the beginning of the 20C, are surrounded with beautiful subtropical gardens. Far too much building has been allowed on the hillsides of Taormina in recent years, but in spite of the passage of time, the little town is still a fascinating place to explore, and not being subject to earthquakes, the medieval churches and palaces, the tiny streets, the Roman remains, have not lost their magic.

Practical information

Getting there
By train

Taormina and Giardini **station** is on the busy line which runs along the coast from Syracuse via Catania to Messina. The station, on the seafront and next to the coast road (SS 114) is built in an eclectic Romanesque-Gothic style, with two battlemented towers. From the station, blue buses (*SAIS-INTERBUS*) and taxis will take you up the hill to the town centre (along via Pirandello; 5km).

By bus

From the bus terminal in via Pirandello, services run by *SAIS-INTERBUS* to the railway station of Taormina, Giardini Naxos, Mazzarò, Castelmola, the Alcantara Gorge and the towns on the foothills of Etna, as well as services to Catania (and Catania airport) and Messina.

Coach excursions (it is preferable to book the day before) in summer run by *CIT*, *SAIS* and *SAT* from the bus terminal to Etna, Syracuse, Piazza Armerina and Enna, Agrigento, Palermo and Monreale, and the Alcantara Gorge. Alternatively, **taxis** can be hired at a

reasonable price for the excursion to Etna.

By car

A pleasant approach, but with hairpin bends, is by the via Pirandello (described below). Another approach road has been built to link up with the Catania–Messina motorway exit (Taormina Nord). This leaves the main coast road (SS 114) near Mazzarò and goes up partly on a viaduct past the huge Lumbi car park to enter Taormina near the stadium and join via Pirandello. A third approach road at the opposite end of the town, leads off from the SS 114 in the locality of Villagonia between Giardini Naxos and the railway station. It terminates at Porta Catania, beside the Excelsior Hotel. A car park has been under construction for many years beneath the town which will have two entrances, at Lumbi and below the Excelsior Hotel, and when finally completed should solve the traffic problems, but so far only the Lumbi part is finished.

To leave the town from Porta Catania (or the Circonvallazione) the best route is to take the via Roma (from piazza S. Domenico), one-way down, and rejoin via Pirandello via via Bagnoli Croce. The new road to Villagonia can also be used as an exit from the town.

Parking

The steep, narrow streets around the town, most of them one-way, are usually congested with traffic, and parking is impossible, even in winter (only residents are allowed to park within the city). The main street (corso Umberto I) is totally closed to traffic at all times; you are therefore obliged to park outside the gates. The car park known as **Lumbi** (☎ 0942/24345), on the northern approach road from the motorway, is the only place where space is almost always available. It charges an hourly tariff. A minibus service (free of charge) operates from Lumbi to Porta Messina. A convenient, but small, car park is in via Pirandello, next to the Hotel Miramare. There is another useful car park at **Mazzarò**, on the coast at the foot of the hill, connected by cableway to Taormina (in 5 minutes; terminus on via Pirandello not far from Porta Messina). Access is allowed to hotels, and most of the large hotels have their own car parks (signposted along the complicated one-way systems).

Cableway

Cableway from the foot of the hill at Mazzarò (car park) to outside Porta Messina in 5 minutes. **Note. The cableway sometimes closes in winter and also whenever the wind is strong.**

 Information offices

Azienda Autonoma, Palazzo Corvaja, ☎ 0942/23243. *Azienda Autonoma*, 54 Via Tisandro, Giardini Naxos, ☎ 0942/51010. Taormina on line: ✉ www. gate2taormina.com. Giardini Naxos on line: ✉ www.aast_giardini.naxos.it.

Where to stay
Hotels

The principal hotels provide transport from the station; they also have car parks. Many hotels are in quiet positions with fine gardens and views. Among the 60 or so hotels are:

☆☆☆☆☆ (L) *Timeo*, 59 via Teatro Greco, ☎ 0942/23801, 📠 0942/628501, ✉ www.framon-hotels.com. Luxury, old hotel; understated elegance; the very best in Sicily.

☆☆☆☆☆ *San Domenico*, piazza S. Domenico, ☎ 0942/613111, 📠 0942/625506, ✉ www.thi.it. An old convent; ambassadors, royalty and ageing film stars stay here. Internet point.

☆☆☆☆ *Excelsior Palace*, 8 via Toselli, ☎ 0942/23975, 📠 0942/ 23978. Traditional old hotel close to Porta Catania.

☆☆☆☆ *Miramare*, 27 via Guardiola Vecchia, ☎ 0942/23401, 📠 0942/626223. Just below town, with gorgeous views of the Straits.

☆☆☆☆ *Monte Tauro*, 3 via Madonna delle Grazie, ☎ 0942/24402, 📠 0942/24403. Modern structure, very comfortable, good restaurant.

☆☆☆☆ *Villa Diodoro*, 75 via Bagnoli Croce, ☎ 0942/23312, 📠 0942/23391. Another famous old hotel, next to public gardens.

☆☆☆☆ *Villa Paradiso*, 2 via Roma, ☎ 0942/23922, 📠 0942/625800. Small hotel, incomparable views.

☆☆☆ *Isabella*, 58 corso Umberto, ☎ 0942/23155, ✉ www.gaishotels.com.

☆☆☆ *Villa Schuler*, 2 via Bastione, ☎ 0942/23481 & 0942/23841. One of the nicest little hotels in town, attentive service. Also has appartments to rent.

☆☆☆ *Villa Sirina*, contrada Sirina, ☎ 0942/51776, 📠 0942/51671, ✉ www.villasirina.tao.it. On the hill between the hospital and the station. Garden and pool, good restaurant.

☆☆ *Victoria*, 81 corso Umberto, built in 1885, but recently refurbished, ☎ 0942/23372, 📠 0942/623567, ✉ www.albergovictoria.it.

☆ *Cableway*, piazzale Funivia, ☎ 0942/24739. Very convenient position at the bottom station of the cableway, rooms rather spartan but the restaurant is excellent.

☆ *La Prora*, 111 via Pirandello, ☎ & 📠 0942/23940. At the bottom of the hill near Cape Taormina, car park, good restaurant and pizzeria; hotel open summer only.

Bed and breakfast

Villa Sara, 55 via Leonardo da Vinci, ☎ 0942/28138.

Youth hostel

Taormina's Odyssey, 2 traversa A, via G. Martino, ☎ 0942/24533.

Farmhouse accommodation

The nearest farmhouses to Taormina are:

Gole Alcantara, contrada Sciara, Motta Camastra, ☎ 0942/985010 📠 0942/985264. Close to the beautiful Alcantara Gorge, camping possible, organic produce.

Gregorio, 272 via Cesare Battisti, contrada Calcare at Furci Siculo, ☎ & 📠 0942/794461. A small lemon farm, very difficult to find, but very pretty rooms, no restaurant, babysitter available.

Rooms and apartments

These are available to let all over the town. For information see the list provided by the *Azienda Autonoma Tourist Office*.

Hotels in the environs of Taormina

TAORMINA-MAZZARÒ The sea resort of Taormina-Mazzarò (described below) at the foot of the hill (cableway or road) also has numerous hotels including:

☆☆☆☆ *Capo Taormina*, 105 via Nazionale, ☎ 0942/572111, 📠 0942/223104.

☆☆☆☆ *Ipanema*, 242 via Nazionale, ☎ 0942/24720, 📠 0942/625821.

☆☆☆☆ *La Plage*, via Nazionale a Isolabella, ☎ 0942/626095, 📠 0942/625850. Little huts right on the beach in front of the beautiful island, good restaurant.

☆☆☆☆ *Mazzarò Sea Palace*, 147 via Nazionale, ☎ 0942/612111, 📠 0942/626237.

☆☆☆☆ *Villa S. Andrea*, 137 via Nazionale, ☎ 0942/23125, 📠 0942/24838, www.framon-hotels.com.

SPISONE ☆☆☆☆ *Caparena*, 189 via Nazionale, ☎ 0942/652033, 📠 0942/36913, ✉ www.gaishotels.com. Spacious. On a sandy beach.

SANT'ALESSIO SICULO (6km north of Cape Taormina), a simple inn, *La Scogliera*, 421 via Nazionale S.Alessio Siculo, close to sea (rocks). All rooms with bath but very basic; excellent homemade food, Sicilian breakfast with granita.

GIARDINI NAXOS There are many good hotels at the resort of Giardini Naxos (see below), 4km west of Cape Taormina.

☆☆☆☆ *Caesar Palace*, via Cuba Porticato, ☎ 0942/643131, 📠 0942/643141, ✉ www.parchotels.it. Close to motorway exit of Giardini Naxos. Brash new hotel with enormous swimming pool and good restaurant.

☆☆☆☆ *Hellenia Yachting*, 41 via Jannuzzo, località Recanati, ☎ 0942/51737, 📠 0942/54310. Refined, good restaurant, beach and pool.

☆☆☆☆ *Sant'Alphio*, via Recanati, ☎ 0942/51383. Nice garden and pool.

☆☆☆ *Nike Hotel*, 27 via Calcide Eubea, Schisò, ☎ 0942/51207, 📠 0942/56315, ✉ www.tao.it/nike. Quiet position on lava rock bay, clean and simple.

CASTELMOLA ☆☆☆☆ *Villa Sonia*, 9 via Porta Mola, Castelmola, ☎ 0942/28082, 📠 0942/28083, ✉ www.hotelvillasonia.com. Superb position on top of the mountain. Pool, sauna, gymnasium. This hotel has an exceptionally good restaurant, worth a visit in its own right.

Campsites

Campsites on the sea to the north at Letojanni, see p 422.

S. Leo (Capo Taormina) ☎ 0942/24658. Very spartan.

Eating out
Restaurants

€€€ *Casa Grugno*, via S. Maria de' Greci, ☎ 0942/21208, near San Domenico, currently the most fashionable restaurant in town; genial Austrian chef; a typical dish is prawns in crunchy vermicelli nests with orange sauce.

€€€ *Da Lorenzo*, 12 via Roma, ☎ 0942/23480. Very high standard.

€€€ *Duomo*, 11 vicolo deglo Ebrei, ☎ 0942/625656. Rub shoulders with the celebrities.

€€€ *La Giara*, 1 via La Floresta, ☎ 0942/625083. Ava Gardner and friends really lived it up here in the 1950s, and it is still an excellent restaurant.

€€ *Grotta Azzurra*, 2 via Bagnoli Croce, ☎ 0942/23505.

€€ *Grotta di Ulisse*, 3 salita Denti, ☎ 0942/625253. Live Sicilian music. Closed Tues in winter.

€€ *La Botte*, piazzetta S. Domenica, ☎ 0942/24198. Good Sicilian antipasti.

€€ *La Griglia*, 54 corso Umberto, ☎ 0942/23980. The owner, Giorgio, takes good care of his guests. Closed Tues.

€€ *La Piazzetta*, 5 via Paladini, ☎ 0942/626317. Good food in a stunning little square just off the main street. Closed Mon in winter.

€ *Porta Messina*, ☎ 0942/23205. Simple local dishes and excellent pizza. Closed Tues in winter.

MAZZARÒ €€ *Il Barcaiolo*, ☎ 0942/625633. On the beach at Mazzarò,

summer only. Tiny family-run restaurant for delicious fish; better dinner than lunch. But beware, there are 120 steps to reach it. Don't forget the midge repellent.

GIARDINI NAXOS *Angelina*, ☎ 0942/51477. By the docks. Superlative spaghetti with clams.

Cafés, pastry shops, ice cream parlours and pubs

TAORMINA *Giuseppe Chemi*, 112 corso Umberto and *Antonino Chemi*, 102 corso Umberto, are excellent pastry shops.

Vico dei Sapori, 13 via teatro Greco serves very good ice cream, and the best *cassata siciliana* and *cannoli di ricotta*. They have a shop offering fine olive oils and wines, spaghetti sauces and pasta. Another excellent ice cream parlour is *Gelatomania*, 7 corso Umberto, for delectable *Ferrero Rocher* ice cream.

O'Seven, 6 largo La Farina. If desire for Guinness is overwhelming while people-watching along main street. Serves delicious salads.

GIARDINI NAXOS *Maharaja*, 12 via Tisandro. Very pleasant spot on the seafront for an after-dinner drink. Music.

Oasi bar, 31/D Via Jannuzzo, Recanati. Luciano bakes fresh cookies daily, good homemade soup.

Picnics

Good places to picnic: in the public gardens; in the environs, at the archaeological site of Naxos.

Beaches

Mazzarò, right in front of the cablecar station, is a popular beach. **Isola Bella** is also nice; turn right outside cablecar station, five minutes' walk, pass under the railway through entrance to La Plage Hotel. **Spisone**, just beneath the motorway exit for Taormina, is the best of all—a sandy beach with crystal clear water. Turn left outside cablecar station, then ten minutes' walk. There is a very

pleasant lido hidden away here called
La Dolce Vita, ☎ 0942/24056, relatively quiet even in mid-summer; good
lunches, and twice a week there is also
dinner with music and the opportunity
for night swimming. Tour guides, hotel
and restaurant employees, shopkeepers
come here—they should know. At
Giardini Naxos the beach is long and
sandy with plenty of lidos and free
stretches as well. Tucked away at the
extreme north end is *Il Cantone del
Faro* at **Sirina**, with a restaurant, pizzeria and bar; they also rent apartments,
☎ & 📠 0942/56832,
✉ ilcantonedelfaro@hotmail.com.

Annual festivals

Parade of Sicilian carts along
corso Umberto (May or
September). **International Film
Festival** (end of June or early July).
"**Taormina Arte**" **Festival**, from June–
September at the Greek Theatre. Drama,
concerts and ballet, with top performers.

Internet points

Internet Café, 214 corso Umberto.
Internet Planet, salita Humboldt.

Foreign language newspapers, stamps, phone cards

Newsagent at the railway station for
periodicals; *Mr Frank*, 9 corso Umberto,
Taormina, has those and everything else.
Naxos News, 20/A via Zara (Giardini
Naxos town centre).
Alfredo D'Amico, next to Hellenia
Yachting Hotel (Recanati area). Alfredo
has a wide selection of opera videos and
classical music CD's. Open summer only.

Anglo-American church

St George's, via Luigi Pirandello (open
every Sunday morning, ☎ 0942/
23859).

History

Tauromenium, probably founded by the Sicels, and then inhabited by the survivors of the destruction of Naxos (see below) by Dionysius of Syracuse in 403
BC, was enlarged in 358 under Andromachus, father of the historian Timaeus.

It was favoured by Rome during the early days of occupation, and suffered
in the Servile War (134–132), but forfeited its rights as an allied city by taking the part of Pompey against Caesar. In 902 it was taken by the Saracens,
then again in 965 when the theatre was destroyed. Count Roger conquered
the town in 1078. Here the Sicilian Parliament assembled in 1410 to choose
a king on the extinction of the line of Peter of Aragon.

The town was visited and described by numerous travellers in the 18C and
19C, and the famous view of Etna from the theatre was painted countless
times. John Dryden came here in 1701, William Hamilton in 1769, Henry
Swinburne in 1778, and Wolfgang Goethe in 1787. John Henry (later
Cardinal) Newman stayed in the town as a young man in 1833. In 1847
Edward Lear spent four or five days in what he described as 'Taormina the
Magnificent'. In 1850 W.H. Bartlett complained that 'anywhere but in Sicily
a place like Taormina would be a fortune to the innkeepers, but here is not a
single place where a traveller can linger to explore the spot'. In 1863 the
painter Count Otto Geleng settled in Taormina and stayed here until his death
in 1939. He married a local girl, became deputy mayor, and founded a nursery school. Florence Trevelyan, daughter of Lord Edward Spencer Trevelyan
(cousin of the historian), came to Taormina in 1881 and married the local
doctor Salvatore Cacciola in 1890. She planted olives and cypresses and exotic

trees on the hillside and created a lovely garden (now the public gardens) as well as dedicating herself to charitable works among the poor of the town.

Taormina was first connected to Messina by railway in 1866 and a year later the line to Catania was inaugurated. In 1874 the first hotel, the Timeo (still open, a fine and luxurious place), was opened in the town, and it became internationally known as a winter resort soon after the first visit of the Kaiser (Wilhelm II) in 1896. The Kaiser returned in 1904 and 1905 with a large retinue, and set the fashion for royal visitors, many of whom came here in secret under false names. In 1906 Edward VII wintered at the S. Domenico Hotel and George V made a private visit in 1924. Before World War I the town had a considerable Anglo-American, German, and Scandinavian colony, including the impoverished Baron Wilhelm von Gloeden (1896–1931), who took up photography here, his studio becoming one of the sights of the town. The painter Robert Kitson built a villa for himself here where he lived from 1905 onwards. Kitson was also concerned with the poverty of the local inhabitants and encouraged Mabel Hill, another English resident, to set up a lacemaking school in the town. The writer Robert Hitchens arrived by car in Taormina in the winter of 1910, the first time a car had reached the town. The Anglican church was built in 1922. D.H. Lawrence and his wife Frieda lived here from 1920–23.

From the 1920s onwards Taormina became fashionable amongst the famous and wealthy as a place to visit, and to spend the winter. The town attracted the attention of allied aircraft in July 1943 when it temporarily became Field-Marshal Kesselring's headquarters. In the 1950s it also became known as a bathing resort and for its film festival. Famous visitors in this period include Truman Capote, who wrote *Breakfast at Tiffany's* and *In Cold Blood* while here, Cecil Beaton, Jean Cocteau, Osbert Sitwell, Salvador Dalí, Orson Welles, John Steinbeck, Tennessee Williams, Rita Hayworth, Greta Garbo and Cary Grant. The town centre is still intact, but there has been plenty of new building on the surrounding hillside. It is a favourite destination for cruise ship passengers since the construction of the motorway has made it more accessible.

The easiest route into town is from the motorway exit straight to **Lumbi** (where there is a large car park), with few hairpin bends, but it is still possible to use the **via Pirandello** which branches off from the main road (SS114) at Cape Taormina and winds up the hill past lovely gardens. It passes the little 15C church of **SS. Pietro e Paolo** (open only for services), the ruins of the Kursaal and a series of late Roman Byzantine tomb-recesses in the wall below the former convent of S. Caterina. Shortly after the junction with via Bagnoli Croce (one-way down from the town) it passes a little **belvedere** with a fine view of Isola Bella and Mazzarò. Beyond the bus terminal, on the right (no. 24), surrounded by a garden of date palms, is the Anglo-American church of **St George's**, built by the British community in 1922, with lava decoration on the exterior. It contains British and American funerary monuments, and memorials to the victims of the two world wars. Beyond the cableway station via Pirandello terminates outside Porta Messina, at the entrance to the town.

Entering **piazza Vittorio Emanuele**, the site of the ancient agora and the Roman forum is now a favourite meeting place, with shady trees and taxis. The two coffee bars on the left are ideal for people-watching and good for coffee,

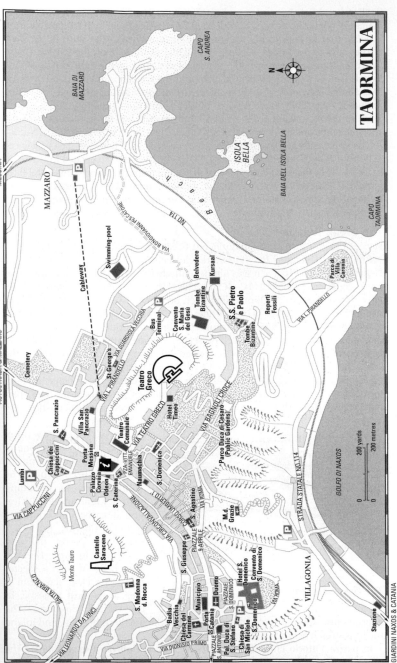

TAORMINA

Sicilian breakfast, ice cream or hot chocolate. The *Shaker Bar* was Tennessee Williams' favourite: he used to order a glass of whisky and then replenish it from a bottle that he kept in his pocket, bought at a cheap wine store in the back streets, and sit for hours, reading or talking. From here on the left via Teatro Greco leads past a congress hall opened in 1990, and (on the right) the large Villa Papale (no. 41), once Palazzo Cacciola and the residence of Florence Trevelyan (see above). At no. 8 is a shop, *Ricordi Siciliani*, selling unusual souvenirs, including beautifully made replicas of Greek and Roman pottery and Etruscan jewellery. Here, and at no. 19, you will find you will find the traditional naif pictures of saints and madonnas painted on glass by Sandra Buffa of Santa Ninfa.

The street ends at a group of cypresses covered with bougainvillea beside the delightful *Hotel Timeo*, with its pergola, the first hotel to be opened in the town in 1874, by Francesco Floresta (see p 408). Illustrious visitors to this hotel have included Winston Churchill and the writers André Gide, Tennessee Williams (who wrote *Streetcar named Desire* and *Cat on a Hot Tin Roof* here), Thomas Mann and Somerset Maugham.

The Greek Theatre

Here is the entrance to the magnificent Greek Theatre (open daily, 09.00–1 hr before sunset), famous for its remarkable scenic position. First erected in the Hellenistic period (4C BC), it was almost entirely rebuilt under the Romans when it was considerably altered (1C–3C AD). This is the largest ancient theatre in Sicily after that of Syracuse (109m in diameter; orchestra 35m across). The cavea, as was usual, was excavated in the hillside; above the nine wedges of seats, a portico (partially restored in 1955) ran around the top (a few stumps of the 45 columns in front survive). The scena is well preserved; it must have had a double order of columns, the four now visible were erected during restoration carried out in the 19C. The outer brick wall is pierced by three arched gates; the inner wall was once cased with marble. The foundations of the proscenium, or stage, remain, together with the parascenia, or wings, and traces of porticoes at the back (perhaps shelters from the weather). The theatre was famous for its acoustics—try testing them.

The celebrated view from the top of the cavea, one of the most breathtaking in Sicily, has been painted by countless artists, including Gustav Klimt and Paul Klee, and described by countless writers: Goethe, in 1787, exclaimed 'Never did any audience, in any theatre, have before it such a spectacle.' On a clear day Etna is seen at its most majestic. In the other direction the

The Greek theatre

Aspromonte Mountains of Calabria extend to the northern horizon, and inland the hills stretch behind Castelmola.

In piazza Vittorio Emanuele (see above) stands **Palazzo Corvaia** (15C; the central tower is Saracen and goes back to the 10C), with mullioned windows and a 15C side-portal in Gothic-Catalan form. Inside the courtyard is a staircase with very worn reliefs of Adam and Eve. The limestone ornamentation with black and white lava inlay is characteristic of Taormina. The building houses the tourist information office. The great hall, meeting-place in 1410 of the Sicilian Parliament, and other rooms, now house an interesting **museum of local crafts** (open daily, 09.00–13.00, 16.00–18.00), donated by local antique dealer and antiquarian Giovanni Panarello. The collection offers a synthesis of Sicilian handicrafts from the 16C–20C.

Room 1 Pieces of Sicilian carts, puppets, puppet-show posters. A section is dedicated to shepherds: items coming from the Peloritan Mountains and Calabria, made of wood and horn (collars for cows and sheep, spoons, bowls, flasks and kegs, walking sticks and spindles). Engraved with geometric and fertility symbols, the decorations were also for recognition of property. The herdsmen and shepherds were very proud of their collars, and if they sold their animals, the collars never went with the sale. The spindles are usually decorated with a female figure. These, and decorated whalebones for corsets, were loving gifts from the shepherds to their women. There is also a good collection of anthropomorphic pottery from Caltagirone, Collesano, Patti and Seminara (Calabria), especially flowerpots representing men's or women's faces. There is a series of little religious statuettes made of wood or papier mâché, good luck charms for babies, and crucifixes in silver, ivory, wood and bone; paintings on glass.

Room 2 A collection of the traditional Christmas cribs, made of ivory, coral, mother-of-pearl. The religious paintings on the wall of the parliament hall are of the 16C and 19C.

The 17C church of **S. Caterina** has three large white stucco Baroque altars and a painting on the high altar of the *Martyrdom of St Catherine* (16C) oil on panel, by Jacopo Vignerio . In the floor of the nave, parts of a Hellenistic temple have been revealed. A 15C statue of *St Catherine* stands on a plinth with stories of her life. The macabre underground funerary chamber of 1662 is at present closed.

Behind the church are the scant remains of the **Odeon** or Teatrino Romano, incorporating part of the preceding Hellenistic temple. Built in the 1C AD, it could hold 200 people. Excavations nearby have revealed public baths of the Imperial Roman period and traces of the Forum.

Outside **Porta Messina**, at the lower end of a large piazza busy with traffic, is **S. Pancrazio** (open for services only), built on the ruins of a 4C BC Greek temple to Isis, Zeus and Serapis, whose cella is still traceable.

A further delight offered by this beautiful town, after visiting the Greek Theatre is a stroll along **corso Umberto I**. This is the place to shop for sweetmeats, elegant clothes and shoes, antiques, locally produced pottery and jewellery. Along the way are medieval doorways, flower-filled balconies and stepped alleyways. It is only about 700m along corso Umberto I from Porta Messina to Porta Catania but there are plenty of distractions: at no. 42 is the pretty doorway and tiny rose window of the deconsecrated church of S. Maria del Piliere. Beyond no. 100 steps (via Naumachia) lead down to the so-called Naumachia, a long brick wall (122m) with niches (formerly decorated with statues) of late Roman date, now supporting a row of houses. Behind it is a huge cistern (no admission): it is thought to have been a monumental nymphaeum or a gymnasium. Between nos 133 and 135 is Vicolo Stretto, said to be the narrowest street in Italy.

On the other side steps lead down (see the map) to via Bagnoli Croce and the beautifully kept public gardens, **Parco Duca di Cesarò**. The gardens are a blaze of colour at all times of the year, with many different varieties of flowering plants and a vast array of Mediterranean and exotic trees. They were created in 1899 by Florence Trevelyan Cacciola (1852–1907), whose bust (a copy of her funerary monument) has been placed on the left of the main entrance on via Bagnoli Croce, presented to the town in 1922 by the Duke of Cesarò. The most elaborate of the delightful Victorian follies here is the pagoda at the far end which resembles a beehive (but is inhabited by birds), with a maze of wooden terraces, antique fragments and lava decoration. In Florence Trevelyan's day the gardens were known, after this construction, as 'The Beehives'. There are now also aviaries, a children's playground and tennis courts, and in 1992 a reproduction of a human torpedo, used in 1941 to sink the British war ships *Queen Elizabeth* and *Valiant* in the port of Alexandria, was installed here as a memorial to local sailors who lost their lives in service.

The corso Umberto I opens into **piazza IX Aprile**, where there is a superb view south across to the sea and Etna. The date refers to April 1860 when the people of Taormina rebelled against the authority of the Bourbons. House martins animate the rooftops. Several cafés here have tables outside, including the *Mocambo*, one of the most famous cafés in the town, once noted for its exclusive clientele, scene both of clamorous fights among the famous and of several scandalous love affairs. It now has a slightly decadent atmosphere.

On the left is the former church of **S. Agostino** (1448), now the library, with a Gothic doorway, and to the right, approached by a pretty flight of steps, stands the 17C church of **S. Giuseppe**, which has a heavily decorated Rococo stucco interior. Beyond the Clock Tower (?12C; restored 1679), is the so-called Borgo Medioevale. The corso is lined with many little medieval palaces, with doors and windows where supposedly Saracenic influences linger among the 15C details of the Gothic-Catalan doorways and windows. The first house on the left (no. 154) has two columns from the Roman theatre. At no. 185 is the former church of S. Giovanni (1533), which is now a club for war veterans and is full of trophies and photographs. Beyond no. 209 a wide flight of steps leads up to Palazzo Ciampoli built in 1412 and restored after war damage.

Opposite the Town Hall (18C) is the **Duomo** (S. Nicola di Bari), founded in the 13C, with battlements, and two lovely side portals (15C and 16C). The façade has a late rose window and portal of 1636. In the **interior**, with six monolithic antique pink marble columns, are a painting of the *Visitation* by Antonino Giuffrè (1463) and a polyptych by Antonello de Saliba (1504), from the former church of S. Giovanni, both in the south aisle. In the chapel at the end of the south aisle, there is a delicate tabernacle dated 1648, and an early 16C *Madonna and Child* in marble. In the north aisle, first altar, there is a *Madonna enthroned with saints* (in poor condition) by Alfonso Franco; on the second altar, a 16C statue of *St Agatha* and on the third altar, *Adoration of the Magi*.

In the piazza is a charming fountain of 1635. The bizarre figure on the top recalls the symbol of Taormina with the bust of an angel on the body of a bull (adapted here as a pregnant female centaur with only two legs). Said to have been found in the ruins of the Theatre, it is probably a Baroque pastiche.

Steps on the right of the fountain ascend past a small black and white Roman mosaic (right; within an enclosure) and (left) the rebuilt church of the Carmine with a pretty campanile. More steps lead up to (left) the Porta Cuseni (or Saraceni), the name given to the village outside the walls. Outside the gate steps (the salita Castelmola) continue up to via Dionisio I which leads right to the **Badia Vecchia**, with its large crenellated tower with fine mullioned windows and black and white intarsias, now the antiquarium or the **Museo Archeologico di Taormina** (open daily 09.00–13.00, 16.00–19.00, Sun & PH mornings only, ☎ 0942/632028). The museum has a collection of objects found during excavations around the theatre and nearby; some fragments of sculpture in marble, a list carved in stone of the magistrates of Taormina from the 2C–1C BC, the financial stone tablets of *Tauromenium*, and a bronze Byzantine sword found recently on the sea bed close to Isola Bella. From here via Leonardo da Vinci leads past a wall in front of cypresses, bougainvillea and plumbago to **Casa Cuseni** (no. 7). The villa was built by Robert Kitson, a painter, in 1907. It later became a pensione, run by his niece, Daphne Phelps, author of *A House in Sicily*. On the opposite side of piazza Duomo, a street descends to the convent of **S. Domenico** (first opened as a hotel in 1894), which has a late 16C cloister. Field-Marshal Kesselring set up his headquarters here in July 1943, and many of his staff were killed by an allied air raid which destroyed the church.

Corso Umberto I ends at **Porta Catania** or Porta del Tocco (1440), with the Aragon family emblem on the outside. Across the walls here there was the Jewish Ghetto (the Jews were forced to leave Sicily and all the Spanish possessions in 1492) with narrow alleys and the interesting **Palazzo Duchi di Santo Stefano**, with Gothic Catalan forms. According to some experts, the large tower was built by the Normans and completely restored in the 14C–15C. The garden and upper floors have a permanent display of works by the Sicilian sculptor Giuseppe Mazzullo, born in Graniti, a village near Taormina (d. 1988), while the lower floor (with four cross vaults) is used for exhibitions (08.30–13.30, 16.00–19.00). This area of the town suffered badly during the air raids of July 1943 (see above), when the little 14C church of S. Antonio (Gothic portal) was damaged. The church contains a crib made in 1953, which is modelled on the town. The neo-Saracenic *Hotel Excelsior*, built in the 1920s, has a wonderful view from the terrace.

Walks in the vicinity of Taormina

There are a number of pretty walks (with signposted paths; see map p 413) from the town down to the coast at Mazzarò, Spisone and Villagonia. Above the town paths lead up to the Madonna della Rocca, the castle, and Castelmola. They all have good views and lead through luxuriant vegetation.

Outside the Parco Duca di Cesarò (public gardens; see above) a narrow road with steps descends past a plaque (1908) which records the work of Mabel Hill (1866–1940), who came to set up an embroidery school in the town to revive the traditional methods of making Taormina lace, and who, with the painter Robert Kitson (see above), took an interest in local social conditions between the wars. Beyond a modern hotel (*Monte Tauro*) built on the steep hillside, a lane continues down to the coast at **Villagonia** near the railway station.

Steps lead down from the other end of the public gardens (beside the *Villa Diodoro* hotel) to via Pirandello which can then be followed downhill to the coast by steps linking the loops in the road.

A path descends from the Belvedere on via Pirandello to Mazzarò (see below) opposite Cape S. Andrea. Another path, off the approach road from Mazzarò and the motorway, starts near the stadium and well-tended cemetery, part of which is reserved for non-Catholics and the town's foreign community (open 08.00–12.00, 14.00–16.00 except Friday; Sun & PH 09.00–12.00). The path descends to **Spisone** beach.

Via Roma, which runs from the public gardens to S. Domenico, although open to cars, provides magnificent views over luxuriant vegetation and precipitous ravines to the sea.

Above the town, from the Circonvallazione, a path (signposted) leads up through trees to the **Madonna della Rocca** and the Castello (see also below), from which there are wonderful views. The return can be made by the 738 steps that link the serpentine loops of the Castelmola road (described below). Monte Ziretto (579m) is also a fine viewpoint.

Environs of Taormina

Castelmola

From the Circonvallazione above Taormina the Castelmola road (with many hairpin bends) climbs up. A turning (right) leads to the Madonna della Rocca and the Castello (398m), with a ruined keep, unfortunately closed.

Castelmola (550m) is a small village with a dwindling population, on top of a rock with a ruined Byzantine castle, high above Taormina. In the little square, with a view from the terrace of Etna and the bay of Naxos, the *Caffè San Giorgio* was founded in 1907 and has an interesting collection of autographs in the visitors' book. The village is well known for its almond wine, which was invented at the San Giorgio. Another picturesque café is in piazza Duomo, the *Caffè Turrisi*. The façade of the parish church of S. Giorgio, reconstructed in Gothic style, opens onto a balcony with another wonderful view. The view is still better from **Monte Venere** or Veneretta (884m), reached by a long footpath from the cemetery of Castelmola.

Mazzarò

Mazzarò is a pretty bathing resort on Capo S. Andrea beneath the hill of Taormina, well supplied with hotels (see above). Offshore is the **Isola Bella**, of great natural beauty, now run as a nature reserve by the World Wildlife Fund. In the 19C the Bourbon government sold the island to Florence Trevelyan for 5000 liras. She built a house on it and later it came into the hands of the Bosurgi family, and was finally acquired by the Sicilian region in 1987. Off **Capo Taormina** 35 Roman columns lie submerged: they are unworked quarried stone, probably destined for a temple or the portico of a villa, which must have been lost in a shipwreck. Footpaths (signposted) and a cableway mount from Mazzarò to Taormina.

Giardini Naxos

Giardini, 4km south of Cape Taormina, once a quiet fishing village, with a long main street parallel to the sea, was developed in the 1960s into the large holiday resort of Giardini Naxos. The wide bay is now lined with hotels, flats and restaurants from Capo Schisò as far as the railway station of Taormina Giardini, and new buildings have been erected wherever possible. There are no signposts to

Giardini Naxos from Taormina: the older city seems to try to ignore its existence. From this bay, Garibaldi, with two steamboats and 4200 men, set out on his victorious campaign against the 30,000 Bourbon troops in Calabria (19 August 1860).

The point of the cape, **Capo Schisò**, was formed by an ancient lava flow which can still be clearly seen at the water's edge here, by the little harbour. This was a natural landing place for the navigators rounding the 'toe' of Italy from the East, and it was the site of the first Greek colony of *Naxos* which has been excavated here. From the sea front there is a view of Taormina, with Castelmola above to the left.

Excavations of Naxos and the Archaeological Museum

By the modern harbour wall is the entrance to the excavations of Naxos and the Museo Archeologico (site and museum open daily, 09.00–19.00 in summer, 09.00–16.00 in winter, ☎ 0942/51001). The entrance is through a pretty, beautifully kept little garden, in which an ancient lava stream is still visible. An old Bourbon fort here has been restored to house the **Archaeological Museum** which has a good collection displayed chronologically on two floors and is well labelled. Recent finds on the site include pottery of 8C BC coming from the island of Naxos in the Ionian Sea, the first tangible proof that at least some of the first settlers came from there, and gave the name to this first colony on Sicily.

Ground floor Neolithic and Bronze Age finds from the Cape (Stentinello ware, etc.); Iron Age finds from the necropolis of Mola including geometric style pottery.

First floor Terracottas and architectural fragments from a sanctuary at S. Venera (6C BC); material found in the area of the ancient city including a fine antefix with polychrome decoration, and Attic pottery; a little altar dating from around 540 BC decorated with sphinxes in relief; a statuette of a goddess (end of 5C BC); a rare marble lamp from the Cyclades found in the sea (end of 7C BC); finds from a tomb near S. Venera of the 3C BC, including four pretty vases for perfume and a glass bowl; bronze objects (helmet of 4C BC, etc.). In the garden, beyond the lava flow, a little museum of underwater finds has been arranged in a small fort. It contains anchors (7C–4C BC) and amphorae dating from various periods.

The fascinating **excavations** (well signposted) in the fields to the south are reached from the garden through a green gate. A path, lined with bougainvillea, leads through the peaceful site of the ancient city.

> The foundation date of the Greek settlement (Chalcidians from Euboea and Ionians from Naxos) is thought to be 734–3 BC. It was the first Greek colony on the island, closely followed by Syracuse and Megara Hyblaea. The town surrendered to Hippocrates of Gela (495) and to Hieron of Syracuse in 476. It was finally destroyed by Dionysius I in 405–4. Excavations were first carried out here in 1953, and digs continue in the area of the city. Exceptionally fine Greek coins, dating from 410–360 BC have been found here, many of them bearing the head of Silenos, often associated with the god Dionysos.

On the right a path leads across a field planted with lemon trees to a stretch of Greek walls. The main area of excavation is about 15 minutes' walk from the museum in a beautiful orchard with lemon trees, palms, olives, orange trees, eucalyptus and medlar trees; between the trees flower bougainvillea, hibiscus and jasmine. Prickly pear, agave and oleander plants also flourish here.

There is an impressive stretch of **city walls** in black lava (c 500m) parallel to a line of eucalyptus trees. The **West Gate** is near a charming little olive tree raised on two circular terraces. A path leads to the original entrance to the **area sacra**, and remains of the 7C and 6C, including part of the walls, an altar and a **Temenos of Aphrodite**. A simple temple, constructed towards the end of the 7C, was built over by a larger temple at the end of the 6C. Under cover, two kilns are preserved, a circular one for water jars, and a rectangular one for tiles; both were in use during the late 6C and 5C BC. Beyond is the sea gate with a fine polygonal lava wall. The high wall, behind a row of cypresses, which blocks the view of the sea, was built during excavation work.

The Alcantara Gorge

From Giardini Naxos a road leads inland along the river valley of the Alcantara (*el qantara*, meaning bridge in Arabic) which has numerous lemon groves. Near Motta Camastra the **Gole Alcantara** are signposted. Beside the car park is a lift (open daily) which descends into the Alcantara Gorge, an unexpectedly deep cleft of basalt prisms, now a protected area. This was originally formed by a lava flow which was eroded by the river forming a narrow gorge in hard basalt. Waders can be hired to explore the gorge, which can also be reached by a path off the main road (signposted Strada Comunale). There are a restaurant and coffee bar by the lift, and a shop selling organic produce, including liqueurs, jams, olive oil and honey, from the nearby farm. The valley is now protected as a Regional Park.

THE PELORITAN MOUNTAINS

The Monti Peloritani, on the northeastern tip of the island, were once thickly forested. The highest peak is the Montagna Grande (1374m). The southern slopes are barren and every drop of the scanty water supply is utilised by means of aqueducts from springs, and subterranean channels in the broad *fiumare*, conspicuous features of the countryside also on the northern slopes. These wide, flat-bottomed torrent beds filled with gravel, similar to the wadis of the Middle East, are usually waterless. In flood time the water descends these channels in spate, carrying a considerable quantity of alluvial matter. Although the mountains are for the most part inaccessible, there are a number of remote little upland villages reached by steep roads from the coast between Taormina and Messina, and between Messina and Tindari. The most interesting are **Forza d'Agrò** on the eastern coast, and **S. Lucia del Mela** and **Castroreale** on the northern coast. The church of **SS. Pietro e Paolo** near Casalvecchio Siculo is of great interest. Some of the most beautiful scenery on the island can be seen on the road which runs inland over the Peloritans from Castroreale Terme via Novara di Sicilia to Francavilla di Sicilia.

Practical information

Getting there
A road and railway from Messina run along both the north and east coasts at the foot of the Peloritan Mountains. Country bus services run by *SAIS-INTERBUS* from Messina (see Messina) and Taormina (from the via Pirandello bus terminal

and from the railway station) to Forza D'Agrò, Santa Teresa di Riva, Alì Terme, Scaletta Zanclea, and local buses from Santa Teresa di Riva to Savoca and Casalvecchio.

Information office

APT Messina, ☎ 090/674236.

Where to stay
Hotels

LETOJANNI ✩✩✩✩ *Park Hotel Lido Silemi*, 1 via Silemi, località Silemi, ☎ 0942/36229, 🖷 0942/652094. On the beach; comfortable.
✩✩✩ *Albatros*, via Luigi Rizzo, ☎ 0942/37560. Clean and central, with beach over the road; management very obliging.
✩✩✩ *Antares*, Poggio Mastropietro, ☎ 0942/36477, 🖷 0942/36095. Perched on hill dominating the Straits.
✩✩✩ *S. Pietro*, via Luigi Rizzo, ☎ 0942/36081. Just right for families; central.
✩✩ *Da Peppe*, 345 via Vittorio Emanuele, ☎ 0942/36159, 🖷 0942/36843. This is a simple little hotel, but the restaurant is renowned; the fish soup (*zuppa di pesce*) is exceptional.
FORZA D'AGRÒ ✩✩✩✩ *Baia Taormina*, via Nazionale, ☎ 0942/756292, 🖷 0942/756603. Close to castle of Sant'Alessio, with shuttle buses to the beach and Taormina.
ALÌ TERME ✩✩✩ *La Magnolia*, 18/A via Lungomare, ☎ 0942/716377/701814, 🖷 0942/701815, 🖳 www.italiabc.it/az/magnolia. The roads in this area are a bit hectic but this little hotel is quite a find: family-run, with good food and Sicilian wine cellar. Just over the road is the wide beach (shale and sand).

Campsites

LETOJANNI ✩✩✩ *Eurocamping Marmaruca*, località Marmaruca, ☎ 0942/36676.
✩✩ *Paradise International*, località Melianò, ☎ 0942/36306.
SANT'ALESSIO SICULO ✩✩ *La Focetta Sicula*, località Torrente d'Agrò, ☎ 0942/751657.

Eating out
Restaurants

LETOJANNI €€€ *Da Nino*, 29 via L. Rizzo, ☎ 0942/36147. Excellent fish dishes.
€€€ *Da Peppe*, 345 via Vittorio Emanuele, ☎ 0942/36159. Excellent fish, people come from miles around.
€€ *Il Ficodindia*, via Appiano, località Mazzeo, ☎ 0942/36301. Typical Peloritan dishes.
€€ *Mezza Luna*, 48 via L.Rizzo, ☎ 0942/37020. Reliable service.
GALLODORO A hilltop village above Letojanni. €€ *Noemi*, ☎ 0942/37338. Superb Sicilian food. Come here for an unforgettable gastronomic experience. Set menu—fixed price includes everything.
FORZA D'AGRÒ €€ *Il Giardinetto*, via Belvedere, ☎ 0942/721074.
€€ *L'Abbazia*, 2 piazza Giovanni XXIII, ☎ 0942/721168. Very pleasant.
SAVOCA €€ *La Pineta*, 3 via Pineta, ☎ 0942/761094. Country food.
ITALA €€ *Antica Pietrarossa*, 29 via Provinciale, ☎ 090/953171. Very good pasta dishes.

Coffee bar and ice cream parlour

LETOJANNI, *Niny Bar*, piazza Durante. Excellent ice cream; their speciality is *granita arcobaleno* (rainbow sorbet), with alternating layers in a glass of fresh fruit sorbet—lemon, peach, mulberry, strawberry and pineapple.

The southern slopes between Taormina and Messina

Letojanni (5km from Taormina; railway station, population 2400) is a thriving holiday resort, with good hotels, a sandy beach, and many bars and restaurants. Paragliding, hang gliding and microlight flying are all possible with courses offered by award-winning pioneer flyer Angelo D'Arrigo, ☒ www.etnacenter.net. Above the resort of Letojanni just to the north of Taormina is **Mongiuffi Melia**, characteristic of the hill villages on the southern slopes of the Peloritans, with several sanctuaries of the Madonna to which pilgrimages are organized in summer.

Forza d'Agrò is a charming little medieval city, overlooking the privately owned Arab Norman castle at Cape Sant'Alessio, from which the views extend along the straight coastline towards Messina, across the straits to Calabria and south to Taormina. Above the piazza a lane leads up to circular steps which ascend through a 15C Gothic Catalan archway, Arco Durazzesco, in front of the church of S. Trinità, with a 15C façade and campanile. It stands next to the former 15C Augustinian convent, with a cloister. There is a fine view of the coast from the terrace behind the church. Out of the other side of the piazza a narrow road leads through the village past the Baroque Chiesa Madre, with a fine 16C façade. Opposite is a charming abandoned old house with pretty balconies. The road continues past attractive old houses covered with flowering plants to the castle which was strengthened at the end of the 16C by a double circle of walls, and which was used for many years as the cemetery.

Savoca and Casalvecchio

From S. Teresa Riva, the largest coastal town (population 8500) between Messina and Taormina, a byroad runs inland to **Savoca**, a village on a saddle between two hills, with a rich artistic and historical heritage. In a private house at the entrance to the village is the *Bar Vitelli*, with a pretty terrace, which has a collection of local artisans' tools and photographs taken when Francis Ford Coppola shot some scenes of the *Godfather* films here. It is best to park here and walk up through the old gate past the 15C church of S. Michele with two pretty portals dating from the early 16C. Near here, a little **Museum of Popular Art** has recently opened (09.30–12.30, 17.00–22.00; Sun & ph 17.00–22.00). Beyond the church of S. Nicolò, usually known as S. Lucia (with a 16C bust of St Lucy above the portal), the road continues up to the Chiesa Madre, built in the 12C and restored in the 15C. By the church is a house with a Gothic Catalan double window. From here the remains of the 17C church of the Immacolata and the ruins of the Norman castle can be seen. Outside the town in the church of the **Cappuccini** are catacombs (crypt, daily 09.00–13.00, 15.00–17.00; ☎ 0942/761245; contribution expected) which preserve the mummified bodies, fully dressed, of citizens who lived here in the 18C, and which were unfortunately vandalised with green paint a few years ago.

The road continues over cultivated hills and valleys up to **Casalvecchio**, charmingly situated on the slopes of a hill. Next to the Chiesa Madre a little diocesan museum has recently been opened. The narrow street continues through the village. 700m beyond, a very narrow road (in places single track) leads left (signposted) and descends through lovely countryside to the old Basilian monastery of **SS. Pietro e Paolo d'Agrò**. The imposing tall Norman church (unlocked by the custodian at the neighbouring farm; tip suggested) is in a beautiful peaceful spot near the Fiumara d'Agrò. Begun in 1116, it is extremely well preserved both inside and out. An inscription over the door relates how Gerardo il Franco dedicated it to Sts Peter and Paul for the Basilian monks in 1172; it was probably also restored at this time. Built of brick and black lava the exterior has splendid polychrome decoration. The Byzantine interior also shows Arab influence in the stalactite vaulting and the tiny domes in the apse and nave. The stucco was removed in this century from the walls to reveal the attractive brickwork. The columns made from Sardinian granite appear to be Roman in origin. It is possible to return to the coast road from here along a very rough road on the gravel bed of the wide torrent (*fiumara*).

Alì Terme, 23km from Messina, population 2500, is famous for its thermal baths and mineral water springs, used since the 18C for the treatment of various ailments, such as rheumatism, gynaecological problems, skin and respiratory complaints. From here the Calabrian coastline is in full view. A byroad leads inland to **Fiumedinisi** where the Chiesa Madre has a wooden statue of *St Lucy* by Rinaldo Bonanno (1589) and a painting of the *Madonna of the Rosary* by Agostino Ciampelli.

Itala (population 1800) is built on the side of a valley with lush vegetation. Above the village a road (very narrow in places) continues uphill and then left past ancient olive trees and lemon groves to the well preserved church of **S. Pietro**. It is preceded by a delightful little courtyard with a garden and palm trees. The priest who has the key lives in the house by the church. The church was built in 1093 by Count Roger in thanksgiving for the Norman victory over the Arabs and has a handsome exterior with blind arcading and a little dome.

Scaletta Zanclea has a long narrow main street (still the main coast road); fishing boats are kept in the alleyways which lead down to the sea under the railway line. The street is particularly busy in the mornings when fresh fish is sold from stalls here. In the upper town the remains of the 13C Castello Ruffo lie beneath Mount Poverello (1279m), one of the highest of the Peloritans.

Mili S. Pietro is in a pretty wooded valley with terraced vineyards and orange groves. On the outskirts of the village (by the school) a primitive little Norman church of **S. Pietro** (1082), founded by Count Roger as a burial place for his son Jordan, killed in battle, can be seen just below the road to the left. Steps descend to the ruins of a house, from which the church can be reached under the arch to the left. It is now in urgent need of restoration and the very interesting vaulted interior is closed (key at the parish church in the village).

Messina to the Badiazza and Monti Peloritani

The road is well signposted from the centre of Messina (Colle S. Rizzo, Portella Castanea, S. Maria Dinnamare and Badiazza). Off the SS 113, a very poor road (almost impassable in places) leads right (signposted) past S. Andrea, a little church built in 1929, and poor houses to the head of the valley. Here, in a group of pine trees, is **La Badiazza** (also called S. Maria della Scala or S. Maria della Valle). This fine 13C church (abandoned) belonged to a ruined Cistercian convent and has an interesting exterior with lava decoration.

The main road continues uphill to enter all that remains of the forest which once covered the slopes of the Peloritan Mountains. Thick pinewoods survive here. The road sign indicating Palermo (250km) is a reminder that this was the main road to Palermo before the motorway was built. At **Colle S. Rizzo** (460m) is a crossroads. From here a spectacular road (signposted Santuario di Maria SS. di Dinnamare) leads for 9km along the crest of the Peloritan range to a height of 1130m. The first stretch is extremely narrow and dangerous but further on the road improves. The views on either side are breathtaking: on the right Milazzo can be seen and on the left the toe of Italy. There are delightful picnic places. Beyond a television mast is a car park (signposted). The church of Maria SS. di Dinnamare, built in the 18C and restored in 1886, was rebuilt in 1899. The aerial view, one of the most remarkable in Sicily, takes in the whole of Calabria, the port of Messina and the tip of Punta Faro. On the other side the Aeolian Islands, including Stromboli (beyond Milazzo) and Mount Etna, can be seen.

From the Colle S. Rizzo crossroads (see above) the road signposted to Castanea leads through fine pinewoods (with views down of the port of Messina, and to the left of the Aeolian Islands, and the motorway in the hills). In spring **Monte Ciccia** (609m) is on the migratory route from Africa to central Europe for thousands of birds, especially honey buzzards. On the approach to the village of **Castanea delle Furie** is an unusual, castellated villa. Castanea, apart from its beautiful name, has a typical medieval town plan and some lovely old churches. The road continues down to Spartà past olives and pines. As the road nears the sea there is a wonderful view of Stromboli.

Northern slopes between Messina and Castroreale Terme

Getting there
By bus
Country bus services run by *AST* (office in Messina, 156 via Primo Settembre, ☎ 090/662244) from Messina (bus stop in viale San Martino, Corso Cavour, viale Boccetta) to **Barcellona** and **Terme Vigliatore**.

Where to stay
Hotels
SCALA-TORREGROTTA ✰✰✰ *Redebora*, 73 via Sicilia, ☎ 090/9981182, 🖷 090/9910900. TERME VIGLIATORE ✰✰✰ *Il Gabbiano*, località lido Marchesana, ☎ 090/9782343, 🖷 090/9781385.
Farm accommodation
RODÌ-MILICI *Villa Laura*, contrada Trappeto, ☎ 090/9741226-9741015. Large farm with olive grove and riding stables. Tennis, swimming pool, bowls and many other activities.

Eating out
Restaurants
SANTA LUCIA DEL MELA €€ *Pellegrino*, 10 piazza Milite Ignoto, ☎ 090/935092.
€€ *La Forchetta del Castello*, contrada Filicusi, ☎ 090/935186.
RODÌ-MILICI €€ *I Vicerè*, contrada Trappeto, ☎ & 🖷 090/9741226. Farm restaurant which serves home-grown produce.
MONTALBANO ELICONA €€ *La Sciarbonata*, contrada Roccaro, ☎ 0941/679455.
NOVARA DI SICILIA €€ *Azienda Agrituristica Girasole*, 49 contrada Greco, ☎ 0941/650812.
€ *La Pineta*, 159 via Nazionale, ☎ 0941/650522. Simple trattoria offering delicious food, home-grown fruit and vegetables, grilled lamb, home-made sausages, excellent house wine. Pizza is served in the evenings, and in summer at their open-air pizzeria by the castle. Closed Mon.

The coast road follows almost exactly that of the Roman consular route (via Valeria) which joined Messina to *Lilybaeum*. At sea off Venetico, Agrippa defeated the fleet of Pompeius at the battle of Naulochos (36 BC). At the inland village of **Roccavaldina** there is a remarkably well preserved 16C pharmacy, complete with its jars, in piazza Umberto I.

S. Lucia del Mela (population 5200) was a place loved by Frederick II of Swabia and Frederick II of Aragon. A narrow road leads up to the fine **Chiesa Madre** (if closed ring at no. 3 via Cappuccini, the priest's house), which is of medieval origins with a lovely 15C portal and an interesting interior. In the south aisle, the first altarpiece of *The martyrdom of St Sebastian* (in poor condition) is attributed to Zoppo di Gangi; on the second altar is a painting of *St Mark the Evangelist* by Deodato Guinaccia (1581) and a statuette of the *Ecce Homo* attributed to Ignazio Marabitti. In the south transept, *St Blaise* by Pietro Novelli is situated. In the chapel to the right of the sanctuary there is a marble statue of *St Lucy* (1512). The high altarpiece of the *Assumption* is by Fra' Felice da Palermo (1771). In the chapel to the left of the sanctuary is an unusual little sculpted *Last Supper* in the frontal of the altar attributed to Valerio Villareale. The altarpiece in the left transept is by Filippo Iannelli (1676), and on the third north altar is an 18C Crucifix. The font dates from 1485.

Also in the piazza is **Palazzo Vescovile** (Bishop's Palace), the priest has the key, with a little collection of works of art. Other churches of interest (open only for services) include: SS. Annunziata with a campanile of 1461 and a painting of the *Madonna and Child* of c 1400, and S. Maria di Gesù (or Sacro Cuore) with a *Crucifix* by Fra Umile da Petralia. The road leads up to the Castle built by Frederick II of Aragon when he repopulated the town with a colony of Lombards in 1322. All that remains of the old structures is a triangular-plan tower and a round keep. Now it houses the seminary and the sanctuary of the Madonna della Neve (1673) with a *Madonna and Child* by Antonello Gagini.

A mountain road (surfaced as far as Calderado) leads into the Peloritan Mountains from S. Lucia del Mela as far as **Pizzo Croce** (1214m). The beautiful **Scifo Forest** here, with chestnuts, oaks and ash has recently been preserved with the help of the local division of the WWF.

Barcellona is a busy agricultural centre (population 40,000), famous for its nurseries of ornamental and flowering plants and fruit trees, mostly citrus. Founded in the 17C, it has some interesting churches, such as the Chiesa Madre, and the church of S. Giovanni, and an important museum of popular art, the Museo Etnostorico 'Nello Cassata', 10 contrada Manno (open 09.00–13.00, 16.00–19.00; Mon am only. ☎ 090/9761883), run by the European Institute of Ethnology. From Barcellona a narrow road leads up to the **Parco Jalari**, where the theme is water and stone. There are over 70 pretty stone buildings and fountains, and 30,000 trees. Accommodation is available, also a restaurant, and a shop with local farm produce. For information, ☎ 090/9746245, 🖷 090/9746700, ✉ www.parcojalari.com.

Castroreale is an upland town (population 3560), once the favourite residence of Frederick II of Aragon from whose castle (1324; now in ruins) it gets its name.

Despite damage in the earthquake of 1978 the little town is unusually well pre-served thanks to the efforts of its inhabitants. The numerous churches contain 16C–17C works of art.

The **Chiesa Matrice** contains a *St Catherine* by Antonello Gagini (1534). A *Crucifix* on a pole as high as the Chiesa Matrice is carried in procession through the little town on Good Friday. From piazza dell'Aquila there is a fine view of the fertile plain. The corso leads to the church of the Candelora, with a 17C carved wooden high altarpiece.

In via Guglielmo Siracusa is the church of **S. Maria degli Angeli** (open on Sunday and in the month of August) which contains a gallery with interesting paintings and two sculptures (*St John the Baptist* by Andrea Calamech, 1568; and a *Madonna* by Antonello Freri, 1510). Further on is the fine **Civic Museum** (open 09.00–12.00, 15.00–18.00, except Wed afternoon), housed in the restored former Oratorio di S. Filippo Neri, with a charming balcony decorated with prancing horses and lions above the doorway. The collection of sculpture and paintings comes from local churches.

In room 1 there are Crucifixes, including a painted one dating from the 14C–15C. Room 2 contains Antonello da Saliba's *Madonna and Child enthroned with angels*, and a sarcophagus with the *effigy of Geronimo Rosso* by Antonello Gagini (1507). Room 3 contains *St Lawrence and stories from his life* by Frate Simpliciano. In room 4 are 17C paintings. Upstairs: vestments, precious books, ceramic tiles, 18C paintings, including works by Fra Felice da Sambuca (1733–1805) and an 18C–19C silver Cross from the Chiesa Matrice are dis-played.

At the end of the street are the churches of S. Marina which is empty, and S. Agata, with a charming *Annunciation* by Antonello Gagini, dated 1519. South of the town, by the cemetery, is the church of S. Maria di Gesù which dates from the 15C.

At the top of the town a circular tower survives of the castle founded by Frederick II of Aragon in 1324.

Terme Vigliatore is a thermal resort with a spring called Fonte di Venere, used for the treatment of gastrointestinal and liver ailments, as well as for skin and respiratory diseases. At **S. Biagio**, west of the town, are the remains of a large Roman villa of the 1C AD (open daily 09.00–13.00), with some rooms, a large peristyle, and part of the baths. The rooms, protected by a plastic roof, have black and white mosaics, mostly geometric, but one floor has a lively fishing scene, with dolphins, swordfish and other fish still found off the coast here. The main hall has a fine opus sectile pavement.

Inland near **Rodì-Milici**, is the site of ancient *Longane*, a Sicel town of some importance, which was no longer inhabited by the 5C BC. Traces of the walls sur-vive and the foundations of a sacred building.

From Castroreale a road runs inland across the western side of the Peloritans (rising to a height of 1100m), connecting the Tyrrhenian coast with the Ionian Sea at Naxos. There is very little traffic and some of the best scenery on the island. It follows the wide **Mazzarrà** and **Novara valleys** on the beds of which are extensive citrus fruit plantations and some 'pillbox' defences from World War Two. Mazzarrà S. Andrea is surrounded with nurseries. Gravel is extracted from the grey waterless riverbed, beside which oranges are grown. A few lovely old abandoned farmhouses survive here.

Novara di Sicilia (675m), the ancient *Noae*, refounded by the Normans who populated it with Lombards, is now a quiet little town below the main road. From largo Bertolami, with a bronze statue of *David* by Giuseppe Buemi (1882), via Duomo leads up to the 16C Cathedral. In the right aisle is a wooden statue of the *Assumption* by Filippo Colicci. In Via Bellini there is a beautiful little 19C opera house. Carnival time here is fun; the local cheeses, called *maiorchini*, are rolled through the streets. The cafés in Novara serve *gelato di cedro*, made with citrons—large knobbly lemons with very thick peel and practically no flesh inside. The zest is particularly aromatic so the peel is candied and used in many Sicilian confectionery recipes.

The fantastic bare horn-shaped **Rocca Novara** (1340m) stands at the end of the Peloritan range. The pass of **Sella Mandrazzi** (1125m) is surrounded by thick woods of pine and fir. The view extends to the coastline and the sanctuary of Tindari on its promontory, beyond the conspicuous Rocca Novara.

The scenery is particuarly fine in this area, and picnic places are provided. From here the mountain road descends through deserted country which provides pasture for sheep and goats. On a clear day there is a spectacular view of Etna, and of the river torrents on the hillsides.

The road continues to descend and there are now some vineyards, persimmon trees and prickly pears. It crosses a bridge before reaching the junction with the road from Moio Alcantara (p 381), near an abandoned villa. The Francavilla road continues left along the side of the valley and then descends through orange groves to **Francavilla di Sicilia**. Above the cemetery on the outskirts is the well signposted **Convento dei Cappuccini**, (17C) where the church has a beautiful 15C *Madonna with Child* attributed to the school of Antonello da Messina, the 17C funerary monument of the Ruffo family, and interesting 17C and 18C works. A Greek sanctuary was excavated in the town in 1979–84 and the votive statues found here are now displayed in the archaeological museum of Syracuse. Among the objects discovered are *pinakes*, pictures made of terracotta relating to the cult of Persephone, which it was previously thought were unique to Locri in Calabria. The Alcantara Gorge and Giardini Naxos on the coast are described on pp 420 and 418.

Another very winding minor road leads southwest from Terme Vigliatore to **Montalbano Elicona**, a little hill town (900m), in a fine position surrounded by woods, with a castle (1302–11) built by Frederick II of Aragon, open for exhibitions and concerts.

MILAZZO AND THE AEOLIAN ISLANDS

The interesting town of Milazzo is the port for the Aeolian Islands, seven beautiful islands of volcanic origin off the north coast of Sicily. Two of the volcanoes, Vulcano and Stromboli, are still active. The scenery is breathtaking and there are important archaeological remains; accommodation ranges from comfortable hotels to rooms with families, always very clean and sometimes even with air conditioning.

Milazzo

Milazzo, population 32,100, is the main port for ferries and hydrofoils for the Aeolian Islands. It stands on the isthmus of a narrow peninsula on the northeast coast of the island in the province of Messina. It is an old city with considerable charm. Unfortunately, it suffers from the presence of an oil refinery and power station on the outskirts, but the beaches are lovely and the citadel is unusual.

Practical information

 Getting there
By sea to the Aeolian Islands

Information on hydrofoil or catamaran and car ferry services are on p 431.

By train

3km from the centre. Services on the Messina–Palermo line; information ☎ 090/9296052, ✉ www.fs-on-line.it.

By bus

Inter-city bus services run by *Giuntabus* from the port to Messina in 50 mins (in connection with hydrofoils from the Aeolian Islands) and to Catania airport (once a day, April–September only), ☎ 090/673782, 🖷 090/ 679677.

Car hire

Maggiore-Budget, 35 via dei Mille, ☎ 090/9287821.
Mylarum 2, 18 via XX Luglio, ☎ 090/ 9224262, 🖷 090/9284000.

Parking

Garage Mylarum 2, 18 via XX Luglio, ☎ 090/9224262.
Central, 60 via Cumbo Borgia, ☎ 090/ 9282472.
These two reliable companies will pick up your car from the pier, garage it and then deliver it on your return from the islands by request.

 Information office
Azienda Autonoma, 20 piazza Duilio, ☎ 090/9222865, 🖷 www.aastmilazzo.it, ✉ info@ aastmilazzo.it.

 Where to stay
Hotels

☆☆☆ *Eolian Park*, 25 via Cappuccini, ☎ 090/9286133, 🖷 090/9282855. Rather incongruous round building near the Castle; swimming pool, wonderful views.
☆☆☆ *Garibaldi*, 160 lungomare Garibaldi, ☎ 090/9240189, 🖷 090/ 9240196, ✉ email hotel_garibaldi@ virgilio.it. Charming little hotel in the fishermen's quarter, with air conditioning.
☆☆☆ *Riviera Lido*, via Panoramica C.da Corrie, ☎ 090/9283456, 🖷 090/ 9287834, ✉ www.milazzonline.it/ rivieralido. On the cape with its own beach; good restaurant, air conditioning.
☆☆ *La Bussola*, 29 via XX Luglio, ☎ 090/9221244, 🖷 090/9282955.
☆☆ *Jack's*, via Col. Magistri, ☎ & 🖷 090/9283300. Clean rooms, near port.

Campsites

☆ *Villaggio Turistico Cirucco*, Capo Milazzo, ☎ 090/9284746.
☆ *Villaggio Turistico Riva Smeralda*, Capo Milazzo, ☎ 090/9282980.
Agriturist, Capo Milazzo, ☎ 090/ 9282838.

 Eating out
Restaurants

€€ *L'Agora*, via Duomo Antico (by the Castle), ☎ 090/9283131. Pub serving very good food. Closed Tues in winter.
€€ *Il Covo del Pirata*, lungomare

Garibaldi, ☎ 090/9284437. Typical restaurant and pizzeria. Closed Wed.

€€ *Marina del Porto*, 17 via Francesco Crispi. Pleasant restaurant and pizzeria on the seafront. Serves (unusual for Sicily) deep-pan pizzas in the evenings. Closed Wed.

€€ *Al Pescatore*, 119 lungomare Garibaldi, ☎ 090/9286595. Very popular. Closed Tues.

€€ *Al Piccolo Casale*, 12 via R. D'Amico, ☎ 090/9224479. Fashionable. Excellent fish; also pizzeria.

€€ *Salamone a Mare*, via Panoramica, ☎ 090/9281233. On the cape; legendary fish dishes. Closed Mon.

€€ *La Tonnara*, 1 via Tono, ☎ 090/9288724. Open-air restaurant and pizzeria with music; summer only.

€€ *L'Ugghiularu*, 101 via Acqueviole, ☎ 090/9284384. Traditional dishes. Closed Wed.

€€ *La Vecchia Cucina*, 17 via Ryolo, ☎ 090/9223070. Closed Mon.

€ *Don Ciccio*, via M. Nardi, corner via Umberto. Tasty pasta dishes.

€ *La Casalinga*, via D'Amico, ☎ 090/9222697. Homely cooking.

Pastry shops, ice cream parlours, sandwich bars, pubs

L'Agora, via Duomo Antico, near the castle. Sandwich bar and snacks.

Alexander, 50 via Veneto. Cakes; ice cream.

Caffè Antico, piazzetta S.Gaetano.

Sandwich bar.

Cream Caramel, 16 via Tenente La Rosa. One of the best pastry shops.

Nicotina, 113 lungomare Garibaldi. Almond biscuits.

Scalinata del Castello Borgo Antico and *Taverna del Gattopardo* are two friendly open-air pubs on the stairs leading up to the castle.

Washington, lungomare Garibaldi. Immensely popular for ice cream and confectionery.

Leisure and sport
Diving centre

FIPSAS, 6 piazza C.Battisti, ☎ 090/ 9288540.

Internet points

Buffetti, 46 via Col.Magistri.

Centro Servizi Milazzese, 105 lungomare Garibaldi.

Cities on line, via Colonnello Bertè.

Mail Box, 7 via dei Mille.

Foreign language newspapers, phone cards, stamps

All of these and other useful articles can be found at the newsagent in front of the ferry-boat dock; also at *Massimo*, 149 via Umberto (with a wider selection of newspapers), and *Filoramo*, 7 piazza Caio Duilio.

History

Milazzo was the ancient *Mylai*, founded by Greeks from Zancle (Messina) in 716 BC. Here Duilius defeated the Carthaginians in a sea battle (260 BC), and here in 1860 Garibaldi successfully assaulted the castle, garrisoned by Bourbon troops, promoting J.W. Peard, a Cornish volunteer, to the rank of colonel on the field. Its castle shows the strategic importance the town had in the past, from Norman times, then during the Swabian, Angevin, Aragonese, Spanish and Bourbon occupations.

The town is divided into the old, higher area (**Borgo Antico**) and the low-lying modern one (**Piano**), which is now the centre. The road for the centre passes the port, where the boats and hydrofoils for the Aeolian Islands dock. In via Crispi is the neo-classical Municipio built at the end of the 19C by Salvatore Richichi. On the other side of the building (reached through the courtyard) is piazza Caio

Duilio, with a horrible copy made in 1990 of the Fontana del Mela (the original of 1762 by Giuseppe Buceti was destroyed in World War Two). Here is the pleasant red façade of the former convent of the Carmelitani (16C; restored), with the Azienda Autonoma information office. Next to it is the Baroque façade of the Carmine (1574; rebuilt in 1726–52), and, on the other side of the square, Palazzo Proto which was Garibaldi's headquarters for a time in 1860 (see above). In via Pescheria, behind the Post Office, fresh fish is sold in the mornings from stalls in the street.

The marine parade (lungomare Garibaldi), planted with trees, is a continuation of via Crispi along the sea front. The 18C church of S. Giacomo is well sited at a fork in the road which leads to the **Duomo Nuovo** (1937–52), which contains paintings by Antonello de Saliba and Antonio Giuffrè, and sculptures attributed to the Gagini school. Further on, via Colombo leads away from the sea past two little Art Nouveau villas, Villino Greco and Villa Vaccarino, now surrounded by unattractive buildings.

From piazza Roma via Impallomeni leads up towards the castle past the Baroque 18C church of **S. Francesco di Paola**, which contains six paintings of miracles of the saint by Letterio Paladino. The Archaeological Antiquarium 'Domenico Ryolo' (open daily 09.30–13.00, summer 17.00–20.30, winter 15.00–18.30, ☎ 090/9222374) houses in six rooms a large collection of material found in the necropoli surrounding the city. The various burials shed interesting light on life and death in the area from the 8C BC to the 1C BC, and show the evolution of Greek and Roman influence on the population. Terracotta vases were widely used for burying the dead, who were interred in the foetal position, or cremated. The presence of pottery from all over the Mediterranean demonstrates the role of ancient Mylai, an important harbour at the centre of the trade routes of the time. The old Women's Prison, built in 1816 and abandone around 1960 has at last been put to good use.

From here the 17C church of the Immacolata and the church of S. Rocco with its crenellated top can be seen above on the left. Just short of here, on the right, is the closed church of S. Salvatore (18C) by G.B. Vaccarini.

Picturesque low houses and open-air cafés (in the summer) surround the double walls of the **Castle** (open 09.00–12.00, 14.30–15.30, (17.00–19.00 in summer); closed Mon, ☎ 090/9221921) built by the Arabs in the 10C–11C on the site of the Greek acropolis, enlarged by Frederick II in 1239, then by the Aragonese in the 14C, by Charles V in the 16C and restored in the 17C. The Spanish walls date from the 16C and enclose a large area used for theatrical performances and concerts in the summer. Here are the remains of the Palazzo dei Giurati, used as a prison in the 19C, and the Duomo Antico (recently restored), an interesting building of the late 17C, attributed to Camillo Camilliani or possibly Natale Masuccio. It was abandoned when the new cathedral was begun in 1937 (see above). In the same area a Gothic doorway leads to the oldest structures of the castle: the imposing Arab-Norman keep and a great hall known as the Sala del Parlamento. From the castle, a flight of steps leads to the Church of the Rosary, built in the 16C and restored in the 18C. The convent by the church housed the Inquisition.

The narrow peninsula of **Cape Milazzo** is simply called *il capo* by the local people. The road threads its way through olive groves and prickly pears to a point where steps go down to the Sanctuary of St Anthony of Padua, a little church

(1575) built in a cave where the saint took refuge after a shipwreck in January 1221. A path continues to a lighthouse and down to a stony beach and the crystal clear sea. It is a beautiful spot, but crowded on summer weekends with bathers. From the cape the view (on a clear day) encompasses all the Aeolian Islands, and also Mount Etna.

The Aeolian Islands

Lipari, Salina, Vulcano, Stromboli, Filicudi, Alicudi and Panarea, together with some rocky islets, form the archipelago known as the Aeolian Islands. Their name derives from Aeolus, the mythical guardian of the winds, 'whose home was on Lipara, a floating island of sheer cliff, within which the winds were confined. He had six sons and six daughters, and they all lived together in a palace surrounded by a brazen wall...' as Robert Graves informs us in his *Greek Myths*. Incidentally, this description of Lipari and of its Citadel is still remarkably accurate. This volcanic area marks the point where the African plate meets the European, folds over and forces itself under the opposing plate. The resulting crease is the point where the magma forming the volcanoes which are now the islands came to the surface. Only two of them, Vulcano and Stromboli are still active. The islands are very small but each one has its own identity and its own particular beauty. It is worth noting that it gets very crowded on Lipari, Panarea and Vulcano in July and August.

Several prehistoric sites have been excavated on the islands, and the Regional Archaeological Museum housed in the Citadel of Lipari is one of the most important collections of its kind in Europe.

The local style of architecture is perfect for the islands: small cubes made of blocks of lava, plastered on the outside with white pumice, with characteristic little round windows like portholes; a flat roof for drying grapes, figs, pumpkins or tomatoes; a veranda (*'u bagghiu*) in front which is the main living area, under a pergola supported by white columns (*'e pulera*); an open air oven for baking bread, and a cistern underneath the house for storing every precious drop of rain water. Unfortunately, modern buildings made of reinforced concrete and hollow bricks have appeared in recent decades, but now the archipelago has been declared a World Heritage Site by the UNESCO, so a closer check will be kept on the various civic administrations and their building programmes.

Practical information

Getting there and getting around
By sea

The most convenient starting point in Sicily for the islands is Milazzo. Throughout the year ferries, hydrofoils and catamarans operate from this port to the islands. For up-to-date information on shipping lines, timetables, tariffs and bus services to and from ports consult: ✉ www.bookingitalia.it.

Car ferries from Naples. An overnight ferry run by *Siremar* leaves twice a week, calling at Stromboli, Panarea, Salina, Lipari, Vulcano and Milazzo.

Car ferries from Milazzo run by *Siremar* and *NGI* leave about five times a day from Milazzo.

Hydrofoils or catamarans from Reggio Calabria and Messina are run by *SNAV* to Vulcano, Lipari and Salina.

Hydrofoils from Palermo and Cefalù run by *SNAV* in summer to Alicudi, Filicudi, Salina, Vulcano and Lipari, although the timetables are subject to change.

Hydrofoils from Naples to Stromboli, Panarea, Salina, Lipari and Vulcano are also run by *SNAV*.

Information and tickets in Milazzo
NGI, 26 via dei Mille (the port), ☎ 090/ 9283415.

Siremar via dei Mille ☎ 090/9283242, ✉ www.siremar.it.

SNAV, 32 via dei Mille ☎ 090/ 9287821, ✉ www.snavali.com.

Sailing times Timetables vary annually and according to season, and all sailings are subject to sea conditions; the time of departure should always be checked locally since in rough weather services are suspended. Some ticket offices on the islands open only 30 minutes before sailing.

Ferry and hydrofoil ticket offices on the islands:
Vulcano
Siremar, porto Levante, ☎ 090/ 9852149-9852217
SNAV, porto Levante, ☎ 090/9852230
NGI, porto Levante, ☎ 090/9852401
Lipari
Siremar (hydrofoils), Marina Corta, ☎ 090/9812200
Siremar (ferries), Marina Lunga Sottomonastero, ☎ 090/9811312
SNAV, Marina Corta, ☎ 090/9880266
NGI, Marina Lunga Sottomonastero, ☎ 090/9811955
Salina
Siremar, porto, S.Marina Salina, ☎ 090/9843004
Siremar, porto, Rinella, ☎ 090/ 9809170
SNAV, porto, S.Marina Salina, ☎ 090/ 9843003

SNAV, porto, Rinella, ☎ 090/9809233
Panarea
Siremar, porto, ☎ 090/983007
SNAV, porto, ☎ 090/983009
Stromboli
Siremar, porto di Scari, ☎ 090/986018
SNAV, porto di Scari, ☎ 090/986003
Filicudi
Siremar, porto, ☎ 090/9889960
SNAV, porto, ☎ 090/9889984
Alicudi
Siremar, ☎ 090/9889795
SNAV, ☎ 090/9812370

Inter-island communications

All the islands are connected by ferry and hydrofoil services; the services to Panarea, Stromboli, Alicudi and Filicudi are less frequent. The ferries are slower and often less direct than the hydrofoil service, but are comfortable and provide an opportunity of seeing the coastal regions of the islands. The hydrofoils are relatively more expensive and less reliable, as they cannot sail in rough weather. Fishing boats may be hired on all the islands, and the trip around the coast of the islands is strongly recommended.

Cars on the islands

Cars are allowed on Lipari, Vulcano, Filicudi and Salina; car ferries run from Milazzo and Naples (see above). However, visitors are not advised to take a car as distances are short and local transport good. It is a good idea to garage your car at Milazzo or Naples; the attendant will pick it up for you and then bring it back on your return. Some car hire services operate on Lipari, Vulcano and Salina. On the other islands small motor vehicles are used to transport luggage, and on Alicudi and Stromboli, mules and donkeys. On Lipari and Vulcano vespas and bicycles can also be hired at the port.

Buses on the islands

Lipari Buses from Marina Lunga to Canneto (every hour) and to the pumice

quarries and Acquacalda (every 2hrs);
to Quattrocchi, Pianoconte, and
Quattropani (every 2hrs); there is also a
tour of the island three times a day in
summer (information and tickets: *Urso*,
29 via Cappuccini, ☎ 090/9811262).
Vulcano A few buses a day from the
port to Piano.
Salina Buses from Santa Marina Salina
and Rinella to Leni, Pollara, Malfa and
Lingua.

Information office
*Azienda Autonoma del
Turismo delle Isole Eolie*,
202 corso Vittorio Emanuele, Lipari
(☎ 090/9880095), ✉ www.netnet.it/
aasteolie.
Panarea on line: ✉ www.amapanarea.it.
Salina on line: ✉ www.isolasalina.com.

Where to stay
Hotels, rooms to rent, and
bed-and-breakfast accommo-
dation are now to be found on all of the
islands; prices tend to be higher than
elsewhere in Sicily. Not all of these
structures have air conditioning; we
have indicated this service with (A/C). It
is essential to book in advance in the
summer months, and advisable to do so
at all times of the year. Many hotels and
restaurants close down completely from
November to March.
Hotels
LIPARI ✫✫✫ *Meligunis* (A/C), 7 via
Marte, ☎ 090/9812426, 📠 090/
9880149, ✉ villameligunis@netnet.it.
Right in the heart of the old city, beautiful rooms, atmosphere, and a rooftop
terrace.
✫✫✫ *Augustus* (A/C), 16 vico Ausonia,
☎ 090/9811232, ✉ villaaugustus@
tin.it. Just off the main street, with a
garden.
✫✫✫ *Carasco*, Porto delle Genti, ☎ 090/
9811605, ✉ carasco@tin.it. On the
sea; diving centre.
✫✫✫ *Gattopardo*, 67 via Diana, ☎ 090/

9811232, 📠 090/9812233,
✉ gattopardo@netnet.it. A 19C villa in
a beautiful sub-tropical garden, with little Aeolian cottages.
✫✫✫ *Giardino sul Mare* (A/C), 65 via
Maddalena, ☎ 090/9811004, 📠 090/
9880150, ✉ www.netnet.it/conti.
Cottages in beautiful gardens going
down to the sea; swimming pool.
✫✫ *Enzo il Negro* (A/C), 29 via Garibaldi,
☎ 090/9813163, 📠 090/9812473.
Everyone knows Enzo! His rooms are
spotlessly clean and there is a beautiful
rooftop terrace for breakfasts.
✫✫ *Oriente* (A/C), 35 via Marconi,
☎ 090/9811493, 📠 090/9880198,
✉ hoteloriente@netnet.it. Very comfortable hotel with garden.
✫✫ *Poseidon* (A/C), 7 via Ausonia,
☎ 090/9812876, 📠 090/9880252,
✉ Poseidon@netnet.it.
At Canneto ✫✫✫ *Casajanca* (A/C), 115
Marina Garibaldi, Canneto, ☎ 090/
9880222-9813244, 📠 090/9813003,
✉ www.netnet.it/casajanca. Interesting
and comfortable little hotel run by the
daughter of a poet.
VULCANO ✫✫✫✫ *Les Sables Noirs*
(A/C), Porto Ponente, ☎ 090/9850,
📠 090/9852454, ✉ www.
framon-hotels.com. The most prestigious hotel on Vulcano.
✫✫✫ *Arcipelago* (A/C), this is in a quiet
position on Vulcanello, with a breathtaking view embracing all seven islands,
☎ 090/9852002, 📠 090/53153.
✫✫✫ *Conti*, Porto Ponente, ☎ 090/
9852012/13, 📠 090/9880150,
✉ www.netnet.it/conti. This pleasant
hotel is on the beach of black sand.
✫✫✫ *Garden*, Porto Ponente, ☎ 090/
9852106, 📠 090/9852359. Good
service, close to beach,
✫✫ *Agostino*, 1 via Favaloro, Porto
Levante, ☎ 090/9852342. Close to
dock.
SALINA ✫✫✫ *Bellavista*, 8 via
Risorgimento, Santa Marina Salina;
panoramic position in pretty village,

☎ 090/9843009.

✳✳✳ *Signum*, 11 via Scalo, Malfa; Aeolian style architecture, peaceful position, ☎ 090/9844222, 📠 090/9844102.

✳✳ *L'Ariana*, 1 via Rotabile, località Rinella, Leni; panoramic position, Excellent restaurant, ☎ 090/9809075, 📠 090/ 9809250.

PANAREA ✳✳✳ *Cincotta*, via S. Pietro, ☎ 090/983014, 📠 090/983211. Right on the brink of the cliff, homemade ice cream, disco, close to harbour.

✳✳✳ *Lisca Bianca*, 1 via Lani, ☎ 090/983004, 📠 090/983291, ✉ liscabianca@liscabianca.it. Panoramic position in front of harbour; good restaurant for not too heavy dishes.

✳✳✳ *La Piazza*, via S. Pietro, ☎ 090/983154, 📠 090/ 983003, ✉ www.hotelpiazza.it. Surrounded by vegetation; all rooms with view.

✳✳ *Raya*, via S. Pietro, località Costa Galletta, ☎ 090/983013, 📠 090/983103, ✉ htlraya@netnet.it. Perched on a hill dominating the port; exclusive clientele.

STROMBOLI ✳✳✳ *Hotel Tesoriero*, a/c, 3 via Lani, ☎ 090/983098, ✉ www.hoteltesoriero.it. Attractive little hotel facing Stromboli.

✳✳✳ *Hotel Villaggio Stromboli*, via Regina Elena, ☎ 090/986018, 📠 090/986258, ✉ villaggiostromboli@netnet.it. On the beach, pleasantly old fashioned.

✳✳✳ *La Sciara*, via Soldato Cincotta, ☎ 090/986121, 📠 090/986284, ✉ lasciara@milazzo.peoples.it. Large garden and beautiful swimming pool.

✳✳✳ *La Sirenetta* (A/C), 33 via Marina, ☎ 090/986025, 📠 090/986124, ✉ lasirenetta@netnet.it. One of the oldest hotels, recently restored; diving centre.

✳ *Locanda Burbablù* (an inn), 17/19 via Vittorio Emanuele, ☎ 090/986118, 📠 090/986323. This is also a very famous restaurant; the breakfasts are

good too.

FILICUDI ✳✳✳ *Phenicusa*, via Porto, ☎ 090/9889946, 📠 090/9889955.

✳ *La Canna*, 43 via Rosa, ☎ 090/9889956, 📠 090/9889966, ✉ vianast@tin.it. This is an excellent choice on Filicudi. The hotel is in an ideal location, it has a pool and the restaurant is superb.

ALICUDI ✳ *Ericusa*, via Perciato, ☎ 090/9889902, 📠 9889671.

Bed and breakfast

LIPARI ✳ *Casa Vittorio*, 15 vico Sparviero, ☎ & 📠 090/9811523.

✳ *Diana Brown*, 3 vico Himera, ☎ 090/9812584, 📠 090/9813213. Nice rooms, very central.

✳ *Residence La Giara*, via Barone, ☎ & 📠 090/9880352. Apartments to rent.

At Canneto ✳ *Giallo Rosso* (A/c), Marina Garibaldi ang. Via Risorgimento, Canneto, ☎ 090/9811298, 📠 090/ 9811358.

At Acquacalda Lipari *A Casa di Cerasella*, via Mazzini, ☎ 090/9821113. They also have a fast motor boat for visiting the other islands.

SALINA ✳ *Il Delfino*, 19 via Garibaldi, Lingua, ☎ 090/9843024. This is also a very good restaurant for fish soup and grilled squid.

PANAREA ✳ *La Sirena* (A/c), via Drautto, ☎ 090/983012, 📠 090/9880069.

STROMBOLI ✳ *Casa del Sole*, via Soldato Cincotta, ☎ & 📠 090/986017.

At Ginostra ✳ *Ginostra B&B*, via S.Vincenzo, ☎ 090/9811787.

Karola Hauffmann, Ginostra, ☎ 090/9812423. Karola stays open year round.

Farmhouse accommodation

LIPARI ✳✳✳ *Tivoli*, 17 via Quartara, Quattropani, Lipari, ☎ & 📠 090/9886031. The farm raises poultry, pigs and rabbits; there are vineyards and olive trees; bowls and volleyball.

Apartments/rooms to rent

SALINA ☆ *Residence Santa Isabel*, 12 via Scalo, Malfa, ☎ & 🖨 090/9844018.

PANAREA ☆ *Albatros* (da Pina) (A/C), via S.Pietro, ☎ 090/983030, 🖨 090/983147.

FILICUDI ☆ *Villa La Rosa*, 24 via Rosa, ☎ & 🖨 090/9889965.

ALICUDI Numerous rooms to rent in private houses.
La Casa dell'Ibiscus, ✉ www.alicudi.net, ibiscus@alicudi.net. Typical old Aeolian house to rent: sleeps four.

Campsites

LIPARI ☆☆ *Baia Unci*, località Canneto, Lipari, ☎ 090/9811909-9812527, 🖨 090/9111715.

Eating out
Restaurants

LIPARI €€€ *Filippino*, piazza Mazzini, ☎ 090/ 9811002. One of the best known restaurants in Italy, of the 'Buon Ricordo' chain; memorable *ravioli di cernia* (fish ravioli).

€€€ *Al Pirata*, salita S. Giuseppe, ☎ 090/9811796. Fashionable and in a lovely setting.

€€ *Blue Moon*, 21 piazza Mazzini, ☎ 090/9811756. Definitely a new rival for the best restaurants on the islands.

€€ *Le Macine*, at Pianoconte, ☎ 090/9822387. Superb creative Aeolian cuisine.

€€ *La Nassa*, 36 via G.Franza, ☎ 090/9811319. Friendly, family-run establishment.

€€ *La Piazzetta*, 13–17 piazza Luigi D'Austria, ☎ 090/9812522. In a pretty square, ideal for people-watching; also pizzeria.

€ *Il Pescecane*, 223 via Vittorio Emanuele, ☎ 090/9812706. Good salads and pizza.

€ *La Trattoria D'Oro*, 28–32 via Umberto, ☎ 090/9812591. There is an inexpensive set menu; they also make a delicious sauce for pasta using tattlers (a kind of squid), called *ragu di totani*. Service is slow.

VULCANO €€€ *Da Maurizio*, via Porto Levante, ☎ 090/9852426. One of the best restaurants of the archipelago.

€€€ *Vincenzino*, via Porto Levante, ☎ 090/9852016. Spaghetti with shrimps and capers are excellent.

€€ *Don Piricuddu*, 33 via Lentia, ☎ 090/9852424. Mixed grills and salads.

€€ *Il Diavolo dei Polli*, at Piano; in the heart of the island, ☎ 090/9853034. Specialises in grilled meat, such as chicken, kid, or rabbit.

€€ *Il Palmento*, Porto Levante, ☎ 090/9852552. Also a pizzeria.

€ *'A Zammarra*, Hotel Conti. Pleasant pizzeria on the beach; open only in summer.

SALINA €€€ *Portobello*, Santa Marina Salina; famous for *spaghetti al fuoco* (fiery spaghetti) and a dessert made of fresh ricotta with honey, pine nuts and currants, ☎ 090/9843125.

€€ *Franco*, via Belvedere, ☎ 090/9843287. Franco is very proud of his spaghetti with sea urchins.

€€ *Il Gambero*, at Lingua, ☎ 090/9843049. For shrimps and grilled squid.

€€ *Mamma Santina*, 40 via Sanità, ☎ 090/9843054. An unusual salad of fresh mint and capers is on the menu here.

PANAREA €€ *Cusiritati*, at the port, ☎ 090/983022. Friendly atmosphere.

€€ *Da Pina*, via San Pietro, ☎ 090/983030. Pina is an institution, innovative and imaginative. Her *gnocchi di melanzane* (aubergine dumplings) are unique.

STROMBOLI €€ *Barbablù*, 17/19 via Vittorio Emanuele, ☎ 090/986118. Very unusual menu; booking essential.

€€ *Ai Geki*, 12 via Salina, ☎ 090/986213. Open year round; a favourite with local people.

€€ *Punta Lena*, 8 via Marina, ☎ 090/986204. On a panoramic terrace overlooking Strombolicchio; excellent grilled vegetables.

€ *Da Luciano*, via Roma. Restaurant and pizzeria.

At **Ginostra** ask for *Immacolata Petrusa*, very famous, ☎ 090/9812305.

FILICUDI €€ *Da Nino sul Mare*, ☎ 090/9889984. A terrace overlooking the sea; good spaghetti with lobster.

€ *Villa La Rosa*, 24 via Rosa, ☎ 090/9889965. Well prepared Aeolian dishes.

Cafés, pastry shops and ice cream parlours

LIPARI *Pasticceria Subba*, piazzetta Monfalcone.

Open-air cafés at Marina Corta for Sicilian breakfast, aperitifs, ice cream and sorbets. *Caffè Vela* for rubbing elbows with the jet set. The owner, Carlo, has won prizes for his superb Aeolian salads. Robert De Niro, Dustin Hoffman, Prince William and Caroline of Monaco have been seen here.

SALINA At Lingua, *Da Alfredo* opposite the pier, for scrumptuous fresh fruit sorbets: watermelon, peach or fig.

VULCANO *Ritrovo Remigio* at Porto Levante.

Annual festivals

LIPARI **Our Lady of Portosalvo**, a fishermen's celebration, 18 July; **San Bartolomeo**, the patron saint, 24 August.

SALINA At Leni, **Madonna del Terzito**, very colourful and heartfelt, 23 July.

Foreign language newspapers, phone cards, stamps

LIPARI The bookshop at Marina Corta; *Mimmo Belletti*, 9, via Garibaldi, also 203 corso Vittorio Emanuele.

Boat trips and rental

LIPARI *Regina*, ☎ & 📠 090/9822237, 🖂 www.navigazioniregina.com organize terrific excursions round the islands.

Da Massimo, ☎ 090/9811714 or 338/3694404. Massimo can be found at Marina Corta. Motor boat and dinghies for hire.

STROMBOLI *Antonio Caccetta*, vico Salina 10, ☎ 090/986023 or 339/5818200. Organizes boat trips round the island.

Stromboliana, Porto Scari, ☎ 090/986390, 📠 090/986396, 🖂 www.stromboliana.it, provides many services including boat excursions and fishing trips for tattlers.

Donkey service

STROMBOLI At Ginostra Hully Stulges, an ex-psychologist from Bavaria, has nine donkeys, ☎ 090/9812423.

Volcano treks

STROMBOLI *Magmatrek*, via Vittorio Emanuele, ☎ & 📠 090/9865768, 🖂 www.magmatrek.it.

Handicrafts

LIPARI Adriana Salvini, 5 via Marte, ☎ & 📠 090/9813767, makes attractive jewellery from obsidian, the black glass-like volcanic stone.

History

The islands were important in ancient times because of the existence of obsidian, a hard volcanic glass used as a tool and exported throughout the Mediterranean. The earliest traces of settlement found belong to the Stentinello culture of the Neolithic age. In the Middle Bronze Age the islands were on the main trade routes between the Aegean Islands and the Western Mediterranean. The Greeks colonised Lipari in c 600 BC, and in the following centuries the islands were attacked by the Athenians and the Carthaginians. They fell to Rome in 252 BC. From then on their history has been closely related to that of Sicily.

Vegetation and wildlife

The islands are all of volcanic origin; Stromboli is still one of the world's most active volcanoes, but the slopes on the opposite side to the lava flows are fertile and cultivated with vineyards. Vulcano is also active; it smells strongly of sulphur and there is little cultivated land. This is the island where shepherds pasture their sheep and goats. In spring when the broom is in flower it is breathtakingly beautiful: yellow flowers and yellow sulphur contrast against the deep blue sea and sky. Alicudi and Filicudi still show signs of the patient terracing which was carried out for many centuries to preserve the tiniest drop of water. Now the cultivations are abandoned, and the *maquis* is taking over again. Salina, with its two extinct volcanic cones, is the greenest and the most fertile of the group. It has forests and extensive vineyards, and its inhabitants make every effort to protect their patrimony from summer wildfires. Lipari, unfortunately, is frequently damaged by fire, probably sometimes deliberately—not everyone likes the idea of the Aeolians being a protected area. The administration of Lipari has however repaired the island's ancient tracks, which are ideal for gentle trekking. Little Panarea is a gem, with lots of wild flowers and pretty houses set in the vegetation.

Birds on their migratory flights frequently stop to rest on the Aeolians. Some of the rocky islets around the larger islands are important nesting spots for Eleonora's falcon (*Falco eleonorae*), a small, dark bird of prey, now extremely rare, which lays its eggs late in the spring so that its young can prey on the flocks of migrating birds flying south in late summer. Flamingoes often stop to rest on the salt pan of Salina, at Lingua. The kestrel, sparrow hawk and buzzard are also present as nesting species.

Among the mammals, there are plenty of bats of various species, rabbits and the common dormouse. Capers grow everywhere, even on sheer rock faces. Fish are abundant and varied. Flying fish can often be seen in the summer, and also groups of dolphins, playing together close to shore.

Lipari

Lipari (37 sq km), the chief island of the group and about 40km from Milazzo on the Sicilian mainland, has become a popular summer resort. About half of its 8580 inhabitants are concentrated in the lively and attractive little port of Lipari. The citadel commands the shore above the town, and separates the two harbours.

The town has low houses, with balconies decorated with plants, and charming narrow streets. There are numerous pastry shops, bars and restaurants, and pleasant little shops selling local specialities. At **Marina Corta** the hydrofoils dock beside the picturesque church of the Anime del Purgatorio. Another attractive church close by is S. Giuseppe at the top of a ramp. Outside the church fishermen are often at work mending their nets, their colourful fishing boats pulled up on the quay beside a solitary palm tree, watched over by the statue of the patron saint, Bartholomew.

Via Garibaldi winds uphill through the town. It passes a wide, scenic flight of steps constructed at the beginning of the 20C up to the citadel, framing the façade of the Duomo at the top (the second approach to the castle hill is described below). Via Garibaldi ends in piazza Mazzini with a garden and some charming houses by the neo-Gothic town hall. The 18C church of S. Francesco has pretty marble altars. Steps lead down to the crypt which was the burial place for the islanders before the cemetery (which can be seen nearby) was opened.

The route from piazza Mazzini to the Citadel or Acropolis leads through impressive 16C Spanish fortifications, with double gates and an entrance tunnel which incorporate classical fragments. The hill is a very peaceful spot, attractively planted with oleanders, prickly pear and ivy. On the summit there are archaeological remains as well as five churches, public gardens and an archaeological museum.

Regional Archaeological Museum

The Museo Archeologico is arranged in four separate buildings (open daily 09.00–14.00; 15.00–19.00; Sun & PH 09.00–13.00, 15.00–19.00; one or more of the buildings can sometimes be closed if there is a lack of custodians; ☎ 090/9880174).

The superb collection, beautifully displayed in chronological sequence (with labels also in English), contains finds from Lipari and other islands in the Aeolian group (as well as from Milazzo and southern Italy). Beyond the cathedral (described below) is the former Palazzo Vescovile (early 18C), with an attractive portal and balconies, which houses the first section dedicated to prehistory.

Upstairs Rooms 1–3 contain Neolithic finds from Lipari, including painted vases, Serra d'Alto style pottery (resembling southern Italian forms), and red pottery of the Diana style, so called because discovered nearby in an area known as contrada Diana. Room 4 has finds dating from c 3000 BC, from Piano Conte, and room 5 contains early Bronze Age material from Capo Graziano on Filicudi. Room 6 displays objects found here on the castle hill belonging to the Capo Graziano (1800–1400 BC) and Milazzese (c 1400–1250 BC) cultures, showing Greek influences. Notable are the vessels on tall pedestals, thought to have been used from a sitting position on the floor.

Ground floor The display continues on the ground floor. The Ausonian culture (from southern Italy) is represented in rooms 7–9; the finds made on the castle hill show the influence of the Italian mainland, and the vessels have a great variety of strangely shaped handles. Here also are the remains of a small cooking device, and a large terracotta pot, the repository of over 2cwt of bronze objects of the 9C BC. There are signs of a violent destruction of Lipari in the 9C BC, and the island appears to have remained uninhabited for the next three centuries.

The last room 10 illustrates the Greek and Roman period on Lipari. The large restored **Attic vase**, used for mixing water and wine, has an exquisite delicate black-figure decoration on the rim showing the *Labours of Hercules* and (inside) a frieze of ships. It is attributed to the 'Painter of Antimenes' (540–30 BC). The couchant lion (c 575 BC) carved from volcanic rock, probably guarded a votive deposit. Also here are a Roman statue of a girl of the 2C AD, found in the bishop's palace, and a statuette of Asklepios (4C BC). A case displays Hellenistic and medieval ceramics. A door leads out to the garden which contains sarcophagi from contrada Diana (see below) and the Epigraphic Pavilion (not always open) which contains funerary inscriptions of 5C–1C BC.

Pavilion On the other side of the cathedral is the pavilion, mostly dedicated

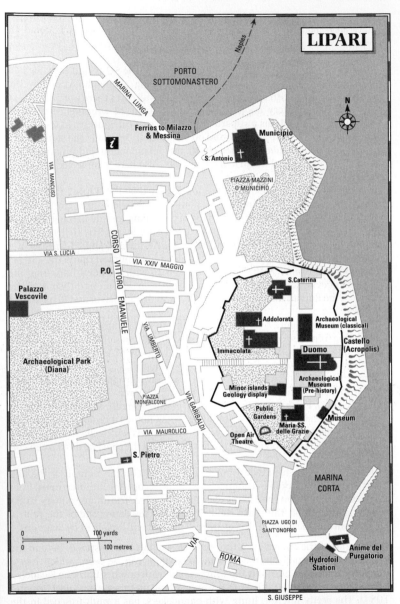

to the Classical period. On the left are three rooms (**16–18**) with finds from Milazzo displayed in chronological sequence from the Middle Bronze Age to the 3C BC, with the reconstruction of a burial site, with the burial pots in the position they were found. On the other side of the entrance **room 20** has a superb collection of terracotta and stone sarcophagi from Lipari, including the stone example in the centre (found in contrada Diana) which is perfectly preserved. It is thought to have been made by the sculptor in 2C–1C BC as his own tomb. In **room 19** beyond is a reconstruction of the piazza Monfalcone necropolis (1125–1050 BC) in Lipari.

First floor Room 21: Attic red-figure kraters of the 5C BC and early Sicilian and Campanian red-figure vases (4C BC) including a splendid krater by the 'Painter of Adrasto' with columns (c 450 BC). In wall cases there are 5C BC grave goods, and Attic pottery on a white ground. **Room 22** contains more vases (350–30 BC). **Room 23** has a superb display of theatrical figurines in terracotta, statuettes (early 4C–mid-3C BC) found on Lipari (note especially the statuettes of dancers, and *Andromeda with her child*), and a fascinating and unique collection of tragic masks and theatrical terracottas. Also here is some very fine gold jewellery.

In **room 24** brightly coloured vases are displayed by the '**Lipari Painter**', a master who excelled in the representation of the female figure. The southern Italian vases include a krater with Dionysus watching a nude acrobat and two actors, and a bronze hydra with a female bust (early 5C BC). The Hellenistic gold jewellery includes a ring of the 4C BC with a female nude. **Room 25** consists of a reconstruction of part of the necropolis of Lipari at contrada Diana (6C–3C BC) with pithoi and situlae. Stairs lead up to **room 26** with the latest finds from the hill showing evidence of the destruction of Lipari in 252 BC, and then sporadic finds from the Roman and Norman periods, as well as medieval and Renaissance ceramics.

Downstairs in **room 27** is a section devoted to underwater archaeology, with finds dating from 2000 BC to the 5C BC, fished up off Capistello (Lipari), and near Filicudi and Panarea, including a magnificent display of amphorae. There are also finds from the wreck of a 17C Spanish warship.

Opposite the pavilion with the prehistoric section, a group of simple old houses display prehistoric finds from the minor islands: Panarea (from the Calcara and Milazzese sites), Filicudi and Salina. In the entrance are three huge pithoi from Portella on Salina. Next door is a building which houses a geological display on three floors with diagrams, maps, reliefs and models which illustrate volcanic activity and the formation of the Aeolian Islands. In the courtyard is a small collection of epigraphs.

Outside, the extensive excavations begun in 1950 on the summit of the hill, have revealed a remarkable sequence of levels of occupation, uninterrupted from the Neolithic Age when the islands were first inhabited. The unique pottery strata (reaching a depth of 9m) make the acropolis the key dating site of the central Mediterranean. The different levels are well labelled and explained by diagrams.

The exterior of the church of S. Caterina (closed) has been restored. Beyond the excavations the small church of the Addolorata can be seen, which has a Baroque façade, and next to it the Immacolata, with another Baroque façade.

The **Duomo** (open 10.00–12.00) was first built on this site by Count Roger (c 1084). The pretty interior, hung with chandeliers, has a vault frescoed in the 18C. On the side altars are 18C reliquary busts in gilded wood. In the north transept is a *Madonna of the Rosary*, attributed to Girolamo Alibrandi, and a statue in silver of *St Bartholomew* which dates from 1728. The statue, together with an elaborate silver reliquary of a boat, is carried in procession through the streets on 24 August, 16 November, 13 February and 5 March. The Benedictine cloister has been restored. Dating from 1131, with later additions, it has vaulted walks, and columns of different shapes and sizes (some of them Doric, and some re-used from Roman buildings), and primitive capitals with animals and birds.

The last church on the hill is **Maria SS. delle Grazie** (closed), with a fine restored façade, reached down a few steps in a little garden. On the other side of the road are public gardens (with fine views) which have a large number of Greek and Roman sarcophagi. These were found in the necropolis of contrada Diana (late 5C and 4C BC), at the foot of the acropolis (now covered by the modern town). There is also a little open-air theatre here, built in 1978.

The main road of the town is **corso Vittorio Emanuele**. On the far (west) side is Palazzo Vescovile, eventually to be restored as the seat of a Diocesan Museum. Beside it is the archaeological zone of **contrada Diana** where two Roman hypogea were found, and where excavations revealed part of the Greek walls (5C–4C BC) of the ancient city, and Roman houses. It is now very overgrown and is no longer open regularly to the public.

A road (26.5km) encircles the island. It leads north from Lipari via Canneto to traverse magnificent huge white cliffs of pumice, with deep gallery quarries. The loading jetties protrude into the sea, here washed clean by the pumice stone. Beyond Porticello the road crosses remarkable red and black veins of obsidian, some of which reach the sea. The beaches are covered with pumice and obsidian, and some of the paths in the villages are cut out of obsidian. A road connects Acquacalda with Quattropani. At Piano Conte lava battle axes and Bronze Age weapons have been found. Near the coast (reached by a byroad) are the ancient hot springs of S. Calogero with remains of Roman baths. An ancient tholos has come to light here. The road returns to Lipari past the viewpoint of Quattrocchi.

Monte S. Angelo (594m; view), in the centre of the island, is an extinct stratified volcano of unusual form.

Vulcano

Vulcano (21 sq km; population 717) is the most southerly of the isles (separated from the southern tip of Lipari by a channel less than 1km wide) and easily reached from the Sicilian mainland (see above) or by frequent hydrofoil services from Lipari (and by local boat excursions). It is of outstanding interest because of its geological structure, its spectacular volcanic landscape with black lava rocks on the sea and black lava beaches. The last volcanic eruption occurred from 1898 till 1890. It has simple houses mostly built in the 20C in a disorderly way. It is deserted out of season but very crowded in summer. Many northern Italians have their summer houses here. A characteristic of Vulcano is the strong smell of sulphur, especially in the area around the port. You get used to it after a while.

The boats dock at **Porto di Levante** near the makeshift quay used by the hydrofoils. A road with simple shops and a few cafés leads to **Porto di Ponente** with mud pools on the beach fed by hot springs. The fine black lava beach nearby, with a number of hotels, is crowded in summer.

In the other direction from the port a straight road leads across the plain at the foot of the volcano. A narrow path (signposted; about 1km from the port) leads up across the fine volcanic soil and rocks to the top of the crater (375m), called **Fossa Grande**, in about 1hr. The route can be damaged and almost impassable after heavy rain, but is normally quite easy (although sturdy shoes are necessary).

There is a remarkable view of the inside of the crater, and the rim steams constantly with sulphurous vapours. On a clear day all of the Aeolian Islands can be seen from here. You can follow the path right around the rim (in about 1hr).

Most of the islanders live in the upland plain of the island known as **Piano**, 7km from the port (reached by a few buses every day). Here there is one inn and bar, a shop, a church and a school: most of the fields have now been abandoned, and some of the houses are now only used in summer. The Piano road passes close to the volcano and at the top of the hill by the first house on the corner a byroad leads left. Another turn left leads to the edge of a cliff with a number of caves and a view of the coast. The road continues gently uphill past a road on the left for **Gelso**, with some restaurants open in summer and good sea bathing. Another byroad leads to **Capo Grillo** which has the best panorama on the island. The Piano road ends in front of the parish church destroyed by an earthquake in 1978 and rebuilt in 1988.

On the northern tip of the island is **Vulcanello**, a volcanic cone which rose out of the sea in 183 BC. Near the Faraglione della Fabbrica, a high rock with alum quarries, are the hot springs of **Acqua Bollente** and **Acqua del Bagno**. Between Vulcano and Lipari are some striking basalt stacks, including the Pietralunga, an obelisk of rock, 72m high.

Salina

Salina, 4km northwest of Lipari, is the highest of the islands (962m), and is formed by two twin volcanic cones and the saddle between them (27 sq km). The shape of **Monte dei Porri** is one of the most perfect mountain cones in the world. It has been identified with Homer's Siren Island, and was anciently called *Didyme*. Its population (2300) is divided into several picturesque villages: **S. Marina**, **Malfa** and **Leni**. The island is famous for its malvasia wine. Capers are also grown here. The island is very green and lovely walks can be taken on the two mountains, the Monte dei Porri (mountain of leeks) and the Fossa delle Felci (glen of the ferns) which has chestnut woods. The attractive old houses and the fine scenery are now protected thanks to an enlightened local administration. On the east coast, near the S. Marina lighthouse, a Middle Bronze Age village has been excavated (not open to the public), and traces of Roman houses have been found on the island (those at the north end of the *lungomare* can be seen). After the Arab conquest of the Aeolian Islands in 838 the island remained virtually uninhabited until the 16C. The island was the setting for the Oscar-winning film *Il Postino*, which describes an episode in the life of Pablo Neruda.

Malvasia wine

This exquisite wine was once so much in demand that almost all the available land on the Aeolian Islands, including the tiny islet of Basiluzzo, was dedicated to its production. The industry supported a population (in 1880) of over 32,000 people, while today there are only 12,000 inhabitants in the archipelago. Most of the wine was exported, some of it to England where it was called Malmsey. In 1881 a terrible blight hit the islands and destroyed almost all the vines; at least 20,000 islanders emigrated to Australia. New incentives for Malvasia came in the 1960s, when a young architect, Karl Hauner, was invited to spend a few days painting on Salina, and he tasted the wine! *Hauner* is still the name to look for when buying this delectable nectar; the winery is now run by his son Carlo. Made from white Malvasia grapes (95 per cent) and black Corinth (5 per cent), after harvesting the bunches are left to wither in the sun on wicker trays for 10 days before being pressed. Sweet but not cloying, it is best drunk chilled for a surprising aperitif. It is thought that the Greeks first planted vines here in the 5C BC.

Panarea

Panarea lies to the northeast (15km from Lipari), towards Stromboli. Its natural beauty and the style of the local architecture has been carefully preserved by its 317 inhabitants. However, its hotels and restaurants, now frequented by famous and wealthy Italians, are a lot more expensive than those on the other islands. It is 3.5 sq km in area. Electricity was only brought to the island in 1982. Near the fishing harbour hot spring water mixes with the sea.

A walk (c 30 mins) leads to a naturally defended promontory on the southern tip of the island. On this superb site the **Bronze Age village** of the Milazzese culture (probably inhabited in the 14C BC), with 23 huts, was excavated in 1948. Mycenaean ceramics and native vases showing Minoan influences were brought to light (now in Lipari Museum, see above).

At the opposite end of the island, near the last houses on the coast, a path descends to the shore at **Calcara** where the fumaroles emit sulphureous gases. Nearby are traces of Neolithic pits made from boulders and volcanic clay, probably used for offerings. A Greek wreck was found offshore here in 1980, and from then until 1987 some 600 pieces of ceramics were recovered from its cargo of precious terracotta vases (5C–4C BC), some of which are now exhibited in the Lipari Museum.

In the sea near the island the beautifully coloured rocks of Lisca Bianca and Basiluzzo (with many traces of Roman occupation) provide a foreground to the ever-changing view of Stromboli.

Stromboli

Stromboli (12.5sq km; c 28km from Lipari) is the most famous island of the archipelago on account of its continual volcanic activity. It consists of a single cone (926m); the present active crater is 200m below the summit. It has been abandoned several times after severe eruptions, but is now again increasing in population (407), and is popular with tourists. Strong activity in December 2002 caused a tsunami, and considerable damage. The population was evacuated for several days.

The main village of Stromboli, **S. Vincenzo**, is on the northeast coast. The boats also call at **Ginostra**, an attractive small group of houses on a rocky headland on the southwest tip of the island, still without electricity. The construction of a port here in 1991 was blocked in an attempt to preserve the beauty of the coast, so when the sea is rough the fishermen still have to ferry the passengers ashore to the tiny harbour of Pertuso, the smallest in the world. Ginostra has about 30 permanent inhabitants, of whom ten are originally from Germany. Eruptions occur on the northwest side of the volcano and are not visible from either of the villages. The cone should be ascended with a guide (c 3hrs) as it is extremely dangerous to trek on the volcano without one, but an easy footpath from Stromboli (S. Vincenzo) ascends as far as the Semaforo (c 1hr 30 mins), from which point the explosions can usually be seen. Normally a small eruption occurs at frequent intervals; on days of unusual violence the spectacle (best seen at night from the sea) of the volcanic matter rushing down the Sciara del Fuoco into the sea is particularly impressive.

Off the northeast coast is the striking rock of **Strombolicchio**, a steep block of basalt (43m).

Filicudi

The remote and picturesque island of Filicudi (9.5 sq km) lies 19km west of Salina. Anciently called *Phoenicoesa*, it has 301 inhabitants. It has recently become a fashionable place to visit. The landscape is pretty despite the construction of a road in the 1970s which destroyed the terraces. Two prehistoric villages have been excavated on Capo Graziano; on the point (Montagnola) 12 huts were uncovered showing evidence of rebuilding before their destruction in the Milazzese period, while just inland, three oval huts yielded Bronze Age vases. Off the cape in 1975 a hoard of Bronze Age ceramics was found on the site of a shipwreck.

Alicudi

The most westerly isle is Alicudi. Its 5 sq km support a dwindling population of 102 inhabitants, several of whom are originally from Germany. It is a particularly beautiful island, with terraces and attractive local architecture. It has only had electricity since 1990.

TINDARI AND THE NEBRODI MOUNTAINS PARK

The ancient site of Tindari is in a very fine position on the sea. The Nebrodi Mountains Park is a protected area with suberb mountain scenery. S. Marco d'Alunzio is an interesting little hill town in the area and there are many others. A great place for trekkers and birdwatchers.

Practical information

Getting there

Tindari is just off the main coast road and motorway between Messina and Palermo. The Nebrodi Mountains Park is approached by fine mountain roads from the north coast from Capo d'Orlando and S. Agata di Militello.

Information offices

APT Messina, ☎ 090/674271-674236.
Aziende Autonome local offices:
Capo d'Orlando, 67 via Piave, ☎ 0941/912784-912517, ✉ www.

aastcapodorlando.it.
Patti, 11 piazza Marconi, ☎ 0941/241136.
Tindari, 15 via Teatro Greco, ☎ 0941/369184.
NEBRODI MOUNTAINS PARK
Main office at **Caronia**, 126 via Ruggero Orlando, ☎ 0921/333211, ✉ parconebrodi@legacy.it.
Information offices at **Alcara Li Fusi**, 1 via Ugo Foscolo, ☎ 0941/793904, and at **Cesarò** (Strada Nazionale), ☎ & 🖹 095/696008.
Pro Loco tourist office at S. Marco d'Alunzio, ☎ 0941/797339.

Where to stay
Hotels

PATTI ✰✰✰ *La Playa*, 3 via Playa, ☎ 0941/361398.

✰✰ *Villa Romana*, contrada Praia, ☎ 0941/361268.

GIOIOSA MAREA ✰✰✰ *Capo Schinò Park Hotel*, contrada Capo Schino, ☎ 0941/301144, ▤ 0941/30116.

CAPO D'ORLANDO ✰✰✰ *La Tartaruga*, Lido S. Gregorio, ☎ 0941/955012, ▤ 0941/955056, ▨ www.agatirno.it/tartaruga. Comfortable hotel on sea front with a very good restaurant; part of the 'Buon Ricordo' chain.

✰✰✰ *Il Mulino*, 46 via Andrea Doria, ☎ 0941/902431, ▤ 0941/911614. Another excellent small hotel with good restaurant.

S. AGATA DI MILITELLO ✰✰✰ *Roma Palace*, via Nazionale, ☎ 0941/703516, ▤ 0941/703519.

Farmhouse accommodation

This province is particularly suitable for holidays in the countryside.

✰✰✰✰✰ *Casali di Margello*, contrada Margello, San Salvatore di Fitalia; very high standard accommodation in lovely restored oil mill and hamlet, spring water, superlative home-produced food and excellent Sicilian wine list, beautiful countryside for trekking and horseriding, swimming pools, also bowls, archery; ☎ & ▤ 0941/486225, ▨ www.casalidimargello.it.

✰✰✰ *Casa Migliaca*, contrada Migliaca, Pettineo, ☎ & ▤ 0921/336722, ▨ www.casamigliaca.com. At the far end of the province near Pettineo, a lovely old farmhouse where guests are encouraged to become part of the family; meals are served in the old farm kitchen and the farm produces olive oil.

✰✰✰ *Santa Margherita*, contrada Santa Margherita, Gioiosa Marea, ☎ 0941/39703, ▤ 0941/301237, ▨ www.agriturismosantamargherita.it. Close to the sea and very well organized for guests.

✰✰✰ *Il Vignale*, contrada Pado, Longi, ☎ & ▤ 0941/485015. In the heart of the Nebrodi Park, ideal for birdwatchers, close to the Rocche del Crasto (griffon vultures and golden eagles), but only for serious nature lovers; the building, an ancient silk mill which sleeps six, is on the wooded mountainside above the village of Longi, where the owners live, there is no telephone on the premises, self-catering only, the track is difficult after rain.

Antico Casale di Lisycon, contrada Lisicò, S. Angelo di Brolo, ☎ & ▤ 0941/533288, ▨ agrinatura@hotmail.com. An old farming village entirely restored, in the woods, with its own spring of pure water, home-made bread.

Casa Scaglione, contrada Spaditta, San Piero Patti, ☎ 0941/661730, ▤ 095/442133, ▨ www.anbba.it/bb/spaditta. Not far from Patti, in the Nebrodi Mountains. An 18C hazelnut farm. Open summer only.

Villa Mara, contrada Zucco, Reitano, ☎ & ▤ 0921/338286, ▨ roniceta@libero.it. A hazelnut farm and olive grove within the Park boundaries.

Villa Nicetta, contrada Nicetta, Acquedolci, ☎ & ▤ 0941/726142. Very old fortified farmhouse with its own church; many activities on offer, including horseriding, trekking, organic food; it is possible to take part in harvesting, sheep milking, etc.

Mountain refuge

✰✰ *Villa Miraglia*, SS 289, Cesarò, ☎ & ▤ 0957/732133, ▨ info@villamiraglia.it; in the heart of the Nebrodi Mountains Park, at a height of 1500m is this welcoming refuge with a good restaurant specialising in traditional mountain fare. Very cosy; horseriding possible.

Eating out
Restaurants

CAPO D'ORLANDO
€€€ *La Tartaruga*, Lido S. Gregorio,

☎ 0941/955421. A 'Buon Ricordo' restaurant, excellent local dishes.
GALATI MAMERTINO €€ *Antica Filanda*, contrada Parrazzi, ☎ 0941/434715.
S. MARCO D'ALUNZIO € *La Fornace*, 115 via Cappuccini, ☎ 0941/797297. Grills and pizza.

Annual festivals

S. FRATELLO The ancient **Festa dei Giudei** is celebrated here on Maundy Thursday and Good Friday in traditional costume.
ALCARA LI FUSI The summer solstice

(24 June) is celebrated in the village with the pagan **Festa del Muzzuni**. The '*muzzuni*' is a large glass bottle, or earthenware jar, one for each of the town quarters. On the evening of the 23rd the jars are richly decorated with silk scarves, gold jewellery and ears of wheat, and carried to the altars by young, unmarried girls. The altars are draped with the brightly coloured '*pezzare*', hand woven rugs. The statue of St John the Baptist is carried in procession through the streets, blessing the *muzzini*, thus guaranteeing prosperity and fertility to every part of the town.

Tindari

On the headland of Capo Tindari (230m) there is a conspicuous church and the excavations of the ancient city of Tyndaris founded in the 4C BC. The road leads to a car park below the huge Sanctuary which was built in 1957–79 to house a seated statue of the Black Madonna of Byzantine style which has been greatly venerated since the 10C (pilgrimage on 8 September). The statue, recently restored and divested of its white silk robe, is made of painted cedar wood from Lebanon and was probably made in the Middle East in the 7C or 8C. The structure of the new church encloses the old 16C Sanctuary, on the seaward side, with a portal of 1598 (the custodian has the key). From the terrace in front of the church there are splendid views of the Aeolian Islands. The currents in the shallows at the foot of the cliffs produce beautiful formations of sand and gravel and areas of temporary marshland of great interest to naturalists.

From the car park a path and steps lead up to a road in front of a small group of houses with a little bar and restaurant which leads to the entrance to the impressive **ruins of Tindari** (open daily 09.00–1hr before sunset).

The ancient city of *Tyndaris* was founded by Dionysius the Elder in 396 after his victory over the Carthaginians. Tyndaris remained an ally of Syracuse until taken by the Romans in 254. A large part of the city slipped into the sea during an earthquake caused by the eruption of Vesuvius in AD 79 and then by another earthquake in AD 365. Excavations begun in the 19C, were resumed from 1949–64, and are still in progress.

A path leads down through a little garden to the excavations in a grove of olives and pines planted with bougainvillea and prickly pear. The beautiful, peaceful site overlooks fields with olive trees on a cliff directly above the sea. To the right, along the **Decumanus Maximus** (main street), are the remains of Roman buildings, including a series of tabernae (shops), two private houses (with peristyle and mosaics), and a bath house with black and white mosaics. At the end of the decumanus is the **Basilica**, once called the Gymnasium, but now thought to have been a monumental entrance to the agora (the area now covered by houses and souvenir shops). Its façade, which collapsed in Byzantine times, was restored in 1956. It is an unusual building with barrel vaulting across the main road of the city: formerly dated in the 1C BC it is now thought to have been built in the 4C AD.

To the left of the entrance is the large **theatre**, a Greek building adapted by the Romans for use by gladiators. The Greek walls (3C BC), obscured by vegetation on the seaward side, survive in a good state of preservation to the south (beside the approach road below the sanctuary), extending, with interval towers, for several hundred metres on either side of the main gate, a dipylon with a barbican.

The small **museum** has a reconstruction of the theatre's monumental stage and backdrop, and finds from the site, including two fragments of Hellenistic statues of winged victories, 4C BC and 1C BC statuettes, a colossal head of the emperor Augustus (1C), vases, reliefs, a capital of 1C BC and a theatrical mask.

Patti (population 11,500), a short distance west of Tindari, is an important agricultural town on a hill, damaged by an earthquake in 1978. In the **cathedral** of Norman origin is the Renaissance *tomb of Adelaide* (d. 1118), queen of Count Roger, who was the first king of Sicily. She died of leprosy. The 16C painting of the *Madonna enthroned with Child* is by Antonello de Saliba.

Patti is renowned for its potteries; an old proverb says 'if you want a tasty dish, cook it in a pot from Patti'.

During the construction of the motorway from Messina part of a large **Roman villa** (4C AD) was uncovered here in 1973 (follow the signs for Marina di Patti and the motorway: the entrance to the site is beneath the motorway viaduct; open daily 09.00–1hr before sunset). This large villa (about 20,000 sq m) was made up of three main structures, with three different orientations. On the western side there are the remains of walls relating to rooms. The main structures centre on a large peristyle with the remains of a pillared portico; on the north east side part of a thermal bath complex has been brought to light. The villa also contains a few polychrome mosaics with geometric and floral designs as well as hunting scenes.

Gioiosa Marea is a seaside resort built in the 18C after an earthquake destroyed the old town of Gioiosa Guardia (or Gioiosa Vecchia), the fascinating ruins of which survive high up (828m) on a hill beyond the motorway. A winding road leads up to the old town, from where there is a wonderful view of the coast and the Aeolian Islands. Vulcano is only 19km offshore.

Capo d'Orlando is another seaside resort (population 12,000) with a rocky promontory and sandy beaches, off which Frederick II of Aragon was defeated in 1299 by Roger of Lauria, commanding the allied fleets of Catalonia and Anjou. The promontory, already occupied in the Greek era, is noted for its sudden storms. It is crowned by a 14C castle and the 16C sanctuary of Maria Santissima.

Just outside the town, at 44 contrada Vina, is a very interesting little museum, the **Fondazione Famiglia Piccolo di Calanovella** (open daily, 10.30–12.30, 16.00–19.00, summer evenings 17.00–20.00, ☎ 0941/957029), the house and garden of the Calanovella family, now protected as a foundation instituted by the last descendants. The beautifully well-kept rooms and gardens are a poignant testimony to the lives led by these artistic, withdrawn and proudly Sicilian aristocrats in the middle of the 20C, and to an era that was drawing to a close. Baron Lucio Piccolo, a prize-winning poet, was a cousin of Giuseppe Tomasi di Lampedusa, and encouraged him to write his famous novel, *Il Gattopardo* (*The Leopard*) while his sister Agata Giovanna was a keen gardener and botanist,and their brother Casimiro, a gifted photographer who also painted watercolours.

Now and again they would all indulge in a seance. In the garden is the cemetery for their cats and dogs. To the east, at **Lido di S. Gregorio**, there is a beautiful sandy beach and a little port. Nearby are the **Terme di Bagnoli** (open 09.00–1hr before sunset), surrounded by a little garden. These were Roman baths, part of a private villa built in the late 4C or 5C AD. Eight rooms have been unearthed, some of which were dislodged in an earthquake.

The Nebrodi Mountains Park

The Parco dei Nebrodi is a protected area of great natural beauty in the Nebrodi Mountains, which stretch from the Peloritans on the east to the Madonie Mountains on the west. They have an average height of 1200–1500m and are the largest forested area to survive on the island. The remarkable landscape changes constantly. The trees include oak, elm, ash, beech, holm oak, cork, maple and yew, and are especially fine in the Caronia forest. The forests are home to the porcupine, the wildcat and the pine marten; the last wolves disappeared in the 1920s. At Rocche del Crasto, one of the highest peaks of the Park near Longi, there are golden eagles and griffon vultures, besides the lanner falcon and the peregrine falcon. The griffon vultures come from Spain, and are taking part in a long-term programme of reintroduction which has met so far with considerable success. There has always been a colony of griffons in this area, but they were accidentally killed in 1965. These mountains have abundant water, with many streams, small lakes and springs. The upland plains provide pastureland for numerous farm animals which roam free (with bells), including cows, horses, sheep, goats and black and white pigs. The S. Fratello breed of horses (identified by their characteristic rounded noses) are now protected and allowed to run wild here. Delicious ricotta, cheeses and salted hams are made by the local farmers.

Monte Soro (1847m) is the highest peak of the Nebrodi. The Biviere di Cesarò (1200m) is a lovely little natural lake with interesting birdlife (including herons, black-winged stilts and great white herons on migration), and a spectacular view of Etna. Nearby Lago Maulazzo is an artificial lake constructed in the 1980s for irrigation but never put into operation. In this area are numerous turkey oaks, maple trees and beech woods, and wild mushrooms (especially the delicious boletus) abound. In spring there are beautiful wild flowers and the hillsides are covered with broom, and the colours in autumn are spectacular. The tiny towns and villages here all have something particular to offer. **Tortorici**, for example, is famous for its hazelnut biscuits called *pasta reale* and its skilful craftsmen. Church bells and bagpipes are still made here. The annual feast of St Sebastian involves a dramatic procession of barefooted faithful who carry the statue of *Sammastianuzzu* through the river in full flood (20 January). At Mistretta they make unique biscuits of white marzipan, which are baked until pale gold in colour. The pastry shop is *Antonino Testa*, 2 via Libertà.

A road leads from Capo d'Orlando across the eastern Nebrodi Mountains to Randazzo below Etna. It passes **Naso**, a small town of 5300 inhabitants, which has 15C–17C tombs in the church of the Minori Osservanti (now known as the church of Santa Maria del Gesù). The church contains a monument to Artale Cardona (d. 1477) in Gothic Renaissance style; the Cardona family were once lords of Naso. Other churches in Naso are the church of SS. Salvatore, the Chiesa Matrice and the church of S. Cono which has a 17C chapel with marble intarsia walls, and the reliquary of S. Cono, the patron saint of Naso.

Floresta (1275m) is the highest village in Sicily, with winter sports facilities. The road reaches a summit level of 1280m before descending in full view of Etna to Randazzo (described on p 379).

At **Frazzanò** Count Roger built the Basilian monastery and church of S. Filippo di Fragalà (11C), with three high apses, a large transept and a poly-chrome exterior of red bricks and local stone (open daily 09.00–13.00, 15.00–19.00, ☎ 0941/959137). A seat of learning, the monastery had an important library which was dispersed in 1866. Among the few remnants saved and now in Palermo, is the oldest document yet found in Europe written on paper, an edict sent by Queen Adelaide to the abbot in 1099. From here the road leads up to the ancient centres of Longi and Galati Mamertino which has just reintroduced roe deer onto its land. Galati Mamertino has some notable works of art, including two marble statues of the *Madonna* attributed to the school of Gagini in the Chiesa Madre, and a *Crucifx* by Fra Umile di Petralia, thought by scholars to be his finest, in the church of S. Caterina.

At **S. Marco d'Alunzio** Robert Guiscard built the first Norman castle in Sicily in 1061 (it survives in ruins at the top of the hill). The interesting little hill town (pop-ulation 2500) has 22 churches built of a distinctive local red marble (called *rosso di S. Marco*). At the entrance to the town on a spectacular site overlooking the sea, is the **Temple of Hercules**, dating from the Hellenistic era: on the red marble base-ment a Norman church (now roofless) was built. Later a Baroque portal and win-dows were added. Above the road on the right is the church of the **Aracoeli**, with a Baroque portal. The interior, including the columns, has local red marble decora-tions. On the south side a marble altar has a gilded wooden statue of *St Michael Archangel*, and another chapel has a fine red marble altarpiece.

Via Aluntia continues past (left) the deconsecrated 12C church of S. Maria dei Poveri (used for exhibitions) and then descends past the town hall and a fountain. On the left is the **Chiesa Matrice** (S. Nicolò) built in 1584. It has a very unusual triumphal arch with large marble sculptures and an 18C organ. On the north side, the fourth chapel has a 16C painting of the *Madonna of the Rosary* in a fine frame, and the fifth chapel a wooden 16C processional statue of the *Immacolata*.

A road leads uphill to the left past the tiny church of S. Giovanni and then down to the side of the hill where **S. Giuseppe** has a lovely portal. There is a fine view of the sea from here. On the left of the façade is the entrance to the **Diocesan Museum** (open on request: parish office, ☎ 0941/797045), inaugu-rated in 1996. In the vestibule are the original capitals from the portal of the church, as well as vestments and statues. The rest of the collection is arranged in the church which has a lovely red, grey and blue pavement and decorative stuc-coes. The quaint collection of miscellaneous objects includes a sculpture of the *Madonna dell' Odigitria* by Giuseppe Li Volsi (1616), statues, reliquaries, and church furniture.

Higher up in the town is the tiny church of **Maria SS. delle Grazie** with a delightful carved high altar with a statue of the *Madonna and Child with the young St John*, and, on either side, two imposing tombs of the Filangeri family, one with an effigy (1481) and the other in red marble (1600). Opposite, built on the rock, is the church of S. Basilio. Beneath S. Teodoro there is a Byzantine chapel with interesting remains of frescoes. A short distance south of S. Marco d'Alunzio, by the church of S. Teodoro is the Badia Nica housing the very inter-esting **Museum of the Byzantine and Norman Cultures** (open daily 09.00–

13.00, 15.30–19.00; 96 via Ferraloro, ☎ 0941/797719) with a collection of frescoes removed from the many churches of the town, and displayed with admirable clarity.

S. Agata di Militello is a seaside resort (population 12,700), from which climbing expeditions may be made in the Nebrodi Mountains Park. Palazzo Gentile houses a museum relating to the Nebrodi, for admission enquire at the town hall.

Alcara li Fusi is a little mountain village beneath the Rocche del Crasto (1315m). The mountain, where golden eagles still nest, can be explored on foot to see the **Grotta del Lauro** (1060m), one of the most interesting caves in Sicily. Excursions into the Nebrodi Park can be organized from here (information at the Town Hall, ☎ 0941/793010, 🖷 0941/793735).

A picturesque road leads south from S. Agata di Militello through the Nebrodi mountains past **S. Fratello**, a Lombard colony founded by Adelaide, queen of Roger I, with a 12C Norman church.

Caronia is in a beautiful forest of the same name. The town preserves a privately owned Norman castle. On the outskirts the site of the Greek and Roman colony of *Kalacte* has been identified. A mountain road leads across the Nebrodi to the hill town of **Capizzi**, one of the highest villages in Sicily. The road joins the beautiful SS120 south of the Nebrodi from Nicosia to Randazzo. It passes the village of Cerami: after his victory at the Battle of Cerami in 1063, Roger I presented four Saracen camels to Pope Alexander II in Rome. East of Troina (described on p 271) the road traverses rugged country with a superb view of Etna, passing below Cesarò, where the remains of its castle can be seen.

On the coast at the west end of the Nebrodi is **S. Stefano di Camastra** (population 5200). It is noted for its fine ceramics, which are made and sold in potteries on the outskirts (most of which are east of the town on the road towards Messina). Local ware is also sold in numerous shops in the town.

A pretty road leads inland through the Nebrodi passing **Mistretta** (950m), an attractive old town (population 6000), with some good Baroque and Rococo buildings, on the site of the ancient *Amestratus*. At the entrance to the town is the 16C church of **S. Giovanni** with a fine flight of steps and a portal carved in 1534. The 17C **Chiesa Matrice** (St Lucy), has some beautiful statues of the Gagini school and two interesting side portals carved in the 14C and 15C respectively. The carved south portal of the church has been ascribed to Giorgio da Milano (1493).

This magnificent mountain road continues south to Nicosia, described on p 274.

At the northwestern corner of the province of Messina is Castel di Tusa. A road leads inland above the wide torrent bed of the Tusa river to the pretty little hill town of **Tusa**, which has interesting sculptures in its Chiesa Matrice. The vast incongruous modern sculptures which were set up in the riverbed were ordered to be demolished by a court ruling in 1991, and again in 1993, but fortunately they are still here and now much appreciated. It is now called *Fiumara d'Arte*. The same artists have designed 16 rooms of the *Hotel Atelier sul Mare* (4 via C.Battisti, Castel di Tusa, ☎ 0921/334295, 🖷 0941/334283, ✉ www.ateliersulmare.com).

Off the road to Tusa is the site of **Halaesa** on a hill. A road leads up from the gate on the byroad to the car park beside the restored convent and church and custodian's house. The attractive site (open daily 09.00–1hr before sunset), with ancient olives and almond trees, commands a fine view of the pretty Tusa valley, the little towns of Tusa and (on the other side of the valley) Pettineo and on a clear day, the Aeolian Islands.

Halaesa was founded in the 403 BC by Archonides, dynastic ruler of Herbita. The most conspicuous remains are those of the Agora (partly protected by a roof), which preserves part of its marble wall panelling and brick paving on the west side, and the walls of the city (a stretch further uphill is strengthened by buttresses). On the hillside below, looking towards the sea, was the theatre, and there were two temples at the top of the hill. Excavations begun in 1952–56 were interrupted in 1972 and have never been resumed.

Cefalù and the Madonie Mountains to the west, in the province of Palermo, are described on pp 133 and 139.

Glossary

Abacus, flat stone in the upper part of a capital

Acroterion, an ornamental feature on the corner or highest point of a pediment

Aedicule, small opening framed by two columns and a pediment, originally used in classical architecture

Agora, public square or market-place

Ambo, (pl. ambones) pulpit in a Christian basilica; two pulpits on opposite sides of a church, from which the gospel and epistle were read

Amphiprostyle, temple with colonnades at both ends

Amphora, antique vase, usually of large dimensions, for oil and other liquids

Antefix, ornament placed at the lower corner of the tiled roof of a temple to conceal the space between the tiles and the cornice

Antis, *in antis* describes the portico of a temple when the side-walls are prolonged to end in a pilaster flush with the columns of the portico

Architrave, lowest part of the entablature, horizontal frame above a door

Archivolt, moulded architrave carried round an arch

Atlantes, (or *telamones*) male figures used as supporting columns

Atrium, forecourt, usually of a Byzantine church or a classical Roman house

Badia, (*abbazia*) abbey

Baglio, from the medieval word *Ballium* meaning a large fortified building. It is now usually used to describe the warehouse of a wine distillery

Baldacchino, canopy supported by columns, usually over an altar

Basilica, originally a Roman building used for public administration; in Christian architecture, an aisled church with a clerestory and apse, and no transepts

Borgo, a suburb; street leading away from the centre of a town

Bottega, the studio of an artist; the pupils who worked under his direction

Bouleuterion, council chamber

Bozzetto, sketch, often used to describe a small model for a piece of sculpture

Bucchero, Etruscan black terracotta ware

Caldarium or **calidarium**, room for hot or vapour baths in a Roman bath

Campanile, bell-tower, often detached from the building to which it belongs

Camposanto, cemetery

Capital, the top of a column

Cardo, the main street of a Roman town, at right-angles to the Decumanus

Caryatid, female figure used as a supporting column

Cavea, the part of a theatre or amphitheatre occupied by the row of seats

Cella, sanctuary of a temple, usually in the centre of the building

Chiaroscuro, distribution of light and shade, apart from colour, in a painting

Chiesa Matrice, (or *Chiesa Madre*) parish church

Chthonic, dwelling in or under the ground

Ciborium, casket or tabernacle containing the Host

Cipollino, onion-marble; a greyish marble with streaks of white or green

Cippus, sepulchral monument in the form of an altar

Cista, casket, usually of bronze and cylindrical in shape, to hold jewels, toilet articles, etc., and decorated with mythological subjects

Console, ornamental bracket

Crenellations, battlements

Cuneus, wedge-shaped block of seats in an antique theatre

Cyclopean, the term applied to walls of unmortared masonry, older than the Etruscan civilisation, and attributed by the ancients to the giant Cyclopes

Decumanus, the main street of a Roman town running parallel to its longer axis

Diorite, a type of greenish coloured rock

Dipteral, temple surrounded by a double peristyle

Diptych, painting or ivory tablet in two sections

Duomo, cathedral

Entablature, the part above the capital (consisting of architrave, frieze and cornice) of a classical building

Ephebos, Greek youth under training (military or university)

Exedra, semicircular recess

Ex-voto, tablet or small painting expressing gratitude to a saint

Fiumare, wide flat-bottomed torrent-bed filled with gravel, usually waterless

Forum, open space in a town serving as a market or meeting-place

Fresco, (*affresco*) painting executed on wet plaster. On the wall beneath the *sinopia* is sketched, and the *cartone* is transferred onto the fresh plaster (*intonaco*) before the fresco is begun, either by pricking the outline with small holes over which a powder is dusted, or by means of a stylus which leaves an incised line on the wet plaster. In recent years many frescoes have been detached from the walls on which they were executed

Frigidarium, room for cold baths in a Roman bath

Fumarole, volcanic spurt of vapour (usually sulphurous) emerging from the ground

Gigantomachia, contest of Giants

Graffiti. design on a wall made with an iron tool on a prepared surface, the design showing white. Also used loosely to describe scratched designs or words on walls

Greek cross, cross with arms of equal length

Hellenistic, the period from Alexander the Great to Augustus (c 325–31 BC)

Herm, (pl. hermae) quadrangular pillar decreasing in girth towards the ground, surmounted by a bust

Hexastyle, temple with a portico of six columns at the end

Hypogeum, subterranean excavation for the interment of the dead (usually Etruscan)

Intarsia, inlay of wood, marble, or metal

Kore, maiden

Kouros, boy; Archaic male figure

Krater, antique mixing-bowl, conical in shape with rounded base

Kylix, wide shallow vase with two handles and short stem

Latomiae, the limestone quarries of Siracusa, later used as prisons, and now tropical gardens

Loggia, covered gallery or balcony, usually preceding a larger building

Lunette, semicircular space in a vault or ceiling, often decorated with a painting or a relief

Marmi mischi, inlay decoration of various polychrome marbles and pietre dure, used in church interiors

in the 17C and 18C

Medallion, large medal, or a circular ornament

Megalith, a huge stone (often used as a monument)

Megaron, an oblong hall (usually in a Mycenean palace)

Metope, panel between two triglyphs on the frieze of a temple

Monolith, single stone (usually a column)

Narthex, vestibule of a Christian basilica

Naumachia, mock naval combat for which the arena of an amphitheatre was flooded

Nymphaeum, a sort of summer-house in the gardens of baths, palaces, etc., originally a temple of the Nymphs, and decorated with statues of those goddesses

Octastyle, a portico with eight columns

Odeion, a concert hall, usually in the shape of a Greek theatre, but roofed

Ogee, (arch) arch shaped in a double curve, convex above and concave below

Oinochoe, wine-jug usually of elongated shape for dipping wine out of a krater

Opisthodomos, the enclosed rear part of a temple

Opus sectile, mosaic or paving of thin slabs of coloured marble cut in geometrical shapes

Ossuary, deposit of or receptacle for the bones of the dead

Palazzo, any dignified and important building

Pantokrator, the Almighty

Pax, sacred object used by a priest for the blessing of peace, and offered for the kiss of the faithful, usually circular, engraved, enamelled or painted in a rich gold or silver frame

Pediment, gable above the portico of a classical building

Pendentive, concave spandrel beneath a dome

Peripteral, temple surrounded by a colonnade

Peristyle, court or garden surrounded by a columned portico

Pietà, group of the Virgin mourning the dead Christ

Piscina, Roman tank; a basin for an officiating priest to wash his hands before Mass

Pithos, large pottery vessel

Podium, a continuous base or plinth supporting columns, and the lowest row of seats in the cavea of a theatre or amphitheatre

Polyptych, painting or tablet in more than three sections

Predella, small painting attached below a large altarpiece

Presepio, literally, crib or manger. A group of statuary of which the central subject is the Infant Jesus in the manger

Pronaos, porch in front of the cella of a temple

Propylon, propylaea. Entrance gate to a temenos; in plural form when there is more than one door

Prostyle, edifice with columns on the front only

Pulvin, cushion stone between the capital and the impost block

Putto, figure of a child sculpted or painted, usually nude

Quadriga, four-horsed chariot

Rhyton, drinking-horn usually ending in an animal's head

Situla, water bucket

Squinch, arched space at the angle of a tower

Stamnos, big-bellied vase with two small handles at the sides, closed by a lid

Stele, upright stone bearing a monumental inscription

Stereobate, basement of a temple or other building

Stilted arch, round arch that rises vertically before it springs

Stoa, porch or portico not attached to a larger building

Stoup, vessel for Holy Water, usually near the west door of a church

Stucco, plasterwork

Stylobate, basement of a columned temple or other building

Tablinum, room in a Roman house with one side opening onto the central court-yard

Telamones, see *Atlantes*

Temenos, a sacred enclosure

Tepidarium, room for warm baths in a Roman bath

Tessera, a small cube of stone, terracotta, marble, glass, etc., used in mosaic work

Tetrastyle, having four columns at the end

Thermae, originally simply baths, later elaborate buildings fitted with libraries, assembly rooms, gymnasia, circuses, etc

Tholos, a circular building

Tondo, round painting or bas-relief

Transenna, open grille or screen, usually of marble, in an early Christian church

Triclinium, dining-room and reception room of a Roman house

Triglyph, blocks with vertical grooves on either side of a metope on the frieze of a temple

Trinacria, the ancient name for Sicily derived from its triangular shape

Triptych, painting or tablet in three sections

Tympanum, area above a doorway or the space enclosed by a pediment

Villa, country house with its garden

Xystus, an exercise court; in a Roman villa the open court preceding the triclinium

Plan of Greek Temples

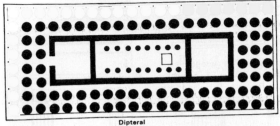

Dipteral
(Octastyle)

Parts of Greek Temple

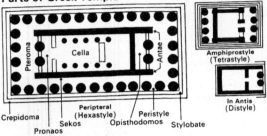

Pteroma

Cella

Antae

Amphiprostyle
(Tetrastyle)

In Antis
(Distyle)

Crepidoma Pronaos Sekos Peripteral
(Hexastyle) Peristyle
Opisthodomos Stylobate

Walls

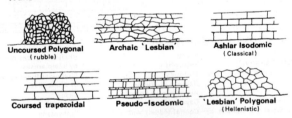

Uncoursed Polygonal
(rubble)

Archaic 'Lesbian'

Ashlar Isodomic
(Classical)

Coursed trapezoidal

Pseudo-Isodomic

'Lesbian' Polygonal
(Hellenistic)

Greek Theatre

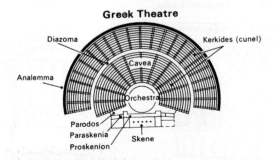

Diazoma

Kerkides (cunel)

Cavea

Analemma

Orchestra

Parodos
Paraskenia Skene
Proskenion

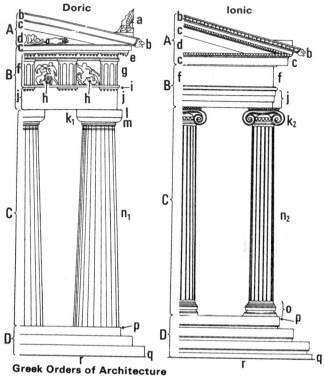

Doric

Ionic

Greek Orders of Architecture

A. Pediment
B. Entablature
C. Column
D. Crepidoma
a. Acroterion
b. Sima
c. Geison or Cornice
d. Tympanum
e. Mutule & Guttae

f. Frieze
g. Triglyphs
h. Metope's
i. Regulae & Guttae
j. Architrave or Epistyle
k_1 Capital (Doric)
k_2 Capital (Ionic) with Volutes
l. Abacus
m. Echinus

n_1 Shaft with flutes separated by sharp arrises.
n_2 Shaft with flutes separated by blunt fillets
o. Bases
p. Stylobate
q. Euthynteria
r. Stereobate

Corinthian Capital

Pergamene Capital

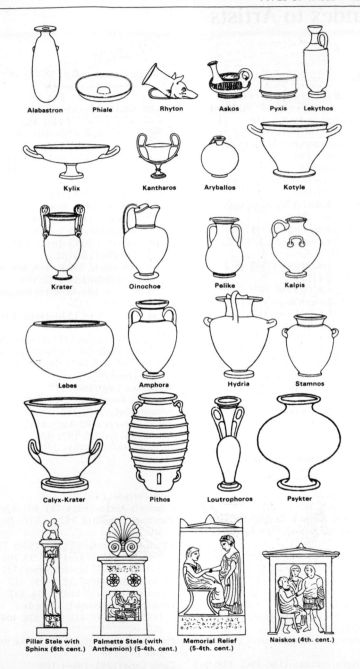

Alabastron Phiale Rhyton Askos Pyxis Lekythos

Kylix Kantharos Aryballos Kotyle

Krater Oinochoe Pelike Kalpis

Lebes Amphora Hydria Stamnos

Calyx-Krater Pithos Loutrophoros Psykter

Pillar Stele with Sphinx (6th cent.) Palmette Stele (with Anthemion) (5-4th. cent.) Memorial Relief (5-4th. cent.) Naiskos (4th. cent.)

Index to Artists

W

X

Z

Index

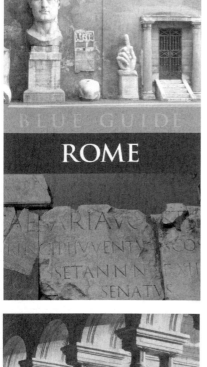

- **the connoisseur's guide to Rome, packed with information about the history and artistic heritage of this magnificent city.**

- **for a city best explored on foot, the Blue Guide provides more than 30 detailed walks, accompanied by a comprehensive colour street atlas site plans, and ground plans of museums and monuments.**

- **hotel, restaurant and café suggestions; detailed informtion on public transport.**

Alta Macadam
8th edition
528pp
ISBN 0–7136–6276–X
£15.99

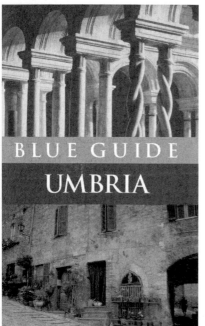

- **a comprehensive guide to one of Italy's most beautiful regions.**

- **detailed descriptions of numerous unspoilt medieval towns and villages, and the countless art treasures in churches and museums.**

- **the best routes to take through Umbria's rolling hills, covered with olive trees and vineyards.**

- **where to stay and eat, and all the practical advice you'll need to make the most of your visit.**

Alta Macadam
4th edition
320pp
ISBN 0–7136–6277–8
£13.99